TOURISM RESEARCH

Cover photographs courtesy of The Image Bank / Getmar 2000.

Printed in Singapore

ISBN 0 471 34255

GAYLE JENNINGS

Central Queensland University

John Wiley & Sons Australia, Ltd

First published 2001 by
John Wiley & Sons Australia, Ltd
33 Park Road, Milton, Qld 4064

Offices also in Sydney and Melbourne

Typeset in 10.5/12 pt New Baskerville

© Gayle Jennings 2001

National Library of Australia
Cataloguing-in-publication data

Jennings, Gayle, 1955–.
Tourism research.

Includes index.
ISBN 0 471 34255 6.

1. Tourism — Research. I. Title.

338.4791

Cover photograph: Courtesy of The Image Bank/Dominic Rouse

Printed in Singapore

10 9 8 7 6 5 4 3 2 1

CONTENTS

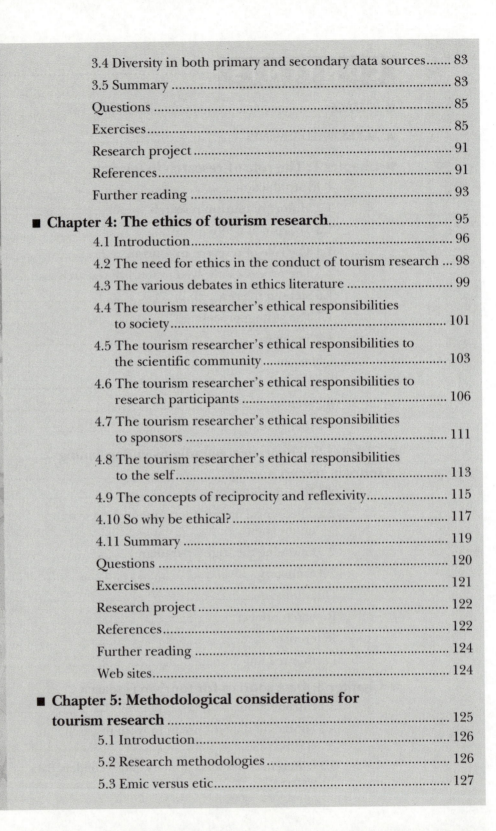

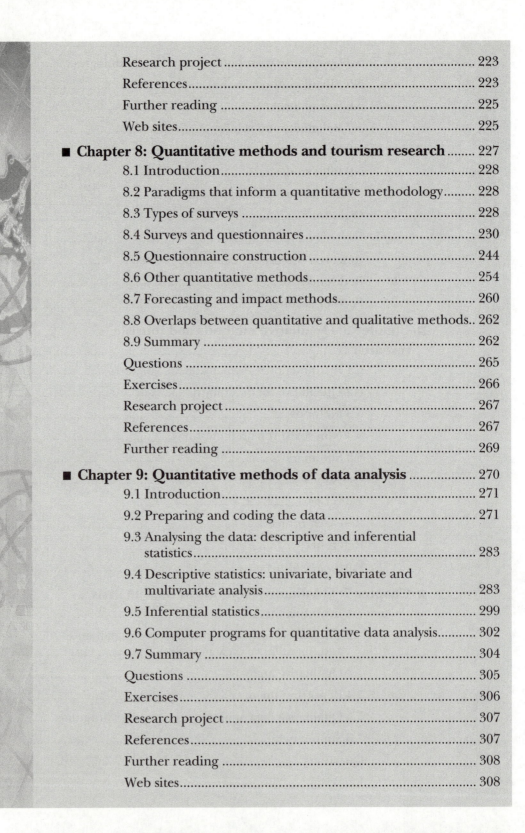

PREFACE ···

Welcome to tourism research. This textbook aims to develop your understanding of the skills involved in tourism research. The text is based on seven conditions of learning: immersion, demonstration, approximation, expectation, responsibility, practice and feedback.[1]

Working through this textbook, you will be 'immersed' in models and 'demonstrations', providing you with a base upon which you can develop your skills and knowledge about tourism research. Throughout the chapters, Industry Insights offer additional examples and/or models, and quotes present other viewpoints in regard to tourism research and the research process. Remember that you may be required to read beyond this textbook for sources to support your approaches and decision making in regard to your own research project — accessing special topic tourism books, tourism and hospitality journals and periodicals, specific tourism and hospitality research related Web sites and related disciplinary literature and information sources to further assist your engagement in the research process.

Ultimately, you are 'responsible' for 'engaging' in the research process and in assuming appropriate ethical behaviour in the conduct of your research. Only you can orchestrate this. This textbook, your lecturer and/or tutors and other resource materials are there to facilitate your learning. As you engage in textbook tasks, and practise your research skills, you will receive 'feedback' on your 'approximations' or interpretation of the various models used in research from your teachers, lecturers or tutors. Ensure you use the feedback to constructively develop your skills and knowledge.

The textbook will engage you in a small-scale research project. Generally, you should clear your research projects with your lecturers, as each tertiary institution has specific requirements related to the conduct of research that must be followed when proposing and conducting research. You should also note that this textbook is based on an overriding assumption that you have a background in tourism theories, concepts, models and frameworks, but have little or no knowledge of the act of conducting research. As you work through this textbook, you will need to draw on this previous knowledge base as you engage in your research project work. For those unfamiliar with basic concepts, models, frameworks and theories utilised in tourism, the first chapter will provide you with some background and a list of references upon which you can further extend your knowledge base.

The text deliberately introduces the qualitative methodology chapters before the quantitative methodology chapters, as they tend to receive least attention in the teaching agenda. The structure of the text ensures flexibility irrespective of whether a quantitative or qualitative methodology is presented first.

Furthermore, the textbook draws on contemporary as well as seminal and key writings. You might consider some of the latter dated; however, do not discount the importance of these seminal works. Many are the source documents upon which others have developed more recent interpretations. As a researcher, you

---

1. Cambourne, Brian. 1988. *The Whole Story: Natural Learning and the Acquisition of Literacy in the Classroom.* Auckland: Ashton Scholastic.

should supplement these seminal works with more current publications such as journal articles, especially academic e-journals, which will provide the most up-to-date information on tourism research for you to access.

Finally, two case studies are presented at the end of the book in chapter 12 to exemplify the incorporation of the key themes in the preceding chapters.

A brief note about the use of the plural pronoun 'their' with a singular noun, such as 'researcher' — this was the publisher's requirement instead of the alternating use of 'she' or 'he'. You should familiarise yourself with the non-sexist language policy of your own institution when preparing your work assignments associated with this text and follow that policy.

I hope as you engage in your studies in tourism research that you are both challenged and rewarded as your skill and knowledge levels build. Best wishes with your studies.

Note to lecturers and tutors

In preparing this textbook, decisions of what to include or not include were influenced by three key points. Firstly, this is a beginning research textbook and cannot be all things to all people, especially given the coverage of theoretical paradigms, qualitative and quantitative methodologies and the writing process associated with research within a twelve week teaching period. There will be lecturers and tutors who use qualitative and/or quantitative methods who will not necessarily find all of the methods of data collection or analysis that they use included. As educators, such researchers can complement the material presented in this textbook with their own experience, knowledge and expertise. Secondly, chapter contents were selected to achieve a balanced representation of themes for a week's worth of learning. Thirdly, some comparisons in the textbook are presented using the opposing ends of continua. Lecturers and tutors should reinforce alternatives that may be achieved by the mixing of methods.

Gayle Jennings 2001

ACKNOWLEDGEMENTS ....

The impetus for writing this book was borne out of immense frustration at not being able to locate a suitable text for use in the research in tourism classes in which I was teaching. A number of tourism texts were available; however, they tended to avoid discussions of the theoretical paradigms that inform research processes and the quantitative research methodology was favoured over the qualitative methodology. I sought a text that introduced students to theoretical paradigms so that their research process would be informed and guided by these theoretical frameworks, and that also presented qualitative and quantitative methods in equal measure and grounded research discussions in tourism within an Australian context. Apparently, others shared my frustration.

I was first encouraged by Maureen Martin at John Wiley to write this text. The development of the book has been a challenge. I would like to acknowledge Darren Taylor's understanding, support and encouragement, and the moral and professional support, as well as technical suggestions, of Catherine Spedding and Caroline Hunter, my copy editors. The reviewers of chapters — Sue Beeton (La Trobe University), Chris Cooper (University of Queensland), Kay Dimmock (Southern Cross University), Christine Lee (Monash Gippsland) and Barry O'Mahony (Victoria University of Technology) — offered critical feedback and served to improve the development of the text. In the end, the final product is my responsibility. I hope, however, that they find that collectively their comments have been incorporated in the text.

My thanks also to Les Killion, Central Queensland University, for allocating me to the *Research in Tourism* course, which initially placed me on the path to writing this text. Colleagues in the School of Marketing and Tourism and in the Faculty of Business and Law at Central Queensland University also provided support and encouragement to me while I was involved in this endeavour.

To the students who have shared the journey of learning in research in tourism over the years, my thanks also — you fashioned the need and the overall structure and content of this text.

Finally, my thanks go to my family and friends who have been supportive and have not complained about my absence in their lives while I worked on this textbook — you are all long-suffering and much loved.

The author and the publisher would like to thank the following copyright holders, organisations and individuals for their permission to reproduce copyright material in this book. The acknowledgements listed below are in addition to those that appear on particular pages in the text.

Figures

Fig. 1.1: from Weaver & Opperman, *Tourism Management*, John Wiley & Sons Australia, p. 7; fig. 5.1: from Patton, *Qualitative Evaluation and Research Methods*, p. 195. Reprinted by permission of Sage Publications; fig. 5.2: adapted from De Vaus, D., *Surveys in Social Research 4th Edition*. Reproduced with permission of Allen & Unwin, www.allen-unwin.com.au: fig. 6.2: from *The Action Research Planner* by Kemmis & McTaggart. Deakin University Press, 1988. Reproduced with permission of R. McTaggart; fig. 7.3: Erik Cohen 'Who is a tourist?', from *Sociological Review*, U22 (1974), p. 534, diagram 1, © The Editorial Board of Sociological Review; fig. 7.6: Atlasti.de, reproduced with permission of Thomas Muhr; figs 7.7, 7.8: Research Ware, Inc.; fig 8.1, map 1 (p. 402), 9.1, 10.7 (appendices list): © GBRMPA: reproduced with permission of Great Barrier Reef Marine Park Authority; figs 8.2, 8.3: Commonwealth of Australia copyright, reproduced by permission; fig. 8.4: from Ritchie & Goeldner, *Travel, Tourism & Hospitality Research* 2nd ed. © 1994 John Wiley & Sons, Inc. Reproduced with permission; fig. 9.2: 'Franchise Fees Survey; from Frazer & Lawley', *Questionnaire Design & Administration: A Practical Guide*, John Wiley & Sons Australia, p. 56. Reproduced with permission of the authors; fig. 9.3: Graduate Careers Council of Australia, Graduate Destination Survey 2000; fig. 9.4: Techneos

Systems Inc.; fig. 9.5: Distance Education Centre, University of Southern Queensland; fig 9.7 (a–d): reproduced with permission of Bureau of Tourism Research; fig. 9.7 (e): from ABS 3201.1 Australian Demographic Trends, p. 28. Commonwealth of Australia copyright reproduced with permission; fig. 10.6: Australian Tourist Commission; fig. 10.7 (lists of tables, figures and maps): from *Voyage from the Centre to the Margins: An Ethnography of Long-term Ocean Cruisers*, Gayle Jennings. Thesis, Murdoch University, 1999; fig. 10.8: *AAPG Bulletin* v50/9 (Sept. 1966), p. 1992, 'Geological Notes, A Scrutiny of the Abstract, II' by Kenneth K. Landes © AAPG. Reprinted by permission of the AAPG whose permission is required for further use.

Text

Pp. 1, 18, 112: from Ritchie & Goeldner, *Travel, Tourism & Hospitality Research* 2nd ed. © 1994 John Wiley & Sons, Inc. Reproduced with permission; pp. 14 & 435: from Neuman, W. L., *Social Research Methods*, 4th ed., © 2000 Allyn & Bacon. Reprinted with permission; tables 3.1, 3.2: from ABS Cat. 3401.0 — Overseas arrivals and departures. Commonwealth of Australia copyright reproduced by permission; tables 3.4 and 3.5, industry insight, p. 252: reproduced with permission of Bureau of Tourism Research; p. 90: from Russell, Mary, *The Blessings of a Good Thick Skirt*, 1994, pp. 33–4, © Harper Collins Publishers, Ltd, reproduced with permission; pp. 100, 207–8, 219, 324: from Miles & Huberman, *Qualitative Data Analysis, 2nd ed. An Expanded Sourcebook*, pp. 289, 111, 119, 239, 316, 298–9. Reprinted with permission of Sage Publications; p. 134: from Patton, *Qualitative Evaluation and Research Methods*, pp. 188–9. Reprinted with permission of Sage Publications; p. 147 (formula), table 5.4: from *Educational and Psychological Measurement* 30/1970, pp. 607–10. Reprinted with permission of Sage Publications; table 5.5: reproduced from Ticehurst and Veal, *Business Research Methods: A Managerial Approach* © Pearson Education Australia, 1999; table 6.1, pp. 161, 196–7, 203: from Denzin & Lincoln, *Handbook of Qualitative Research*, pp. 224–5, 434, 439, 218. Reprinted with permission of Sage Publications; table 8.1: from Frey, *Survey Research by Telephone*, p. 76. Reprinted with permission of Sage Publications; p. 243: from Frazer & Lawley, *Questionnaire Design & Administration: A Practical Guide*, John Wiley & Sons Australia, p. 3; industry insight, p. 250 : adapted from 'A framework for monitoring community impacts of tourism' by Faulkner and Tideswell. *Journal of Sustainable Tourism* vol. 5, no. 1, 1997, p. 18, table 3. Reproduced by permission of the authors; table 9.7: from Sarantakos, S., *Social Research* 2nd ed., 1998. Reproduced with permission of Macmillan Education Australia; p. 330: Commonwealth of Australia copyright, reproduced by permission; pp. 331–2 (industry insight): from Hall and Johnston, *Polar Tourism: Tourism in the Arctic and Antarctic Regions*, John Wiley & Sons, 1995. Reproduced with permission of John Wiley & Sons, Limited; pp. 348, 357 & 365: from Glesne, C., *Becoming Qualitative Researchers* 2nd ed., © 1999 by Allyn & Bacon. Reprinted with permission; pp. 360 (industry insight), 431: © ANZALS. The Australian and New Zealand Association for Leisure Studies was established in 1991 to provide academics, researchers and professionals with an interest in leisure research and scholarship with opportunities to enhance the profile of leisure studies in the South Pacific Region; pp. 417–27: from Weaver & Opperman, Tourism Management, John Wiley & Sons Australia, pp. 420, 422, 423; pp. 428–30: from NHMRC, *National Statement on Ethical Conduct in Research Involving Humans: Principles of Ethical Conduct*. © Commonwealth of Australia copyright. Reproduced with permission; selected glossary terms: From Weaver, D., *Tourism Research*, John Wiley and Sons Australia, Ltd and Sekeran, U., *Research Methods in Business*, John Wiley & Sons, Inc., New York.

Every effort has been made to trace the ownership of copyright material. Information that will enable the publisher to rectify any error or omission in subsequent editions will be welcome. In such cases, please contact the Permission Section of the publisher, which will arrange for the payment of the usual fee

1

The role of
research in tourism

'[O]ver the last fifteen years ... world competition in tourism has grown dramatically as more and more countries and regions realize both the desirability and the necessity of including tourism as a major component of their social and economic structure. During this period, the tourism industry has been gradually "getting its act together" by becoming a more cooperative and more coordinated force. In parallel, and on another front, progress has been made in developing research techniques which improve the reliability of travel and tourism data, thus enhancing our understanding of consumer behavior and consumer spending patterns in tourism. While much progress yet remains to be accomplished, there is little doubt that the level of sophistication in tourism research is much higher than it was and that there will be continued pressure for even more rigorous information gathering, analysis and interpretation systems.'

(Ritchie & Goeldner 1994, p. xiii)

LEARNING OBJECTIVES

After studying this chapter, you should be able to:

- discuss the nature of tourism as a 'discipline'
- understand the role of research in tourism
- distinguish between the various types of research
- outline the steps involved in the research process
- identify the phases of the writing process as applied to tourism research.

1.1 INTRODUCTION

As a student of tourism research, you have a significant role to play both in the rigour of data collection, analysis and interpretation as well as in the development of the sophistication of tourism research. In undertaking this subject, you will acquire knowledge and skills to conduct and evaluate tourism research. As a consequence, you will be able to contribute to the development of the sophistication and the rigour of tourism research.

To assist you in acquiring your knowledge and skills, this textbook is conceptually divided into three sections. In the first section, discussion focuses on the role of research in tourism, the theoretical underpinnings of tourism research, data sources for tourism research and the ethics of tourism research. In the second section, you will learn about the methodological considerations for tourism research, in particular qualitative and quantitative methods of data collection and analysis. This section also considers the use of computer programs in tourism research. The third section outlines the role of the writing process in tourism research. You will be presented with information regarding the writing of research proposals, reports and journal articles as well as guidelines for presenting seminars and poster papers. Finally, the textbook concludes with some reflections on the future of tourism research.

This chapter is the first of four chapters that discuss various aspects of the research process. The chapter introduces some background information regarding the history of tourism research, the development of tourism from a field of study to a 'discipline' and the impact of this development on tourism research. The role of research in tourism is also discussed. The various types of research are identified and the latter part of the chapter explains the research process using a series of steps as well as the various phases of the writing process as it applies to tourism research.

1.2 HISTORY OF TOURISM RESEARCH

Initially, the study of tourism — that is, tourism research — was predicated to the counting of numbers and the determination of economic benefits. This occurred because tourism, a service industry, was viewed as an economic development tool both at a national and international level, particularly for those regions or nations with minimal or no primary or technological resources. For many years, boosterism and the economic tradition (Getz 1987) were the predominant planning approaches adopted for tourism development. Both are founded on economic paradigms. As a consequence, research focused on tourism as an economic activity, in particular the economic advantages and disadvantages of tourism (Crompton & Richardson 1986; Helber 1988).

More recently, however, attention has turned to the nature of the tourist, the tourist experience and, circa the Brundtland Report (World Commission on Environment and Development 1987), the social, environmental and economic impacts of tourism, as well as training and educational needs. Interest has also shifted from the supply side (e.g. the tourism industry sectors and government) to the demand side of tourism (the tourists).

> In the Australian context, recent trends provide an indication of the potential role of tourism as a key focus of future economic development. However, tourism research is not well represented in the national research effort and it is apparent that this potential will not be realised unless national research capabilities are upgraded to meet the challenges of this increasingly complex and competitive area of economic activity. Nor will it be possible to manage the social, economic and environmental impacts of tourism in a manner that is consistent with the principles of sustainability unless decision making is informed by rigorous and ongoing research (Bushell, Faulkner & Jafari 1998, p. 6).

As you can see, there is some similarity between this quote and the quote at the start of the chapter, and by studying tourism research you are contributing to the improvement of the research capabilities of Australian tourism. The following Industry Insight discusses another way you can contribute to the development of tourism within Australia.

INDUSTRY INSIGHT

The Council of Australian Tourism Students (CATS) is one avenue by which you can contribute to the development of tourism within Australia. The council aims to:

- ensure CATS is represented at tertiary institutions offering tourism programs
- provide a collective voice for tourism students both during and after their studies have concluded
- improve the employment prospects for graduating tourism students
- facilitate the Tourism Council of Australia to maintain the standards and quality of tourism education
- organise various activities and provide services to assist tourism students.

Source: *Tourism Queensland (2000, p. 39)*

Given the rapid growth of tourism during the twentieth century and the predominant view of tourism as an economic activity, it is no surprise to learn that the study of tourism postdates the phenomenon of tourism itself. Or further, that the disciplinary nature of tourism commenced as a fragmented and multidisciplinary approach rather than an integrated and interdisciplinary one or a synthesised holistic discipline of study.

In reality, tourism is only just emerging as a discipline in its own right. Its beginnings are founded in other disciplines such as economics, geography, sociology, social psychology, social anthropology, marketing and history. These and other disciplines enabled an understanding of tourism to be achieved in the absence of a specific 'tourism' discipline. Resultantly, tourism, as a 'discipline', has evolved over time by drawing on other disciplines to inform its research processes and its theoretical frameworks. However, some would question whether tourism is yet a 'discipline' in its own right. The problematic nature of tourism centres on whether it is a multidisciplinary and/or an interdisciplinary field of study.

Przeclawski (1993, p. 11) has noted that multidisciplinary research involves the study of tourism from an individual discipline's theoretical and methodological paradigms ('concepts and methods'), with the result that the findings are discipline specific and unable to be synthesised except superficially. An interdisciplinary approach, on the other hand, is one in which tourism phenomena are studied using various disciplinary perspectives, although they are grounded in the same sampling procedures, the same sites and the same methods to facilitate the accumulation of a comprehensive information set about the phenomena (Przeclawski 1993).

There have been various arguments as to whether tourism should be multidisciplinary or interdisciplinary in nature. See, for example, the discussions by Jafari (1977), Leiper (1981), Stear (1981), Przeclawski (1993), Echtner and Jamal (1997) and Tribe (1997). To reiterate a past perspective:

> tourism is usually viewed as an application of established disciplines, because it does not possess sufficient doctrine to be classified as a full-fledged academic discipline (Bodewes 1981, p. 37).

Leiper (1989) suggests there is a need for the establishment of a central ground. This ground should be interdisciplinary based, as the use of a multidisciplinary approach rather than an interdisciplinary approach is counterproductive to the development of a tourism discipline. A multidisciplinary approach is fragmented with unconnected findings. By utilising an interdisciplinary approach, 'interdisciplinary triangulation' can be achieved (Janesick 1994, p. 251). 'Interdisciplinary triangulation' enables other disciplines to inform the research process and thereby broaden both the understanding of method and data. An interdisciplinary approach is also promulgated by Weaver and Oppermann (2000, p. 7), who provide a useful illustration of the evolution of tourism studies towards discipline status (see figure 1.1).

While there appears to be a desire to move towards an interdisciplinary approach within tourism literature discussions, the future, as indicated in

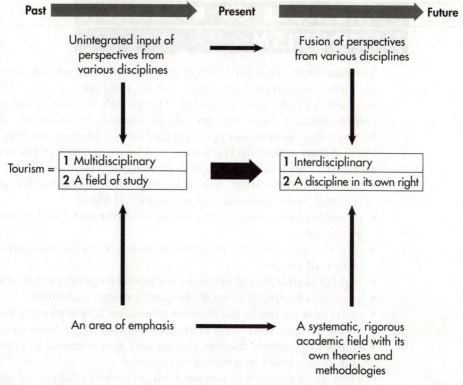

Figure 1.1
The evolution of tourism studies towards discipline status

Past → Present → Future

Unintegrated input of perspectives from various disciplines

Fusion of perspectives from various disciplines

Tourism =

| 1 Multidisciplinary |
| 2 A field of study |

| 1 Interdisciplinary |
| 2 A discipline in its own right |

An area of emphasis

A systematic, rigorous academic field with its own theories and methodologies

Source: *Weaver & Oppermann (2000)*

Weaver and Oppermann's illustration, is still a long way off. Tourism research has yet to move substantially beyond the descriptive and applied nature of much of its research. Although Jafari (1989) identified tourism (and by default tourism research) as currently applying a knowledge-based approach, it is far from being evenly distributed or evidenced as a major paradigmatic shift (Kuhn 1962). Essentially, a knowledge-based approach is one based more on scientific rigour and the development of tourism theories and concepts and less on descriptive research. After approximately 30 years of development as a field of study, it is timely for tourism to make such a paradigmatic shift to a knowledge-based approach and informed research. No longer is it acceptable for the discipline to engage only in descriptive research (counting numbers and describing the activities of tourists). The challenge for the discipline is to move towards a more rigorous and academic profile, one in which:

• applied research is informed by theory and in its turn critiques the theoretical constructs upon which it draws

• the development of 'intellectual depth and sophistication' (Smith 1988, p. 182) is translated by researchers for use in practice.

Only in this way will the discipline develop and mature. Tourism has already developed theoretical concepts peculiar to tourism itself, and needs to continue this process. As a future researcher in tourism you have a role to play in this process.

The latter half of the twentieth century saw tourism spread quite rapidly over the globe. Now, in the twenty-first century, most parts of the globe are touched by tourism in one way or another. The growth in tourism has precipitated a complementary need for growth in tourism information. Subsequently, research has become an important tool for the tourism industry both nationally and internationally. It is a tool used by private and public sectors alike to gather data on a variety of aspects of tourism. Tourism research:

- provides information for planning and management at the local, regional, state, national and international levels
- provides information on the social, environmental and economic impacts of tourism
- offers insights into the motivations, needs, expectations and levels of satisfaction of tourists
- highlights educational needs for commercial operators and service providers
- generates temporal views of the past, present and future
- offers data for use in the business sphere, such as marketing and promotion
- allows comparisons to be made and policies to be developed
- enables operators, tourism bodies and governments to evaluate tourism and its outcomes in a variety of contexts.

The role of research in tourism is all pervasive in the overall tourism system.

■ 1.4.1 Industry sectors *and research needs*

Each of the sectors involved in tourism and the related hospitality industry has its different knowledge and data needs. The following discussions, while not extensive or complete, serve to demonstrate the diversity of information needs.

Tourism attractions

Tourism attractions can be either natural (e.g. Karijini National Park, Uluru, Kata Tjuta, the Flinders Ranges, the Great Barrier Reef) or built (e.g. Melbourne Exhibition Centre, National Parliament House, the Darling Harbour complex, the town of Richmond in Tasmania). They can also be human-based (e.g. the Tjabiki Dance Company or the Melani folk festival) or special events linked to sport and/or celebrations and festivals (e.g. the Henley on Todd Regatta, the Darwin to Ambon Yacht Race, the Birdsville Races, the Melbourne Cup, the Olympic Games, the Moomba Festival, the Gay and Lesbian Mardi Gras, the Melbourne Comedy Festival). Attractions can be business related (such as conferences, meetings and exhibitions) or experientially based (such as bungy jumping, sky diving, whitewater rafting, tramping, climbing or touring).

Although it might appear that there are six discrete categories of attractions, the reality is that there is often overlap between the categories. An attraction may constitute several types, for example experiential, business related and natural, as evidenced in a business meeting that includes whitewater rafting in a natural environment as part of a team-building exercise. Or, for example, a special event that is culturally based and presented in a built environment, such as a Melanesian dance festival conducted in a resort precinct. However, the purpose here is not to develop another tourism attraction typology — popular typologies are already described in tourism literature, for example Mill and Morrison's (1998) typology of tourist attractions (scope: primary or secondary destinations; ownership: public, private or non-profit; permanency: event or site; drawing power: local, state, regional, national, international) and Clawson's (1963) classification of resource bases (nature-based, intermediate and user-oriented sites). The intent is to demonstrate the diversity of attractions and, as a consequence, the diversity of information needs. This sector's needs include information about:

- destination (attraction) images
- the competitiveness of a tourism product (attraction)
- the quality of the service delivery by staff
- site visitation patterns
- the quality of educational components offered during a tourism experience
- current and potential target markets
- social, cultural, environmental and economic impact assessments
- the location of a tourism product in the destination life cycle (Butler 1980)
- strategies for future planning and marketing, or an understanding of the consequences of legislative and statutory changes.

The transport sector

The transport sector includes public and private transport networks and services such as buses, taxis, hire cars, trains, ferries, cruise liners, planes, helicopters and sea planes, as well as local forms of transportation such as animal transportation modes and bicycle-derived forms. This sector requires information on, for example:

- the development and evaluation of pricing strategies
- the determination of demand elasticities, income and price elasticities
- data regarding quality control
- scheduling
- safety and security issues
- usage trends and patterns
- customer expectations and satisfaction
- seasonality impacts
- environmental and social impacts
- target markets
- competitiveness within the transport sector
- management issues
- future forecasting of transport needs
- the effectiveness of innovations and technological advancements.

The hospitality sector

The hospitality sector primarily includes the food and beverage and accommodation industries. Some of the hospitality sector's data requirements include a need for information on:

- quality evaluation and client needs in regard to services, amenities, facilities and their layout

- the functionality and aesthetics of room designs in accommodation facilities
- an evaluation of menu changes and menu contents
- stock control
- health and safety issues
- education and training requirements
- pricing strategies
- the effectiveness of yield management techniques
- the effectiveness of loyalty programs
- the development and monitoring of market profiles
- the evaluation of marketing strategies
- competitors and their products
- the development and review of strategies regarding cost-efficiency improvements
- an evaluation of management and policies
- the implications of legislative and statutory changes such as tax systems
- the benefits and costs of tour packaging and product clustering
- a longitudinal knowledge of usage patterns and trends.

Tourism bodies

Tourism bodies may consist entirely of public or private representatives or a mixture of personnel from the public and private sectors. They can also operate at several levels — local, regional, state, national or international (Mill & Morrison 1998). The research requirements of tourism bodies are not dissimilar to those of the sectors noted above. Tourism bodies, for example tourist associations, may be interested in gathering information on:
- a destination's image
- the identification of major generating regions
- the identification of market segments
- the development of sociodemographic profiles
- the identification of community attitudes
- the assessment of social, cultural, environmental and economic impacts
- the resultant strategies for ameliorating, amplifying, modifying or curtailing such impacts
- the evaluation of future development needs in regard to infrastructure, superstructure, facilities and amenities
- investment requirements and strategies.

Government

The various levels of government (local, state, national and international through various trade agreements) also require data in their roles. Governments may assume the roles of coordinators, planners, legislators/regulators, entrepreneurs and stimulators of tourism — investments and markets (International Union of Official Travel Organisations (IUOTO) 1974) — as well as interest protectors (Davis, Wanna, Warhurst & Weller 1993). Consequently, governments need:
- to establish data sets to monitor incoming and outgoing visitation patterns and to keep track of residents and visitors alike
- to gather data on visitor numbers and activities in order to manage natural and built environments in a sustainable way

- to quantify visitor numbers and establish visitor patterns for planning and management purposes
- data on visitor numbers to provide and maintain infrastructure and public facilities to support both local communities and visitors
- to know about expenditure patterns to regulate or stimulate investment
- data to determine associated taxes or to implement legislation and statutory requirements to maintain standards of construction and/or quality of life for residents or tourists
- to assess social, cultural, environmental and economic impacts
- to determine the effectiveness of overseas advertising and promotional campaigns.

Tourists

A plethora of typologies exist that describe the range of tourist and/or traveller types. There are interactive models and the cognitive-normative models (Murphy 1985). Examples of interactive models include: Cohen's (1972) fourfold typology of tourist experiences and roles — the organised mass tourist, the individualised mass tourist, the explorer and the drifter; Smith's (1978) sevenfold classification including the explorer, elite, offbeat, unusual, incipient mass, mass and charter tourist; and Pearce's (1982) 15 traveller types — tourist, traveller, holiday maker, jetsetter, businessman [sic], migrant, conservationist, explorer, missionary, overseas student, anthropologist, hippie, international athlete, overseas journalist and religious pilgrim. The cognitive-normative models are exemplified by Plog's (1974) psychographic continuum, which ranges between psychocentricism (non-adventurous folk) and allocentricism (adventurous folk).

Data requirements relating to tourists include:
- developing typologies in association with market segmentations and psychometric profiles
- finding out and understanding tourists' motivations, to assist in providing quality tourist experiences, appropriate amenities, facilities and services, planning, development and maintenance of tourism spaces, and marketing campaigns
- obtaining data on socioeconomic backgrounds, generating areas, expectations, values and attitudes.

The community

Tourism spaces can be situated within community settings, for example the staging of the Sydney 2000 Olympics, the development of the Iwaski coastal resort (now rebranded as Rydges Capricorn International Resort) at Yeppoon, Queensland or the development of heritage tourism in the historic village of Richmond, Tasmania. As a consequence of tourism spaces entering community settings, a need for community research arises and usually falls into two categories:
- research associated with community participation in tourism planning and development
- research to establish social and cultural impacts.

Tourism may be introduced into a community intentionally through planning or unintentionally, such as when a film location becomes a tourist site (e.g. Barwon Heads, Victoria, the setting for the television series 'Seachange'). Consequently, the introduction of tourism spaces in communities behoves various tourism-related agencies and sectors to:

- identify community attitudes to development
- assess social, cultural, environmental and economic impacts and develop strategies for sustainable tourism development
- implement or review legislative requirements and inform policy development.

Doxey's (1975) irridex (which notes that residents move from euphoria, to apathy, to annoyance and then to antagonism in their attitudes towards increasing tourist numbers) provides a useful theoretical lens to determine community attitudes to tourism development.

The environment

While the environment has been partially covered in the discussion on attractions, it is worthwhile reiterating some research requirements peculiar to tourism and the environment. Budowski (1976) identified three relationships between tourism and the environment: conflict, coexistence and symbiosis. Research can facilitate the movement towards and the establishment of a symbiotic relationship. Such research would include:

- environmental audits
- the identification of preservation and conservation values
- the conduct of environmental impact assessments
- the monitoring of environmental impacts and amelioration strategies
- the identification of issues and the subsequent development of legislative requirements and policy development
- the determination of carrying capacities, limits of acceptable change and recreational and tourism opportunity spectra
- economic values such as use values associated with the environment
- the identification and monitoring of attitudes to user-pays pricing strategies.

Tourism and hospitality operators and companies

This group may need:

- information about visitor needs and wants in order to provide better services, facilities or amenities
- data to maintain or improve market share
- data in regard to the performance of their tourism operations in order to increase efficiencies and profits.

All sectors of the overall tourism system have their specific research needs. Some of the information needs of attractions, transportation, the hospitality sector, tourism bodies, government, tourists, communities and the environment have been highlighted, but naturally there will be overlaps between the sectors. An example of a merging of interests is demonstrated in the following Industry Insight.

1.4.2 **Specific roles** *of tourism research*

The purposes of research in tourism can be summarised as:
• constructing and testing theory
• profiling, inventory making and collecting baseline data
• assessing social, cultural, environmental and economic impacts
• identifying educational needs
• assisting in planning and management activities
• contributing to monitoring and evaluation
• providing a temporal perspective — past, present and future trends.

The interests and disciplinary backgrounds of writers are usually reflected in the lists they construct as to the purpose or role of tourism research. Three other lists are provided for you to consider, and these are summarised in figure 1.2. McIntosh, Goeldner and Ritchie (1995, pp. 403–4) describe six uses of tourism research within a business context:
• identifying problems
• providing market information
• minimising operational wastages
• identifying new profitable resources
• facilitating sales promotion
• fostering goodwill.

Veal (1997, p. 7) defines nine roles for research associated with planning and managing tourism:
• establishing the terms of reference
• conducting an environmental appraisal
• consulting with stakeholders
• setting goals and objectives
• determining and assessing different action strategies
• selecting the most appropriate action strategy
• implementing the appropriate action strategy
• monitoring the action strategy's implementation
• establishing feedback and response mechanisms.

Gunn (1994, pp. 4–5) describes four commonly used approaches to tourism research and their functions or purpose:
- describing and inventory
- testing
- predicting, forecasting
- modelling, simulating.

Figure 1.2 illustrates the functions and purposes of tourism research described in this section. It enables you to compare the viewpoints presented in this textbook with the viewpoints of McIntosh, Goeldner and Ritchie, and Veal and Gunn.

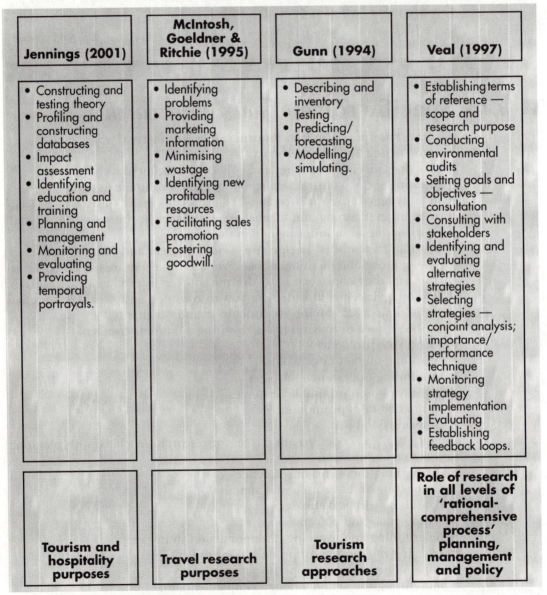

Jennings (2001)	McIntosh, Goeldner & Ritchie (1995)	Gunn (1994)	Veal (1997)
• Constructing and testing theory • Profiling and constructing databases • Impact assessment • Identifying education and training • Planning and management • Monitoring and evaluating • Providing temporal portrayals.	• Identifying problems • Providing marketing information • Minimising wastage • Identifying new profitable resources • Facilitating sales promotion • Fostering goodwill.	• Describing and inventory • Testing • Predicting/forecasting • Modelling/simulating.	• Establishing terms of reference — scope and research purpose • Conducting environmental audits • Setting goals and objectives — consultation • Consulting with stakeholders • Identifying and evaluating alternative strategies • Selecting strategies — conjoint analysis; importance/performance technique • Monitoring strategy implementation • Evaluating • Establishing feedback loops.
Tourism and hospitality purposes	**Travel research purposes**	**Tourism research approaches**	**Role of research in all levels of 'rational-comprehensive process' planning, management and policy**

■ **Figure 1.2** *Purposes, functions and roles of tourism and hospitality research*

The next section of this chapter moves beyond the identification of information needs and the purpose or role of research in tourism to a consideration of how the information may be acquired.

THE PROCESSES INVOLVED IN TOURISM RESEARCH

Conducting research is a twofold activity. First, you undertake the research process in order to gather data or information. Second, you use the writing process to move you from the construction of research aims or hypotheses related to your information needs to the development of your data collection tool(s) and then to the reporting of your findings. Both processes are overviewed in turn.

■ 1.5.1 The research *process*

Research is an activity that gathers information on a phenomenon using scientific rigour and academic acumen. Within the social sciences, various classification systems exist to describe the types of research that can be undertaken. For example, research may be described as pure or applied; or as exploratory, descriptive, explanatory, causal, comparative, evaluative or predictive. Research can also be described as being qualitative or quantitative or mixed method research. All these descriptors can be confusing to a person who is engaging with research literature/texts for the first time. Essentially, each of the classifications refers to a finer lens of definition. The descriptors pure and applied refer to the primary function or purpose of research. The descriptors exploratory, descriptive, explanatory, causal, comparative, evaluative and predictive are related to the type of information required. The terms qualitative and quantitative and mixed method relate to the type of methodologies used to gather the information required. These varying levels of abstraction are highlighted in figure 1.3.

■ **Figure 1.3**
Types of research

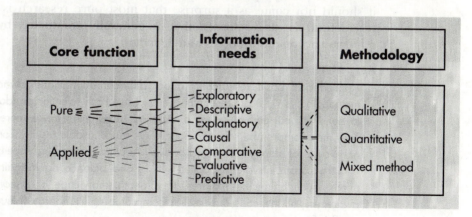

Core functions of research

Essentially, there are two primary divisions in the types of research — pure research and applied research. Each type of research has its own function and purpose and contributes differently to understanding the phenomenon of tourism. However, while this textbook is focused on the discipline of tourism, the following discussion relates equally to other social sciences.

Pure research

Pure research is sometimes referred to as basic research. It is research from which theories, frameworks and models are constructed. Pure or basic research advances our knowledge of the world. In the field of tourism, examples of theories or theoretical constructs include the destination life cycle (Butler 1980), Doxey's irridex (1975), Clawson's recreation experience (1963), which was later modified by Killion (1992) to demonstrate the travel experience, and the quasi-theoretical push-pull motivation models (see, for example, Dann (1977) or Gray's (1970) wanderlust and sunlust classification). Pure research takes time and addresses broad issues that may have no immediate application by the tourism industry.

Pure research can also be undertaken to test existing theories in order to confirm, modify or reject them. For example, what motivates people to travel opens up the potential to test Maslow's (1943) hierarchy of needs or Csikszentmihalyi's (1974) flow theory in a tourism context. Both theories, although drawn from the field of social psychology, contribute to the interdisciplinary understanding of tourist motivations. Some other theories that have been externally derived and tested in a tourism context are McCarthy and Perreault's (1999) four Ps from the marketing literature and the sociological theories relating to alienation and anomie (Durkheim 1952) used to formulate the quasi-theoretical push-pull motivation model. Another example is the recreation opportunity spectra (Stankey & Wood 1982) modified into the tourism opportunity spectra by Butler and Waldbrook (1991).

Pure research can be exploratory, descriptive or explanatory in nature. However, as the purpose of pure research is to explain how the world works, it should not come as a surprise that most pure research is explanatory research. It is also research that is generally conducted by academics, scholars and research bodies and agencies.

Applied research

Applied and basic researchers adopt different orientations toward research methodologies ... Basic researchers emphasize high scientific standards and try to conduct near-perfect research. Applied researchers make more trade-offs. They may compromise scientific rigor to get quick, usable results. Compromise is no excuse for sloppy research, however. Applied researchers squeeze research into the constraints of an applied setting and balance rigor against practical needs. Such balancing requires an in-depth knowledge of research and an awareness of the consequences of compromising ·standards (Neuman 2000, pp. 24–5).

As the term denotes, applied research involves some element of application of the findings into practice, whether that practice is planning, development, problem solving, issue identification, improvement of services, amelioration of impacts or comparison of pricing policies.

Essentially, most tourism research is located in the applied research field; however, that is not to downplay the role of pure research. As noted above, it is from pure research that the theories we use in tourism or tourism-related disciplines are primarily derived. Applied research is generally research that is designed to gather information relating to a problem, issue or planning need. This type of research is undertaken by academics, scholars, research agencies, government agencies and bodies at the local, regional and national level, tourism organisations and associations, tourism operators, tourism industry sector associations, and the community. Researchers who engage in data collection for applied research may be working for a sponsor or a client, as is illustrated by the following Industry Insight.

INDUSTRY INSIGHT

A study of recreational usage patterns in Shoalwater Bay and adjacent waters was conducted by Jennings (1998). The study was commissioned by the Great Barrier Reef Marine Park Authority (GBRMPA) to obtain data on recreational usage patterns in the study area. The findings assisted GBRMPA planners and managers during public participation phases and in the development of draft management plans for the area.

All research must be undertaken in an ethical manner. This is especially relevant for applied research, as the client may angle for a bias in the research design or reporting. Researchers are bound by ethical standards and such angling is not acceptable. Researchers must be responsible to themselves, the scientific community, the public and their sponsors in conducting ethical research. There is further discussion of research ethics in chapter 4.

Just as pure research draws on several approaches, that is exploratory, descriptive and explanatory research, so too does applied research. However, applied research draws on a wider range of approaches: exploratory, descriptive, explanatory, causal, comparative, evaluative and predictive (all of these terms are explained below). This does not mean to imply that each of these approaches is mutually exclusive. Research may be both descriptive and explanatory. For example, a study might aim to determine the influence of sociodemographics on travel motivations to a major tourist attraction. One sub-aim of the study would be to determine the sociodemographic profiles of visitors to the tourist attraction (a descriptive approach). A second sub-aim would be to determine the motivations of the tourists in selecting that attraction (an explanatory approach). Then the researcher would test for any relationships between the tourists' sociodemographic profiles and their motivations for selecting the tourist attraction (a causal approach). The research could also be descriptive and comparative. For example, sociodemographic profiles and visitation patterns may be developed in regard to domestic tourists who visit rural tourism attractions in New Zealand and North America. The sociodemographic profiles are then compared to identify similarities and differences between the two groups of domestic tourists. While these examples demonstrate possible research projects with several data requirements, research projects may in fact have multiple data requirements. For example, in the descriptive, comparative research project described above, an explanatory element could be added to the study by explaining the reasons for the similarities and differences between the two groups. Subsequently, you should be aware that research approaches may be singular, dual or multiple in nature.

In the main, the decision regarding the overall approach adopted in the research process is primarily informed by the type of knowledge the researcher wants to acquire. This is best illustrated with examples. The researcher may wish to explore the patterns of visitation to various exhibits in a cultural museum in order to develop a large-scale research project to improve visitor interaction with exhibits. Consequently, the researcher would engage in exploratory research. The researcher may wish to describe the sociodemographics of visitors to an attraction or region over a specific time period in order to develop appropriate promotional and marketing materials. This type of research would adopt a descriptive approach. The researcher may seek to explain the reasons for a drop in visitation levels to a tourism region in order to take appropriate action to re-establish its market share, in which case the research design would be predicated to explanatory or causal research. Alternatively, the researcher may wish to compare visitation patterns in two similar tourist regions over time in order to understand reasons for differences (a comparative approach) and to develop and establish benchmarks and/or baseline data regarding the development of competitive edge strategies for future comparative research. The researcher may wish to evaluate the effectiveness of a 10-week training program developed to improve front office servicing of customers in a hotel. In this case, the research would be predominantly evaluative in nature. However, in order to evaluate, the researcher needs to incorporate a temporal framework to the research design. There needs to be a 'before' and 'after' set of data collected (that is pre- and post-test/data sets) in order to determine if any change has occurred as a result of the training program. Finally, the researcher may wish to draw on data that has been collected over a period of years to determine or forecast future visitation patterns (predictive research). Subsequently, approaches to research can also have a temporal nature, pre- or post-, or past, present and future data collection requirements. Each of the examples demonstrates the seven main approaches that can be taken in tourism research. These approaches are described below in terms of their use value and possible data sources.

Approaches to research based on information requirements

There are seven approaches to research based on information requirements and these are discussed below. You should bear in mind, however, that researchers may use a singular, dual or multiple approach. The specific research information needs will determine which of these approaches will be selected. To date, the majority of tourism research has been founded on descriptive research. However, as tourism is now a discipline with some 30 years experience, there is a need to move beyond the essentially descriptive nature of its research profile into more analytical research approaches in order to better understand the phenomenon of tourism and to develop and modify theoretical constructs with which to firmly ground tourism as a discipline in its own right.

Exploratory research

Exploratory research is conducted when very little or no data exist on the tourism phenomenon being investigated. Findings from exploratory research can be used to develop a more extensive research project. Generally, exploratory research is not published. Rather, it serves to establish possible categories and concepts suitable for use in further research, in determining the feasibility of a major study or in understanding that which exists in areas related to the study topic. Exploratory research can draw on secondary sources, expert opinions and observations (these and other methods mentioned below are described in more detail in chapters 5, 6 and 8). In the main, exploratory research is informed by a qualitative methodology, due to the flexibility of data collection approaches such a methodology affords and the fact that exploratory research is not based on random sampling and representation of a study's population (these terms are discussed in chapter 5). The qualitative methodology is explained later in this section and in more detail in chapter 5.

Descriptive research

Descriptive research enables the researcher to describe the tourism phenomenon under study. It does not attempt to explain the reasons for the phenomenon. Basically, descriptive research is interested in 'who' and 'what', although Neuman (2000, pp. 21–2) states that exploratory research covers 'what' and descriptive research covers 'who' and 'how'. However, it is this author's opinion that the 'how' moves the researcher into explanation and therefore is linked to the 'why' of a phenomenon — the essence of explanatory research. Essentially, descriptive research provides a 'picture' (Neuman 2000, p. 21) of the tourism phenomenon.

A considerable amount of tourism research findings are founded in this approach. For example, descriptions of tourism patterns and behaviours, such as sociodemographic profiles, statistics on inbound and outbound travel, purpose of travel, duration of stay, mode of transport, type of accommodation used, activities engaged in and patterns of expenditure, are helpful for the planning and management of tourism. As Gunn (1994, p. 4) comments:

One approach in tourism is merely to describe, not to prove new relationships or to demonstrate the value of new practices. While some scholars denigrate the value of descriptive research, tourism knowledge is in such a stage of infancy that descriptive research is valuable and necessary today. The many facets of the complicated phenomenon called tourism have not even been described adequately. Basic inventory and description are often helpful in decision making.

Descriptive research contributes to the development of tourist profiles, tourist or traveller typologies, descriptions of travel experiences, steps in tourism decision-making processes, spatial distribution patterns of tourist movements/flows and tourism developments, tourism inventories and baseline databases upon which to measure future changes in tourism trends and impacts. Subsequently, descriptive research is used in the planning and development of tourism policy making and the establishment of baselines for the future monitoring and evaluation of tourism trends and patterns using evaluative research processes. Descriptive research can also provide information that will either support or debunk existing tourism theories and concepts or suggest modifications to the theories and concepts. For example, Killion's (1992) travel experience (based on Clawson's recreation experience) involves the following phases: planning and anticipation, travel to site, on-site activities, return travel and recollection. The phases are a circular rather than a linear process. The model reflects a travel experience based on one primary destination rather than multiple destinations. Descriptive research into independent travellers suggests that the model requires modification to take into account multiple destinations within the overall travel experience.

Descriptive research may be developed using quantitative, qualitative or mixed method methodologies (these are described later in this chapter and also in chapters 5, 6 and 8).

Explanatory research

While Gunn (1994) has suggested that tourism is still in its infancy, there are others who believe it has progressed beyond that stage (see, for example, the previous discussion and references related to tourism as a discipline). As the term explanatory research suggests, the main aim of this approach is to explain the 'how' and 'why' of the tourism phenomenon under study. Explanatory research is similar to causal research as the researcher is trying to find the cause to explain a specific tourism pattern or behaviour described by descriptive research or outlined in an exploratory research study. However, causal research depends exclusively on hypotheses, whereas explanatory research does not.

Explanatory research may use either quantitative or qualitative methodologies or a mixed method approach.

Causal research

Causal research may be generated from either exploratory or descriptive research. Causal research is unambiguously linked to the use of a quantitative methodology and involves the use of variables and the construction of hypotheses to support or reject causal relationships between two or more variables. For example, a researcher may consider the following statement: the lowering of airfares to capital cities in the low season will increase visitation rates to those cities. In this statement, the researcher has hypothesised a relationship between the cost of airfares and visitation rates to capital cities. The statement is a hypothesis describing a causal relationship between two variables, an independent variable, the lowering of airfares (the cause variable), and the dependent variable, the increase in visitation rates (the effect variable). The researcher would design data collection and analysis tools to either support or reject the hypothesis and thereby support or reject the proposed causal relationship between the two variables. If the hypothesis is supported, the information might be used by airlines to alter pricing strategies to increase yields during the low season. If the hypothesis is rejected, the airlines might engage in further research to determine how to improve yields on routes to capital cities during the low season.

Comparative research

Comparative research involves comparing research study units across time and space as well as between the study units themselves, for example comparing domestic tourism patterns in Australia in the 1900s, 1930s, 1950s, 1970s and 1990s, or comparing tourist settings or regions (both are considered spaces), such as international tourist patterns in Melbourne and Perth. Comparisons can also be conducted between tourists' experiences based on gender, age, education or income levels. Other comparative studies might determine the similarities and differences between tourist profiles, such as domestic and international tourists, the differences and similarities in expenditure patterns between business tourists and the visiting friends and relatives market, or the impacts of gaming facilities on local residents in two different locations such as Townsville and Launceston. Primarily, in comparative research, the researcher is concerned with identifying the similarities and differences between the sites, groups or patterns under study.

Comparative research may use either qualitative, quantitative or mixed method methodologies. The outcomes of comparative research can assist with planning and development strategies and policies, legislative requirements, marketing programs and campaigns, ameliorating impacts, training and educative program development and community consultation processes.

Evaluative research

Evaluative research is primarily applied research rather than theory-building research, as the researcher is interested in determining the outcomes of changes in strategies, practices and planning, and legislative mechanisms. Evaluative research may be based on either summative or formative evaluation strategies. Formative evaluation is undertaken as an ongoing activity, whereas summative evaluation is primarily undertaken at the end of the process to determine the success or otherwise of a strategy or the introduction of a change mechanism or activity. Evaluative research draws on quantitative, qualitative or mixed method methodologies.

An example of evaluative research would be a formative evaluation of marine transportation impacts in a previously non-utilised marine area. Other examples are formative and summative evaluations of public participation in tourism development in the planning phase and, if the development is approved, formative and summative evaluations of the implementation and establishment phases of the development; a summative evaluation of a staff development program to improve front-office service in a lodging facility; and a summative evaluation of traffic flows in a tourist enclave due to the introduction of roundabouts and improvements in road signage.

Predictive research

Predictive research aims to provide information concerning future events. Forecasting also comes under predictive research. There are various time periods involved in predictive research: the short term (one to two years), the medium term (two to five years), the long term (five to 10 years) and futurism (more than 10 years) (Mill & Morrison 1998). Predictive research is essentially based on judgments, even when mathematical modelling is used, and forecasting is primarily based on expert opinions and judgments — these judgments are only as good as the experts who make them.

Predictive research draws on descriptive research and may use either quantitative, qualitative or mixed method methodologies. Predictive research is used to assist decision making and planning, and development processes.

Approaches to research based on the methodology used

Once the approach (or approaches) has been determined in regard to the information needs of a research project, an appropriate methodology has to be selected and suitable tools for data collection (and analysis) have to be chosen. In the previous section, reference was made to qualitative, quantitative and mixed method methodologies. These methodologies are governed by specific paradigms (positivism, interpretive social sciences, critical theory, feminist perspectives, postmodernism and chaos theory) that will be discussed in detail in chapter 2. The paradigms are mentioned briefly here so that you may start associating them with the relevant methodologies. Essentially, a paradigm is 'a basic set of beliefs that guides action, whether of the everyday garden variety or action taken in connection with a disciplined inquiry' (Guba 1990, p. 17). In this text, the 'disciplined inquiry' is the conduct of tourism research.

Primarily, there are two distinct approaches that inform the gathering of data in any research project — the qualitative approach and the quantitative approach. The qualitative approach is grounded in the interpretive social sciences paradigm and sits comfortably with the more recently espoused feminist approaches to the conduct of research. The qualitative methodology gathers information as text-based units, which represent the social reality, context and attributes of the tourism phenomenon under study. The methodology is inductive in nature.

The qualitative approach is the complete antithesis of the quantitative approach, which takes the tourist experience, event or phenomenon and abstracts it to the level of numerical representation. A quantitative research approach is grounded in the positivist social sciences paradigm that primarily reflects the scientific method of the natural sciences. Such a paradigm adopts a deductive approach to the research process.

In practice, some research is conducted using a mixture of both qualitative and quantitative approaches. Subsequently, a third approach is generated by the combination of these two approaches and is often referred to as the mixed method approach.

This section provides a brief introduction to the two major methodologies that will inform the conduct of your research, as well as mixed methods, and chapter 5 expands upon this discussion.

Qualitative methodology

Research that is informed by a qualitative methodology is grounded in the interpretive social sciences, is inductive in nature and is based on textual representations of the phenomenon under study. It also has some synergies with critical theory, feminist research and postmodern approaches. Qualitative or inductive research commences in real-world settings, that is in the empirical social world, where data about the tourism phenomenon are gathered, then analysed, and theoretical constructions are either generated or modified (refer to figure 1.4).

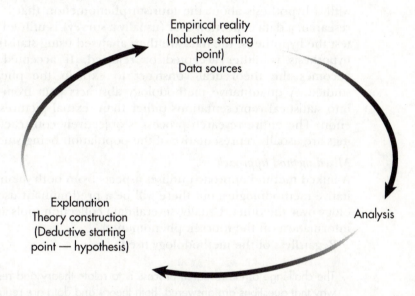

■ **Figure 1.4**
Inductive and deductive processes

Empirical reality
(Inductive starting point)
Data sources

Analysis

Explanation
Theory construction
(Deductive starting point — hypothesis)

Consider the following quote in relation to the inductive process demonstrated in figure 1.4: 'Inductive theorizing begins with a few assumptions and broad orienting concepts. Theory develops from the ground up as the researchers gather and analyze the data' (Neuman 2000, p. 61). In particular, data are generally gathered from the perspective of the insider being studied, such as the tourist, the local resident, the tourism association volunteer or manager, the room cleaner or the tour guide. Research that utilises a qualitative methodology will draw on data collection methods such as participant observation, in-depth interviews and/or focus groups. These methods are detailed in chapter 6. As a consequence of its overlying paradigm, qualitative research is subjective since it relies on the texts and discourses of participants and involves small numbers of participants in the research process by nature of gathering in-depth information, sometimes referred to as 'thick descriptions'. Moreover, qualitative research, because of the small numbers of participants, does not assume to represent the wider population. Qualitative research enables researchers to highlight detailed and in-depth snapshots of the participants under study. In reality, qualitative research provides a slice of life from those participants being studied.

Quantitative methodology

Quantitative research is grounded in the positivist social sciences paradigm that primarily reflects the scientific method of the natural sciences. Such a paradigm adopts a deductive approach to the research process. As such, it commences with theories or hypotheses about a particular tourism phenomenon, gathers data from the real-world setting and then analyses the data to support or reject hypotheses. 'Researchers who adopt a more deductive approach use theory to guide the design of a study and the interpretation of results. They refute, extend, or modify the theory on the basis of results' (Neuman 2000, p. 61).

The difference between a quantitative and qualitative methodology is demonstrated in figure 1.4. Essentially, a deductive approach commences with a hypothesis about the tourism phenomenon that is the focus of the research, a data collection tool (usually a survey) is utilised to gather data to test the hypothesis, the data are then analysed using statistical tools and the hypothesis is either accepted or rejected. If accepted, the hypothesis becomes the theoretical construct to explain the phenomenon being studied. A quantitative methodology abstracts data from the participants into statistical representations rather than textual pictures of the phenomenon. The entire research process is objectively constructed and the findings are usually representative of the population being studied.

Mixed method approach

A mixed method approach utilises aspects from both quantitative and qualitative methodologies, but there will be a predominant use of one methodology over the other. Usually, several data collection tools are used to gather information on the tourism phenomenon.

Regardless of the methodology used:

> The challenge of the research process is to relate theory and research in such a way that questions are answered. Both theory and data are required ... The end result of the research process is neither theory nor data but knowledge ... The research process is a disciplined way of learning about ourselves and our world (Bouma 1996, p. 18).

1.6 STEPS IN THE RESEARCH PROCESS

Various writers have suggested a variety of models for the process of undertaking research. For the purposes of this textbook, the following model has been adopted due to its more simplistic nature — identify the research topic, develop the research design, implement the research design and report the findings (see figure 1.5 and following discussion).

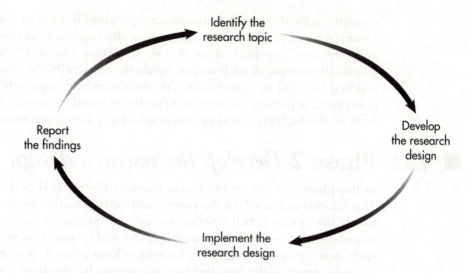

■ Figure 1.5
The research process

- Identify the research topic
- Develop the research design
- Implement the research design
- Report the findings

You will note that the process is presented as a circular path. The reason for this is that the report of the research findings may lead the researcher onto another research project based on those findings or, alternatively, the report may lead other researchers into a research process informed or influenced by the reported findings. Furthermore, the conclusion of one research project will influence future research as the researcher consolidates and develops their research skills and knowledge. It should also be noted that researchers may be working on several research projects at the one time.

The model presented in figure 1.5 compares with the seven-stage process described by Neuman (2000) — that is, choose a topic, focus the research question, design the study, collect the data, analyse the data, interpret the data and inform others. It also compares with Weaver and Oppermann's (2000) model involving seven phases (problem recognition, question formulation, identification of data, data collection, data analysis, data presentation and data interpretation) and Veal's (1992) four steps (preparation and planning, investigation, analysis and writing up/presentation of the results). However, Veal (1997) extended the four phases into an eight-phase model by breaking down the four phases into smaller sub-phases.

■ 1.6.1 Phase 1 *Identify the research topic*

This is essentially the initial phase of any research project. Research topics may arise from the personal interest of the researcher, as a direction from a supervisor, from a client's briefing paper, from the identification of a problem (e.g. complaints from customers regarding quality of service, congestion at a tourist destination, antagonistic host communities, continual falls in profit or competitive edges), from an information gap or from government planning requirements (e.g. social or environmental impact assessments). Once identified, the research topic may be presented as a research aim and associated objectives, or as a hypothesis or hypotheses. For example, a local tourist organisation might identify a fall in visitation rates. Undertaking a preliminary investigation, the organisation can use an aim and objectives approach since it does not know why visitation rates have fallen. An example of such an aim would be: to identify the factors that have resulted in a fall in visitor numbers. An alternative approach might be to generate a hypothesis or several hypotheses based on anecdotal evidence, such as: the highway diversion has resulted in a fall in visitation numbers.

1.6.2 **Phase 2** *Develop the research design*

In this phase, the researcher has to consider the method of data collection. The information needs of the project will determine the methodology upon which the research will operate — that is, qualitative or quantitative or mixed method — the type of sampling that will be undertaken and the pilot study development. Using the information from phase 1, several models can be constructed to develop the research design for the tourist organisation. In the first example, based on the research aim to identify the factors that have resulted in a fall in visitor numbers, the researcher might decide to hold a focus group (see chapter 6) of former visitors based on the records of tourism operators. In the second example, using the hypothesis that the highway diversion has resulted in a fall in visitation numbers, the researcher might choose to undertake a telephone survey (see chapter 8) of former visitors.

1.6.3 **Phase 3** *Implement the research design*

Implementing the research design is focused on two major activities: data collection and data analysis. Both activities are associated with ethical issues relating to permission to conduct the study and to the researcher acting ethically during data collection and analysis. Also in this phase, the researcher will be involved in running a pilot of the study. The pilot is in a sense a trial run of the data collection tools (and analysis) using the same sample population that will be used in the final study. Implementing the research design involves 'field work' and completing the data collection (in the above examples, either running a focus group or conducting a telephone survey, and commencing and completing the data analysis).

1.6.4 **Phase 4** *Report the findings*

The fourth phase involves the preparation of the final report and the presentation of the findings in written and/or oral form. The final report might be complemented by written reports such as media releases, posters, and issues or position papers, and oral reports such as conference presentations and seminars. As noted above, the output from this phase may generate further research projects for the researcher or contribute to other researchers identifying research topics.

The entire research process is linked to the writing process. In formulating background notes, research proposals, literature reviews, questionnaires, interview schedules, reports and various other genres associated with disseminating the findings from research (such as media releases, newsletters, articles, position papers, issues papers, letters and journal articles), you will be engaged in composing, from the Latin meaning 'put together' (Macrorie 1980, p. 1). Specifically, you will be engaged in the writing process. Several models of the writing process exist. Murray (1982, p. 15) has identified three stages in the writing process — pre-writing, writing and rewriting. Graves (1984) also uses three phases — rehearsal (pre-writing), composing and post-writing (all activities after the first draft is completed). Macrorie (1980, p. 297) uses a four-phase model — collecting, imitating, revising and writing. In a sense, they are all describing the same process, one in which one-shot writing is rarely the norm. The development of quality writing requires drafting and redrafting to clarify meaning and once that is done the writer's attention then, and only then, should turn to proofreading. The structure of the writing process differs between writers — you may have a similar or different method to those identified above. However, successful writing needs to be drafted and revised several times rather than composed the night before an assignment is due or a milestone is to be met.

This textbook adopts the following writing process: rehearsal, repetitions of drafting and revising, proofing and publishing (either in the written or oral form — that is, going 'public'), as illustrated in figure 1.6.

■ Figure 1.6
The writing process

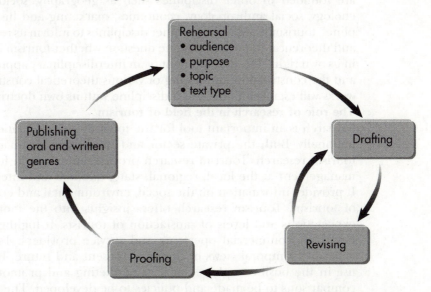

In the rehearsal stage, the writer brainstorms, lists, engages in stream of consciousness writing, outlines a structural plan of the writing, and collects relevant data, models of the genre to be written and other resources to assist the writing process. In this stage, the writer should also be mindful of their audience, as well as the purpose of the writing, the topic and the text type — that is, the genre (Bean & Bouffler, 1987). During the drafting and the revising stages, the writer's key focus should be on clarifying their intent to ensure that the text clearly conveys their meaning. In the proofing stage, the writer attends to the issues of punctuation, syntax and grammar. The publishing stage involves the writer producing either personally or professionally the final document in polished form for dissemination to the appropriate audiences.

As you are guided through your study by this textbook, you will be familiarised with the process of writing as it relates to research proposal writing, data collection tool construction, report writing, poster designs and oral presentation modes. Each of these genres associated with research has specific functions and has attendant tone, tenor and modes for conveying your message to your audience or readers. The specificities of each genre are discussed towards the end of this textbook in chapters 10 and 11. If you are in the beginning phases of the research process, the writing of a research proposal will be in the forefront of your mind. You might like to scan through chapter 11 to familiarise yourself with some of the details related to the writing of a research proposal in order to move you into the rehearsal stage for this writing task.

1.8 SUMMARY

The nature of tourism as a 'discipline'

Tourism is only just emerging as a discipline in its own right. Its beginnings are founded in other disciplines such as geography, sociology, social psychology, social anthropology, economics, marketing and history. As a 'discipline', tourism draws on these other disciplines to inform its research processes and theoretical frameworks. Some question whether tourism is yet a discipline in its own right. The development of an interdisciplinary approach to research and the construction and testing of various theoretical constructs and frameworks will establish tourism as a discipline with its own doctrine.

The role of research in the field of tourism

Research is an important tool for the tourism industry nationally and internationally. Both the private sector and the public sector are interested in tourism research. Tourism research provides information for planning and management at the local, regional, state, national and international levels. It provides information on the social, environmental and economic impacts of tourism. Tourism research offers insights into the motivations, needs, expectations and levels of satisfaction of tourists. It highlights educational needs for commercial operators and service providers. Tourism research generates temporal views of the past, present and future. It offers data for use in the business sphere, such as marketing and promotion, and allows comparisons to be made and policies to be developed. The role of research in tourism is all pervasive in the overall tourism system.

The various types of research

Depending on the overall function, information needs or methods used, research can be classified into various categories: research may be pure or applied; it may be exploratory, descriptive, explanatory, causal, comparative, evaluative or predictive; and it may also be classified based on the methodology to be used — qualitative, quantitative or mixed method.

The steps involved in the research process

Various writers have suggested a variety of models for the process of undertaking research, but this textbook adopts the following model due to its more simplistic nature: identify the research topic, develop the research design, implement the research design and report the findings.

The phases of the writing process as applied to tourism research

The structure of the writing process differs between writers. This textbook adopts the following writing process: rehearsal, drafting and revising, proofing and publishing.

Questions

1.1 Is tourism a discipline in its own right, or is it a multidisciplinary aggregation or an interdisciplinary field of study? Explain your answer.

1.2 List the various functions and purposes of tourism research that you consider important for the state or territory in which you live. Explain your answer.

1.3 Identify some of the specific information needs of governments, tourism operators and communities hosting tourists in your local area.

1.4 If you were asked to prepare the next five-year tourism plan for your local community or area, which types of research would you undertake and why?

1.5 Provide examples from your local area to demonstrate each of the seven types of research that could be conducted in tourism — exploratory, descriptive, explanatory, causal, comparative, evaluative and predictive.

1.6 Look up one of the academic tourism journals and identify an example of research that uses (a) a qualitative methodology, (b) a quantitative methodology and (c) mixed method methodology. Discuss the examples with your peers at the next tourism class and seek feedback from your tutor.

1.7 Outline the steps involved in the research process and demonstrate each phase using an example drawn from an electronic journal or government Web site.

1.8 Why is knowledge of the writing process appropriate to the conduct of research?

1.9 Consider a tourism attraction in your local area. What do you believe are its major information needs and why?

RESEARCH PROJECT

You are encouraged to engage in the research process by undertaking a small-scale research project while you study this text. Given the various examples of research possibilities presented in this chapter, look around your local area for a possible 'topic' to study. Make a list of possible topics, undertake preliminary investigations to determine how easy it is to gather information on each of the topics — consider literature sources, Web sites, access to settings and the feasibility of the topic being studied in a term or semester. Discuss your topics in the next tutorial to gain feedback from your peers and tutors. You will need your tutor and/or lecturer's approval to conduct your research as universities and educational institutions (as well as other bodies) are bound by ethical guidelines and standards and so, as a consequence, are you. Chapter 4 details the ethical issues associated with tourism research if you wish to know more about ethics at this point in time.

REFERENCES

Bean, Wendy & Bouffler, Christine. 1987. *Spell by Writing*. Rozelle: Primary English Teachers Association.

Bodewes, T. 1981. 'Development of Advanced Tourism Studies in Holland', *Annals of Tourism Research*, vol. 8, no. 1, pp. 35–51.

Bouma, Gary, D. 1996. *The Research Process*. Third Edition. Melbourne: Oxford University Press.

Budowski, G. 1976. 'Tourism and Conservation: Conflict, Coexistence or Symbiosis'. *Environmental Conservation*, vol. 3, no. 1, pp. 27–31.

Bushell, Robyn, Faulkner, Bill & Jafari, Jafar. 1998. *Tourism Research in Australia, Mobilising National Research Capabilities*. Canberra: Bureau of Tourism Research.

Butler, R. 1980. 'The Concept of a Tourism Area Cycle of Evolution: Implications for Management of Resources'. *Canadian Geographer*, vol. 24, pp. 5–12.

Butler, R. W. & Waldbrook, L. A. 1991. 'A New Planning Tool: The Tourism Opportunity Spectrum'. *The Journal of Tourism Studies*, vol. 2, no. 1, May, pp. 2–14.

Clawson, Marion. 1963. *Land and Water for Recreation: Opportunities, Problems and Policies*. Chicago: Rand McNally.

Cohen, Erik. 1972. 'Toward a Sociology of International Tourism'. *Social Research*, vol. 39, pp. 164–82.

Crompton, L. J. & Richardson, S. L. 1986. 'The Tourist Connection Where Public and Private Leisure Services Merge'. *Parks and Recreation*, October, pp. 38–44, 67.

Csikszentmihalyi, Mihaly. 1974. *Flow: Studies of Enjoyment*. Chicago: University of Chicago.

Dann, Graham. 1977. 'Anomie and Ego-Enhancement'. *Annals of Tourism Research*, vol. 4, no. 4, pp. 184–94.

Davis, G., Wanna, J., Warhurst, J. & Weller, P. 1993. *Public Policy in Australia.* Second Edition. Sydney: Allen & Unwin.

Doxey, G. 1975. 'A Causation Theory of Visitor-Resident Irritants, Methodology, and Research'. *Conference Proceedings of the Travel Research Association.* San Diego, pp. 195–8.

Durkheim, Emile. 1952. In Finifter, A. W. 1972. *Alienation and the Social System.* New York: John Wiley & Sons.

Echtner, C. & Jamal, T. 1997. 'The Disciplinary Dilemma of Tourism Studies'. *Annals of Tourism Research,* vol. 24, pp. 868–83.

Getz, D. 1987. 'Tourism Planning and Research: Traditions, Models and Futures'. Paper presented at The Australian Travel Research Workshop, Bunbury, Western Australia, 5–6 November.

Graves, Donald. 1984. 'The Child, the Writing Process, and the Role of the Professional'. In Graves, D. *A Researcher Learns to Write: Selected Articles and Monographs.* Exeter: Heinemann Educational Books, pp. 16–25.

Gray, Peter. 1970. *International Travel: International Trade.* Lexington, MA: Lexington Books.

Guba, E. G. 1990. 'The Alternative Paradigm Dialog'. In Guba, E. G. (Ed.) *The Paradigm Dialog.* Newbury Park: Sage.

Gunn, Claire. 1994. 'A Perspective on the Purpose and Nature of Tourism Research Methods'. In Ritchie, J. R. B. & Goeldner, C. R. (Eds.) *Travel, Tourism and Hospitality Research: A Handbook for Managers and Researchers.* Second Edition. New York: John Wiley & Sons.

Helber, L. E. 1988. 'The Roles of Government in Planning in Tourism with Special Regard for the Cultural and Environmental Impact of Tourism'. In McSwain, D. (Ed.) *The Roles of Government in the Development of Tourism as an Economic Resource.* Seminar Series, No. 1. Townsville: Centre for Studies in Travel and Tourism, James Cook University, pp. 17–23.

International Union of Official Travel Organisations (IUOTO) 1974. 'The Role of the State in Tourism'. *Annals of Tourism Research,* vol. 1, no. 3, pp. 66–72.

Jafari, J. 1977. 'Editor's Page'. *Annals of Tourism Research,* vol. 5, pp. 6–11.

Jafari, J. 1989. 'An English Language Literature Review'. In Bystrzanowski, J. (Ed.) *Tourism as a Factor of Change: A Sociological Study.* Vienna: Centre for Research and Documentation in Social Sciences, pp. 17–60.

Janesick, V. J. 1994. 'The Dance of Qualitative Research Design'. In Denzin, N. K. & Lincoln, Y. S. *Handbook of Qualitative Research.* Thousand Oaks: Sage, pp. 209–19.

Jennings, Gayle. 1998. *Recreational Usage Patterns of Shoalwater Bay and Adjacent Waters.* Research Publication No. 50, Townsville: Great Barrier Reef Marine Park Authority.

Killion, Les. 1992. *Understanding Tourism. Study Guide.* Rockhampton: Central Queensland University.

Kuhn, Thomas. 1962. *The Structure of Scientific Revolutions.* Chicago: University of Chicago Press.

Leiper, N. 1981. 'Towards a Cohesive Curriculum in Tourism: The Case for a Distinct Discipline'. *Annals for Tourism Research*, vol. 8, no. 1, pp. 69–74.

Leiper, N. 1989. *Tourism and Tourist Marketing*. Homewood, Ill: Richard D. Irwin.

Macrorie, Ken. 1980. *Telling Writing*. Rochelle Park, NJ: Hayden Book Company.

Maslow, A. H. 1943. 'A Theory of Human Motivation'. *Psychological Review*, vol. 50, pp. 370–96.

McCarthy, William D. & Perreault, E. Jerome. 1999. *Basic Marketing: A Global Managerial Approach*. Thirteenth Edition. New York: Irwin/McGraw-Hill.

McIntosh, R. W., Goeldner, C. R. & Ritchie, J. R. B. 1995. *Tourism: Principles, Practices, Philosophies*. Seventh Edition. New York: John Wiley & Sons.

Mill, R. C. & Morrison, A. M. 1998. *The Tourism System*. Third Edition. Dubuque, IO: Kendall/Hunt.

Murphy, P. E. 1985. *Tourism: A Community Approach*. New York: Methuen.

Murray, D. M. 1982. *Learning by Teaching: Selected Articles on Writing and Teaching*. Montclair, NJ: Boyton/Cook.

Neuman, W. L. 2000. *Social Research Methods, Qualitative and Quantitative Approaches*. Fourth Edition. Boston: Allyn & Bacon.

Pearce, P. L. 1982. *The Social Psychology of Tourist Behaviour*. Oxford: Pergamon Press.

Plog, S. C. 1974. 'Why Destination Areas Rise and Fall in Popularity'. *The Cornell Hotel and Restaurant Administration Quarterly*, vol. 14, no. 4, February, pp. 55–8.

Przeclawski, Krzysztof. 1993. 'Tourism as the Subject of Interdisciplinary Research'. In Pearce, D. G. & Butler, R. W. (Eds.) *Tourism Research, Critiques and Challenges*. London: Routledge, pp. 9–13.

Ritchie, J. R. B. & Goeldner, C. R. 1994. *Travel, Tourism and Hospitality Research: A Handbook for Managers and Researchers*. New York: John Wiley & Sons.

Smith, S. L. J. 1988. 'Defining Tourism: A Supply Side View'. *Annals of Tourism Research*, vol. 15, no. 2, pp. 179–90.

Smith, Valene. 1978. *Hosts and Guests: The Anthropology of Tourism*. Oxford: Basil Blackwell.

Stankey, G. H. & Wood, J. 1982. 'The Recreation Opportunity Spectrum: An Introduction'. *Australian Parks and Recreation*, February, pp. 6–14.

Stear, Lloyd. 1981. 'Design of a Curriculum for Destination Studies'. *Annals of Tourism Research*, vol. 19, pp. 85–95.

Tourism Queensland. 2000. *Queensland Tourism Industry Directory*.

Tribe, John. 1997. 'The Indiscipline of Tourism'. *Annals of Tourism Research*, vol. 24, pp. 638–57.

Veal, Anthony. 1992. *Research Methods for Leisure and Tourism: A Practical Guide*. Harlow: Longman.

Veal, Anthony. 1997. *Research Methods for Leisure and Tourism: A Practical Guide*. Second Edition. London: Pearson Professional.

Weaver, David & Oppermann, Martin. 2000. *Tourism Management*. Brisbane: John Wiley & Sons.

FURTHER READING

Babbie, E. 1995. *The Practice of Social Research*. Seventh Edition. Belmont: Wadsworth Publishing Company.

Cambourne, Brian. 1984. 'The Origins of Teachers' Doubts About 'Naturalising' Literacy Education and Some Suggestions for Easing Them'. In *Reading: 1984 and Beyond, Selected Key Papers of the 10th Australian Reading Conference 1984*, vol. 2, pp. 17–39.

Elbow, Peter. 1981. *Writing with Power: Techniques for Mastering the Writing Process*. New York: Oxford University Press.

Smith, Frank. 1981. *Demonstrations, Engagement, and Sensitivity: A Revised Approach to Language Learning*. Language Arts.

Wallace, Walter. 1971. *The Logic of Science in Sociology*. Chicago: Aldine-Atherton.

Williamson, J. B., Barry, S. T. & Dorr, R. S. 1982. *The Research Craft*. Boston: Little, Brown.

World Commission on Environment and Development. 1987. *Our Common Future* (also known as the Brundtland Report). London: Oxford University Press.

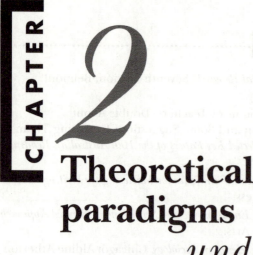

CHAPTER 2

Theoretical paradigms
underpinning tourism research

'[P]aradigms ... can be characterized by the way their proponents respond to three basic questions, which can be characterized as the *ontological*, the *epistemological*, and the *methodological* questions. The questions are these:

1   *Ontological:* What is the nature of the 'knowable'? Or, what is the nature of 'reality'?
2   *Epistemological:* What is the nature of the relationship between the knower (the inquirer) and the known (or knowable)?
3   *Methodological:* How should the inquirer go about finding out knowledge?'

(Guba 1990, p. 18)

LEARNING OBJECTIVES

After studying this chapter, you should be able to:

■ describe the major theoretical paradigms that inform tourism research

■ discuss the differences between each of the theoretical paradigms

■ explain the consequences of these differences for the conduct of tourism research.

The majority of tourism research textbooks do not address the theoretical paradigms that underpin tourism research. Consequently, the purpose of this chapter is to introduce you to the various theoretical paradigms that can inform tourism research. These paradigms are positivism, an interpretive social sciences approach, a critical theory orientation, feminist perspectives, a postmodern approach and a chaos theory orientation. Each of the paradigms has ramifications for the conduct of tourism research. As a researcher, it is important for you to understand the basic tenets of each of the paradigms. This understanding will ensure that when you design your own research project, you will be able to maintain consistency between the approach being adopted for your data collection and the subsequent construction of 'knowledge' from your data.

This chapter provides an overview of the paradigms. It does not provide a detailed account of each paradigm, as this is beyond the scope of this textbook. You are, however, directed to the references and suggested readings provided at the end of this chapter to further your own understanding of each of the paradigms.

The chapter begins by defining the term 'paradigm' and then outlines the differences between the terms 'paradigm', 'methodology' and 'methods'. The latter two are sometimes used interchangeably; however, as you will read, 'methodology' and 'methods' do mean different things. The chapter then draws on the three questions presented in Guba's (1990) quote (see page 32) to describe each paradigm, particularly in regard to how each views:

- the real world, that is its ontological basis
- the relationship between the researcher and the subject or object of the research, that is its epistemological basis
- data collection and knowledge construction, that is its methodological basis.

The following three questions, based on Guba's three questions (1990), are used to organise the description of each paradigm:

1. How is the world perceived? (Ontological basis)
2. What is the relationship between the researcher and the subjects or objects of research? (Epistemological basis)
3. How will the researcher gather data/information? (Methodological basis).

The consequences of each paradigm for tourism research and potential areas of research using each paradigm are also included immediately following the description of each paradigms. You should be aware from the outset, and this will be reiterated later in the chapter, that a researcher will not necessarily explicitly state the paradigm informing their work. However, it should be implicitly reflected in the structure, implementation and reporting of the entire research process.

The term 'paradigm' was introduced in chapter 1, as were the interpretive social sciences paradigm, the feminist perspectives paradigm and the positivist paradigm. You will recall from chapter 1 that a paradigm is 'a basic set of beliefs that guides action, whether of the everyday garden variety or action taken in connection with a disciplined inquiry' (Guba 1990, p. 17).

Sarantakos (1998, p. 30) distinguishes between a paradigm, a methodology and the methods used in a study. A methodology 'is a model, which entails theoretical principles as well as a framework that provides guidelines about how research is done in the context of a particular paradigm' (Sarantakos 1998, p. 32; see also Stanley & Wise 1990, p. 26). Guba (1990) sees the term 'methodology' as part of the structure that constitutes a paradigm (reread the quote at the beginning of this chapter to refresh your memory). On the other hand, methods are 'the tools or instruments employed by researchers to gather empirical evidence or to analyse data' (Sarantakos 1998, p. 32; see also Stanley & Wise 1990, p. 26). Thus, a paradigm is the overlying view of the way the world works; the methodology is the complementary set of guidelines for conducting research within the overlying paradigmatic view of the world; and the methods are the specific tools of data collection and analysis a researcher will use to gather information on the world and thereby subsequently build 'theory' or 'knowledge' about that world. The terms and their definitions are summarised in table 2.1.

■ **Table 2.1**
Summary of terms and their definitions

TERM	DEFINITION
Paradigm	A set of beliefs
Ontology	The nature of reality
Epistemology	The relationship between the researcher and the subjects/objects
Methodology	The set of guidelines for conducting research
Method	The tools for data collection and analysis

Having explained the difference between paradigms, methodologies and methods you should be able to see how each is related to the other. Bear these relationships in mind as you progress through the chapter and ensure that you use the terms appropriately in your research writing. This is important, so that you can convince your readers that you have the knowledge and skills to conduct and report your research.

In the past, the dominant paradigm of social sciences research was positivism. Essentially, positivism is grounded in the physical sciences and this paradigm 'views' the world or reality as very organised or structured and based on rules that guide actions in both the natural and the social world. Over time, other paradigms have arisen that challenge this view, such as the interpretive social sciences paradigm, conflict theory and chaos theory orientation. These paradigms differ and question the ontological, epistemological and methodological premises of positivism. Our discussion now turns to each of these paradigms.

■ 2.2.1 Positivist *paradigm*

Positivism has its roots in the work of René Descartes (1596–1650) and his Cartesian paradigm, as well as the work of Isaac Newton (1642–1727) and his Newtonian physics paradigm of scientific inquiry. The adoption of positivism as a means to understand the social world is credited to Auguste Comte (1798–1857). As a paradigm, positivism embraces a view of the world as being guided by scientific rules that explain the behaviour of phenomena through causal relationships. This world view can be further explained by examining positivism's ontological, epistemological and methodological bases.

1. How is the world perceived? (Ontological basis)

As already noted, positivism is founded in the physical sciences where the natural world is perceived as being organised by universal laws and truths. The social world is similarly perceived as being organised by universal laws and truths. In such a world, human behaviour is therefore predictable, because it is governed by external forces (the universal laws and truths that explain causal relationships). Subsequently, human behaviour can be shaped and controlled once causal relationships have been determined. A positivist approach to social inquiry is sometimes described as a behaviourist approach because it sets out to explain behaviour using causal relationships. Basically, positivism is nomothetic — it is founded upon observable or testable facts from which generalisations can be made to develop theories to explain behaviour or relationships in the natural and social worlds — that is, to explain 'reality'.

2. What is the relationship between the researcher and the subjects or objects of research? (Epistemological basis)

The relationship between the researcher and the subjects or objects is one that is objective and value free. The researcher is assumed not to impact on or influence the results or findings in a research project. The conduct of research follows strict procedures to ensure objectivity and value-free interpretations. As a consequence, other researchers should be able to replicate the same piece of research and obtain the same findings.

3. How will the researcher gather data/information? (Methodological basis)

A positivist researcher will use the methodology of the physical sciences, such as 'controlled experiments' and repeatable procedures that will achieve the same results each time the 'experiment' is conducted. The research process is objective and value free due to the specificity of the procedures that must be followed and because the researcher assumes a position that detaches them from the subjects or objects or setting being studied.

The researcher usually commences with a hypothesis, which has been deductively derived and based on empirically validated facts. The process of deduction involves the testing of theories about the way the natural and social worlds operate. Using a theory, the researcher will generate a hypothesis that is then tested to determine the veracity of the theory for explaining a specific behaviour or phenomena. That is, theory is deduced and then tested in the empirical world.

'An empirical statement or theory is one which can be tested by some kind of evidence drawn from experience' (Abercrombie, Hill & Turner 1988, p. 86) or based in the real world. A researcher operating from a positivist paradigm will primarily use quantitative methods. The methods of data collection include questionnaires, observation, documentary analysis and experiments and quasi-experiments. (These methods are explained in chapters 3 and 8.) Analysis will be conducted using statistical calculations and the units of study will subsequently become numeric representations. Analysis of data gathered using a quantitative methodology is discussed in chapter 9.

Language or terms associated with a positivist research process include hypotheses, variables, probability (random) sampling, descriptive statistics, measures of association, inferential statistics, measures of central tendency and mathematical formulae that enable the researcher to generate theories about the world. These terms are explained in chapters 5, 8 and 9.

Consequences of a positivist paradigm for tourism research

A positivist paradigm, when applied to tourism research, predicates the explanation of a tourism behaviour, event or phenomenon to being based on causal relationships. These relationships would be discerned by the observation or testing of facts from which generalisations would be made, which in turn would be extrapolated to explain any future occurrence of the behaviour, event or phenomenon. A tourism researcher working within a positivist paradigm deductively derives facts about tourism. Specifically, the tourism researcher commences their study from a 'theory' that demonstrates causal relationships. The researcher uses a quantitative methodology and subsequently develops a hypothesis. Data would then be gathered using, say, questionnaires, and then analysed using mathematical formulae. Samples would be selected to be representative of the population being studied as well as randomly selected. Results would be recorded in numerical representations and statistical tests would be used to determine the veracity of the hypothesis and its applicability to the wider population or tourism phenomenon under study.

A glance through conference proceedings or tourism journals in your library will quickly inform you that most tourism research has been grounded in the positivist paradigm.

During March 2000, the third in a series of annual studies to determine and monitor community attitudes to international tourism was conducted. The study was informed by a positivist paradigm. A representative sample of 1171 Australian residents over the age of 14 was surveyed. The sample was representative in terms of age, gender and geographic location. Data collected were analysed using statistical formulae.

Some of the key findings were:
- 94% of respondents support international tourists visiting Australia
- 97% consider inbound tourism advantageous to Australia
- 96% believe international tourism is important to Australia's economy
- 78% support government funding for the overseas promotion of Australia as a tourist destination
- 90% would like to see more people coming to Australia for a holiday.

Source: *Australian Tourist Commission (2000)*

Some potential areas of tourism research informed by a positivist paradigm

The Industry Insight above provides an example of the positivist paradigm applied to tourism research and community attitudes. Some other potential areas for research are outlined below.

The first example is drawn from consumer behaviour studies. A consumer behaviour researcher might wish to determine the effect that changes in the price of holiday packages have on consumer behaviour. The researcher might hypothesise that the more expensive the price of a package, the fewer the number of tourists wishing to buy the package. Or, the cheaper the price of the package, the greater the number of tourists wishing to buy the package. To test the hypothesis or hypotheses, the researcher would generally prepare a scenario describing the contents of the holiday package and the destination(s) and then construct questions to measure responses to various changes in the price of the holiday package. In order for the findings to be extrapolated to the empirical world, the questionnaire would be administered to a representative random sample of potential holiday purchasers following strict procedures that we will consider in chapter 5.

The second example is drawn from environmental impact studies. A researcher might be engaged to determine the impacts of a tourism resort and marina complex development at the mouth of an estuarine river. The researcher hypothesises that the construction of a groyne wall will change the course of the river. To test the hypothesis, the researcher could construct various models using computer simulations representing a number of different structures and positions of the groyne wall and the effects on the river flow under a variety of flow conditions. For example, the researcher might consider high and low tide patterns, flood tides and simulations based on historical data of the river course patterns. The outcome would be to determine the most feasible structure and location for the groyne wall. Undoubtedly, the researcher would also consider impacts on the ecosystems as well as social and economic impacts.

Other potential areas for research include:
- tourism forecasting and modelling
- social impact studies
- economic impact studies
- marketing research studies
- hospitality satisfaction studies.

To summarise, the positivist paradigm is deductive in nature, that is based on theories concerning causal relationships that can be empirically tested (in the real world or using models of the real world). It is a paradigm in which the researcher uses a quantitative methodology and maintains a position of objectivity throughout the research process. Positivist interpretations are value free and statistically tested and can be generalised to all other similar sets of behaviour, events or tourism phenomena.

■ *2.2.2* **Interpretive social sciences** *paradigm*

The interpretive social sciences paradigm is based on the work of Max Weber and his term 'verstehen' or empathetic understanding. How is verstehen achieved? 'Empathic or appreciative accuracy is attained when, through sympathetic participation, we can adequately grasp the emotional context in which the action took place' (Weber 1978, p. 5).

As a paradigm, the interpretive social sciences paradigm (also known as the constructivist paradigm) 'assumes a relativist ontology (there are multiple realities), a subjectivist epistemology (knower and subject create understandings), and a naturalistic (in the natural world) set of methodological procedures' (Denzin & Lincoln 1994, pp. 13–14). Immediately, you should be able to see that this paradigm differs from the positivist paradigm, as this paradigm asserts that:
- there are multiple explanations or realities to explain a phenomenon rather than one causal relationship or one 'theory'
- the research process should be subjective rather than objective.

As you progress through this section, you will also become aware of several other differences between the interpretive social sciences and the positivist paradigm, such as:
- the use of a qualitative methodology instead of a quantitative methodology
- data are collected from an insider's perspective rather than from an outsider's perspective
- data are collected in their real world or natural setting as opposed to being collected under 'experimental' conditions.

You may have found Denzin and Lincoln's description of the interpretive social sciences paradigm somewhat complex in nature, so the paradigm is now examined using our three questions.

1. How is the world perceived? (Ontological basis)

The interpretive social sciences paradigm considers the world is constituted of multiple realities. The interpretive social sciences researcher assumes an inductive approach to research, and commences their study in the empirical world in order to develop explanations of phenomena. These generalisations are used as the basis for 'theory' building and generation. This contrasts with the positivist paradigm, which utilises a deductive approach, commencing with 'theory' and then testing the 'theory' in the empirical world.

2. What is the relationship between the researcher and the subjects or objects of research? (Epistemological basis)

In order to achieve 'verstehen', the researcher is obliged to enter the social setting and become one of the social actors acting in that social setting (Blumer 1962). This action is recommended so as to:

> ... catch the process of interpretation through which [the actors] construct their actions ... To catch the process, the student must take the role of the acting unit whose behaviour he [sic] is studying, since the interpretation is being made by the acting unit in terms of objects designated and appraised, meanings acquired, and decisions made, the process has to be seen from the standpoint of the acting unit ... To try to catch the interpretative process by remaining aloof as a so-called 'objective' observer and refusing to take the role of the acting unit is to risk the worst kind of subjectivism — the objective observer is likely to fill in the process of interpretation with his [sic] own surmises in place of catching the process as it occurs in the experience of the acting unit which uses it (Blumer 1962, p. 188).

Thus, in the interpretive social sciences paradigm, the relationship between the researcher and subject (or, to use the terminology of the interpretive social sciences paradigm, 'social actors', 'respondents', 'participants' or 'interviewees') is subjective rather than objective, as is the case in the positivist paradigm.

3. How will the researcher gather data/information? (Methodological basis)

To gather knowledge from the empirical world, a researcher informed by the interpretive social sciences paradigm will use a qualitative methodology. The methods of data collection would include, for example, participant observation, in-depth interviews, case studies, focus groups and appreciative inquiry (see chapter 6). A researcher operating in this paradigm seeks to understand phenomena from an insider's perspective rather than an outsider's perspective, as is the case in the positivist paradigm. The insider's view, or the 'emic perspective', allows for the identification of multiple realities (Fetterman 1989, p. 31) since the views of all social actors are taken into account and are equally valued. Thus, unlike positivism, exceptions are included rather than discounted.

The language of the interpretive social sciences paradigm includes terms such as ideographic view, participants, respondents, emic perspective, reflexivity, reciprocity, grounded theory analysis, content analysis and triangulation. These terms are explained in chapters 5, 6, and 7.

Consequences of an interpretive social sciences paradigm for tourism research

The use of the interpretive social sciences paradigm in tourism research means that the researcher has to become an 'insider' and subsequently experience the phenomena, or become one of the social actors within the tourism system being studied. The insider's view is perceived as providing the best lens to understand the phenomena or social actors being studied and means that the researcher will need to be in the 'field setting' for some time in order to acquire this understanding and to be accepted.

The interpretive social sciences paradigm is appropriate for the study of travel experiences, hospitality experiences, host–guest interactions, tourism and hospitality workers' experiences, and host/residents' experiences.

The interpretive social sciences researcher will need to be familiar with the tenets of qualitative methodology in order to successfully gain 'knowledge' from the study setting. Furthermore, the researcher will need to be aware that when using an interpretive social sciences paradigm, the people studied will not be representative of the wider population — the findings of a study are specific to those who participated. However, in undertaking tourism research using an interpretive social sciences paradigm, the researcher will acquire an in-depth knowledge of the tourism phenomena or experience that is grounded in the empirical world — a world where there are multiple realities rather than one 'truth' to explain tourism phenomena. These understandings will be expressed in text-based rather than numerical representations. The reporting of the findings or theory would also be interspersed with quotes from the people being studied.

The Industry Insight opposite provides an example of the use of the interpretive social sciences paradigm in tourism research.

Some potential areas of tourism research informed by an interpretive social sciences paradigm

The possibilities for undertaking tourism research using an interpretive social sciences paradigm are extremely diverse. For example, a researcher might choose to conduct research into:

- the cruise ship experience, by studying the workers' perspectives or the travellers' perspectives by either working aboard the cruise ship or becoming a cruise ship passenger, respectively — data would be gathered using participant observation, as well as in-depth interviewing with colleagues or passengers
- host–guest interactions, by becoming part of the host community and observing and gathering data through in-depth interviews or focus group studies
- customer service evaluation, by becoming a customer in the various sectors of the hospitality industry, and supplementing this participant observation with in-depth interviews of other customers.

To summarise, the interpretive social sciences paradigm is founded in the real-world setting of social action. The paradigm requires the researcher to become part of the social group being studied, to be subjective and to use a qualitative research methodology. As a result, knowledge of the world is thereby constructed inductively.

Westerhausen has studied independent travellers in Asia using an interpretive social sciences paradigm. Data were gathered emically using participant observation and interviews. Westerhausen travelled as an independent traveller on several extended periods throughout the course of his research. By constantly comparing themes in the analysis phase, he found:

- Western independent travel is a mass phenomenon
- Western independent travel provides existential, life-altering experiences
- Western independent travellers are a viable market for a sustainable tourism product
- development of the Western independent traveller market is being undermined by outside influences and sectors
- other tourism sectors and non-local operators are 'cannibalising' independent traveller destinations
- the 'cannibalisation' of such destinations is 'unnecessary and undesirable' for sustainable tourism.

Source: *Westerhausen (1999)*

■ 2.2.3 Critical theory *paradigm*

The critical theory paradigm is grounded in the work of Karl Marx and the need to conduct research that will free oppressed groups from oppression and thereby change their social circumstances. Critical theory has synergies with the interpretive social sciences paradigm but not with positivism. Both the critical theory and interpretive social sciences paradigms differ from positivism because they are grounded in real-world settings and view people as thinking and acting persons rather than as people following defined rules and procedures. Another difference between positivism and critical theory is that critical theory asserts that research should cause some change. Researchers adopting a critical theory paradigm criticise positivism for maintaining the status quo due to its ontological perspective of a stable and structured society following rules that both regulate and guide behaviour. Critical theory also criticises the interpretive paradigm for valuing all points of view as being equal rather than using research to further the cause of minority groups. Researchers operating under a critical theory paradigm see inquiry as a means to benefit the world and change conditions, particularly for the oppressed.

1. How is the world perceived? (Ontological basis)

Critical theory portrays the world as being complex and organised by both overt and hidden power structures. Subsequently, the world involves oppression, subjugation and exploitation of minority groups who lack any real power. The social world is perceived as being orchestrated by people and institutions in power positions who try to maintain the status quo and subsequently their positions of power.

2. What is the relationship between the researcher and the subjects or objects of research? (Epistemological basis)

The critical paradigm adopts a position 'between subjectivism and objectivism' (Sarantakos 1998, p. 40). Essentially, the outcome of scientific research using this approach is to effect change in the conditions of those being studied. As a consequence, the research process involves interaction between the researcher and the minority group being studied. The researcher's values are an important part of the research process as the entire process is about the transformational change of the social setting being studied (Guba & Lincoln 1994, p. 110). As in the interpretive social sciences paradigm, the relationship is a subjective one. Thus, the researcher's empathy with the minority group and the researcher's commitment to changing the social circumstances of those being studied is paramount to achieving the required transformational changes to the minority group being studied. In the end, the findings of the researcher should empower the minority group to effect social change to improve its social circumstances.

3. How will the researcher gather data/information? (Methodological basis)

The critical theory paradigm emphasises the need to get below the surface to the real meaning of social interactions and the power plays that are implicit in social interactions. You will see that a similar emphasis is referred to in the postmodern section of this chapter. To get below the surface, the critical theorist researcher will predominantly use a qualitative methodology. Furthermore, as outlined above, the process is subjective and, as a consequence, the process is also value laden. Methods used by a critical theorist researcher would include, for example, participant observation, in-depth interviewing, focus groups, Delphic panels and appreciative inquiry in order to expose the oppression, subjugation and exploitation of the minority group being studied. These terms are explained in chapter 6.

Consequences of a critical theory paradigm for tourism research

The use of the critical theory paradigm in tourism research means that the interests or needs of minority groups will be identified and data collected in order to open up or improve the provision of tourism opportunities, experiences and services for those minority groups. During the course of data collection, the researcher may experience conflict with those in power positions and their willingness to divulge information or to make changes. Despite the possibility of some conflict from power groups, the researcher will be concerned with making significant changes for the minority group. Consequently, the researcher has to help challenge the taken-for-granted assumptions and values held by those in power with regard to the minority group and its access or lack of access to travel experiences, opportunities and services. Minority groups that a critical theorist researcher may undertake tourism research for include single parents, sole carers, people with physical disabilities, people with intellectual disabilities, people from lower socioeconomic backgrounds, senior citizens, gays, lesbians, women, residents in host communities, employees in developing nations, and governments in developing nations or small island states.

The following Industry Insight highlights the use of the critical theory paradigm in tourism research.

INDUSTRY INSIGHT

Hanson (1997) has undertaken a study of 300 heterosexual women sex workers. The women were aged between 25 and 45 and lived in New Zealand. Using in-depth interviews and observations collected during visits to sex work locations, Hanson was able to determine the contribution these women were making to tourism, particularly, sex tourism. She also was able to illuminate the women's marginalisation as well as the non-recognition of the industry within the wider economy, government and tourism industry.

Source: *Hanson (1997)*

Some potential areas of tourism research informed by a critical theory paradigm

Remember that the critical theorist is trying to get below the surface and understand the social setting from the position of a person in the minority group being studied, as opposed to those in power. Furthermore, the researcher will use methods associated with a qualitative methodology to gather the data to effect social change. One example of potential research is outlined below, followed by some suggestions for other possible tourism research topics.

The first example is a generic one — the study of a host community in a developing nation experiencing negative impacts from tourism as a result of several multinational corporations' involvement in tourism enterprises in the host community. Essentially, the host community may feel as if it is being treated as a 'plantation economy' — that is, an economy in which the 'spoils' of tourism are not being enjoyed by the host community but rather by the multinational corporations, which are not based in the host nation. Once the specific host community in a developing nation has been chosen (sometimes the nation may be selected because of the researcher's interests or contacts or because of an intermediary), the researcher will enter the host community. The research process, however, will take time because the researcher has to become immersed in the host community and gain acceptance within the community. The use of a community member as a mediator may prove necessary. Through participant observation and in-depth interviewing the researcher will be able to determine the negative impacts of the involvement of the multinational corporations in tourism enterprises upon the host community. The findings from the research would then be used to effect transformational changes to current practices in relation to the host community and tourism. Basically, the researcher in such a study would be required to champion the cause of the host community to facilitate change and empower the host community. Note that the findings would be particular to the location being studied and would not be considered as being representative of other locations. Other similar studies would need to be undertaken to establish any comparative links.

Some other possible examples of critical theory research applied to tourism include studies of:

- host–guest interactions, particularly where the hosts are the minority and are being overwhelmed by tourism numbers so that they feel their location is becoming a tourism precinct rather than an integrated community
- the negative social impacts of tourism on the host community, particularly where the negative impacts are being overlooked by those in positions of power such as governments and tourism developers and operators
- the relationship between those in power, such as tourism developers and/or governments, and those without power, such as local business operators or resident groups, particularly in regard to tourism planning and development
- indigenous hospitality workers and their working conditions in developing nations
- the exploitation of children in sex tourism
- social pathologies resulting from tourism developments upon minority groups such as the unemployed, women or children
- the impacts of vertical integration by overseas companies within host nations and their impacts on indigenous companies
- the impacts of mega-events such as the Olympic Games on various sectors within the host community and their living conditions.

To summarise, the critical theory paradigm is concerned with undertaking research that will effect transformational change for minority groups who, without the researcher and the knowledge generated by the research, would be unable to change the practices of those in power. Like the interpretative social sciences paradigm, the critical theory paradigm primarily uses a qualitative methodology, the relationship between the researcher and the minority group(s) being studied is subjective and knowledge is generated from the real world. However, the critical theory paradigm differs from the interpretive social sciences paradigm as the former does not see all 'realities' as equal. Instead, the critical theory paradigm focuses on oppressed, subjugated or exploited groups and works to champion their cause.

■ *2.2.4* **Feminist perspectives** *paradigm*

Sarantakos (1998) groups feminist perspectives within the critical theory paradigm. Neuman (2000), on the other hand, identifies both 'feminist' and postmodern approaches as emergent approaches and discusses them separately from positivism, interpretive social sciences and critical theory paradigms. This textbook follows Neuman's treatment of 'feminism' and postmodernism as emergent approaches/paradigms and discusses them as separate 'paradigms'. In adopting this approach, it is acknowledged that there are similarities between the interpretive and critical theory approach and some of the tenants of 'feminist research'. The term 'feminist research' is used generically here (Hirsch & Fox Keller 1990, p. 2) as there are 'multiple feminist perspectives' (Reinharz 1992, p. 241), four of which will be discussed in the following section.

The similarities between the interpretive social sciences and critical theory paradigms and the feminist perspectives paradigm are particularly associated with the sharing of knowledge and experiences between social actors and researchers (that is, the epistemological basis of the paradigms). Moreover, similarities between the paradigms' ontological and methodological viewpoints occur when the:

> feminist critique of conventional social sciences methods intersects with the Marxist and interpretive criticisms at the points where their methodologies reflect women's experience. The idea of grounding inquiry in concrete experience rather than in abstract categories is reflected in women's historical identification with the concrete, everyday life of people and their survival needs (Westkott 1990, p. 62).

1. How is the world perceived? (Ontological basis)

There are basically four feminist perspectives: the radical feminist perspective, the Marxist and socialist perspective, the liberal feminist perspective and the postmodern perspective. Each has its own specific view of the world.

- The radical feminist perspective views society as patriarchal. Men occupy the ruling class positions and women the subject class positions. These positions are reified through the institution of the family, an institution that exploits women through their provision of free labour in the domestic domain, such as home and child care. This exploitation is variously attributed to biological or cultural circumstances.
- Marxist and socialist feminist perspectives are based on the work of Engels and Marx. Engels (1972) suggested that the subordination of women was a result of historical circumstances that were related to material (private property) and economic reasons. This differs from the view expressed by Marx who, according to Barrett (1988, p. 189), considered that the differences between women and men were biologically based and that the family unit was a 'natural' unit. Engels accounted for the inequality of family units based on the ownership of private property.

- The liberal feminist perspective attributes the oppression of women to the culture and attitudes of individuals and not to the structures and institutions of society (Haralambos & Holborn 1991, p. 536). Liberal feminists purport that, through education, women should be able to achieve equality of the sexes as a result of partnership in the means of production and coequality in legislative and statutory matters (Taylor Mill 1970, p. 95).
- '[P]ostmodern feminists similarly attempt to criticize the dominant order, particularly its patriarchal aspects, and to valorize the feminine, woman, the Other' (Tong 1989, p. 223). However, in formulating and expressing their criticisms, postmodern feminists are constrained by the phallologo-centric nature of text/language itself (Tong 1989, pp. 217, 223). The phallologocentric nature of text/language refers to the fact that language is masculinist in nature and creation.

There are some similarities between each of the feminist perspectives, such as:

- the view that the world is mediated by gendered constructions and these constructions have served to subjugate women and position them in the role of 'other'
- the dominant hegemony is patriarchy and women have been rendered invisible in the social construction of reality, primarily due to their association with the domestic sphere rather than the public sphere
- power relations between men and women are subsequently unequal and as a result women are oppressed by men.

Another principle reflected in feminist thought is that 'all scientific knowledge is always, in every respect, socially situated' (Harding 1991, p. 11). Haraway (1988) describes this as 'situated knowledges' to reiterate the nature of multiple realities existing within the one social setting. Thus, the theories developed from feminist perspectives are reflexive — that is, their meanings are reflections of their social constructions (Sarantakos 1998, p. 51). The similarity with the ontological view of the interpretive social sciences is also therefore evident.

2. What is the relationship between the researcher and the subjects or objects of research? (Epistemological basis)

The researcher and the women being studied are subjects together, jointly generating knowledge. This is sometimes referred to as the researcher and women participants being co-researchers. Thus, the relationship, as in the interpretive social sciences and critical theory paradigms, is subjective in nature. The relationship also exhibits reciprocity, in that there is mutual sharing of experiences between the researcher and the women being studied.

3. How will the researcher gather data/information? (Methodological basis)

The principles of feminist methodology listed below are based on those promulgated by Cook and Fonow (1990, pp. 72–80):

- acknowledgment of 'the pervasive influence of gender' by (1) correcting the silencing of women's voices by analysing women's experiences, (2) recognising the social knowledge has been primarily framed by men

about men and (3) locating the researcher whose gender influences the 'research act'
- a 'focus on consciousness-raising' of the researcher and the research subjects as well as use of consciousness-raising techniques in the research process
- a 'rejection of the subject/object separation' in the research act (see also Harding 1991, pp. 138–63; Westkott 1990, pp. 60–1)
- 'examination of ethical concerns' (Cook & Fonow 1990, pp. 72–80)
- 'emphasis on empowerment and transformation' (Cook & Fonow 1990, pp. 72–80).

Again, as in the interpretive social sciences and critical theory paradigms, there is a predilection to qualitative research methods.

The following Industry Insight highlights a tourism research project that used a feminist perspectives paradigm.

INDUSTRY INSIGHT

In 1998 and 1999, a study of farm tourism operations in Central Queensland was conducted. The study was informed by the Marxist and socialist perspective and utilised a qualitative methodology and the following methods: participant observation, semi-structured interviews and documentary analysis.

The study found that:
- farm tourism impacts on women's workloads, farm-family interactions, farm operations, and farm financial resource allocations and reallocations
- in moving outside their more traditionally identified 'domestic' spheres of work, farm women still meet with resistance from the dominant patriarchal hegemony
- women's experiences in farm tourism in Central Queensland have similarity with women engaged in tourism work on a global level. Their work is essentially rooted in the domestic sphere and access to more public positions is either mediated or denied by men.

Source: *Jennings & Stehlik (1999)*

Consequences of a feminist perspectives paradigm for tourism research

The use of a feminist perspectives paradigm will challenge the dominant patriarchal hegemony that pervades tourism research. Until recently, most studies have been androcentric in nature and have not taken into account the gender bias prevalent in most tourism research. Women's roles or experiences in tourism in the main have been understudied, and they have been generally rendered 'invisible' (Cook & Fonow 1990). The use of a feminist perspectives paradigm will start to redress this situation and provide a balanced gender perspective to knowledge construction in tourism.

Some potential areas for tourism research using a feminist perspectives paradigm

One such example involves the study of business women's travel experiences. In order to understand business women's travel experiences, a research project could be developed that would enable the researcher to engage in participant observation of travel as a business woman as well as to conduct focus groups and in-depth interviews with business women.

Some other possible areas of tourism research using a feminist paradigm include:

* barriers to women's participation in the tourism system
* women's participation rates in high-level management positions in tourism and hospitality organisations
* an investigation into women's occupational levels in the tourism and hospitality industries
* opportunities for women in developing countries to obtain overseas education scholarships or support for tourism training
* policies regarding women and tourism.

To summarise, the feminist perspectives paradigm involves the world view that women are the subject class and men the ruling class, and that subsequently women have been oppressed and subjugated. There are four major feminist perspectives: radical feminism, Marxist and socialist feminism, liberal feminism and postmodern feminism. The relationship between feminist researchers and the women they are studying is subjective and based on reciprocity. The methodology aims to correct the silencing of women's voices, and emphasises consciousness-raising, empowerment and transformation (Cook & Fonow 1990). The methods used are drawn from a qualitative methodological framework.

■ 2.2.5 Postmodern *paradigm*

Basically, postmodernism is the counterpoint to modernism. Modernism is associated with the advent of industrialisation, capitalism, state government, urbanisation and knowledge growth (Punch 1998, p. 144). In regard to knowledge and the Western ontological view of the world, modernism:

* asserts truth as immutable facts
* valorises progress
* expresses humanist tendencies
* is based on a strong reliance on science and knowledge (Neuman 2000, p. 83).

On the other hand, postmodernism:

* asserts that there is no one truth that describes social phenomena; all phenomena are different
* views the world as chaotic, one without patterns and predicability, without linkages to the past or to the future.

Consequently, postmodernists question the veracity of immutable truths expressed by modernists. In particular:

> The core of postmodernism is the doubt that any method or theory, discourses or genre, tradition or novelty, has a universal and general claim as the 'right' or the privileged form of authoritative knowledge. Postmodernism suspects all truth claims of masking and serving particular interests in local, cultural, and political struggles. But postmodernism does not automatically reject conventional methods of knowing and telling as false or archaic. Rather, it opens those standard methods to inquiry and introduces new methods, which are also, then, subject to critique.
>
> The postmodernist context of doubt distrusts all methods equally. No method has a privileged status (Richardson 1994, pp. 517–18).

Therefore, as was the case of the feminist perspectives paradigm, you need to be aware that in using the term a postmodern paradigm, the term is used generically. It is generically applied because as postmodern positions assert, there is no one truth and no one definition of postmodernism. Instead, there is a 'plurality of different postmodern theories and positions' (Kellner 1990, p. 257). This is also intimated in Richardson's quote and in the fact that one of the feminist perspectives discussed above is called post-modern feminism, which indicates it is one of a number of postmodern viewpoints as well as one of a number of feminist perspectives.

1. How is the world perceived? (Ontological basis)

Postmodernists perceive that there is no one truth but multiple interpretations of reality. In their opinion, grand theories can no longer be promulgated as the world is in a constant state of change and differentiation. The rapid change the world is experiencing is being facilitated by the processes of 'monocentric organization-disorganization, hyperdifferentation-dedifferentiation, hyper-rationalization and hypercommodification' (Crook, Pakulski & Waters 1992, p. 220). Furthermore, as Urry (1990, p. 85) notes, the postmodern world is one in which reality ('the referents of signification') is being replaced by 'signs or representations'. He further says, '[e]verything is a copy, or a text upon a text, where what is fake seems more real than the real' (Urry 1990, p. 85).

2. What is the relationship between the researcher and the subjects or objects of research? (Epistemological basis)

The postmodernist perspective is extremely subjective and postmodernists acknowledge their subjectivity in the course of conducting and writing up 'research outputs'. The 'researcher' cannot be withdrawn from the research context or site. The researcher is also an actor in the research process, as indicated in the quote by Richardson above. As such, the researcher describes their experience and the resultant 'knowledge' as but one view of the social world. The research findings can be presented in a variety of genres apart from scientific research reports or scientific articles. Genres such as novels, films and dramatic representations may be used, and this is another aspect of postmodernism — it breaks down boundaries between disciplinary areas and investigations (Richardson, 1994, p. 517).

3. How will the researcher gather data/information? (Methodological basis)

> Postmodern approaches lend themselves to methodologies and research techniques that allow us to discern how definitions of truth and reality are continually being revised through the richness of context. For many postmodernists ... this translates into research methods which focus on talk and text as sources of 'data' ... The research act itself is seen as socially constructed and key concerns are the issue of inter-subjectivity and reflexivity (Symon & Cassell 1998, pp. 2–3).

The researcher gathers information by questioning and, as Richardson noted, the researcher questions the methods and tries to design new ways to gain knowledge. The postmodernist deconstructs (breaks down) the social phenomenon or object of inquiry to determine its core essence. Several researchers may obtain different end points. All are equally valid within a postmodern paradigm. Furthermore, postmodernists work with descriptions rather than abstractions (Neuman 2000, p. 84).

Some of the language used in postmodern research includes subjectivity, discourses, discourse analysis, reflexivity, subject and self, and deconstruction (Richardson 1994). These terms are explained in chapters 3, 5 and 6.

Consequences of a postmodern paradigm for tourism research

If we reconsider Richardson's quote above, then the postmodern paradigm enables researchers to investigate tourism phenomena by questioning methods, theories, discourses, genres and facts in regard to whose interests are being served within local, cultural and political conflicts. If we adopt a poststructuralist approach that focuses on 'language, subjectivity, social organization, and power' (Richardson 1994, p. 518), postmodernism enables us to particularly investigate the language we use to describe phenomena. For as Richardson notes, '[l]anguage does not "reflect" social reality, but produces meaning, [and thereby] creates social reality'(1994, p. 518).

Essentially, a postmodern paradigm encourages tourism researchers to question tourism reality and to realise that there is a variety of explanations rather than just one truth or 'grand theory'. A postmodern paradigm enables us to move beyond and below the surface meanings of language and tourism phenomena. By applying the ontological, epistemological and methodological premises of postmodernism, we are able to investigate postmodern tourism phenomena such as the rise in popularity of lifestyle packages, the 'McDonaldisation' of tourism experiences, the globalisation of tourism services and products, issues of authenticity, the commodification of culture, post or mass tourism, and virtual reality tourism (see, for example, the Industry Insight opposite).

Postmodernism also allows researchers to be more creative in their reporting of research beyond the standard use of scientific reports and journal articles, narratives and documentaries, and to clearly identify the author as 'I' within 'reports'. Such subjectivity of the researcher is important in order for audiences to understand the researcher's description of the tourism phenomenon being deconstructed and presented.

INDUSTRY INSIGHT

Fiefer's (1985) work, *Going Places*, identifies three features of the postmodern tourist. According to Fiefer, the postmodern tourist:

- can enjoy tourist experiences without leaving home via simulations, such as videos or television programs
- desires change and choice in tourist experiences to prevent boredom setting in
- is aware that tourism experiences are inauthentic or contrived and that the overall experience is only a 'game' or 'games' with many textual interpretations.

Source: *Fiefer (1985)*

Some potential areas of tourism research informed by a postmodern paradigm

Urry's book *The Tourist Gaze* (1990) is an example of postmodern 'research' into tourism. The book describes the attributes of postmodern tourism and the sources of its development from a modern world. Eco's *Travels in Hyper-Reality* (1986) is another example. Bearing in mind that Ryan (1997, p. 18) states that postmodern texts 'deconstruct the grand design of systems', other possible 'research' areas include:

- the 'McDonaldisation' of tourist experiences
- the globalisation of tourism
- virtual tourism
- the examination and description of 'authentic travel experiences', especially given that Baudrillard (1983, p. 155) notes that '[w]e are presently living with a minimum of real sociality and a maximum of simulation'.

To summarise, the postmodern paradigm has no parallels with positivism, the interpretive social sciences and critical theory paradigms or radical, Marxist/socialist or liberal feminism. It does, however, have some synergies with the postmodern feminist perspective. Essentially, postmodernism rejects 'claims of totality, certainty, and methodological orthodoxy' (Lather 1990, p. 330).

■ *2.2.6* **Chaos theory** *paradigm*

The conceptualisation of chaos theory is attributed to Edward Lorenz. Lorenz was a meteorologist who, when trying to repeat a weather pattern simulation in 1961, discovered that changing the number of decimal points in an equation that would generate the simulation altered the results of the sequences or patterns. His discovery is known as the 'butterfly effect', which can be explained as follows:

> the flapping of a single butterfly's wing today produces a tiny change in the state of the atmosphere. Over a period of time, what the atmosphere actually does diverges from what it would have done. So, in a month's time, a tornado that would have devastated the Indonesian coast doesn't happen. Or maybe one that wasn't going to happen, does (Stewart n.d., p. 141).

Chaos theory can also be classified as an emergent paradigm (like feminist perspectives and postmodernism), particularly within tourism inquiry. However, chaos theory is very quickly being challenged by complexity theory. Both chaos theory and complexity theory are derived from work in the physical sciences, mathematics and artificial intelligence. The ramifications of both theories challenge the assumptions inherent in the paradigms discussed above for explaining the world — that is, the nature of reality or the operation of the world. While chaos theory tries to describe the world using non-linear dynamics, complexity theory suggests the world is akin to 'a model of complex systems that go through a rapid transition from chaos to order by self-organising' (Rubinstein & Firstenberg 1999, p. 34). What specifically is the difference between chaos theory and complexity theory?

> The simple answer is that chaos deals with situations such as turbulence … that rapidly become highly disorganised and unmanageable. On the other hand, complexity deals with systems composed of many interacting agents. While complex systems may be hard to predict, they may also have a good deal of structure and permit improvement by thoughtful intervention (Axelrod & Cohen 1999, p. xv).

As researchers, you need to be aware that the literature relating to chaos theory and complexity theory is more extensive in the natural sciences and artificial intelligence areas than within the social sciences. Both chaos theory and complexity theory are applied using metaphoric dimensions within the social science areas.

Returning to chaos theory itself, this paradigm is the complete antithesis to positivist viewpoints. You will recall that positivism purports that the world is governed by laws and causal relationships. As a consequence, the world has a sense of predicability about it. For example, if it has been proven that when 'a' is added to 'b' then 'c' will occur, then it is assumed that in every instance, when 'a' is added to 'b' then 'c' will occur and this becomes an immutable fact. Any minor deviations from the established 'law' or 'fact' or 'theory' are deemed to be irregularities, are not considered as important and are subsequently ignored by positivist researchers. Chaos theory researchers, on the other hand, see that any minor changes in a system are important. They are important because it is perceived that these minor changes can have significant impacts as they aggregate and amplify over time. The difference between the two paradigms lies in the fact that in a positivist paradigm, stable linear relationships are observed and explained, whereas the chaos theory paradigm purports that systems are unstable and non-linear — that is, they are observed as dynamic. A frequently used definition of chaos theory is 'the qualitative study of unstable aperiodic behavior in deterministic nonlinear dynamical systems' (Donahue 1999, p. 1).

1. How is the world perceived? (Ontological basis)

The world is made up of unstable, non-linear dynamic, ever-changing systems rather than stable (static) linear systems. The metaphor of chaos/disorder, unpredictability and turbulence is applied to explain the social world based on the metaphoric use of 'chaos' (see the Industry Insight on page 54). The world is unpredictable and cannot be ordered; small events can make significant unexpected impacts.

2. What is the relationship between the researcher and the subjects or objects of research? (Epistemological basis)

The relationship is similar to the relationship between the researcher and the subjects or objects in the positivist paradigm. The relationship is still based on scientific experiments and mathematical equations as the keystone to scientific inquiry, but chaos theory uses fractal geometry that focuses on non-linear, non-integral systems and descriptive algorithms (Donahue 1999, p. 4), rather than Euclidean geometry and its focus on linear, integral systems. The researcher, however, remains objective and value free.

In the social sciences areas, chaos theory challenges the epistemological position of inquiry, especially when using a qualitative methodology. The researcher may change the setting altogether — remember small events can have significant impacts. The nature of inquiry using chaos theory is dynamic — it is 'like walking through a maze whose walls rearrange themselves with every step you take' (Gleik, in Patton 1990, p. 82). Researchers need to spend time in the field and ensure that the disorder experienced in the field is not forced into patterns or explanations (Patton 1990, p. 83).

3. How will the researcher gather data/information? (Methodological basis)

The researcher will use open systems and descriptive algorithms to explain the world that is perceived as dynamic and ever changing. Within the social sciences, '[n]onlinear dynamics raise questions about how we bring order to what we observe ... [chaos theory offers] a new set of metaphors for thinking about what we observe, how we observe, and what we know as a result of our observations. Chaos theory challenges our need for order and prediction, even as it offers new ways to fulfill those needs. While much chaos research is highly mathematical, making sense of results seems to depend heavily on metaphors' (Patton 1990, p. 82).

Furthermore, within the social sciences, researchers will gather data by learning to observe, describe and value chaos (Patton 1990, p. 83) rather than forcing the data into ordered and patterned explanations.

Consequences of chaos theory for tourism research

Chaos theory enables the tourism system to be analysed as a dynamic system rather than a steady state or predictable system. It is particularly applicable to the management and planning of tourism, and the impacts of tourism, especially given the 'butterfly effect' discovered by Lorenz.

INDUSTRY INSIGHT

Russell and Faulkner investigated the use of chaos theory to explain the development of tourism on the Gold Coast. They charted the historical impacts of some individual entrepreneurs and their actions in setting off changes to the direction of tourism development on the Gold Coast.

Source: *Russell & Faulkner (1998)*

Some potential areas of tourism research informed by the chaos theory paradigm

The use of chaos theory in tourism research has tended to focus on tourism development or management. McKercher (1999) advocates that the use of chaos theory is more applicable to the understanding of the tourism system than a positivist approach. According to McKercher, a positivist approach that is closed and ordered does not tend to explain the functioning of the tourism system. He sees the tourism system as being fluid and ever changing and operating in an open system rather than a closed system, as is the case with a positivist paradigm.

Researchers intent on using the chaos theory paradigm need to understand the paradigm and its associated implications for research. In the past, researchers and students have appropriated the vocabulary for use in a metaphorical sense, including the term 'chaos'. It is important to understand the difference between the metaphorical and technical meanings associated with the terms and vocabulary used in chaos theory (Symptoms of Chaos, n.d.). Furthermore, chaos theory is being challenged by complexity theory and researchers need to address this challenge when outlining their preference of chaos theory over complexity theory as a paradigm to inform tourism research.

CHOOSING THE 'RIGHT' PARADIGM

In the main, tourism research has been predicated to a positivist paradigm. Other paradigms are beginning to be applied, but the driving force behind the paradigm that informs any research process is usually dependent on the background and training of the researcher.

In the past, the emphasis has been on the quantitative methodology, which is part of the positivist paradigm. It is only more recently, in the quest for knowledge as to 'why' tourism phenomena are occurring, that a qualitative methodological paradigm has been sought to get at the deeper meanings people attribute to tourism and tourism experiences, events and phenomena.

Obviously, there are advantages and disadvantages associated with each of the paradigms, but the paradigm adopted should take into account the nature of the tourism system that is being studied. For example, if a government wants to know what will happen when a user-pays system is implemented in a tourism area, then a positivist paradigm could be applied in order to gain an understanding of the resultant drop-off in visitation levels and the subsequent reduction in revenue. Or, if a government wants to understand the social impacts of a mega-event on the lifestyles of local residents, then an interpretive social sciences paradigm should be applied. On the other hand, if people with a disability want to achieve greater access to modes of travel, then a critical theory paradigm is more appropriate. An understanding of women's travel and tourism experiences behoves the use of a feminist perspectives paradigm. Given the degree of radical change that is associated with the process of postmodernisation and, for example, consumerism of packaged 'lifestyles' in which tourism plays a role by offering diverse lifestyle packages, then a postmodern paradigm would be more appropriate for the research focus. Finally, to understand the effects of small changes and the possible effects when amplified over time, the chaos theory paradigm might be considered.

Alternatively, one topic could be investigated using a variety of paradigms. For example, residents' attitudes to increasing tourist numbers could be investigated using the following paradigms:
* positivism
* the interpretive social sciences
* critical theory
* feminist perspectives paradigm.

Table 2.2 provides an overview of each of the paradigms presented in this chapter. First, the ontology, epistemology and methodology of each paradigm are outlined. Then, a hypothetical example is provided to demonstrate the application of each paradigm in relation to a single research focus. This enables you to see how a study can be considered using different paradigms to study the same thing.

■ **Table 2.2** *An overview of the paradigms that inform tourism research*

	POSITIVISM	INTERPRETIVE SOCIAL SCIENCES	CRITICAL THEORY	FEMINIST PERSPECTIVES	POST-MODERNISM	CHAOS THEORY
Ontology	Universal truths and laws	Multiple realities	Complex world organised by overt and hidden powers	World mediated by gendered constructions; men have power	World is complex and constantly changing; infinite interpretations	World is unstable, non-linear and dynamic
Epistemology	Objective	Subjective	Between objective and subjective	Subjective	Subjective	Objective
Methodology	Quantitative	Qualitative	Predominantly qualitative	Predominantly qualitative	Questioning and deconstruction, qualitative forms	Quantitative and qualitative if used metaphorically
Hypothetical example drawn from tourism: new management has taken over the running of the regional tourism association and wants to develop a database of visitation patterns.	The researcher might gather statistical data on visitation patterns from all available sources, such as accommodation venues, tourist attractions and transportation networks, and collate this into a database. The database would establish the factual (objective) arrangements of visitor patterns based on available statistics.	The researcher might decide to interview key people, such as tourism operators, local residents and local government personnel in the region, to ascertain their perceptions of visitor patterns over the time period being studied. This would develop knowledge of visitor patterns based on the subjective viewpoints of those who are interviewed.	The researcher might choose to investigate the visitor patterns of minority groups such as the aged, the disabled or lower socioeconomic groups.	The researcher might choose to focus on the visitation patterns of single mothers, business women, retired women or women with disabilities, or the role of women in decision making regarding visitation to the region.	The researcher might choose to examine visitation patterns by analysing the types of packages offered (i.e. the variety of tourist experiences that are commodified) through an investigation of promotional materials.	The researcher might focus on the development of descriptive algorithms to demonstrate what past changes in visitation patterns will mean for the future by factoring them in and focusing on the changes rather than disregarding them as anomalies.

Major theoretical paradigms that inform tourism research

There are six theoretical paradigms that a researcher can use when undertaking tourism research: a positivist approach, an interpretive social sciences approach, a critical theory approach, a feminist perspectives, a postmodern approach and a chaos theory orientation.

Positivism is grounded in the physical sciences. This paradigm sees the natural and social world as governed by laws that make the real world a closed system, which is stable and patterned so behaviour and events may be predicted. Scientific inquiry is objective and value neutral and uses a quantitative methodology.

An interpretive social sciences paradigm is grounded in the social world of the social actors and their everyday lives. This paradigm perceives that social actors are in control of their actions rather than pursuing their lives regulated by rules and actions without any agency of their own. Scientific inquiry in this paradigm is subjective and value laden. Researchers primarily use a qualitative methodology.

Critical theory paradigm uses a mid-point between subjectivism and objectivism and sees the social world as constrained by rules. However, these rules are able to be changed by actors and their actions. Scientific inquiry in this paradigm should elicit transformational change and the purpose of the research is to change the social circumstances of those being studied. Primarily, qualitative research methodology is applied.

The feminist perspectives paradigm aims to make visible the real world experience of women and to break the dominant hegemony that is patriarchal in nature. This paradigm draws on interpretive, critical and postmodern paradigms. Some question whether this is a paradigm or a perspective. Essentially, a qualitative methodology is adopted and the researcher and the researched are subjects together.

The postmodern paradigm debunks grand theory, sees the world as constructed of multiple realities and perceives that no one perspective has priority over another. The aim of the postmodern paradigm is to deconstruct the surface features of phenomena and get to the underlying core reality. A variety of means are used including qualitative methodology.

The chaos theory paradigm sees the world as made up of open, dynamic, ever-changing systems that are non-linear in nature. Scientific inquiry is based on descriptions of algorithms, and social sciences research uses chaos theory as a metaphor. Small changes can result in large-scale outcomes. Chaos theory is being challenged by complexity theory as way of explaining the world.

The difference between the theoretical paradigms

Each of the paradigms has its particular ontological, epistemological and methodological viewpoints. Positivism is rooted in the physical sciences and uses objective and value-free scientific procedures. Similarly, chaos theory has a mathematical orientation. However, the view of the system as closed as in a positivist paradigm is not supported in the chaos theory paradigm, which asserts that systems are open and dynamic. Chaos theory uses descriptive algorithms to demonstrate iterative changes within systems. The interpretive, critical, feminist and postmodern paradigms are all subjective; however, their ontological views differ.

The consequences of the difference between the theoretical paradigms for the conduct of tourism research

Each of the paradigms will determine the way the researcher will consider a research topic and design the methods for data collection. In the preparation of the research process, the researcher will demonstrate their understanding of the paradigms and the need for the research purpose, methodology and methods of data collection to be complementary.

Questions

2.1 In your own words, what is a paradigm and how would you explain the terms ontology, epistemology and methodology?

2.2 Of the six paradigms outlined in this chapter, which most closely reflects your view of the world (ontology), your relationship between the knower and the known (epistemology) and your methodology?

2.3 Why is it important to have an understanding of the various paradigms for a scientific inquiry?

2.4 For the six theoretical paradigms outlined in this chapter, design possible research questions that parallel each of the ontological, epistemological and methodological viewpoints consistent with each paradigm. Be prepared to discuss your matching of questions and paradigms in class.

2.5 In your opinion, is one paradigm's approach better than the others? Justify your opinion.

2.6 Why is it necessary for a researcher to ensure that research projects are informed by the 'right' theoretical paradigm?

RESEARCH PROJECT

By now, you should have discussed with your tutor or lecturer a possible research project. Discuss the paradigm that you believe is underpinning your research topic with your peers and seek feedback from your tutor to verify that you have identified the appropriate paradigm for your project.

REFERENCES

Abercrombie, N., Hill, S. & Turner, B. S. 1988. *The Penguin Dictionary of Sociology.* Second Edition. Harmondsworth: Penguin Books.

Australian Tourist Commission. 2000. *Community Attitudes to International Tourism.* http://www.atc.net.au/intell/market/survey.htm.

Axelrod, Robert & Cohen, Michael D. 1999. *Harnessing Complexity: Organizational Implications of a Scientific Frontier.* New York: The Free Press.

Barrett, Michéle. 1988. *Women's Oppression Today: The Marxist/Feminist Encounter.* Revised Edition. London: Verso.

Baudrillard, Jean. 1983. *Seduction.* Translated by Brian Singer. New York: St Martins Press.

Blumer, Herbert. 1962. 'Society as Symbolic Interaction'. In Rose, A. (Ed.) *Human Behaviour and Social Processes: An Interactionist Approach.* Boston, MA: Houghton Mifflin.

Cook, Judith A. & Fonow, Mary Margaret. 1990. 'Knowledge and Women's Interests'. In McCarl Nielsen, Joyce (Ed.) *Feminist Research Methods, Exemplary Readings in the Social Sciences.* Boulder, CO: Westview Press.

Crook, Stephen, Pakulski, Jan & Waters, Malcolm. 1992. *Postmodernization: Change in Advanced Society.* London: Sage.

Denzin, Norman K. & Lincoln, Yvonna S. 1994. 'Introduction: Entering the Field Of Qualitative Research'. In *Handbook of Qualitative Research.* Thousand Oaks: Sage, pp. 1–17.

Donahue, Manus J. 1999. Chaos and Fractal Phenomena. http://www.iglobal.net/pub/camelot/chaos/chaos.htm.

Eco, Umberto. 1986. *Travels in Hyper-Reality.* London: Picador.

Engels, Friedrich. 1972. *The Origin of the Family, Private Property and the State.* London: Lawrence & Wishart.

Feifer, M. 1985. *Going Places.* London: Macmillan.

Fetterman, David. M. 1989. *Ethnography, Step By Step.* Applied Social Research Methods Series, Volume 17. Newbury Park: Sage.

Guba, Egon G. 1990. *The Paradigm Dialog.* Newbury Park: Sage, pp. 17–27.

Guba, E. G. & Lincoln, Yvonna, S. 1994. 'Competing Paradigms in Qualitative Research'. In Denzin, Norman K. & Lincoln, Yvonna S. *Handbook of Qualitative Research.* Thousand Oaks: Sage, pp. 105–17.

Hanson, Jody. 1997. 'Sex Tourism as Work in New Zealand: A Discussion with Kiwi Prostitutes'. In Oppermann, Martin. *Pacific Rim Tourism.* Oxford: CAB International.

Haralambos, Michael & Holborn, Martin. 1991. *Sociology, Themes and Perspectives.* Third Edition. London: Collins Educational.

Haraway, Donna. 1988. 'Situated Knowledges: The Science Question in Feminism and the Privilege of Partial Perspective'. *Feminist Studies,* vol. 14, p. 3.

Harding, Sandra. 1991. *Whose Science? Whose Knowledge?* Milton Keynes: Open University Press.

Hirsch, Marianne & Keller, Evelyn Fox (Eds) 1990. 'Introduction: 4 January 1990'. In *Conflicts in Feminism*. New York: Routledge.

Jennings, Gayle & Stehlik, Daniela. 1999. The Innovators are Women: The Development of Farm Tourism in Central Queensland, Australia. 1999 International Society of Travel and Tourism Educators Annual Conference, Vancouver, 4–7 November.

Kellner, Douglas. 1990. 'The Postmodern Turn: Positions, Problems, and Prospects'. In Ritzer, George (Ed.) *Frontiers of Social Theory: The New Syntheses*. New York: Columbia University Press, pp. 255–86.

Lather, Patti A. 1990. 'Reinscribing Otherwise: The Play of Values in the Practices of the Human Sciences'. In Guba, Egon G. (Ed.) *The Paradigm Dialog*. Thousand Oaks: Sage, pp. 315–32.

McKercher, Bob. 1999. 'A Chaos Approach to Tourism'. *Tourism Management*, vol. 20, no. 4, pp. 425–34.

Mill, Harriet Taylor. 1970. 'Enfranchisement of Women'. In Mill, John Sturt & Mill, Harriet Taylor. *Essays on Sex Equality*. Chicago: University of Chicago Press, pp. 89–122.

Punch, Keith. 1998. *Introduction to Social Research, Quantitative and Qualitative Approaches*. London: Sage Publications.

Neuman, W. Lawrence. 2000. *Social Research Methods, Qualitative and Quantitative Approaches*. Fourth Edition. Boston: Allyn & Bacon.

Reinharz, Shulamit. 1992. *Feminist Methods in Social Research*. New York: Oxford University Press.

Richardson, Laurel. 1994. 'Writing: A Method of Inquiry'. In Denzin, Norman, K. & Lincoln, Yvonna S. *Handbook of Qualitative Research*. Thousand Oaks: Sage, pp. 516–29.

Rubinstein, Moshe F. & Firstenberg, Iris R. 1999. *The Minding Organization: Bring the Future to the Present and Turn Creative Ideas into Business Solutions*. New York: John Wiley & Sons.

Russell, Roslyn & Faulkner, Bill. 1998. Movers and Shakers: The Chaos Makers of the Gold Coast. Paper presented at the Eighth Australian Tourism and Hospitality Research Conference: Progress in Tourism and Hospitality Research, Gold Coast, Queensland, 11–14 February.

Ryan, Chris. 1997. 'The Chase of a Dream, the End of Play'. In *The Tourist Experience: A New Introduction*. London: Cassell, pp. 1–24.

Sarantakos, Sotirios. 1998. *Social Research*. Second Edition. South Melbourne: Macmillan Education.

Stanley, Liz & Wise, Sue. 1990. 'Method, Methodology and Epistemology in Feminist Research Processes'. In Stanley, L. (Ed.) *Feminist Praxis: Research, Theory and Epistemology in Feminist Sociology*. London: Routledge, pp. 20–60.

Stewart, Ian. n.d. Does God Play Dice? The Mathematics of Chaos, p. 141. Quoted in History of Chaos. http://tqd.advanced.org/3120/text/c-his1.htm.

Symon, Gillian & Cassell, Catherine (Eds) 1998. 'Reflections on the Use of Qualitative Methods'. In *Qualitative Methods and Analysis in Organizational Research: A Practical Guide*. London: Sage, pp. 2–9.

Symptoms of chaos. n.d. http://www.vanderbilt.edu/AnS/psychology/cogsci/chaos/workshop/Symptoms.html.

Tong, Rosemarie. 1989. *Feminist Thought: A Comprehensive Introduction.* London: Routledge.

Urry, J. 1990. *The Tourist Gaze. Leisure and Travel in Contemporary Societies.* London: Sage.

Weber, Max. 1978. In Roth, Guenther & Wittich, Claus (Eds.) *Economy and Society: An Outline of Interpretive Sociology.* Volume 1. Berkeley: University of California Press.

Westerhausen, Klaus. 1999. Western Travellers in Asia: A Mobile Subculture in Search of a Home. Unpublished PhD thesis. Murdoch University.

Westkott, Marcia. 1990. 'Feminist Criticism of the Social Sciences'. In McCarl Nielsen, Joyce. (Ed.) *Feminist Research Methods: Exemplary Readings in the Social Sciences.* Boulder, CO: Westview Press.

FURTHER READING

Caplan, Paula J. & Caplan, Jeremy B. 1999. *Thinking Critically About Research on Sex and Gender.* Second Edition. New York: Longman.

Eichler, Margrit. 1991. *Nonsexist Research Methods: A Practical Guide.* New York: Routledge.

Gleik, James. 1987. *Chaos: Making a New Science.* New York: Penguin.

Kumar, Ranjit. 1996. *Research Methodology: A Step-By-Step Guide for Beginners.* South Melbourne: Addison Wesley Longman.

McCarl Nielsen, Joyce (Ed.) 1990. *Feminist Research Methods: Exemplary Readings in the Social Sciences.* Boulder, CO: Westview Press.

Patton, Michael Q. 1990. *Qualitative Evaluation and Research Methods.* Second Edition. Newbury Park: Sage, pp. 82–4.

Roberts, Helen (Ed.) 1981. *Doing Feminist Research.* London: Routledge.

Seidman, Steven. 1994. *Contested Knowledge: Social Theory in the Postmodern Era.* Oxford: Blackwell.

Stanley, Liz (Ed.) 1990. *Feminist Praxis: Research, Theory and Epistemology in Feminist Sociology.* London: Routledge.

Wearing, Betsy. 1998. *Leisure and Feminist Theory.* London: Sage.

3

Data sources for
tourism research

'While it is the case that the major and sometimes only data collection instrument utilized in naturalistic inquiry is the inquirer him- or herself, the sources that instrument utilizes may be both human and nonhuman. Human sources are tapped by interviews and observations, and by noting nonverbal cues that are transmitted while those interviews or observations are under way. Nonhuman sources include documents and records, as well as the unobtrusive informational residue (conventionally called unobtrusive "measures") left behind by humans in their everyday activities that provides useful insights about them.'

(Lincoln & Guba 1985, pp. 267–8)

LEARNING OBJECTIVES
After studying this chapter, you should be able to:

■ list the possible sources of primary and secondary data for use in tourism research
■ describe the major primary data sources for tourism research
■ discuss the advantages and disadvantages of using primary data sources for the conduct of tourism research
■ describe the major secondary data sources for tourism research
■ discuss the advantages and disadvantages of using secondary data sources for the conduct of tourism research
■ locate key sources of secondary data relevant to Australia
■ outline the process of documentary analysis
■ have a rudimentary understanding of content analysis
■ explain the difference between primary and secondary data sources
■ appreciate the diversity in both primary and secondary data sources.

𝓘NTRODUCTION ······································

Chapter 2 introduced you to the major paradigms that inform tourism research processes: positivism, the interpretive social sciences approach, critical theory orientation, feminist perspectives, postmodernism and chaos theory orientation. The chapter also provided you with examples of possible research projects appropriate for each of the paradigms. You will recall that each of these approaches involved the researcher directly gathering data from the 'subjects' or 'study units' involved in the tourism phenomenon under study. Essentially, all the research projects were based on primary data collection. Primary data collection is the term used to describe any data that are collected by a researcher directly from subjects or study units associated with the tourism phenomenon being researched. This is not the only way to gather data, however, for as the introductory quotes indicate, you can gather data from textual documents, other pre-existing data sources and the data already collected by other researchers. These types of data are called secondary data sources. The term reflects the fact that the data sources are 'second-hand' sources — that is, they have been collected first-hand by another researcher and are being used as 'second-hand' information by a second researcher not associated with the initial study.

This chapter focuses on the various sources of data that are relevant to tourism research. Specifically, the chapter provides you with information regarding primary and secondary data, and the advantages and disadvantages of each. It also provides you with a list of important secondary tourism data sources, as well as describing how to analyse secondary data sources using both quantitative and qualitative methodologies. The analysis of primary data sources using qualitative and quantitative methodological constructs is discussed in chapters 7 and 9, respectively, and so is not addressed in this chapter.

𝓢OURCES OF DATA FOR USE IN TOURISM RESEARCH: AN OVERVIEW ·····

Researchers are able to access two types of data sources: primary and secondary. Primary data sources are those that are collected first-hand by the researcher for use in their research project. Primary data include, for example, responses to questionnaires, interview texts and observations. Secondary data sources are those that have been produced by someone else for primary usage and are then used by another researcher not connected with the first project. Secondary data include, for example, statistical records, government documents, diaries and letters, and research data conducted by other researchers.

■ 3.2.1 Primary data sources *for tourism research*

Each of the paradigms discussed in chapter 2 use primary data for tourism research. The primary data are generated using the appropriate methodological framework and associated methods for data collection and analysis. Within a quantitative methodology, primary data are collected using the methods of scientific experimentation, modelling, mathematical formulae and questionnaires. Within a qualitative methodology, primary data are collected using observation, in-depth interviews, focus groups, the Delphi technique and case studies (these methods are described in detail in chapters 6 and 8). Regardless of the paradigm informing the research process, primary data are always collected first-hand by the researcher for the specific purpose of understanding the tourism phenomenon being studied.

Advantages and disadvantages of using primary data sources

There are various advantages and disadvantages of primary data collection that researchers have to weigh up against the paradigm being used and any external constraints. External constraints that may impact on the research process include time, personnel and finances available to conduct the research.

Advantages

The key advantage of primary data is that the data have been collected for the specific purposes of the researcher's current project. Subsequently, if the relevant scientific guidelines and protocols have been followed correctly, the data will have relevance and recency. Primary data collection also enables the researcher to target the specific population (study units) desired for the study rather than making compromises by widening, narrowing or adjusting the target population or study units as sometimes occurs when using secondary data sources.

The second advantage is that, as the data have been gathered first-hand, the data are unlikely to be confounded by unknown conditions and actions that may bias the data, such as researcher bias. A researcher using a positivist paradigm could choose, for example, to report only the data that support the research hypothesis rather than the data that do not support it. On the other hand, the existence of such bias is a possibility when using secondary data sources, although the 'second-hand' user will probably not be aware of such biasing factors. Consequently, the possibility of bias by other researchers is countered in primary data collection as the 'primary' researcher is responsible for the entire research process, and it is assumed that this researcher is operating within an ethical framework and following the appropriate scientific protocols.

Finally, in working with primary data sources the researcher does not inherit the methodological errors that could exist in some secondary data sources.

The advantages of primary data then are:
- relevance
- recency
- appropriate 'population' studied
- lack of other researcher bias
- lack of inherited methodological errors.

Disadvantages

Primary data collection involving human participants is considered reactive research. The participants in most cases are aware that they are being studied. As a consequence, the participants may change their behaviours, opinions, attitudes or values. When this happens, the data do not reflect the real world or the participants' points of views. As well as being reactive research, primary data collection with human participants is intrusive, as people have to expend time and energy in responding to the researcher's data collection tools. Data collection can also occur at inconvenient times or places for both researcher and participants, especially for tourists and visitors. Research into tourism generally occurs when people are on holidays or travelling. Being asked to participate in a study may be the anathema of the experience tourists and visitors are seeking. Consequently, researchers have to be prepared for people refusing to participate in research studies. On the other hand, people on holidays may be quite happy to participate in research as they have the time and are interested in the topic.

Other disadvantages of primary data collection, whether using human or non-human study units, are related to resource costs. Primary data collection is time-consuming in both data collection and analysis. It is resource-expensive: personnel need to be trained and data collection instruments need to be produced. There could also be associated travel and accommodation costs, telephone, facsimile and Internet costs, as well as laboratory and computer costs.

The disadvantages of primary data collection are then its:

- reactive nature
- obtrusive nature
- time-consuming nature
- resource-expensive nature in regard to personnel, finances, research materials and technical equipment and hardware.

The specific advantages and disadvantages of each of the main methods used by quantitative and qualitative methodologies in tourism research are expanded upon in chapters 6 and 8, respectively.

■ 3.2.2 Secondary data sources *for tourism research*

As noted in the introductory quote by Goeldner, researchers often forget to exhaust all possible secondary data sources before embarking on their own primary data collection and analysis. Secondary data sources can vary in nature from statistical sources to documentary sources. Documentary sources generally may be classified as cultural products or artefacts (Reinharz 1992). Examples of such products and artefacts are diaries, newspapers, magazines, photographs, advertising posters, video clips, films, meeting minutes, visitor record books and souvenirs.

While primary data collection, essentially with human participants, is considered reactive, obtrusive and intrusive, secondary data collection is described as non-reactive, unobtrusive (not noticeable) and non-intrusive. There is no interaction with study participants. There is also no intrusion as the data have already been collected and exist in the diverse repository of our cultural products and documents. Secondary data sources can be used as the basis for an entire research project. When this occurs, the researcher is said to be conducting 'desk research' (Kosters 1994, p. 159).

A useful classification system for cultural documents is provided by Sarantakos (1998, pp. 274–5). As you read through the list, remember that the word 'document' does not simply refer to text-based items — it also describes audiotape recordings, videotape recordings, films and artefacts such as paintings and posters (Jorgensen 1989, pp. 92–3). Sarantakos' list has five components:

- *Public documents* These include statistical documents and reports, for example the World Tourism Organization's inbound and outbound tourism statistical reports (see appendix 1), the Australian Bureau of Statistics' 'Overseas Arrival and Departures' profiles (see tables 3.1 and 3.2 for examples of such statistical data) and government census reports. Public documents also include government reports and documents, for example the 'National Cruise Shipping Strategy' (Commonwealth Department of Tourism 1995a), and newspapers, magazines, journals and other print media, for example the travel section in the *Australian* or the Qantas in-flight magazine, *The Australian Way*. Various literary genres also fall into the realm of public documents, such as travel books (e.g. Eric Newby's stories *The Big Red Train Ride, A Short Ride in the Hindu Kush* and *Round Ireland in Low Gear*, Patsy Adam-Smith's *Footloose in Australia* or Mary Russell's collection of stories about women travellers reported in *The Blessings of a Good Thick Skirt*). Another genre is the travel guide, such as those by Lonely Planet, Periplus Editions, Fromm and the 'Let's Go' series. All these examples are classified as public documents because they are easily accessed in the public domain. However, that does not mean that there is no cost associated with acquiring them — some are free; others are not. Other examples of public documents are shown in tables 3.2 and 3.3.

■ **Table 3.1** *Overseas arrivals and departures, Australia — top 10 source countries, year ending 30 June 1999*

COUNTRY OF BIRTH	1979 RANK ORDER (NO.)	PROPORTION (%)	1989 RANK ORDER (NO.)	PROPORTION (%)	1999 RANK ORDER (NO.)	PROPORTION (%)
United Kingdom	3	9.1	2	13.5	1	13.0
Indonesia	10	1.4	8	3.2	2	7.4
United States of America	2	10.4	3	9.5	3	7.4
New Zealand	1	45.8	1	20.4	4	6.8
Japan	5	4.9	4	8.8	5	6.3
China (excluding Taiwan)	22	0.5	6	3.9	6	5.7
Singapore	12	0.8	9	2.4	7	5.0
Malaysia	4	6.6	5	7.3	8	5.0
India	14	0.8	20	0.9	9	4.7
Hong Kong (SAR of China)	6	1.9	7	3.6	10	4.7
Total	—	82.2	—	73.5	—	66.0

Source: *ABS (1999)*

■ Table 3.2 *Overseas arrivals and departures, Australia —*
top 10 source countries*, main reason for journey, year ending 30 June 1999

	BUSINESS		VISITING FRIENDS, RELATIVES		HOLIDAY		ALL LONG-TERM EMPLOY-MENT		EDUCATION		VISITORS	
COUNTRY OF BIRTH	1979 (%)	1999 (%)	1979 (%)	1999 (%)	1979 (%)	1999 (%)	1979 (%)	1999 (%)	1979 (%)	1999 (%)	1979 (no.)	1999 (no.)
United Kingdom	9.9	15.8	7.5	5.2	12.2	22.7	34.5	37.4	2.5	4.3	3 096	15 577
Indonesia	4.3	1.3	6.2	1.3	0.6	0.6	5.6	2.7	46.5	88.1	484	8 891
United States of America	17.8	33.1	1.2	1.6	1.7	9.0	16.2	25.3	5.1	8.3	3 543	8 881
New Zealand	1.8	9.7	6.0	12.2	14.4	8.3	55.5	48.3	3.5	6.4	15 589	8 139
Japan	31.7	24.5	5.1	2.2	1.1	14.8	8.4	9.5	7.4	30.8	1 657	7 613
China (excluding Taiwan)	11.6	9.6	1.8	9.6	2.4	1.7	30.5	7.1	31.7	60.5	164	6 853
Singapore	5.7	3.6	1.8	0.7	0.0	1.4	13.1	5.4	66.4	80.7	282	6 027
Malaysia	0.4	1.7	0.6	1.2	0.3	1.0	3.5	5.6	88.4	86.0	2 251	5 986
India	5.0	2.8	6.1	2.5	1.8	1.1	18.7	10.2	24.1	76.0	278	5 610
Hong Kong (SAR of China)	0.8	2.0	0.9	0.7	0.3	0.8	1.7	2.5	87.2	90.2	658	5 600
All countries	7.1	11.2	5.7	4.2	9.2	8.5	34.2	17.6	15.5	45.3	34 064	119 892

*Based on 1998–99 ranking.   **Source:** *ABS (1999)*

- *Archival documents* These documents record or provide an historical insight into the tourism phenomenon chosen for study. Archival documents include public records and historical data.
- *Personal documents* These documents are written with specific audiences in mind, including the self. Personal documents contain 'personal' information or details about the author, and examples include diaries, personal letters, personal emails and autobiographies. Access to personal documents may be easy if they are located in the public domain (e.g. published autobiographies), or they may be inaccessible or regulated by a 'gatekeeper' (someone who has control over the documents and their accessibility). As with public documents, personal documents may be acquired free of charge or there may be some administrative fee or cost associated with their acquisition.
- *Administrative documents* These documents are generated in the business environment and are associated with the public and private sectors as well as the non-profit sector. Administrative documents include annual reports, memoranda, meeting notes and agenda, business correspondence and in-house documentation. Usually, these documents are accessed by permission from the auspicating body or via a 'gatekeeper'. Again, there may be costs associated with accessing and using these documents. There may also be sanctions against their use.
- *Formal studies and reports* These documents are produced for and by the public, private and non-profit sectors. The documents may have conditions or restrictions placed on them in regard to the dissemination of their contents to the wider public domain. This is especially true if the documents are produced as 'commercial-in-confidence' or 'in-house' reports. As with other document types, there can be costs associated with their acquisition.

There are two other parameters for classifying documents, and these focus on the temporal and original nature of the documents (see Sarantakos 1998 who reports on Becker 1989 and Stergios 1991). The temporal nature of documents is twofold: they can be either contemporary or retrospective.

- *Contemporary documents* are produced at or around the same time that the tourism phenomenon being studied occurs — for example, documents produced at the time of the World Expo in Australia in 1988.
- *Retrospective documents* are produced after the tourism phenomenon has occurred — for example, the production of documents relating to the 1988 World Expo in the current decade or year.

In regard to the originality of the text in documents, documents may be considered either primary or secondary.

- *Primary documents* are written from first-hand accounts — for example, the reporting of the Sydney Olympic Games Opening Ceremony in the *Weekend Australian* by a sports journalist attending the event.
- *Secondary documents* are written from second-hand accounts — for example, a report about the Sydney Olympic Games Opening Ceremony based on first-hand accounts written in a number of newspapers by a person who only read those papers and did not actually attend the Opening Ceremony.

Advantages and disadvantages of using secondary data sources

As with primary data sources, there are advantages and disadvantages of using secondary data sources. Some of these have already been alluded to in the section on secondary data sources, but the specific advantages and disadvantages are addressed below.

Advantages

There are a number of advantages to using secondary data sources for tourism research. The following discussion is informed by Becker (1989), Berger, Wolf and Ullman (1989), Puris (1995, in Sarantakos 1998), Babbie (1995) and Lincoln and Guba (1985).

- Secondary data sources enable researchers to go back in time to re-examine tourism phenomena. This is known as 'retrospectivity' and it is not something a primary data source can do. Secondary data sources used in this way enable the prediction or forecasting of future events, trends and patterns. They also allow for comparisons to be made between data sets over time.
- Secondary data sources are usually much quicker to access, as well as being easy to access. This is true if the documents are located in the public domain. For example, many reputable secondary sources are available via the Internet.
- Some secondary data sources are free and others, if accessed through the public domain, may have minimal costs.
- Since there is no interaction between the researcher and the writer or producer of the document, the data collected are spontaneous and are not mediated by the interaction between the researcher and the

researched. For example, diaries and personal letters contain spontaneous expressions relating to travel experiences that may be toned down or changed if it was known that the text would be used for research.

- Sometimes, secondary data sources are the only available way to access tourism data, such as the International Visitor Survey (IVS) produced by the Bureau of Tourism Research (BTR). All legal visitors to Australia must complete an entry card, and the data from these cards are used to analyse international visitor arrivals. Similarly, departure cards completed by Australian residents provide data on overseas travel by Australians.
- Secondary data sources, especially those produced by governments and commercial research institutions, usually meet high research standards and therefore are of a high quality. Refereed journals have a higher quality than general magazine articles, which may lack the scientific standards of research and reporting.
- With secondary data, there is a possibility of re-testing the data to determine the credibility of the original research. The data can also be used as a comparative data set for temporal, cultural or geographical analysis with other secondary data studies.
- There is also the possibility of analysing previously collected data stored in databases with a different question in mind. This saves the researcher time and money by not having to replicate studies (Babbie 1995, p. 275).
- Secondary data sources are a 'rich source' of data, since they are produced in the 'natural language of the setting' (Lincoln & Guba 1985, p. 277) — that is, using the language of the participants rather than that of the researcher.
- Secondary data sources are non-reactive. Study units are unaware that the data are being used so there is no intrusion and no inconvenience, although this may not be the case for the person providing access to the data, such as the gatekeeper.

Thus, the advantages of secondary data sources may be summarised using the following key terms: retrospectivity, quick and easy accessibility, low cost, spontaneity, sole source point, high quality, possibility of retesting (Becker 1989; Berger, Wolf & Ullman 1989; Puris 1995, in Sarantakos 1998, p. 277), secondary analysis (Babbie 1995), richness (Lincoln & Guba 1985) and non-reactivity.

Disadvantages

The disadvantages of secondary data sources primarily relate to accessibility issues, methodological issues and a lack of complete knowledge of the process under which the documents were produced. The nature of some cultural documents also can prevent a representative analysis being undertaken. These points are explained below.

- Some secondary documents may not be easy to locate — being fragile, they may be stored in a museum, library or private collection. These locations may not be near the researcher, or the documents may be secured or protected by a gatekeeper who does not wish to allow the researcher access to the documents.

- Some secondary documents may not be in complete sets or may be incomplete. This is especially true of administrative documents. In non-profit associations, for example, accessing complete data sets may be problematic. Sometimes, the lack of personnel to carry out administrative tasks may mean that some documentation is not undertaken. Alternatively, documentation may be incomplete because it has been misplaced during a changeover of new executive members and/or unexpected departures of executive members who may accidentally take any documentation with them.
- Some secondary documents may be too fragile to access or have restrictions placed on their use because of their fragility (Killion 1998, pp. 3–9).
- If the secondary data are statistical or related to research, there may be some methodological problems that the original writer has written out of the documentation. There could also be problems such as coding errors, falsification of responses and fabrication of data. (These issues are discussed further in chapter 4.)
- The secondary data researcher may also not be able to detect if there is any apparent bias in documentary data, though feminist writers would say that most documentation is biased since it has been produced by a dominant patriarchal hegemony and most texts have been created as 'male-stream' texts.
- Secondary data do not always address the exact 'question' or 'problem' the current researcher is trying to address (Punch 1998).
- Secondary data may have issues associated with validity (accuracy) and reliability (dependability of measures) (Kumar 1996, p. 125). This is particularly a problem when the researcher wants to re-analyse the secondary data sets.
- Some cultural documents such as songs or ballads (depicting journey and travel) may change as they are handed down through the generations. As a result, their validity — accuracy in telling the past — is questionable (Burns 1997, p. 392).
- There is always a question of reliability with secondary documents. The 'secondary' researcher does not always know how and why the original documents were produced or the cultural setting in which they were produced. As Tuchman (1994, p. 321) comments: 'Ask questions of all data, primary and secondary sources. Do not assume that anything about data is "natural," inevitable, or even true.'
- Secondary documents such as personal documents and literary genres may not be representative of the wider population, being only specific to the person who wrote them. However, this does not discount their worth. From a quantitative methodological perspective, lack of representativeness may be problematic, but for a qualitative methodology this would not be a problem as representativeness is not the aim (the focus is on understanding issues and attitudes). For example, the travel tales of Newby (1958, 1978, 1987) are not representative of all the people who travelled through the same areas as the author. However, he does provide us with insights into the modes of travel, facilities, amenities and travel experiences associated with specific times and geographical locations.

Similarly, the tales of women travellers in Russell's *The Blessings of a Good Thick Skirt* (1994) are not representative. Each tale is about individual women travellers from different time periods. The tales, however, provide us with information regarding the challenges pioneering women travellers had to face and, as Russell terms it, 'their world' of experience.

- Since the nature of the documentation varies, comparison between documents is not always possible. However, this does provide a point for triangulation and mixed method research, as feminist researchers would suggest. In a positivist paradigm, comparisons could not be made as the methods or scope (time, place, subjects or study units) may not be included in the secondary documentation.

The disadvantages associated with secondary data sources can be summarised using the following key terms: possible problematic access, incompleteness, fragility, questionable reliability, possible methodological problems, bias (including 'malestream' bias), applicability to current research, validity and reliability, questionable representativeness and problematic comparisons.

■ 3.2.3 **Problems** *with census data*

Before moving on to consider key sources of secondary data relevant to the Australian setting, some additional disadvantages of working with statistical data, especially census data, should be discussed. You may be wondering what census data have to do with tourism research. Census data are national data sets that provide researchers with information about the national population. The data collected span many criteria, including gender, age, religious affiliation, marital status, nationality, birthplace, current place of residence, educational background and qualifications, employment details, dwelling details, income and vehicle ownership. This information can assist tourism researchers in determining the sociodemographics of host communities at (potential) tourism destinations. It can provide information concerning population characteristics that can then be used in developing market segments to assist with marketing, particularly advertising strategies. Knowledge of national population demographics can also assist in further research possibilities and the subsequent development of government policies, guidelines or strategies, such as the report on seniors in Australia (Golik 1999).

There are five key disadvantages to using census data. Killion (1998) identifies these disadvantages as related to:

- *The temporal constraints of census data*: census data, like other cultural artefacts and documents, provide only a snapshot image in time. The data provide information about the nation's population on the night of the census collection. However, like other secondary data, census data enable researchers to gain an historical overview of the nation's population trends by drawing on and comparing past census data reports.
- *The passage of time*: census data are collected every five years. However, there is a time delay between the collection, analysis and reporting of the

data. Killion suggests that up to two years may pass before census data are released, and social and population circumstances may change during that period. This can make decision making based on census data problematic because of the data's lack of ability to accurately reflect the characteristics of the current population.

- *The scale of measurement*: census data are reported at a national, regional or statistical division, or local and subdivisions. The lower-scale measurements can be problematic, as they may not reflect regional or local tourism boundaries. Furthermore, the clustering of intervals for categories may not fit other statistical categories (or vice versa). For example, the age categories for the Australian population are recorded as: under 5 years, 5–14 years, 15–19 years, 20–24 years, 25–29 years and so on, in increasing five-yearly intervals (www.statistics.gov.au/D3110124/ 24ca.htm). These categories do not compare with those used in the Domestic Tourism Monitor (Bureau of Tourism Research 1996, p. 55), which uses the following intervals: 14–17 years, 18–24 years, 25–39 years, 40–54 years, and 55 years and over. Thus using census data for some tourism research projects or for comparative analysis can be problematic.
- *The changes in boundaries that can occur*: census boundaries are sometimes redefined and this creates problems when comparing different data sets from different years.
- *The periodic nature of the data*: census data are only available periodically following census dates. It is not an annual data collection process due to the nature of the scale associated with data collection and analysis.

Furthermore, in regard to general statistical sources, some categories may change over time, such as the tourist accommodation statistical database exemplified below:

From December quarter 1993, hotel, motel and guest house establishments with fewer than 5 rooms have been formally excluded from the scope of this collection. The calculation method for site occupancy rate for caravan parks has changed as from September quarter 1992. Occupancy measures from September quarter 1992 are therefore not comparable with those from previous periods (ABS 1997).

These changes in classification, as well as a lack of commonality between measures (such as the different age intervals noted previously), confound the ease with which the plethora of secondary data may be utilised for comparative purposes and secondary analysis. Another issue is raised by Taylor (1994), who notes that there can also be problems because tourism data are subsumed within other data sets and there is a lack of standardisation of definitions:

Central Statistical Agencies usually collect and disseminate a great deal of data directly relative to the operation of the tourism industry. The basic problem in the use of these data is the lack of a clearly defined tourism industry within standard industrial classifications.

3.2.4 **Key sources** *of secondary data relevant to Australia*

Possible sources for statistical data include, but are not the exclusive purvey of, the following:

World Tourism Organization (WTO)

Pacific Asia Travel Association (PATA)*

Office of National Tourism (Australia)*

Australian Bureau of Statistics (ABS)*

CSIRO — Tourism

New Zealand Tourism Board (NZTB)

New Zealand Department of Conservation

New Zealand Tourism Policy Group

Bureau of Tourism Research (BTR)*

Australian Tourist Commission (ATC)

Tourism Council Australia (TCA)

Tourism Queensland

Tourism New South Wales (TNSW)

Canberra Tourism

Tourism Victoria

Tourism Tasmania

South Australian Tourist Commission (SATC) and Office of Tourism Industry Development

Northern Territory Tourist Commission (NTTC)

Western Australian Tourist Commission (WATC)

Regional tourism associations

Local tourism associations

Local councils and shires

Government departments such as the Great Barrier Reef Marine Park Authority, Department of Environment, Department of Sports

Host farm associations

Australian Farm and Country Tourism (AFACT)

Australian Federation of Travel Agents

Ecotourism Association of Australia*

Association of Australian Convention Bureaux (AACB)

Meetings Industry Association of Australia (MIAA)

National Restaurant and Caterers Association

Each source marked with an asterisk is presented in appendix 2 with a Web address active at the time of print and some background information on the source. Table 3.3 presents an overview of the sources of Australian tourism statistics that have relevancy to your studies. You should also be aware that each Web site has links to other related Web sites that may be relevant to your research. Follow these links to make sure that you exhaust all possible sources of data pertinent to your research. Remember to bookmark these sites as you 'surf the Web' for ease of access in the future.

SURVEY/ PUBLICATION TITLE	FREQUENCY	DESCRIPTION	KEY DATA ITEMS	
International Visitor Survey (IVS)	Ongoing Quarterly and annual	Survey of the characteristics, behaviour and expenditure of international visitors to Australia	Characteristics of visitors	Country of residence Nationality Age/sex Occupation Reasons for visit
			International itinerary	Stopovers Time away from home Previous visits to Australia
			Australian itinerary	Length of stay City of arrival/ departure Transport used Region of stay Accommodation used Places/attractions visited Sports, entertainment and cultural activities
			Travel arrangements	Inclusive package tour Travel party Prepaid arrangements Type of booking agent Information sources
			Expenditure	Average visitor expenditure Average item expenditure
			Reactions	Satisfaction Dissatisfaction
Source: Bureau of Tourism Research				
Domestic Tourism Monitor (DTM)	Ongoing Quaerterly and financial year	Survey of level of domestic travel, and characteristics/ behaviour of domestic tourists Basis of reporting: trips visits nights	Characteristics of travellers/non-travellers (people)	Age/sex Occupation/income/life cycle Origin
			Travel behaviour	Origin and destination Purpose of trip Duration of trip Transport used Accommodation used Month returned from trip
			Market shares	Share of trips generated by state/territory received
Source: Bureau of Tourism Research				

SURVEY/ PUBLICATION TITLE	FREQUENCY	DESCRIPTION	KEY DATA ITEMS	
Domestic Tourism Expenditure Survey (DTES)	Full survey 1992 Some data on overnight trips in 1993–94 and 1994–95	Survey of expenditure of domestic travellers	Overnight trips	Origin by destination Primary purpose of trip Itemised expenditure
			Day trips	Type of day trip Itemised expenditure by origin/purpose
Source: Bureau of Tourism Research			Australian component of overseas trips	Item expenditure by purpose/origin
Forecast	Ongoing *Forecast* magazine half-yearly	Latest forecasts provided by the Tourism Forecasting Council	Forecasts currently available: Domestic trips	Business and non-business
			Domestic nights	Purpose Hotels, motels and guest houses State and purpose
			International arrivals	Origin
			International visitor nights	Origin Hotels, motels and guest houses
			International visitor expenditure	Origin Direct and prepaid
Source: Tourism Forecasting Council, c/-Commonwealth Department of Industry, Science and Tourism			Resident departures	Purpose
Overseas Arrivals and Departures (OAD)	Ongoing Monthly, quarterly, annual	Profile of level and characteristics of travellers to and from Australia	Number of overseas visitors arriving/departing by	Purpose of journey Country of residence Age/sex Port of arrival/ departure
			Number of Australian resident departures by	Purpose of journey Country of intended stay Intended length of stay Age/sex
Source: Australian Bureau of Statistics				Port of departure

(continued)

SURVEY/ PUBLICATION TITLE	FREQUENCY	DESCRIPTION		KEY DATA ITEMS
Survey of Tourist Accommodation (STA)	Ongoing Monthly data, published quarterly	Census of supply, and levels of utilisation, of selected tourist accommodation	Hotels/motels and guest houses with facilities by local government area	Establishments/capacity/ employment Room nights sold Occupancy rates Takings
			Holiday flats and units by statistical local area	Entities/capacity/ employment Unit occupancy rates Takings
			Caravan parks by selected statistical area	Establishments/capacity Site occupancy rates Takings
			Visitor hostels by statistical division	Establishments/capacity/ employment Bed occupancy rates Takings
Source: Australian Bureau of Statistics				
Service Industries Surveys (SIS)	Irregular	Survey of structure and activities of key sectors of the tourism industry Survey conducted in 1986–87 and 1991–92 1991–92 survey covered: hospitality industry car hire theme parks/ attractions	Number of enterprises Employment, wages, and salaries Turnovers and selected expenses Value added Net operating surplus Commodity or activities	
Source: Australian Bureau of Statistics				
International Scheduled Air Transport	Ongoing Annual and financial year Some monthly	Air traffic to and from Australia	International passengers by operator Operator market shares Airline passenger capacity and utilisation International airport traffic and aircraft movements (inbound and outbound) City pairs (inbound and outbound) Freight movements by city pairs (inbound and outbound)	
Source: Commonwealth Department of Transport and Regional Development				

SURVEY/ PUBLICATION TITLE	FREQUENCY	DESCRIPTION	KEY DATA ITEMS	
Air Transport Statistics — Domestic Airlines	Ongoing Annual and financial year Some quarterly	Airline operations in Australia	Industry performance (by carrier)	Operational performance Passengers/cargo carried Passenger/cargo kilometres Capacity available Load factors
			Airport statistics City pair statistics Fleet details	Inbound/outbound
Source: Commonwealth Department of Transport and Regional Development				
Yearbook of Tourism Statistics and related publications	Ongoing Yearly	World tourism statistics and individual countries	Visitor numbers and origin Receipts Accommodation used in selected countries	
Source: World Tourism Organization				

Source: *Bureau of Tourism Research*

There are a variety of documentary sources such as:

- National tourism policies, for example *Tourism: A Ticket to the 21st Century* (Office of National Tourism 1998)
  Specific tourism strategies include:
- National Ecotourism Strategy (Commonwealth Department of Tourism 1994b)
- National Rural Tourism Strategy (Commonwealth Department of Tourism 1994a)
- Draft National Aboriginal and Torres Strait Islander Tourism Industry Strategy (Aboriginal and Torres Strait Islander Commission 1994)
- A National Strategy for the Meetings, Incentives, Conventions and Exhibitions Industry (Commonwealth Department of Tourism 1995b)
- National Cruise Shipping Strategy (Commonwealth Department of Tourism 1995).

There are also a variety of tourism journals, which report research projects, including:

- *Journal of Tourism Research*
- *Annals of Tourism*
- *Tourism Management*
- *Journal of Tourism Studies*
- *Journal of Sustainable Tourism*
- *Tourism Economics*
- *Asia Pacific Journal of Tourism Research*
- *Tourism Geographies*

- *Festival Management and Event Tourism*
- *International Journal of Hospitality and Tourism Administration*
- *Current Issues in Tourism.*

Appendix 3 contains an extended list of tourism-related journals as well as hospitality journals. You might also consider looking up and reading Sheldon's (1990) study into the quality of academic journals. Although dated, you might consider the comments made in this article as you conduct your own research. However, when looking for data you should not restrict yourself to just tourism and hospitality-based journals. Remember, tourism is an interdisciplinary phenomenon. Consequently, tourism articles are published not only in tourism and hospitality journals, but also in discipline-specific journals, so you should investigate other related journals in the disciplines of geography, social psychology, business, sociology and women's studies to name a few.

When looking for secondary data sources, you may find the following checklist, developed by Langley (1987, p. 50), useful as it is equally applicable to all tourism secondary sources you might access: 'Have you:
- Found the most relevant [data] to your research?
- Made sure you understand them fully?
- Discussed what they show?
- Used them in a way that adds to your research?
- Acknowledged their source?
- Discussed ways in which they might be unreliable?'

■ *3.2.5* **The process** *of documentary research*

The process of accessing documents and images is one that requires organisation and a structured plan, so that all the required documents are gathered together by the appropriate time. Like any scientific method, there are rules or guidelines that must be followed. The following guidelines are based on the writings of Sarantakos (1998, p. 276). You can use these guidelines when you need to develop a literature review for your research proposal and for your final research report. A literature review is an important component of any research undertaking. It identifies the current state of research in the field of study and provides background information on other studies and their findings and statistics. When a literature review is conducted will depend on the researcher's operating paradigm, methodology and method of analysis. In a positivist paradigm, the literature review will be undertaken prior to any data collection. The data collection will be guided by the literature review. However, in an interpretive social sciences paradigm or a feminist perspective paradigm, the literature review may be undertaken after data collection. This would be especially the case if the researcher were using grounded theory analysis, which is 'grounded' (derived) in the everyday world of the people being studied and what they perceive as issues or worth researching. Prior to conducting grounded theory analysis, the researcher would conduct a methodological literature review. Literature searches and reviews are discussed in detail in chapter 10.

1. Locating pertinent documents or artefacts

The researcher has to search a wide variety of sources such as library catalogues, journal indexes and databases (including electronic records and hard copy databases) in the public domain, as well as contacting experts about other possible sources of documents, artefacts or images. The following Industry Insight considers the use of library indexes and databases.

INDUSTRY INSIGHT

Tertiary institutions offering tourism programs will generally provide guides for researchers regarding secondary data sources that are disciplinary based. For example, at Central Queensland University, the following guide is provided.

Journal databases
Electronic journal indexes are excellent tools for finding citations (references) of suitable articles; most indexes also provide abstracts of articles and some databases provide the full text of articles, which you can print as you are searching the database. Databases particularly relevant for tourism studies are:

- *ABI/Inform (full text, available on Proquest)*
- *APAIS (available on WinSPIRS and WebSPIRS)*
- *ATI (Australian Tourism Index, available on WinSPIRS and WebSPIRS)*
- *Emerald (full text from 1994 onwards)*
- *Expanded Academic (full text, available on Infotrac)*

Researchers are able to link immediately from the highlighted Web sites to the electronic databases and journals.

Source: *http://www.library.cqu.edu.au/faculty/business/tourism.htm*

During this phase, the researcher may also examine bibliographies in other related works. In locating suitable documents and determining whether to include them in the research process, the researcher will be influenced by the availability and accessibility of the documents. Remember, availability and accessibility were two of the disadvantages of using secondary data sources. If the documents are not available locally, the researcher will need to consider whether they can be accessed in the time frame apportioned to the research project. For printed documents, the researcher will have to investigate whether they are still in print or in a readable format (e.g. in the language of the researcher). If the search is not proving fruitful, the researcher may have to broaden the search descriptors and use lateral thinking processes to exhaust all possibilities.

2. Organising and analysing the documents

During this phase, the researcher ensures that there is some methodological fit between the secondary source documents and their own research project. The researcher will need to consider the type of research and methodology being used. If using a quantitative methodology, the researcher may replicate tables and graphs, or categories from previous questionnaires and surveys, for use in the current project. If using a qualitative methodology, the researcher may use content analysis/discourse analysis. And if using feminist content analysis, the researcher may use textual deconstruction. Content analysis and deconstruction are addressed in the next section.

3. Evaluating the information

Using set criteria derived from the purpose of the study, the researcher has to evaluate the materials collected, and this is dependent on the type of study, specifically the methodology used and whether the data are available.

4. Interpreting the data

The interpretative process (i.e. the analysis of data derived from the documents) will depend on whether the documents are to be analysed quantitatively or qualitatively. Specifically, the secondary data may be analysed statistically or textually. Furthermore, the reporting of the 'findings' will result in either deductive or inductive statements, respectively.

■ *3.2.6* **Analysis** *of secondary data*

As already noted, secondary data can be analysed using a qualitative or a quantitative methodology. Both methodologies draw on content analysis as the tool for this process. There are, however, other analytical methods that could be used and these are described in chapters 7 and 9. In this chapter, however, our emphasis is on content analysis. The term 'content analysis' has a number of different names in other disciplines:

> Sociologists tend to use the term 'content analysis', historians the term 'archival research', and philosophers and students of literature the term 'textual analysis' or 'literary criticism'. Different disciplines also apply different interpretive frameworks to the analysis of cultural artefacts. Discourse analysis, rhetoric analysis, and deconstruction are additional terms that refer to the examination of texts (Reinharz 1992, p. 148).

Quantitative content analysis

Quantitative content analysis entails four elements: frequency, direction, intensity and space (Sarantakos 1998 and Neuman 2000). Each of these elements is discussed in turn below.

Frequency

This refers to the number of times a word, phrase or image appears. For example, in advertising for holiday resorts, how many times do senior citizens appear in the images used? How many times are romantic 'young heterosexual couples' used to advertise holiday packages? How many times is the phrase 'the adventure of a lifetime' used in advertising a specific tourism product? How many times is the word 'resort' used to advertise accommodation venues?

Direction

Neuman (2000) uses the term direction, while Sarantakos (1998) uses the term evaluation. In both cases, the term refers to the positivity or negativity of the text or image being studied. In textual documents, the determination of positivity and negativity may be decided using lists of adjectives or descriptors about the aspect being studied. For example, in attempting to determine how women travellers are accepted within a specific destination, a researcher might examine reports in newspapers and apply the descriptors of positivity such as 'welcomed' and 'included' or the descriptors of negativity such as 'shunned', 'abused', 'spat on', 'ignored'.

Intensity

The direction (the positivity or negativity) of the text or images can also be measured by their intensity, that is their strength of direction along a continuum of positivity or negativity. For example, one travel reporter may report a restaurant's service as excellent, while another may report the service as good. Obviously, there is a difference in the strength in these evaluations — one is strongly towards the positive end of the service continuum and the other is only midway towards the positive end. In visual images, intensity may also be measured by the use of black and white images and colour images, or by placement within the foreground or background.

Space

Space generally refers to the amount of space allocated to the text or images in a document. For the text, the number of words or the number of paragraphs and pages can be counted. Sometimes, standard measurements (e.g. square centimetres) are used to calculate the actual physical space allocated to the text or images. An alternative/additional option is to consider the location of the text or images in the document — for example, do the images appear on the first page or in a right-hand corner towards the end of the document? If you consider that tourism promotional materials are conveyed using radio and television, then space becomes a measure of elapsed time. An example of measuring space would be examining travel magazines to determine the amount of space devoted to family holidays by undertaking a content analysis of the visual images. The researcher would have to consider several aspects regarding space, such as the size and shape of the images, their positioning on the page and their overall placement in the document. The first practical exercise at the end of the chapter engages you in the use of content analysis in a positivist paradigm.

For content analysis to be effective, the researcher has to clearly identify the unit of study so that no ambiguity exists in its interpretation and develop an effective coding system. This means that the categories used have to be 'mutually exclusive' (each unit can only be coded into one category) and exhaustive (all units must have a category into which they can be coded). As Neuman (2000) comments, there are also issues of validity and reliability that have to be addressed. Validity and reliability are discussed in chapter 5. Crandell (1994) provides an overview of content analysis of text documents and statistics that you may find helpful.

Qualitative content analysis

Qualitative content analysis is used by the interpretive social sciences paradigm, the critical theory paradigm and the feminist perspectives paradigm. It can also be used in tourism research informed by these paradigms. As with quantitative content analysis, the method of qualitative content analysis has scientific protocols. The protocols are not unlike those Dey (1993) notes in regard to qualitative data analysis. In his chapter focusing on 'Creating categories', he outlines the process:

> The process of finding a focus for the analysis, and reading and annotating the data, leads on naturally to the creation of categories ... Ideas must be sifted, their import assessed, their relevance evaluated. Some may be discarded. Others may suggest key concepts through which to understand the data (Dey 1993, pp. 99–100).

As Dey intimates, it is through the data that the categories or taxonomies are created. In the case of quantitative content analysis, the categories are predetermined — as Lincoln and Guba (1985) note, this is rarely the case with qualitative content analysis. Lincoln and Guba also suggest some further sources for reading on content analysis:

> The naturalistic inquirer will rarely enjoy the luxury of an a priori taxonomy, but when it occurs the analytic modes are well spelled out in such standard content analysis source works as Holsti (1969), Krippendorff (1980), and Rosengren (1981). If the documents are dissimilar, an especially useful approach is the case aggregation method outlined by Lucas (1974a, 1974b). An extended illustration of the latter is given in Guba and Lincoln (1981). When the taxonomy is to emerge in (be grounded in) the data themselves, the method of constant comparison outlined by Glaser and Strauss (1967) is applicable (Lincoln & Guba 1985, p. 278).

Aspects of content analysis such as aggregation, constant comparison or successive approximation are detailed in chapter 7. Content analysis is also a specific tool used by feminist researchers and is called feminist content analysis (Reinharz 1992). It is also a method of analysis for 'postmodern' researchers. An example of the way feminist content analysis is undertaken using a deconstructionist analytic method is given by Martin:

> I deconstruct and reconstruct ... [the] story from a feminist viewpoint, examining what it says, what it does not say, and what it might have said. This analysis highlights suppressed gender conflicts implicit in ... [the] story and shows how apparently well-intentioned organizational practices can reify, rather than alleviate, gender inequalities (Martin, in Reinharz 1992, p. 149).

A practical application of qualitative content analysis is presented in the practical exercises for this chapter. You should also investigate the references and further readings to further extend your understanding of content analysis.

3.3 | DIFFERENCES BETWEEN PRIMARY AND SECONDARY DATA SOURCES

Having considered both primary and secondary data sources, we now move on to the major differences between the two sources. The key difference lies in the relationship of the researcher to the original data collection process. With primary data sources, the researcher has first-hand association with the data, whereas with secondary data sources, the researcher has second-hand association with the originally collected data. Primary data are generally collected using observation, interviews and questionnaires and are analysed using a variety of quantitative and qualitative methods and analysis (discussed in chapters 6, 7, 8 and 9). Secondary data are usually collected following scientific guidelines and the collection process is often called desk (top) research or documentary research. Secondary data are analysed using content analysis or textual analysis or deconstruction. Content analysis can be applied within a quantitative or a qualitative methodology.

3.4 | DIVERSITY IN BOTH PRIMARY AND SECONDARY DATA SOURCES

The range of secondary data sources is wide; no wonder that Goeldner (1994) among others laments that researchers do not exhaust secondary data sources prior to embarking on primary data collection. Depending on the type of data required, primary and secondary data can both be utilised in quantitative and qualitative methodologies and by the various paradigms that inform tourism research. In your role as a researcher, you have available to you a plethora of statistical sources, journal articles, historical archives, cultural archives and documentary texts to assist you in your future research projects.

3.5 | SUMMARY

Possible sources of primary and secondary data for use in tourism research
Researchers can source either primary or secondary data. Primary data are collected from participants or study units directly involved in the tourism

phenomenon being studied. Secondary data have already been collected by a previous researcher/researchers — a second researcher then accesses that data for their research.

The major primary data sources for tourism research

The major primary data sources are data collected through observation, interviews, group panels and questionnaires.

The advantages and disadvantages of using primary data sources for the conduct of tourism research

The advantages of primary data are: relevance, recency, appropriate population studied, lack of other researcher bias, and lack of methodological errors. The disadvantages of primary data are its reactive, obtrusive, time-consuming and resource-expensive nature.

The major secondary data sources for tourism research

The major sources, based on Sarantakos' classificatory system, are public documents, archival documents, personal documents, administrative documents, and formal studies and reports.

The advantages and disadvantages of using secondary data sources for the conduct of tourism research

The advantages of secondary data sources can be summarised using these key words: retrospectivity, quick and easy accessibility, spontaneity, low cost, sole source point, high quality, possibility of retesting, non-reactivity, secondary analysis and richness. The disadvantages are: possible problematic access, incompleteness, fragility, questionable reliability, possible methodological problems, bias, applicability to current research, validity and reliability, questionable representativeness, and problematic comparisons.

The key sources of secondary data relevant to Australia

Relevant statistical sources include: World Tourism Organization (WTO), Pacific Asia Travel Association (PATA), Office of National Tourism (Australia), Australian Bureau of Statistics (ABS), New Zealand Tourism Board (NZTB), Bureau of Tourism Research (BTR), Australian Tourist Commission (ATC), Tourism Council Australia (TCA), CSIRO — Tourism.

The process of documentary analysis

Documentary analysis involves identifying and locating relevant documents and materials, gathering and analysing those documents and materials, evaluating the relevancy of the documents and materials to the research study, and interpreting and reporting the findings from the overall analysis.

The rudiments of content analysis

Quantitative content analysis involves determining the frequency, direction, intensity and space associated with the variable(s) the researcher has selected for study. Data are gathered and analysed in regard to these four aspects, and then a report is compiled. Qualitative content analysis involves locating the data, developing categories arising from the data, assessing the relevance and strength of the categories and reporting the findings.

The difference between primary and secondary data sources

The key difference between primary and secondary data sources is associated with the researcher's role in gathering the original data. The researcher has first-hand association with primary data sources and second-hand association with secondary data sources (someone else collected the d̶ ̶ ̶ ̶ ̶ ̶ ̶ ̶esearcher is using it second-hand). Primary data research with humans or animals is considered reactive, intrusive and obtrusive; on the other hand, secondary data research is considered non-reactive, non-intrusive and unobtrusive.

The diversity in both primary and secondary data sources

The use of primary or secondary data depends on the research project, the overlying paradigm and any external factors such as time and monetary constraints. For tourism researchers, data sources are extensive. Primary data may be gathered by using observation, interviews, panel groups or questionnaires. Secondary data may be gathered from cultural documents and artefacts accessible in the private, public and non-profit sectors. All researchers need to investigate secondary data sources, if only to write a literature review providing background information relating to the research project. On the other hand, some researchers will conduct research using only secondary data sources. Regardless of the guiding paradigm of the research process, both primary and secondary data sources are diverse in nature and have their own specific methods for collection and analysis. The researcher's role is to ensure that they are aware of the diversity and choose the best methods to gather the data.

Questions

3.1   What are the main advantages and disadvantages of primary data sources?

3.2   What are the main advantages and disadvantages of secondary data sources?

3.3   Define the two types of data sources, then describe when you might use each type of source and why.

3.4   Of the secondary data sources available to you in Australia, which would you access, and why?

3.5   In your opinion, is the diversity in data sources problematic for researchers? Explain your answer.

EXERCISES

This chapter commences the first of the practical exercise sections that will be used to assist you in applying the knowledge you have gained from this textbook.

Exercise 3.1

Examine the following statistics provided by the Bureau of Tourism Research (see tables 3.4 and 3.5). Based on this data, write a 100-word description of the current state of tourism within Australia. In your description [text obscured] the data from the two sets of figures. You should also check to see that more recent statistics have not been released since this textbook has been published, and if they have, then use them. This material could be used in your own research project if you are conducting your study in Australia. It would enable you to provide some of the background information regarding tourism and perhaps some comparative discussion points to return to after you have analysed your own data.

■ **Table 3.4** *International visitors* by country of residence, 1990–97*

COUNTRY OF RESIDENCE	1990	1991	1992	1993	1994	1995	1996	1997
New Zealand	382 400	441 500	412 300	463 400	439 100	490 700	609 600	621 100
Japan	459 600	510 800	604 900	641 000	687 000	737 900	766 600	766 000
Hong Kong	49 500	56 800	66 600	83 000	98 400	117 300	137 600	136 600
Taiwan	n.a.	32 600	58 900	100 400	132 300	138 300	144 800	138 900
Thailand	17 800	22 800	30 900	42 300	60 200	72 500	80 500	61 800
Korea	n.a.	n.a.	n.a.	n.a.	105 700	160 600	216 200	220 500
Malaysia	41 600	43 300	54 100	70 500	83 200	94 400	118 200	125 800
Singapore	65 700	74 700	99 300	130 100	158 800	168 500	185 900	201 300
Indonesia	29 500	32 400	39 500	61 000	90 400	107 600	129 900	138 200
China	n.a.	n.a.	n.a.	n.a.	n.a.	n.a.	52 300	63 800
Other Asia	109 300	73 500	88 300	121 400	77 300	102 800	74 400	88 700
United States	240 100	259 000	249 400	266 800	273 700	287 900	299 200	309 800
Canada	50 700	50 800	45 800	47 600	51 100	55 000	57 800	60 800
United Kingdom	272 100	258 200	282 300	301 800	329 800	335 400	347 200	387 800
Germany	71 800	75 200	86 100	102 300	114 900	119 800	120 700	124 500
Other Europe	177 900	171 900	178 000	199 500	236 800	258 800	291 400	319 400
Other countries	97 400	113 100	129 400	152 300	165 900	174 500	197 500	209 100
TOTAL	2 065 400	2 216 600	2 425 800	2 783 400	3 104 600	3 422 000	3 829 800	3 974 000

* Visitors aged 15 years and over.
Data for Middle East countries are included in Other Asia in 1989 and 1990 and in Other countries from 1991 onwards.
Data for Ireland are included in the United Kingdom from 1989 to 1994 and in Other Europe in 1995.

Source: *Bureau of Tourism Research (1999a)*

■ Table 3.5 *International visitors by main purpose of journey, 1990–97*

MAIN PURPOSE	1990	1991	1992	1993	1994	1995	1996	1997
Holiday	1 153 900	1 327 500	1 489 000	1 730 900	1 933 400	2 047 800	2 290 000	2 302 500
Visiting relatives	407 100	426 600	440 000	475 200	540 600	631 600	704 100	737 100
Business	231 100	221 500	236 100	267 800	320 800	360 400	391 700	436 100
Convention	41 900	34 700	27 700	44 000	50 800	69 600	98 900	126 800
Other	231 300	206 300	232 900	265 400	259 000	312 500	345 100	371 500

Changes in purpose of journey categories from September 1994 mean that data after that date are not strictly comparable with data for earlier periods.

Source: *Bureau of Tourism Research (1999b)*

Exercise 3.2

(a) Go to your local tourism information centre and assess the current image portrayed by your local/regional tourist association's print media advertising strategy. You will need to gather all the print media that are specifically produced by the association and used to promote your local area/region. (This means that you should not include individual operators' print media in the study.)

In practice, depending on the number of documents you have collected, you may choose to study all the documents or a randomly selected sample (sampling procedures are outlined in chapter 5). However, for the purpose of this exercise, choose just one document that has sufficient images (at least 20) to practise the skills associated with content analysis. In this exercise, the emphasis is on developing the skills associated with using the four measures of quantitative content analysis (frequency, direction, intensity and space), rather than on sampling techniques, as this is not discussed in detail until chapter 5.

(b) Glance through the document so that you have an idea of the types of images that are presented, then classify (categorise) these images. One way to do this is to classify the images according to the subjects of the composition — for example, human and non-human subjects.

In the human set, you could include subcategories such as individuals, twosomes, family groups (parents/carers and children), extended family groups (parents/carers, children and grandparents/carers) and other groups (here you may consider differentiating between small, medium and large-scale groups). In the non-human set, you would need to differentiate between built (you might consider attractions, accommodation, restaurants, facilities and amenities), natural (terrestrial and marine) and mixed (natural and built). Some images may be composed of human and non-human subjects, so you will have to decide which is the main subject (it will be in the foreground, not the background).

There are, of course, other ways to classify the images. You might consider the type of tourist experience being engaged in, such as urban tourism, rural tourism, adventure tourism, marine tourism and sport tourism. You could also do a gender analysis or an age analysis. Or you could choose to analyse all these variables (gender, age, type of tourist experience). Regardless of how you decide to classify the images, you need to define each of the categories so others will understand your coding (classifying) of the categories and sub-categories. Again, however, for the purposes of this exercise, we will apply the human/non-human classification system and use the coding matrix that follows.

(c) Before moving on to the next stage, define the following terms. Some are self-explanatory, such as 'individuals', but you will need to indicate whether you mean the subject is composed of sets of individuals or that one person is the subject of the image. You also need to advise how you will account for and define a local as opposed to a visitor. Terms: individuals; twosomes; family groups; extended family groups; other groups; built settings — attractions, accommodation, restaurants, facilities and amenities; natural settings — terrestrial and marine; and mixed (natural and built) settings.

(d) Next you need to develop a coding matrix. Figure 3.1 shows how a coding matrix might be developed from the preceding discussion.

■ **Figure 3.1**
Example of a coding matrix

Document name: _____
Researcher: _____
Date:

SUBJECT	TALLY	TOTAL
Human subjects		
Individual		
Twosome		
Family group		
Extended family group		
Other groups		
Non-human subjects		
Attractions		
Built		
Natural		
Mixed		

Accommodation		
5 star		
4 star		
3 star		
2 star		
Budget		
Food and beverage		
Hotels		
Bars		
Restaurants		
Fast foods		
Facilities/amenities		
Post office		
Banks		
Hospitals		
Transportation		
Air		
Bus		
Train		
Hire car		
Other		

(i) Undertake a frequency count of the categories you have identified and note the count in the matrix. Write a 100-word paragraph describing the outcomes of your coding (your findings) and discuss this with your tutorial peers and/or tutor.

(ii) To measure direction, you could analyse what has been placed in the foreground and what has been placed in the background. The 'foreground' images are the 'positive' images and the 'background' images are the 'negative' images as they are not the subject of the overall image. You could also consider age and activity and the types of 'positive' and 'negative' images used — for example, are older people presented in a non-active setting (i.e. a negative image that is the result of stereotyping) or in an 'active' setting (i.e. a positive image that is the result of non-stereotypical imaging)?

(iii) To measure intensity, you could determine the use of black and white versus colour images.

(iv) Space is self-explanatory — it is the physical area taken up by certain images. For example, you may find that the number of active elderly people is small (less than 10), represented by two black and white images that take up 15 cm^2 of space within a document of 1000 cm^2, whereas there may be 70 non-active elderly people represented by 10 colour images that take up 100 cm^2 of space within the same document. What could you infer from two such findings?

Exercise 3.3

Examine the following two passages carefully.

'The first *climbed* ascent [of Mont Blanc] by a woman ... was made by a French mountaineer, Henriette D'Angeville, in 1838. A highly organized climber, she was the first woman fully to plan her own ascent. Shackled as all women were in those days by their clothes, she nevertheless managed to struggle upwards in a long skirt — with a pair of brightly checked trousers underneath. Modesty was not a virtue with which Henriette was overfamiliar, which may explain why one male commentator described her disparagingly as "a thwarted maiden lady in her forties". She gained the maximum publicity for the climb, dramatically announcing that she had made her will before setting out. The news of her successful three-day ascent — brought down from the summit by carrier pigeon — was celebrated by a burst of cannon fire' (Russell, 1994, p. 91).

'Margery Kempe, voluble, energetic, given to hearing voices and seeing visions, was born in 1373 and at the age of forty set out on a five-month journey to Jerusalem. Margery was obsessed with holiness — her own and everyone else's ...

'Margery Kempe holds an important position in the history of women travellers. Like many before and after her, she took to the whole paraphernalia of travel with the noisy delight of a drake getting her [sic] first sight of water. Although a matron of comfortable means, she stoically endured hardship, danger and illness during the two years she was away from home. Despite the unchristian behaviour of her companions, who cut up her clothes, stole her bed sheets and walked too fast for her, she displayed a dogged determination to complete what she had set out to do. Like many women travellers, however, she enjoyed a privileged position in her own society and it was this which enabled her confidently to deal with officials and critics alike.

In one major aspect, however, she differed from most of the women travellers who were to follow her. She was both ill-educated and ill-prepared to benefit intellectually from her experiences. She died in 1438, untouched by the ripples of humanism and radical religious thinking that were beginning to disturb, yet again, the relatively calm pond of English society. She left behind, however, a record of her travels and the final irony in her tale is that this unique book — the earliest autobiographical travel account still in existence to be written in the vernacular — had to be dictated, for this most exuberant and talkative of women travellers could neither read nor write' (Russell, 1994, pp. 33, 34).

The qualitative content analysis that will used here is based on Strauss and Corbin's (1990) selective coding and will follow this path: 'A (conditions) leads to B (phenomenon), which leads to C (context), which leads to D (action/interaction/ including strategies), which then leads to E (consequences)' (Strauss & Corbin 1990, pp. 124–5).

(a) In the two passages, what do you think is the key theme, storyline or issue associated with these women? Write you answer in a paragraph of approximately 50 to 100 words.

(b) What were the 'conditions' that led the women to pursue their travel experiences?

(c) How would you describe the 'phenomenon' of their travel experiences?

(d) What were the social 'contexts' in which the two women were living and the attitudes to women pursuing the paths these two women took?

(e) What 'action/interaction/strategies' did the women use to achieve their travel goals given the constraints they confronted?

(f) What were the 'consequences' of their actions?

(g) Using your responses to these questions, write a second paragraph that synthesises your answers without using the descriptors from Strauss and Corbin (1990).

The tasks in this activity have only used two passages, which is too small a basis to make any emphatic statements about the experiences of all women.

RESEARCH PROJECT

What are your initial thoughts about using primary data collection in your own research project? Make a list of all possible secondary data sources you will need to examine for your own research. Remember to think about public documents, archival documents, personal documents, administrative documents, and formal studies and reports. What secondary statistics will you access, if any? Why?

REFERENCES

Aboriginal and Torres Strait Islander Commission. 1994. *Draft National Aboriginal and Torres Strait Islander Tourism Industry Strategy.* Canberra: Aboriginal and Torres Strait Islander Commission.

Adam-Smith, Patsy. 1973. *Footloose in Australia.* Sydney: Seal Books.

Australian Bureau of Statistics (ABS). 1997. 'Tourist Accommodation: Queensland at a Glance'. http://statistics.gov.au/D3110124/24ee.htm.

Australian Bureau of Statistics (ABS). 1999. 'Overseas Arrivals and Departures, Australia, October 1999'. Catalogue No. 3401.0. http://www.abs.gov.au. websitedbs/D3110122.NSF/66b4effdf36063e24a25648300177cd5/.

Babbie, Earl. 1995. *The Practice of Social Research.* California: Wadsworth.

Bureau of Tourism Research (BTR). 1996. Domestic Tourism Monitor, 1994–95. Canberra: Bureau of Tourism Research.

Bureau of Tourism Research (BTR). 1999a. 'International Visitors by Country of Residence, 1990–97'. http://www.btr.gov.au/statistics/Datacard/dc_ivs_x_purpose.html.

Bureau of Tourism Research (BTR). 1999b. 'International Visitors by Main Purpose of Journey, 1990–97'. http://www.btr.gov.au/statistics/Datacard/dc_ivs_x_purpose.html.

Bureau of Tourism Research (BTR). Sources of Australian Tourism Research.

Burns, Robert. 1997. *Introduction to Research Methods.* Third Edition. South Melbourne: Longman.

Commonwealth Department of Tourism. 1994a. *National Rural Tourism Strategy.* Canberra: Australian Government Publishing Service (AGPS).

Commonwealth Department of Tourism. 1994b. *National Ecotourism Strategy.* Canberra: Australian Government Publishing Service (AGPS).

Commonwealth Department of Tourism. 1995a. *National Cruise Shipping Strategy.* Canberra: Australian Government Publishing Service (AGPS).

Commonwealth Department of Tourism. 1995b. *A National Strategy for the Meetings, Incentives, Conventions and Exhibitions Industry.* Canberra: Australian Government Publishing Service (AGPS).

Crandell, Louise. 1994. 'The Social Impact of Tourism on Developing Regions and its Measurement'. In Ritchie, J. R. Brent. & Goeldner, Charles R. (Eds) *Travel, Tourism, and Hospitality Research: A Handbook for Managers and Researchers.* New York: John Wiley & Sons, pp. 413–23.

Dey, Ian. 1993. *Qualitative Data Analysis: A User-Friendly Guide for Social Scientists.* London: Routledge.

Goeldner, Charles R. 1994. 'Travel and Tourism Information Sources'. In Ritchie J. R. Brent. & Goeldner, Charles R. (Eds) *Travel, Tourism, and Hospitality Research: A Handbook for Managers and Researchers.* New York: John Wiley & Sons, pp. 81–90.

Golik, Ben. 1999. *Not Over the Hill. Just Enjoying the View, Summary Report: A Close-up Look at the Seniors Market for Tourism in Australia.* Office of Ageing.

Jorgensen, Danny L. 1989. *Participant Observation: A Methodology for Human Studies.* Applied Social Research Methods Series, Volume 15. Newbury Park: Sage.

Killion, Les. 1998. *Research in Tourism, Study Guide.* Rockhampton: Central Queensland University Distance Learning Centre.

Kosters, Martinus J. 1994. 'Tourism Research in European National Tourist Organizations'. In Ritchie J. R. Brent. & Goeldner, Charles R. (Eds) *Travel, Tourism, and Hospitality Research: A Handbook for Managers and Researchers.* New York: John Wiley & Sons, pp. 155–64.

Kumar, Ranjit. 1996. *Research Methodology: A Step-By-Step Guide for Beginners.* Sydney: Longman.

Langley, Peter. 1987. *Doing Social Research: A Guide to Coursework.* Ormskirk, Lancashire: Causeway Press.

Lincoln, Yvonna S. & Guba, Egon, G. 1985. *Naturalistic Inquiry.* Newbury Park: Sage, pp. 267–8.

Office of National Tourism. 1998. *Tourism: A Ticket to the 21st Century.* Canberra. http://www.tourism.gov.au/publications/ticket/contents/html.

Neuman, W. Lawrence. 1994. *Social Research Methods, Qualitative and Quantitative Approaches.* Third Edition. Boston, MA: Allyn & Bacon.

Neuman, W. L. 2000. *Social Research Methods, Qualitative and Quantitative Approaches.* Fourth Edition. Boston, MA: Allyn & Bacon.

Newby, Eric. 1978. *The Big Red Train Ride.* London: Picador.

Newby, Eric. 1958. *A Short Walk in the Hindu Kush.* London: Picador.

Newby, Eric. 1987. *Round Ireland in Low Gear.* London: Picador.

Punch, Keith. 1998. *Introduction to Social Research, Quantitative and Qualitative Approaches.* London: Sage.

Reinharz, Shulamit. 1992. *Feminist Methods in Social Research.* New York: Oxford University Press.

Russell, Mary. 1994. *The Blessings of a Good Thick Skirt: Women Travellers and their World.* London: Flamingo.

Sarantakos, Sotirios. 1998. *Social Research.* Second Edition. South Melbourne: Macmillan Education.

Sheldon. P. J. 1990. 'Journals in Tourism and Hospitality: The Perceptions of Publishing Faculty'. *The Journal of Tourism Studies*, vol. 1, no. 1, May, pp. 42–8.

Strauss, Anselm & Corbin, Juliet. 1990. *Basics of Qualitative Research, Grounded Theory Procedures and Techniques.* Newbury Park: Sage.

Taylor, Gordon D. 1994. 'Research in National Tourist Organizations'. In Ritchie, J. R. Brent & Goeldner, Charles R. (Eds) *Travel, Tourism, and Hospitality Research: A Handbook for Managers and Researchers.* New York: John Wiley & Sons, pp. 147–54.

Tuchman, Gaye. 1994. 'Historical Social Science: Methodologies, Methods, and Meanings'. In Denzin, Norman K. & Lincoln, Yvonna S. (Eds) *Handbook of Qualitative Research.* Thousand Oaks: Sage, pp. 306–23.

Weaver, David & Oppermann, Martin. 2000. *Tourism Management.* Brisbane: John Wiley & Sons.

FURTHER READING

Glaser, Barney & Strauss, Anselm. 1967. *The Discovery of Grounded Theory.* Chicago: Aldine.

Guba, Egon & Lincoln, Yvonna. 1981. *Effective Evaluation.* San Francisco: Jossey-Bass.

Holsti, O. R. 1969. *Content Analysis for the Social Sciences and Humanities*. Reading, MA: Addison-Wesley.

Krippendorff, Klaus. 1980. *Content Analysis*. Beverley Hills, CA: Sage.

Office of National Tourism. n.d. 'Where to Find Tourism Data'. http://www.tourism.gov.au/FactsandFigures/FindTourismData.doc.

Patton, Michael Q. 1990. *Qualitative Evaluation and Research Methods*. Second Edition. Newbury Park: Sage, pp. 82–4.

Rosengren, Karl. E. (Ed.) 1981. *Advances in Content Analysis*. Beverley Hills, CA: Sage.

Weber, R. P. 1990. *Basic Content Analysis*. Second Edition. Quantitative Applications in the Social Sciences Series, Volume 49. Newbury Park, CA: Sage.

4

The ethics of
tourism research

'Ethics (from the Greek *ethos*, "character") is the systematic study of value concepts — "good", "bad", "right", "wrong" — and the general principles that justify applying these concepts.

'Thus, the ethics of social research is not about etiquette; nor is it about considering the poor hapless subject at the expense of science or society. Rather, we study ethics to learn how to make social research "work" for all concerned. The ethical researcher creates a mutually respectful, win-win relationship with the research population; this is a relationship in which subjects are pleased to participate candidly, and the community at large regards the conclusions as constructive. Public policy implications of the research are presented in such a way that public sensibilities are unlikely to be offended and backlash is unlikely to occur.

'In contrast, an ethically insensitive researcher may leave the research setting in pandemonium. The ensuing turmoil may harm the researcher, his or her institution, and even the cause he or she seeks to promote.'

(Sieber 1992, p. 3)

LEARNING OBJECTIVES

After studying this chapter, you should be able to:

- understand the need for ethics in the conduct of tourism research
- overview the various debates in ethics literature
- discuss the tourism researcher's ethical responsibilities to society
- describe the tourism researcher's ethical responsibilities to the scientific community
- outline the tourism researcher's ethical responsibilities to research participants
- explain the tourism researcher's ethical responsibilities to sponsors
- be aware of the tourism researcher's ethical responsibilities to the self
- understand the concepts of reciprocity and reflexivity
- explain the need to be ethical.

*I*NTRODUCTION

This chapter concludes the first section of this textbook on the research process. Chapters 1–3 have focused on the role of research in tourism, the theoretical paradigms underpinning tourism research and data sources for tourism research. These chapters have provided you with background information regarding the overall context of undertaking research activities in the global phenomenon of tourism. This chapter informs you of the 'moral' and 'professional' guidelines that you are required to use during the course of any research project or study. Table 4.1 overviews some of the ethical and political questions to consider during the course of any research project, and these are discussed in more detail later in the chapter.

■ **Table 4.1**
Ethical and political questions to consider in tourism research

RESEARCH ISSUES	ETHICAL AND POLITICAL QUESTIONS
Research project design	• Does the researcher have the necessary skills to conduct the research project? • What are the researcher's qualifications? • What previous experience has the researcher had in tourism research? • Does the researcher have any references from previous clients?
Client	• Who is sponsoring the research? • Who will benefit from the research? • Who will be able to access the data and the findings? • How will confidentiality be maintained if there is a researcher–client relationship? • How does the client envisage their role during the course of the research? • Does the researcher have autonomy, or is the project conditionally based on client expectations or specific findings?
Accessibility	• Who are the gatekeepers to the participants? • Do the gatekeepers have a vested interest in the research, and if so, what is that interest? • What methods will be used to gain access to the participants? Do these methods protect the rights of the individual? • Is deception planned for use? If so, is it warranted? • Are incentives being used and will these influence responses?
Intellectual freedom	• Who owns the research process and all its outputs? • Does the researcher have to sign a confidentiality clause? If so, why?

RESEARCH ISSUES	ETHICAL AND POLITICAL QUESTIONS
Data collection	• Does the research protect the rights of the individual? • Will informed or written consent be used? • Is there any duplicity associated with the data collection? If so, why? • What sampling methods will be used? • How is the data to be collected? Is this the best method, given the circumstances of the research? • What happens when the researcher gains 'guilty knowledge'? • What happens if the researcher gets 'dirty hands'? • Have aspects of reflexivity been considered? • Has reciprocity been included in the research design?
Data analysis	• How will the data be interpreted? • Who will interpret the data? • How will confidentiality be maintained? • Where will data be stored and for how long before being destroyed? • Will others be permitted access to the data for secondary analysis? If so, what measures will be used to protect the participants?
Reporting the findings	• Have a variety of genres (forms of writing) been considered for the reporting of the findings, so that all stakeholders in the research process may access and understand the findings? • Who owns the report (clients, researchers, participants)? • Have the participants been informed of all the possible uses of the research findings? • Have the participants been informed of all the possible audiences who may be informed of the research findings? • Who controls the further use of the report and data collected? • What will happen if the findings are censored? Where should the moral obligations of the researcher lie — with the participants or with the client?

Source: *Based on Minichiello, Aroni, Timewell & Alexander (1995, p. 193)*

As indicated by the introductory quote and table 4.1, ethics for the tourism researcher, and indeed any researcher, is associated with a variety of stakeholder groups: society; government; the scientific community; the research participants; sponsors or clients; and the researcher (Neuman 2000). These six groups represent all the major stakeholders involved or affected by any tourism research. Tourism research occurs in a social context and the findings are usually applied to that wider social context rather than just the research setting. Subsequently, researchers need to be aware of the consequences of their data collection and research findings for society, governments and the scientific community. In your reading, you will come across other lists of stakeholders — for example, Kumar (1996) identifies only three stakeholders: participants; researchers; and funding bodies. However, this chapter uses the six stakeholder groups to organise the discussion of the 'moral' and 'professional' guidelines and responsibilities (i.e. the ethical practices and concerns) of tourism research. Simultaneously, the chapter addresses ethical issues regarding each of the stakeholder groups.

4.2 THE NEED FOR ETHICS IN THE CONDUCT OF TOURISM RESEARCH

Today, researchers in the Western world are required to follow ethical guidelines in the conduct of research. Within Australia, the key ethical guidelines that inform any research are primarily derived from the National Health and Medical Research Council (NHMRC) guidelines and standards of research (see appendix 4). Such guidelines have been instituted to protect the rights of individuals (human subjects) and, in the case of research of non-human subjects, the rights of non-human subjects. The NHMRC guidelines have been developed as a reaction to past unethical practices in which the rights of humans and non-human participants have not been protected or valued.

Most Western ethics guidelines originate from the Nuremberg Code (Neuman 2000, p. 101). The Nuremberg Code was developed and used in the course of investigations and hearings dealing with Nazi war crimes, particularly the conduct of medical experiments on concentration camp inmates (see www.ushmm.org/research/doctors/code_expl.htm; and Neuman 2000, pp. 101–2). Although the Nuremberg Code is associated directly with medical experiments, it has been applied to the wider context of social research (i.e. any research involving human participation) (Neuman 2000, p. 102). Other codes that also influence the research process are the 1948 Universal Declaration of Human Rights (United Nations) and the 1964 Declaration of Helsinki (Neuman 2000, p. 102).

Codes of ethics usually entail the following key items:
- voluntary participation by the individual
- informed consent given by the participant after being provided with either oral or written information about the research
- the right of the individual to refuse to answer any questions or perform any actions
- the right of the individual to withdraw from the research at any time during its conduct
- the right of the participant not to be deceived regarding any aspect of research (purpose, sponsor or usage of the findings)

- the right of the participant not to be harmed during any stage of the research, as well as after the research has concluded
- the right of the individual to have any personal information or data treated as either confidential or anonymous as befits the circumstances of the research
- the right of research participants to access the research findings.

There are fuller codes of conduct regarding research ethics, and the additional components of such codes will be presented during the discussion of each of the stakeholder groups and the associated ethical issues and guidelines for each group. Within Australia, various professional associations and other related disciplinary areas have codes of conduct for research, for example:

- the Australian and New Zealand Association for Leisure Studies (ANZALS)
- the Australian Sociological Association (TASA)
- the Australian Psychological Association (APA).

As most of you will be using this text in association with formal studies, you should be aware that most universities and tertiary institutions have their own codes or guidelines for the ethical conduct of research. In 1990, the Australian Vice-Chancellors Committee (AVCC) released *Guidelines on Responsible Practices in Research and Problems of Research Misconduct,* along with a recommendation that individual institutions establish their own ethical guidelines for the conduct of research (Sarantakos 1998, p. 22). Familiarise yourself with the guidelines of your institution so that you follow your institution's requirement. If you are not engaging in formal study, you can still locate ethical guidelines, such as the one presented in appendix 4 or those of the above professional associations. However, be aware, as Stake (1995, p. 58) comments, that such guidelines 'are not perfect, sometimes [being] more concerned about limiting liability than about the well-being of the individuals' who will be involved in the research. Furthermore, Stake advocates that research should be 'non-hortatory, resisting exploitation of the specialist's platform' (Stake 1995, p. 48).

4.3 THE VARIOUS DEBATES IN ETHICS LITERATURE

Essentially, the literature on ethics can be divided into two categories (K. Punch 1998). The first relates to the production of sets of guidelines for the ethical conduct of research. The second relates to texts that discuss the issues associated with research and the ways to deal with such issues — see, for example, the writings of Maurice Punch (1986, 1994) and Sieber and Sorensen (1992), or the edited works by Sieber (1982) and Stanley and Sieber (1991). Miles and Huberman (1994) provide an overview of five theoretical positions that may inform the discussion of ethics and ethical issues based on the work of Deyhle, Hess and LeCompte (1992 in Miles & Huberman 1994, p. 289) (see following page).

A *teleological* theory judges actions according to primary ends, good in themselves (e.g., the presumed value of knowledge resulting from research). A *utilitarian*, pragmatic approach judges actions according to their specific consequences — benefits and costs — for various audiences: the researcher, the researched, colleagues, the public. A *deontological* view invokes one or more universal rules (e.g., Kant's categorical and practical imperatives, which boil down to: (a) Would I like this action to be applied to everyone — including me? and (b) Will I treat every person I encounter as an end, and not as a means to something I want?). A *critical theory* approach judges actions according to whether one provides direct benefits to the researched and/or becomes an advocate for them. A *covenantal* view judges actions according to whether they are congruent with specific agreements made with others in trusted relationships.

These theoretical positions regarding ethics pervade the paradigms that inform tourism research to differing degrees. This will not be examined here, but such a discussion is included in the review questions at the end of this chapter. The following sections examine the issue of ethics in relation to various stakeholder groups and present additional components and/or guidelines for the conduct of ethical tourism research. Note that ethical responsibilities exist prior to, during and after the research process has been completed. Figure 4.1 provides a visual overview of a researcher's responsibilities to stakeholders.

■ **Figure 4.1**
Ethics,
stakeholders
and the
research
process

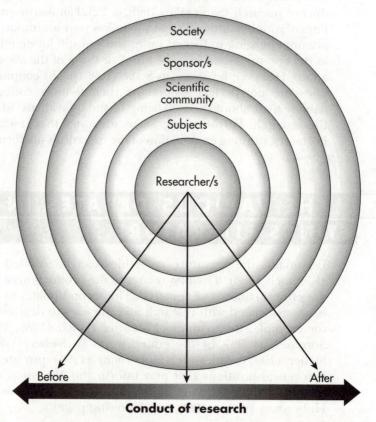

THE TOURISM RESEARCHER'S ETHICAL RESPONSIBILITIES TO SOCIETY

As stated earlier, tourism research generally occurs in everyday social settings, unless, for example, a researcher is using a laboratory setting to study an individual's physiological responses to various tourism stimuli, to conduct mathematical permutations or to model real-world scenarios. In all cases, regardless of whether the research setting is located in the real world or in a laboratory setting, the tourism researcher has responsibilities to society. Many codes of ethics are founded on the Nuremberg Code, the Universal Declaration of Human Rights and the Declaration of Helsinki. The protection of individual rights is a moral and social responsibility that is internationally recognised in the Western world, and is guided by these international code and declarations. Therefore, it is expected that every researcher has a responsibility to ensure that they protect the rights of individuals (and non-human subjects) participating in their research.

Moreover, returning to the premise that most tourism research occurs in everyday social settings, the researcher needs to ensure that the research does not alter adversely the everyday experiences of participants and other members of society. This is an important issue, especially for tourism researchers who are trying to gather data from people involved in an activity, the very nature of which is to get away from the intrusions of everyday life. Primarily by engaging in touristic experiences, tourists hope to suspend 'their normal everyday life', to escape, to be challenged, to have fun, to learn or to relax in another everyday setting. Imagine then, for example, that you are a tourist tramping through backcountry when your path is intercepted by an intrepid researcher. Or that you are relaxing under the shade of a tree in a tranquil setting and a tourism researcher appears beside you. Would you be willing to participate in their study? Why or why not? How can tourism research be achieved when it is in essence the antithesis of the overall touristic experience? Too much intrusion will result in societal rejection of tourism research and may lead to a possible flow-on of non-participation in any research undertaking or study.

For example, during 1999, in a particularly popular coastal tourism location in a neighbouring country, tourists were bombarded by supposed tourism researchers on what seemed like every corner of the main precinct and into neighbouring streets. The intensity of the data gathering by competing 'research teams' was so great that tourists were receiving multiple requests for participation in research and, as a consequence, were becoming aggressive, angry, rude and were choosing not to enter the precinct since in the course of walking half a kilometre they were being intercepted by at least three if not four 'researchers'. The action of these researchers had ramifications for tourism operators in the precinct — they were losing customers. Word-of-mouth quickly spread to other tourists not to bother to go to the precinct as they would only be hassled. This example serves to emphasise the need for ethical conduct in the real-world setting, as it has ramifications not only for the tourists but also for other members of the community or social setting.

In some societies, there are gatekeepers who prevent the 'overexamination' of tourists and communities alike. Governments may assume this role at the national level and at the local level. At an international level, non-national researchers may have to apply to conduct research in various countries (e.g. in Vietnam, Indonesia and Papua New Guinea). Moreover, in some countries, national researchers also have to gain the approval of government to undertake research. At a more local level, tourism operators, park managers, motel/hotel managers, tourism associations and presidents of various clubs such as fishing, rock climbing and adventure clubs or student associations are the gatekeepers who may or may not allow you access to their clients or constituents depending on your research aims and methods and the potential use of the findings. These gatekeepers are all trying to protect the interests of their clients or constituents and/or their way of operating their facilities or services.

Sometimes, well-intentioned research may not be allowed to proceed or access to potential participants will be denied because gatekeepers perceive that the researcher may alter the status quo of operations or interfere with the overall quality of life of their constituents, or the research may generate negative touristic experiences.

Gatekeepers may also act to protect the rights of constituents by refusing access because of past manifest intrusions into everyday life, sacred ceremonies and traditional cultural events. For example, the Hopi Reservation, Arizona (United States) has specific rules regarding visitation, such as a prohibition of photography, videotaping and audiotaping, and sketching. Permits must be obtained for visitation to archaeological sites. Similarly, research must be sanctioned and approved based on its benefits to the Hopi People.

Tourism research that involves community participation or consultation, or social or environmental impact assessment places the researcher firmly in the eye of society and has subsequent concomitant social and moral responsibilities. With such research, the researcher will undeniably become involved in political situations. Various stakeholder groups may try to manipulate the outcomes of the research. Some stakeholder groups may even place pressure on the researcher to present findings in one particular light. The researcher, however, is obliged to act ethically and to report the facts or findings as they are, without any manipulation by the researcher (or by outside influences). We will consider such manipulation later in the section on the researcher's responsibility to sponsors and clients.

Table 4.2 provides a checklist of the researcher's ethical responsibilities to society. When using the checklist, if any responses differ from those indicated, then the research design needs to be reconsidered with respect to its ethical framework. In some cases, there may be political ramifications, and this may be especially true of research informed by either (though not exclusively) a critical theory or feminist paradigm. If there are political ramifications, then there also needs to be some discussion regarding the social 'good' of the research.

■ Table 4.2
*Checklist of
the
researcher's
ethical
responsibilities
to society*

QUESTION	YES	NO
1. Does the research design apply the principles of the Nuremberg Code, the Declaration of Helsinki, the Universal Declaration of Human Rights or the NHMRC guidelines?	X	
2. Is the research moral and socially responsible?	X	
3. Will everyday life experiences be adversely altered?		X
4. Will others be adversely affected during the course of the research?		X
5. Have gatekeepers been apprised of the research?	X	
6. Has access been sought through gatekeepers?	X	
7. Are there any possible political ramifications of the research?		X
8. Is there any potential for manipulation of the research design?		X
9. What is the social 'good' of the research?	Explain the 'good' here:	

4.5 THE TOURISM RESEARCHER'S ETHICAL RESPONSIBILITIES TO THE SCIENTIFIC COMMUNITY

The tourism researcher belongs not only to the tourism and hospitality research community but also to the larger scientific community comprising all disciplinary areas. As a member of both communities, the tourism researcher is obliged to follow rules for the ethical conduct of research. Any misconduct in relation to the rules of ethical conduct affects not only the individual tourism researcher but also the reputation of all members of the wider scientific community. In order to ensure that all researchers act in an ethical manner, various disciplinary areas have developed their own codes of ethics. The code of conduct for the Australian and New Zealand Association for Leisure Studies (ANZALS) is presented in appendix 5 and discussed in the following Industry Insight.

The Code of Ethics of the Australian and New Zealand Association for Leisure Studies (ANZALS) (see appendix 5) was developed from the Australian Sociological Association and the Sociological Association of Aotearoa. The code aims to cover ethical issues in teaching and research as well as ethical issues associated with professional behaviour and the role of ethics in publications. The code posits an ethical statement, which is followed by specific guidelines regarding ethical responsibilities to research participants, the conduct of contractual research, teaching and student research. The code also addresses ethical issues associated with publication, acknowledgment of sponsorship, and specific procedures and conventions for ANZALS to deal with breaches in ethical behaviour or conduct in any of the aforementioned areas.

Such codes of ethical conduct for research ensure that the researcher conducts ethically responsible research with respect to the treatment of individuals, the methodology used and the soundness of the findings.

Part of the process of maintaining ethical practices within the scientific community is the use of peer reviews. Peer reviews involve other qualified researchers assessing the quality and feasibility of research proposals, as well as the quality and integrity of research reports. In particular, a peer reviewer will aim to determine whether the researcher whose work is being reviewed will or has treated the participants ethically by protecting and respecting participants' rights as humans or protecting and respecting the rights of non-human participants. A peer reviewer will also seek to determine whether the researcher has the appropriate research skills and theoretical knowledge to conduct the research, whether the methodology is the most appropriate for the collection of data, and whether the data collection and analysis are appropriate and, of course, ethical. In the case of research reports, the peer reviewer will seek to determine whether the findings are truthfully presented and that there is no evidence of bias.

If the researcher wishes to publish their research in one of the tourism and hospitality journals, their submission will usually be peer reviewed. The use of the peer review process maintains the integrity and quality of tourism and hospitality research and thereby ensures that the reputation of individual researchers and the scientific community is maintained.

Essentially, the ethical responsibilities of a tourism researcher to the scientific community relate to three issues: the protection of the right of the individual (or non-human participant); the protection of the reputation of the scientific community; and the production of ethical research.

Table 4.3 provides a checklist of the researcher's ethical responsibilities to the scientific community. As with the researcher's ethical responsibilities to society, should any of the responses on the checklist differ from those indicated, then the peer reviewer would have to question the overall ethical nature of the proposed research if reviewing a research proposal or the research project if reviewing a report or an article. Depending on the extent of the mismatch to the responses on the ethics checklist, the researcher being reviewed may be requested to explain or, in extreme cases, may be banned from membership of professional associations or publicly exposed.

■ **Table 4.3**
Checklist of the researcher's ethical responsibilities to the scientific community

QUESTION	YES	NO
1. Does the research design apply the principles of the Nuremberg Code, the Declaration of Helsinki, the Universal Declaration of Human Rights or the NHMRC guidelines?	X	
2. Is the research morally and socially responsible?	X	
3. Is the researcher appropriately skilled to conduct the research?	X	
4. Have all sources been appropriately acknowledged and referenced?	X	
5. Has access to participants been appropriately sought?	X	
6. Is the methodology appropriate for the research aims/hypotheses?	X	
7. Has the data collection process respected the rights of the human/ non-human participants?	X	
8. Are the data measures reliable?	X	
9. Is the data analysis valid?	X	
10. Are the findings substantiated?	X	
11. Is there any evidence of bias?		X
12. Has there been any manipulation of the research design?		X
13. What is the social 'good' of the research?	Explain the 'good' here:	

THE TOURISM RESEARCHER'S ETHICAL RESPONSIBILITIES TO RESEARCH PARTICIPANTS

The primary issue for researchers is the protection of the rights of both human and non-human participants. Essentially, the researcher has to ensure that, in the course of any research project, the participants do not experience any harm. While the discussion here focuses on human participants rather than non-human participants, unless otherwise stated you should be able to identify similarities with respect to ethical conduct for both types of participants.

Harm can be defined in four ways — physical harm, psychological harm, legal harm and other harm (Neuman 2000, pp. 92–5) — and these are discussed below.

■ 4.6.1 Physical *harm*

The prevention of physical harm has its roots in the Nuremberg Code, although this is not to suggest that, with the instigation of the Nuremberg Code, the Declaration of Helsinki and the Universal Declaration of Human Rights, there have not been research projects that have harmed participants or have been unethical. In the last half of the twentieth century, complaints were made regarding the alleged use of military personnel as 'guinea pigs' (i.e. non-voluntary or uninformed research participants) in the conduct of research into chemical and pharmaceutical products. American blood banks are also alleged to have continued to use AIDS-affected blood with the knowledge that the blood was infected with the AIDS virus. Both alleged instances are unethical and immoral and outside the guidelines of the aforementioned code and declarations.

Within the sphere of tourism and hospitality research, it is the researcher's responsibility to ensure that the participants, the research assistants and the researcher come to no physical harm. In particular, issues related to occupational health and safety have relevance for the conduct of tourism research.

Consider, for example, the positioning of participants and researchers in relation to potentially dangerous physical situations, such as trying to conduct an exit survey in a narrow doorway when hundreds of weary passengers are trying to disembark from a ferry at the end of a long day trip. Or the issues associated with the interruption of concentration when tourists are executing demanding tasks in the research setting, such as trying to conduct an interview with a tourist who is learning how to abseil just before they make their final safety check and manoeuvre over the edge of a precipice. Tourism research should never place participants or research workers in situations that are physically dangerous or harmful.

4.6.2 Psychological *harm*

Tourism research should never cause participants to experience anxiety or embarrassment, or generate feelings of inferiority or stress. There may be some circumstances in which such feelings might be utilised in the research setting, although the reasons for their use would have to be well justified. Furthermore, the participants would have to be informed of the purposes of the research and would have to maintain the right to withdraw at any stage of the research. Examples of situations in which a researcher may inadvertently cause psychological harm include:

- asking and/or badgering an illiterate person to complete a questionnaire
- asking and/or badgering a non-English speaking person to participate in an interview or complete a questionnaire using English
- making comments in response to questions or statements such as 'You must know the meaning of that word, everyone knows that!', 'You mean you are on the dole!', or 'Is that all the schooling you had?'
- hectoring a participant for a response when one is not forthcoming
- displaying non-verbal behaviours of impatience or inattention such as pen tapping or foot tapping when a participant is thinking about a response, or not paying attention to a participant during an interview.

4.6.3 Legal *harm*

In the course of conducting some research, a researcher may come across information that will put them in a compromising situation. In particular, a researcher may come across information that identifies illegal activities. For example, researchers who are conducting research into sex tourism in other countries may become aware of illegal child sex tours (in terms of the Australian legal system). Or researchers who are studying casual tourism employment patterns may become aware of part-time or casual tourism workers who are receiving cash in hand payments and accessing social service payments or, in the case of non-Australian residents, who are working without a work permit or visa. Before embarking on research projects that may potentially place the researcher in a compromising situation, the researcher must clearly determine what their responses will be and what they see their role to be. As a researcher, you must clearly know your role. If you have stated that you will protect the rights of the participants, then your records of illegal behaviour must be protected, otherwise you will be breaking the trust of the participants and this can undermine future research (Neuman 2000, p. 95). Neuman (2000) comments that you have to make this decision bearing in mind the consequences to other people who may be affected by the information — for example, in the case of sex tourism, the children who are involved in sex tourism.

4.6.4 Other *harm*

In the conduct of research, there are other potential avenues of harm for participants or others associated indirectly with any research. For example, evaluative research may indicate a need for downsizing, which could actively lead to the loss of jobs and incomes for tourism and hospitality personnel. Comparative research may indicate that one provider is better than another, which could lead to loss of contracts for one supplier and subsequent losses of income with wider-reaching impacts associated with multiplier effects in communities. Evaluation of attractions or facilities may result in their closure and subsequent loss of jobs because of occupational and health and safety issues or breaches of standards that are highlighted. Again, the researcher needs to protect the rights of individuals but also be aware of the flow-on harmful effects that their research may have. Stake (1995, p. 60) advises that '[t]he researcher should leave the site having made no one less able to carry out their responsibilities'.

Table 4.4 provides a checklist for monitoring the researcher's ethical responsibilities to research participants with respect to the avoidance of harm. Again, responses contrary to those indicated in the checklist require deep reflection by the researcher and strong justification for non-compliance.

■ Table 4.4
Checklist of the researcher's ethical responsibilities to research participants

QUESTION	YES	NO
1. Does the research protect the rights of the participants?	X	
2. Is the research moral and socially responsible?	X	
3. Has the researcher anticipated all the risks associated with the location for the data collection?	X	
4. Has the researcher anticipated all the risks associated with the involvement of research participants?	X	
5. Has the researcher anticipated all the risks associated with the involvement of research assistants?	X	
6. Has the researcher anticipated all the risks associated with the research in regard to non-participants?	X	
7. Is there any physical harm associated with this research?		X
8. Is there any psychological harm associated with this research?		X
9. Is there any legal harm associated with this research?		X
10. Is there any other harm associated with this research?		X
11. Is the researcher prepared to terminate the research if there is any risk?	X	

■ *4.6.5* **Informed** *consent*

Two direct outcomes of the Nuremberg Code are voluntary participation and informed consent by research participants. '[Informed consent] is the most fundamental ethical principle that is involved [in research]. Participants must understand the nature and purpose of the research and must consent to participate without coercion' (Burns 1997, p. 18).

Glesne (1999, pp. 116–17) adds several other dimensions to the concept of informed consent. Participation should be voluntary based on a participant's knowledge of research processes and the consequences of those processes on the participant's wellbeing, as well as the freedom to withdraw from the research process. David de Vaus (1995, p. 334) provides a more extensive checklist in regard to informed consent. He advocates that informed consent needs to provide the participants with knowledge of:

1. the research purpose and processes
2. any potential risks or harm
3. the benefits of the research
4. how the participants were chosen
5. the ability to ask questions concerning the research
6. the voluntary nature of their participation
7. the identity of the researcher and sponsor
8. how the findings will be used.

Researchers may either provide their potential participants with an informed consent letter (see figure 4.2 on page 110), or they may read the letter to the potential participants. Some research projects may also require written consent, in which case the researcher would provide an informed consent letter similar to that used in figure 4.2, but would add a statement that the participant has read and understood the text and agrees to participate as per the conditions noted in the letter.

There are two other issues regarding informed consent and data collection on individuals: privacy, specifically anonymity, and confidentiality. Sometimes, the two latter terms are used interchangeably. However, they mean two different things:

> Anonymity means that the researcher will not and cannot identify the respondent … Confidentiality simply means that the researcher can match names with responses but ensures that no one else will have access to them (de Vaus 1995, p. 337).

Why offer anonymity and confidentiality? De Vaus (1995, p. 337) suggests four reasons for assuring confidentiality; however, they also apply to assuring anonymity. Apart from protecting participants' rights, assuring anonymity and confidentiality will:

1. enhance the nature and veracity of responses
2. encourage involvement
3. enhance the sample size and its representation of the overall study population
4. ensure the participants' privacy is not compromised.

Whether you are offering anonymity or confidentiality, any assurances you give must be honoured.

■ Figure 4.2
*An example
of a form
letter used to
provide
informed
consent*

Coast West Tourism and Recreation Research Centre
Coast West University
The Peninsula

May 2001

Dear _____,

A study of the recreational use of Sunshine Bay is being undertaken by Jenna Chang from Coast West University for the Coast West Marine Park Advisory Group. The study seeks to determine the number of users, types of recreational use and areas of use, as well as the opinions of current users regarding activities appropriate for the area. The information gathered in the study will assist park managers to plan for the future management of Sunshine Bay.

As a registered permit-holder and user of the Sunshine Bay area, you are invited to participate in this study. Your participation is voluntary. If you agree to participate in the study, please return your completed questionnaire in the reply paid envelope. Any information you provide will be anonymous. To ensure this, you are asked not to record your name anywhere on the questionnaire.

If you are interested in the results of this study, they will be published in various print media after July, including recreational magazines.

If you have any concerns regarding your participation or the questionnaire please contact Jenna Chang, Coast West Tourism and Recreation Research Centre, Coast West University, The Peninsula. Telephone: CWU-5888 3333 between the hours of 9.00 a.m. and 5.00 p.m. Monday to Friday.

Jenna Chang

■ *4.6.6* **Deception** *and covert research*

Informed consent requires that research participants are fully apprised of the nature of the research in which they are participating. Deception occurs when participants are deceived about some aspect of the research. For example, the true identity of the sponsor may be masked or the overall research purpose may be couched in ambiguous terms or purposefully misrepresented. The reason for such deception is usually based on the premise that had the participants been made aware of the real identity of sponsor or the purpose of the research, then their responses would have been influenced by that knowledge. Deception of this nature must be approved by research peers, the scientific community and/or ethics review panels. Ethics review panels are involved in reviewing applications for ethical clearance for the undertaking of research.

Covert research, on the other hand, involves research in which the participants are not informed or aware of their participation. As Patton (1990) notes, there are two diametrically opposing opinions regarding the use of covert research in the scientific community. One opinion rejects the use of covert research and the other supports it. These views are best portrayed by the opinions of Shils (1959, in Patton 1990) and Douglas (1976, in Patton 1990), respectively. Shils rejects the use of 'observations of private behavior, however technically feasible, without the explicit and fully informed permission of the person to be observed', as it is 'morally obnoxious ... manipulation' (Shils 1959, in Patton 1990, p. 210).

Douglas, on the other hand, comments:

> All competent adults are assumed to know that there are at least four major problems lying in the way of getting at social reality by asking people what is going on and that these problems must be dealt with if one is to avoid being taken in, duped, deceived, used, put on, fooled, suckered, made the patsy, left holding the bag, fronted out and so on. These four problems are (1) misinformation; (2) evasions; (3) lies; and (4) fronts (Douglas 1976, p. 57, in Patton 1990, p. 210).

As a researcher, you have to make your own decisions regarding covert research and the use of deception. This should be determined by weighing the 'moral' good such research will do for society against how such covert activities and deception infringe on the rights of humans. It also needs to be sanctioned by an appropriate body from your discipline, profession or organisation.

4.7 THE TOURISM RESEARCHER'S ETHICAL RESPONSIBILITIES TO SPONSORS

As already stated, all research must be undertaken in an ethical manner. This is especially relevant in undertaking applied research, as the client or sponsor may angle for a bias in the research design or reporting. Researchers are bound by ethical standards and such angling is not acceptable. Researchers must be responsible to themselves, the scientific community, the public and the sponsors for the conduct of ethical research.

When working for a client or sponsor, there are essentially two types of research: conditional and non-conditional. Conditional research has limitations placed upon it. These limitations may be time, money, personnel or research design constraints. Individually or in combination, these constraints will influence the overall research design, including ethical considerations. Researchers have to determine whether such constraints will result in ethical or unethical behaviour and outcomes. This does not mean to suggest that all conditional research is unethical. Conditional research requires that the specific limitations of the study have to be noted, but such limitations do not imply that the research is unethical. Non-conditional research has no constraints imposed on it and is the rarer option associated with working with sponsors or clients. This type of research allows the researcher autonomy in the development of the time lines and the research design that are used.

When working for sponsors and clients, it is essential that contracts are established to clearly delineate the areas of responsibility for each party. Researchers should ensure that the issue of intellectual property rights is addressed. In some contracts, the researcher signs over the research material and all associated intellectual property rights to the sponsor or client. The researcher then has to seek permission from the sponsor or client to use the data. In other cases, part of the contract may require the researcher to sign a 'secrecy clause', as the researcher may be collecting information of a 'commercial-in-confidence' nature.

■ *4.7.1* **Deception**

A sponsor may request the researcher to withhold the sponsor's identity (the above discussion on deception has relevance here as well). A sponsor may also seek to have the purpose of their research masked. Babbie (1990, p. 344) offers some guidance. He notes that researchers cannot always be fully cognisant of how their research will be used. Once the research is completed for a sponsor, it may be used for other analytical purposes to which the researcher is not privy and so therefore cannot inform the participants. However, in regard to research purposes, Babbie makes the following four points:

1. ensure the purpose is stated in a form that will not affect the reliability of the results
2. ensure you tell the participants all you can about the purposes when such information will not influence participants' responses
3. present the purposes in general rather than specific formats
4. untrue purposes should never be constructed.

Some advertising conversion research studies use deception. For example, Woodside and Ronkainen recommend:

> The identification of a state or location as the sponsor of the study should be avoided. To desensitize respondents, the questionnaire should be used to collect data on travel behavior with respect to competing travel destinations. Furthermore, the letter accompanying the questionnaire should not refer to the fact that the respondent is known to have written for travel information. Recent conversion studies have been conducted by independent research agencies identified as the sponsor of the study. However, no direct test has been reported to substantiate this proposition (Woodside & Ronkainen 1994, p. 550, in Ritchie & Goeldner 1994).

Woodside and Ronkainen appear to support Douglas' perspective on covert research.

■ 4.7.2 Incentives

Sometimes, sponsors or clients may seek to use incentives to encourage participation in a study. If this is the case, researchers need to ensure that the sponsor is going to follow through with the provision of such incentives. However, incentives are considered by some researchers to be bribes. How ethical then is their use? How can a researcher be sure that the participant has responded because of genuine interest and provided truthful responses, as opposed to participating in order to receive the incentive and giving responses not reflecting their true position?

Subsequently, ethical responsibilities to sponsors relate to the researcher ensuring that the sponsor's intent is ethical. The researcher needs to question the ramifications of participating in conditional research and research that uses incentives, as well as deception and covert research. If the researcher becomes aware of duplicity by the sponsor, then the researcher should be prepared to withdraw from the research and possibly expose the sponsor for unethical practices (using counsel or based on legal advice).

4.8 THE TOURISM RESEARCHER'S ETHICAL RESPONSIBILITIES TO THE SELF

> Ethics define what is or is not legitimate to do, or what 'moral' research procedure involves (Neuman 2000, p. 90).

This section considers the issues that relate to the researcher and the legitimate conduct of research. There is some overlap here between the expectations of ethical practices by the scientific community and other stakeholder groups. That being said, for the tourism researcher, ethical responsibilities are associated primarily with the design, conduct and reporting of the research. There are three key issues that need to be considered: professional misconduct (see Neuman 2000 and Sarantakos 1998); power relations (see Sieber 1992 and Neuman 2000); and politics (Babbie 1995 and Neuman 2000).

■ 4.8.1 Key issues *for the researcher*

As a member of the scientific community, a researcher has to ensure that they do not engage in any research misconduct. The key types of misconduct are research fraud (research falsification) and plagiarism (Neuman 2000, p. 91). Research fraud is the fabrication of data and the subsequent false reporting of those data by a researcher or research team. It also includes the misrepresentation of research design, in particular the methods used. Plagiarism involves a researcher claiming another researcher's work to be their own or using another writer's text as their own. The issue of plagiarism will be outlined in more detail in chapter 10. Both types of misconduct are 'amoral' and unethical.

The researcher must also not abuse the power position associated with the conduct of research. In the opening quote Sieber reminds us of the power position between the researcher and the 'subject'. The power the researcher has over the participants or 'subjects' is associated with the researcher's academic qualifications or education, perceived knowledge levels and research training, as well as their access to confidential data. The researcher must not abuse their relationship with the subjects: to do so will impact on the rights of the participants, the scientific community and the researcher.

Babbie (1995, p. 461) provides insight into the difference between politics and ethics: 'the ethics of social research deals more with the methods employed, and the political issues are more concerned with the substance and use of research'. In reality, '[a]ll research is political from the micro-politics of interpersonal relationships, through the politics of research units, institutions and universities, to those of government departments and finally to the state' (Bell & Newby 1977, pp. 9–10, in Oakley 1981, p. 54).

An example of politics is provided by Caplan and Caplan (1999, p. 108), who suggest the following list of questions that could be used when reading sex-difference research to determine political agendas. Although framed for consideration of research between different sexes and genders, the questions are equally applicable to other research, as the questions try to determine the individual political bias of the researcher.

1. What were the researcher's reasons for conducting the research?
2. Does the wording of the research questions contain any bias?
3. Does the research design exhibit any flaws or methodological problems?
4. Were the data interpreted without any evident bias?
5. Are there any other possible explanations for the findings proffered?

■ 4.8.2 Relationships *between the researcher and the participants*

Different paradigms provide different relationships (the epistemological position) between the researcher and the participants or 'subjects'. Positivist and chaos theory paradigms have an objective relationship; the other paradigms are subjective in nature. The beginning of this chapter briefly introduced the theoretical perspectives of teleological, utilitarian, deontological, critical theory and covenantal views to ethics. Flinders (1992, in Miles & Huberman 1994, p. 289) presents another view regarding approaches to ethics. Flinders identifies four types of approaches to ethics: relational ethics (associated with attachment, respect and caring); utilitarian ethics (as applied in positivism); deontological ethics (viewing the researcher and the researched as collaborators); and ecological ethics (associated with understanding the local culture and avoiding detachment). Each of these four approaches has ramifications for three main areas of the overall research process: accessing participants, collecting the data and reporting the findings (see table 4.5).

■ Table 4.5
*The effects of
the four
ethical
approaches
on three
main areas
of the
research
process*

	UTILITARIAN APPROACH	DEONTOLOGICAL APPROACH	RELATIONAL APPROACH	ECOLOGICAL APPROACH
Accessing participants	Informed consent	Reciprocity	Collaboration	Cultural sensitivity
Collecting the data	Avoidance of harm	Avoidance of wrong	Avoidance of imposition	Avoidance of detachment
Reporting the findings	Confidentiality	Fairness	Confirmation	Responsive communication

Source: *Based on Flinders (1992, in Miles & Huberman 1994, p. 289)*

We can further consider the relationship between the researcher and the researched based on the methodology used. Stake (1995, p. 103) in particular discusses the role of the researcher in qualitative research and 'how much will the researcher be her- or himself? ... Often, the researcher will be pressured to be more the evaluator, the scientist, or the therapist than he or she wants to be. Others will help negotiate the role. The role should be an ethical choice, an honest choice.'

As Jorgensen (1989, p. 68) notes for those engaging in participant observation: '[I]n participating, you should be sensitive to ethical issues, politics, and complications regarding your self-concept.' Furthermore, researchers have to be ready to deal with the morals associated with any illegal or unethical activities they may uncover in the course of their research. They have to decide whether they will position themselves as a 'freelance undercover informant' or a 'scientist' (Neuman 2000, p. 95). As Fetterman (1989) notes, there are two possible outcomes of undertaking research: 'guilty knowledge' and 'dirty hands'. Guilty knowledge refers to 'confidential knowledge of illegal or illicit activities' and dirty hands refers to 'situations in which the ethnographer cannot emerge innocent of wrong doing' (Fetterman 1989, p. 135). Again, the researcher has to decide on the role to be played.

4.9 THE CONCEPTS OF RECIPROCITY AND REFLEXIVITY

Over the past 50 years or so, the number of social studies and surveys being conducted has increased substantially, and to some extent they have become a part of everyday life. That being said, it still cannot be disputed that studies and surveys are an intrusion into the everyday lives of individuals. The increase in the number of social surveys and studies has generated two views: acceptance of such studies and surveys as part of everyday life; and rejection of such studies as being a bother and gross intrusion into people's lives.

As has happened in the past, some people who participate in studies and surveys today are often not apprised of the outcomes of the research findings. Subsequently, the issue of reciprocity has developed. This has certainly been an issue for interpretive social sciences, conflict theory and feminism paradigms, but has not always been the purveyance of all paradigms. In today's world, people want something back for participating in research. In the section dealing with the tourism researcher's responsibilities to the sponsor, we touched on the issue of incentives and payment. Fetterman (1989) suggests that this type of reciprocity is perhaps the least preferred by researchers as there is always a question mark concerning the person's participation. Did they participate for the sake of the study or for the sake of the payment? Furthermore, how much did the payment 'shape the person's responses or recommendations throughout the study?' (Fetterman 1989, p. 135).

Rather than payment, reciprocity can involve participants being informed or offered a copy of the research findings in an accessible and understandable form. The reciprocity here is directly linked to the participants providing information and the researcher providing a summation of all the participants' information back to the participants. Reciprocity, as some feminist researchers (such as Oakley and Bell Hooks) comment, can also occur during the course of the research process. For example, Oakley (1981, p. 49) notes:

> I had found, in my previous interviewing experiences, that an attitude of refusing to answer questions or offer any kind of personal feedback was not helpful in the traditional goal of promoting 'rapport'. A different role, that could be termed 'no intimacy without reciprocity', seemed especially important in longitudinal in-depth interviewing.

Obviously, such involvement on the part of the researcher in the research process would not be condoned by researchers operating from a positivist paradigm, as this type of reciprocity would be considered to alter the objective nature of the research process. And such an accusation would be correct from a positivist viewpoint. However, from the interpretive social sciences, critical theory, poststructuralist/postmodern and especially feminist perspectives, such objectivity is the antithesis of the social construction of reality. The role of the researcher within the overall research process and the notion of objectivity and subjectivity bring us to the concept of reflexivity.

Reflexivity refers to 'the sense of seriously locating [oneself] in [one's] research' (Williams 1990, p. 254). Consequently, reflexivity also involves subjectivity, especially the social situatedness of the self. Harding (1991, pp. 162–3) comments on the nature of reflexivity:

> [I]ndividuals express 'heartfelt desire' not to harm the subjects they observe, to become aware of their own cultural biases, and so on, but such reflexive goals remain at the level of desire rather than competent enactment. In short, such weak reflexivity has no possible operationalization, or no competency standard, for success.
>
> A notion of strong reflexivity would require that all the objects of inquiry be conceptualized as gazing back in all their cultural particularity and that the researcher, through theory and methods, stand behind them, gazing back at his [sic] own socially situated research project in all its cultural particularity and its relationships to other projects of his [sic] culture — many of which (policy development in international relations, for example, or industrial expansion) can only be seen from locations far away from the scientist's actual daily work.

As well as being a feminist issue, reflexivity is also a concern of the interpretive social sciences (especially ethnographic studies), critical theory and the poststructuralist 'form' of postmodernism. Harding (1991) also posits that reflexivity is a problem for those scientists operating within a positivist paradigm, as their understanding is 'artificially restricted to the micro processes of the laboratory and research community', particularly because of the positivist tendencies to 'isolat[e] research communities from the larger social, economic, and political currents in their societies' (Harding 1991, p. 162).

Another perspective on reflexivity is provided by Marcus (1994, pp. 568–73), who identifies four types of reflexivity:
1. 'subjectivist reflexivity', often associated with feminist writing and also anthropology
2. 'objectified reflexivity', based on the writing of Bourdieu
3. 'reflexivity as a politics of location' (see the work of Myers 1988)
4. 'subjectivist, experiential reflexivity', primarily espoused in feminism.

Subjectivist reflexivity socially situates the researcher within the study. An objectified form of reflexivity is presented in the writings of Bourdieu (1990a, in Marcus 1994, p. 570): 'An objectified form of reflexivity, [refers to] making an object of that which shapes your knowledge, never giving into a romantic subjectivist fantasy.' Subjectivist, experiential reflexivity is similar to presenting an autobiography. For example:

> I chose to begin by locating myself as a participant within the subculture of long-term ocean cruising. I did this in order to demonstrate that 'my vantage point' is grounded on 'the same social relations that structure the everyday world experiences' (Cook & Fonow 1990, p. 73) of the cruisers I had studied. Furthermore, I needed to emphasise that my own experience was and is gendered by my being a woman who had participated in the subculture of long-term ocean cruisers and who now lives in the margins of that subculture. A subculture which has traditionally been dominated by men. In locating myself, I acknowledge my 'biases and preconceived notions about how people behave and what they think' (Fetterman 1989, p. 11). I also acknowledge my subjectivity. My subjectivity, as already stated, is situated in my biography: a white, middle-class, Anglo-Celtic Australian woman who chose to study white, middle class, Western women and men in heterosexual relationships in the process of pursuing a cruising lifestyle' (Jennings 1999, pp. 17–18).

In addressing issues of reciprocity and reflexivity, researchers are forced to identify their relationship to participants in the conduct of research and to acknowledge the role they subsequently play in the process of research.

4.10 $\mathcal{S}$O WHY BE ETHICAL?

Essentially, tourism researchers need to be ethical to ensure that they protect the rights of the individuals (including non-humans) who participate in their research and to protect the standing of the scientific community. It also ensures that knowledge is advanced based on findings that have been ethically determined and, as a consequence, these findings should assist the further development or enhancement of society (see the Industry Insight below). For researchers, being ethical means knowing that they can live with themselves because they have acted both morally and professionally throughout the research process. All paradigms are required to consider ethics. However,

> No paradigm is without ethical problems, but the problems that plague construc-tivism [the interpretive social sciences paradigm] are radically different from those that engage the attention of conventional postpositivist [derived from posi-tivism] researchers. The emphasis on face-to-face interaction, on faithfully repre-senting multiple, constructed, and often conflicting realities, and on maintaining privacy and anonymity while utilizing extensive word-for-word, natural language quotations in case studies as well as the case studies in general are all problems typically faced by the emergent-paradigm [interpretive social sciences and con-flict theory] inquirer (Lincoln 1990, p. 83).

INDUSTRY INSIGHT

Within Australia, the Bureau of Tourism Research (BTR) conducts tourism research in order that government agencies and the Australian tourism industry may make informed decisions regarding tourism patterns, potential tourism developments, tourism servicing, marketing and the monitoring of tourism trends. BTR disseminates its research findings using a variety of genres and media such as data cards, research reports, conference pro-ceedings, research papers and statistical data presented in hard copy on paper or in electronic format, accessed through the Bureau's Web site (www.btr.gov.au).

The role of BTR in providing timely information regarding tourism trends is significant. However, the significance of BTR's research is related to more than just the timeliness of its data outputs — it is also related to the overall credibility of its research. BTR has prepared a draft charter (see www.btr.gov.au/charter/charter.html) regarding its research activities. The charter incorporates issues related to the conduct of research in an ethical manner. Specifically, the draft charter states that BTR places high value on:
• being honest, ethical and professional
• being helpful, courteous and considerate
• acting with care and diligence.

Source: *http://www.btr.gov.au/charter/charter.html*
(downloaded 8 March 2000)

The need for ethics in the conduct of tourism research

The need for ethical guidelines in regard to the conduct of tourism research has developed from the Nuremberg Code, the Universal Declaration of Human Rights, the Declaration of Helsinki and numerous professional, disciplinary and institutional codes of ethics regarding the protection of human and non-human participants. Codes of ethics usually discuss voluntary participation, informed consent and the right of the participant to refuse to respond or the right to withdraw, as well as the right not to be deceived or to be harmed in any way. Issues pertaining to confidentiality, anonymity and access to findings are also included.

The various debates in ethics literature

Ethics literature has two foci: ethical guidelines and ethical issues. There are five theoretical positions with respect to the discussion of ethics: teleological theory; utilitarian, pragmatic approach; deontological view; critical theory approach; and covenantal view.

The tourism researcher's ethical responsibilities to society

The tourism researcher's responsibilities to society are founded in the Nuremberg Code, the Universal Declaration of Human Rights, the Declaration of Helsinki and the resultant codes of ethics for the conduct of research using human and non-human participants. The main issues for the researcher include the protection of the rights of the individual and the intrusion into the everyday lives of the various participants in the tourism phenomenon under study.

The tourism researcher's ethical responsibilities to the scientific community

Ethical conduct in regard to the wider scientific community is related to three issues: the protection of the right of the individual; the protection of the reputation of the scientific community; and the production of ethical research.

The tourism researcher's ethical responsibilities to research participants

Obviously, the protection of human and non-human rights is the researcher's primary responsibility. Research should not cause physical, psychological, legal or other harm. Research participation should be voluntary and based on informed consent. Anonymity and confidentiality assurances must be honoured. Deception and covert research are essentially unethical and require sanctioning by an auspicating body or ethics panel.

The tourism researcher's ethical responsibilities to sponsors

Researchers need to ensure that sponsors request ethical research studies. Research carried out on behalf of sponsors may be conditional (with limitations on time, money or research design) or non-conditional. Some researchers may be requested to use incentives or deception. The merits of incentives and deception have to be weighed against the 'social' good of the research.

The tourism researcher's ethical responsibilities to the self

A researcher must avoid any misconduct (fabrication/falsification or plagiarism), use of power or political manipulation of data, although some research has a political agenda (e.g. research informed by the critical theory orientation or feminist paradigms).

The concepts of reciprocity and reflexivity

Reciprocity means giving something back to the participants, and reflexivity means locating oneself in one's research. Marcus (1994) identifies four types of reflexivity: subjectivist; objectified; located politically; and subjectivist, experiential.

The need to be ethical

Researchers need to be ethical to protect research participants from harm. They also need to be ethical to ensure that the standing of the scientific community is protected and that the research findings are derived in a morally and professionally responsible way.

Questions

4.1 Which of the five theoretical positions regarding ethics is aligned with each of the paradigms informing tourism research? Explain your answer.

4.2 What are the main ethical issues for the researcher in relation to the scientific community?

4.3 Why is plagiarism such an issue for the scientific and wider community?

4.4 Can a researcher always ensure reciprocity and reflexivity in tourism research?

4.5 If a tourism researcher is only concerned with the research setting and its outcomes, what do you think might be some of the ramifications for society?

4.6 Is there any time when you would consider using deception in a tourism research study? Explain your answer.

4.7 What are the primary ethical issues in regard to the tourism researcher's responsibilities to participants?

4.8 Is there any time when you think it would be appropriate to present your findings as directed by a sponsor? Explain your answer.

4.9 What do you believe are your moral responsibilities for the conduct of tourism research?

4.10 Reflect on the various paradigms that inform tourism research. Is ethics an issue for all paradigms?

4.11 Do you think that tourism researchers should be guided by a professional code of ethics, or should tourism researchers be individually responsible for the conduct of ethical research?

Exercise 4.1

Devise your own checklist regarding ethics and research participants. Compare it with the checklists of other members in your class or with a professional tourism/hospitality body or association.

Exercise 4.2

Consider the following hypothetical scenario.

One enterprising 'resort' owner (the term 'resort' is used loosely here) has decided to try to increase the number of his clientele by conducting market research. Other 'resort' operators have also incorporated the idea into their marketing strategy. Concurrently, the majority of individual 'resort' owners in a tourism precinct have decided independently of each another to conduct the same type of market research. Each of the managers wants to determine the sociodemographics of the tourists, their length of stay in the area and their current accommodation venue.

Each of the managers prepares a questionnaire that enables them to collect such information. The questionnaires are to be given out by young unemployed people in the local area. The men are required to be well dressed in smart shirts, long trousers, shoes and socks, while the women are required to be dressed in national costume. The young people are told that they will only be paid for fully completed questionnaires. They are informed that the study is to gather general information about the tourists who come to the area. They are also told that each respondent will be placed into a draw for a free holiday (although none of the resort managers intends to honour this). In order to be eligible for the 'free' draw, tourists must provide their room number in the personal details section.

Each resort manager sees the questionnaire as a way to locate tourists who can then be approached and encouraged to change accommodation venues. The young people who have been employed to gather the data are not informed that each resort manager will use the data to visit all the respondents in the area in an attempt to get them to move their accommodation to their resort venue.

During the course of the first week of data collection, 11 young people are on the streets approaching tourists. The data collection is particularly concentrated in the evenings when the tourists are moving about looking for places to eat. Each tourist is bound to encounter at least three interviewers in the course of trying to get to a restaurant. Furthermore, on the way home they are likely to encounter another or the same interviewer and, in the case of the latter, to be approached again.

Those tourists who do not answer the questionnaire completely are harangued by the young interviewers to complete all the details. The tourists are followed or chased by the interviewers in an effort to coerce them to comply.

(a) In your opinion, what are the main ethical issues associated with this hypothetical scenario?

(b) What do you consider are the primary ethical issues that have not been addressed?

(c) What are the possible consequences of this research for society, the scientific community, the participants, the stakeholders and the researchers?

RESEARCH PROJECT

With respect to your own research project, what are the key ethical issues that you must address regarding:

- your ethical responsibilities to society?
- your ethical responsibilities to the scientific community?
- your ethical responsibilities to research participants?
- your ethical responsibilities to sponsors? (if applicable — if not, your responsibilities to the institution where you are studying?)
- your ethical responsibilities to yourself?
- reciprocity and reflexivity?

What strategies will you use in your research design to ensure that you are meeting your responsibilities to all of the stakeholder groups? How will you address reciprocity and reflexivity? When you have constructed your responses, review table 4.1 and consider whether you have addressed all the relevant issues.

REFERENCES

Babbie, Earl. 1990. *Survey Research Methods*. Second Edition. Belmont: Wadsworth.

Babbie, Earl. 1995. *The Practice of Social Research*. Seventh Edition. Belmont: Wadsworth.

Burns, Robert. 1997. *Introduction to Research Methods*. Third Edition. Melbourne: Longman.

Caplan, Paula J. & Caplan, Jeremy B. 1999. *Thinking Critically About Research on Sex and Gender*. New York: Longman.

de Vaus, David. 1995. *Surveys in Social Research*. Fourth Edition. Sydney: Allen & Unwin.

Douglas, Jack. 1976. *Investigative Social Research: Individual and Team Field Research*. Beverley Hills, CA: Sage.

Fetterman, David. M. 1989. *Ethnography, Step by Step*. Applied Social Research Methods Series, Volume 17. Newbury Park: Sage.

Flinders, D. J. 1992. 'In Search of Ethical Guidance: Constructing a Basis for Dialogue'. *Qualitative Studies in Education*, vol. 5, no. 2, pp. 101–16.

Glesne, Corrine. 1999. *Becoming Qualitative Researchers: An Introduction.* Second Edition. New York: Longman.

Harding, Sandra. 1991. *Whose Science? Whose Knowledge?* Milton Keynes: Open University Press.

Jennings, Gayle. 1999. Voyages from the Centre to the Margins: An Ethnography of Long-Term Ocean Cruisers. Unpublished PhD dissertation. Murdoch University.

Jorgensen, Danny. 1989. *Participant Observation: A Methodology for Human Studies.* Applied Social Research Methods Series, Volume 15. Newbury Park: Sage.

Kumar. Ranjit. 1996. *Research Methodology: A Step-By-Step Guide for Beginners.* South Melbourne: Longman.

Lincoln, Yvonna S. 1990. 'The Making of a Constructivist: A Remembrance of Transformations Past'. In Guba, Egon G. (Ed.) *The Paradigm Dialog.* Newbury Park: Sage, pp. 67–87.

Marcus, George. 1994. 'What Comes (Just) After 'Post'? The Case of Ethnography'. In Denzin, Norman K. & Lincoln, Yvonna S. (Eds) *Handbook of Qualitative Research.* Thousand Oaks: Sage, pp. 563–74.

Miles, Matthew B. & Huberman, A. Michael. 1994. *Qualitative Data Analysis: An Expanded Sourcebook.* Second Edition. Thousand Oaks: Sage.

Minichiello, Victor, Aroni, Rosalie, Timewell, Eric & Loris Alexander. 1995. *In-Depth Interviewing.* Second Edition. Melbourne: Longman.

Myers, F. 1988. 'Locating Ethnographic Practice: Romance, Reality, and Politics of the Outback'. *American Ethnologists*, vol. 15, pp. 609–24.

Neuman, W. L. 2000. *Social Research Methods, Qualitative and Quantitative Approaches.* Fourth Edition. Boston, MA: Allyn & Bacon.

Oakley, Ann. 1981. 'Interviewing Women: A Contradiction in Terms'. In Roberts, Helen (Ed.) *Doing Feminist Research.* London: Routledge, pp. 30–61.

Patton, Michael. Q. 1990. *Qualitative Evaluation and Research Methods.* Second Edition. Newbury Park: Sage.

Punch, Keith. 1998. *Introduction to Social Research, Quantitative and Qualitative Approaches.* London: Sage.

Punch, Maurice. 1986. *The Politics and Ethics of Fieldwork.* Beverley Hills, CA: Sage.

Punch, Maurice. 1994. 'Politics and Ethics in Qualitative Research'. In Denzin, N. K. &. Lincoln, Y. S. (Eds) *Handbook of Qualitative Research.* Thousand Oaks, CA: Sage, pp. 83–97.

Sarantakos, S. 1998. *Social Research.* Second Edition. South Melbourne: Macmillan.

Shils, Edward. 1959. 'Social Inquiry and the Autonomy of the Individual'. In Lerner, D. (Ed.) *The Human Meaning of the Social Sciences.* Cleveland, OH: Meridian.

Sieber, J. E. (Ed.) 1982. *The Ethics of Social Research: Surveys and Experiments.* New York: Springer-Verlag, pp. 151–66.

Sieber, Joan E. 1992. *Planning Ethically Responsible Research: A Guide for Students and Internal Review Boards.* Applied Science Research Methods Series, Volume 31. Newbury Park: Sage.

Sieber, J. E. & Sorensen, J. L. 1992. 'Ethical Issues in Community-Based Research and Intervention'. In Edwards, J., Tindale, R. S., Heath, L. & Posavac, E. J. (Eds) *Social Psychology Applications to Social Issues. Volume 2: Methodological Issues in Applied Social Psychology.* New York: Plenum.

Stake, Robert E. 1995. *The Art of Case Study Research.* Thousand Oaks: Sage.

Stanley, B. & Sieber, J. E. 1991. *The Ethics of Research on Children and Adolescents.* Newbury Park, CA: Sage.

Williams, Anne. 1990. 'Reading Feminism in Fieldnotes'. In Stanley, Liz. (Ed.) *Feminist Praxis.* London: Routledge, pp. 253–61.

Woodside, Arch & Ronkainen, Ilkka. 1994. 'Improving Advertising Conversion Studies'. In Ritchie, J. R. Brent & Goeldner, Charles R. (Eds) *Travel, Tourism and Hospitality Research: A Handbook for Managers and Researchers.* Second Edition. New York: John Wiley, pp. 545–57.

FURTHER READING

Bailey, K. D. 1988. 'Ethical Dilemmas in Social Research. A Theoretical Framework'. *American Sociologist,* vol. 19, pp. 121–37.

Barber, B. 1976. 'The Ethics of Experimentation with Human Subjects'. *Scientific American,* vol. 234, no. 2, pp. 25–31.

Bulmer, M. (Ed.) 1982. *Social Research Ethics.* London: Macmillan.

Homan, Roger. 1991. *The Ethics of Social Research.* London: Longman.

Kimmel, A. 1988. *Ethics and Values in Applied Social Research.* Beverley Hills: Sage.

Lee, Raymond. 1993. *Doing Research in Sensitive Topics.* Newbury Park, CA: Sage.

Levine, R. J. 1986. *Ethics and Regulation of Clinical Research.* Baltimore, MD: Urban & Schwarzenberg.

Sapsford, R. & Abbott, P. 1996. 'Ethics, Politics and Research'. In Sapsford, R. & Jupp, V. (Eds) *Data Collection and Analysis.* London: Sage, pp. 317–42.

Wadeley, A. 1991. *Ethics in Research and Practice.* Leicester: British Psychological Society.

WEB SITES

The Royal Windsor Society for Nursing Research. The Declaration of Helsinki. www.windsor.igs.net/~nhodgins/helsinki.html (downloaded 6 March 2000).

United States Holocaust Memorial Museum. The Nuremberg Code. www.ushmm.org/research/doctors/Nuremberg_Code.htm (downloaded 6 March 2000).

Universal Declaration of Human Rights. www.udhr50.org/UDHR/udhr.HTM (downloaded 6 March 2000).

5

Methodological
considerations for
tourism research

'Both qualitative and quantitative approaches have their strengths
and weaknesses, and advantages and disadvantages. "Neither one
is markedly superior to the other in all respects" (Ackroyd & Hughes
1992: 30). The measurement and analysis of the variables about
which information is obtained in a research study are dependent
upon the purpose of the study. In many studies you need to combine
both qualitative and quantitative approaches.'

(Kumar 1996, p. 12)

LEARNING OBJECTIVES
After studying this chapter, you should be able to:

- discuss the different research methodologies that can be used in tourism research
- describe the difference between an emic and an etic approach to data collection
- explain the differences between qualitative and quantitative methodologies
- explain the use of a mixed method approach
- distinguish between the various types of sampling
- outline the need for reliability and validity in relation to qualitative and quantitative research
- understand the various types of triangulation and their purpose in tourism research
- discuss the role of pilot studies in the process of conducting tourism research.

5.1 INTRODUCTION

This chapter sets the scene for chapters 6 to 9 in which qualitative and quantitative methods of data collection and analysis are discussed in detail. Initially, this chapter highlights the major differences between the quantitative (positivistic or hypothetico-deductive) and the qualitative (non-positivistic or holistic-inductive) approaches to research. It also considers the use of mixed methods. The chapter then moves on to discuss sampling, and reliability and validity issues associated with qualitative and quantitative research. The use of triangulation in research, and the need for pilot studies to be conducted prior to engaging in data collection, are also addressed.

5.2 RESEARCH METHODOLOGIES

In chapter 1 you were introduced to an essentially binary classification of research methodologies: qualitative and quantitative methodologies. A third type was also suggested: the mixed method approach. By now, you should be aware that qualitative and quantitative methodologies are located at opposite ends of a continuum regarding world views, that is ontological positions. A qualitative methodology is associated with the paradigms of the interpretive social sciences, critical theory orientation, postmodernism and feminism. These paradigms may be clustered together and described as the holistic-inductive paradigm. They are holistic because the paradigms study the whole phenomenon and all its complexity (in this case, tourism) rather than breaking the phenomenon into component parts and studying discrete variables and causal relationships (Patton 1990). On the other hand, a quantitative methodology is associated with the paradigms of positivism and chaos theory. However, chaos theory intersects with qualitative research if the 'metaphoric' aspect of chaos is applied (Patton 1990). In the main, these two paradigms may be overviewed as hypothetico-deductive, although chaos theory is non-linear in nature, whereas positivism is linear. Both, however, describe the world as numeric representations (unless a metaphoric focus is adopted in the case of chaos theory).

Between the holistic-inductive and hypothetico-deductive paradigms lies the mixed method approach. The mixed method approach merges, in different ways and degrees, the methods used by quantitative and qualitative methodologies. All three types of methodologies are discussed in further detail later in the chapter.

5.2.1 Selecting *the 'right' methodology*

In undertaking any research and selecting the methodology, the researcher has to consider the nature of the setting being studied or the 'question' being asked, as well as any possible limitations on the study, such as time and resources. Resources may be human or monetary resources, or research tools such as computers or computer-assisted telephone interviewing laboratories (CATI systems). There also needs to be a match between the study topic and methodology. For example, a research question that seeks to determine the size of the visiting friends and relatives market in an area would use a quantitative methodology, not a qualitative methodology, because the focus is on quantification. However, if the research question looked at the nature of the visiting friends and relatives market, then a qualitative methodology might be used to determine the nature of the market. And if the research question looked at the size and nature of the visiting friends and relatives market, then a mixed method approach might be used.

When considering the approach that may be used in a research project, the researcher has three options:

- a quantitative methodology
- a qualitative methodology
- a mixed method approach.

The choice centres on the nature of the research topic, the setting, the possible limitations and the underlying theoretical paradigm that informs the research project (hypothetico-deductive or holistic-inductive).

5.3 EMIC VERSUS ETIC

The terms 'emic' and 'etic' are founded in the discipline of anthropology and are especially associated with the qualitative methodological tool of ethnography. Ethnography is 'the art and science of describing a group or culture' (Fetterman 1989, p. 11). Pike (1954) is credited with coining the terms emic and etic (Pelto & Pelto 1978, p. 54). The terms describe two quite distinct approaches to data collection and subsequently the researcher's role in the study setting, as well as the analysis of data. According to Pike (1954, in Pelto & Pelto 1978, pp. 54–5):

... an Emic [approach] is in essence valid for only one language (or one culture) at a time ... It is an attempt to discover and to describe the pattern of that particular language or culture in reference to the way in which the various elements of that culture are related to each other in the functioning of the particular pattern, rather than an attempt to describe them in reference to a generalized classification derived in advance of the study of that culture.

An etic analytical standpoint ... might be called 'external' or 'alien', since for etic purposes the analyst stands 'far enough away' from or 'outside' of a particular culture to see its separate events, primarily in relation to their similarities and their differences, as compared to events in other cultures, rather than in reference to the sequence of classes of events within that one particular culture.

Etic criteria have the appearance of absolutes, within the range of sensitivity of the measuring instrument (or the expertness of the analyst); emic criteria savor more of relativity, with the sameness of activity determined in reference to a particular system of activity.

Today, the terms have come to be used to describe researchers' epistemological positions — emic (insider) and etic (outsider) — in relation to the collection and analysis of data.

■ 5.3.1 Emic *perspectives*

Essentially, the emic perspective is associated with the holistic-inductive paradigm, particularly the interpretive social sciences paradigm (Fetterman 1989). The interpretive social sciences paradigm is premised on the belief that the insider's view provides the best lens to understanding the phenomenon being studied, because the insider's view, or the 'emic perspective', allows for the identification of multiple realities (Fetterman 1989, p. 31). Furthermore, an 'emic perspective' asserts that:

> ... cultural behaviour should always be studied and categorized in terms of the inside view — the actors' definition — of human events. That is, the units of conceptualization ... should be 'discovered' by analyzing the cognitive processes of the people studied, rather than 'imposed' from cross-cultural (hence, ethnocentric) classifications of behavior (Pelto & Pelto 1978, p. 54).

Consequently, as Blumer (1962) has noted, the researcher is obliged to enter the social setting and become one of the social actors in that social setting.

■ 5.3.2 Etic *perspectives*

The etic position is linked to positivism (Fetterman 1989) and carries with it a structured systematic set of 'rules' to interpret the study setting from an outsider's perspective. Rather than study the social setting as a holistic system greater than the sum of the parts, eticists break the system down into smaller units.

The work of Harris (1964) adopts an etic approach. In particular, Harris' research focuses on 'actones'. Actones are the smallest unit of analysis and are defined as 'a behavioral bit consisting of the body motion and environmental effect which rise above the threshold of the observer's auditory and visual senses' (Harris 1968, p. 37). Such a system of observation becomes problematic when there are several social actors within the study setting, and the use of video cameras becomes necessary to capture all the action and verbal texts. Verbal texts in Harris' opinion should not be used as the main source of data, because verbal texts may belie a social actor's real behaviour patterns. This is the complete antithesis of the position stated by Thomas and Thomas (1928, p. 572) that '[i]f [women and] men define situations as real, they are real in their consequences'. Harris uses actones as building blocks to develop a representation of the study setting or phenomenon. The actones can be linked together to create 'episodes' that can be developed into 'episode chains', and then into 'scenes' and 'serials' and thus the representation of the phenomenon within the overall setting or social system.

5.3.3 Mixing *emic and etic perspectives*

As is the case with qualitative and quantitative methodologies, a mixed method approach may be used regarding emic and etic perspectives. As Fetterman (1989) comments, a researcher may adopt an emic approach to data gathering and analysis, but there comes a time when the researcher has to stop being one with the field and make sense of the data by adopting the mantle of a researcher/interpreter, an 'outsider' rather than an 'insider'. With this stepping back, the researcher generally utilises both emic and etic perspectives, since the writing of the final depiction of the study phenomenon is constructed using the researcher's voice, which is now no longer an insider's voice but a scientific voice (albeit based on the participants' voices and confirmations). In any ethnographic research, various mixes of emic and etic perspectives may be used. However, Fetterman (1989, p. 32) advocates that 'good ethnography requires both emic and etic perspectives'.

5.4 QUALITATIVE VERSUS QUANTITATIVE METHODOLOGIES

There are often debates about which methodology (qualitative or quantitative) is best. However, rather than debate which is the better method of the two, the discussion should look at which methodology (and theoretical paradigm) is the most suitable for the researcher's purpose.

5.4.1 Qualitative *methodology*

As noted above, a qualitative methodology is associated with the holistic-inductive paradigm. Research informed by a qualitative methodology will have the following attributes:

- an inductive approach that establishes the nature of truth by being grounded in the real world
- an ontological view that sees the world as consisting of multiple realities
- a subjective relationship between the researcher and the participants, that is a subjective epistemology
- the researcher is essentially viewed as an insider by the study participants
- the research design is unstructured in order to respond to the field setting and therefore the research design emerges in the course of field work; the research design is also study-specific since it is grounded in the setting being studied
- the researcher is interested in emblematic themes that arise during the course of the study
- the sampling method is non-random, with every person in the study population not having an equal chance of selection

- data are represented as textual units rather than numeric representations
- data analysis is focused on eliciting key themes and motifs associated with the participants being studied
- representation of the findings is usually in 'narrative' form, with the researcher writing in the first person and using an active voice
- the research report reflects a 'slice of life' from the study setting and is specific to that study setting only.

The following Industry Insight provides an example of the use of a qualitative methodology in tourism research.

INDUSTRY INSIGHT

In 1999/2000, the Market Research Unit of the Australian Tourist Commission commissioned innovative research informed by a qualitative methodology in order to determine the role of the Internet in consumers' travel destination decision making (Milica Loncar, ATC, 2001, personal communication). In particular, the research used the qualitative method of focus groups accompanied by a Web-browsing exercise. As noted in the ATC's 1999–2000 *Annual Report*:

'The overall objective of the research was to better understand consumer needs, expectations and preferences for Internet travel sites and to help understand the Internet's role in the traveller's motivational and decision-making cycle. Findings from this research will be used in the further development of australia.com.'

Source: *Australian Tourist Commission (2000)*

Most tourism research uses a quantitative methodology, and this is discussed in the following section.

5.4.2 Quantitative *methodology*

A quantitative methodology is associated with the positivistic or hypothetico-deductive paradigm. Research informed by a quantitative methodology will have the following attributes:

- a deductive approach that establishes the nature of truth by testing hypotheses
- an ontological view that sees the world as consisting of causal relationships
- an objective relationship between the researcher and the participants, that is an objective epistemology
- the researcher is essentially viewed as an outsider by study participants

- the research design is structured, systematic and replicable
- the researcher identifies and tests relationships between variables
- the sampling method is random, with every person in the study population having an equal chance of selection
- data are represented numerically
- data analysis is predicated to statistical analysis
- representation of the findings is based on statistical tables and graphic representations and the report text is written in the third person, using a passive voice
- the report provides findings from the sample that may be generalised to the wider study population.

The following Industry Insight provides an example of the use of a quantitative methodology in tourism research.

INDUSTRY INSIGHT

The International Visitor Survey (IVS) conducted by the Bureau of Tourism Research (BTR) uses a quantitative methodology. The survey is conducted at Australia's major international airports and involves approximately 12 000 international visitors each year aged 15 years and over who are departing Australia. The people surveyed must have stayed more than 24 hours and less than 12 months. Interviews are conducted using probability sampling (randomly selected passengers on randomly selected flights). The survey produces quarterly reports and an annual report. Data on the following information is gathered: visitor characteristics (such as country of residence, age, reasons for visit); international itinerary (such as stopovers and number of previous visits to Australia); itinerary in Australia (such as duration of stay, port of arrival and departure, transportation and accommodation used, attractions visited); travel arrangements (such as type of travel party, how travel was organised); expenditure; and satisfaction with visit. The survey is conducted as an interview by trained researchers. For further details contact the Bureau of Tourism Research in Canberra or visit www.btr.gov.au.

■ 5.4.3 Differences *between qualitative and quantitative methodologies*

Qualitative researchers believe that rich descriptions of the social world are valuable, whereas quantitative researchers, with their etic, nomothetic commitments, are less concerned with such detail (Denzin & Lincoln 1994, p. 6).

The differences between the two methodologies can be listed using, for example, the specific research approach (deductive or inductive), the ontological view (hypothesis based or grounded in the real world), the epistemological view (objective (etic) or subjective (emic)), the presentation of concepts (variables or themes), the research design (structured, systematic, replicable or unstructured, emergent, study specific), the representation of data (numeric or textual), the analytical approach (statistical or thematic), the representation of the findings (statistical tables, graphs or narrative), the voice of the researcher (third person passive or first person active) and the reflection of the real world (representative or slice of life). Table 5.1 outlines the major differences between the two methodological perspectives.

■ Table 5.1
Main differences between qualitative and quantitative methodologies

	QUALITATIVE	QUANTITATIVE
Research approach	Inductive	Deductive
Ontological view	Multiple realities	Causal relationships
Nature of truth	Grounded in the real world	Hypothesis testing
Epistemological view	Subjective	Objective
Researcher situatedness	Emic (insider)	Etic (outsider)
Research design	Unstructured Emergent Study specific	Structured Systematic Replicable
Research focus	Themes	Variables
Participant selection	Non-random	Random
Representation of data	Textual	Numeric
Analysis	Themes, motifs	Statistical analyses
Representation of findings	Narrative	Statistical tables and graphs
Voice of the researcher	First person, active	Third person, passive
Reflection of the real world	Slice of life	Representative

The following Industry Insight discusses the use of the two methodologies in tourism research.

Roger Riley and Lisa Love (2000) conducted an examination of the status of qualitative research in tourism by examining the *Journal of Travel Research*, the *Annals of Tourism Research, Tourism Management* and the *Journal of Travel and Tourism Marketing*. Each journal was studied from the date of its commencement to 1996. The researchers found that positivism was the dominant paradigm. The study also found that those journals linked to informing industry published more hypothetico-deductive research than holistic-inductive research. The requirement to write in the third person and to utilise the 'classical scientific mode' — introduction, literature review, methodology, findings, discussion and conclusion — forced qualitative researchers to adopt a positivist reporting persona. Consequently, such report formats misrepresent the way that qualitative data is reported and presented. This can only add to the confusion of researchers seeking models to present their qualitative findings if they seek only tourism journal articles as models. Other models exist outside tourism and this is sometimes why holistic-inductive researchers seek to publish their qualitative studies in non-tourism journals. Riley and Love (2000, pp. 182–3) comment: '[I]t is important to remember that the tourism industry is economically-driven, and thus has a clear place for quantification. At the same time, because there are other ways of knowing, it must have an equally clear place for qualitative research.'

5.5 MIXED METHODS

The concept of mixed methods was introduced in chapter 1, and refers to the mixing of both quantitative and qualitative methodologies in varying ways and degrees. There are differing stances held with regard to mixed methods. The extremes range from support to non-support for the mixing of methods. The supporters suggest that mixing methods enables the 'deficiencies' of both qualitative and quantitative methodologies to be overcome. Non-supporters suggest that, as the two methodologies are founded in specific paradigms with differing ontological and epistemological views, mixing methods results in mixing theoretical world views that are contradictory to each other.

Using the two descriptors introduced in chapter 1 — deductive and inductive approaches or paradigms — we can cluster positivism and chaos theory orientation as the deductive or hypothetico-deductive paradigm and interpretive social sciences, critical theory orientation, feminist perspectives and postmodernism as the inductive or holistic-inductive paradigm. Patton (1990, p. 195) provides a model that overviews the possible ways of mixing 'methods' based on such a division of paradigms (see figure 5.1).

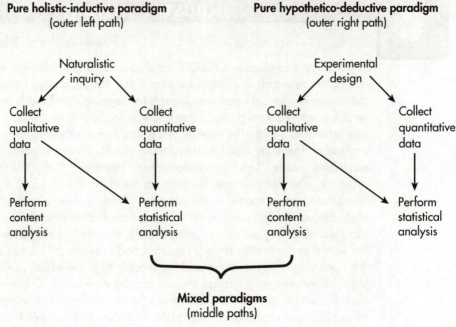

■ Figure 5.1
Pure and mixed research approaches

Pure holistic-inductive paradigm
(outer left path)

Pure hypothetico-deductive paradigm
(outer right path)

Naturalistic inquiry

Experimental design

Collect qualitative data

Collect quantitative data

Collect qualitative data

Collect quantitative data

Perform content analysis

Perform statistical analysis

Perform content analysis

Perform statistical analysis

Mixed paradigms
(middle paths)

Source: *Patton (1990, p. 195)*

Mixed methods are also a component of triangulation, particularly methodological triangulation, which is discussed later in the chapter. The term 'methodological triangulation' is introduced here as it has relevance to the discussion of mixed methods. As Patton (1990, pp. 188–9) comments:

> [methodological] [t]riangulation can include borrowing and combining parts from pure methodological approaches, thus creating mixed methodological strategies. To accomplish this it is necessary to separate the measurement, design, and analysis components of the hypothetico-deductive (quantitative/experimental) and holistic-inductive (qualitative/naturalistic) paradigms ... The ideal-typical qualitative methods strategy is made up of three parts: (1) qualitative data, (2) a holistic-inductive design of naturalistic inquiry, and (3) content or case analysis. In the traditional hypothetico-deductive approach to research, the ideal study would include (a) quantitative data from (b) experimental (or quasi-experimental) designs and (c) statistical analysis.
>
> A variety of mixes are possible — mixes of measurement, design, and analysis.

Sieber (1973) also comments that mixed methods can assist with data collection, data analysis and research design. In regard to research design, Miles and Huberman (1994) see the application of mixed methods as having four possible combinations:

• the simultaneous and integrated collection of qualitative and quantitative data during the field work phase

- qualitative field work undertaken alongside a multiwave survey, with the first wave survey informing the field worker of focal points for observation — similarly, field work may refine survey foci in future waves
- alternation between qualitative exploratory research that informs the construction of a quantitative data collection tool — for example, a questionnaire — followed by further qualitative field work to achieve a deeper understanding of the quantitative findings
- a quantitative starting point such as a survey used to determine the focal points for a qualitative study, which may be followed up by a quantitative study to clarify conflicting findings.

While the first two combinations use quantitative and qualitative methodologies contemporaneously, the latter two are really a succession of research projects each informed by the findings of the former, and as such, are more like multistage research utilising complementary methodologies throughout. Miles and Huberman (1994, p. 41) propose that the questions researchers need to focus on when considering the linking of methods (i.e. the use of mixed methods) are 'should it be done, how will it be done, and for what purposes'.

Another set consisting of three types of mixed methods is suggested by Creswell (1994). In the first type, Creswell identifies a two-stage research process of data collection utilising quantitative and qualitative methods independently of each other. The integration of mixed methods occurs at the analysis stage and is reported in the findings and discussion of the written research report. The second type is structured using a dominant paradigm with the incorporation of an alternative paradigm — for example, a positivist-based research project that incorporates the use of open-ended questions (a qualitative approach) to gain further understanding of the phenomenon being studied. The third type is a research project similar to the first type explained by Patton (1990), in which both quantitative and qualitative methodologies are integrated throughout all phases of the research project. However, 'Guba and Lincoln (1988) have argued that the internal consistency and logic of each approach, or paradigm, mitigates against methodological mixing of different inquiry modes and data-collection strategies' (Patton 1990, p. 193)

How can a paradigm be at once deductive and inductive, or hypotheses focused and open to emergent data (Patton 1990)? Trow (1970, p. 149, in Patton 1990, p. 196) suggests we should 'get on with the business of attacking our problems with the widest array of conceptual and methodological tools that we possess and they demand. This does not preclude discussion and debate regarding the relative usefulness of different methods for the study of specific problems or types of problems.'

The argument should not be about which paradigm is superior, but rather what is the best means to achieve the aims of the research. For example, a researcher conducting primarily a quantitative study of tourist satisfaction levels may choose to mix methods by including some open-ended questions in order to elicit the reasons behind some of the choices tourists made in their responses.

Greene, Caracelli, and Graham (1989) suggest that the adoption of mixed methods in a research project should be based on consideration of the differences between methods and the reasons for using each, the focal point of the study, the key paradigm informing the study and the actual operationalisation of the research process. Punch (1998) supports a similar view and indicates that there is a multiplicity of mixes depending on whether or not the qualitative and quantitative methodologies and methods will have 'equal weight', whether they will be conducted in an integrated or separate manner, and whether they will be used in a sequential manner or not. Bryman (1988 and 1992, in Punch 1998, p. 247), for example, supports the notion of a multiplicity of mixes by suggesting 11 combinations of mixes beyond those proposed by Miles and Huberman (1994) and Cresswell (1994).

5.6 SAMPLING

Before discussing the different types of sampling that can be used in tourism research, it is useful to explain several key terms to ensure that you understand what each means. In the following definitions, each term is exemplified with a common theme to demonstrate the differing levels of definition associated with the terms.

- *Population* A population comprises all the study subjects (tourists, visitors, hosts, family, friends, employees, managers) or study units (attractions, transport providers, accommodation facilities) that are the focus of the research project (Ticehurst & Veal 1999, p. 160). Example: all five-star accommodation facilities in Australia.
- *Target population* The target population is the units in the population that the researcher wishes to target for study (Neuman 2000, p. 201). Example: all five-star accommodation facilities in Victoria.
- *Sample* A sample is a selection of subjects or units from the overall population (Sarantakos 1998, p. 139). Example: all five-star accommodation facilities located in the central business district (CBD) in Melbourne, Victoria.
- *Sampling* Sampling is the means by which subjects or study units from the target population are included in the research project (Sarantakos 1998, p. 139). Example: in this case, as the number of facilities would not be large, a saturation survey would be undertaken, that is all five-star facilities in the CBD would be included.
- *Sampling ratio* A sampling ratio is '[t]he ratio of the size of the sample to the size of the target population' (Neuman 2000, p. 201). Example: the number of five-star accommodation facilities in the CBD divided by the number of five-star accommodation facilities in Victoria.
- *Sample frame* A sample frame is a list that represents all members or units of a study population (Neuman 2000, p. 201), such as electoral roles and telephone directories, as well as passenger lists, hotel guest lists and client databases. Example: accommodation listing from Tourism Victoria or the *Yellow Pages*.

- *Sample unit* A sample unit is an individual subject or study unit drawn from the overall study population and included in the sample. Example: one of the five-star accommodation facilities selected.

In the latter definition, the use of the term 'subject' is not consistent with the language of a qualitative methodology:

> In quantitative studies, those researched are commonly called *subjects*. Qualitative researchers tend to be uncomfortable with the term *subject* because it implies the *acting on* rather than the *interacting with* that at best characterizes qualitative inquiry. Therefore, I use the following terms somewhat interchangeably ... *research participants, respondents, interviewees* and *researched*, as well as the term *others* as suggested by postmodernists (Glesne 1999, p. xii).

As researchers, we have the option to study either all of the study units or participants or only some of the study units or participants. If a researcher chooses to study all of the study units or participants, then they are using a saturation sample (used with small populations) or a census (used with large populations) — that is, all possible units are included in the study. If, however, the population of study units is too large to study given the time, human and budgetary resources available (see below), then the researcher may choose to study a sample of the entire population. In choosing the latter path, the researcher may use systematic (probability) sampling (each study unit has an equal opportunity to participate) or non-systematic (non-probability) sampling (each study unit does not have an equal opportunity to participate).

Reasons why researchers may choose to sample populations include:
- the population may be too large to study in its entirety within the research time frame
- the population may be difficult to access given its geographical distribution, especially if face-to-face contact is desired
- the human resources available to work on the research project may be insufficient to study the entire population
- the amount of money available for the research project may be limited and insufficient to study the entire population.

There are a number of advantages in sampling a population, including:
- the time required for data collection is reduced
- the human resources required for data collection and analysis are reduced
- the costs of the overall research budget are lower as fewer units are studied
- the costs of expendable items such as material resources, computer banks and questionnaire production are lower
- other related costs, such as paying experts for their opinions, training researchers and travelling time, are lower
- the study is completed in a shorter time, so data analysis can occur more quickly and findings become available earlier
- systematic sampling enables the findings to be generalised to the entire population

- the researcher(s) studies fewer members of the population, so more time can be spent with each member to gather more information and/or to follow up to increase response rates
- members of the population who are not part of the study are not targeted — the researcher(s) can hone in on the target population (e.g. five-star accommodation facilities in Victoria as opposed to the whole of Australia).

There are also some disadvantages in choosing to sample the population, including:

- difficulties associated with determining the size of the sample
- knowing whether the targeted study unit has actually participated
- the generation of queries from the sample participants
- accessibility to and availability and currency of sampling frames
- defining the sampling unit
- the need for greater organisation in regard to administration and planning than non-systematic (non-random) sampling (Sarantakos 1998).

When sampling a population, there are some principles the researcher needs to observe. According to Sarantakos (1998), subjects or study units must:

- be systematically and objectively selected
- be unambiguously defined
- be listed only once in the population
- not be interchanged
- not be discarded
- be selected without bias
- be selected using ethical and scientifically justified processes.

There are two classificatory systems for sampling: non-random (non-probability) sampling and random (probability) sampling. Non-random sampling is generally associated with qualitative research methods (inductively based paradigms), whereas random sampling is generally associated with quantitative research methods (deductively based paradigms). However, for various reasons, such as research approach and limited resources (time and money), non-random sampling may be used for quantitative research.

■ 5.6.1 Non-probability *sampling*

With non-probability or non-random sampling, as both terms suggest, each unit of the population being studied does not have an equal chance of being included in the study. There are a number of non-random sampling approaches: convenience sampling, purposive sampling, snowball sampling, expert sampling and quota sampling (Sarantakos 1998; Neuman 2000).

Convenience sampling

Convenience sampling has several synonyms — accidental, haphazard, chunk and grab sampling (Sarantakos 1998, p. 151) — all suggesting the focus is not on a systematic selection process. Convenience sampling refers to the selection of participants for a study based on their proximity to the researcher and the ease with which the researcher can access the participants. These types of samples are not representative of the population from which they are drawn. Furthermore, the sample has a temporal frame to it — the sample only reflects those study units convenient to the researcher at the time the study was conducted. Such sampling lacks the ability to reflect other time periods. Since the sample is also based on the researcher's selection procedures, the result may be that all the study units (if a human sample) are the same age, gender or race because these are the people the researcher feels most comfortable approaching.

Another issue related to convenience sampling is that it may not enable the researcher to study the real focus of the research study. For example, the researcher may choose to study the types of water-based activities tourists engage in over a long weekend. Let us assume that there are 11 beaches in the study area and that they are all long distances apart and not easy to access. The nearest beach to the researcher is a surfing beach, so the researcher chooses it as the study location. As a result, the sample will be biased, because the researcher will mainly be making contact with people who like to surf. While the beach is convenient, it may not reflect the diversity of water-based activities available at other beach locations in the area.

Although convenience sampling is often used because it enables quick collection of data without the expense of a more systematic selection process, it is 'the least desirable' of the sampling methods as it is 'neither purposeful nor strategic' (Patton 1990, pp. 180 and 181).

Purposive sampling

Purposive sampling is also referred to as judgmental sampling since it involves the researcher making a decision about who or what study units will be involved in the study. The researcher uses their knowledge to determine who or what study units are the most appropriate for inclusion in the study based on the potential study units' knowledge base or closeness of fit to criteria associated with the study's focus. For example, the researcher may wish to identify the types of leadership styles exhibited by management in a hotel chain. To save time and money, the researcher might decide to purposively target all senior managers, as opposed to middle and junior managers or staff, since the researcher wants to conduct a study using a qualitative methodology using participant observation (this method will be described in chapter 6). In making this decision, the researcher may have figured that the other managers and staff will still be included in the study through the use of participant observation, as the senior managers will from time to time have to engage with these other groups.

Snowball sampling

Snowballing sampling has several other names — chain referral, reputational or network sampling (Neuman 2000, p. 199) or rhizome sampling (Stehlik 1999). Snowball sampling is used with difficult to reach participants because the researcher may not be informed about formal or informal 'network connections'. Once the researcher has identified one member of the population, other members are identified by this member and then by the next participants contacted until all the participants have been contacted. The researcher could use snowball sampling, for example, to study extreme adventure tourists. These tourists are primarily independent tourists who are not dependent on the tourism industry to organise their extreme adventure travel experiences. Consequently, there are no readily available sampling frames, only informal networks of association between the extreme adventure tourists themselves.

Expert sampling

Expert sampling only involves people who the researcher identifies as 'experts'. These people have specialist knowledge with which to make informed opinions or comments. Such samples are used in focus groups and Delphic sessions (these types of methods are discussed in detail in chapter 6). For example, the researcher may use expert sampling of tourism association managers to forecast possible scenarios regarding various tourism planning strategies and their consequences.

Quota sampling

Quota sampling involves the researcher calculating a set number of participants for inclusion in the sample based on some predetermined 'variables' (attributes or characteristics) inherent in the overall study population, such as gender and age. However, once the number of sample units has been calculated for each variable being considered, the selection process is by convenience. Quota sampling differs from stratified sampling (a random sampling technique) in that the latter divides the population into strata by random selection and the former determines the numbers in each strata then follows up with convenience sampling. Sarantakos (1998) suggests that we could describe quota sampling as non-random proportional stratified sampling. It is also described as mixed sampling (Kumar 1996) or quasi-random sampling.

■ *5.6.2* **Probability** *sampling*

In random/probability samples, each unit of the population being studied has an equal chance of being included in the sample — that is, the selection of units is determined by chance and each unit is therefore randomly selected. The decision regarding how many units to include in the study is primarily determined by the level of confidence the researcher wishes to achieve in regard to generalising their findings to the wider population. The decision can also be influenced by the amount of time, money and human resources the researcher has available. There are various tables available to researchers to assist in decision making regarding sample size in probability samples. Examples of such tables are presented later in the chapter. There are a number of random sampling approaches: simple random sampling, systematic sampling, stratified random sampling and multistage cluster sampling.

Simple random sampling

In simple random sampling, every unit has an equal chance of being selected. Sarantakos (1998) outlines a number of simple random sampling techniques: lottery, computer, name, date of birth and number methods.

Lottery method

The lottery method requires a sampling frame — that is, a list of all the units or members of the population. Examples of tourism sampling frames range from hotel guest lists, caravan registration lists and passenger lists, to telephone lists of specific populations such as tourist operators and accommodation venues in an area, to membership listings of tourism organisations and associations. In the lottery method, units are selected randomly from, for example, a container that holds all the possible units or members of the population.

Computer method

Random samples may be generated by computer programs. The researcher has to have access to a sampling frame, such as a passenger list, an accommodation listing, an attractions list, or a list of club or association members. Each individual entry on the sampling frame is assigned a number. The number of random numbers to be selected is determined and then the sample units are identified by the computer program.

Name method

The name method involves generating the sample based on alphabetical listings of participants' first names or family names or alphabetical listing of attractions, accommodation facilities or tourism company names. Using the alphabet as the organiser for the selection of the sample units, as well as the simple random lottery method, the alphabetical letter is determined for sample selection. Participants or study units associated with that letter become the second sampling frame. From this second sampling frame, individual sample units are selected using either the lottery method, a table of random numbers (see appendix 6) or computer-generated listings. There may be several iterations of the selection of alphabetical letters.

Date of birth method

With this method, the sampling frame is constructed using participants' date of birth and selection follows the same procedure as the name method, only birth dates are used instead. A birth date is randomly selected, and all records for that date listed in the sampling frame are then assigned a number and the simple random sampling procedure (the lottery method, a table of random numbers or computer generation) is repeated. Again, there may be several iterations of this process.

Number method

This method of sampling requires the sampling frame to be numerically organised, such as the site numbers in a caravan park listing listed 1 to 300, occupants of hotel rooms by room numbers from 1 to 550 or vehicle registration numbers from 000 to 999. The selection of a number between 0 and 9 is randomly determined using the lottery method, a table of random numbers or computer generation. However, prior to selecting the number, the researcher has to determine where in the sample unit's numerical representation the randomly selected number will appear, such as the first number, the middle number or the last number. For example, the researcher may be using a sampling frame of room numbers in a hotel, and has determined in advance that the randomly selected number will be associated with all of the last numbers in the room number listing. The researcher randomly selects 4, so all room numbers in the hotel ending with 4 will be included in the sample (rooms 4, 14, 24, 34, ... 104, etc.).

Systematic sampling

Whereas in the previous sampling procedures the selection of a participant or study unit was independent of other selections, in systematic random selection, the selection of one unit is dependent on the previous unit. As lists or files of names are generally used for the sampling frame, the method is also known as the file method.

First, the researcher has to assign numbers to the sampling frame, and then the researcher has to determine the sampling interval using the sampling fraction. For example, from a list of 1000 cruise ship passengers the researcher wishes to select 500 passengers.

The sampling fraction is $k = N/n$

where k is the sampling fraction, N is the number of units in the target population and n is the number of units in the sample.

The sampling fraction equals the number of units in the target population divided by the number of units in the sample. Given the above example,

$k = 1000/500 = 2$

Thus, the sampling fraction is 2 — that is, every second name.

The researcher still has to determine the random starting point using a simple random sample method. Then the researcher adds k to that number and so on until the 500 units have been selected.

However, there can be problems with this method. For example, let us say the cruise ship is setting sail as a 'heterosexual couples' cruise and the cruise company has a policy of listing the male partner before the female partner. The list would look something like this:

1. Mr Chang
2. Ms Chang
3. Mr Vygotsky
4. Ms Vygotsky
5. Mr Verdi
6. Mrs Verdi
7. Mr Chermside
8. Mrs Chermside

and so on. Let us assume that the starting point is 2 — given that the sampling fraction is 2, the researcher will be selecting every second name. What will happen to the sample of cruise ship passengers? It will be biased, as they will all be women. A better method in this case would be to use a simple random sample method since the researcher has already allocated each passenger a number.

Stratified random sampling

This is a more complicated form of random or systematic sampling. The population is divided into strata, and these strata make up the final sample in the study. Strata may be divided based on gender, economic status, age, country of origin or telephone prefixes and/or exchanges, for example.

The steps in stratified sampling involve:
- dividing the population into a number of strata
- developing sampling frames for each strata
- developing samples from each strata
- merging the individual samples into one listing.

For example, assume a hypothetical research project — a telephone survey of Localtown residents' holiday patterns. In column 1 in table 5.2, the telephone number prefixes associated with the Localtown exchanges are identified. There are 1000 telephone numbers in each prefix (column 3). Assume that the telephone company that provided the telephone listing has informed us of the number of residential and business numbers associated with each prefix (column 4 identifies the number of residential numbers in each prefix). Since we know the total number of residential numbers (2800), we can determine the number of residential numbers we need to call in each prefix (strata) to ensure a proportionate representation of residential numbers throughout each strata (see column 5). Column 5 is determined by dividing the number of residential numbers in each prefix by the total number of residential numbers in Localtown (2800), and expressing the answer as a percentage. We now know the percentage of our overall sample size that must be drawn from each of the prefixes (strata). For example, if our sample size is 1000, we would call 36 numbers in the prefix 49390, 71 numbers in prefix 49391, and so on.

To determine our starting number in each prefix or strata, we can use the lottery system, a table of random numbers or computer generation. Then we need to determine our sampling fraction (see systematic sampling above). Once the sampling fraction and starting number have been determined, each subsequent number that is selected is based on the corresponding previous number as a result of using the sampling fraction. Since the prefixes for Localtown include both residential and business numbers, the number dialled may be a business number. Researchers have to predetermine how to deal with such instances. Often, the strategy is to dial the next number until a residential number is dialled (there may be several reiterations of this process until the researcher is successful in dialling a residential number). The researcher then returns to the original starting number, adds the sampling fraction and arrives at the next number.

In reporting the methodology used in a study, the sampling procedures must be described clearly. Thus, you must outline how you dealt with the above issues so that another researcher may replicate your study.

PREFIXES	EXCHANGE NAME	NUMBER OF TELEPHONES	NUMBER OF RESIDENTIAL NUMBERS	% REPRESENTATION
49390	Localtown	1000	100	3.6
49391	Localtown	1000	200	7.1
49392	Localtown	1000	800	28.6
49393	Localtown	1000	500	17.9
49394	Localtown	1000	200	7.1
49395	Localtown	1000	300	10.7
49399	Localtown	1000	700	25.0
TOTAL		7000	2800	100.0

In stratified random sampling, a researcher has to remember to consider proportionate or disproportionate sample sizes. The above example sampled seven exchanges in proportions equal to the population — had we been sampling disproportionately, the results would not have represented the population. Sometimes, disproportionate sample sizes are used when the results of a strata may yield insignificant results. For example, in a study of all visitors to a tourist destination, the proportion of interstate visitors may be quite small compared to intrastate visitors. If the researchers are concerned about interstate visitors' perceptions and needs, they may decide to increase the size of units drawn from the interstate strata and decrease the number of intrastate visitors.

Multistage cluster sampling

This method of sampling is used when researchers want to study clusters in geographical areas. As an example, assume another hypothetical study — the study of residents' attitudes to the development of a casino/resort in the city Tourville. The research design involves a face-to-face interview with adult residents using random sampling. Since Tourville has a population of one million, not all residents can be included, so a sample must be undertaken. The researcher wants to ensure that all suburbs have an equal chance of being involved in the study, so the following procedure is applied. Geographically, the city is divided into suburbs or postcode precincts, and a sample of suburbs or postcode precincts is selected. Next, the researcher randomly samples a number of blocks within each of the randomly selected suburbs. Within each of these selected blocks, the researcher randomly selects households for incorporation in the study, and then randomly selects one resident from within each household who will be invited to participate in the study. See figure 5.2 for a visual portrayal of this process. Stage 1 involves the identification of suburbs or postal precincts and the selection of a random sample from those suburbs or postal precincts. In stage 2, suburbs are divided into blocks, which are then randomly sampled. The process continues to street and household level and finally to individual participants.

■ Figure 5.2
Example of multistage cluster sampling

Stage 1

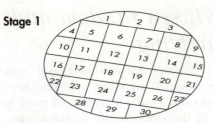

Divide 'Tourville' into suburbs or postcode precincts. Select a random sample from the 30 suburbs.

Stage 2

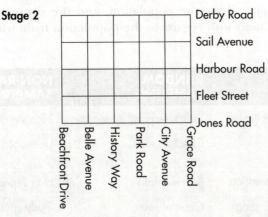

Derby Road
Sail Avenue
Harbour Road
Fleet Street
Jones Road

Beachfront Drive
Belle Avenue
History Way
Park Road
City Avenue
Grace Road

Divide suburbs into blocks. Select a random sample of blocks.

Stage 3

1. 21 City Avenue	8. 6 Grace Road	15. 108 Jones Road
2. 23 City Avenue	9. 8 Grace Road	16. 61 Fleet Street
3. 25 City Avenue	10. 10 Grace Road	17. 63 Fleet Street
4. 27 City Avenue	11. 100 Jones Road	18. 65 Fleet Street
5. 29 City Avenue	12. 102 Jones Road	19. 67 Fleet Street
6. 2 Grace Road	13. 104 Jones Road	20. 69 Fleet Street
7. 4 Grace Road	14. 106 Jones Road	

Select households randomly, from a sampling frame developed from each of the households within each of the selected blocks.

Stage 4

Prepare a sampling frame devised from each selected household by listing all adult residents in that household. The grid below is then used to select individual participants.

Grid for selecting individuals in multistage sampling

ASSIGNED NUMBER OF ADDRESS	TOTAL NUMBER OF ELIGIBLE PERSONS					
	1	2	3	4	5	6 OR MORE
1 or 2	1	1	2	2	3	3
3	1	2	3	3	3	5
4 or 5	1	2	3	4	5	6
6	1	1	1	1	2	2
7 or 8	1	1	1	1	1	1
9	1	2	3	4	5	5
10 or 11	1	2	2	3	4	4
12	1	1	1	2	2	2

Source: *de Vaus (1995)*

5.6.3 Differences *between random and non-random sampling*

The differences between random (probability) and non-random (non-probability) sampling are outlined in table 5.3. The key differences are associated with the method used for the selection of participants (or units), the degree chance plays in the opportunity to participate, the degree to which the sample reflects the population, and the degree to which study findings can be used with regard to the population from which the sample was drawn.

■ **Table 5.3**
The basic *ferences between* *random* *robability) and* *non-random* *ion-probability)* *sampling*

	RANDOM SAMPLING	NON-RANDOM SAMPLING
Selection of participants	Structured and systematic	Non-structured
Opportunity to participate	Equal chance	Unequal chance
Reflexivity of population	Representative	Non-representative
Applicability of findings	Generalisable	Study-group specific

5.6.4 Sample *size*

Often, novice researchers ask 'How large should a sample be?' (quantitative methodology) or 'For how long do I collect data from participants?' (qualitative methodology). In responding to these questions, the following need to be considered:

• the overall size of the population
• the nature of the population (homogeneous or heterogeneous)
• the accessibility of the population (easy or difficult to access).

Sometimes, the questions are rhetorical, especially when working with a population where a census or saturation survey is possible. Generally, however, quantitative methodologies are associated with large sample sizes, to obtain a high degree of accuracy and to ensure findings are representative of the population being studied. On the other hand, qualitative methodologies usually focus on smaller sample sizes, since the intent is to gather in-depth information, rather than less in-depth information from a large number of participants or study units.

Other considerations that influence the size of a sample are the amount of time available to conduct the study, the amount of money available to fund the study and the number of personnel allocated to the study. These considerations are issues for both quantitative and qualitative methodological frameworks.

Sample size: quantitative methodologies

How large should a sample be? If the researcher has sufficient resources, a census may be possible. However, research of this type is generally not the rule for most tourism research, as census-based research is usually undertaken at the national level by agencies with very large resources. On the other hand, if the study population is unique, such as a small, local sea kayaking club, a saturation survey may be possible — that is, all members of the population may be studied. If a census or saturation sample is not used, then sample size is sometimes determined in relation to the overall size of the study population, although this process is criticised by various researchers. Ticehurst and Veal (1999, p. 164), for example, dispute the argument that the size of a sample should bear some relationship to the overall size of the study population, such as the sample being 10% or 20% of the population. They assert that it is the size of the sample that is important when using probability sampling.

Alternatively, Neuman (2000, p. 217) reports the following rules of thumb:

- for populations under 1000, researchers should sample 30% of the population
- for populations over 10 000, researchers should sample a minimum of 10% of the population
- for populations over 100 000, researchers should sample 1% of the population.

In determining absolute sample sizes, statisticians have developed tables that can assist in determining sample size and the degree of confidence that the findings from the study reflect the whole population. Table 5.4 provides researchers with sample size when the population number is known. This table was developed by Krejcie and Morgan (1970) using the formula:

$$s = \frac{\chi^2 NP(1-P)}{d^2(N-1)} + \chi^2 P(1-P)$$

Table 5.5 provides confidence levels for varying sample sizes. There are other ways of determining the size of a sample, such as using the formula shown above.

However, looking at tables 5.4 and 5.5, you can see that, as Ticehurst and Veal suggest, the percentages outlined by Neuman can be problematic. This is especially evident if you look at table 5.5 and note the confidence levels associated with small sample sizes that might be associated with populations less than 1000 in number. The smaller the sample size, the less confident a researcher can be regarding the application of the findings to the wider population. Another general rule of thumb can be noted from table 5.4 — that is, with small populations, the sample size needs to be large. Furthermore, by cross-referencing to table 5.5, at the lower sample size points, you can see that small changes in sample size yield higher degrees of accuracy (see, for example, the difference between sample sizes of 50, 80 and 100 — their respective confidence levels for a finding of 50% are 13.9%, 11.0% and 9.8%). Neuman (2000, p. 217) also recognises that increasing the size of small samples provides large benefits in accuracy. Alternatively, with large populations, small samples are not problematic, because larger samples do not improve the degree of confidence to any great extent (see, for example, the difference in confidence levels between samples of 1000, 2000, 4000 and 10 000 in table 5.5).

N*	S†	N	S	N	S	N	S	N	S
10	10	100	80	280	162	800	260	2 800	338
15	14	110	86	290	165	850	265	3 000	341
20	19	120	92	300	169	900	269	3 500	346
25	24	130	97	320	175	950	274	4 000	351
30	28	140	103	340	181	1000	278	4 500	354
35	32	150	108	360	186	1100	285	5 000	357
40	36	160	113	380	191	1200	291	6 000	361
45	40	170	118	400	196	1300	297	7 000	364
50	44	180	123	420	201	1400	302	8 000	367
55	48	190	127	440	205	1500	306	9 000	368
60	52	200	132	460	210	1600	310	10 000	370
65	56	210	136	480	214	1700	313	15 000	375
70	59	220	140	500	217	1800	317	20 000	377
75	63	230	144	550	226	1900	320	30 000	379
80	66	240	148	600	234	2000	322	40 000	380
85	70	250	152	650	242	2200	327	50 000	381
90	73	260	155	700	248	2400	331	75 000	382
95	76	270	159	750	254	2600	335	1 000 000	384

*N is the population size.
†S is sample size.

Source: *Krejcie & Morgan (1970, pp. 607–10, in Sarantakos 1998, p. 163)*

SAMPLE SIZE	PERCENTAGES FOUND FROM SAMPLE ('RESULTS')					
	50%	40 OR 60%	30 OR 70%	20 OR 80%	10 OR 90%	5 OR 95%
50	13.9	13.6	12.7	11.1	8.3	*
80	11.0	10.7	10.0	8.8	6.6	*
100	9.8	9.6	9.0	7.8	5.9	4.3
150	8.0	7.8	7.3	6.4	4.8	3.5
200	6.9	6.8	6.3	5.5	4.2	3.0
250	6.2	6.1	5.7	5.0	3.7	2.7
300	5.7	5.5	5.2	4.5	3.4	2.5
400	4.9	4.8	4.5	3.9	2.9	2.1
500	4.4	4.3	4.0	3.5	2.6	1.9
750	3.6	3.5	3.3	2.9	2.1	1.6
1000	3.1	3.0	2.8	2.5	1.9	1.3
2000	2.2	2.1	2.0	1.7	1.3	1.0
4000	1.5	1.5	1.4	1.2	0.9	0.7
10 000	1.0	1.0	0.9	0.8	0.6	0.4

* Confidence interval > 5.0.

Interpretation of table: for example, for a sample size of 400, a finding of 30% is subject to a confidence interval of ±4.5 (that is to say, we can be 95% certain that the population value lies in the range 25.5% to 34.5%).

Source: *Ticehurst & Veal (1999, p. 166)*

Sample size: qualitative methodology

For how long should you collect data from participants? One suggestion is that data should be collected until a 'qualitative isomorph' (Ford 1975) is reached. And more specifically, when a 'qualitative informational isomorph' is achieved — that is, when 'redundancy with respect to information' occurs (Lincoln & Guba 1985, pp. 233–4). This is also referred to as theoretical sampling, essentially a cyclical process of data collection and analysis that continues until no new data are found, only confirmation of previous 'theories' (Punch 1998, p. 167).

In using convenience or purposive sampling, the researcher decides when enough participants or units have been sampled. This occurs when there is redundancy in regard to data. The cut-off is not predetermined, but emerges as an outcome of the research process and concurrent data analysis. With qualitative research, it is the 'quality', not the 'quantity', of the data that determines the sample size (Sarantakos 1998).

If mixed methods are used, then the researcher may use random sampling techniques and complementary sample size determination to ensure that representativeness is achieved, rather than an in-depth view of a slice of life from the study population.

5.7 RELIABILITY AND VALIDITY

When engaging in research, whether it is research that uses a quantitative or a qualitative methodology, the researcher must address issues of reliability and validity. Essentially, the researcher must check that the questions and measures being used to gather data are reliable and valid. Although used together, reliability and validity have quite different meanings, as outlined in the following discussion.

■ 5.7.1 Quantitative *methodology*

Within the hypothetico-deductive paradigm, 'Reliability is a matter of whether a particular technique, applied repeatedly to the same object, would yield the same result each time' (Babbie 1990, p. 132), whereas 'Validity refers to the extent to which an empirical measure adequately reflects the real meaning of the concept under consideration' (Babbie 1990, p. 132). To highlight the difference between the two terms, a valid measure of time can be obtained from a chronometer, which determines minutes and seconds. However, a reliable measure will not be obtained if we use our own chronometers (our wristwatches), as these are subject to differences. A reliable and valid measure would be achieved using a stopwatch that has been calibrated to Greenwich Mean Time.

There are several types of validity: face validity, criterion-related validity, content validity and construct validity (Babbie 1990, pp. 133–4). Face validity refers to the fact that the concept being measured is being done so appropriately, that is 'on the face of it' (Sarantakos 1998, p. 79). For example, an interviewer-completed questionnaire intending to establish tourist satisfaction at a specific tourist attraction is said to have face validity if the interviewer poses questions relating to levels of satisfaction with the facilities, amenities, services and the attraction itself. If no questions are asked about satisfaction levels, then the questionnaire has little face validity.

Criterion-related validity is associated with establishing measures that will be able to predict future outcomes in relation to specific criteria. This is particularly used to determine a participant's potential behaviour or ability. For example, an extreme adventure tourism operator may ask potential clients to complete a questionnaire that is aimed at determining the ability of clients to participate in the range of activities successfully. In particular, some cruise ship companies sailing to Antarctica have a series of questions that potential customers must complete in order to determine whether the clients will adapt to the Antarctic environment and meet its challenges successfully. This validity measure is also called predictive validity.

Content validity refers to the use of measures that incorporate all of the meanings associated with a specific concept. For example, if we are endeavouring to describe the travel experiences (Clawson 1963) of a market segment and only ask about 'travel to' and 'on-site' experiences, then our instrument has low content validity. This is because it does not present questions that enable us to describe the 'planning phase', the 'return travel phase' or the recollection phase', or travel experiences that involve multiple stopovers and/or primary destinations.

Construct validity is associated with a measure encapsulating several indicators that are theoretically sound. For example, if we wanted to study motivation we could use Maslow's (1943) hierarchy of needs to provide various indicators for motivation, such as survival, belongingness, self-esteem and self-actualisation.

The issues of validity and reliability are particularly important in the construction of survey questions and you should consider this as you work through chapter 8.

■ 5.7.2 Qualitative *methodology*

Within the holistic-inductive paradigm, 'Perfect validity entails perfect reliability but not the converse; perfect validity is theoretically impossible. Herein lies the paradox of the qualitative tradition' (Kirk & Miller, 1986, p. 71). There are a number of types of reliability: quixotic, diachronic and synchronic. 'Quixotic reliability' is achieved when the selected method of observation constantly provides the same outcome (Kirk & Miller 1986, p. 41). 'Diachronic reliability' relates to the immutable nature of an observation over time (Kirk & Miller 1986, p. 42). 'Synchronic reliability' refers to the comparability or synergy of observations occurring contemporaneously (Kirk & Miller 1986, p. 42).

Researchers should be aware that: 'Reliability and validity are by no means symmetrical. It is easy to obtain perfect reliability with no validity at all ... Perfect validity, on the other hand, would assure perfect reliability, for every observation would yield the complete and exact truth' (Kirk & Miller, 1986, p. 20).

'Triangulation is not a tool or a strategy of validation, but an alternative to validation' (Denzin & Lincoln 1994, p. 2). Thus, triangulation is not used in order to correct any bias or to improve validity (Blaikie 1991, p. 115), for that is not the purpose of triangulation (Denzin 1989a, 1989b, p. 244; Fielding & Fielding 1986, p. 33; Flick 1992, p. 194). Triangulation is used because 'no single method ever adequately solves the problem of rival causal factors … Because each method reveals different aspects of empirical reality, multiple methods of observations must be employed' (Denzin 1978, p. 28). Triangulation is also a feminist methodological strategy.

Denzin (1978) identifies four types of triangulation:

- data triangulation
- investigator triangulation
- theory triangulation
- methodological triangulation.

Researchers concerned with data triangulation draw on various sources of data in the research process. Investigator triangulation refers to the employment of several researchers or evaluators in a study. Theory triangulation involves researchers using several theories or perspectives to analyse data. Methodological triangulation involves researchers using several methods to gather data relevant to a study.

Janesick (1994, p. 251) suggests a fifth type of triangulation: interdisciplinary triangulation. Janesick believes that other disciplines can inform the research process and thereby broaden understanding of the method and data.

An example of the use of triangulation is given below:

In this study, I have relied on data triangulation, investigator triangulation, theory triangulation, methodological triangulation and interdisciplinary triangulation. Specifically, I have used a variety of data sources: my own autobiographical materials, participant observations, cruising yachtspersons, and secondary sources, particularly cruising literature and academic and non-academic studies of cruising folk. I have worked with several different researchers, as I consider that the cruisers who participated in the study of long-term cruisers were in fact co-researchers and several cruisers have acted as evaluators of my data analyses. I have also drawn on several perspectives/theories to interpret the data, such as work/leisure theories from sociology, motivation theories from social psychology and tourism studies, and various feminist perspectives. Consequently, in undertaking theory triangulation, I also applied interdisciplinary triangulation as I drew upon the disciplines of sociology, social anthropology, social psychology and tourism to inform my study. Finally, I used methodological triangulation, specifically the use of both qualitative and quantitative methods. By applying the five types of triangulation in my study, I was able to 'add rigor, breadth, and depth' to my study (Denzin & Lincoln 1994, p. 2; Flick 1992, p. 194) (Jennings 1999, p. 29).

*P*ILOT STUDIES

Pilot studies are a part of both qualitative and quantitative research. In both types of research, the researcher develops a tool or tools for gathering data. Before going into the field to gather the data, the researcher must check that the tools work. In this case, the researcher runs a 'dress rehearsal' of the data collection process. If the researcher has developed an observation schedule, then the researcher must go out into the field and test it to see that the criteria that have been developed are measurable and able to be notated. If the researcher has developed an interview schedule, then the schedule has to be tested to ensure that the questions are appropriately framed in order to acquire the required data. The pilot study also enables a 'pilot testing' of the analytical tools.

*S*UMMARY

The different research methodologies that can be used in tourism research
Primarily, there are two classifications for research methodologies: qualitative and quantitative methodologies. Qualitative methodologies are predicated to the interpretive social sciences, critical theory, feminist perspectives and postmodern paradigms. The use of qualitative methodologies ensures that these paradigmatic positions can gain in-depth knowledge of, in this case, the tourist phenomena being studied. The resultant data provide rich and thick descriptions for analysis. The use of a quantitative methodology is predicated to positivist and chaos theory paradigms, wherein tourism phenomenon are considered to be either linear-causal or non-linear chaotic in nature and able to be numerically measured.

The difference between an emic and an etic approach to data collection
An emic approach is associated with the interpretive social sciences, critical theory, feminist perspectives and postmodern paradigms. The research foci are generated by the participants and the experiences of the insiders, with subjectivity being paramount. The etic approach is associated with the positivist paradigm and quantitative methodology. The research foci are determined by the researcher and data are gathered from an outsider's viewpoint, with objectivity being paramount.

The differences between qualitative and quantitative research
The differences between qualitative and quantitative research methodologies are summarised in table 5.1.

The use of mixed methods
Over time, there has been a merging of qualitative and quantitative methodologies. Mixed methods have evolved in order for researchers to gain fuller insights into study phenomena, in this case tourist phenomena, by drawing on features from both methodologies.

The various types of sampling
All researchers have to decide whether to study the entire population or to study just some of the population. Limitations of time, money and human resources will influence the choice of sampling used. Sampling is primarily

either non-probability or probability based. Non-probability sampling includes convenience, purposive, snowball sampling and expert sampling. Non-probability sampling includes simple random sampling (lottery method, first name, date of birth or computer-generated methods), stratified sampling, cluster sampling and multi-stage sampling. Quota sampling, a quasi-random sampling method, is also used.

The need for reliability and validity in relation to qualitative and quantitative research

For both qualitative and quantitative methodologies, there is a need for reliability and validity. With qualitative methodologies, reliability and validity are associated with ensuring that what is being attempted to be 'measured' is actually measured. There are various types of reliability: quixotic, diachronic and synchronic. With quantitative methodologies, reliability and validity are also associated with measuring appropriately what is being measured. There are various types of validity: face, criterion-related, construct and content.

The various types of triangulation and their purposes in tourism research

Denzin (1978) identifies four types of triangulation: data triangulation; investigator triangulation; theory triangulation; and methodological triangulation. Janesick (1994) suggests a fifth type: interdisciplinary triangulation.

The role of pilot studies in the process of conducting tourism research

Pilot studies enable researchers to check that their methods are credible before entering the field or commencing data collection. Pilot studies clarify question wording, structure and design, and enable a trial of the analysis processes.

Questions

5.1 Which paradigm(s) would use a qualitative methodology and why?

5.2 Which paradigm(s) would use a quantitative methodology and why?

5.3 Develop a table that outlines the key differences between emic and etic perspectives.

5.4 Is the debate between the use of a qualitative methodology and a quantitative methodology a clear-cut debate? Justify your opinion.

5.5 Does the use of 'mixed methods' fit with the major paradigms that inform tourism research? Justify your opinion.

5.6 Construct a diagram that outlines the match of paradigms, methodologies and sampling techniques.

5.7 Explain the nature of reliability and validity in regard to a qualitative methodology.

5.8 Explain the nature of reliability and validity in regard to a quantitative methodology.

5.9 Define the five types of triangulation presented in this chapter.

5.10 Are pilot studies important to the research process? Explain your answer.

EXERCISES

Exercise 5.1
A local tourism organisation is trying to understand the nature of the contribution of the visiting friends and relatives market to the local economy. What methodological framework would you use and why? Write a summary of 100–200 words outlining and justifying your methodological approach.

Exercise 5.2
A tourism-related government agency wants to determine the national population's attitude to the establishment of a large-scale marine park in southern Australian waters. What sampling method would you use to determine the population's attitude and what sampling frame would you use? In 250 words, explain your choice of sampling method and sampling frame.

RESEARCH PROJECT

Your research project requires you to clearly consider the methodological approach you will take. Write a brief summary of 500–750 words outlining your selected methodology. Ensure you address the following questions and justify your responses:

- Are you using a quantitative, qualitative or mixed method approach?
- Where do you stand in regard to emic or etic perspectives?
- What type of sampling do you intend to use and why?
- How will you address reliability and validity issues?
- What role does triangulation have in your research project?

As you prepare your summary, you need to link the methodology to the over-riding paradigm that informs your research. Which paradigm are you drawing on? In chapter 2, you were informed that each paradigm has a specific onto-logical, epistemological and methodological perspective. As you prepare your research project, you need to keep in mind the need for complementarity between your chosen paradigm's ontology, epistemology and methodology.

REFERENCES

Australian Tourist Commission. 2000. *New Century, New World Annual Report 1999–2000.* http://www.atc.net.au/about/annual/annual.htm (downloaded 12 March 2001).

Babbie, Earl. 1990. *Survey Research Methods.* Belmont: Wadsworth.

Blaikie, Norman W. H. 1991. 'A Critique of Triangulation in Social Research'. *Quality and Quantity,* vol. 25, pp. 115–36.

Blumer, Herbert. 1962. 'Society as Symbolic Interaction'. In Rose, A. (Ed.) *Human Behaviour and Social Processes: An Interactionist Approach.* Boston, MA: Houghton Mifflin.

Bryman, A. 1988. *Quantity and Quality in Social Research.* London: Unwin Hyman.

Bryman, A. 1992. 'Quantitative and Qualitative Research: Further Reflections on their Integration'. In Brannen, J. (Ed.) *Mixing Methods: Qualitative and Quantitative Research.* Aldershot: Avebury, pp. 57–78.

Clawson, Marion. 1963. *Land and Water for Recreation: Opportunities, Problems and Policies.* Chicago: Rand McNally.

Creswell, J. W. 1994. *Research Design: Qualitative and Quantitative Approaches.* Thousand Oaks: Sage.

Denzin, Norman. 1978. *The Research Act: A Theoretical Introduction to Sociological Methods.* New York: McGraw-Hill.

Denzin, Norman. 1989a. *The Research Act: A Theoretical Introduction into Sociological Methods.* Second Edition. New York: McGraw-Hill.

Denzin, Norman. 1989b. *Interpretive Interactionism.* Newbury Park: Sage.

Denzin, Norman & Lincoln, Yvonna. 1994. 'Introduction: Entering the Field of Qualitative Research'. In Denzin, Norman & Lincoln, Yvonna. *Handbook of Qualitative Research.* Thousand Oaks: Sage, pp. 1–17.

de Vaus, D. A. 1995. *Surveys in Social Research.* Fifth Edition. Sydney: Allen & Unwin.

Fetterman, David. M. 1989. *Ethnography, Step by Step.* Applied Social Research Methods Series, Volume 17. Newbury Park: Sage.

Fielding, Nigel G. & Fielding, Jane L. 1986. *Linking Data.* Qualitative Research Methods Series, No. 4, Newbury Park, CA: Sage.

Flick, U. 1992. 'Triangulation Revisited: Strategy of Validation or Alternative?' *Journal of the Theory of Social Behaviour,* vol. 22, pp. 175–98.

Ford, Julienne. 1975. *Paradigms and Fairy Tales: An Introduction to the Science of Meanings.* Volume 1. London: Routledge & Kegan Paul.

Glesne, Corrine. 1999. *Becoming Qualitative Researchers: An Introduction.* Second Edition. White Plains, NY: Longman.

Greene, J. C., Caracelli, V. J. & Graham, W. F. 1989. 'Toward a Conceptual Framework for Mixed-Method Evaluation Designs'. *Educational Evaluation and Policy Analysis,* vol. 11, no. 2, pp. 255–74.

Guba, Egon & Lincoln, Yvonna. 1988. 'Do Inquiry Paradigms Imply Inquiry Methodologies?' In Fetterman, David (Ed.) *Qualitative Approaches to Evaluation in Education: The Silent Scientific Revolution.* New York: Praeger, pp. 89–115.

Harris, Marvin. 1964. *The Nature of Cultural Things.* New York: Random House.

Harris, Marvin. 1968. *The Rise of Anthropological Theory.* New York: Crowell.

Janesick, Valerie. 1994. 'The Dance of Qualitative Research Design'. In Denzin, Norman & Lincoln, Yvonna. *Handbook of Qualitative Research.* Thousand Oaks: Sage, pp. 209–19.

Kirk, Jerome & Miller, Marc. 1986. *Reliability and Validity in Qualitative Research.* Newbury Park: Sage.

Krejcie, R. V. & Morgan, D. W. 1970. 'Determining Sample Size for Research Activities'. *Educational and Psychological Measurement,* vol. 30, pp. 607–10.

Kumar. Ranjit. 1996. *Research Methodology: A Step-By-Step Guide for Beginners.* South Melbourne: Longman.

Lincoln, Y. S. & Guba, E. G. 1985. *Naturalistic Inquiry.* Newbury Park: Sage.

Loncar, Milica. 2001. The Manager, Market Research Unit, Australian Tourist Commission (personal communication, 12 March 2001).

Maslow, Abraham. 1943. 'A Theory of Human Motivation'. *Psychological Review,* vol. 50, pp. 370–96.

Miles, Matthew B. & Huberman, A. Michael. 1994. *Qualitative Data Analysis: An Expanded Sourcebook*. Second Edition. Thousand Oaks: Sage.

Neuman, W. L. 2000. *Social Research Methods, Qualitative and Quantitative Approaches*. Third Edition. Boston, MA: Allyn & Bacon.

Patton, Michael Q. 1990. *Qualitative Evaluation and Research Methods*. Second Edition. Newbury Park: Sage.

Pelto, Pert J. & Pelto, Gretal H. 1978. *Anthropological Research: The Structure of Inquiry*. Second Edition. London: Cambridge University Press.

Pike, Kenneth. 1954. *Language in Relation to a Unified Theory of the Structure of Human Behavior*, Volume 1, California: Summer Institute of Linguistics.

Punch, Keith F. 1998. *Introduction to Social Research*. London: Sage.

Riley, Roger W. & Love, Lisa L. 2000. 'The State of Qualitative Tourism Research'. *Annals of Tourism Research*, vol. 27, no. 1, pp. 164–87.

Sarantakos, S. 1998. *Social Research*. Second Edition. South Melbourne: Macmillan.

Sieber, S. D. 1973. 'The Integration of Fieldwork and Survey Methods'. *American Journal of Sociology*, vol. 78, no. 6, pp. 1335–59.

Stehlik, D. 1999. From Snowball to Rhizome. Feminist Rural Research and the Challenge to 'Credibility'. Paper presented at the International Conference 'Issues of Rigour' in Qualitative Research, Melbourne, 8–10 July.

Thomas, William I. & Thomas, Dorothy Swaine. 1928/1970. *The Child in America: Behavior Problems and Programs*. New York: Alfred A. Knopf.

Ticehurst, Gregory W. & Veal, Anthony J. 1999. *Business Research Methods: A Managerial Approach*. Australia: Longman.

Trow, Martin. 1970. 'Comment on "Participant Observation and Interviewing: A Comparison"'. In Filstead, W. J. *Qualitative Methodology*. Chicago: Markham.

FURTHER READING

Brannen, J. (Ed.) 1992. *Mixing Methods: Qualitative and Quantitative Research*. Aldershot: Avebury.

Bureau of Tourism Research (BTR). International Visitor Survey. Annual and quarterly reports available. www.btr.gov.au.

Caplan, Paula J. & Caplan, Jeremy B. 1999. *Thinking Critically About Research on Sex and Gender*. New York: Longman.

Denzin, Norman K. & Lincoln, Yvonna S. (Eds) 1994. *Handbook of Qualitative Research*. Thousand Oaks: Sage.

Hammersley, M. 1992. 'Deconstructing the Qualitative-Quantitative Divide'. In Brannen, J. (Ed.) *Mixing Methods: Qualitative and Quantitative Research*. Aldershot: Avebury, pp. 39–55.

Minichiello, Victor, Aroni, Rosalie, Timewell, Eric & Alexander, Loris. 1995. *In-Depth Interviewing*. Second Edition. Melbourne: Longman.

Ritchie, J. R. Brent & Goeldner, Charles R. (Eds) 1994. *Travel, Tourism and Hospitality Research: A Handbook for Managers and Researchers*. Second Edition. New York: John Wiley & Sons.

Roberts, Helen. (Ed.) 1981. *Doing Feminist Research*. London: Routledge.

Sudman, Seymour. 1976. *Applied Sampling*. New York: Academic Press.

6

Qualitative methods

and tourism research

'The hegemony of one research style deprives social scientists of a variety of other research strategies that have equal, and possibly superior, claims to the mantle of "science" ... The complexity of the world around us demands the deployment of a variety of techniques and strong intellectual and methodological discipline, not a commitment to the hegemony of a single research modality.'

(Whyte, Greenwood & Lazes 1991, p. 19)

LEARNING OBJECTIVES

After studying this chapter, you should be able to:

- discuss the criteria that define qualitative methods
- discuss the theoretical positions that inform qualitative methods
- understand the nature of exchanges in interviews
- describe the principles of unstructured/in-depth interviews and the advantages and disadvantages of using in-depth interviews
- explain the processes involved in semi-structured interviews and the advantages and disadvantages of semi-structured interviews
- distinguish between the various types of participant observation
- outline the nature of focus groups and the advantages and disadvantages of using focus groups
- describe the different approaches that may be used for longitudinal studies
- provide an overview of the Delphic method
- understand the various types of case study and the advantages and disadvantages of using case studies
- discuss the role of action research as a qualitative research method
- describe the nature of documentary research
- reflect on the role of non-sexist research methods.

INTRODUCTION

Tourism and hospitality research have tended to be influenced by the hypothetico-deductive paradigm. This chapter introduces alternatives to the observance of such a single research modality. In particular, the chapter presents a variety of qualitative research methods. As discussed in chapter 5, qualitative research methods are predicated on the tenets of a qualitative methodology. These tenets are: an inductive approach; an ontological view that recognises multiple realities; truths/evidence grounded in the real world; a subjective epistemology; an emic (insider's) perspective; an emergent research design that has a thematic focus; non-random participant selection; the collection of textual data that are analysed for themes and motifs; and representation of the research findings in a narrative format written in the first person that represents a slice of life of the social setting under study. Any deviation from these tenets suggests a mixing of methods.

This chapter focuses on qualitative methods that follow these tenets. A qualitative methodology is associated with the holistic-inductive paradigm (interpretive social sciences, critical theory, feminist perspectives and post-modern paradigms). The main methods (tools) of data collection are interviews, participant observation, focus groups, Delphi techniques, case studies, action research and documentary methods. There are other methods, such as the biographical method that studies and reports on a person's life (see Smith 1994), but this chapter concentrates on the main methods. Each method is defined, outlined and then its advantages and disadvantages are considered.

QUALITATIVE METHODOLOGY

The key principle of a qualitative approach to data collection and analysis is that '[i]f it is our serious purpose to understand the thoughts of a people, the whole analysis of experience must be based on their concepts, not ours' (Boas 1943, p. 314). This is achieved through 'verstehen' (Weber 1978) — that is, empathetic understanding (see chapter 2). There are a number of theoretical positions that inform the use of a qualitative methodological framework in research design. Some of these theoretical positions include symbolic interactionism, phenomenology, heuristic inquiry, ethnomethodology and ethnography. Background information about each of these positions is presented in the following subsections to give you a rudimentary understanding of each.

■ 6.2.1 Symbolic *interactionism*

Symbolic interactionism is founded on the works of Thomas (1928), Mead (1934) and his concept of the 'looking glass' image of self, and Blumer (1962 and 1969). Symbolic interaction looks at how humans act in relation to events, objects and others based on a system of meanings associated with each. Such meanings are generated by social interaction, and meanings are modified over time through further social interactions. One of the methods Blumer used to look at symbolic interactionism was group discussions and interviews in the research process (Patton 1990, p. 76). According to Blumer, symbolic interactionism is based on three premises:

> [F]irst, that 'human beings act toward things on the basis of the meanings that the things have for them' [Blumer 1969, p. 2]; second, that the meanings of things arise out of the process of social interaction; and third, that meanings are modified through an interpretive process which involves self-reflective individuals symbolically interacting with one another (Denzin 1992, p. xiv).

There are a diversity of forms of symbolic interactionism with an equally diverse number of interpretive and qualitative methodological approaches (Denzin 1992, pp. xiv–xv), such as ethnography, grounded theory (Glaser & Strauss 1967), participant observation, feminist perspectives, interviewing and conversational analysis (Maynard 1987).

■ 6.2.2 Phenomenology

Phenomenology is firmly grounded in the subjective meanings that social actors construct to explain their social reality. Phenomenology is attributed to the work of Husserl and his student Schutz (1972). 'By phenomenology Husserl ([1913] 1960) meant the study of how people describe things and experience them through their senses' (Patton 1990, p. 69). In particular, '[p]henomenological research focuses on the ways in which social actors make situations meaningful. It focuses on the way people interpret the actions of others, how they make sense of events and how, through communication, they build worlds of meaning' (Bouma 1996, p. 178). The chief method used by phenomenologists is participant observation.

One type of phenomenological research is heuristic inquiry. A work that exemplifies this approach is Maslow's (1943, 1956, 1966) hierarchy of needs used in tourism motivation studies.

■ 6.2.3 Heuristic *research*

'The uniqueness of heuristic inquiry is the extent to which it legitimizes and places at the fore [the] personal experiences, reflections, and insights of the researcher' (Patton 1990, p. 72). The process of heuristic research involves six phases: initial engagement, immersion, incubation, illumination, explication and creative synthesis (Moustakas 1990). Methods used in heuristic research include conversational interviews, semi-structured interviews and standardised open-ended interviews (Moustakas 1990, p. 47). Interviews are also supplemented with the use of personal documents such as journals and diaries (Moustakas 1990, p. 49).

■ 6.2.4 Ethnomethodology

Ethnomethodology is grounded in the work of Garfinkel (1967), who also coined the term, and Zimmerman (1971). Ethnomethodology is an extension of the work of Schutz applied to everyday life. From an ethnomethodological perspective, there is no order to social life, only that ascribed by the social actors. Essentially:

> [e]thnomethodology gets at the norms, understandings, and assumptions that are taken for granted by people in a setting because they are so deeply understood that people don't even think about why they do what they do (Patton 1990, p. 74).

The methods that ethnomethodologists use are in-depth interviews and participant observation (Patton 1990, p. 74).

■ 6.2.5 Ethnography

'Ethnography is the art and science of describing a group or culture' (Fetterman 1989, p. 11). The conduct of an ethnography is guided by several principles (Burns 1997; Fetterman 1989; Harding 1991):
- a focus on understanding and interpretation
- a focus on process or negotiation of meanings
- research undertaken in natural settings
- social phenomena studied within the social context in which they occur, in order that a holistic perspective is gained
- emic and etic perspectives jointly utilised
- the identification of multiple realities/perspectives
- the use of multiple methods that include participant observation and interviewing
- non-judgmental positioning.

Furthermore, in reporting their findings, ethnographers are required to detail their 'ethnographic presence' in order to indicate to the reader how close they were to the people being studied. Consequently:

> ethnographers openly describe their roles in events during the fieldwork (Fetterman 1989, p. 116).

Table 6.1 demonstrates how two of these theoretical positions may be applied to qualitative research in tourism. It also introduces other theoretical positions (grounded theory, ethnoscience and qualitative ethology) that could be applied and references for you to pursue if you are interested in reading more about them. You should notice particularly the types of research 'questions' posed and subsequent research focus, the participants involved in the study, comments on sample size, the methods used for data collection, the other sources of data that might be accessed in the study, and the type of findings or results that would eventuate.

■ Table 6.1 *Overview of some theoretical positions applied to qualitative research in tourism*

STRATEGY	TYPE OF RESEARCH QUESTIONS	RESEARCH QUESTION/ FOCUS	PARTICIPANTS/ INFORMANTS[a]	SAMPLE SIZE[b]	DATA COLLECTION METHODS	OTHER DATA SOURCES	TYPE OF RESULTS	MAJOR REFERENCES
Phenomenology	Meaning questions — eliciting the essence of experiences	What is the meaning of arriving home?	Travellers arriving home; phenomen- ological literature; art, poetry and other descriptions	Approximately six participants	In-depth conversations	Phenomen- ological literature; philosophical reflections; poetry; art	In-depth reflective description of the experience of 'what it feels like to come home'	Bergum (1991), Giorgi (1970), van Manen (1984, 1990)
Ethnography	Descriptive questions — of values, beliefs, practices of cultural group	What is the arrival gate like when an international plane arrives?	Travellers, families, others who observe the setting, such as … rental car personnel, cleaning staff, security guards, etc.	Approximately 30–50 interviews	Interviews; participant observation; other records, such as airport statistics	Documents; records; photography; maps; genealogies; social network diagrams	Description of the day-to-day events at the arrival gate of the airport	Ellen (1984), Fetterman (1989), Grant & Fine (1992), Hammersley & Atkinson (1983), Sanjek (1990), Spradley (1979), Werner & Schoepfle (1987a, 1987b)
Grounded theory	'Process' questions — experience over time or change, may have stages and phases	Coming home: reuniting the family	Travellers, family members	Approximately 30–50	In-depth interviews observations	Participant observation; memoing; diary	Description of the social psychological process in the experience of returning home	Chenitz & Swanson (1986), Glaser (1978, 1992), Glaser & Strauss (1967), Strauss (1987), Strauss & Corbin (1990)
Ethnoscience	Classificatory questions — descriptive	What are types of travellers?	Those who observe the setting daily — … rental car personnel, cleaning staff, security guards, etc.	Approximately 30–50	Interviews to elicit similarities and differences of travellers, card sorts		Taxonomy and description of types and characteristics of travellers	
Qualitative ethology		What are the greeting behaviours of travellers and their families?	Travellers and their families	Units — numbers of greetings — 100–200	Photography, video; coded	Videotaped; note- taking	Description of the patterns of greeting behaviours	Eibl-Eibesfeldt (1989), Morse & Bottorff (1990), Scherer & Ekman (1982)

Source: *Morse (1994 pp. 224–5)*

[a] Examples only.
[b] Number depends on saturation.

Methods are the tools used to gather empirical data (Sarantakos 1998, p. 32; Stanley & Wise 1990, p. 26). As tools of data collection, Wolcott reflects that:

> [I]n the past two decades, qualitative methods … have come to be widely known and accepted. There is no longer a call for each researcher to discover and defend them anew, nor a need to provide an exhaustive review of the literature about such standard procedures as participant observation or interviewing (Wolcott 1990, p. 26).

This is still the case today. The next section considers the different methods used to gather data within a qualitative methodological framework.

■ 6.3.1 Interviews

Interviews have been likened to conversations — they are 'merely one of the many ways in which two people talk to one another' (Benney & Hughes 1970, p. 191). Dexter (1970, p. 149) elaborates a little further on the nature of interviews as conversations; he sees interviews as conversations with a purpose. However, Oakley considers these views of interviews as simplistic. For her, interviews are pseudo-conversations that traditionally have set rules to follow (Oakley 1981, p. 32). Interviews need to be established on 'a relationship of mutual trust', otherwise the outcomes of the interview will be 'particularly dismal' (1981, p. 56). Furthermore, Oakley (1981, p. 41) notes that interviews should be 'non-hierarchical', with the interviewer adding 'his or her own personal identity in the relationship'. As noted in chapter 4, Oakley (1981) also considers that interviews are an exchange, as interviewers must engage with the participant to establish rapport, and there is 'no intimacy without reciprocity'.

'No intimacy without reciprocity' is demonstrated in the following interview transcription. A fictitious name has been used to protect the identity of the participant:

Interviewer: There are some people who would like to do what you are doing but never do it. Why do you think they don't go?

Rowena: You share!

Interviewer: You want me to share my thoughts?

Rowena: Yes, it is only fair. You are being very professional asking questions. Now I want to know what you think!

Interviewer: I think it is because they do not feel they can leave the safety of land, and the security of a land-based life.

Rowena: I disagree. You mention both. I think the reasons for men are different to women. The men do not go because …

The above interaction between the interviewer and participant is contrary to the view purported by Ticehurst and Veal (1999, p. 100) that '[t]he interviewer is meant to listen and encourage the respondent to talk — not to engage in debate'. By not engaging, the interview may have been terminated by the interviewee had the inverviewer not shared their thoughts.

Sometimes, interviews may become a site for personal reflection by interviewees. As Patton (1990, pp. 353–4) notes: 'The process of being taken through a directed, reflective process affects the persons being interviewed and leaves them knowing things about themselves that they didn't know — or at least were not aware of — before the interview.'

The nature of the interview as a reflective process is demonstrated in the following excerpt from an interview transcript:

Interviewer. Okay, that's all of the interview. Are there any comments or suggestions you want to comment about it?

Victor. No, not really. It's just difficult to answer the questions spontaneously. There are a lot of questions that you want a lot of the reasons for doing things, but I never really actually ... I know I must be doing things for a reason, but I've never really tried to identify the reason and consciously consider why I'm doing it.

Interviewer. So do you think I am asking people things that are difficult to respond to?

Victor. Yeah, in a way, but I suppose personally I've never really tried to analyse why I'm doing things.

There are various types of interviews, ranging from structured interviews to unstructured interviews. Table 6.2 outlines the differences between the types of interviews. Each type of interview has its own particular ontological, epistemological and methodological position. This chapter discusses the two qualitative-oriented types of interviews: unstructured interviews (or depth or in-depth interviews) and semi-structured interviews.

■ **Table 6.2**
The differences between the various types of interviews

	STRUCTURED INTERVIEWS	SEMI-STRUCTURED INTERVIEWS (FOCUSED INTERVIEWS)	UNSTRUCTURED INTERVIEWS
Ontology	Closed world view — universal truths and reality	Multiple realities	Multiple realities
Epistemology	Objective (subjects and study units)	Subjective (participants and phenomenon)	Subjective (participants and phenomenon)
Methodology	Quantitative	Qualitative	Qualitative
Examples	Standardised interviews; surveys; opinion polls; interviewer-completed questionnaires	In-depth interviews; surveys; group interviews (focus groups)	In-depth interviews; group interviews (focus groups)
Format	Fixed schedule; short responses	Topic/theme lists generally open-ended questions	Oral/life histories; conversational
Duration	Short — 10 to 30 minutes	Medium to long — 1 hour or more	Medium to long — 2 hours or more; several sessions

Unstructured or in-depth interviews

The interview is an exchange between the interviewer and the interviewee and, as noted above, it is like a conversation. The interviewer should not dominate the conversation, as the purpose is to elicit the views of the interviewee. However, the interviewer may have to be ready to become a subject together with the interviewee, especially if the research has a feminist methodological basis or the interviewee makes reciprocity demands. In unstructured interviews, control by the interviewer is minimal, as the interviewee is really leading the interview with their thoughts.

Essentially, there is no formal interview schedule. The interviewer has an idea about themes or issues, and may also have a list of topics relevant to the themes or issues, and these are merely used as a guide. The 'real' guide to the issues or themes is vested in the interviewees and they end up leading the interview by order of their thoughts and reflections on the topic. Therefore, there is no set order of questions. The interaction between the interviewer and the interviewee is fluid; the interviewer may occasionally manage the interaction to return the interviewee to the topic should the discussion diverge from it.

In-depth interviewing is sometimes combined with other methods, such as participant observation. The combination of interviewing and participant observation serves to add to the richness of the data collected:

> ... in-depth interviewing focuses on, and relies on, verbal accounts of social realities. This is somewhat different from participant observation, which relies on participation in, and observation of, behaviour or action in the context in which it occurs. It is often argued (Taylor & Bogdon 1984) that the participant observer is in a better position than the interviewer to gain access to the everyday life of the informant or group of informants because the participant observer directly experiences the social world which the informant inhabits, rather than simply relating second-hand accounts (Minichiello, Aroni, Timewell & Alexander 1995, pp. 69–70).

Moreover, in combining participant observation and interviewing, any distortions and discrepancies can be discovered — that is, methodological triangulation may be achieved.

Advantages and disadvantages

The advantages of in-depth interviews are associated with the ontological and epistemological perspectives of the interpretive social sciences paradigm. The disadvantages are founded in the critiques of the interpretive social sciences paradigm as opposed to the use of a positivist paradigm.

Advantages

Some of the advantages include:

- in-depth interviews enable the interviewer to gather 'rich' data and 'thick' descriptions (Geertz 1973) of the social world being studied — in so doing, the multiple realities that explain the social world are elucidated

- by establishing a subjective relationship between the interviewer and the interviewee, rapport and trust are able to be established and this facilitates the interaction and the depth of discussion on the research 'topic'.

Disadvantages

Some of the disadvantages include:

- the data cannot be extrapolated to the wider population — the data collected in qualitative research are only true of the people who participated
- the subjective nature of the interaction, as opposed to the objective nature in a positivist approach, raises queries over reliability and validity for some positivist critics
- there is a large investment in time and personnel in gathering such data — in-depth interviews range from two hours duration up to a total of 10 hours or more over several sessions.

To overcome some of these disadvantages, some researchers may choose to use semi-structured interviews.

Semi-structured interviews

Semi-structured interviews can be used by both qualitative and quantitative methodologies. The focus of this chapter is on qualitative methods — quantitative semi-structured interviews are described in chapter 8. Semi-structured interviews remain within the genre of a conversation; however, the interviewer has a prompt list of issues that focus the interaction. The list adds some structure to the interview, although the ordering of the discussion about the issues on the list may vary between interviews. As with unstructured interviews, semi-structured interviews are fluid in nature and follow the thinking processes of the interviewee. An example of a semi-structured interview prompt list is presented in figure 6.1. Generally, semi-structured (and unstructured) interviews start with grand tour questions (Spradley & McCurdy 1972, p. 63) in order to make interviewees feel comfortable, as well as to set the context for the interview.

■ **Figure 6.1**
Example of a semi-structured interview prompt list

TRAVEL EXPERIENCES WITHIN AUSTRALIA

- ■ Background travel experiences (grand tour type of question)
- ■ Present travel experience
  - — who with?
  - — how able to travel now?
  - — duration of travel
  - — why Australia?
  - — what activities?
  - — satisfaction
    - • destinations
    - • activities
    - • people (hosts)
- ■ Future plans
- ■ Other comments

Advantages and disadvantages

As with in-depth interviews, the advantages and disadvantages of semi-structured interviews are associated with the paradigm informing the methodology and thence the method, particularly the ontological and epistemological perspectives of inductive paradigms as opposed to deductive paradigms.

Advantages

The advantages of semi-structured interviews include:

- multiple realities can be determined since the semi-structured interview does not constrain the participant to following the interviewer's a priori reasoning
- the subjective epistemological viewpoint enables rapport to be established
- the method's usefulness in gathering data on complex issues and sensitive issues, as the interviewer can take time to establish rapport and move towards the examination of such issues, whereas in a structured interview, the objective nature of the epistemological positioning of the researcher works against such issues being examined in any great depth
- detailed information regarding attitudes, opinions and values may be elicited as opposed to using scales that tend to reduce the interviewee's experiences to numeric positions along a continuum
- the questions are not objectively predetermined and presented, so the interviewer is able to ask for further clarification and detail and pursue these issues without negatively affecting the quality of the data collected
- interview probes can be altered to follow the path the interviewee is focused on pursuing
- queries can be clarified, which is generally not the case when an interviewer is operating from an objective epistemological perspective, as such explanations are considered to add researcher bias to the data collection process
- verbal and non-verbal cues can be recorded and included in the analysis
- follow-up questions can be framed to further extend responses
- the semi-structured schedule provides a more relaxed interview setting.

Disadvantages

There are several disadvantages of semi-structured interviews when compared to a more positivist data collection approach. Most of the disadvantages are associated with the epistemological approach being a subjective one. The disadvantages include:

- using different interviewers results in differences in researcher-interviewee interactions and this may reduce the comparability between data collected by different researchers and interviewees
- the interviewees are able to interpret reality rather than the interviewer (the interviewee leads the interaction and the interviewer follows)
- this style of interviewing is closer to unstructured than structured interviewing, so critics of the approach focus on the reliability and validity of the data collected and the variability in epistemological interactions
- replication is impossible since the social interaction between the interviewer and the interviewee is a snapshot view of interaction influenced by

the type of day, the setting of the interview and the social circumstances surrounding both the interviewer and the interviewee

- semi-structured interviews take much longer than structured interviews — semi-structured interviews can be up to one to two hours in duration or three to five hours with breaks, or they can be run as a series of interviews over several days, weeks or months
- data may be useless if the interviewer has not developed good interviewing skills and does not probe and follow leads given by the interviewee that the interviewee does not subsequently elaborate upon
- rapport is necessary to gather the complexity and sensitivity of data in a trusting environment — time and personal investment must be expended by the interviewer and interviewee to do this, and much time may be spent prior to the interview as the interviewer and the interviewee get to know each other
- the researcher may manipulate the data and bias the data by only pursuing one particular line of prompting.

Sometimes, in semi-structured interviews, several or more people may be interviewed at the one time. The following section comments about interviewing heterosexual couples together. Larger groups are discussed later, in the section on focus groups.

Interviewing heterosexual couples together

Sometimes, researchers choose to interview heterosexual couples together. There are varying attitudes to the appropriateness of this for data collection. Reinharz (1992, p. 41) reports that the 'sociologist Lillian Rubin wrote that involvement in the women's movement showed her the need to interview husbands and wives separately and privately because "women tend to discuss their feelings about their lives, their roles, and their marriages [relationships] more freely when men are not present"'. Reinharz goes on to say that Wajcman also agrees with Rubin 'that separate interviews are preferable, although fruitful discussions can occur if both spouses [partners] are present. Interviewing husbands and wives [partners] separately has the disadvantage of obscuring how interaction occurs in the couple. The views the researcher hears expressed separately may rarely be expressed when the couple is together' (Reinharz 1992, p. 41).

Women interviewing men

Feminists state that '[w]omen stand in the position of "the Other" to men of the dominant groups' (Harding 1991, p. 134), and this has an effect on the interview exchange. The reverse situation of men interviewing women also reinforces the 'other' position, with the men being associated with the dominant group in society or the power group. Essentially, the existence of obvious gender empathy will impact on heterosexual interview situations. Age, educational qualifications and profession can also be associated with power positions in interviews. This is exemplified in Jennings' (1999) reflections of time in the field gathering data on long-term ocean cruisers.

During my fieldwork, I was tested by the men, to see if I knew anything about cruising or whether I was just an academic. Questions would include passages undertaken, type of boat, what sort of electrical system, solar power, type of refrigeration, engine, gear box, and various other technical systems and questions. Having sailed through Indonesia, an area into which most cruisers were heading, also assisted as I was able to share cruising information, some language terms regarding boats and charts if necessary. This was part of the reciprocity of the exchange of information resulting from the study.

Reciprocity was mentioned earlier in the chapter. Another example of reciprocity is provided in the following Industry Insight.

INDUSTRY INSIGHT

The following excerpts from interview transcriptions from Jennings (1999) demonstrate reciprocity in action:

Paulo: I think you've [the interviewer] been more informative to us!
[Because the interviewer answered the following questions]
'How many sailboats do you think you could get anchored in there without ... is it big enough for a lot of boats?'
'Is it secure?'
'Any problems with safe anchorage for an island?'
'24 hours a day there's somebody sitting on the boat?'
'How do you feel about the cyclone season up here?' (Paulo)
'Do you know anything about going out the Endeavour Channel from Cape York instead of going on up to Thursday Island? ... I was just ... If you've got an extra minute, let me show you what I had in mind. ... Let's see. From Cape York from over here somewhere you can go up Thursday Island and on out. One of these routes, anyway. I was wondering about just going straight out Endeavour Straight here. Out this way. Some people said this was poorly surveyed and shifting sands and it's not a good idea, but I think I've not talked with anyone who's really knowledgeable, or who has done it.' (Joshua)
'I know that this is kind of diverting, but what is the tonnage of your boat?' (Gemma)
'Were you a sailor as a child or did you ...?'
'So what kind of boat do you have?' (Heidi)

Jennings (1999) provided inside information regarding future sailing routes and anchorages to the cruisers who were interviewed in her study and the cruisers provided information regarding their independent travel-based lifestyles. There was an exchange and sharing of information by all parties concerned.

Some hints for interview etiquette

Regardless of the type of interview conducted (in-depth, semi-structured or structured), there are a number of protocols of which the interviewer needs to be aware:

- always arrange the appointment to suit the interviewee
- check that you have all the interview materials working and organised before you arrive
- always arrive on time
- be flexible — life events may mean that an interviewee is unable to fulfil their commitment to you on the specific day — remember you are operating in different time and schedule settings, and while your research may be top priority for you, it may be a minor priority for the interviewees in the overall schema of their lives
- consider your overall appearance — for example, if you are interviewing people on a beach, it would be wise not to appear in professional dress; on the other hand, if you are interviewing business executives, it would be wise to wear professional dress
- be aware of cultural protocols or codes of conduct
- be conscious of social justice principles
- remember the ethical rights of the interviewee
- check that the interviewees understand their rights
- pay attention to the interviewee throughout the interview session — do not get distracted by events outside the interview setting
- ask permission to take notes or to audiotape or videotape the session
- arrange a time to have the interviewee check or comment on the interview transcript if possible
- use probes and prompts to elicit further information
- do not manipulate the interviewee to present information in one light only — this biases the data
- check the comfort level of the interviewee
- be prepared to break off the interview if necessary
- advise the interviewee when approaching midpoint and especially near the end
- ensure you formally close the interview, as often other disclosures may arise after the interview has finished that the interviewee does not want recorded and this request must be honoured.

■ 6.3.2 Participant *observation*

Participant observation involves 'intensive fieldwork in which the investigator is immersed in the culture under study' (Patton 1990, p. 67). Within the research literature, participant observation has been described in a variety of ways. Junker (1960), Gold (1969), Gans (1982), and Adler and Adler (1987) have variously presented either a four- or a three-role model for participant observation field work. Junker (1960) has identified four roles: the 'complete observer', the 'observer as participant', the 'participant as observer' and the 'complete participant'. Gold has similarly identified four roles. Gans has identified three roles: the total researcher, the researcher participant and the total participant. Adler and Adler have also identified three roles: peripheral membership, active membership and complete membership. Table 6.3 provides a comparison of these roles based on their etic or emic perspective. These perspectives are based on Lewins' (1992) work.

■ Table 6.3
A comparison of role models for participant observation field work

LEWINS 1992	JUNKER 1960	GANS 1982	ADLER AND ADLER 1987
Etic	Complete observer	Total researcher	Peripheral membership
	Observer as participant	Researcher participant	Peripheral membership
Emic	Participant as observer	Researcher participant	Active membership
	Complete participant	Total participant	Complete membership

Source: *Based on Lewins (1992), Junker (1960), Gans (1982), Adler & Adler (1987)*

Steps in participant observation

There are a variety of steps involved in participant observation (Sarantakos 1998, pp. 209–10):

• consider the research purpose
• decide which type of participant observation will be used
• seek ethical clearance
• negotiate access to the study setting if necessary
• engage in exploratory observation of the site and its usage patterns and flows
• design the research methodology
• conduct a pilot study
• enter the field
• analysis the data
• report the findings using several genres for the client and the participants.

Runcie (1976) has outlined four stages for participating in a social setting in which the researcher has not previously been a member:

• In stage one, the researcher may be treated suspiciously, especially if the research purpose has not been clearly articulated to the participants. Generally, the interactions between the researcher and the participants will be superficial. Participants may exhibit some hostility to the researcher, as not all members of the study group may wish to participate and thus some may refuse to cooperate.

• The second stage is associated with establishing the observer/observed relationship. The researcher may be considered a 'provisional' member of the group. During this stage, the researcher will probably have to reiterate the ethics being followed, such as that all data are confidential and how confidentiality will be ensured, before participants will divulge information to the researcher. The participants will manage the interactions — what will be discussed and if they will discuss anything at all with the researcher.

• The third stage is defined by the researcher being granted 'categorical' membership of the group. Rapport is well established, and the researcher and participant roles are well defined. In this stage, the researcher is able to gather data while participating as a group member.

- The final stage is the departure stage. The researcher has completed all the necessary observation (a qualitative informational isomorph has been reached) and must withdraw from the study setting. This can be a difficult time for the researcher and the group, as both will have established relationships and friendships. Some participants will want to maintain contact to ensure that the observation made was correct or appropriate.

Advantages and disadvantages

The advantages and disadvantages noted below will vary depending on the type of participant observation involved.

Advantages

The advantages of participant observation include that it:

- examines interactions and behaviours in real-world settings
- enables researchers to become aware of how the participants construct and describe their world
- provides first-hand information
- provides information when other data collection methods are less effective — for example, routes taken around museum exhibits, length of time spent at interpretive signs in a national park
- may highlight behaviours/events that the observed may not wish to discuss — for example, interactions, behaviours
- is time-efficient
- is not associated with complicated data collection methods
- is cost-effective, as several methods are simultaneously being used (observation and interviewing)
- enables a wide range of data to be collected, as the researcher is in the study setting for an extended time period.

Disadvantages

The disadvantages of participant observation include that it:

- does not work well with large groups, as the observer can only be in one location or one setting at one time
- does not have a temporal comparability, as it is focused on the present; past or future settings are unable to be observed
- is not appropriate for opinions and attitudes unless coupled with interviewing, as the researcher cannot observe attitudes and opinions — such an approach being etic in nature
- may not gather complete information sets, as some events may be taboo for observation
- may be associated with observer bias, selective observations and interpretations (consider the perspective of a critical theory-oriented researcher or a feminist researcher, both of whom are trying to change the real-world circumstances of the people being studied)
- has no controls for researcher bias — as a participant, the researcher may go 'native', thereby losing objectivity
- does not provide quantifiable generalisations on results

- may result in misinterpretation of interactions or phenomena if analyses are not revalidated by the participants
- may cause changes in behaviour due to the participant observer's presence as noted by Runcie
- may result in difficulty in comparability if several observers are in the 'field'
- means that replication is impossible, because once the act has occurred, it is over
- is associated with subjective interpretations by observers.

■ 6.3.3 Focus *groups*

Focus groups may be described as focused or semi-structured group interviews (Minichiello, Aroni, Timewell & Alexander 1995). Instead of interviewing participants individually, study participants are interviewed together. Focus groups are used when an interviewer wants to determine points of view, opinions and attitudes towards tourism-related concepts such as destination image, product testing, attitudes and values associated with host–guest interactions, and the attitudes and values of local residents to tourism developments. Focus groups can also be used to gather data for forecasting. Forecasting involves gathering data upon which the researcher is able to predict future events and issues. As noted earlier in this textbook, forecasts can be short term (one day to two years), medium term (two to five years), long term (five to 15 years) and futuristic (more than 15 years) (Mill & Morrison 1998).

Focus groups are used when the facilitator believes that the interaction between group members will add to the richness of the data collected, as a result of the group members questioning, clarifying, challenging and discussing their positions in regard to the focus of the discussion. Interactions between participants are important, because such interactions can cause a participant to reflect and further develop or clarify their position. As with interviews, focus groups enable the researcher to gather data in more detail than they would have been able to collect had all the participants been involved in a survey. Interactions can occur between participants as well as through orchestration by the facilitator.

To ensure that focus groups are workable, their size needs to be limited. Focus groups usually involve eight to 12 people. Larger numbers than this result in the interactions of members being constrained and/or limited. In larger groups, the interaction becomes more formalised and less free flowing and the facilitator has to work hard to ensure that all the participants contribute. For example, a focus group involving 20 people with a duration of one hour would average three minutes per person — not enough time to ensure in-depth discussion.

In order for focus groups to gather relevant data successfully, an experienced facilitator is required. In particular, a focus group facilitator needs to be versed in group process skills, such as ensuring:
- all people's views are respected
- all people have equal time to contribute
- no one dominates the session
- emotions do not get out of hand.

The facilitator should also possess a knowledge of group roles, and the ability to probe and delve deeper into issues using questions and points of clarification.

There are various ways that a novice researcher can learn how to facilitate a focus group, such as shadowing another facilitator, establishing a mentoring or coaching relationship with an experienced facilitator, gaining training in process consultancy skills, and practising and rehearsing focus group sessions and receiving feedback from expert observers.

Focus groups require some pre-screening to ensure that the people who participate have the characteristics of the population they are drawn from. Quota sampling techniques may be used to ensure the range of demographic features of the study population is reflected in the focus group participants. Focus group composition may also require further screening to ensure that the group does not contain biased positions. For example, a focus group of residents who are going to discuss a tourism development needs to contain participants who are for, against and undecided about the tourism development, otherwise the group could be constituted of participants who are all either for or against the development.

Focus groups may be a one-off event or they may be used to constitute a longitudinal study — that is, a study that allows researchers to gather data from the same participants over a period of time. The latter method requires participants to commit to participate for a set period of time. Sometimes, incentives are used to ensure prolonged participation — for example, meals and transport are paid for by the researcher or the research client.

The study group may be a cross-section or a representative sample of a set group. The success of focus groups depends on:
- the selection of appropriate persons from the study population
- a comfortable setting that ensures the engagement of all participants
- the skills of the facilitator to generate dialogue between the participants (LaPage 1994).

Advantages and disadvantages

There are a number of advantages and disadvantages associated with the use of focus groups as a qualitative research method. Some of these are outlined below.

Advantages
Focus groups enable:
- participants to interact with others in order to clarify individual positions
- some degree of flexibility to follow unexpected trends or issues
- the generation of multiple realities by participants
- a subjective interaction between facilitator and participants that establishes rapport and results in the development of 'rich' data.

Disadvantages
The disadvantages of focus groups are primarily related to the facilitator's skills. If the facilitator is not well skilled, then focus groups may:
- be dominated by strong personalities
- diverge from the focus of attention

- present a biased perspective
- be constituted of participants who do not reflect the variety of views of the study population.

■ 6.3.4 **Longitudinal** *studies*

Longitudinal studies involve the study of the same people or a similar sample of people over a set period of time. Data may be collected using interviews, focus groups, participant observation and the documentary method (explained later in the chapter). Longitudinal studies may also be conducted using quantitative methods; however, as this chapter focuses on qualitative methods, only those methods associated with a holistic-inductive paradigm are discussed. Neuman (2000) identifies several types of longitudinal studies: panel studies, time series studies, trend studies and cohort analysis. He also includes case studies as a method of data collection for longitudinal studies. The differences between these types of longitudinal study are shown in table 6.4.

■ Table 6.4
Types of longitudinal studies

TYPE OF STUDY	CHARACTERISTICS	TOURISM EXAMPLE
Panel study	Same group of people over time	Identifying a group of people who represent a specific sociodemographic market segment and studying their holiday patterns over an extended period of time.
Time series	Different individuals over time, although one of the criteria remains constant, such as the study setting	An integrated resort determining the changing market segments that use the resort.
Trend studies	Research over time with different subjects	Studying residents to determine their domestic and international travel patterns.
Cohort analysis	Participants have an experience that is similar within a set time period	Identifying flight crew intakes trained during a specific year and then studying them throughout their employment to discuss working conditions.
Case study	Intense observation or data collection over the short or long term	Studying a small seaside community located close to a major tourism precinct over a 20-year period using a variety of qualitative research methods such as focus groups, participant observation, interviews and the documentary method.

Purpose of longitudinal studies

The purpose of longitudinal studies is to track trends and patterns over time using a comparable study group constituted of either the same people or people with the same attributes. Longitudinal studies seek to ascertain a long-term understanding of:

- social impacts of tourism development associated with host communities as well as tourists
- environmental impacts, by gathering data from people with relevant knowledge or experiences
- effects of social and economic changes on travel behaviour
- changes in travel experience behaviour
- trends or patterns in on-site activities of various market segments
- changes or trends in regard to tourism destinations
- forecasting future events.

Advantages and disadvantages

As with other methods, a variety of advantages and disadvantages have to be considered by the researcher regarding the use of longitudinal studies.

Advantages

The main advantage of longitudinal studies is the gathering over time of extensive data that is rich in nature and allows a fuller picture to be achieved, as opposed to a snapshot of one set of people in one instance in time. Changing circumstances such as age, income levels, social conditions and environmental conditions can be considered to provide an understanding of the complexity of travel behaviours and impacts over time.

Disadvantages

To ensure that longitudinal studies involve the same people over time, researchers must maintain extensive records and regular contact with the participants so that they do not become 'lost' to the researcher. Such record keeping may be expensive. Incentives that are sometimes used to maintain participation may be deemed to bias the data collected. Sarantakos (1998) notes the following disadvantages:

- persuading potential participants of the importance of the study and their participation
- learning how to deal with 'drop-outs' in studies within a constant sample of participants over time
- researcher bias in participant selection.

■ 6.3.5 Delphi techniques

There are a variety of names for this approach — Delphi interviews, Delphi technique, Delphic poll, executive judgment method or knowledgeable panel method. The source of this method is based in the tradition of the ancient Greeks, who asked the gods for the future directions. It was also used during World War II in the 1940s to predict future events (Sarantakos 1998).

The RAND Corporation is credited with introducing the method as a forecasting tool when other data such as historical records or trend data were unavailable (Killion 2001). The technique involves the repeated interviewing of experts until a consensus has been reached. Experts are drawn from technical fields, academic literature and peers who have expertise in the topic being studied. The researcher is the focal point, aggregating the data from successive interviews and disseminating them to participants for further reflection and opinion gathering.

Advantages and disadvantages

The advantages and disadvantages of this technique reflect similarities with other methods, as well as some different ones.

Advantages

The advantages include:

- the Delphic method enables geographically dispersed experts to participate in the study without the expense of bringing the participants face-to-face in a focus group
- participants can put forward their points of view without being influenced by the face-to-face interaction that occurs in a focus group: since there is no contact between the participants (all information is gathered through the researcher), the participants do not know each other and respond to the data gathered on the basis of the data rather than on the basis of who produced the data or commented on the data
- no travel expenses are incurred as the researcher contacts the participants in their own geographic locations — it is a cost-effective way to gather data from participants without having to bring people together in a focus group
- information may be added throughout the process (Ritchie 1994)
- since data are gathered in a sequential manner, the Delphic method is appropriate for phased planning exercises (Ritchie 1994).

Disadvantages

The Delphic method has similar disadvantages to focus groups and some longitudinal studies, such as:

- there is a problem of maintaining panel participation for the duration of the iterations
- it is a time-consuming method as there are several iterations that must be performed until consensus is reached
- the panel size may prove to be too unwieldy
- the panel composition may exhibit researcher bias.

■ 6.3.6 Case *studies*

According to Yin (1994, p. 13):

A case study is an empirical inquiry that
- investigates a contemporary phenomenon within its real-life context, especially, when
- the boundaries between phenomenon and context are not clearly evident.

Stake (1995, p. xi), on the other hand, defines a case study as 'the study of the particularity and complexity of a single case, coming to understand its activity within important circumstances'.

Case studies are sometimes confused with ethnography or participant observation (Yin 1994). However, they are not the same. In fact, case studies incorporate the use of participant observation and ethnography as part of the repertoire of methods that may be used to gather data on a specific case or set of cases.

The literature suggests a number of different types of case studies, and these are outlined in table 6.5. This list is not mutually exclusive — for example, a single case study can also be an intrinsic or an instrumental case study. Similarly, a multiple case study (or a collective case study) can also be an intrinsic or an instrumental case study. Furthermore, the research approach can also be linked into the case study type, such as a single intrinsic case study that is exploratory or a multiple and instrumental case study that is explanatory.

■ **Table 6.5**
Types of cases studies applicable to tourism

TYPE OF CASE STUDY	DESCRIPTION
Exploratory (Yin 1994)	The study 'explores' single or multiple cases of the tourism phenomenon to discover uniqueness or characteristics, since no pre-existing data exist in the public arena. The 'what' is determined.
Descriptive (Yin 1994)	The study collects evidence to enable the researcher to describe either a single case or multiple cases. The 'who', 'what' and 'where' are determined.
Explanatory (Yin 1994)	The study seeks to determine 'how and why' the single case or multiple cases operate as they do.
Single (Yin 1994)	Only one case is studied holistically, such as one tourism organisation, one tour operation, one transportation company or one tourism event. The case selected may be critical, unique, extreme or revelatory.
Multiple (Yin 1994)	Several cases are studied holistically. The cases studied may be similar in nature or different in nature.
Intrinsic (Stake 1995)	Cases are studied that hold particular interest for the researcher.
Instrumental (Stake 1995)	Cases are studied in order to achieve secondary ends, e.g. studying an organisation such as a hotel to determine the impact of a change in pricing rates.
Collective (Stake 1995)	A number of cases are studied during the course of the one project — similar to Yin's (1994) multiple case study.

Source: *Yin (1994) and Stake (1995)*

Data collection for case studies operating within the holistic-inductive paradigm and the hypothetico-deductive paradigm are based on multiple methods. Case studies informed by the holistic-inductive paradigm use the documentary method, participant observation and interviewing. Subsequently, qualitative case studies use methodological triangulation.

Steps in case study design and data collection

The following list outlines the steps involved in case study design and data collection:

- identify the issue(s) or research theme(s)
- determine the type of case to be used (see table 6.5)
- select the case or cases
- negotiate access to the case setting
- enter the setting or commence data collection
- gather the data (using the documentary method, participant observation, interviewing)
- analyse the data using, for example, categorical aggregation and aggregative interpretation (which are discussed in chapter 7)
- check the findings with case study members
- leave the case setting
- report the data (discussed in chapter 10).

As noted in chapter 4, ethical considerations apply before, during and after the case study has been conducted.

Advantages and disadvantages

There are a number of advantages and disadvantages associated with case studies.

Advantages

The following advantages are associated with case study research:

- in-depth data is collected on a single case or multiple cases
- evidence is grounded in the social setting being studied
- study members can check the data for 'accuracy and palatability' (Stake 1994, p. 115)
- member checking may remove researcher bias
- methodological triangulation is used.

Disadvantages

The disadvantages of case study research are associated with the holistic-inductive paradigm being used:

- the case study focus is emergent — as the study progresses, the focus is refined, that is it uses 'progressive focusing' (Stake 1994), rather than the research focus being clearly stated at the outset. This may extend the amount of resources that are required to conduct the study, especially time and money
- the research process is subjective as opposed to objective
- evidence may be denied for reproduction based on the use of member checking

- the researcher may not act ethically and consequently data collection, analysis and findings may contain bias
- findings are specific to the case study
- findings are not able to be generalised to other cases.

■ 6.3.7 **Action** *research*

There are various ways to instigate change in an organisation. Change is a process, but it is also associated with a particular research approach — action research. Action research is primarily grounded in a problem-solving approach (Burns 1990, 1997; Kemmis & McTaggart 1988; Whyte 1989). In essence, action research involves a group of people with a common interest within an organisation devising a plan to improve some aspect of operation or practice. The plan is subsequently implemented, monitored and reflected upon, which may result in another iteration of the action research process. The action research spiral illustrated in figure 6.2 reflects the process associated with action research.

■ **Figure 6.2**
The action research spiral

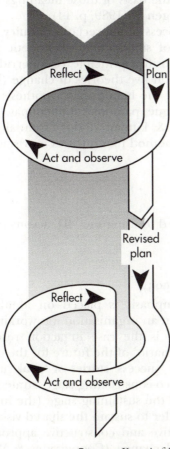

Source: *Kemmis & McTaggart (1988, p. 11)*

Such an approach is at odds with Lewin (1948), who first coined the term 'action research'. In action research, the 'distinction between research and action becomes quite blurred' (Patton 1990, p. 157). This can militate against allowing action research to achieve what Lewin described as the benefits of action research — a contribution to knowledge (theory), as well as the betterment of human conditions (practice) (Lewin 1948).

There are several approaches to action research: cooperative inquiry, participatory action research and action inquiry (Reason 1994). However, all share the following characteristics:

- ontology — reality is individually and collectively known (Reason 1994)
- epistemology — experiential learning arising from participation with others and self-reflexive directed actions
- methodology — essentially qualitative, although mixed methods may be used.

The differences between the three approaches are found in their ideology, intellectual tradition and practice (Reason 1994). Cooperative inquiry was developed by Heron (1971) and is founded on the tenets of humanistic psychology, especially self-determination and small group behaviour. Participatory action research has a political agenda, particularly empowerment and sharing power. The approach is considered a liberationist one (Fals-Borda & Rahman 1991), although it is criticised for not considering the micro issues of negative group behaviours and the need for leadership training and development. Action inquiry is research into practice based on individualism and elitism and is criticised for ignoring the 'common people' (Reason 1994, p. 335).

An overall criticism of action research is provided by Cooperrider and Srivastva (1987), who argue that action research based on problem solving is unidimensional and operates from a deficit-based model, which consequently limits socio-organisational transformation. As an alternative, Cooperrider and Srivastva propose that organisational change using appreciative inquiry overcomes the shortcomings of action research as the former is multidimensional in nature, addresses both theory and practice, and operates from a non-deficit model. This latter point is important, for as Cooperrider and Srivastva note, through 'our choice of method we largely recreate the world we later discover' (p. 129). Such a perspective is supported by the sociologically based interpretive paradigm where '[i]n the course of daily life, people make sense of the world around them; they give it meaning and they interact on the basis of those meanings (Schultz 1967; Blumer 1969; Denzin 1978)' (Jorgensen 1989, p. 14).

Five principles inform the process of appreciative inquiry: the constructionist principle, the principle of simultaneity, the poetic principle, the anticipatory principle and the positive principle (Cooperrider & Whitney 1996). The process is also based on five theories of change (Bushe 1998a): the social construction of reality, the heliotropic hypothesis (Cooperrider 1990), organisational inner dialogue, paradoxical dilemmas (Bushe 1998b) and appreciative process (Bushe & Pitman 1991). Essentially, appreciative inquiry is a qualitative research method that involves four stages:
• appreciating
• envisioning
• co-constructing
• sustaining.

The four stages are also referred to using the '4D' acronym:
• discover (appreciate)
• dream (envision)
• design (construct)
• destiny (sustain) (Hammond 1996).

In the appreciating stage, emphasis is placed on identifying success stories or 'peak' experiences when an organisation was working well, rather than focusing on 'problems' as is the case in action research. In the envisioning stage, a 'best case scenario' of the future for the organisation is developed, based on the positive 'success' stories or 'peak' experiences — that is, its positive history. In the co-constructing stage, strategies are collectively designed for the future. In the sustaining stage (the final stage), the strategies are implemented in order to sustain the shared vision.

Appreciative inquiry is a positive and constructive approach to organisational development and social change (Cooperrider & Whitney 1996) and has the potential to be applied within the tourism industry to manage organisational change and assist community development processes. The following are some of the possible applications of appreciative inquiry for the tourism industry:

- transformational change of travel organisations and tourism associations
- shared visioning within the wider community
- strategic planning
- team development
- focus group research
- evaluation
- monitoring of visions and mission statements.

Advantages and disadvantages of action research

The advantages are similar between the types of action-oriented processes for organisational change.

Advantages

The advantages of action research include:

- its participatory nature
- its real-world context
- the vested interest of participants in the research process outcomes
- the ownership of the outcomes by the participants
- its focus on finding solutions to problems (cooperative inquiry, participatory action research and action inquiry)
- a positive rather than a problem-based world view (appreciative inquiry)
- its focus on empowerment of participants
- its focus on improving organisational practices, conditions and processes.

Disadvantages

The disadvantages of action research relate to:

- the outcomes being site or organisation specific
- the time involved in engaging in the process
- the use of the deficit model (cooperative inquiry, participatory action research, and action inquiry).

■ 6.3.8 Documentary *method*

In chapter 3, the process of documentary research was presented as part of the overall discussion of secondary data sources. In particular, the documentary method is associated with the use of 'mute evidence' such as written texts and cultural artefacts (Hodder 1994). As noted in chapter 3, documents and records are different (Lincoln & Guba 1985). Documents are personal in nature whereas records are public domain texts. You will recall this differs from Sarantakos' description of documents also presented in chapter 3.

Advantages and disadvantages

The advantages and disadvantages of secondary data sources have already been discussed in chapter 3, so only a selection is presented here. Refer to chapter 3 for the entire list.

Advantages

The advantages of the documentary method include:

- it uses non-intrusive research processes
- it enables the past and the present to be studied, thereby providing an 'historical insight' (Hodder 1994, p. 393).

Disadvantages

The disadvantages of the documentary method include:

- it maintains an epistemological position as an outsider and is 'etic' in nature
- the data record the past and not the future
- the researcher is separated from the authors of the texts in most circumstances
- there is difficulty in checking the insider's perspective, as most texts are historical in nature
- iterative readings of texts and analyses will produce different interpretations.

6.4 NON-SEXIST RESEARCH METHODS

Regardless of whether you use a qualitative or a quantitative methodology, social justice principles must be embedded in your research design, including your methodology and methods for data collection. One principle of social justice that was not specifically addressed in chapter 4 on ethics is the avoidance of sexism in research methods. Eichler (1988 and 1991) provides a guide for researchers to ensure that their research is not diffused with sexism. The use of non-sexist research methods is the purview of all researchers, not only feminist researchers. Using Eichler's (1988) original text, the following four aspects must be considered by researchers with respect to their methods:

- the avoidance of androcentricity (a male only viewpoint)
- the avoidance of overgeneralisation (the study of one sex, with the findings presented as representing both sexes)
- the avoidance of gender insensitivity (the non-consideration of the role of gender in research findings)
- the avoidance of double standards (using different methods to deal with the same phenomenon, in this case the category of sex — male or female — through the use of language, concept development, research method, data interpretation and the presentation of the findings).

Researchers should be aware that sexism may not be overt in its practice and that 'dominant groups generally do not like to be told about or even quietly reminded of the existence of inequality' (Miller 1976, pp. 6–8). Eichler (1988 and 1991) provides an extensive checklist to guide researchers in the use of non-sexist research methods.

SUMMARY ··

The criteria that define qualitative methods

The key research methods used are interviews, participant observation, focus groups, longitudinal studies, Delphi techniques, case studies, action research and the documentary method. These methods are informed by the holistic-inductive paradigm that reflects multiple realities, a grounding in real-world settings, a subjective epistemology, an emic perspective, an emergent research design, non-random participant selection, textual data sources, thematic analysis, and narrative 'reports' written in the first person and using the active voice that portray a slice of life from the study setting.

Theoretical positions that inform qualitative methods

The theoretical positions that inform qualitative methods include: symbolic interactionism (founded on the work of Thomas, Mead and Blumer); phenomenology (founded on the work of Husserl and Schutz); heuristic research (see the work of Moustakas); ethnomethodology (founded on the work of Garfunkel and Zimmerman); and ethnography (see Fetterman).

The nature of exchanges in interviews

Interviews are like conversations, and involve the establishment of rapport, reciprocity and personal reflection by the interviewee(s). Interviews can be unstructured, semi-structured or structured.

The principles of unstructured/in-depth interviews and the advantages and disadvantages of using in-depth interviews

Unstructured interviews seek to identify the multiple realities of the social world being studied. In-depth interviews are subjective in nature, allow for rich and in-depth data to be collected and may involve several sessions. Unstructured interviews do not have a formal interview schedule or set of questions and are long in duration. Unstructured interviews are akin to a conversation. The advantages and disadvantages of unstructured interviews are related to the holistic-inductive paradigms' ontological, epistemological and methodological perspectives.

The processes involved in semi-structured interviews and the advantages and disadvantages of semi-structured interviews

Semi-structured interviews have a little more structure than unstructured interviews, because the researcher has a prompt list of themes that directs their engagement with the interviewees. Like unstructured interviews, semi-structured interviews aim to gather rich data and detailed descriptions of the tourism setting being studied. Interviews are also long and may involve several sessions. The advantages and disadvantages of unstructured interviews are related to the holistic-inductive paradigms' ontological, epistemological and methodological perspectives.

The various types of participant observation

Junker (1960) identifies four roles for participant observation: complete observer, observer as participant, participant as observer, complete participant. Gans (1982) identifies three roles: total researcher, researcher participant and total participant. Adler and Adler (1987) define three roles: peripheral membership, active membership and complete membership.

These roles can be organised into emic and etic roles depending on the degree of participation of the researcher. For example, emic roles are participant as observer, researcher participant, active membership and complete membership. The more etic roles are complete observer, observer as participant, total researcher and peripheral membership. Runcie (1976) proposes four stages in participant observation.

The nature of focus groups and the advantages and disadvantages of using focus groups

Focus groups are focused or semi-structured group interviews and are used to elicit opinions and attitudes. Focus groups require skilled facilitators and are best run with eight to 12 people. Focus group members should be pre-screened to determine suitability regarding study population criteria. Focus groups may be constructed using quota sampling.

The different approaches that may be used for longitudinal studies

Longitudinal studies examine the same sample of people or a similar sample of people over time. Types of longitudinal study include panel studies, time series studies, trend studies, cohort analysis and case studies. Data may be collected using focus groups, participant observation, interviews and the documentary method.

An overview of the Delphic method

The Delphic method is also known as Delphi interviews, the Delphi technique, the Delphic poll, the executive judgment method and the knowledgeable panel method. The Delphic method involves repeated interviewing and sharing of gathered data until a consensus is reached.

The various types of case study and the advantages and disadvantages of using case studies

Case studies may be exploratory, descriptive, explanatory, single, multiple (a collective case study), intrinsic or instrumental in nature. In-depth data can be obtained from one case or a set of cases. The advantages of case studies include that the findings are generated through the use of methodological triangulation and member checking, and the findings are grounded in the tourism setting being studied. The disadvantages arise from the lack of objectivity of the researcher, the lack of generalisability of the findings and the possibility of researcher bias. In addition, case studies are time-consuming.

The role of action research as a qualitative research method

Action research assists in organisational change. Action research involves planning, implementing, monitoring and reflecting. There are three types of action research: cooperative inquiry, participatory action research and action inquiry. Action research has been criticised for its deficit model focus and for not remaining true to Lewin's use of action research to achieve both theory and practice outcomes. Appreciative inquiry is an alternative to action research and operates on a positively framed focus to change. Appreciative inquiry involves four phases: appreciating, envisioning, co-constructing and sustaining.

Nature of the documentary method

The documentary method uses 'mute evidence' and involves the analysis of personal (and public) documents. Chapter 3 details this method in more detail.

Non-sexist research methods

There are four aspects that must be considered by researchers in regard to non-sexist research methods: androcentricity, overgeneralisation, gender insensitivity and double standards.

Questions

6.1 Provide a brief summary of the qualitative methods presented in this chapter.

6.2 Explain the key differences between unstructured interviews and semi-structured interviews.

6.3 Apply either Junker, Gans or Adler and Adler's model of participant observation to exemplify the applicability of participant observation to conducting research in a tourism or hospitality context.

6.4 When would you include focus groups in your research design and why?

6.5 Describe the differences between the use of focus groups and the Delphi technique.

6.6 Consider the various types of case studies a researcher may use. Is one better than the others for a tourism context? Justify your responses.

6.7 What are the key differences between action research and appreciative inquiry?

6.8 Do you think the documentary method is appropriate to the study of tourism and hospitality phenomena? Justify your answer.

6.9 Should a researcher operating within a qualitative methodological framework use several qualitative methods? Explain your position.

6.10 Write a short paragraph (200 words) describing the main points a researcher needs to consider to ensure that they use non-sexist research methods.

EXERCISES

Exercise 6.1

A heritage museum is concerned that not all its exhibits are drawing visitors. Some of the staff also believe that some of the exhibits do not hold the attention of visitors for very long.

(a) Using participant observation as your principal method of data collection for an exploratory research project, prepare a rough draft of your research design. A floor plan of the museum is provided in figure 6.3 on page 186. What else do you need to know?

(b) Describe the limitations and advantages of using observation as your primary method of data collection in this exercise.

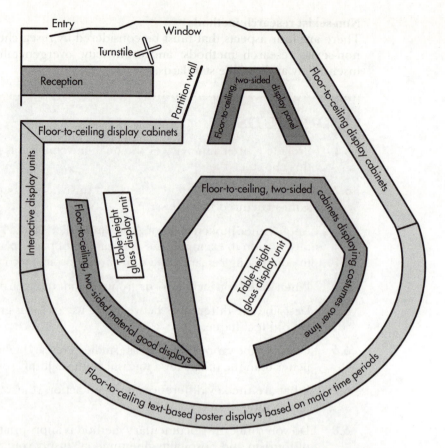

■ Figure 6.3
Floor plan of the museum

Entry

Window

Turnstile

Reception

Partition wall

Floor-to-ceiling, two-sided display panel

Floor-to-ceiling display cabinets

Floor-to-ceiling display cabinets

Interactive display units

Floor-to-ceiling, two-sided material good displays

Table-height glass display unit

Floor-to-ceiling, two-sided

Table-height glass display unit

cabinets displaying costumes over time

Floor-to-ceiling text-based poster displays based on major time periods

Exercise 6.2

State managers of a national park network want to determine the effectiveness of the education component of visitors' park experiences. The education component has been running as it is for four years in all parks and involves guided tours by indigenous and non-indigenous rangers, self-guided tours, interpretive signage, pamphlets and brochures. Using an instrumental case study approach, prepare a first draft of your research design. To ground your research design, choose a state with which you are familiar.

(a) Discuss the limitations and advantages of using observation as your primary method of data collection.

(b) What else would you need to know? How will you acquire that knowledge or information?

Exercise 6.3

The government has called for expressions of interest from researchers to conduct a national study into the effects of ageing on domestic tourism patterns from 2005 to 2020.

(a) Outline a qualitative research project that would enable you to achieve the information the government requires.

(b) Outline your approach and methods.

(c) Consider the challenges and benefits of your approach.

RESEARCH PROJECT

Imagine that you had more time and other resources such as personnel and assured monetary support. If you are using essentially a hypothetico-deductive paradigm, how could you (a) reshape your own research project to incorporate a mixed method approach and (b) reframe your project using a holistic-inductive paradigm and qualitative methods? If you are using a holistic-inductive paradigm, what other qualitative methods could you incorporate to generate methodological triangulation?

REFERENCES

Adler, Patricia A. & Adler, Peter. 1983. 'Shifts and Oscillations in Deviant Careers: The Case of Upper-Level Drug Dealers and Smugglers'. *Social Problems*, vol. 31, pp. 195–207.

Benney, Mark & Hughes, Everett C. 1970. 'Of Sociology and the Interview.' In Denzin, Norman K. (Ed.) *Sociological Methods: A Source Book*. Chicago: Aldine Publishing Company.

Blumer, Herbert. 1962. 'Society as Symbolic Interaction.' In Rose, A. (Ed.) *Human Behaviour and Social Processes: An Interactionist Approach*. Boston, MA: Houghton Mifflin.

Blumer, Herbert. 1969. *Symbolic Interactionism*. Englewood Cliffs, NJ: Prentice-Hall.

Boas, Franz. 1943. 'Recent Anthropology'. *Science*, vol. 98, pp. 311–14, 334–7.

Bouma, Gary D. 1996. *The Research Process*. Third Edition. Oxford: Oxford University Press.

Burns, Robert B. 1990. *Introduction to Research Methods*. Melbourne: Longman.

Burns, Robert B. 1997. *Introduction to Research Methods*. Third Edition. South Melbourne: Longman.

Bushe, Gervase. R. 1998a. 'Five Theories of Change Embedded in Appreciative Inquiry'. Paper presented at the 18th Annual World Congress of Organisational Development, Dublin, Ireland, 14–18 July. http://www.bus.sfu.ca/homes/gervase/5theories.html.

Bushe, Gervase. 1998b. 'Appreciative Inquiry in Teams'. *Organization Development Journal*, vol. 16, no. 3., pp. 41–50.

Bushe, Gervase & Pitman, T. 1991. 'Appreciative Process: A Method for Transformational Change'. *Organization Development Practitioner*, vol. 23, no. 3, pp. 1–4.

Cooperrider, David L. 1990. 'Positive Image, Positive Action: The Affirmative Basis of Organizing'. In Srivastva, Suresh & Cooperrider, David L. (Eds) *Appreciative Management and Leadership: The Power of Positive Thought and Action in Organisations*. San Francisco: Jossey-Bass, pp. 91–125.

Cooperrider, D. L. & Srivastva, Suresh. 1987. 'Appreciative Inquiry in Organisational Life'. *Research in Organizational Change and Development*, vol. 1: 129–69.

Cooperrider, David & Whitney, Diana. 1996. *Appreciative Consultation: A Constructive Approach to Organisation Development and Social Change.* The Appreciative Inquiry Workshop, Taos, New Mexico, October 1996. Boulder, CO: Perpetual Motion Unlimited.

Denzin, Norman K. 1992. *Symbolic Interactionism and Cultural Studies.* Oxford: Blackwell.

Dexter, Lewis, A. 1970. *Elite and Specialized Interviewing.* Evanston: Northwestern University Press.

Eichler, Margrit. 1988. *Non-Sexist Research Methods.* Sydney: Allen & Unwin.

Eichler, Margrit. 1991. *Non-Sexist Research Methods: A Practical Guide.* New York: Routledge.

Fals-Borda, O. & Rahman, M. A. (Eds) 1991. *Action and Knowledge: Breaking the Monopoly with Participatory Action Research.* New York: Intermediate Technology/Apex.

Fetterman, David. M. 1989. *Ethnography, Step By Step.* Applied Social Research Methods Series, Volume 17. Newbury Park: Sage.

Gans, Herbert J. 1982. 'The Participant Observer as a Human Being: Observation on the Personal Aspects of Fieldwork'. In Burgess, Robert G. (Ed.) *Field Research: A Sourcebook and a Field Manual.* Boston, MA: Allen & Unwin, pp. 53–61.

Garfinkel, Harold. 1967. *Studies in Ethnomethodology.* Englewood Cliffs, NJ: Prentice-Hall.

Geertz, Clifford. 1973. *The Interpretation of Cultures.* New York: Basic Books.

Glaser, Barney G. & Strauss, Anselm L. 1967. *The Discovery of Grounded Theory.* Chicago: Aldine.

Gold, Raymond L. 1969. 'Roles in Sociological Field Observation.' In McCall, George J. & Simmons, J. L. (Eds) *Issues in Participant Observation: A Text and Reader.* Reading: Addison Wesley, pp. 30–8.

Hammond, Sue A. 1996. *The Thin Book of Appreciative Inquiry.* CSS Publishing.

Harding, Sandra. 1991. *Whose Science? Whose Knowledge?* Milton Keynes: Open University Press.

Heron, J. 1971. *Experience and Method: An Inquiry into the Concept of Experiential Research.* Surrey, UK: University of Surrey, Human Potential Research Project.

Hodder, Ian. 1994. 'The Interpretation of Documents and Material Culture'. In Denzin, Norman K. & Lincoln, Yvonna S. *Handbook of Qualitative Research.* Thousand Oaks: Sage, pp. 393–402.

Husserl, Edmund. 1960. *Cartesian Meditations: An Introduction to Phenomenology.* Translated by Dorion Cairns. The Hague: Martinus Nijhoff.

Jennings, Gayle 1999. Voyages from the Centre to the Margins: An Ethnography of Long-Term Ocean Cruisers. Unpublished PhD thesis. Murdoch University.

Jorgensen, Danny L. 1989. *Participant Observation: A Methodology for Human Studies.* Applied Social Research Methods Series, Volume 15. Newbury Park: Sage.

Junker, Buford. H. 1960. *Fieldwork: An Introduction to the Social Sciences.* Chicago: University of Chicago Press.

Kemmis, S. & McTaggart, R. 1988. *The Action Research Planner.* Third Edition. Melbourne: Deakin University Press.

Killion, G. L. 2001. *Research in Tourism Study Guide.* Rockhampton: Central Queensland University.

LaPage, Wilbur F. 1994. 'Using Panels for Travel and Tourism Research'. In Ritchie, J. R. Brent & Goeldner, Charles R. (Eds) *Travel, Tourism and Hospitality Research: A Handbook For Managers and Researchers.* Second Edition. New York: John Wiley & Sons, pp. 481–6.

Lewin, K. 1948. 'Action Research and Minority Problems'. In Lewin, K. (Ed) *Resolving Social Conflicts.* New York: Harper & Row.

Lewins, Frank. 1992. *Social Science Methodology: A Brief but Critical Introduction.* South Yarra: Macmillan Educational.

Lincoln, Yvonna S. & Guba, Egon G. 1985. *Naturalistic Inquiry.* Newbury Park: Sage, pp. 267–8.

Maslow, Abraham H. 1943. 'A Theory of Human Motivation'. *Psychological Review,* vol. 50, pp. 370–96.

Maslow, Abraham. 1956. 'Self-Actualising People: A Study of Psychological Health'. In Moustakas, Clarke (Ed.) *The Self.* New York: Harpers & Brothers, pp. 160–94.

Maslow, Abraham H. 1966. *The Psychology of Science.* New York: Harper & Row.

Maynard, Douglas, M. 1987. 'Language and Social Interaction'. *Social Psychological Quarterly,* vol. 50, pp. v–vi.

Mead, Herbert. 1934. In Morris, C. (Ed.) *Mind, Self and Society.* Chicago: University of Chicago Press.

Mill, Robert C. & Morrison, Alistair. 1998. *The Tourism System: An Introductory Text.* Third Edition. Dubuqu, Ia: Kendal Hunt.

Miller, Jean Baker. 1976. *Toward A New Psychology of Women.* Boston, MA: Beacon Press.

Minichiello, Victor, Aroni, Rosalie, Timewell, Eric & Alexander, Loris. 1995. *In-Depth Interviewing.* Second Edition. Melbourne: Longman.

Morse, Janice. 1994. 'Designing Funded Qualitative Research'. In Denzin, Norman K. & Lincoln, Yvonna S. (Eds) *Handbook of Qualitative Research.* Thousand Oaks: Sage, pp. 220–35.

Moustakas, Clark. 1990. *Heuristic Research, Design, Methodology, and Applications.* Newbury Park: Sage.

Neuman, W. L. 2000. *Social Research Methods, Qualitative and Quantitative Approaches.* Fourth Edition. Boston: Allyn & Bacon.

Oakley, Anne. 1981. 'Interviewing Women: A Contradiction in Terms.' In Roberts, Helen (Ed.) *Doing Feminist Research.* London: Routledge, pp. 30–61.

Patton, Michael Q. 1990. *Qualitative Evaluation and Research Methods.* Second Edition. Newbury Park: Sage.

Punch, Keith F. 1998. *Introduction to Social Research.* London: Sage.

Reason, Peter. 1994. 'Three Approaches to Participative Inquiry'. In Denzin, Norman K. & Lincoln, Yvonna S. (Eds.) *Handbook of Qualitative Research.* Thousand Oaks: Sage, pp. 324–39.

Reinharz, Shulamit. 1992. *Feminist Methods in Social Research.* New York: Oxford University Press.

Ritchie, J. R. Brent. 1994. 'The Nominal Group Technique: Applications in Tourism Research'. In Ritchie, J. R. Brent & Goeldner, Charles R. (Eds) 1994. *Travel, Tourism and Hospitality Research: A Handbook for Managers and Researchers.* Second Edition. New York: John Wiley & Sons.

Ritchie, J. R. Brent & Goeldner, Charles R. (Eds) 1994. *Travel, Tourism and Hospitality Research: A Handbook for Managers and Researchers.* Second Edition. New York: John Wiley & Sons.

Runcie, J. F. 1976. *Experiencing Social Research.* Illinois: Homewood Hills.

Sarantakos, S. 1998. *Social Research.* Second Edition. South Melbourne: Macmillan.

Schutz, Alfred. 1932/1972. *The Phenomenology of the Social World.* London: Heinemann.

Smith, Louis. 1994. 'Biographical Method'. In Denzin, Norman K. & Lincoln, Yvonna S. (Eds) *Handbook of Qualitative Research.* Thousand Oaks: Sage, pp. 286–305.

Spradley, James P. & McCurdy, David W. 1972. *The Cultural Experience: Ethnography in Complex Society.* Chicago: Science Research Association.

Stake, Robert E. 1995. *The Art of Case Study Research.* Thousand Oaks: Sage.

Stanley, Liz & Wise, Sue. 1983. *Breaking Out: Feminist Consciousness and Feminist Research.* London: Routledge & Kegan Paul.

Thomas, William. I & Thomas, Dorothy Swaine. 1928/1970. *The Child in America: Behaviour Problems and Programs.* New York: Alfred A Knopf.

Ticehurst, Gregory W. & Veal, A. J. 1999. *Business Research Methods: A Managerial Approach.* Australia: Longman.

Weber, Max. 1978. In Roth, Guenther & Wittich, Claus (Eds) *Economy and Society: An Outline of Interpretive Sociology.* Volume 1. Berkeley: University of California Press.

Whyte, W. F. 1989. 'Advancing Scientific Knowledge Through Participatory Action Research'. *Sociological Forum*, vol. 4, no. 3, pp. 3–38.

Whyte, W. F., Greenwood, D. J. & Lazes, P. 1991. 'Participatory Action Research, Through Practice to Science in Social Research'. In Whyte, W. F. (Ed.) *Participatory Action Research.* Sage Focus Editions, Volume 123. Newbury Park: Sage.

Wolcott, Harry F. 1990. *Writing Up Qualitative Research.* Qualitative Research Methods Series, Volume 20. Newbury Park: Sage.

Yin, Robert. 1994. *Case Study Research, Design and Methods.* Second Edition. Applied Social Research Methods Series, Volume 5. Thousand Oaks: Sage.

Zimmerman, Donald. 1971. 'The Practicalities of Rule Use'. In Douglas, J. D. *Understanding Everyday Life.* London: Routledge & Kegan Paul.

FURTHER READING ....

Bergum, V. 1991. 'Being a Phenomenological Researcher'. In Morse, J. M. (Ed.) *Qualitative Nursing Research: A Contemporary Dialogue*. Newbury Park, CA: Sage, pp. 55–71.

Chenitz, W. C. & Swanson, J. M. 1986. *From Practice to Grounded Theory*. Menlo Park, CA: Addison-Wesley.

Eibl-Eibesfeldt, I. 1989. *Human Ethology*. New York: Aldine de Gruyter.

Ellen, R. F. (Ed.) 1984. *Ethnographic Research*. London: Academic Press.

Fetterman, D. M. 1989. *Ethnography: Step by Step*. Newbury Park, CA: Sage.

Giorgi, A. 1970. *Psychology as a Human Science: A Phenomenologically Based Approach*. New York: Harper & Row.

Glaser, B. G. 1978. *Theoretical Sensitivity*. Mill Valley, CA: Sociology Press.

Glaser, B. G. 1992. *Basics of Grounded Theory Analysis*. Mill Valley, CA: Sociology Press.

Glaser, B. G. & Strauss, A. L. 1967. *The Discovery of Grounded Theory: Strategies for Qualitative Research*. Chicago: Aldine.

Gold, Raymond L. 1958. 'Roles in Sociological Field Observation'. *Social Forces*, vol. 36, pp. 217–23.

Grant, L. & Fine, G. A. 1992. 'Sociology Unleashed: Creative Directions in Classical Ethnography'. In LeCompte, M. D., Millroy, W. L. & Preissle, J. (Eds) *The Handbook of Qualitative Research in Education*. New York: Academic Press, pp. 405–46.

Green, H., Hunter, H. & Moore, B. 1990. 'Application of the Delphi Technique in Tourism'. *Annals of Tourism Research*, vol. 17, pp. 270–9.

Hammersley, M. & Atkinson, P. 1983. *Ethnography: Principles in Practice*. London: Tavistock.

Hughes, C. C. 1992. ' "Ethnography": What's in a Word — Process? Product? Promise?' *Qualitative Health Research*, vol. 2, pp. 451–74.

Miles, Matthew B. & Huberman, A. Michael. 1994. *Qualitative Data Analysis: An Expanded Sourcebook*. Second Edition. Thousand Oaks: Sage.

Morse, J. M. & Bottorff, J. L. 1990. 'The Use of Ethology in Clinical Nursing Research'. *Advances in Nursing Science*, vol. 12, no. 3, pp. 53–64.

Polyani, M. 1962. *Personal Knowledge*. Chicago: University of Chicago Press.

Sanjek, R. (Ed) 1990. *Fieldnotes: The Makings of Anthropology*. Albany: State University of New York Press.

Scherer, K. R. & Ekman, P. 1982. *Handbook of Methods in Nonverbal Behavior Research*. Cambridge, UK: Cambridge University Press.

Spradley, J. P. 1979. *The Ethnographic Interview*. New York: Holt, Rinehart & Winston.

Srivastva, Suresh & Cooperrider, David L. 1990. *Appreciative Management and Leadership: The Power of Positive Thought and Action in Organisations*. San Francisco: Jossey-Bass.

Strauss, A. L. 1987. *Qualitative Analysis for Social Scientists*. New York: Cambridge University Press.

Strauss, A. L. & Corbin, J. 1990. *Basics of Qualitative Research: Grounded Theory Procedures and Techniques.* Newbury Park, CA: Sage.

van Manen, M. 1984. 'Practicing Phenomenological Writing'. *Phenomenology + Pedagogy,* vol. 2, pp. 36–69.

van Manen, M. 1990. *Researching the Lived Experience.* London: University of Western Ontario.

Werner, O. & Schoepfle, G. M. 1987a. *Systematic Fieldwork: Foundations of Ethnography and Interviewing.* Volume 1. Newbury Park, CA: Sage.

Werner, O. & Schoepfle, G. M. 1987b. *Systematic Fieldwork: Ethnographic Analysis and Data Management.* Volume 2. Newbury Park, CA: Sage.

7

Qualitative methods
of data analysis

'Data analysis involves organizing what you have seen, heard, and
read so that you can make sense of what you have learned.
Working with the data, you describe, create explanations, pose
hypotheses, develop theories, and link your story to other stories. To
do so, you must categorize, synthesize, search for patterns, and
interpret the data you have collected.'

(Glesne 1999, p. 130)

LEARNING OBJECTIVES
After studying this chapter, you should be able to:
- reiterate the differences between qualitative and quantitative data
  analysis
- understand that qualitative data analysis occurs during three phases of
  research projects
- outline and use a number of qualitative data analysis methods
- discuss various computer programs available to qualitative
  researchers.

7.1 INTRODUCTION

In previous decades, qualitative data analysis has been criticised for its nebulous practices — practices that were less than public and often only fleetingly referred to in research reports, articles and documents (Neuman 2000). These practices have, however, become more overt and are now treated explicitly in research reports. Furthermore, qualitative data analysis has become more systematised, with numerous publications outlining and describing the various types of qualitative data analysis available to qualitative researchers (Miles & Huberman 1994, p. 1).

In several chapters at the beginning of this textbook, various representations of the differences between qualitative and quantitative research methodologies were presented. These were reiterated in detail in chapter 5. However, prior to commencing the focus of this chapter — the discussion of qualitative data analysis methods — it is timely to further expand upon the differences between qualitative and quantitative research methodologies as they pertain to data analysis. At the same time, similarities between the two methodologies are also outlined. Such an approach will enable you to consolidate your previous understanding and further ground your knowledge regarding the differences and similarities in qualitative and quantitative data analysis. Moreover, such an understanding and knowledge is important to assist you in justifying your own chosen methods for data (collection and) analysis.

7.2 DIFFERENCES AND SIMILARITIES BETWEEN QUALITATIVE AND QUANTITATIVE DATA ANALYSIS

Given that you should have already developed an understanding of the key differences between qualitative and quantitative methodologies, the key differences and similarities between both in regard to data analysis are presented in table form. Table 7.1 outlines the differences and similarities between qualitative and quantitative data analysis and draws primarily on the work of Neuman (2000, pp. 418–19).

As can be seen from the table, qualitative data analysis is grounded in an inductive approach that builds theory from the empirical data collected during the research process. These data are not abstracted into numerical representation; rather, they maintain congruence with the form in which they were collected — an ideographic form. As a consequence, themes and motifs are generated by comparison between data and inferences are made. The researcher explicitly states the analytical method(s) used and attempts to represent the findings that are error-free.

■ Table 7.1

*Differences
and
similarities
in
qualitative
and
quantitative
data
analysis*

	QUALITATIVE	QUANTIATIVE
Differences	Text-based analysis to identify themes and motifs.	Numeric analysis using statistical formulae.
	Inductive approach.	Deductive approach.
	Generates theory from empirical data and evidence.	Tests hypotheses.
	Analysis begins with data collection.	Analysis begins when all data are collected (data coding may begin earlier, although analysis cannot be completed until all data are collected).
	Data analysis is grounded in the real world and maintained in the form the data were collected, e.g. conversations that have been transcribed or visual images that have been digitised.	Data analysis is abstracted from the real world using numbers and statistical representation.
Similarities	Analysis involves inferences founded in empirical (ideographic) data.	Analysis involves inferences founded in empirical (numerical) data.
	Method(s) of analysis are made visible to readers through the research design.	Method(s) of analysis are made visible to readers through the research design.
	Comparisons are made between empirical data to identify differences and similarities.	Comparisons are made between empirical data, particularly covariance between variables.
	Analysis attempts to be error-free.	Analysis attempts to be error-free.

Also noted in the table is the fact that data analysis can commence as soon as the data are collected. Miles and Huberman (1994) also iterate this perspective. They state that qualitative data collection and analysis are not two discrete entities of the research process, as is often the case in quantitative analysis. Miles and Huberman see the process of data collection and analysis as overlapping. Furthermore, qualitative research analysis is often linked to sample size. Recall from chapter 5 that sampling within a qualitative methodology continues until a 'qualitative isomorph' (Ford 1975) or a 'qualitative informational isomorph' (Lincoln & Guba 1985) is reached, and that this state is also known as 'theoretical sampling' (Punch 1998). A qualitative informational isomorph is reached when there is redundancy in information being identified in the data and no new information is being found. Thus, in order to determine when redundancy has been achieved, the researcher has to have been engaging in constant and comparative data analysis. Consequently, analysis occurs throughout the data collection phase as well as after the data have been collected.

During data collection, researchers may commence making memos to themselves, as well as considering preliminary conceptual units or categories (Miles & Huberman 1994). In analysis, researchers may engage in content analysis, constant comparative analysis, matrix building, mapping, successive approximation, domain analysis, taxonomy building, ideal type identification, event-structure building and modelling (Dey 1993; Huberman & Miles 1994; Miles & Huberman 1994; Punch 1998; Glesne 1999; Neuman 2000). It is important to note that researchers will also focus on negative evidence, as such evidence has implications for the authenticity of any 'theory' being constructed from the empirical data (Strauss & Corbin 1998; Neuman 2000). Regardless of the type of analysis that is conducted, whether it is qualitative or quantitative, Huberman and Miles (1994) provide us with a reminder of our obligations as researchers:

> The conventions of quantitative research require clear, explicit reporting of data and procedures. That is expected so that (a) the reader will be confident of, and can verify, reported conclusions; (b) secondary analysis of the data is possible; (c) the study could in principle be replicated; and (d) fraud and misconduct, if it exists, will be more trackable. There is an added, internal need: keeping analytic strategies coherent, manageable, and repeatable as the study proceeds. That is, the reporting requirement encourages running documentation from the beginning. In our view, the same needs are present for qualitative studies, even if one takes a more interpretive stance (Huberman & Miles 1994, p. 439).

Do not forget to record and report your methods of analysis so that they are clearly and explicitly stated, and openly available to reviewers and/or readers.

7.3 QUALITATIVE ANALYSIS

> A qualitative researcher analyzes data by organizing it into categories on the basis of themes, concepts, or similar features. He or she develops new concepts, formulates conceptual definitions, and examines the relationships among concepts (Neuman 2000, p. 420).

Qualitative data analysis, as Neuman has just suggested, involves the organisation of like categories as well as the development of relationships and process models based on constant comparison of the text-based data. Specifically, according to Miles and Huberman (1994), there are three aspects of analysis: data reduction, data displays and conclusion drawing/verification. Data reduction is associated with the distillation of rich data into identifiable categories, themes and concepts. Data displays are the ideographic presentations of the categories, themes and concepts. These may range from maps, taxonomies, matrices and models to visual (and textual) portrayals of the distillation of constantly reoccurring themes and motifs and relationships and processes found in the rich data. By constantly comparing data against other data, qualitative 'theory' is built and this is the third aspect of analysis — conclusion drawing/verification.

Qualitative 'theory' has several constructions:

- "grand theory" ... a congeries of a few major, well-articulated constructs
- a "map" aiming to generalize the story (or stories) told about a case (Rein and Schön 1977)
- a predicted pattern of events, to be compared with what is actually observed (Yin 1991)
- a model, with a series of connected propositions that specify relations, often hierarchical, among components (Reed & Furman 1992)
- a network of nonhierarchical relationships, expressed through statements defining linkages among concepts (Carley 1991) (Huberman & Miles 1994, p. 434).

At this point, it is important to note the difference between 'grand' and 'substantive' theory. Grand theory is theory that is derived 'from a study of a phenomenon examined under many different types of situations' (Strauss & Corbin 1990, p. 174). On the other hand, substantive theory is theory that has been derived from 'the study of a phenomenon situated in one particular situational context' (Strauss & Corbin 1990, p. 174).

In verifying 'theory', Huberman and Miles (1994, p. 434) advise that researchers need to be aware of how 'they are construing "theory" as analysis proceeds, because that construction will — consciously or not — inevitably influence and constrain data collection, data reduction, data display, and the drawing and verification of conclusions'. In other words, researchers need to be open to the data to ensure that they do not 'force' the data (Glaser 1992).

Having identified three aspects of data analysis and five types of 'theory', we now overview ways to reduce, display and conclude/verify qualitative data. A number of data analysis methods enable researchers to do just that: memos, coding, content analysis, constant comparative analysis, successive approximation, domain analysis, ideal types, event-structure analysis, matrices, taxonomies, typologies, conceptual trees, mind maps, grounded theory analysis and the zoom model. Each of these methods is detailed in the sections below, before we move on to discuss computer programs and their applications in qualitative data analysis.

■ 7.3.1 Memos

Memos are messages researchers make to themselves during the course of research design, particularly during data collection and analysis. Memos may be constructed:

- using oral recorders if in the field (such recordings are transcribed later)
- using pen and paper to produce diary and field notes (notes are used to supplement transcriptions and observations)
- in memo and annotation sections in software programs
- as hard copy in exercise books or notebooks or in file card systems.

Essentially, memos serve to assist the researcher throughout the analysis phase. Memos can record an observation, a reflection or a comment to pursue a new direction of questioning or data collection/analysis. Memos can also record a 'eureka' discovery — an unexpected finding or concept arising during field and analytical work. For example, the following memo was noted in an exercise book from a research project conducted by Jennings (1999):

> This interviewee commented on having to pass through an initiation process, check van Gennep's (1960) *Rites of Passage*, London, Routledge & Kegan Paul regarding liminaries. This could be useful for explaining the rites of passage or transition into the subculture.

In fact, this memo influenced the subsequent writing up of the research, as reflected in the following excerpt taken from the final report:

> To draw upon social anthropology, my own experience enabled me to success-fully pass through the 'rites of initiation' (van Gennep, 1960, pp. 11, 20) to become a full member of the subculture, that is the 'preliminaries', the separation from mainstream society, the 'liminaries', the threshold rites, and the 'post limi-naries', the aggregation rites (Jennings 1999, p. 32).

When making memos, it is important to date them and to identify the set-ting and/or context in which the thought was produced, so that you can track your thinking throughout your research.

■ 7.3.2 Coding

Codes are tags or labels for assigning units of meaning to the descriptive or inferential information compiled during a study. Codes usually are attached to 'chunks' of varying sizes — words, phrases, sentences, or whole paragraphs, connected or unconnected to a specific setting. They can take the form of a straightforward category label or a more complex one (e.g. a metaphor) (Miles & Huberman 1994, p. 56).

An example of the use of a metaphor for coding is drawn from a study of long-term ocean cruisers by Jennings (1999). 'Caught in the irons' is a nautical term used by sailing folk to describe three types of situations. First, the term describes a situation where a boat has moved into a 'no go' zone — that is, the boat has come up to face the same direction from which the wind is coming. As a result, the wind passes over the sails at an insufficient angle to enable the boat to make any forward motion or to move off the direction of the wind. Second, the term means the use of a leg shackle as punishment to encourage conformity aboard vessels. Third, the term refers to being stuck in a relationship in which one 'cannot' get out. To maintain the 'naturalism' of the analysis, the metaphor 'caught in the irons' was derived from the setting in which it emanated and was used to code text that identified relationships that were at odds with each other.

Codes used by researchers may be either descriptive, interpretive or pattern based (Miles & Huberman 1994). Descriptive codes name the chunk of data being analysed, and interpretive codes follow a deeper level of analysis and make inferences. Pattern codes are produced from further progression of analysis beyond interpretive codes. Pattern codes identify themes, processes and relationships.

Figure 7.1 illustrates text that has been coded using descriptive, interpretive and pattern codes.

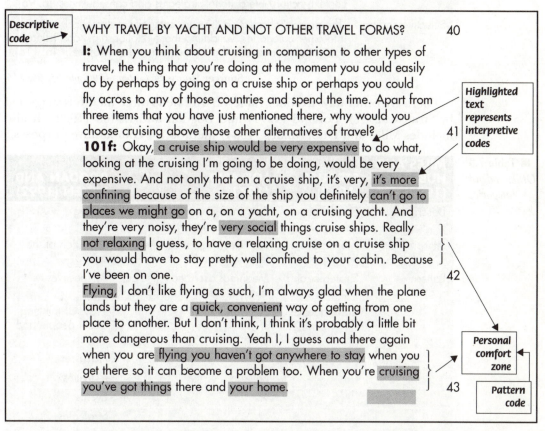

■ **Figure 7.1** *Example of descriptive, interpretive and pattern codes*
Source: *Unpublished raw data from Jennings (1999)*

Alternatively, Strauss (1987) identifies three phases of coding and, by inference, three types of coding: open coding, axial coding and selective coding (see table 7.2). Open coding occurs during the first phases of analysis — that is, during data collection. The researcher reviews the data and searches for reoccurring words, themes or concepts. This type of coding is preliminary coding. Open coding may drive further data collection and/or movement into other coding processes. The code may describe a word or a theme contained in a series of paragraphs. Axial coding refers to coding that arises out of the initial open coding. Axial coding involves the researcher in deeper analysis by searching for relationships between the open codes. Axial coding may progress the researcher onto selective coding. Selective coding involves the examination of some codes over and above others.

■ Table 7.2
Strauss'
(1987) three
types of
coding

CODE TYPE	DEFINITION
Open coding	'The process of breaking down, examining, comparing, conceptualizing, and categorizing data' (p. 61).
Axial coding	'A set of procedures whereby data are put back together in new ways after open coding, by making connections between categories. This is done by utilizing a coding paradigm involving conditions, context, action/interactional strategies and consequences' (p. 96).
Selective coding	'The process of selecting the core category, systematically relating it to other categories, validating those relationships, and filling in categories that need further refinement and development' (p. 116).

Source: *Strauss & Corbin (1990, pp. 61, 96, 116)*

There are other ways to code. Table 7.3 overviews three methods suggested by Strauss (1987), Lofland (1971) and Bogdan and Biklen (1992). It also includes Miles and Huberman's (1994) method for comparative purposes.

■ Table 7.3
Other coding
categories

MILES AND HUBERMAN (1994)	STRAUSS (1987)	LOFLAND (1971)	BOGDAN AND BIKLEN (1992)
Descriptive	Conditions	Acts (non-routine actions, short term in nature)	Setting
Interpretive	Interactions among actors	Activities (regular actions, long term in nature)	Definition of the setting
Pattern	Strategies and tactics	Meanings ascribed to the acts and actions by the actors	Perspectives
	Consequences	Participation	Ways of thinking about people and objects
		Relationships	Processes
		Settings	Activities
			Events
			Strategies
			Relationships sand social structure
			Methods

Researchers need to be aware that coding can be overdone. You can code to such a micro level of detail that you 'cannot see the forest for the trees', especially if you have not been keeping memos of what you are trying to achieve with the coding process you are conducting. Therefore, make sure you keep a map of the path you are trying to follow with your codes (this is addressed in more detail in the section on mapping later in the chapter). Furthermore, overcoding can move you from a qualitative paradigm to a quantitative one. In overcoding, you usually reduce your data to such a level of abstraction that they lose their meaning and connection with the original context or setting from which they emanated. Your use of such overcoding turns to number counting (how many times the code appears rather than what the code means). If this happens, then you have situated yourself in a quantitative paradigm and its associated ontological, epistemological and methodological consequences.

Codes may be developed using:

- oral recorders
- pen and paper lists
- the margins of textual data to record codes
- file cards to record and organise codes
- computer programs to create and manage coding.

See figure 7.2 for examples of various coding techniques.

Pen and paper lists

- What influenced you to go cruising?
- Why travel by yacht and not other travel forms?
- The boat as home
- Package tourism vs cruising

Using margins of documents

I: When you decided to go cruising, did you have any specific reason, why you wanted to go, if I asked you why you are going cruising what would you answer back to me?

317f: Because [laughs] we are a bit further down the track and if we don't go cruising now we will never go. So we need to go while we have our strength and our body fitness and while we can still enjoy it. And I suppose while we've got the motivation to do it because I suppose that as you get on you don't want to do these things. You don't want to do these things, you want to grow roses, well we don't want to do that yet, we don't want to grow roses or whatever people do in gardens. [Laughs]

318m: It's a bit of an adventure as well isn't it darling, doing this sort of thing.

317f: Yes. It's a great experience, a great adventure.

(margin notes: AGE NOW GO ADVENTURE*)*

File card systems

Why go cruising?

Advantages of cruising
- In control

Disadvantages of cruising
- Seasickness

Why travel by boat and not other travel forms?
- Cost (see transcripts . . .)
- Comfort (see transcripts . . .)
- Environmental bubble (see transcripts . . .)

Computer programs

(1)	/why go cruising?
(1 1)	/why go cruising?/freedom (escape)
(1 1 1)	/why go cruising?/freedom/male
(1 1 2)	/why go cruising?/freedom/female
(1 2)	/why go cruising?/belonging
(1 2 1)	/why go cruising?/belonging/male
(1 2 2)	/why go cruising?/belonging/female
(1 3)	/why go cruising?/fun
(1 3 1)	/why go cruising?/fun/male
(1 3 2)	/why go cruising?/fun/female
(1 4)	/why go cruising?/power
(1 4 1)	/why go cruising?/power/male
(1 4 2)	/why go cruising?/power/female
(1 5)	/why go cruising?/survival
(1 5 1)	/why go cruising?/survival/male
(1 5 2)	/why go cruising?/survival/female

Created with NUD*IST STAND-ALONE V. 2.3.1.

■ **Figure 7.2** *Examples of different types of coding techniques*
Source: *Unpublished raw data and field notes from Jennings (1999)*

Qualitative data analysis using codes is time-consuming, and involves reflection by the researcher. Such reflections need to be recorded, which again reinforces the need for memos (discussed above).

■ 7.3.3 Content *analysis*

> Content and narrative analysis struggle continuously with the problem of context or the embeddedness of a text or story within personal or group experience (Manning & Cullum-Swan 1994, p. 474).

Content analysis has already been discussed in chapter 3, so it is reviewed here only briefly. You were also reintroduced to content analysis (albeit implicitly) in chapter 6 during the discussion of the documentary method. Qualitative content analysis is predicated on four concepts (Sarantakos 1998, p. 284):

* openness
* communicativity
* naturalism
* interpretivity.

All four relate to the ontological, epistemological and methodological viewpoints of the theoretical paradigm informing the research, as you will see from the following discussion. In qualitative content analysis:

* The researcher is free to investigate the texts without any 'a priori' theory or concepts to direct them. Thus, the researcher is 'open' to discover what the textual units being studied reveal. The data will not be forced in any way by 'a priori' theory, as may be the case in quantitative content analysis.
* The researcher is responsible for analysing the contents of the 'communication' texts and explaining their meanings based on the social setting or context from which they were drawn.
* The researcher analyses the content in its holistic form and setting so that the data reflect real-world settings, events and texts rather than abstractions of the real-world setting, as is the case in quantitative content analysis.
* The interpretation is embedded in the real world and so must be explained within the context of the real world — the meaning of the text is explained based on the setting from which it was drawn rather than some other objectively derived analysis.

Qualitative content analysis may be conducted in a number of ways (Sarantakos 1998). First, the analytical units are determined by organising the units based on their classification type, such as letters, interview transcriptions and organisational administrative documents, and their appropriateness to the study topic, question or problem (Sarantakos 1998). Then the units are analysed either semantically and/or syntactically or holistically linking parts of the texts to the intent of the overall document (Sarantakos 1998; Danner 1979, in Sarantakos 1998). Alternatively, the text may be analysed using categories associated with 'actions, effects of expressions and principles that will allow statements about the emotional and cognitive background as well as about the behaviour of the communicators' (Sarantakos 1998, p. 284). The text may then be analysed using summation, explanation, structuration or objective hermeneutics (Mayring 1983, 1985, 1988, in Sarantakos 1998). These are explained in the table 7.4.

■ **Table 7.4**
Types of content analysis

TYPE OF CONTENT ANALYSIS	EXPLANATION
Summation	The data being analysed are reduced into categories that integrate and generalise the major themes of the documents.
Explanation	The text is explained based only on the content of the documents or in conjunction with documents not included in the original units of analysis.
Structuration	The data are ordered according to a predetermined set of categories or an order determined through the texts themselves.
Objective hermeneutics	The data are analysed using objective and subjective methods to explain the nature of the textual interactions and their consequences and interpretations.

Source: *Mayring 1983, 1985, 1988, in Sarantakos (1998, pp. 284–5)*

Content analysis can also be conducted using computer software, specifically using key word searches, although the interpretation of the content analysis and the theory building lie with the researcher — the program cannot do this for the researcher. As with any computer software, the program will only be as 'good' as the researcher using it in regard to the ability to analyse, interpret and theorise. Computer programs are discussed later in the chapter.

■ *7.3.4* **Constant** *comparative analysis*

Constant comparative analysis allows the researcher to develop grounded theory. A grounded theory is one inductively derived from the study. Data collection, analysis, and theory are related reciprocally. One grounds the theory in the data from statements of belief and behavior of participants in the study … It is basically opposite to the use of theory in the quantitative paradigm. Instead of proving a theory, the qualitative researcher studies a setting over time and develops theory grounded in the data (Janesick 1994, pp. 218–19).

For researchers involved in grounded theory development, constant comparative analysis is but one of two processes used in coding through which the development of grounded theory is able to obtain its 'precision and specificity' (Strauss & Corbin 1990, pp. 62–3). The other process is asking questions (Strauss & Corbin 1990). Questioning is discussed in the next section on successive approximation. Constant comparative analysis enables researchers to develop categories through constantly comparing coded data. As a result, like-coded data are identified and verified through their repetitive presence and by the process of theoretical sampling. When naming coded data concepts, Strauss and Corbin (1990, pp. 68–9) advise researchers not to use 'borrowed concepts' as they often carry preconceived or loaded meanings. Instead 'in vivo' concepts are recommended. Glaser (1978, p. 70) and Strauss (1987, p. 33) coined the term 'in vivo', meaning concepts that are named by the study participants themselves in their own words, rather than researcher-contrived concept terms. Constant comparative analysis is not unlike successive approximation.

■ 7.3.5 Successive *approximation*

Successive approximation is similar to constant comparative analysis. It is also similar to open, axial and selective coding (Neuman 2000), the methods of coding used in grounded theory analysis. According to Neuman (2000), the researcher is able to refine their analysis by successively repeating the coding and categorising processes; commencing with the first tentative codes through to the repeatedly modified and examined codes that emerge as concepts, relationships and 'theory'. Through successive approximation, 'the evidence and theory shape each other' (Neuman 2000, p. 427). As noted above, constant comparative analysis is one of two processes used in coding, the other being questioning. Questioning is also part of successive approximation — questions are asked to determine the fit of the concepts or theory to the evidence as it amasses. Any contradictions set off a further set of data collection and concept building and testing. The aim of successive approximation, as with all qualitative data analysis, is to ensure a 'goodness of fit' of the theory to the data.

■ 7.3.6 Domain *analysis*

Domain analysis is founded in the work of James Spradley (Neuman 2000). Spradley (1980) used domains as the main classifying unit for describing cultural settings. Within cultural settings, various domains can be determined. Domains are primarily organising ideas or concepts. Specifically, '[c]ultural domains are categories of meaning'(Spradley 1980, p. 88) that include three components — a 'cover term' (name), 'included terms' (subcategories of the domain) and a 'semantic relationship' (is a kind of) (Spradley 1980, p. 89). For example, a cruise is a kind of holiday, holiday being the 'domain' and cruise the 'included term'. The semantic relationship allows for the inclusion or exclusion of items into a domain. For example, taking the domain 'holiday', sitting an exam would probably not be considered by most people to be a holiday, in which case, sitting an exam is not a kind of holiday — the relationship between exams and holidays does not allow for inclusion. There are a number of relationships evident in domains. Table 7.5 outlines those identified by Spradley (1980) — examples have been provided using the concept of a holiday as the overall domain.

RELATIONSHIP	SEMANTIC RELATIONSHIP	EXAMPLE
Strict inclusion	A is a kind of B	A cruise is a kind of holiday.
Spatial	A is a place in B	The duty-free shop is a place in the international airport.
	A is a part of B	The check-in counter is a part of the international airport.
Cause–effect	A is a result of B	Catching an international flight is a result of purchasing a ticket.
Rationale	A is the reason for doing B	Theft is the reason for wearing a money belt.
Location-for-action	A is a place for doing B	The restaurant is a place for dining out.
Function	A is used for B	A bus is used for transporting holiday-makers.
Means–end	A is the way to do B	Saving hard is the way to afford a holiday.
Sequence	A is a step (stage) in B	The 'travel to' phase is a stage of the travel experience'.
Attribution	A is a characteristic of B	Wearing Hawaiian shirts is a characteristic of resort holiday-makers.

Source: *Based on Spradley (1980, p. 93)*

Spradley (1980, pp. 89–91) identifies three types of domain: folk domains, mixed domains and analytic domains. Folk domains utilise the language of the cultural setting being studied — for example, in the south-eastern islands of Papua New Guinea, the term 'dim-dim' is used to describe a 'white-skinned person'. Mixed domains incorporate folk terms and researcher-assigned terms — the researcher generates a term where there is no relevant folk term. For example, among researchers in the preceding example, the term 'expatriate' might be used to describe non-indigenous persons. Of course, subcategories would be required to identify the different nations from which the expatriates are drawn. Analytic domains utilise the language of the researcher rather than the people or setting being studied — they are derived by the researcher and from existent theories, for example the concept of 'host and guest' described by Valene Smith (1978) to describe the tourist–resident interaction.

There are a number of steps involved in conducting domain analysis (Spradley 1980, pp. 93–99):

- choose a semantic relationship, for example:
  1. *Semantic relationship*: strict inclusion
  2. *Form*: A is a kind of B
  3. *Example*: a bus tour is a kind of holiday
- organise a domain analysis worksheet (see example below)

INCLUDED TERMS	SEMANTIC RELATIONSHIP	COVER TERMS
_____	(is a kind of)	_____
_____		_____
_____		_____

- choose a selection of data
- examine the data for 'cover terms' and 'included terms' that match the 'semantic relationship'
- re-examine the data for other semantic relationships
- prepare a catalogue of identified domains.

Domain analysis is an ongoing process — as the researcher collects new data, they have to ensure that the analysis fits all contexts of the setting being studied. Domains can also be described using taxonomies. Taxonomies are described later in the chapter.

◼ 7.3.7 **Ideal** *types*

The use of ideal types in qualitative data analysis is founded in the work of Max Weber (Neuman 2000, p. 431). 'Ideal types are models or mental abstractions of social relations or processes. They are pure standards against which the data or "reality" can be compared. An ideal type is a device used for comparison, because no reality ever fits an ideal type' (Neuman 2000, p. 431). Ideal types can be used to highlight the difference between cases or to accentuate the sameness between cases. When highlighting differences, specifically identifying contrasting contexts (Neuman 2000, p. 432), the ideal type is used as a counterpoint to illuminate unusual contextual contrasts in the setting or phenomenon being studied. On the other hand, when using ideal types to accentuate sameness, that is organising data to demonstrate similarity through analogy, the ideal type aids the organisation of data conceptually and systematically based on the ideal type (Neuman 2000).

◼ 7.3.8 **Event-structure** *analysis*

The acronym ESA stands for event-structure analysis (Neuman 2000, p. 432). This type of analysis organises data into events following a chronological order. However, it is different to storytelling or narratives, as event-structures demonstrate the linkages between events prior to their occurrence. Consequently, ESA is more analytical than a narrative retelling of events, because ESA attempts to identify the causal relationships. Apart from event-structure analysis, there are other time-related ways of analysing (and displaying) data. These include event listings, event-state networks, activity records, decision modelling and time-ordered matrices (Miles & Huberman 1994). These are outlined in table 7.6. While these are analytical methods, they are more oriented to data displays, which in essence are displays of data reduction that result from analytical processes used by the researcher.

■ **Table 7.6**
Time-related displays of data analysis

TYPE OF DISPLAY	DEFINITION
Event listing	'An event listing is a matrix that arranges a series of concrete events by chronological time periods, sorting them into several categories' (p. 111).
Event-state network	An event-state network charts the relationship between events and causes for the events.
Activity record	An activity record visually represents the specific steps involved in undertaking an activity. Visual representation is facilitated by the use of arrows to move the steps from one to the next. The activity is recorded in serial form, following the 'and then' formulae of recounts of events. An activity record is explicit in regard to its time sequence and sequential order. (See also the work of Werner & Schoepfle 1987 and Werner 1992.)
Decision modelling	These displays represent plans of actions and thought processes guiding those actions. In their best form, they contain the bare essentials of the flow processes engaged in decision-making.
Time-ordered matrix	'A time-ordered matrix . . . has its columns arranged by time period, in sequence, so that you can see when particular phenomena occurred. The basic principle is chronology. The rows depend on what else you're studying' (p. 119).

Source: *Miles & Huberman (1994, pp. 111–19)*

■ *7.3.9* **Matrices**

Matrices essentially involve the crossing of two or more dimensions or variables (often with subvariables) to see how they interact. They lend themselves well to a variable-oriented analysis and can be expanded to a more holistic case-oriented style (Miles & Huberman, 1994, p. 239).

Matrices can be developed using a number of organisational methods. Miles and Huberman (1994) provide the following checklist to consider in the construction of matrices:

• Is the matrix going to represent descriptive or explanatory data?
• Is the matrix going to represent partially or fully ordered data (using, for example, temporal organisers, degrees of strength and/or intensity of activities, or hierarchical organisers)?
• Is the matrix going to be time-ordered or non-sequentially constructed?

- Is the matrix representing categories and, if so, how will they be organised and separated?
- Is the matrix design going to be two, three or more than three ways in direction?
- Is the matrix design at the cell level going to contain quotes, summaries, explanations, judgments or various mixes of these contents?
- Is the matrix to represent data from single or multiple cases?

Networks are an alternative to matrices:

> Networks are not dimensional in the same sense [as matrices], but involve a series of nodes connected by links. They lend themselves well to a case-oriented, syntagmatic approach that recreates the 'plot' of events over time, as well as showing the complex interaction of variables. They give us the kinds of narratives that tend to get chopped up analytically in matrices (Miles & Huberman 1994, p. 239).

■ 7.3.10 **Other** *methods of analysis and display*

In addition to the above methods of analysis and display, taxonomies, typologies, conceptual trees, mind maps/semantic webs and sociograms may also be used to assist researchers in analysing (and displaying) empirical data.

Taxonomies are developed from domain analysis and visually represent the subcategories of a category either in tabular form or in diagrammatic form. For example, the domain 'holiday' may be represented in table form thus:

DOMAIN	DOMAIN SUBTYPES
Holiday	Bus tour
	Resort holiday
	Visiting friends and relatives
	Shopping holiday
	Boat cruise
	Train trip

Typologies are also developed from domains. Figure 7.3 illustrates a typology developed using Cohen's (1972) description of the tourist's experiences and roles.

■ **Figure 7.3**
Typology of traveller roles

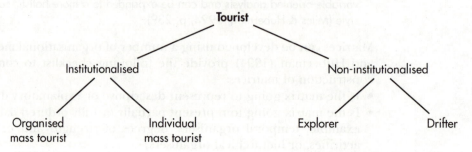

Source: *Cohen (1974, p. 534)*

Conceptual trees are another means to display analysed data. A conceptual tree represents diagrammatically categories and subcategories using 'branches' to move into further levels of definition regarding the categories and subcategories. Figure 7.4 illustrates the conceptual tree Cohen developed to represent the definition of a tourist.

■ Figure 7.4
A conceptual tree for the definition of the tourist role (Cohen 1974)

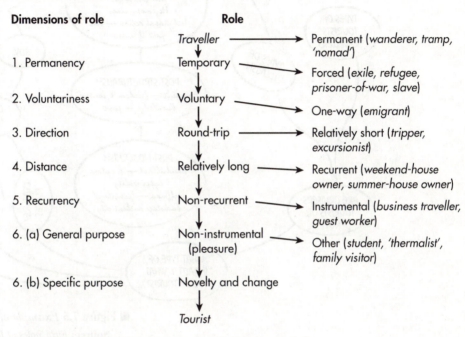

Dimensions of role	Role
	Traveller → Permanent (*wanderer, tramp, 'nomad'*)
1. Permanency	Temporary → Forced (*exile, refugee, prisoner-of-war, slave*)
2. Voluntariness	Voluntary → One-way (*emigrant*)
3. Direction	Round-trip → Relatively short (*tripper, excursionist*)
4. Distance	Relatively long → Recurrent (*weekend-house owner, summer-house owner*)
5. Recurrency	Non-recurrent → Instrumental (*business traveller, guest worker*)
6. (a) General purpose	Non-instrumental (pleasure) → Other (*student, 'thermalist', family visitor*)
6. (b) Specific purpose	Novelty and change
	Tourist

Note: 'Thermalist' means one who visits thermal pools/spas.

Source: *Cohen (1974)*

Mind maps display the thinking and reflections of researchers in a visual pattern. Mind maps connect thoughts and identify relationships between data. Mind maps may be referred to as semantic webs. Semantic webs are associated with terms relevant to the data that are linked together to form a web-like construction of data analysis, relationships or conceptual thinking. Figure 7.5 shows an example of a mind map.

Sociograms identify relationships between various people in a social setting. In portraying a sociogram, people involved in the study setting are located at various points on a sheet of paper or on a computer screen using a graphics program. Having observed and recorded interactions in the social setting, the researcher then records the nature, type and number of interactions as linkages between each of the people in the setting. Sociograms can be used to identify key people in a setting, as well as the nature of interactions and types of roles played by participants within the setting. Sociograms can also be devised using qualitatively and quantitatively derived interview data that identifies the nature and/or types of relationships and number of interactions between people in a study setting.

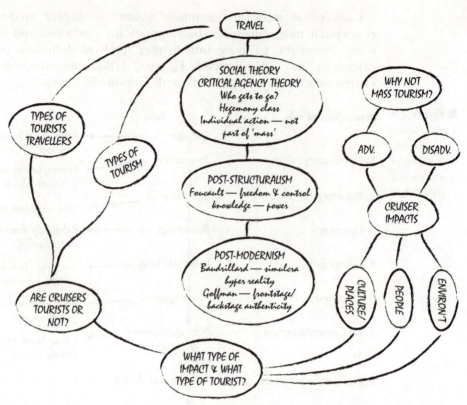

■ Figure 7.5 *Example of a mind map*
Source: *Field notes of Jennings (1993)*

■ *7.3.11* **Grounded theory** *analysis*

[G]rounded theory is both a strategy for research, and a way of analyzing data (Punch 1998, p. 163).

Grounded theory analysis was referred to briefly earlier in the chapter (and in chapter 3), and here we elaborate further on this research method. Specifically, grounded theory is a systematic qualitative research method (Strauss & Corbin 1990, p. 24) that enables the researcher to inductively generate theory from the phenomenon being studied. Grounded theory depends on four criteria: 'fit, understanding, generality, and control' (Strauss & Corbin 1990, p. 23). However, like all qualitative research, '[y]our final theory is limited to those categories, their properties and dimensions, and statements of relationships that exist in the actual data collected' (Strauss & Corbin 1990, p. 112). Consequently, grounded theory is ideographic — it provides a symbolic representation or 'thick' description; and 'limited generalisation is warranted' (Wolcott 1990, p. 30).

Essentially, ' "grounded theory" depends on participant observation … and a method of comparative analysis aimed at constructing theories inductively. The "constant comparative method" of analysis involves four stages: (1) comparing the data applicable to each conceptual category; (2) integrating the categories and their properties; (3) delimiting the emergent theory; and (4) writing up the theory (Glazer [sic] and Strauss 1967, pp. 105–15)' (Jorgensen 1989, p. 113). Furthermore, grounded theory is action based and demonstrates action and change, specifically, 'A (conditions) leads to B (phenomenon), which leads to C (context), which leads to D (action, including strategies), which then leads to E consequences' (Strauss & Corbin 1990, pp. 124–5). The conclusion of the process involves '[v]alidating one's theory against the data [to] complete its grounding' (Strauss & Corbin 1990, p. 133), validity being 'the extent to which it gives the correct answer' (Kirk & Miller 1986, p. 19).

Grounded theory was co-originated by Glaser and Strauss, although they appear to have developed differences in opinion regarding the process of grounded theory. In particular, Glaser (1992, p. 101) contends that Strauss and Corbin present a technique that is 'full conceptual description by a preconceived model', whereas Glaser purports that grounded theory is 'a systematic model of induction and emergence'. According to Glaser (1992, p. 31), for grounded theory to work, the researcher should not begin the literature review prior to gathering the data, because this would cause the researcher to have preconceived ideas about the data to be gathered and may result in data being forced. Glaser (1992, p. 58) also criticises Strauss' comment that the 'personal experience, professional knowledge, and technical literature' assists in analysing the data. Again, Glaser (1992, pp. 56–7) reiterates that this will force the analysis rather than letting it emerge through the use of constant comparisons of the data. Strauss adopts a contrary view to Glaser (see Strauss & Corbin 1990).

■ 7.3.12 The zoom *model*

Pamphilon (1999) has developed a 'zoom model' to analyse oral history stories. Her analytical framework can be explained using a photographic metaphor. The framework contains four levels of analysis:

- The first level, the 'macro-zoom' level of analysis, defines the dominant discourses in texts.
- The second level, the 'meso-zoom' level of analysis, gives clarity to themes and phrases and taken-for-granted assumptions. This level also investigates the silences and absences in textual accounts.
- The third level, the 'micro-level', concentrates on the pauses and the emotions evident in texts. This level in particular highlights 'linguistic incongruence' (de Vault 1990, p. 97) or the inability of language to suitably express a person's experience.
- the last level, the 'interactional' zoom level, focuses on transactions and reactions during in-depth interviewing.

As Pamphilon (1999, p. 3) comments, 'so much can be lost when an oral account is transcribed into text, it is crucial that oral sources are always acknowledged as oral sources'. The role of the researcher in oral interactions is important. As mentioned earlier in this textbook, in non-positivist paradigms, researchers need to identify their personal and 'political' role (MacKinnon 1982, p. 20) in the research act. The interactional level of the zoom model demands that researchers must write themselves into the text.

Reporting the Data

A full discussion of reporting qualitative research is in chapters 10 and 11; however, as Miles and Huberman (1994) note, analysis pervades data collection, and analysis and results. At this stage, it is appropriate to comment on reporting findings based on analysis. As researchers, you should bear in mind that '[d]escription and quotation are the essential ingredients of qualitative inquiry. Sufficient description and direct quotations should be included to allow the reader to enter into the situation and thoughts of the people presented in the report' (Patton 1990, pp. 429–30). Descriptions should be thick rather than thin, as thick description allows further analysis (and verification of your analysis) by the reader.

Qualitative Data Analysis and Computer Programs

> Computers make good friends. No matter how stupid, dull or dumb we may feel, we can still feel smarter than our computer. Computers can do many things, but they cannot think — and we can. Unfortunately, that also means the thinking is up to us. A computer can help us to analyse our data, but it cannot analyse our data. This is not a pedantic distinction: we must do the analysis (Dey 1993, p. 55).

As a researcher you may already be aware that there are a number of software programs available to you to assist you in your data analysis. In using such programs, you should remember that they are only tools, and they are only as 'good' as the person who is using them. Qualitative software programs will not take over your role as the researcher/analyst — you have to effectively use the tools to get the best out of them. This means taking the time to understand how each program works. You should ensure that you become familiar with any program you intend to use well before you reach the data analysis stage — you do not want to be hindered by your lack of knowledge or ability to use a program effectively, as this will lead to project completion delays and personal frustration.

In this chapter, no one particular software program is advocated over another. In discussions with other researchers, you may find that some researchers express biased viewpoints regarding the advantages and disadvantages of software programs. These views may be founded in loyalty to the first program used or may be founded upon an evaluation program. When gathering your own information regarding the use of software programs, you would be wise to query upon what basis other researchers' opinions are founded so your own decision making is informed. Furthermore, you should conduct your own evaluation, and later in the chapter you are provided with guidelines to do this.

■ 7.5.1 **Computer programs** *that assist in data analysis*

This section presents an overview of several of the qualitative data analysis programs available to you, along with some of their features, and a comparison of the programs, so that you can compare their capabilities.

ATLAS.ti

ATLAS.ti can be used with Windows 95 and 98 as well as Windows NT 4.0. The software package is useful for unstructured text-based data. The package allows researchers to engage in ' "VISE": Visualization, Integration, Serendipity and Exploration' (www.atlasti.de/atalsneu.html) in regard to theory building. ATLAS.ti enables researchers to:

- manage data analysis using text-based, graphic, audio and video data
- generate text files, memos and annotations
- select and build codes and compare databases
- support publication using html (see figure 7.6)
- create visual representations of relationships using semantic networks
- build theory (VISE)
- use hypertext linkages.

■ **Figure 7.6**
Example of conversion of analysis units into html

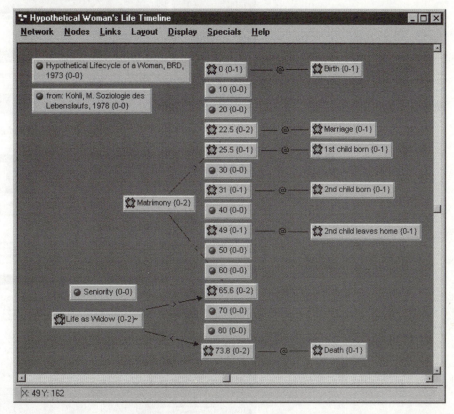

Source: *www.atlasti.de/atlasneu.html*
(example adapted from Kohli, M., Soziologische Texte Luchterhand, 1978, pp. 181 ff)

HyperRESEARCH™

HyperRESEARCH™ version 2.0 is available in Mac and PC formats. Hyper-RESEARCH™ enables researchers to:

- manage data analysis using text-based, graphic, audio and video data
- use code-and-retrieval operations to conduct data analyses, as well as enabling theory building via the Hypothesis Tester' (see figure 7.7)
- generate text files, memos and annotation
- create visual representations of relationships using code maps (see figure 7.8)
- operate one case at a time
- use hypertext linkages.

■ **Figure 7.7**
Example of HyperRESEARCH™ 2.0 Hypothesis Tester

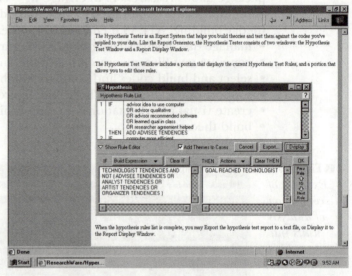

Source: *www.researchware.com/hr20.html*

■ **Figure 7.8**
Example of a code map

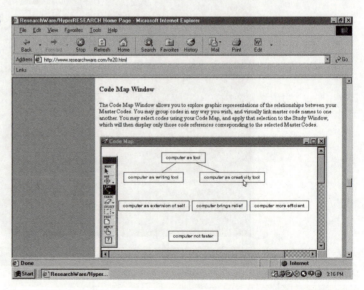

Source: *www.researchware.com/hr20.html*

winMAX

As the name suggests, winMAX operates in conjunction with Windows 95 and later versions, Windows NT and PC platforms. winMAX enables researchers to:

- manage multiple texts
- support text files, memos, qualitative and quantitative procedures and file exchanges (special features for teamwork provided)
- engage in code-and-retrieval and text analysis using Boolean and lexical searches (see figure 7.9) (Boolean searches limit or expand text searches using "or" as well as "and")
- identify relationships and display them visually
- build and test theories.

In 2001 a new program will be released that will provide additional features such as the ability to read .rtf formatted texts, to edit texts and to use invivo coding.

■ **Figure 7.9**
winMAX example of a lexical search operation

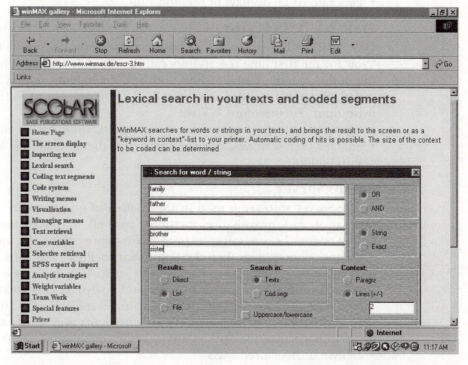

Source: *www.winmax.de/escr-5.htm*

The Ethnograph

The Ethnograph v5.0 operates on a Windows platform. It enables researchers to:

- manage data analysis of multiple text files
- create text files, memos and annotations
- engage in code-and-retrieval including lexical and Boolean searches
- develop code books and definitions
- display code families visually as trees.

QSR NUD*IST 4

The acronym NUD*IST was developed from the following key terms: *Non-numerical Unstructured Data Indexing Searching and Theory* building. QSR NUD*IST is able to handle both text-based data (interview transcripts, field notes, meeting minutes) and non-text based data (photographs, charts, visual images). QSR NUD*IST is designed for efficient data management and for creating and exploring new ideas and theories' (NUD*IST Manual, October 1993, p. 2-1). QSR NUD*IST is available for use with both Mac and PC platforms. QSR NUD*IST assists researchers to:

- manage multiple data inputs including visual and textual data
- use code-and-retrieval and Boolean searches
- develop relationships between data and test those relationships
- build and test theories
- produce data reports accompanied by statistical summaries
- generate visual displays of relationships.

QSR NUD*IST Vivo

QSR NUD*IST Vivo or NVivo operates on both Mac and PC platforms. 'Now for the first time researchers can handle rich data as rich text — with full ability to edit, visually code and link documents as they are created, coded, filtered, managed and searched' (www.qsr.com.au/software/nvivo/nvivo.htm). Furthermore, NVivo:

- supports multiple data sources — text-based, audio, visual and graphic
- enables text searches, code-and-retrieval, theory building and relationship building.

SphinxSurvey

SphinxSurvey software is used in the analysis of questionnaire data in both qualitative and quantitative methods, as well as mixed methods. The SphinxSurvey Lexica software program is more suited for the analysis of qualitative data analysis than the SphinxSurvey Plus[2]. The software program does more than just analyse data. It also assists you, as a researcher, to prepare questionnaires as well as to enter and analyse results created from the survey. The software works on PC platforms using Windows. It has specific hard disk space and free memory requirements and needs a 3.5" floppy drive. In particular, the SphinxSurvey Lexica enables researchers to:

- analyse unstructured texts
- conduct lexical analyses
- create annotations
- generate reports.

Having provided an overview of some of the features of the current software, the next subsections will compare qualitative data analysis software firstly by classifying the software based on their primary features. Then using the work of Miles and Weitzman (1994), an evaluation of software will be presented and some guidelines provided to enable you to make informed decisions about the type of software you might use in your own project.

7.5.2 **Comparison** *of computer software programs for qualitative data analysis*

Qualitative data analysis programs can be categorised based on their capabilities. Richards and Richards (1994), Miles and Weitzman (1994) and Neuman (2000) use similar categories, and these are outlined in table 7.7.

■ **Table 7.7** *Types of qualitative data analysis software programs and some examples*

TYPES OF DATA ANALYSIS SOFTWARE PROGRAMS				
RICHARDS & RICHARDS (1994)	MILES & WEITZMAN (1994)	NEUMAN (2000)	FUNCTIONS OF SOFTWARE	EXAMPLES OF SOFTWARE
Word processors	Word processors	Word processing	Writing, note-making, transcriptions, annotations, memos, simple search and retrieve of strings of text, managing multiple documents and formats, linking and hypertext.	Microsoft Word, Claris Works, Macwrite, Appleworks
Text search packages	Word retrievers	Text retrieval	Text searches, string searches, Boolean searches (and, or, not); faster searching compared to word processors; may permit memos, annotations and statistical reports.	Metamorph, GOfer™, ZylNDEX™, Sonar Professional, The Text Collector, WordCruncher
Relational database management systems	Text-based managers	Textbase managers	As well as text retrieval, can sort and organise data, search finds and file these as records and fields; may use hypertext linkages.	askSam, Folio VIEWS, winMAX, Orbis and ZylNDEX
Hypercard® and Hypermedia			Non-relational database management system, similar to a stack of cards or file cards. Can only view one card at a time, so cannot demonstrate relationships. Hypercard — text storage. Hyperqual — basic code and retrieve program. Hypersoft — modelling HyperRESEARCH — hypothesis testing.	Hypercard®, Hypersoft, HyperRESEARCH™, Story Space™
Code-and-retrieve software	Code-and-retrieve programs	Code-and-retrieve programs	Enable the researcher to code and retrieve text from multiple documents in a database and display the results in the one text document; may support memos, annotations and provide statistical results.	Ethnograph, Kwalitan, ATLAS.ti, winMAX, QSR NUD*IST, QUALPRO, Hypercard®

(continued)

TYPES OF DATA ANALYSIS SOFTWARE PROGRAMS

RICHARDS & RICHARDS (1994)	MILES & WEITZMAN (1994)	NEUMAN (2000)	FUNCTIONS OF SOFTWARE	EXAMPLES OF SOFTWARE
Rule-based theory builders (e.g. Hyper RESEARCH); logic-based systems (e.g. AQUAD, QUALOG); index-based approach (e.g. QSR NUD*IST)	Theory builders	Code-based theory builders	Allow theory building based on codes, logic and/or indexing. Code and retrieval results are further worked to determine relationships that are 'tested' to determine the authenticity of the 'theory'.	ETHNO, QSR NUD*IST, AQUAD, ATLAS.ti, HyperRESEARCH™, QCA
Conceptual network systems	Conceptual network builders	Conceptual network builders	'Theory' is built and tested using graphic representations and networks.	ATLAS.ti, HyperRESEARCH™, QSR NUD*IST, MetaDesign, SemNet, MECA

Several writers have compared software packages (Tesch 1990; Pfaffenberger 1988; Miles & Weitzman 1994; Weitzman & Miles 1995). Table 7.8 provides an overview of the comparison of software programs by Miles and Weitzman (1994) based on the following categories: version, operating system, search and retrieval ability, database management, memoing, data linking, matrix building, network display, theory building and user friendliness. Miles and Weitzman evaluate each program primarily using a three-point scaling system (see key below the table for details of the scales).

■ **Table 7.8** *Miles and Weitzman (1994) comparison of qualitative data analysis programs*

	VERSION	OPERATING SYSTEM	CODING	SEARCH AND RETRIEVAL	DATABASE MANAGEMENT	MEMOING	DATA LINKING	MATRIX BUILDING	NETWORK DISPLAY	THEORY BUILDING	USER FRIENDLINESS
AQUAD	[3.2]	D	■	◐	□	■		◐		■	✓✓
askSam	[5.1]	DW		●	■	□	■				✓✓
ATLAS.ti	[1.0e]	D	■	◐	□	■	■	○	●[a]	■	✓✓✓
Folio Views	[3.0]	DW	■	●	■	■	■	○			✓✓✓
HyperQUAL[b]	[4.3]	Mc	■	○	■	■	■	○			✓✓
HyperRESEARCH™	[1.5]	McW	■	◐	□			○		■	✓✓✓
Inspiration	[4.0]	Mc		○		■	■		●		✓✓✓
Kwalitan	[3.1]	D	■	◐	□	■	□			□	✓✓✓
winMAX[b]	[3.x]	D	■	○	■		■				✓✓
MECA	[1.0]	McDU					■		◐	■	✓✓
Meta Design	[4.0]	McW		○		□	■		●		✓✓

	VERSION	OPERATING SYSTEM	CODING	SEARCH AND RETRIEVAL	DATABASE MANAGEMENT	MEMOING	DATA LINKING	MATRIX BUILDING	NETWORK DISPLAY	THEORY BUILDING	USER FRIENDLINESS
Metamorph[c]	[3.5]	McDUM		●[d]	□	□	■				✓
	[4.0]	McWU	□	●[d]	□	■	■				✓✓
QSR NUD*IST	[2.3]	McWUM	■	●	□		□	◐		■	✓
	[3.0]	Mc	■	●	□	■	□	●	◐	■	✓✓
Orbis[b][e]	[1.0]	DW	□	●	■	□	□	●			✓✓
QCA	[3.0]	D		○			□		◐	■	✓
QUALPRO	[4.0]	D	■	◐	□	□					✓✓✓
SemNet	[1.0.2]	Mc		◐		■	■		●	■	✓✓
Sonar Professional	[8.4]	McW		●	□	■	□			□	✓✓
The Ethnograph	[4.0]	D	■	◐	□	■			○		✓✓
The Text Collector	[1.7]	D		●	□						✓✓✓
WordCruncher	[4.5]	D		◐	□		■				✓
	[Beta]	W		●	□	■	■				✓✓
ZyIndex	[5.0]	DW		●	□	■	■				✓

```
■     = designed for this purpose, as we see it (may be more or less effective)
□     = not really designed for it, but can do at least in a limited way
blank = cannot do this
●     = Strong                          ✓   = not too friendly
◐     = OK                              ✓✓  = fairly friendly
○     = weak                           ✓✓✓ = very friendly
blank = absent
Operation system:  Mc = Macintosh    D = DOS        U = Unix
                   M = Main frame     W = Windows
```

[a] Weaker than Inspiration and MetaDesign on graphics, but can create networks from data.
[b] Reviewed from documentation, so ratings are somewhat speculative.
[c] Based on version 3.5 and a demo of version 4.0, so ratings for 4.0 are somewhat speculative.
[d] For raw text retrieval, in a class by itself.
[e] Available as add-on module for XyWrite 4.0 or Notabene 4.0 word processors. Ratings include word processor features.

Source: *Miles & Weitzman (1994), in Miles & Huberman (1994, p. 316)*

Given the passage of time since the comparison in table 7.8 was made, and the fact that Miles and Weitzman (1994, p. 311) advocate that '[e]xpect the information here to decay as programs are refined and new programs appear', Miles and Weitzman (1994, pp. 313–15) provide the following guiding questions to assist you in your own selection when considering the use of qualitative software:

• What is your current computer skill and knowledge base?
• What type of system are you operating on?
• How compatible is the hardware you will use to the running requirements of the programs?

- What type of project is your research?
- What types of data management are required for the project?
- What types of analysis are required?
- What are the qualitative data analysis programs' characteristics?
- How user-friendly is the program?
- What type of software support are you able to access?

When contemplating using qualitative data analysis software, you should consider the above questions and try out the software before committing. Many of the programs have demonstrations to trial before buying. Also consider whether you are being influenced by 'brand loyalty' rather than effective evaluation based on your needs, the project's needs, the range of software available and its ability to fulfil both your needs and the project's needs.

A comprehensive list of applications for both IBM compatible and Macintosh computers can be found at the CAQDAS Networking Project web site (www.soc.surrey.ac/caqdas/[corrected from original). This site contains links to demonstration versions of most of the available programs (Punch 1998, p. 233).

7.6 SUMMARY

The difference between qualitative and quantitative data analysis

Qualitative data analysis is inductive in nature and involves text-based analysis that identifies themes and motifs that generate theory derived from empirical data. Qualitative data analysis commences with data collection, whereas quantitative data analysis occurs after all the data have been collected, coded and entered into the analytical system. Furthermore, quantitative data analysis is deductive, and uses numerals and statistics to test hypotheses. Both data analysis techniques are, however, predicated on comparisons between and within data, the development of inferences, the clear definition of analytical methods for the reader and attempts to ensure that the findings are as error-free as possible.

Qualitative data analysis occurs during three phases of research projects

Data analysis occurs during data collection, data analysis and data reporting. Furthermore, it involves three activities: data reduction, data display and conclusion drawing/verification.

A number of qualitative data analysis methods

Qualitative researchers may draw upon the following methods: memos, coding, content analysis, constant comparative analysis, successive approximation, domain analysis, ideal types, event-structure analysis, matrices, taxonomies, typologies, conceptual trees, mind maps, grounded theory analysis and the zoom model.

The computer programs available to qualitative researchers

Computer programs may be used to undertake text retrieval, text management, code-and-retrieval, code-based theory building and conceptual network building. Some of the programs used by qualitative researchers include ATLAS.ti, HyperRESEARCH™, winMAX, the Ethnograph, QSR NUD*IST and SphinxSurvey.

Questions

7.1 Although there are similarities between methods of qualitative and quantitative data analysis, there remain differences within these similarities. In the chapter, the similarities were noted as: inferences are made; methods are identified; comparisons are undertaken; and researchers try to be error-free. Outline the key differences that are inherent in qualitative and quantitative perspectives in regard to each of these similarities.

7.2 What do you consider to be the major benefit from simultaneously engaging in data collection and analysis? Are there any challenges related to such engagement?

7.3 Consider each of the various types of data analysis: which do you believe should be a part of every qualitative research project?

7.4 Write a paragraph of approximately 250 words outlining your opinion regarding the use of literal transcriptions to demonstrate themes and motifs in research reports.

7.5 What are the key advantages and disadvantages of using computer software programs for qualitative data analysis?

EXERCISES

Exercise 7.1

Examine the following excerpts from a series of interview transcriptions derived from Jennings' (1999) study into long-term ocean cruisers. Then develop codes as part of an open coding process. Outline your key code categories and explain and justify your codes at this point in time. In the transcripts, the letter 'm' indicates a male speaker and the letter 'f' indicates a female speaker.

322m: Ah, well, I've always liked travelling. I'm not that fussed about stopping in motels and that sort of thing. I travelled around Australia by vehicle about three times. Anyway, I think boating is a means, travelling is the attraction for me. You know I've gotten to like the lifestyle of just living on the boat.

357f: This is hard [turns to her partner, she seeks help 'Do I tell the truth?' He nods.] It is my husband's dream, and I followed. Love is the biggest and the strongest thing, I love him and he wanted to do it, so I followed. When I came on this boat it was like my home. I did courses — navigation and skipper's certificate. We do not feel we have made a mistake; if we have it is the money we have used. But we do not feel we have made a mistake.

364m: When my wife and I were young we had powerboats and we lived up a river, in our home state. Our kids got used to boating at an early stage, all four of them, and eventually we decided at that time we had to get into sailboating, so we did. By the time we got our youngest kid through school, we moved aboard the sailboat and took off to see what we could see of the world.

365f: Well, we started sailing in our home country. 366m decided to build a boat, mainly for the purpose of getting out of our home country and leaving it behind and we did a bit of dinghy sailing just to get the feel of what it was all about and which way the wind was blowing, and then 366m built the boat and I hadn't had much experience in sailing at all and we just set off. 366m had done a few trips, so he had more experience than I had. That was in 1983.

352m: I choose this lifestyle because of the adventure, the lifestyle, and I love beaches.

251f: For me, it's the challenge, it's a personal challenge for me to make landfalls. I've got to do it, I want to do it, it's my goal.

326m: Primarily travel, maybe a little about the lifestyle. We met a lot of people who were in the lifestyle and it appealed to us. And you have the freedom to go where you want when you want.

359f: When I met 360m, he was about to retire and go cruising and it was just never anything which had ever occurred to me before that and then when we first got married, we were going to do just that and then I got pregnant with my youngest son so that put paid to that until he was about two and a half and then we took off.

330m: Me, personally, because the ideal of the lifestyle appeals to me, and the idea of having a long extended holiday instead of working in a dull boring routine job is more appealing.

328m: Control over your life, definitely, and the fact that I'm too lazy to work all my life and I don't see that as a natural lifestyle working for some boss and I just think cruising is the way to go.

357f: To see the world. Scandinavia is a small place. I want to see the world; it's a good way to see the world without being a tourist. You can choose your own way, if you want to go here or there.

Exercise 7.2

Still focusing on the above excerpts, undertake some preliminary axial coding.

Exercise 7.3

In your next non-tourism research tutorial session, develop a diagram that both identifies the main participants in the tutorial discussion and the interaction networks for the first 40 minutes of the tutorial. Bring this back to your tourism class and discuss the methods you used to record the data and how you chose to map the interactions.

Exercise 7.4

This chapter introduced you to some computer programs for tourism research. Over the next week, access the Web sites noted at the end of this chapter, follow the links to the demonstration sites, then conduct your own review of the software packages that are available to you. Alternatively, the class may choose to identify individuals/groups to specifically evaluate software demonstrations and report back at the next class session.

RESEARCH PROJECT ···

Draw a mind map that represents the way you see your final report being constructed at this stage. You might also consider the structure of individual chapters. This activity is appropriate for qualitative, quantitative and mixed method research projects.

REFERENCES ···

Bogdan, R. & Biklen, S. K. 1992. *Qualitative Research for Education: An Introduction to Theory and Methods*. Second Edition. Boston, MA: Allen & Unwin.

Cohen, Erik. 1972. 'Toward a Sociology of International Tourism'. *Social Research*, vol. 39, pp. 164–82.

Cohen, Erik. 1974. 'Who is a Tourist? A Conceptual Clarification'. *Sociological Review*, vol. 22, pp. 527-55.

de Vault, Marjorie. 1990. 'Talking Listening for Women's Standpoints: Feminist Strategies for Interviewing and Analysis'. *Social Problems*, vol. 37, no.1, pp. 99–118.

Dey, Ian. 1993. *Qualitative Data Analysis: A User Friendly Guide for the Social Scientists*. London: Routledge.

Ford, Julienne. 1975. *Paradigms and Fairy Tales: An Introduction to the Science of Meanings*. Volume 1. London: Routledge & Kegan Paul.

Glaser, Barney. 1978. *Theoretical Sensitivity*. Mill Valley, CA: Sociology Press.

Glaser, Barney. 1992. *Emergence Versus Forcing. Basics of Grounded Theory Analysis*. Mill Valley, CA: Sociology Press.

Glesne, Corrine. 1999. *Becoming Qualitative Researchers: An Introduction*. Second Edition. New York: Longman.

Huberman, A. Michael & Miles, Matthew B. 1994. 'Data Management and Analysis Methods'. In Denzin, Norman & Lincoln, Yvonna (Eds.) *Handbook of Qualitative Research*. Thousand Oaks: Sage, pp. 428–44.

Janesick, Valerie. 1994. 'The Dance of Qualitative Research Design'. In Denzin, Norman & Lincoln, Yvonna (Eds) *Handbook of Qualitative Research*. Thousand Oaks: Sage, pp. 209–19.

Jennings, Gayle 1993. Field notes. Unpublished.

Jennings, Gayle 1999. Voyages from the Centre to the Margins: An Ethnography of Long-Term Ocean Cruisers. Unpublished PhD thesis. Murdoch University.

Jorgensen, Danny. 1989. *Participant Observation: A Methodology for a Human Studies*. Applied Social Research Methods Series, Volume 15. Newbury Park: Sage.

Kirk, Jerome & Miller, Marc L. 1986. *Reliability and Validity in Qualitative Research*. Qualitative Research Methods Series, Volume 1. Newbury Park: Sage.

Lincoln, Yvonna & Guba, Egon, G. 1985. *Naturalistic Inquiry*. Newbury Park: Sage.

Lofland, J. 1971. *Analyzing Social Settings: A Guide to Qualitative Observation and Analysis*. Belmont, CA: Wadsworth.

MacKinnon, Catherine A. 1982. 'Feminism, Marxism, Method, and the State: An Agenda for Theory'. In Keohane, Nannerl O., Rosaldo, Michelle Z. & Gelphi, Barbara C. (Eds) *Feminist Theory: A Critique of Ideology*. Chicago: The University of Chicago Press.

Manning, Peter K. & Cullum-Swan, Betsy. 1994. 'Narrative, Content and Semiotic Analysis'. In Denzin, Norman & Lincoln, Yvonna (Eds) *Handbook of Qualitative Research*. Thousand Oaks: Sage, pp. 463–77.

Miles, Matthew & Huberman, A. Michael. 1994. *Qualitative Analysis: An Expanded Sourcebook*. Second Edition. Thousand Oaks, CA: Sage.

Miles, Matthew & Weitzman, Eben. 1994. 'Appendix: Choosing Computer Programs for Qualitative Data Analysis'. In Miles, Matthew & Huberman, A. Michael. 1994. *Qualitative Analysis: An Expanded Sourcebook*. Second Edition. Thousand Oaks, CA: Sage, pp. 311–17.

Neuman, W. Lawrence. 2000. *Social Research Methods: Qualitative and Quantitative Approaches*. Fourth Edition. Boston, MA: Allyn & Bacon.

Pamphilon, Barbara, 1999. 'The Zoom Model: A Dynamic Framework for the Analysis of Life Histories'. *Qualitative Inquiry*, vol. 5, no. 3, special edition.

Patton, Michael, Q. 1990. *Qualitative Evaluation and Research Methods*. Second Edition. Newbury Park: Sage.

Pfaffenberger, B. 1988. *Microcomputer Applications in Qualitative Research*. Beverley Hills, CA: Sage.

Punch, Keith. 1998. *Introduction to Social Research Quantitative and Qualitative Approaches*. London: Sage.

Richards, Thomas & Richards, Lyn. 1994. 'Using Computers in Qualitative Research'. In Denzin, Norman & Lincoln, Yvonna (Eds) *Handbook of Qualitative Research*. Thousand Oaks: Sage, pp. 445–62.

Sarantakos, Sotirios. 1998. *Social Research*. Second Edition. South Melbourne: Macmillan.

Smith, Valene (Ed.) 1978. *Host and Guests: The Anthropology of Tourism*. Oxford: Basil Blackwell.

Spradley, James. 1980. *Participant Observation*. New York: Holt, Rinehart & Winston.

Strauss, Anslem. 1987. *Qualitative Analysis for Social Scientists*. Cambridge, UK: Cambridge University Press.

Strauss, Anselm & Corbin, Juliet. 1990. *Basics of Qualitative Research: Grounded Theory, Procedures and Techniques*. Newbury Park: Sage.

Tesch, R. 1990. *Qualitative Research: Analysis Types and Software Tools*. London: The Falmer Press.

van Gennep, Arnold. 1960. *Rites of Passage*. London: Routledge & Kegan Paul.

Weitzman, Eben & Miles, Matthew. 1995. *Computer Programs for Qualitative Data Analysis*. Thousand Oaks, CA: Sage.

Werner, O. 1992. 'How to Record Activities'. *Cultural Anthropology Methods Newsletter*, vol. 4, no. 2, pp. 1–3.

Werner, O. & Schoepfle, G. M. 1987. *Systematic Fieldwork: Volume 2. Ethnographic Analysis and Interviewing.* Newbury Park, CA: Sage.

Wolcott, Harry F. 1990. *Writing Up Qualitative Research.* Qualitative Research Methods Series, Volume 20. Newbury Park: Sage.

FURTHER READING ....

Boyatzis, Richard E. 1998. *Transforming Qualitative Information. Thematic Analysis and Code Development.* Thousand Oaks, CA: Sage.

Fieldings, Nigel G. & Lee, Raymond M. 1998. *Computer Analysis and Qualitative Research.* Thousand Oaks, CA: Sage.

Gahan, Celia & Hannibal, Mike. 1998. *Doing Qualitative Research Using QSR NUD*IST.* Thousand Oaks, CA: Sage.

Hesse-Biber, S., Dupuis, P. & Kinder, T. S. 1991. 'HyperRESEARCH: A Computer Program for the Analysis of Qualitative Data with an Emphasis on Hypothesis Testing and Multimedia Analysis'. *Qualitative Sociology,* vol. 14, pp. 289–306.

Huber, G. L. & Garcia, C. M. 1991. 'Computer Assistance for Testing Hypotheses About Qualitative Data: The Software Package AQUAD 3.0'. *Qualitative Sociology,* Vol. 14, pp. 325–48.

Kelle, U. (Ed.) 1995. *Computer-Aided Qualitative Data Analysis.* London: Sage.

Mühr, T. 1991. 'ATLAS/ti: A Prototype for the Support of Text Interpretation'. *Qualitative Sociology,* vol. 14, pp. 349–71.

Ragin, C. C. 1987. *The Comparative Method: Moving Beyond Qualitative and Quantitative Strategies.* Berkeley: University of California Press.

Richards, Tom & Richards, Lyn. 1991. 'The NUDIST Qualitative Data Analysis System'. *Qualitative Sociology,* vol. 14.

Sapsford, Roger & Jupp, Victor (Eds) *Data Collection and Analysis.* Thousand Oaks, CA: Sage.

Scott, John. 1998. *Social Network Analysis.* Second Edition. Thousand Oaks, CA: Sage.

Strauss, Anselm & Corbin, Juliet. 1990. *Basics of Qualitative Research, Grounded Theory Procedures and Techniques.* Newbury Park: Sage.

WEB SITES ....

http://www.soc.surrey.ac/caqdas/

http://www.sagepub.com

ATLAS.ti (http://www.atlasti.de/atlasneu.html); demonstration site (http://www.atlasti/de/prerelease.htm)

HyperRESEARCH (http://www.researchware.com/demos.html); demonstration site (http://www.researchware.com/demos.html)

winMAX (http://www.winmax.de)

The Ethnograph (http://www.qualisresearch.com/info.htm); demonstration site (http://www.qualisresearch.com/demo.htm)

QSR NUD*IST (http://www.qsr.com.au/software/nvivo/nvivo.htm); demonstration site (http://www.qsr.com.au/events/Books/publica.htm#QSR NUD*IST 4)

QSR NUD*IST Vivo (http://www.qsr.com.au); demonstration site (http://www.qsr.com.au/software/nvivo/NVDemo.htm)

SphinxSurvey (http://www.lesphinx-developpement.fr/en/download/overview.htm); demonstration site (http://www.lesphinx-developpement.fr/en/download/download.htm)

8

Quantitative methods
and tourism research

'The quantitative approach to research usually involves statistical analysis. It relies on numerical evidence to draw conclusions or to test hypotheses. To be sure of the reliability of the results it is often necessary to study relatively large numbers of people or organisations and to use computers to analyse the data. The data can be derived from questionnaire surveys, from observation or from secondary sources.'

(Ticehurst & Veal 1999, pp. 20–1)

LEARNING OBJECTIVES
After studying this chapter, you should be able to:

- review the ways the hypothetico-deductive paradigm informs both a quantitative methodology and quantitative methods
- overview the different types of surveys from which a researcher may choose
- explain the differences between surveys and questionnaires
- describe the nature of mail surveys
- outline the advantages and disadvantages of telephone surveys
- explain the differences between self-completion and interviewer-completed questionnaires
- state the main issues associated with en-route, on-site, household and omnibus surveys
- identify the main features of e-questionnaires
- understand the key elements in constructing a questionnaire
- describe other quantitative methods such as observation, longitudinal studies, case studies, the Delphic method, the documentary or archival method and experimental and quasi-experimental methods
- review the rudiments of forecasting, social and environmental impact assessments and the nominal group technique
- discuss the overlaps between quantitative and qualitative methods.

8.1 INTRODUCTION

In chapters 6 and 7, qualitative methods of data collection and analysis were presented. This chapter and chapter 9 concentrate on quantitative methods of data collection and analysis. As in chapter 6, only the most widely used quantitative methods are presented here. The chapter reviews the tenets of the hypothetico-deductive paradigm and briefly comments on how the tenets inform a quantitative methodology and methods. The chapter then focuses on surveys, the most commonly used method of quantitative data collection, before briefly discussing other quantitative methods.

8.2 PARADIGMS THAT INFORM A QUANTITATIVE METHODOLOGY

A quantitative methodology is informed by positivist and post-positivist paradigms or the hypothetico-deductive paradigm. The following tenets are associated with a quantitative methodology: a deductive approach; an ontological view that sees the world as consisting of causal relationships; an objective epistemology; the use of an etic perspective (an outsider's perspective); a structured, systematic, replicable research design; the use primarily of random sampling; numerically-based data collection; statistical analyses; the representation of research findings using statistical tables and graphs; reports written in the third person using the passive voice; and findings that are generalisable to the wider population. The main methods of data collection are surveys (questionnaires and structured interviews), longitudinal studies, case studies, the documentary method, observation, impact assessment and quasi-experimental methods. In chapter 6, a discussion of non-sexist research methods was presented. This should be reread in conjunction with this chapter, as it also has relevance to quantitative methods.

8.3 TYPES OF SURVEYS

As noted in chapter 5, quantitative methods dominate tourism and hospitality research, especially the use of surveys. Surveys have their roots in census data collection by 'governments', who used censuses in order to gain an understanding of the number of people in their populations for taxation purposes. Neuman (2000) suggests that the use of surveys as a data collection method increased in the second half of the twentieth century due to six developments:

- developments in information technology (IT), such as computers, which enabled researchers to examine large data sets
- developments in IT that allowed storage of large data sets for later secondary analysis

- the conduct of research as a 'core business' for some public and private sector organisations
- the commitment of governments to funding survey research in order to gather data for decision-making purposes
- the refinement of methodological processes over time, with subsequent improvements in reliability and validity
- the improved skilling of researchers in data collection and statistical methods of data analysis.

Just as there are various approaches to research (exploratory, descriptive and explanatory), surveys can be similarly classified as descriptive, explanatory, predictive and evaluative based on the overall objective(s) of the study (Babbie 1990). Descriptive surveys describe the population and are exemplified by national censuses. However, within tourism and hospitality contexts, descriptive surveys are generally not carried out on such a large scale and rely on the use of probability sampling techniques to reflect the overall population. Descriptive surveys enable researchers to describe the 'who' (demographic characteristics of tourists and visitors), 'what' (activities and destination preferences) and 'how' (social and economic status) of the study population. Most descriptive surveys gather data on gender, age, educational background, occupation or income level, type of travel group, destination, type of transport used, length of stay, type of accommodation used and purpose of trip.

Explanatory surveys are designed to test a hypothesis (a causal relationship). For example, to test the hypothesis that more locals visit Phillip Island in Victoria than non-locals, the researcher would design a survey to collect data on place of residence and visitation patterns to Phillip Island. Through data analysis, the researcher would determine the existence of any relationship between place of residency and visitation patterns to Phillip Island, then either accept or reject the hypothesis. Usually, researchers will test several hypotheses. Continuing on from the Phillip Island example, the hypothesis might be complemented by several other hypotheses, such as length of residency in the local area will decrease visitation to Phillip Island by locals, or proximity to Phillip Island to place of residency will increase visitation for recreational purposes. Based on this set of hypotheses, the researcher would design a survey, collect data on place of residency, length of residency, visitation patterns to Phillip Island, and reasons for visitation (e.g. close to place of residence, recreational purposes, interest in fairy penguins, interest in crafts, location to take visiting friends and relatives).

Predictive and evaluative surveys are used to assist managers to make decisions regarding future patterns/trends or to evaluate a practice, protocol or strategy. Such surveys involve two to three temporal data sets, one that represents the current status and/or past, and one that is future oriented or placed. Predictive surveys make extrapolations about future patterns and trends based on past and current data sets, for example the more Wagga Wagga residents know about regional tourist attractions, the greater the number of those attractions visited by the locals and their visiting friends and relatives. Evaluative surveys compare past strategies against newly implemented strategies to determine their effectiveness. Continuing with the Wagga Wagga example, the researcher might hypothesise that Wagga Wagga residents' knowledge of regional tourist attractions will increase as a result of a weekly 10-minute promotional segment on commercial television. Just as methods can be combined, so too can surveys — for example, a survey may be descriptive and explanatory, or descriptive and evaluative, or some other combination.

8.4 SURVEYS AND QUESTIONNAIRES

The terms 'surveys' and 'questionnaires' are sometimes used interchangeably. However, as Sarantakos (1998) points out, they are quite different:

In general, surveys are methods of data collection in which information is gathered through oral or written questioning. Oral questioning is known as interviewing; written questioning is accomplished through questionnaires (Sarantakos 1998, p. 223).

The following sections discuss mail surveys, telephone surveys, self-completion questionnaires, e-questionnaires, interviewer-completed questionnaires, en-route surveys, on-site surveys, household surveys and omnibus surveys.

■ 8.4.1 Mail *surveys*

Mail surveys use questionnaires to gather data. The questionnaires are mailed to respondents, who then fill in the answers and return the questionnaires to the researcher. Mail surveys thus rely on respondents being literate or conversant with the language used in the questionnaire. Questionnaires are usually three to four pages in length. Longer questionnaires may be used (up to 20 pages in length), although the overall length of the questionnaire can reduce response rates as people may tire from responding to questions. Long questionnaires are successful, however, when the issue or topic being researched is of interest to the respondent.

Mail surveys usually are associated with at least three mail-out processes for the researcher. The first mail-out process consists of four components: a covering letter, a consent form, the questionnaire itself and a return envelope. The return envelope enables the researcher to pay for the cost of returning the questionnaire. This can be done in two ways, and there are two sets of opinions regarding which option is the best. One way is to use stamped envelopes; the other is to use reply-paid envelopes. Stamped envelopes are said to increase response rates, as respondents can see that someone has gone to the trouble to place stamps on the envelopes. A contrary opinion is that stamps increase costs when the envelopes are not returned. If envelopes are not returned, reply-paid envelopes are the better option because the researcher only pays the costs associated with the returned letters, although there are also costs involved with the original mail-out and for stationery consumed.

The second and third mail-out processes may involve the use of a reminder card (see figure 8.1) and the entire resending of the original questionnaire mail-out materials with an updated letter explaining the second or third mail-out. However, this is an expensive strategy, especially if the questionnaire is long (and thus heavy), as the associated mail-out costs will be high.

■ **Figure 8.1**
Example of a reminder card

4 June 1996

Last week a survey was sent to you which asked about your use of Shoalwater Bay and adjacent waters as well as your opinions concerning suitable activities for the area.

If you have already completed and returned the survey, please accept my thanks. If you have forgotten about it and intend to respond, would you please do so and return it today? Your information is important so that the usage patterns of Shoalwater Bay are correctly represented and opinions regarding the suitability of activities are adequately canvassed.

If you have not received a survey or have misplaced it, please telephone me on (079) 309339 and I will forward another to you.

Yours sincerely

Gayle Jennings
Tourism and Leisure Studies

Source: *Jennings (1998, p. 86)*

You can see from figure 8.1 that the reminder card also acknowledges that the respondent may have returned the questionnaire, in which case they are thanked and asked to ignore the request to return the question-naire. In the initial letter of contact, respondents are usually informed about the use of reminder cards and that, because of anonymity assur-ances, all respondents will receive these reminders. If confidentiality has been assured, then the researcher is able to target only those respon-dents who have not returned their questionnaires by matching question-naire code numbers to a respondent database or sampling frame. Reminders are usually sent two weeks and then four weeks after the initial mail-out.

Advantages and disadvantages

As was discussed in chapter 6, some of the advantages and disadvantages of research methods relate to the theoretical paradigms that inform the over-lying methodology. In this chapter, that methodology is a quantitative methodology. As a consequence, the advantages and disadvantages relate to the ontological (world view) of causal relationships, the objective epistemological perspective (i.e. an objective subject–researcher relationship) and methodological perspectives that are reductionist and numeric in nature.

Advantages

The key advantages of mail surveys are the lower personnel and implementation costs associated with survey distribution and collection. This is especially true when compared to interviewer-conducted surveys (see below). In mail surveys, the researcher uses the postal system to disseminate and collect questionnaire materials to and from each respondent/household included in the study. Neuman (2000, pp. 271–2) also notes other advantages — mail surveys:

- are the cheapest method when research is conducted by only one researcher
- enable the researcher to target dispersed geographical areas
- are completed at the respondents' convenience
- can offer anonymity when codes are not used; if codes are used, confidentiality assurances would have to be offered
- remove interviewer bias since the interviewer is not physically present
- can achieve high response rates from well-educated respondents or when there is high interest in the research topic.

Disadvantages

The key disadvantages are associated with the lack of face-to-face contact between the respondent and researcher, which prevents immediate data collection. There are other disadvantages (Neuman 2000, p. 272):

- mail surveys are not always fully completed and returned
- return of surveys can take some time — surveys are usually returned within a two-week time frame from the initial mail-out, but returns may continue for another month
- to increase response rates, reminder cards are used, which adds to the cost, although, on the other hand, reminder cards increase response rates if at least two are used
- use of reminder cards also increases the time component of data collection, that is the duration of the study period
- the absence of the researcher results in a lack of control or assurance that the surveys will be completed
- respondents are unable to seek clarification and this may lead to incomplete answers
- the researcher can never be sure the targeted respondent has actually answered the questions
- the researcher is unable to make observation notes
- the researcher has no way of knowing the literacy level of respondents
- the length of questionnaires restricts the use of visual aids
- open-ended questions do not achieve lengthy written responses
- questions of a complex nature are not responded to well.

■ 8.4.2 Telephone *surveys*

Telephone surveys are primarily structured interviews using closed questions, with an interviewer recording the respondent's answers. Contact with respondents is made using telephone technology. Telephone technology may be further assisted by computer technology, in which case the responses are immediately recorded using software programs that integrate the responses with analysis procedures. As with mail surveys, telephone surveys enable the researcher to increase the geographical spread of the survey while reducing costs when compared with a house-to-house survey. The telephone survey has the added advantage of making voice-to-voice (personal) contact with respondents, which is lacking in mail surveys. Ideally, interviews should be around five to 10 minutes in duration. The suggested time for making calls on weekdays is between 5.30 p.m. and 9.00 p.m. (Weeks, Jones, Folsom & Benrud 1980; Vigderhous 1981; Warde 1986; Weeks, Kulka & Pierson 1987; Frey 1989). During the weekend, telephone calls should be made on Saturdays between 9.00 a.m. and 2.00 p.m. and on Sunday evenings (Frey 1989). Researchers should also be aware of public holidays and important local, state, national or cultural events (e.g. Show Day holidays, Labour Day, Melbourne Cup, football grand finals, Chinese New Year) that may occur during the data collection period. Such events may impact on people's willingness or ability to participate in a telephone survey occurring at the same time as the event.

Advantages and disadvantages

Telephone surveys enable personal contact to be made with respondents and samples may be drawn from a range of geographical regions for a lesser cost than face-to-face interviews conducted by household visits. On the other hand, whereas mail surveys can be conducted by one researcher, telephone surveys require a number of interviewers. These interviewers require training and supervision to ensure proper and ethical conduct, as well as having to be paid, which adds to the cost of the overall survey.

Advantages

There are a number of other advantages of telephone surveys:

- approximately 95% of Western populations can be reached by telephone (Neuman 2000, p. 272)
- computer-assisted technology can be used to reduce implementation and analysis time (Frey 1989)
- telephone surveys are quick in nature (Sarantakos 1998)
- if call-backs are used, a 75–90% response rate can be generated (Frey 1989; Neuman 2000)
- the interviewer is in charge of the question order (Frey 1989; Neuman 2000)
- probes can be used to elicit further information (Neuman 2000)
- the researcher/interviewer can ensure that only one respondent answers the questions.

Disadvantages

There are a number of other disadvantages:
- depending on call rates, telephone surveys can be more expensive than mail surveys
- there is a high cost if long-distance calls are involved
- the infrastructure for telephone stations can be expensive
- there are limited interview times pertaining to the best times for making and gaining responses
- the interviewer may be linked to lessening of anonymity and interviewer bias despite using randomly generated numbers (Neuman 2000)
- telephone surveys cannot use visual aids (Neuman 2000)
- open-ended questions are limited (Neuman 2000), in order to minimise the duration of each call
- the interviewer can only hear disruptions and the tone of voice of the respondent (Neuman 2000) — non-verbal behaviour cannot be observed
- the interviewer is unable to control the interview; the respondent can hang up at any time.

■ 8.4.3 Self-completion *questionnaires*

The following two sections lead on from the discussion of questionnaires in mail surveys and telephone surveys and further highlight the differences between self-completion questionnaires and interviewer-completed questionnaires. The key difference between the two is that self-completion questionnaires, as the term suggests, are completed by the respondent, whereas interviewer-completed questionnaires are administered by the interviewer, who asks the questions, provides the response sets and records the respondent's answers.

Surveys that use self-completion questionnaires engage the participant in responding to and recording responses on the questionnaire. Self-completion questionnaires are used in a variety ways to collect tourism data. For example, immigration departments require residents and non-residents to complete departure and arrival cards. These cards are short question-naires that simultaneously enable the government to keep track of resident and non-resident movements and collect travel data such as length of trip, purpose of trip, port of arrival and port of departure (see figure 8.2). The Industry Insight on page 236 provides an example of a self-completion questionnaire that organisers of special events might use to determine the economic impact of their event within the local area.

Self-completion questionnaires require minimal administration as the participant does most of the work associated with the questionnaire (i.e. reading and responding). Self-completion questionnaires may be distrib-uted to possible respondents or left in a prominent position for completion. The latter option has a lower response rate than the former as there is no personal contact between the researcher and the participant to ensure the return of the completed questionnaire.

■ **Figure 8.2**
Australian outgoing passenger card

Outgoing passenger card • Australia

PLEASE ✗ AND ANSWER **D** OR **E** OR **F**

PLEASE COMPLETE IN ENGLISH
Family/surname

Given names

Passport number

Flight number or name of ship

Country where you will get off this flight

What is your usual occupation?

◆ Nationality as shown on passport

Date of birth   Day   Month   Year

D Visitor or temporary entrant departing
▸ City or State where you spent most time

E Australian resident departing temporarily
▸ In which State do you live?   NSW   Vic   Qld   SA   WA   Tas   NT   ACT   Other
▸ Intended length of stay overseas   Years   Months   Days   OR
▸ Country where you will spend most time abroad
▸ Main reason for overseas travel (✗ one only):
Convention/conference 1   Employment 5
Business 2   Education 6
Visiting friends or relatives 3   Exhibition 7
Holiday 4   Other 8

F Australian resident departing permanently
▸ In which State did you live?   NSW   Vic   Qld   SA   WA   Tas   NT   ACT   Other
▸ What is your country of future residence?

DECLARATION *The information I have given is true, correct and complete.*
YOUR SIGNATURE   Day   Month   Year

TURN OVER THE CARD
English

Are you taking out of Australia AUD$10,000 or more in Australian or foreign currency equivalent?   Yes   No

MAKE SURE YOU HAVE COMPLETED BOTH SIDES OF THIS CARD. PRESENT THIS CARD, ON DEPARTURE WITH YOUR BOARDING PASS AND PASSPORT.

Information sought on this form is required to administer immigration, customs, quarantine, statistical, health, wildlife and currency laws of Australia and its collection is authorised by legislation. It will be disclosed only to agencies administering these areas and those entitled to receive it under Australian law. The leaflet *Safeguarding your personal information* is available at Australian ports and airports.

© Commonwealth of Australia 2000
16 (Design date 11/00)

Source: *Commonwealth of Australia (1998)*

Advantages and disadvantages

As you would expect, there are some similarities between self-completion questionnaires and mail surveys, as well as household self-completion surveys (such as the national census).

Advantages

The advantages of self-completion questionnaires include:

- the participant can complete the questionnaire at their own pace
- if left with the respondent, the questionnaire can be completed at a time convenient to the respondent.

Disadvantages

The disadvantages of self-completion questionnaires include:

- the researcher can never be sure that the targeted person has responded to the questionnaire, unless the researcher has personally handed the questionnaire to the respondent and waited for its completion
- the respondent is unable to seek clarification unless the researcher is present
- the respondent may not understand the language of the questionnaire, resulting in a partially completed or non-completed questionnaire
- lower response rates result if the researcher is not present or a suitable time is not arranged for collection of the completed questionnaire.

Organisers of special events often conduct surveys, particularly self-completion questionnaires, to determine the economic impact of a special event within the local area. An example of such a survey is presented in Figure 8.3. This survey was developed by Ian McDonnell, Johnny Allen and William O'Toole (1999) based on guidelines produced by the National Centre for Culture and Recreation Statistics, Australian Bureau of Statistics in 1997.

[FESTIVAL NAME] VISITORS' SURVEY

The organising committee of the [festival name] is conducting this survey to obtain information on the economic importance of the festival.

Information supplied in this survey will be treated confidentially and the results will be presented only in the form of aggregated data.

You may find it easier to complete this questionnaire at the end of your visit to the festival. However, you may wish to complete this questionnaire during your visit. If so, and you are uncertain of the answer to any question, please give what you consider to be your most likely response.

Thank you for your cooperation.

How to complete this questionnaire:

Answer questions by ticking the appropriate box or by writing in the answer.

Please add any comments you feel are necessary to clarify any of your answers.

Do not complete this questionnaire if you are under 15 years of age.

1. Are you: Male? ☐ Female? ☐
2. What is your age?   Under 15 years (*no more questions*) ☐
   15–24 ☐   25–44 ☐   45–64 ☐   65 or more ☐
3. How many [festival name] performances and events did you attend?
   Number ☐
4. Where do you usually live?
   [Study area] (*no more questions*) ☐
   Elsewhere in Australia ☐   Overseas ☐
5. How many nights did you stay in [study area]?   Nights ☐
6. Would you have come to [study area] this year had the [festival name] not been held?
   Yes ☐   No (*go to question 10*) ☐

7. Was your visit to [study area] during the festival an additional visit especially for the festival?

Yes (*go to question 10*) ☐   No ☐

8. Did you stay longer in [study area] on this visit because of the festival?

Yes ☐   No (*no more questions*) ☐

9. How many more nights did you stay?   Nights ☐

10. *This question is about your estimated expenditure in [study area] during your entire visit.*

Please include all spending made by you and all members of your family (if another member of your family receives a questionnaire, you should still include their expenditure on your questionnaire).

Remember to include payments made by cheque, bankcard and credit cards.

On your visit, how much did you (and your partner/family) spend in [study area] on:

Accommodation? ☐   Meals, food and drink? ☐

Festival tickets? ☐

Other entertainment costs (e.g. nightclubs, movies, museums)? ☐

Transport (e.g. taxi fares, petrol, car hire)? ☐

Personal services (e.g. hairdressing, laundry, medical)? ☐

Other expenditure (e.g. films, souvenirs, books, cigarettes)? ☐

Total expenditure ☐

11. How many people does this expenditure cover?

Number of adults ☐   Number of children ☐

If you require any assistance with this questionnaire, please see one of the interviewers who handed it out. Please hand the completed questionnaire back to the interviewer or post it back in the reply paid envelope supplied. Thank you for your assistance.

■ **Figure 8.3** *Example of a self-completion questionnaire*
Source: *McDonnell, Allen & O'Toole (1999, pp. 282–3)*

■ *8.4.4* **Interviewer-completed** *questionnaires*

Interviewer-completed questionnaires (or face-to-face interviews) can be from half an hour in duration or up to 10 pages of questions. Interviewer-completed questionnaires are akin to structured interviews mentioned in chapter 6. As a consequence, the interviews are rigid in the order of question framing and in the choice of question responses. Questions are generally closed questions to remove any researcher bias.

Interviewer-completed questionnaires can also be subdivided into intercept surveys and household interviews. Within tourism studies, there are essentially two types of intercept surveys: en-route surveys and on-site surveys (see discussion later in the chapter). The term 'intercept' is used since the respondent is 'intercepted' in the course of an activity (Frey 1989) — in this case either travelling to or from a destination or several destinations or while on-site at a destination. Interviewer-completed questionnaires may also be used during house-to-house surveys (household interviews). Interviewer-completed surveys engage the respondent in answering questions posed orally by the interviewer. The respondent does not have to write anything down — this task is completed by the interviewer.

Advantages and disadvantages

The advantages and disadvantages of interviewer-completed surveys are similar to those of telephone surveys.

Advantages

Advantages include:
- the respondent does not have to write anything, so the research is less intrusive than a mail survey or a self-completion survey
- show cards and visual images can be used
- face-to-face interaction can contribute to increased participation
- face-to-face interaction achieves a higher response rate than mail or telephone surveys
- clarification may be sought by the respondent regarding language problems or terms used
- probes may be used by the interviewer to extend responses
- both open-ended and closed questions may be asked
- longer surveys can be used because of the personal engagement between the respondent and the interviewer
- face-to-face interviews allow observations to be included in data collection
- the questionnaire is presented and collected at the same time, so no follow-up is required.

Disadvantages

The disadvantages of interviewer-completed questionnaires include:
- the costs of employing interviewers and training interviewers as well as supervisors can drain the research project budget
- the travel costs associated with transporting the interviewers to the interview sites can also inflate project costs depending on the transportation used and the distance travelled
- the costs associated with supervisors checking the quality of the interview techniques compounds the overall research project budget
- the presence of an interviewer can introduce interviewer bias based on the interviewer's appearance, mannerisms, tone of voice or language used
- respondents may query anonymity or confidentiality claims given that the interviewer is face-to-face with the respondent
- respondents may not find the interception by the interviewer convenient
- if interviewer-completed questionnaires are conducted when a respondent is en-route, this restricts or eliminates call-back at a more convenient time.

■ 8.4.5 **Other** *types of surveys*

This section briefly examines four other types of surveys: on-site surveys, en-route surveys, household surveys and omnibus surveys. Intercept surveys are conducted while the respondent is in the process of engaging in some activity. The two types of intercept survey used in tourism research are on-site surveys and en-route surveys. Intercept surveys use either interviewer-completed questionnaires or self-completion questionnaires. Household surveys occur at the residence of the respondent. Omnibus surveys are conducted through household surveys either using face-to face surveys or telephone surveys.

On-site surveys

Veal (1992, p. 114) suggests that on-site surveys are the most used form of survey in tourism. On-site surveys may be either self-completed or interviewer-completed. The advantages and disadvantages of on-site surveys reflect the advantages and disadvantages discussed above for self-completion questionnaires and interviewer-completed questionnaires. You may recall from chapter 4 that research ethics were discussed and it is useful for researchers to be mindful that on-site surveys may be considered by some potential respondents to be the complete antithesis of the travel experience. In short, as researchers, we have to be able to accept rejections and/or negative responses to our requests for tourists and travellers' participation in our research projects.

En-route surveys

En-route surveys are conducted during the travel experience, primarily the travel-to phase or the return travel phase. These surveys enable trends in travel markets to be kept up-to-date (Hurst 1994). En-route surveys have been used by airlines for some forty years. They are cost-effective, but they do not achieve a census. The process involves selecting a place and time, such as international airports every five years, as well as the schedules, outward-bound passengers, days and times. Finally, consideration is given to the characteristics of the passengers who are to participate — selection may be by gender, age and/or family life cycle. There are a number of issues associated with en-route surveys, and these relate to questionnaire and interview methods. Sampling is also an issue in regard to probability or non-probability samples (refer back to chapter 5 for the advantages and disadvantages of sampling and a discussion of the various sampling methods), as are responses rates and bias. Sometimes, incentives are used to increase the response rate.

Household surveys

Household surveys involve the use of interviewer-completed questionnaires or the delivery and collection of self-completion questionnaires. Data collected in this fashion are not collected during a travel experience since the respondents are at home (although the respondents could be on holidays and staying at home). Household surveys usually collect data regarding attitudes and opinions about travel and tourism products and developments. They also facilitate the monitoring of changes in socioeconomic profiles and travel and tourism trends and patterns. The advantages and disadvantages of household surveys are the same as for interviewer-completed and self-completion questionnaires. There is also an issue with respondents' sharpness of memory and powers of recollection that can add a biasing factor to the data collected. For example, asking a person to recall how much money was spent on accommodation or entertainment while on holidays 10 months ago may be problematic unless the person maintained a diary or kept records of expenditure.

Omnibus surveys

Omnibus surveys may be interviewer-completed or self-completion questionnaires, although they are generally interviewer-completed. Omnibus surveys consist of a set of demographic questionnaires and sets of questions generated by a number of organisations, businesses, agencies or researchers. Omnibus surveys share the cost of implementation between the various contributors to the question sets. They are a means to enable large-scale studies to be completed by clustering a number of questions that are non-related into the one questionnaire design. The sharing of costs for the survey implementation enables each contributor to achieve greater geographical distribution or larger representative sample sizes.

■ 8.4.6 e-questionnaires

In the late twentieth century, the use of electronic communication increased, as did the use of IT by the general public and the private sector. E-commerce, e-travel, e-business and e-marketing are all examples of how IT has and is changing the social, economic and business environments and the way of doing business and transactions. e-questionnaires are a more recent way of collecting data using surveys, in this case questionnaires. e-questionnaires are similar to mail surveys as there is no direct interaction between the researcher and the respondent. However, undernets and real time chat channels can be used to conduct more interactive and open-ended 'interviews', as well as focused group discussions. Furthermore, bulletin boards can be used to study a group with similar interests.

Advantages and disadvantages

The main advantages of e-questionnaires are the scope and speed of contact. The major limitation is the extent to which the population being studied uses IT.

Advantages

The key advantages relate to:

- the ease of conduct of an e-questionnaire (questionnaires can be linked to data analysis programs, as is the case with computer-assisted telephone interviews; however, e-questionnaires do not require the data recording to be completed by an operator — the respondent does that)
- the cost of conduct is minimal
- the speed of data collection is faster than mail, telephone or intercept surveys
- the typing speeds of participants when using real-time keyboard-to-keyboard data collection via chat channels (alternatively, typing speed can slow the interaction and data collection process)
- transmission speeds and quality when using face-to-face data collection via the use of you-see-me–I-see-you connectors (alternatively, if transmission speeds and quality are poor, this will slow the data collection process).

Disadvantages

The main disadvantages are:

- the possibility of data corruption via virus transmission
- the possibility of bogus replies as a result of computer hacking activities
- the possible unreliability of e-lists
- having to gain access to some e-lists via a gatekeeper.

To reiterate, with the improvements in IT, e-questionnaires are becoming an increasingly used tool for tourism research across a variety of sectors.

■ 8.4.7 Comparison *of survey methods*

When a researcher has determined that a quantitative methodology will inform the research process, the researcher has to choose the appropriate method. If the method is a survey, then an overall comparison between surveys is a useful process in which the researcher should engage. In this section, two tables are presented to assist in the comparative process.

Table 8.1, developed by James Frey (1989), compares the differences between administration, sampling and data quality associated with mail, face-to-face, intercept and telephone surveys. While the table is a number of years old, the material is still relevant and does consider the choice of survey method in relation to the overall research process and the decisions a researcher has to make.

Table 8.2, constructed by Frazer and Lawley (2000), includes a comparison of mail, face-to-face, telephone and Internet questionnaires. This table does not present as many criteria as table 8.1, since it focuses only on communication methods.

■ Table 8.1
Comparing four types of survey methods

FACTOR	MAIL	FACE-TO-FACE	INTERCEPT	TELEPHONE
ADMINISTRATION				
1. Cost	1	4	2	2
2. Personnel requirements: interviewers	n.a.	4	4	3
3. Personnel requirements: supervision	2	3	3	4
4. Time for implementation	4	4	1	1
SAMPLE				
5. Sample coverage	3	1	4	1
6. Response rate — general public	4	2	2	2
7. Refusal rate	unknown	3	3	3
8. Non-contact/non-accessibility	2	3	1	2
9. Ability to obtain from elite population	4	1	unknown	2
10. Respondent within household	4	1	n.a.	1
11. Sampling special subpopulation	4	2	4	2
DATA QUALITY				
12. Interview control	n.a.	3	3	1
(a) Control consultation	4	1	2	1
13. Obtaining socially desirable responses	1	4	2	3
14. Item non-response	3	2	2	3
15. Impact of questionnaire length on response	3	1	4	2
16. Confidentiality	4	4	2	3
17. Ability to ask sensitive questions	2	1	3	2
18. Ask complex questions	3	1	2	3
(a) Ability to clarify	4	1	1	2
(b) Use of visual aids	3	1	4	4
19. Use of open-ended questions.	4	1	3	2
(a) Ability to probe	4	1	1	2

Key: 1: = major advantage; 2 = minor advantage; 3 = minor disadvantage; 4 = major disadvantage; n.a. = not applicable.

Source: *Frey (1989, p. 76)*

CRITERIA	MAIL QUESTIONNAIRE	PERSONALLY ADMINISTERED QUESTIONNAIRE	TELEPHONE QUESTIONNAIRE	INTERNET QUESTIONNAIRE
Cost	Low	High	Moderate	Very low
Speed of data collection	Slow	Immediate	Immediate	Fast
Ability to reach geographically dispersed segments	High	Very low	Medium	Very high
Length of questionnaire	Long (4–12 pages)	Long (30–60 minutes)	Medium (10–30 minutes)	Long (4–12 pages)
Questionnaire complexity	Simple only	Simple to complex	Simple only	Simple only
Question complexity	Simple to moderate	Simple to complex	Simple only	Simple to moderate
Hard-to-recall data obtainable	Good	Poor	Moderate	Good
Respondent anonymity	Possible	Not possible	Not possible	Possible
Rapport with respondents	None	High	Moderate	None
Interviewer bias	None	High	Medium	None
Need for interviewer supervision	No	Yes	Yes	No
Response rate	Low	Very high	Moderate	Moderate

Source: *Frazer & Lawley (2000, p. 3)*

■ *8.4.8* **Advantages and disadvantages** *of surveys*

The preceding sections have independently and comparatively considered mail, telephone, self-completion and interviewer-completed questionnaires, en-route, on-site, household and omnibus surveys, and e-questionnaires. To finalise the focus on the various types of surveys that may be used in tourism and hospitality research, the overall advantages and disadvantages of surveys are now considered.

Advantages

According to Sarantakos (1998, pp. 224–5):

- surveys are less expensive than semi-structured or in-depth interviews
- survey data can be collected and processed quickly
- surveys contain uniformity as the same questions are asked and the same responses are provided
- surveys maintain an objective epistemological position
- surveys enable a wider geographical distribution than semi-structured or in-depth interviewing for a lower cost.

Disadvantages

There are a number of disadvantages with surveys that have not been noted already in the preceding subsections:

- closed response sets restrict answers by participants (Killion 1998)
- in-depth data are not gathered (Sarantakos 1998)
- survey responses are essentially a passive activity for respondents that do not require in-depth thought (Killion 1998, Sarantakos 1998)
- surveys may create attitudes where none had previously existed (Killion 1998)
- surveys may create expectations regarding research outcomes (Killion 1998)
- surveys are an intrusive form of data collection (Killion 1998)
- lack of reciprocity, that is unmet promises and inappropriate usage of data, may effect future participation if statements regarding reciprocity are not fulfilled.

8.5 QUESTIONNAIRE CONSTRUCTION

Once the decision regarding type of survey has been made, researchers need to turn their attention to the construction of the interviewer-completed or self-completion questionnaire itself. The construction of a questionnaire is paramount to the success of data collection and analysis. In designing your questionnaire, you need to consider what data you need to collect to effectively fulfil your aims or to test your hypothesis/hypotheses. A hypothesis is 'a predicted answer to a research question' (Punch 1998, p. 39). If you are testing a hypothesis, there will be at least two variables — an independent variable and a dependent variable. In fact, '[t]he language of quantitative research is a language of variables and relationships among variables' (Neuman 2000, p. 126). The independent variable is sometimes referred to as the causal variable (Neuman 2000) or change variable (Kumar 1996). The dependent variable is also referred to as the outcome variable (Kumar 1996). There are other variables, such as extraneous variables (variables that influence the degree of impact of the independent variable on the dependent variable) and intervening variables (variables that need to be present for the independent variable to influence the dependent variable).

Hypotheses in quantitative research can be described as causal hypotheses (Neuman 2000) that state a tentative relationship between variables or research hypotheses (Kumar 1996) that are the focus of your research. Or they may be alternative or null hypotheses, which state the opposite of the causal or research hypotheses. The following example demonstrates these terms for tourism.

Causal or research hypothesis: a decrease in airfares on major domestic sector routes will result in an increase in air ticket purchases for those routes.

The causal variable, change variable or independent variable is: a decrease in airfares on major domestic sector routes

The outcome variable or dependent variable is: an increase in air ticket purchases for those routes

Alternate hypothesis/null hypothesis: there will be no difference in air ticket purchases due to decreases in airfares on major domestic sector routes.

In constructing surveys, first you need to be cognisant of your aims or hypotheses, and then you need to consider the variables you are attempting to study. For example, in descriptive surveys, researchers are testing descriptive hypotheses (Sarantakos 1998, p. 134). Thus, in descriptive surveys, you want to determine the 'who', 'what' and 'how'. In an earlier discussion, age, gender, destination and reason for travel were mentioned — these are key 'variables' in descriptive quantitative research. In explanatory surveys, researchers are testing relational hypotheses (Sarantakos 1998, p. 134) and consideration of independent, dependent, extraneous and intervening variables needs to be undertaken by the researcher.

Essentially, in quantitative research, the researcher attempts to either accept (support, confirm) or reject (not support, not confirm) hypotheses. There is never an ultimate proof (Neuman 2000, p. 129). Hypotheses are accepted or rejected depending on the levels of significance and consideration of Type I or Type II errors (Burns 1997, pp. 107–111). Acceptance or rejection of hypotheses is examined in chapter 9. The remainder of this section focuses specifically on the construction of survey questions.

David de Vaus (1995) has provided a checklist to assist with question wording. Table 8.3 has been constructed based on de Vaus' checklist items. The first column identifies the check item, the second provides a poor example regarding the check item and the third provides an improved example. You should be able to provide a further improvement to the examples in the third column. In addition to considering these 12 questions during question construction, researchers also need to be aware that some questionnaire designs and layouts can induce a 'response set'.

CHECK ITEM	POOR EXAMPLE	IMPROVED EXAMPLE
1. Simple language used	What is your usual mode of transportation that you utilise to reach Fishing Island?	How do you get to Fishing Island?
2. Possible question shortening	Have you been in a situation when you have missed a plane connection?	Have you ever missed a plane connection?
3. Single-focused rather than multiple-focused questions used	In the last 12 months, how often have you visited friends and relatives?	In the last 12 months, how often have you visited friends? In the last 12 months, how often have you visited relatives?
4. Non-leading questions used	Do you think recreational fishing should be allowed at Fishing Island when fishing stocks are declining?	Should recreational fishing be allowed at Fishing Island?
5. Use of 'negatives' (no, not or dis- words) is free from confusion	Sex tourism should not be allowed. Agree or disagree	Sex tourism should be illegal. Agree or disagree
6. Filter question used to determine knowledge base	Do you agree or disagree with the environmental management charge policy?	Are you aware of the environmental management charge? Yes or no If yes, then ask: Do you agree or disagree with the environmental management charge policy? If no, go to Question . . .
7. Definitions provided when necessary	Are you a local?	Do you live within a 40-km radius of the post office?
8. Questions free from ambiguity	Do you agree that resort guests should not not be allowed to swim in the same area as the guests using windsurfers and sailing boats? (This question uses a double negative (should not not) and is multiple in focus, as well as being long.)	Swimming should be allowed in the same area as windsurfing. Agree or disagree Swimming should be allowed in the same area as sailing boats. Agree or disagree

CHECK ITEM	POOR EXAMPLE	IMPROVED EXAMPLE
9. Indirect approach used for sensitive questions	When you are on holidays, how much alcohol do you consume per day?	Please indicate which of the following responses noted on this card matches your alcohol consumption when you are on holidays. Or Some people consume more alcohol on holidays than they normally do at home. Is this also true for you? (If quantities of alcohol consumption are required, there would be a follow-on question.)
10. Temporal frames provided where necessary	How many overnight business trips do you go on?	How many overnight business trips did you go on in the last month?
11. Allowance made for an unframed opinion	What is your opinion to increasing charter flights to Darwin? Agree or disagree	What is your opinion to increasing charter flights to Darwin? Agree, no opinion or (undecided), disagree
12. Categories used to diminish detailed responses	What is your age? ___ years ___ months	What is your age? [ ] 14–17 [ ] 18–24 [ ] 25–39 [ ] 40–54 [ ] 55–69 [ ] 70 and over

■ 8.5.1 Response *sets*

Some survey questions may produce response sets (de Vaus 1995, p. 86). Response sets may be either 'acquiescent response sets', in which the survey respondent agrees regardless of the question, or 'socially desirable response sets', in which the respondent alters their responses to fit what they deem to be socially desirable. For example, the question regarding alcohol consumption in table 8.3 may not be truthfully answered by some respondents — someone who overconsumes may report a lesser amount and a non-drinker may actually report alcohol consumption.

The term 'response set' has an additional meaning. Sarantakos (1998, p. 233) uses the term 'response set' to describe the alternatives provided to respondents when completing a questionnaire. Response sets for questions should be:
• exhaustive
• mutually exclusive
• unidimensional.

'Exhaustive response sets' enable all possible responses by a participant to be recorded. This is achieved by the use of 'Other' as a category. Some researchers request respondents to specify the other category in order to determine whether an additional category or categories should be assigned during the analysis phase. 'Mutually exclusive sets' mean that a respondent can only record an answer in one category. For example, the following sets of categories used to determine annual income levels of tourists are problematic:

```
[ ] Under $10 000
[ ] $10 000–$15 000
[ ] $15 000–$20 000
[ ] $20 000–$30 000
[ ] $30 000–$40 000
[ ] $50 000–$60 000
[ ] Over $60 000
```

The categories are problematic for two reasons. First, the categories are not mutually exclusive in all cases. If you earn $15 000, in which category do you record your income? $10 000–$15 000? Or $15 000–$20 000? Second, given the improved standard of living of many countries or regions, the categories mean that further segmentation of the upper income levels cannot be undertaken — for example, ranges between $60 000 and $900 000 are amassed together.

'Unidimensional response sets' mean that only one dimension or concept is being measured in a question. For example, asking guests to rate their satisfaction levels in regard to housekeeping service should use only one dimension, such as very satisfied to very dissatisfied. The following set of scale categories is not appropriate:

Very satisfied Satisfied Undecided Unacceptable Very unacceptable

The scale uses two concepts — satisfaction and acceptability. Both mean different things and are not comparable measures. Another example drawn from the hospitality industry asks the client to evaluate their experience:

Overall, I thought the service from the staff was:
Excellent ☐   Average ☐   Good ☐   Poor ☐

What is your first impression of the scale used? Are you able to distinguish between average and good? Why or why not? Essentially, average and good are used synonymously, so why include two measures that determine the same measurement?

This discussion has indirectly introduced some of the response sets researchers may use in questionnaire construction. The following section discusses in more detail the various response sets a researcher may use in survey designs.

◼ 8.5.2 **Survey** *response sets*

The most commonly used response sets in tourism and hospitality are checklists, ranking scales, Likert scales, semantic differential scales, Thurstone and Guttman scales, scenarios and open-ended questions.

Checklists

Checklists enable researchers to present a number of categories from which a respondent can select either an unlimited or a limited number of relevant categories. For example, a researcher may be interested in determining the various types of information sources accessed by a tourist to select a particular destination as a holiday choice. The researcher might then construct the following checklist:

Question 10 How did you find out about this attraction? (You may tick more than one answer)
(a) Personal knowledge .... ( )
(b) Relatives .... ( )
(c) Friends .... ( )
(d) Newspapers .... ( )
(e) Tourist brochures .... ( )
(f) Travel agent .... ( )
(g) Televisions ads .... ( )
(h) Radio programs .... ( )
(i) Radio ads .... ( )
(j) Other _____

Ranking scales

Ranking scales ask respondents to rank an entire list or to select and rank a limited number from a list. The following example drawn from Brokensha and Gulberg (1992) asks respondents to rank the five most-enjoyed aspects of a destination:

Question 15 Please identify the top five aspects you most enjoyed at this destination.
(Use each of the numerals 1, 2, 3, 4 and 5 only once. 1 indicates the most-enjoyed aspect and 5 indicates the fifth most-enjoyed aspect.)
Aspects most enjoyed:
(a) People .... ( )
(b) Climate .... ( )
(c) Scenery .... ( )
(d) Wildlife .... ( )
(e) Open spaces .... ( )
(f) Beaches .... ( )
(g) Lifestyles .... ( )
(h) Safe to travel .... ( )

Likert scales

In 1932, Likert developed a rating scale to measure attitudes. The construction of Likert scales involves the generation of a number of items related to a research topic — for example, items related to the social impact of a casino development in a coastal town. Initially, a large number of items are generated in relation to the topic. Statements using those items are then prepared with a five-point response set using, for example, strongly agree, agree, undecided, disagree, strongly disagree. A pilot test of the statements is then constructed to determine their unidimensionality and their internal consistency (Sarantakos 1998). Those statements with unidimensionality and internal consistency are used in the construction of the questionnaire. The following Industry Insight demonstrates the use of a Likert scale.

INDUSTRY INSIGHT

Faulkner and Tideswell (1997) used Likert scales in a study designed to determine resident reactions to tourism on the Gold Coast. A five-point scale ranging from very strongly agree to very strongly disagree was used.

DIMENSIONS	PERCEPTIONS POSITIVE STATEMENTS	1 = Very strongly agree; 5 = Very strongly disagree.				
Economic and employment impacts	Tourism brings important economic benefits to the region	1	2	3	4	5
	Tourism creates employment oppportunities in the Gold Coast region	1	2	3	4	5
Sociocultural impacts	I like to see/meet visitors to the Gold Coast	1	2	3	4	5
	Visitors to the Gold Coast enrich culture of this area	1	2	3	4	5
	Tourism has increased the pride of local residents in their city	1	2	3	4	5
	Tourism has made the Gold Coast a more interesting and exciting place in which to live	1	2	3	4	5
Environment	Tourism has made residents and local public authorities more conscious of the need to maintain and improve the apperance of the area	1	2	3	4	5
	The development of tourism facilities has generally improved the appearance of the area	1	2	3	4	5
	Tourism has contributed to the conservation of our natural assets	1	2	3	4	5

PERCEPTIONS ——————————— DIMENSIONS POSITIVE STATEMENTS	1 = Very strongly agree; 5 = Very strongly disagree.				
Accessibility and quality of life In general, tourism development brings facilities to the region that improve the quality of life of its residents	1	2	3	4	5
Tourism has resulted in a greater range of outdoor and indoor recreational facilities being available to Gold Coast residents	1	2	3	4	5
Tourism has resulted in a greater range of outdoor and indoor recreational facilities being available to Gold Coast residents	1	2	3	4	5
Tourism has resulted in a better standard of services being provided by shops, restaurants and other areas of commerce	1	2	3	4	5
Tourism has resulted in Gold Coast residents having a greater range of choice with regard to shopping facilities, restaurants, etc.	1	2	3	4	5
Public funding and future development The use of public funds for tourism promotion and infrastructure development is justified by the benefits this brings to the community	1	2	3	4	5
Further tourism development is beneficial to the community and should be encouraged	1	2	3	4	5

Semantic differential scales

Semantic differential scales were designed by Osgood, Suci and Tannenbaum (1957). These scales may be used to determine independent and comparative measures of concepts. The scale itself is made up of two opposites. For example, the researcher might ask tourists to locate themselves between the opposites displayed below in relation to the type of holiday desired.

```
active        6  5  4  3  2  1  0   passive
educational   6  5  4  3  2  1  0   non-educational
flexible      6  5  4  3  2  1  0   rigid
guided        6  5  4  3  2  1  0   non-guided
etc.
```

Thurstone and Guttman scales

Other scales that may be used in questionnaire construction are Thurstone scales and Guttman scales. Thurstone scales are used to measure attitudes; however, the scale is dependent upon experts for its construction. Thurstone scales are time-consuming and demanding in judging items relevant for inclusion (Babbie 1990). Guttman scales measure social distance, particularly how close a respondent will allow another type of person to be to them (Sarantakos 1998).

Scenarios

Scenarios or vignettes are used to standardise a context, so that respondents will be prevented from saying their answer depends on whether they have enough money, or whether they have two weeks or three weeks holidays. For example, a scenario or vignette might be:

You are on an income of $30 000 per annum. You are single, you own your own home, you have no credit card debts, and have been granted four weeks paid holiday leave two months from now. Which of the following destinations would you choose?
(a) Thailand   (c) Italy
(b) Japan   (d) United States of America

Open-ended questions

The above response sets are described as closed, because the answers have been predetermined. Another type of question is the open-ended question, and it is posed with space on the questionnaire or sufficient time for the respondent to reply. The open-ended question might be analysed using content analysis procedures described in chapter 3, or the responses might be reduced to categories and numerically coded and analysed. An example of an open-ended question is:

Why did you choose to come to this destination for your holiday?

_____

_____

A closed question that aims to determine the same information posed in the above open-ended question is shown in the following Industry Insight.

INDUSTRY INSIGHT

The Domestic Tourism Monitor uses the following closed question:
Q5 (a) Can you tell me from this card (SHOWCARD 3) the main reason for your trip to (MAIN DESTINATION)?
Q5 (b) Still looking at the card (SHOWCARD 3), what other reasons were there for this trip?
    (i)   Pleasure holiday
    (ii) Visiting friends/relatives
    (iii) Personal reasons
    (iv) Conference/seminar
    (v) Business
    (vi) Working holiday
    (vii) Education/School excursion
    (viii) Other reasons (SPECIFY) _____
    (ix) None/no other

Source: *Bureau of Tourism Research (1996, p. 17)*

8.5.3 Levels *of measurement*

Closed-ended questions are measured at different levels: nominal, ordinal, interval and ratio levels. The nominal measure is associated with the use of words or nouns to classify response sets (nominal measures were presented in the checklist on page 249 and in the Industry Insight opposite). Nominal measures usually include the use of 'other' to ensure all categories have been included.

Ordinal measures classify response sets into groups and then order those groups from the lowest to the highest. The sociodemographic categories of age and income are examples of ordinal measures. Again, the Domestic Tourism Monitor provides examples of these categories:

Age: 14–17, 18–24, 25–39, 40–54, 55 and over.
Income: under $10 000, $10 000–$15 000, $15 000–$20 000,
$20 000–$30 000, $30 000–$40 000, more than $40 000.

You might consider the mutual exclusivity issues with these income categories.

Interval measures are a further development of the ordinal measure. Interval measures contain equal separations between categories, such as 0–15 years, 16–30 years, 31–45 years and 46–60 years. Each category has an interval of 15 years separating the upper and lower limits. Interval measures are also used with calendar time, such as days, weeks and months, distance travelled and duration of stay.

Ratio measures have classificatory categories based on ascending or descending rank order, equal interval spaces and the addition of a zero point as the lowest unit. Interval measures do not necessarily commence at zero (Kumar 1996). Ratio measures are used with demographic variables such as age or income levels or number of people in a travel group.

8.5.4 Pilot *studies*

Pilot studies were discussed in chapter 5. The use of pilot studies is important in both qualitative and quantitative research. Pilot studies enable the researcher to determine that the categories provided for questions are valid and reliable measures, the terms are understandable, the question order flows and how long the tool takes, as well as the suitability of the measures for analysis. Pilot studies should be conducted with respondents who reflect the characteristics of the sample. However, pilot study results are not incorporated into the analysis. Most pilot studies should involve at least 50 participants in order to determine the effectiveness of the tool and its implementation, as well as its analytical capability. Also be aware that the effectiveness of the survey will play a part in the survey response rate.

8.5.5 Response *rates*

Survey response rates reflect how well the researcher was able to achieve responses from all possible participants in a sample (Kviz 1977). There are two ways to determine the response rate for a survey, and both result in response rates being expressed as a percentage. The first method (formula

A) determines the response rate by dividing the number of completed surveys by the number of participants in the sample. The formula is expressed as:

$$\text{Formula A} = \frac{\text{Number of completed surveys}}{\text{Number in sample}} \times 100$$

The second method (formula B) divides the number of completed surveys by the number of participants in the sample who were successfully contacted and either fully completed, partially completed or refused to complete the survey. The formula is expressed as:

$$\text{Formula B} = \frac{\text{Number of completed surveys}}{\text{Number in sample} - (\text{non-contactables})} \times 100$$

Depending on which formula is used, the researcher may provide two images of the survey response rate. For example, the researcher may send out 1200 mail questionnaires, but may receive back 100 with incorrect postal addresses, 100 incomplete questionnaires and 50 refusals to participate, as well as 400 non-returns (and the 100 incorrect addresses and 400 non-returns make 500 non-contactables). Therefore, from the original 1200 questionnaires mailed out, only 550 fully completed and returned questionnaires are obtained. Using formula A, the response rate is 45.8% $\left[\frac{550}{1200} \times 100 \right]$, whereas using formula B, the response rate is 78.6% $\left[\frac{550}{(1200 - 500)} \times 100 = \frac{550}{700} \times 100 \right]$. Thus, formula B provides a better picture regarding response rates.

Researchers often do not indicate which formula they have used (Frey 1989, p. 50), although they should, so that a clear and accurate picture may be presented regarding their findings. According to Frey (1989), the best response rates for telephone and face-to-face surveys using formula B are 70–75%; if formula A is used, then the best response rates are considered to be 40–50%. The best response rates for a mail survey are 25–30% when no reminder cards are used, and up to 50% when two or more reminder cards are used (Frey 1989). Response rates are discussed here rather than in chapter 9 on quantitative analysis because response rates can influence the researcher's choice of the survey method to be used.

8.6 OTHER QUANTITATIVE METHODS

As noted in chapter 6, some qualitative methods have a quantitative equivalent, such as observation, longitudinal studies, case studies, the Delphic method, the documentary or archival method and experimental and quasi-experimental methods. Each of these is briefly discussed on the following pages before describing forecasting and impact assessments.

■ *8.6.1* **Observation**

In chapter 6, various types of participant observation roles were introduced. When the researcher uses a quantitative methodology, observation is classified as the complete observer (Junker 1960), the total researcher (Gans 1982) or as having adopted a peripheral membership (Adler & Adler 1983) role. These are the etic roles within participant observation. Observations can be conducted mechanically by using turnstile counters or infrared beams to count numbers, as well as by using information technology linked to video cameras to observe behaviours.

Observation can also be conducted without participants' knowledge. Here, the researcher must gain ethical clearance from an auspicating body and have good reasons for using such a method. This type of observation is considered non-intrusive (although an extreme invasion of privacy), but this depends on the skill of the observer in ensuring that the observees are not aware that they are being observed. As an example, assume that a park agency wants to determine the effectiveness of interpretive signage in the park area. Ethical approval is granted to monitor the number of park visitors who read the interpretive signs in the park area and to determine how long the park visitors spend reading each of the interpretive signs. To inform park visitors of the study's purpose might inflate the number of people who read or appear to read the signs — it may actually set up a 'socially desirable response set' in the park visitors.

Novice researchers sometimes indicate in their research design that they are going to observe visitor attitudes, satisfaction levels and opinions. In preparing such research designs, researchers need to be especially careful in indicating that they are using etically-based observations to determine attitudes, satisfaction levels and opinions. Essentially, it is almost impossible to determine attitudes, satisfaction levels and opinions without asking some questions to triangulate the data. For example, just because someone is smiling does not mean that person is happy with the current experience — the person could be masking anger, ridiculing someone or something, putting on a socially accepted 'face' or remembering another experience that made them happy. Without talking to the person, there is no way to confirm the person is happy with the current experience and is therefore satisfied.

■ *8.6.2* **Longitudinal** *studies*

As noted in chapter 6, longitudinal studies can be described as panel studies, time series studies, trend studies and cohort analysis studies, as well as case studies. Longitudinal studies may also constitute a mix of these types. Each type can be informed by a quantitative methodology (or a qualitative methodology, see chapter 6). Participants can be selected using probability sampling techniques, causal relationships can be tested, objective respondent–researcher relationships can be maintained and data can be reduced to numerical representations and analysed statistically. Moreover, longitudinal studies can be designed to include etically oriented observations, questionnaires or structured interviews, archival research or experimental or quasi-experimental methods. As each of these methods has already been or will be discussed independently in this chapter, they will not be repeated here. The advantages and disadvantages of longitudinal studies within a quantitative methodology are similar to some of the advantages and disadvantages of qualitative longitudinal studies. Advantages include:

• one group or a similar group is studied over time
• profiles are developed
• relationships between changing sociodemographics and changing travel and tourism patterns and trends can be examined.
The disadvantages include:
• maintaining participation over time
• the need for constant record keeping
• the use of incentives to maintain participation may bias data.
The key differences between the two approaches (quantitative and qualitative) to the conduct of longitudinal studies relate to the overall differences in the paradigms that inform each methodology (see chapter 5).

■ 8.6.3 Case *studies*

As mentioned in chapter 6, case studies may be explanatory, single, multiple, intrinsic, instrumental or collective. As a method of quantitative methodology, case studies involve the use of archival research, questionnaires or structured interviews, observation and/or experimental or quasi-experimental methods. The main difference between quantitative and qualitative case studies is founded in the approaches to data collection and analysis. Quantitative case studies gather data in numerical forms and statistically analyse the data, whereas qualitative case studies gather data in thematic or ideographic forms and analyse the data without reducing them to numerical representations — thick descriptions are used.

The main advantages of quantitative case studies are:
• data are collected using several data sources
• probability sampling and/or statistical tests can achieve a representative picture
• a detailed picture is amassed about one or several cases
• data are collected objectively
• comparisons can be made
• studies can be repeated.
The main disadvantages are:
• findings are reduced to numerical representation and lack in-depth or thick descriptions
• studies may be resource intensive.

■ 8.6.4 The Delphic *method*

The Delphic method was introduced in chapter 6. By using the tenets of a hypothetico-deductive paradigm, the Delphic method can be informed by a quantitative methodology. Essentially, the Delphic method gathers data from experts, usually about future patterns. This can be achieved by using structured interviews or questionnaires. The data are gathered and analysed statistically and the various stages of the Delphic method are repeated until consensus is achieved. Figure 8.4 outlines such a method using a step-by-step approach, from identification of events to be studied, to data collection, analysis and findings. The graph in the figure demonstrates the findings of a Delphic process. The temporal representation is overlaid with medians and interquartile ranges (these are introduced in chapter 9).

STEP	PROCEDURE	
Identify relevant events	Determine events from theoretical models, futures scenarios or literature. Panel members may also suggest events.	
Prepare event statements	Statements must be clear and precise.	
Select and establish panel of experts	Select panellists from area of expertise suggested by the problem — expertise based on contributions to the literature and peer recognition.	
Mail Delphi questionnaire	Questions asked of panel members.	Summary information sent to panel members.
Round 1 questionnaire	Assign probabilities and dates to events. Add events to list. Solicit information on ambiguous statements.	Edit event statements. Prepare response summary distributions showing individual responses.
Round 2 questionnaire	Ask individuals to re-evaluate their round-1 responses based on summary distributions. Ask panellists to provide reasons for changing or not changing their responses if they remain outside interquartile range.	Prepare interquartile response summaries for round-2 questionnaire. Edit reasons given by those outside interquartile range.
Round 3 questionnaire	Ask individuals to evaluate their round-2 responses based on summary information. Ask panellists to provide reasons for changing or not changing their responses if they remain outside interquartile range.	Prepare summaries of interquartile distribution of round-3 questionnaire responses. Edit reasons given by those outside interquartile range.

(*continued*)

STEP	PROCEDURE
Round 4 questionnaire	Give individuals final chance to re-evaluate their round-3 responses based on summary information. Ask panellists to rate their expertise, evaluate desirability of each event, evaluate interactions between events and evaluate social impact of each event.
Other rounds	Questionnaires should continue until a consensus prediction begins to emerge.
Data analysis	Prepare event summaries showing event distribution, probabilities, impacts, desirabilities and interactions. Use median prediction as most probable year of event occurrence. Prepare summaries of interquartile distributions. Prepare futures scenarios.

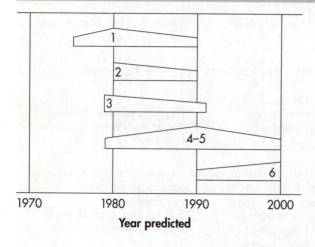

Key to events

1. Different recreation activities allocated specific time periods for the same recreation-management area.
2. Computers used to advise recreationists where to go for recreation.
3. Tax credits to industries that practise pollution control.
4. Consumers accept major cost of pollution control.
5. Most homes have videotape systems.
6. Seven hundred and fifty kilometres is a reasonable one-way distance to travel for a weekend.

■ **Figure 8.4** *The Delphic method*
Source: *Moeller & Shafer (1994)*

■ 8.6.5 **Documentary** *or archival method*

The investigation of documents, artefacts, archival materials and various media is another method that is used by quantitative researchers to obtain data regarding tourism phenomena. Chapter 3 noted that documentary or archival research could be conducted using either a quantitative or qualitative approach. Look again at chapter 3, especially the section on quantitative content analysis, which details the use of frequency, direction, intensity and space when analysing data, and Sarantakos' (1998) stages of documentary research. Crandell (1994) also provides a four-step process for documentary research:

- identify the research questions
- determine the relevant documents, archives and media
- classify items into various categories
- note the frequency of occurrence of categories/variables.

However, this process only measures frequency, and researchers also need to consider direction, intensity and space. The advantages and disadvantages of the documentary method are detailed in chapter 3.

■ 8.6.6 **Experimental** *and quasi-experimental methods*

Various disciplines and sub-disciplines associated with tourism use experimental and quasi-experimental methods to understand travel and tourism phenomena. The following section looks at forecasting and impact assessment, both of which use experimental or quasi-experimental methods. In the forecasting section, examples of statistical and mathematical models are noted with regard to economic aspects of tourism. Social and environmental impacts can similarly be studied using experimental and quasi-experimental methods. The experimental method can be outlined using Kumar's (1996) classifications:

- the after-only method (the study population is studied after an 'intervention' has occurred)
- the pre- and post-test method (the study population is studied prior to and after an 'intervention' has occurred)
- the control method (the population is studied using two similar groups: one group is engaged with the experimental 'intervention' and the other, the control group, is not — the results are then compared)
- the double control method (two control groups are used instead of only one, as in the above method: one is observed prior to the intervention and the other is not — two groups are used to determine if any extraneous variables are operating)
- the comparative method (different strategies or degrees of intervention are used on the study population)
- the matched control experimental method (two groups are identified and individuals in each group are matched with an individual in the other group — as the two groups should be 'identical' in composition, a random determination is then made of which group will be the control group and which the experimental group)
- the placebo method (three groups are determined — an experimental group, a placebo group and a control group — the placebo group believes it is receiving the 'intervention' when in fact it is not).

Marketing also uses a number of these experimental study designs to test and evaluate products and marketing strategies.

The term quasi-experimental is used to describe experiments that vary the classical experimental method which uses pre-tests, post-tests, control groups and random sampling (Neuman 2000). For example, a researcher might not include a pre-test.

■ 8.7.1 Forecasting

Forecasting can be short (up to two years), medium (two to five years) or long term (five to 15 years) (Mill & Morrison 1998). Beyond 15 years, the term 'futurism' is applied (Mill & Morrison 1998). Forecasting involves the use of prediction. The quality of the predictions is dependent on the skill and expertise of those who have constructed or applied the mechanisms for making the predictions (Mill & Morrison 1992). Essentially, forecasting can be conducted using mathematical formulae, statistical methods or expert guesstimates (Mill & Morrison 1992). In particular, formulae or statistical methods are used to determine or evaluate economic feasibility and impacts of various projects. According to Mill and Morrison (1992), a variety of methods are available to researchers:

- Linear, exponential and cyclical methods — these involve the use of extending statistical series to determine short-term forecasts.
- The covariation method — this method is applied when no model exists for a destination on which to make projections. The researcher determines short- and medium-term forecasts based on relationships between variables through consideration of degrees of magnitude or statistical series. Basically, an increase in the magnitude of one variable should result in an increase in the other, and the same variation should occur with decreases.
- The correlation method — this method is used only when experience and reasoning suggest it is appropriate. Correlation is used for short- to long-term forecasts. Variables with relationships may vary similarly or contrarily.
- The summation method — summation involves the weighting of factors and is used for short- to medium-term forecasts. This method is only as good as the individual making the weightings.
- The testing method — this method is not a fully mathematical method. It is an experimental method that attempts to determine a market section that changes ahead of other market sections. The method is used for medium- to long-term forecasts.
- Calculation methods — these methods are generally used to determine short- to medium-term forecasts. There are a variety of methods such as calculation by indices, sales potential, unit sales, elasticity coefficient and models.
- Guesstimates — these may be either individual or group based. The latter use either committees or Delphic panels and can be either short-term or futurism focused.

8.7.2 **Social** *and environmental impact assessments*

Both social and environmental impact assessments can be determined using a quantitative methodology. The chief methods of data collection include observation, surveys, longitudinal studies, case studies, the Delphic method, the documentary or archival method, forecasting and experimental and quasi-experimental methods. The advantages and disadvantages of each of these methods have been discussed elsewhere in the chapter, but it useful to note here the advantages and disadvantages of the overriding methodology. The advantages of a quantitative methodology are associated with: hypotheses or causal relationships that are determined in regard to impacts; the objective nature of the data collection and analysis; and the findings being generalisable based on random sampling techniques and/or statistical tests. The disadvantages are associated with the reductionist nature of the data and the objective relationship between the researcher and the subjects, and the world.

8.7.3 **Nominal** *group technique*

The nominal group technique is used for planning, impact assessment and problem solving (Ritchie 1994, pp. 493–4). The technique involves three phases:
* identification of the problem(s)/issue(s)
* identification of strategies to address the problem(s)/issue(s)
* monitoring of the strategies and recommendations.
  Following are the specific steps of the nominal group technique.
* The issue/problem is selected for study.
* Relevant stakeholders are brought together at a single location.
* The issue/problem is presented to the stakeholders by a moderator.
* The moderator facilitates clarification regarding the issue.
* Individual stakeholders brainstorm data relevant to the issue.
* Stakeholder responses are recorded and displayed clearly. Responses are recorded in a 'round robin' fashion until all responses are exhausted.
* Additional items can be added as result of discussions relating to clarifications after all responses have been recorded.
* After all ideas are posted and clarified, duplications are eliminated.
* All ideas are coded to assist in the selection of the most important ideas.
* Individuals select their choice of the top 10 ideas from all the ideas that are displayed.
* The moderator undertakes the pooling of rankings and the aggregation of rankings.
* The 10 key ideas are identified and at subsequent meetings strategies and monitoring techniques are determined.

The advantages of the nominal group method include: it is a systematic approach; all relevant ideas are listed; and it is possible to gain individual and aggregated measures of ideas. The disadvantages include the fact that a trained facilitator is required to keep the group focused.

8.8 OVERLAPS BETWEEN QUANTITATIVE AND QUALITATIVE METHODS

As has been discussed previously, there are some 'overlaps' in methods of data collection. Observation, interviewing, longitudinal studies, case studies, the Delphic method and archival or documentary research can be used with either a quantitative or qualitative methodological framework. The distinguishing feature that determines whether a case study is quantitative or qualitative is founded in the paradigm that informs the methodology and the inherent ontological, epistemological and methodological perspectives of those governing paradigms. Furthermore, a researcher may choose to mix methods. The choice of methodology and methods is directly linked to the aims, objectives and hypotheses of the research project. A researcher should choose the methodology and the methods based on their appropriateness for the research purpose, rather than debating which methodology is the better methodological position.

8.9 SUMMARY

Ways positivist and post-positivist paradigms inform both a quantitative methodology and quantitative methods

Positivism and post-positivism can be clustered as the hypothetico-deductive paradigm. These paradigms focus on causal relationships, an objective epistemology, an etic perspective, a systematic research design, random sampling, numerical data collection and analysis, statistical representation, and reports written in the third person using the passive voice that are generalisable to the wider population. The main methods of data collection are surveys (questionnaires and structured interviews), longitudinal studies, case studies, the documentary method, modelling, observation and impact assessment methods.

The different types of surveys from which a researcher may choose

Researchers can choose from either written surveys (questionnaires) or oral surveys (interviews) to gather data. Surveys include mail, telephone, intercept (either on-site or en-route), household and omnibus, and e-questionnaires.

The difference between surveys and questionnaires

Surveys collect data through the use of interviews and questionnaires. Interviews gather data using oral communication techniques. Questionnaires gather data through written communication techniques. Interviews and questionnaires are forms of surveys and are not synonymous with surveys.

The nature of mail surveys

Mail surveys are self-completion questionnaires that enable the researcher to target a wide geographical area for a lesser cost than a household survey. Mail surveys involve the use of a covering letter, an ethics consent form, the questionnaire itself and a return envelope. To improve response rates at least two reminders should be used. Mail surveys achieve a response rate of 25–30% without reminders and more than 50% when several reminders are used (Frey 1989).

The advantages and disadvantages of telephone surveys

Telephone surveys, like mail surveys, enable researchers to target a wide geographical area for a fraction of the cost of household surveys. Telephone surveys are quicker than mail surveys with respect to successful calls as there is no time lag in receiving responses unless a call-back later is requested. Telephone surveys enable the interviewer to control the exchange (unless the respondent hangs up) and ensure that the person targeted answers the questions. The disadvantages of telephone surveys relate to call rates, and these can render them more expensive than mail surveys. As is the case with household surveys, interviewers require training and supervision, and this adds to the overall cost of the survey. Visual aids cannot be used, and call times can be intrusive, for example during weekday evenings when meals are being prepared.

The differences between self-completion and interviewer-completed questionnaires

Interviewer-completed questionnaires require the presence of an interviewer, whereas self-completion questionnaires do not. Response rates are lower for self-completion questionnaires compared with interviewer-completed questionnaires due to lack of face-to-face interaction during questionnaire completion. More visual inputs can be used with interviewer-completed questionnaires, such as show cards and visual images, as the interviewer only needs one set as opposed to multiple copies for each participant in self-completion questionnaires.

The main issues associated with en-route, on-site, household and omnibus surveys

En-route, on-site, household and omnibus surveys can use either self-completion or interviewer completed questionnaires. En-route and on-site surveys are intercept surveys and enable the researcher to gather data during the course of a person's travel experience. Household and omnibus surveys can be conducted by interviewers doorknocking or using telephone technology. Household and omnibus surveys gather data on respondents when the respondents are at home and are generally not involved in a travel experience (although the person could be holidaying at home at the time of the survey).

The main features of e-questionnaires

The increase in information technology capabilities and usage, as well as the increased usage of information technology as a means of exchange, has generated an innovation in questionnaire administration. Questionnaires are now being administered using e-technology. By accessing email lists, bulletin boards, user lists and Web sites, researchers can conduct surveys regionally, nationally and internationally for a much reduced cost when compared to mail, telephone and household surveys. e-questionnaires enable a single researcher to gather data on large samples. The administration of the questionnaire is essentially completed by the respondents and the responses can be linked directly to an analysis program. E-questionnaires greatly reduce personnel costs associated with other survey methods.

The key elements in constructing a questionnaire

Researchers should ensure that their questionnaire collects the data they require for their research purpose. The wording of the questions is important — researchers should use simple language; short, single-focused, non-leading, unambiguous questions; filter questions; definitions; temporal frames when appropriate; and categories. Responses sets should be exhaustive, mutually exclusive and unidimensional in nature. Response sets include the use of checklists, ranking scales, Likert scales, semantic differential scales and scenarios. Pilot studies should be used to ensure that the survey is well constructed.

Observation, longitudinal studies, case studies, the Delphic method, the documentary or archival method and experimental and quasi-experimental methods

While surveys are the most frequently used quantitative method, researchers should be aware that there are other methods of data collection such as observation, longitudinal studies, case studies, the Delphic method, the documentary method, and experimental and quasi-experimental methods. These have various advantages and disadvantages and researchers should consider their use in addition to surveys or in association with surveys and, of course, in conjunction with qualitative methods if mixed methods are being used. Observation enables researchers to determine tourist behaviour patterns such as routes taken around an aquarium or hands-on engagement with exhibits in a museum. Longitudinal studies enable researchers to gather quantitative data on travel and tourism patterns over time. Case studies use a variety of methods to gather detailed quantitative data on one or a number of cases. The Delphic method enables researchers to gather quantitative data from a panel of experts. The documentary method allows researchers to use content analysis to measure the frequency, direction, intensity and space of the concepts being studied. Experimental and quasi-experimental methods include the use of the after-only method, the pre- and post-test method, the control method, the double control method, the matched control experimental method and the placebo method.

The rudiments of forecasting, social and environmental impact assessments and the nominal group technique

Forecasting is described as either short, medium, long term or futuristic and is associated with using formulae or 'guesstimates' to determine future events (Mill & Morrison 1992). Statistical methods may be used to determine or evaluate the economic feasibility of various products, such as linear, exponential and cyclical extrapolation, covariance, correlation, summation methods, calculation methods using indices, sales potential, unit sales and elasticity coefficients, as well as models. Social and environmental impact assessments use observation, surveys, longitudinal studies, case studies, the document method or the experimental or quasi-experimental method to gather quantitative data. The nominal group technique uses group and individual brainstorming to identify a problem, generate strategies to rectify the problem and develop procedures to monitor the strategies.

The overlaps between quantitative and qualitative methods

A number of methods (observation, interviewing, longitudinal studies, case studies, the Delphic method and the documentary method) can be used in either a quantitative or qualitative methodological framework. The paradigms that inform the research process will determine the major difference in the application of the methods. The methodology should be chosen based on the best way to achieve the required data, rather than on which methodology is the best.

Questions

8.1 You are preparing to write a research proposal to conduct a large-scale regional survey of domestic tourism patterns. You have decided that the survey should be either a mail survey or a telephone survey, rather than a household survey or part of an omnibus survey. Assume that the budget for the entire research project will support either a mail survey or a telephone survey. Consider the advantages and disadvantages of each survey method and decide which method to use. Write a summary of 500 words, outlining which survey you would use and why.

8.2 What is your opinion regarding the suitability of the suggested telephone contact times noted in this chapter?

8.3 Under what circumstances do you consider that a self-completion questionnaire might turn into an interviewer-completed questionnaire?

8.4 Taking into consideration your own access to IT, describe the research design that you would use to conduct an e-questionnaire of your peers.

8.5 Write a 300-word summary of the main issues a researcher must check for when preparing a questionnaire.

8.6 In your opinion, what are the ethical issues associated with en-route, on-site, household and omnibus surveys?

8.7 You have been asked to conduct a study of the social impacts of a proposed tourism development in your local area as a case study. Outline the type of case study you would use, as well as the data collection methods, and comment on any other aspects of the overall research design that you think you should address, such as ethics, access, time lines and budget.

8.8 In your opinion, what are the advantages and disadvantages of forecasting methods?

8.9 Having considered both qualitative and quantitative research methods, what is your opinion regarding the mixing of methods?

Exercise 8.1

A local tourism association has called upon your expertise to review a questionnaire that a student volunteer has prepared for a family-run resort operating in the area. Consider the questionnaire below and note any aspects that require further attention by the student volunteer.

This is a research study into the facilities and services at the resort complex here. Your help is appreciated thanks a lot. Use ticks and crosses. Leave on your pillow when you've finished.

---

1. What is your sex?
    ( ) Woman   ( ) Male
2. Why is this resort your favourite holiday destination?
3. Who comes with you to the resort and why do they come with you?

- -

- -

4. How well does the service rate at the resort?

		Expectations		
Below		Met		Exceeded
( )	( )	( )	( )	( )

5. Where did you travelled from?
6. What is your income level?

Less than $20 000	( )
$20 000 to $30 000	( )
$30 000 to $40 000	( )
More than $40 000	( )

8. How would you rate the facilities at the destinatoin

	Excellent	Good	Satisfactory	Below Average	Poor
Swimming Pool	( )	( )	( )	( )	( )
Kid's club	( )	( )	( )	( )	( )
Restaurants	( )	( )	( )	( )	( )
Boutiques	( )	( )	( )	( )	( )
Bars	( )	( )	( )	( )	( )

9. How long are you staying?
(a) A few days   ( )
(b) Less than a week   ( )
(c) A week   ( )
(d) Less than two weeks ( )
10. Will you come back again? Yes ( )   No ( )   Undecided ( )
11. What was the best aspect of your stay at the resort?
12. Why was this the best aspect?

- -

- -

13. Any other comments?

Exercise 8.2

You have been asked by a national tourism organisation to prepare a set of 10 questions regarding cruise ship travel patterns by residents for inclusion in an omnibus survey of national households using stratified random sampling. You do not have to worry about including demographic questions, as these are already included in the study and do not count as part of your 10 questions. Prepare your 10 questions and response sets for discussion in tutorials.

RESEARCH PROJECT

Does your research project use a quantitative methodology or a qualitative methodology or a mixed method approach? If it is informed by a qualitative methodology, then assume you have been requested by your client to alter your methodology to use a mixed methods approach. Of the methods presented in this chapter, which would you use to complement your qualitative methodology and why? Furthermore, at what stage of the research process would you incorporate the quantitative method(s) you have just considered introducing? Write a one-page response to these questions.

If your project already uses a quantitative method, assume you have been granted additional funds to add another method to your data collection. Write a one-page summary outlining with method you would choose and why.

If your project is using a mixed method approach, assume that your client has requested that you only utilise a quantitative methodology because the time period for the research has been shortened. How will you amend your project design? Write a one-page response to this question.

REFERENCES

Adler, Patricia & Adler, Peter. 1983. 'Shifts and Oscillations in Deviant Careers: The Case of Upper-Level Drug Dealers and Smugglers'. *Social Problems*, vol. 31, pp. 195–207.

Babbie, Earl. 1995. *The Practice of Social Research*. Belmont: Wadsworth.

Brokensha, Peter & Gulberg, Hans. 1992. *Cultural Tourism in Australia*. Canberra: Australian Government Publishing Service.

Bureau of Tourism Research (BTR). 1996. Domestic Tourism Monitor, 1994–95. Canberra, p. 17.

Burns. Robert. 1997. *Introduction to Research Methods*. South Melbourne: Longman.

Crandell, L. 1994. 'The Social Impact of Tourism on Developing Regions and its Measurements'. In Ritchie, J. R. & Goeldner, C. R. (Eds) *Travel, Tourism and Hospitality Research: A Handbook for Researchers*. Second Edition. New York: John Wiley & Sons, pp. 413–23.

de Vaus, David A. 1995. *Surveys in Social Research.* Fourth Edition. Sydney: Allen & Unwin.

Frazer, Lorelle & Lawley, Meredith. 2000. *Questionnaire Design and Administration.* Brisbane: John Wiley & Sons.

Frey, James H. 1989. *Survey Research by Telephone.* Second Edition. Sage Library of Social Research, Volume 150. Newbury Park: Sage.

Gans, Herbert J. 1982. 'The Participant Observer as a Human Being: Observation on the Personal Aspects of Fieldwork.' In Burgess, Robert G. (Ed.) *Field Research: A Sourcebook and a Field Manual.* Boston, MA: George Allen & Unwin, pp. 53–61.

Hurst, F. 1994. 'Enroute Surveys'. In Ritchie, J. R. & Goeldner, C. R. (Eds) *Travel, Tourism and Hospitality Research: A Handbook for Researchers.* Second Edition. New York: John Wiley & Sons, pp. 453–71.

Jennings, Gayle. 1998. *Recreational Usage Patterns of Shoalwater Bay and Adjacent Waters.* Great Barrier Reef Marine Park Authority.

Junker, Buford H. 1960. *Fieldwork: An Introduction to the Social Sciences.* Chicago: University of Chicago Press.

Killion, G. L. 1998. *Research in Tourism.* Rockhampton: Central Queensland University.

Kumar, Ranjit. 1996. *Research Methodology: A Step-By-Step Guide for Beginners.* South Melbourne: Longman.

Kviz, F. J. 1977. 'Towards a Standard Definition Of Response Rate'. *Public Opinion Quarterly,* vol. 41, pp. 265–67.

Likert, R. A. 1932. 'A Technique of Measurement of Attitudes'. *Archives of Psychology,* vol. 140, pp. 44–53.

McDonnell, Ian, Allen, Johnny & O'Toole, William. 1999. *Festival and Special Event Management.* Brisbane: John Wiley & Sons.

Mill, Robert C. & Morrison, Alistair. 1992. *The Tourism System: An Introductory Text.* Second Edition. Englewood Cliffs, NJ: Prentice-Hall.

Mill, Robert C. & Morrison, Alistair. 1998. *The Tourism System: An Introductory Text.* Third Edition. Dubuque, Ia: Kendall/Hunt.

Moeller, G. H. & Shafer, E. L. 1994. 'The Delphi Technique: A Tool for Long-Range Travel and Tourism Planning'. In Ritchie, J. R. & Goeldner, C. R. (Eds) *Travel, Tourism and Hospitality Research: A Handbook for Researchers.* Second Edition. New York: John Wiley & Sons.

Neuman, W. L. 2000. *Social Research Methods: Qualitative and Quantitative Approaches.* Fourth Edition. Boston: Allyn & Bacon.

Osgood, C. E., Suci, G. J. & Tannenbaum, P. H. (Eds) 1957. *The Measurement of Meaning.* Urbana, Ill: University of Illinois Press.

Punch. Keith F. 1998. *Introduction to Social Research.* London: Sage.

Ritchie, J. R. & Goeldner, C. R. (Eds) *Travel, Tourism and Hospitality Research: A Handbook for Researchers. Second Edition.* New York: John Wiley & Sons.

Sarantakos, Sotirios. 1998. *Social Research.* Second Edition. Melbourne: Macmillan.

Ticehurst, Gregory W. & Veal, Anthony J. 1999. *Business Research Methods: A Managerial Approach.* Australia: Longman.

Veal, Anthony. 1992. *Research Methods for Leisure and Tourism: A Practical Guide.* Harlow: Longman.

Vigderhous, Gideon. 1981. 'Scheduling Phone Interviews: A Study of Seasonal Patterns'. *Public Opinion Quarterly,* vol. 18, pp. 210–12.

Warde, William D. 1986. *Problems with Telephone Surveys.* National Agricultural Statistics Services Staff Report. Department of Agriculture.

Weeks, Michael F., Jones, B. L., Folsom Jnr, R. E. & Benrud, C. H. 1980. 'Optimal Times to Contact Sample Households'. *Public Opinion Quarterly,* vol. 44, pp. 101–14.

Weeks, Michael F., Kulka, Richard A. & Pierson, Stephanie A. 1987. 'Optimal Call Scheduling for a Telephone Survey'. *Public Opinion Quarterly,* vol. 51, pp. 540–9.

FURTHER READING

Dillman, Donald A. 1978. *Mail and Telephone Surveys: The Total Design Method.* New York: John Wiley & Sons.

Foddy, William. 1993. *Constructing Questions for Interviews and Questionnaires.* Cambridge: Cambridge University Press.

Silverman, George. 1994. *Introduction to Telephone Focus Groups.* Market Navigation. http://www.mnav.com/phonefoc.htm, downloaded 22 April 1997.

Tilley, Andrew. 1999. *An Introduction to Research Methodology and Report Writing in Psychology.* Brisbane: Pineapple Press.

Williams, P. W. 1994. 'Frameworks for Assessing Tourism's Environmental Impacts'. In Ritchie, J. R. & Goeldner, C. R. (Eds) *Travel, Tourism and Hospitality Research: A Handbook for Researchers.* Second Edition. New York: John Wiley & Sons, pp. 425–36.

Quantitative methods
of data analysis

'The method of analysis adopted depends on the complexity of the research question. If it involves only one variable, select a method of analysis appropriate for univariate analysis. If the question involves two variables we will use a method designed for bivariate analysis and so on ... Within each level of analysis (univariate, bivariate, multivariate) there is a range of methods of analysis ... The choice between methods is determined in part by the level of measurement of the variables involved: some methods of analysis are appropriate only for variables measured at certain levels (e.g. interval). Having chosen an appropriate method of analysis, the choice of statistics to be used with that particular method is affected by the method of analysis itself and the level of measurement of the particular variables.'

(de Vaus 1995, pp.133–4)

LEARNING OBJECTIVES
After studying this chapter, you should be able to:

- prepare and code data ready for quantitative analysis
- understand the role of descriptive statistics in quantitative data analysis
- explain the procedures to establish measures of central tendency
- describe measures of association
- outline the key elements of inferential statistics
- display quantitative data analysis findings
- overview a range of computer programs available to quantitative researchers.

$\mathcal{I}$NTRODUCTION

In chapter 8, you were introduced to various quantitative methods of data collection such as observation, questionnaires (self-completion and interviewer-completed questionnaires and en-route, on-site, household and omnibus surveys), e-questionnaires, forecasting and impact assessment techniques. This chapter introduces ways to analyse the data collected by these methods. Table 7.1 presented an overview of the similarities and differences between qualitative and quantitative data analysis. You should review the table before continuing this chapter, so that you remain aware of the key distinctions between the two approaches to data analysis. Having re-read table 7.1, there are a number of key points that you should bear in mind as you progress through this chapter. The points are associated with the ontological and epistemological viewpoints of quantitative research and the consequent ramifications on quantitative data analysis. The key points are listed below. Quantitative data analysis:

- involves the use of numbers and statistical formulae
- is predicated to deduction
- tests hypotheses
- usually cannot be conducted until all the data have been collected; however, data entry may commence prior to the collection of all the data
- abstracts the real world into numerical and statistical representations
- involves inferences grounded in empirical numerical data
- clearly articulates the methods in the research reports
- involves comparisons between variables
- aims to be error-free (Neuman 2000, pp. 418–19).

This chapter describes in further detail the methods of analysis that are founded in these points as well as those described by de Vaus (1995) in the opening quote. You will be introduced to univariate analysis, bivariate analysis and multivariate analysis. You will also be familiarised with the conditions regarding the use of the various methods of analysis. These conditions are derived from the level of measurement of the variable(s) being investigated (nominal, ordinal, interval and ratio). You will also be introduced to additional methods of analysis not described by de Vaus but listed in the objectives for this chapter.

$\mathcal{P}$REPARING AND CODING THE DATA

Research projects are designed to collect data relevant to a specific research problem, issue, hypothesis/hypotheses or aim(s). As a result of quantitative data collection, you will have amassed several piles of individual data sets (completed questionnaires or interview response sheets) (Killion 1998). Individually, the raw data sets mean little for tourism decision making and need further attention in order to provide meaning to the aims or hypotheses of your research project. The individual data sets need to be aggregated. In particular, the data need to be organised, coded and entered into either a manually or computer-constructed aggregation or recording system. Such systems enable you to determine patterns in the data and to test relationships between variables. The patterns and the testing of data are usually represented numerically. These representations include tables and graphic forms.

The purpose of this chapter is to familiarise you with the main methods of data analysis in a quantitative paradigm that are associated with aggregation processes. These aggregation processes are linked to statistical analyses. It is important to note that the purpose of this chapter is not to make you a statistics expert. The breadth of information covered in this textbook is too wide to achieve such an end, especially when statistics textbooks, computer programs and courses proliferate in their own right to achieve such aims. Therefore, the aim of the chapter is to introduce you to descriptive statistics, which will enable you to 'describe numerical data' (Neuman 2000, p. 317). You will also be familiarised with inferential statistics (statistics that enable you to test hypotheses and determine the relevance of the findings from the study population to the wider population on the basis of probability sampling). However, prior to making statements about the sample population in relation to the wider population, the data must be coded, entered and cleaned. The following sections outline the procedures and reasons for these three activities.

■ 9.2.1 Coding *data*

Coding data involves three steps: the development of codes (which may occur prior to the data collection process and which may appear on data collection tools); data entry; and data cleaning. You will recall that qualitative data analysis also involves data coding and chapter 7 described a number of ways to code qualitative data (descriptive, interpretive and pattern-based codes, and open, axial and selective coding, for example). Refer back to chapter 7 if you need to refresh your memory.

Coding in quantitative analysis differs from qualitative coding in that the raw data (the information provided by the participants as responses) are turned into numerical representations so that statistical analyses can be conducted on the aggregated data. Figure 9.1 illustrates how raw data is translated into coded data. In this example, the questionnaire included sociodemographic questions, which were asked and answered using textual units (words). A code was developed for each of the response sets in the questionnaire, and numerical codes were assigned for each response. These responses were then turned into a series of numbers, ready to be entered into a computer software program for further statistical analysis once the entire set of raw data had been coded and entered. Statistical analysis is described later in the chapter.

■ **Figure 9.1**
*Example of
how to
translate
raw data
into coded
data*

(a) Questionnaire section commencing sociodemographics

The final part of the questionnaire asks you for some personal details so that characteristics of users from various locations may be determined.

14. What is your gender?
Woman ( )   Man ( )
15. What is your age?
(Please place a tick in the appropriate bracket.)

15–19..................( )	40–44..................( )	65–69..................( )
20–24..................( )	45–49..................( )	70–74..................( )
25–29..................( )	50–54..................( )	75–79..................( )
30–34..................( )	55–59..................( )	80–84..................( )
35–39..................( )	60–64..................( )	85+..................( )

(b) Code book section corresponding to sociodemographics (SPSS software used for data analysis)

14. What is your gender?
Woman ( )   Man ( )

	VAR	**COL(S)**	**CODE**
14	Gender	15	1 (Woman)
			2 (Man)
			9 (Missing)

15. What is your age?

15–19..................( )	40–44..................( )	65–69..................( )
20–24..................( )	45–49..................( )	70–74..................( )
25–29..................( )	50–54..................( )	75–79..................( )
30–34..................( )	55–59..................( )	80–84..................( )
35–39..................( )	60–64..................( )	85+..................( )

	VAR	**COL(S)**	**CODE**
15	Age	16–17	01 (15–19)
			02 (20–24)
			03 (25–29)
			04 (30–34)
			05 (35–39)
			06 (40–44)
			07 (45–49)
			08 (50–54)
			09 (55–59)
			10 (60–64)
			11 (65–69)
			12 (70–74)
			13 (75–79)
			14 (80–84)
			15 (85 + . . .)
			99 (Missing)

(c) Example of questionnaire data entered as coded responses

```
10199999999119999999901021011999991010119999906991999999
05999999999999999999912221112111222211212221112111222211 2
12121112111222211212221112111222211212221112111222211 2
04999999999999209020612299999999999999
```

Source: *Jennings (1998)*

When considering the coding of raw data, Kumar (1996, p. 203) outlines four steps in the coding process: code book preparation; code book checking; data coding; and finally data checking and cleaning. Each of these is discussed below.

Code book preparation

Code books are prepared when the data collection tool does not have codes already assigned on the tool (see figure 9.2, which shows an example of a pre-coded questionnaire). They are also used if raw data are not being directly entered using a scanner (see later in the chapter). Code books consist of a record of all the codes assigned to response set categories for each question in a survey. Figure 9.1 provides an example of an excerpt of a code book. Neuman (2000) suggests making a copy of the code book in case the original is misplaced. This ensures that you have a backup and do not have to commence the coding process all over again. Having copies of code books is especially important if more than one person is involved in data entry: the more people involved, the greater the possibility of materials being misplaced, unless there are very clear procedures in place that are followed prescriptively by all involved.

■ **Figure 9.2**
Example of a
pre-coded
questionnaire

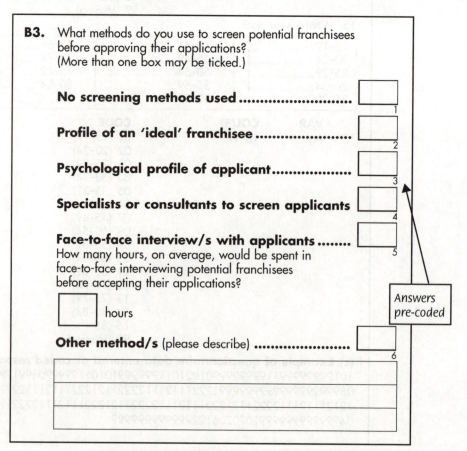

Source: *Frazer & Lawley (2000, p. 56)*

Checking the appropriateness of the code book

Before coding all the raw data, the researcher needs to ensure that the codes have been correctly assigned and that they work. Just as the researcher has to engage in pre-testing or running a pilot of their questionnaire or other data collection tool, so too do they have to undertake a check of the code book. This check is achieved by taking a sample of the questionnaires (or other data collection tool), then entering the responses using the codes in the code book. During this check, the researcher should ensure that there are no anomalies in the codes assigned to response sets, as well as ensuring that appropriate codes have been ascribed to any 'other' categories and open-ended questions.

Coding all the raw data

Once the code book has been checked for any anomalies, the researcher then proceeds to enter all the raw data based on the codes assigned for each set of responses.

Checking and cleaning the data

Coding data requires human involvement (unless raw data responses are scanned using computers; however, even then there can be errors, as discussed below). Humans can make errors no matter how careful they are. Checking and cleaning the data involves examining the coded data for any incorrectly assigned codes and correcting these errors by reviewing the original data.

■ *9.2.2* **Data** *entry*

As already noted above, there are a number of ways that data can be entered. The ease of data entry will depend on the researcher giving full consideration to the data analysis phase in the research design stage. It is possible, for example, to enter data immediately from the questionnaire if data codes are included in the questionnaire design. Otherwise, code books need to be prepared and data entry will require some cross-referencing between the questionnaire and the computer program by the data entry person (which also increases the chances of possible errors in data entry). Data can be entered using:

- transfer sheets
- edge-coding
- direct data entry
- direct data entry by interviewers
- scanners (Babbie 1995, pp. 369–72).

It can also be entered using spreadsheets, as well as being entered manually using pen and paper recording sheets. Each method is briefly overviewed prior to discussing the third phase of data coding, that is data cleaning.

Transfer sheets

Transfer sheets are linked to the use of data cards (Babbie 1995). Data cards use a system of hole-punching in same-sized cards to enable the researcher to determine patterns in data sets. The patterns are determined by pushing a rod (or series of rods) through the data card sets in order to determine which cards fit the pattern determined by the hole (a variable) or holes (variables) selected for examination by the researcher. Each hole is related to response sets associated with specific study variables being studied. After the rod or rods have been passed through the entire data card sets, the researcher is left with a number of cases associated with the pattern being studied (these are the ones now hanging from the rod or rods). Transfer sheets remove the need for the use of holes and rods, and replace them with columns and codes that are transferred to a computer program and subsequently read:

> The traditional method of data processing involves the coding of data and the transfer of code assignments to a transfer sheet or code sheet. Such sheets were traditionally ruled off in 80 columns, but they can be adapted to other data configurations appropriate to the data entry method ... Coders write numbers corresponding to the desired code in the appropriate columns of the sheets. The code sheets are then used for keying data into computer files (Babbie 1995, p. 369).

The use of transfer sheets takes some time, transferring data into codes and onto a transfer sheet and then entering the codes into a computer software program to statistically analyse the coded data. This involves three stages of data handling and the potential for coding errors increases with each stage of handling. That being said, Babbie (1995) suggests that this method is still useful for complex questionnaires. It might be argued, however, that given the recent developments in information technology, the use of transfer sheets for complex questionnaires is now redundant, unless of course there is some economic imperative (and/or lack of information technology skills) for not accessing such technology.

Edge-coding

Edge-coding involves designing a questionnaire with coding data along one side. Codes are recorded in spaces in the margin or in code boxes already organised in the questionnaire. The section of questionnaire shown in figure 9.3 has code boxes in the questionnaire and the margin is used to indicate to the coder into which column the data should be entered. Knowing which column specific data have to be entered into assists the process of data entry. It also assists in the data cleaning and checking processes, as errors in columns can be identified quickly. The appropriate question is determined and the coder returns to the original data to examine where the error occurred and subsequently makes the appropriate changes based on the original data.

6. ABOUT YOU

(a) Sex: Male   ☐ 1
                                           Female   ☐ 2   123

(b) Age at 30 April 2000:   ☐☐   124–5

                                           Years

(c) Place of permanent residence: in Australia   ☐ 1   126
                                   overseas   ☐ 2

                   If in Australia, postcode: ☐☐☐☐   127–30

          If overseas, country .... ☐☐ 132–33

(d) Where were you on 30 April 2000?
                                   in Australia   ☐ 1   134
                                   overseas   ☐ 2

(e) Would you describe yourself as having a disability?
                                   Yes, physical   ☐ 1
                                   Yes, sensory   ☐ 2   135
                                   Yes, other   ☐ 3
                                   No   ☐ 4

(f) Are you an Aborigine or Torres Strait Islander?
                                   Yes   ☐ 1   136
                                   No   ☐ 2

(g) Do you come from a non-English speaking background?
                                   Yes   ☐ 1   137
                                   No   ☐ 2

Source: *Murdoch University Graduate Destination Survey (April 2000)*

Direct data entry

Data entry can be expedited if the questionnaire is designed to enable direct data entry. In this case, there is no need for coders to transfer data onto code cards, transfer sheets or code sheets — the data are entered directly from the questionnaire response sheet into the computer program assigned for the analysis phase. Refer back to figure 9.2 for an example of this — as you can see, the responses are pre-coded to facilitate coding and entry by the researcher or research assistant.

Direct data entry by interviewers

Direct entry of data is generally associated with telephone interviewing and computer-assisted telephone interview (CATI) facilities. Direct coding is also possible through the use of computer-assisted personal interview (CAPI) technology. This technology allows direct entry by the interviewer as well as by respondents themselves. Use of CATI facilities is discussed in the following Industry Insight.

The Centre for Social Science Research (C4SSR), Rockhampton (Qld), has a Population Research Laboratory (PRL). This laboratory is solely organised around the conduct of social surveys. The laboratory uses computer-assisted telephone interview (CATI) and computer-assisted personal interview (CAPI) hardware and software. In 1999, the Centre for Social Science Research conducted the first Central Queensland Social Survey (CQSS), an omnibus survey. This survey of 1200 residents over the age of 16 living within a defined Central Queensland region focused on a number of issues, such as attitudes to local government, health, welfare, information technology and tourism. Using the CATI facilities of the PRL, the CQSS findings about the holiday patterns of Central Queensland residents included:

- 62% of residents had taken a holiday in the previous 12-month period
- the holidays were one or two weeks in duration
- the purpose of most holidays was for pleasure, followed by visiting friends and relatives
- two-thirds of the residents who had a holiday did so in the home state (Qld)

The CATI system enables the telephone interviewers to enter the data directly. In addition, the PRL has a scanner, which enables print-based questionnaire response sheets to be scanned in and then analysed by computer software. The laboratory also uses disk-by-mail DBM and Teleform methods. Once the laboratory has collected the data, it is cleaned by checking code entries.

CAPI technology is associated with hand-held computers, laptop computers and computer kiosks or stations. Of these three types of CAPI hardware, the first enables interviewers the most ease and mobility (and has the lowest cost). The recorders are usually palm-sized and enable researchers to directly record responses in the field and then download the data on return from the field into the base computer ready for analysis. In addition to a direct cable connection, all hand-held computers support connections to the base computer by wired, and in some case wireless, modem. Techneos Systems Inc. has developed Mobile CAPI (MCAPI) software for use on hand-held computers running the Palm® operating system. Figure 9.4 shows the Mobile Interviewer™ software. This product from Techneos is one of a number of MCAPI software programs available to researchers.

Interviewers can use laptop computers to enable direct data entry, but, although laptops are lighter than desktop computers, they are more cumbersome than hand-held computers and can limit the interviewer's mobility. However, laptops can be set up and secured at stations to enable the respondents to enter the data directly for the researcher. Consequently, direct data entry can be completed by respondents as well as interviewers. Usually, the programs are written to prevent respondents (and interviewers) from changing the set-up of the questionnaires — all the respondents (and inter-viewers) have to do is to record their responses. Direct data recording by respondents is also possible using computer kiosks and Internet Web sites. The following Industry Insight exemplifies the use of direct data entry by respondents through their personal computers.

■ **Figure 9.4**
Example of a hand-held computer

Source: *http://www.techneos.com/demo_mi.html*

INDUSTRY INSIGHT

The Travel and Tourism Research Association (TTRA) contracted Triton Tech-nology to conduct an after-event evaluation of the TTRA 2000 conference held in Burbank, California (USA). All TTRA members, whether they attended the conference or not, were sent an email requesting them to complete an e-questionnaire. Several reminders were sent to increase the response rate. The questionnaire was completed by the respondents and therefore employed a respondent-entered analysis procedure. After each TTRA member entered their responses, the program immediately updated the data findings to incorporate these responses.

Scanners

Scanners enable researchers to scan participants' response sheets directly into a computer system for subsequent analysis. The response sheet has to be designed so that scanning is possible and to enable direct coding and subsequent analysis by appropriate software programs. Scanning is faster than direct data entry by coders (i.e. human coders). Figure 9.5 on page 280 illustrates a questionnaire designed for scanning responses.

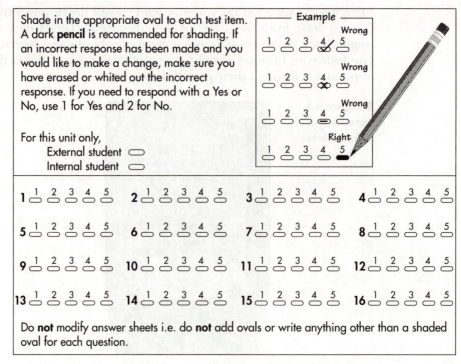

■ Figure 9.5
*Sample
questionnaire
designed for
scanning
responses*

Source: *University of Southern Queensland (1992)*

Manual entry and spreadsheets

Depending on your study, you may choose not to use code books or computer software to assist with your data analysis. You may decide this if your sample is small, and/or you only have a limited number of questions, and the purpose of your study is descriptive. However, such a decision would usually not be the case in most tourism studies. Should you decide that engaging in computer analysis is not warranted, you may choose to use manual coding and entry as a better alternative. In this case, you would enter data into tally sheets (see table 9.1), which would then be developed into frequency distribution reports.

■ Table 9.1
*Example of a
tally sheet*

WHAT IS THE PURPOSE OF YOUR VISIT?	TALLY	TOTAL
Pleasure		
Visiting friends		
Visiting relatives		
Business		
Conference/seminar		
Private reasons		
Other reasons		

The tally sheet in table 9.1 can easily be turned into a frequency distribution table and/or percentage table (described later in the chapter) once you have determined the total count for each category relating to purpose of visit. However, the use of percentages would be questionable here, as presumably the sample size is small since you have decided to proceed along this path. Without reference to the original sample size in the construction of frequency distribution and percentage tables, you may in fact end up presenting misleading information, especially if the information is taken out of context and the sample size is omitted. For example, you may have interviewed only 50 respondents when you know that more than 50 000 people were involved in the activity you were studying. Subsequently, if you find that 50% of your sample engaged in one aspect of the activity you were studying, your findings, if taken out of context by someone else, may be used to suggest that 50% of the entire population was also involved in that aspect of the activity. (Refer back to chapter 5 to re-examine probability sampling, sample sizes and confidence levels.) Care needs to be taken when presenting tables and figures related to your findings: you must ensure that all the information has been provided. The presentation of quantitative research findings is also discussed later in this chapter.

Alternatively, instead of using tally sheets, researchers may decide to use spreadsheet programs and construct formulae to calculate sums or averages of rows and/or columns. The formulae enable the data to be analysed as they are entered. Figure 9.6 shows a Claris spreadsheet and formulae used to determine the expenditure patterns of long-term ocean cruisers while in ports of call. In particular, the spreadsheet uses formulae to calculate sums (totals), average expenditure and annual budgetary expenditure. The latter two were determined using formulae associated with the columns.

	A	...	U	V	W	X	Y	...	DB
1	CRUISING	...	316	318	320	322	324	...	TOTAL
2	**Expenditure items**	...						...	
3	Meat, foodstuff	...	1 500	400	1 600	800	1 200	...	18 644
4	Alcohol (beer, wine, spirits)	...	250		500	400	200	...	4 885
5	Cigarettes and tobacco	...						...	40
6	Clothing and footwear	...			200	200	200	...	2 165
7	Perfumes, cosmetics, toiletries	...	20			20	50	...	610
8	Toys (inc. souvenirs)	...						...	240
9	Books	...		20		100	150	...	1 263
10	Photographic equipment and film	...		35		20	200	...	875
11	Paintings, carvings, sculptures	...						...	100
12	Hand-crafted goods	...		20				...	250
13	Jewellery and gems	...						...	0
14	Postal and telephone costs	...	60	30	100	100	500	...	1 830
15	Public and other transport	...		200	140	100	3 500	...	6 347
16	Accommodation (non-boat)	...					800	...	1 935
17	Travel and leisure pursuits	...	800			1 200	250	...	4 810
18	SUBTOTAL OF ABOVE	...	2 630	705	2 540	2 940	7 050	...	43 994
19		...						...	
20		...	...	...	...	...	...	...	...

■ **Figure 9.6** *Using a spreadsheet to analyse data*
Source: *Jennings (1999)*

■ *9.2.3* **Data** *cleaning*

Data cleaning involves two types of cleaning — possible-code cleaning and contingency cleaning (Babbie 1995). Cleaning data is necessary because of the fact that data entry involves humans and humans are prone to make errors despite their best intentions not to do so. Errors in data entry are associated with coders assigning the wrong codes and respondents making mistakes such as coding two responses instead of only one. Kumar (1996, p. 200) notes that 'even the best investigators can:
- forget to ask a question
- forget to record a response
- wrongly classify a response
- write only half a response or
- write illegibly.'

Similarly, respondents may miss a question, incorrectly respond to a question or respond illegibly making it difficult for the researcher to determine which response has been marked. The next sections look at how such errors can be corrected.

Code cleaning

As previously discussed, specific codes are assigned to various responses sets. Data entry requires the appropriate response set to be recorded with the appropriate code. However, some codes may be incorrectly assigned. To give an example, the following question is part of the Central Queensland Social Survey:

In the last 12 months, have you had a holiday?
1 Yes
2 No
3 Don't know
4 No response

The possible codes that can be used to enter the data for this question are 1, 2, 3 and 4 — the codes are listed down the left-hand side of the responses. When checking data entry, data cleaning is required if any other numeral appears in the code sheets, for example 5 or 6. There are no responses in the example associated with a code of 5 or 6, so if the researcher finds one of these numbers, they would need to revisit the original data if possible and correct the error. If the original data cannot be revisited, which may be the case if the data are recorded during a telephone interview or field interview where there is no opportunity for call-back, the data will be entered as missing.

Contingency cleaning

This type of cleaning relates to the recording of responses that do not follow 'if-then' scenarios (Babbie 1995). Babbie provides the example that an interviewee may be asked how many children they have given birth to. If any men have recorded a number of children, this indicates an error in entry. The 'if-then' scenario is 'if you are a woman, then you have the potential to give birth to a child'. This question could be included in a tourism study if family life cycle and life events are being studied in relation to opportunity to engage in travel. A specific tourism example is exemplified by the following case. A questionnaire asks residents to identify their income level and savings level, as well as their holiday spending. The data would require cleaning if a respondent indicates having spent more than $1500 on souvenirs when their income level and savings are both identified as nil or negative and the person has not been in receipt of a gift or windfall of money. The 'if-then' scenario is that 'if you have no income, no savings or gifts of money, then you will not be able to spend $1500 on souvenirs'. There has been an error in the data entry. Due care and attention are required in questionnaire design, data coding and data entry, for as Babbie (1995, p. 373) states: '"Dirty" data will almost always produce misleading research findings.'

9.3 ANALYSING THE DATA: DESCRIPTIVE AND INFERENTIAL STATISTICS

Having discussed the preparation and aggregation of raw data, this section introduces some of the methods of quantitative data analysis: descriptive statistics and inferential statistics.

Descriptive statistics enable researchers to describe the aggregation of raw data in numerical terms (Neuman 2000, p. 317). Descriptive statistics involve the use of univariate, bivariate and multivariate analysis. These methods of analysis incorporate the use of frequency distributions, percentage tables and measures of central tendency. They also incorporate the use of measures of variation, such as: ranges, percentiles and standard deviation for univariate analysis; cross-tabulation, scattergrams and measures of association such as chi-square, the phi coefficient, Spearman's rho and Pearson's r for bivariate analysis; and chi-square, analysis of variance and multiple regression analysis for multivariate analysis.

Inferential statistics involve consideration of statistical significance, levels of significance and Type I and Type II errors. Each of these is discussed below, along with the methods of displaying the results for each type of analysis.

9.4 DESCRIPTIVE STATISTICS: UNIVARIATE, BIVARIATE AND MULTIVARIATE ANALYSIS

When analysing data, researchers can choose from univariate (one variable), bivariate (two variables) and multivariate (more than two variables) analysis. The number of variables to be analysed at any time will relate back to the aims, objectives or hypotheses of the research project. For example, a research project that aims to describe the sociodemographic characteristics of daytrippers is likely to engage in univariate analysis, as the research is only aiming to describe the variables of age, gender, education, occupation, income, place of residency, and so on of the daytrippers. Alternatively, a research project that aims to determine the effect of age on destination selection will investigate the existence of any relationships between the two variables — age and destinations selected. And a research project that seeks to determine relationships between the sociodemographic characteristics of tourists and the prices of four destination packages will involve the researcher examining multiple variables — sociodemographics (age, gender, etc.), destination packages and the prices of those packages.

■ 9.4.1 Univariate *analysis*

Univariate analysis involves the analysis of one variable at one time. This is easily achieved by representing the frequency distribution associated with a variable. Frequency distributions can be developed using any of the methods of data entry and coding discussed previously in this chapter. Essentially, the frequency distribution portrays the number of responses associated with each of the categories in a response set. Frequency distributions can be used with variables measured at the nominal, ordinal and interval level. You may recall from chapter 5 that nominal levels are associated with categories that have names. Named categories include, for example, a respondent's gender, state of origin, country of origin, attractions visited, type of transport used and accommodation used. Ordinal levels refer to measurements based on ranking systems or the ordering of responses. Ordinal levels are used to identify tourists, customers or residents' attitudes, opinions and behaviours using measures such as very satisfied, satisfied, no opinion, dissatisfied and very dissatisfied. Interval levels use standard measures of units for responses, such as minutes, hours, kilometres, nautical miles and degrees Celsius or Fahrenheit. Such measures are standard because they have global uniformity. In tourism terms, for example, standard measures are used to measure the number of hours taken for a trip, the number of kilometres travelled or the distance in nautical miles to the next destination using water-based transport.

Frequency distributions are portrayed in one of two ways. The first is as a raw count frequency table and the second is as a percentage frequency distribution table. However, before providing you with an example of each table, it is useful to consider Sarantakos' (1998, p. 345) advice regarding table construction. Primarily, tables consist of five components: titles, headings, bodies, marginals and footnotes. When constructing tables, all five components need to be considered.

- *The title should be clear and unambiguously outline the contents of the table.* Tables should be able to stand alone away from any textual explanation and be meaningful in their own right. Therefore, the title should be sufficiently detailed to do this. Providing a title such as 'Number of visitors' does not do this, as it does not tell us, for example, where the visitors were visiting and when they were visiting. A better title would be 'The number of visitors to the Melbourne Botanical Gardens in January 2001'.

This title enables the table to stand apart from the surrounding text and have meaning in its own right.

- *Headings should be used to define the contents of rows and columns.* If headings are not included, readers are obliged to guess at the contents and this may result in them making incorrect conclusions.
- *The body of a table consists of cells that contain either raw count data or percentaged data.* The contents of cells need to be clearly identified in a sub-heading that indicates whether the reader is looking at raw count data or percentage frequency data. Alternatively, this information may be given in the headings ascribed to rows and/or columns.
- *Marginals provide the researcher with cell space in which to record the totals or sums of the rows and/or columns.* The use of marginals removes the need for subheadings or footnotes to inform readers that the contents of the table have been either row or column summed. If marginals are not used, the researcher needs to include subheadings or footnotes to provide this information.
- *Footnotes enable the researcher to add extra information that is important to the reading of the table and its contents.* Footnotes can provide information regarding missing data and descriptions of any 'other' category contents, as well as data sources.

Table 9.2 demonstrates the representation of raw count and percentage frequency distributions. Consider the five requisite components of a table described above as you review the table and its construction.

■ **Table 9.2**
Example of a raw count and percentage frequency distribution table

STATE	RAW COUNT FREQUENCY DISTRIBUTION FREQUENCY (IN '000S)	PERCENTAGE FREQUENCY DISTRIBUTION PERCENTAGE
New South Wales	5 156	36
Victoria	2 561	18
Queensland	3 089	21
South Australia	934	6
Western Australia	568	4
Tasmania	461	3
Northern Territory	309	2
Australian Capital Territory	1 337	9
Total number of trips	14 415	100

Note: Percentage column does not total 100 due to rounding.

Source: *Bureau of Tourism Research (1996, p. 21)*

In table 9.2, a statement regarding column summation was not made as the process is obvious due to the use of double lines to separate the summed cells from the other cells in the columns. It is also obvious because there is a category in the final row of column one indicating the fact that the columns have been summed (Total number of trips). The researcher could present the data from this table as a bar graph or a pie chart. Bar graphs portray each of the categories and their frequency using vertical bars that are separated to show there is no quantitative relationship between each of the measures (Sarantakos 1998). Pie charts enable representation of data to be proportionate to the size of the unit being measured (Sarantakos 1998).

Other methods of representing frequency distributions are polygons, histograms, cartographs and population pyramids. Polygons consist of dots joined by lines and are mostly used with interval data. Histograms are graphs with vertical bars adjoining each other. These can be made into a frequency polygon by joining the midpoints of the bars. Cartographs demonstrate frequencies on a map to visually identify the location and magnitude of the variable being represented (Sarantakos 1998). Population pyramids usually portray two variables (such as sex and age) in comparison to each other using horizontally positioned bars to represent the frequencies. Figure 9.7 shows an example of a bar graph, a pie chart, a polygon, a cartograph and a population pyramid.

Measures of central tendency

The central tendency of a frequency distribution refers to where the scores in the distribution tend to centre, cluster or congregate. There are several ways of measuring the central tendency of frequency distribution (e.g., mean, median and mode) (Tilley 1999, p. 99).

Having organised the coded data into frequency distributions, the researcher is able to comment further on the data by using measures of central tendency. Measures of central tendency are used to enable researchers to report on the results (in this case frequency distributions) as one number. The measures of central tendency — mode, median and mean — are associated with specific levels of measurement. For example, the mode is used with nominal, ordinal and interval levels of measurement. The median is used with levels of measurement that are measured at the ordinal, interval and ratio level but not at the nominal level. The mean is calculated for interval and ratio levels only. Each of these measures of central tendency is described in more detail below.

Mode

The mode of a distribution is the category with the most frequently occurring results. An example will help demonstrate this. Consider the following raw data regarding the type of transport used by domestic travellers to travel to a specific destination, say for our purposes Adelaide. In this hypothetical example, the sample size is extremely small purely for demonstration purposes. The following raw data list represents the types of transport used to travel to Adelaide by the hypothetical study group: plane, private car, bus, train, plane, bus, private car, private car. The mode is the most frequently occurring category, and you should be able to determine this simply by 'eyeballing' (Neuman 2000, p. 317) the list.

However, in most data analysis, the data are too large in number to be 'eyeballed', and need to be aggregated into frequency or percentage distribution tables to identify the mode. If we aggregate our hypothetical data,

(a) A bar graph

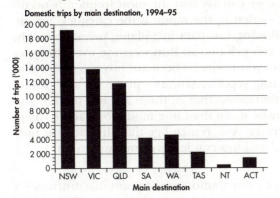

Domestic trips by main destination, 1994–95

Number of trips ('000), y-axis from 0 to 20 000. Main destination (x-axis): NSW, VIC, QLD, SA, WA, TAS, NT, ACT

(b) A pie chart

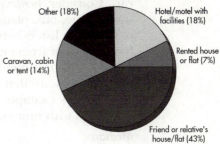

Total visitor nights by type of accommodation used, 1994–95

- Other (18%)
- Hotel/motel with facilities (18%)
- Rented house or flat (7%)
- Friend or relative's house/flat (43%)
- Caravan, cabin or tent (14%)

(c) A polygon

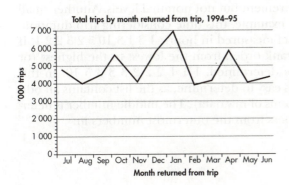

Total trips by month returned from trip, 1994–95

'000 trips, y-axis from 0 to 7 000. Month returned from trip (x-axis): Jul, Aug, Sep, Oct, Nov, Dec, Jan, Feb, Mar, Apr, May, Jun

(d) A cartograph

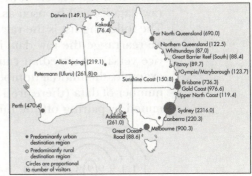

Top 20 destination regions in Australia for inbound visitors, 1996

- Darwin (149.1)
- Kakadu (76.4)
- Far North Queensland (690.0)
- Northern Queensland (122.5)
- Whitsundays (87.0)
- Great Barrier Reef (South) (88.4)
- Fitzroy (89.7)
- Gympie/Maryborough (123.7)
- Alice Springs (219.1)
- Petermann (Uluru) (261.8)
- Sunshine Coast (150.8)
- Brisbane (736.3)
- Gold Coast (976.6)
- Upper North Coast (119.4)
- Perth (470.4)
- Sydney (2316.0)
- Adelaide (261.0)
- Canberra (220.3)
- Great Ocean Road (88.6)
- Melbourne (900.3)
- Predominantly urban destination region
- Predominantly rural destination region
- Circles are proportional to number of visitors

(e) A population pyramid

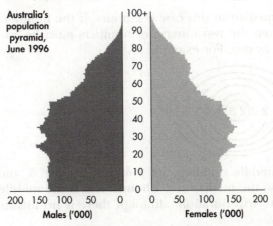

Australia's population pyramid, June 1996

Age axis from 0 to 100+. Males ('000) from 200 to 0; Females ('000) from 0 to 200.

■ **Figure 9.7** *Example of a bar graph, a pie chart, a polygon, a cartograph and a population pyramid*

Source: *BTR (1996, pp. 2, 7, 11); Weaver & Oppermann (2000, pp. 78, 122)*

we get the following frequencies: plane (2), private car (3), bus (2) and train (1). Having aggregated the data, we can say that the most frequently occurring category is the private car — that is, the mode is the category 'private car'. Consider, however, the following raw data list: plane, private car, bus, train, plane, bus, plane, private car, private car. Run your eye over the types of transport listed here. What do you notice? There are two categories that have the most frequently occurring representations – plane (3) and private car (3). This is a bimodal distribution — that is, there are two modes. You need to be aware that there may be more than one mode for a set of categories, as this example demonstrates. Also remember that the mode is only associated with nominal, ordinal and interval levels of measurement.

Median

The median is the middle score of a distribution or the point in a distribution that is identified as having half the cases below it and half above it. The median can be determined in two ways: by organising the raw data into rank order or by using a bar graph. Remember that the median is associated with ordinal, interval or ratio levels of measurement but not nominal levels. Another small raw data list will be used as an example, this time considering trip duration. The following list is the raw data measured in hours: 1 3 1 3 10 5 2 3 2 2 1. If we rearrange the raw data in rank order, from the lowest to the highest (or vice versa), the median can be determined. 1 1 1 2 2 2 3 3 3 5 10. In this example, the middle number is easy to determine, as the list contains an odd number of data (there are 11 items of raw data). The middle number is determined by pairing off the numbers from the outermost numbers in:

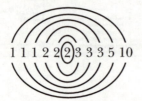

The median in this case is 2 hours. If the number of items of raw data is even, then the two innermost numbers must be added together and then divided by two. For example:

The middle numbers are 2 and 3: 2 + 3 = 5, and 5 divided by 2 = 2.5 hours, so the median is 2.5 hours. This is the middle of the distribution in regard to trip duration, although there is no measure of 2.5 hours in the raw data.

Mean

The mean is the average of the distribution and can only be calculated using levels of measurement involving intervals and ratios. Still working on trip duration, we can use the last set of raw data (1 1 1 2 2 2 3 3 3 3 5 10) to determine the mean of the distribution. The mean duration of travel time is calculated by adding up all the raw data and dividing the total by the number of travellers reporting trip durations (in this case, 12). The calculation is thus: $(3 \times 1) + (3 \times 2) + (3 \times 3) + 5 + 10 = 3 + 6 + 9 + 5 + 10 = 33$, and 33 divided by 12 = 2.75 hours. Therefore, the mean duration of travel time is 2.75 hours. However, as Tilley (1999, p. 124) comments: 'Unlike the [m]edian and [m]ode, the [m]ean is sensitive to the value of every score in the distribution, particularly extreme scores ... Therefore, a change in any one of the scores will cause a change in the value of the [m]ean. This is not necessarily true of the [m]edian or the [m]ode.'

The following examples demonstrate this. Again, the raw data list relates to duration of travel time measured in hours, but this list is different as two additional travellers have been added to the sample, so there are now 14 travellers: 1 1 1 2 2 2 2 2 3 3 3 3 5 10. The mode (the most frequently occurring category) of this distribution is 2 hours; the median is 2 hours (there are two middle scores: 2 and 2, therefore 2 + 2 = 4, and 4 divided by 2 = 2 hours); and the average is 2.85 hours. However, look what happens when the last two travel times are altered from 5 and 10 to 10 and 20, respectively. The mode remains 2 hours, the median remains 2 hours, but the mean changes to 3.9 hours. Alternatively, if these last two travel times are altered from 5 and 10 to 0.5 hours and 0.5 hours respectively, the mode remains 2 hours, the median remains 2 hours, but the mean becomes 1.86 hours. The arithmetic symbol for the mean is X.

How do the measures of central tendency assist the tourism and hospitality industry? What do these statistical calculations tell us? The mode can assist in marketing, as it enables us to determine the most preferred or used category. This can help in possible market identification for travel products or possible untapped markets and potential market diversification. The median enables us to determine the middle point of a distribution and to understand the distribution of the population on either side of the middle point. The average tells us an approximate acceptable value for a category being studied — that is, the average score. Together, the three measures can tell us about the type of distribution being represented by the sample being studied.

At this point, it is necessary to discuss the types of distributions in which raw data aggregations may result. This is important because the type of distribution may be described as either normal or skewed and this will impact on the use of measures of central tendency The type of distribution will also affect decision making regarding how normal or skewed the distribution is.

Types of frequency distributions

Using the measures of central tendency and graphical representation of frequency distributions, researchers can make statements about the nature of frequency distributions. Distributions can be normal or skewed. In normal distributions, the mean, median and mode are clustered around the same point and represent a bell-shaped curve (see figure 9.8(a)). In skewed distributions, the frequencies are not evenly distributed about a central point, but are clustered at one end of the distribution or the other (either clustering around higher or lower scores). In negatively skewed curves, the scores are skewed around the upper values being measured (see figure 9.8(b)), and in positively skewed curves, the scores are clustered around the lower values (see figure 9.8(c)). A further type of distribution is a J-shaped distribution, which results from the inclusion of a large range of high-value scores in the frequency distribution (see figure 9.8(d)).

The use of measures of central tendency in conjunction with each other become problematic in distributions representing negatively, positively or J-shaped curves. In the case of negatively and positively skewed curves, the median is a better measure of central tendency because it is closer to the majority of the scores and the mean does not represent the 'typical' case (Tilley 1999, p. 125). In the case of J-shaped curves, the mode is more appropriate as it is closer to the majority of scores than either the median or the mean (Tilley 1999, p. 125). A discussion of distribution leads into a discussion of measures of variation.

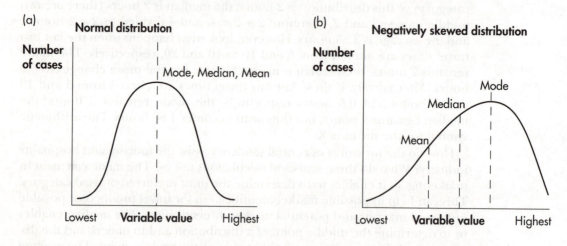

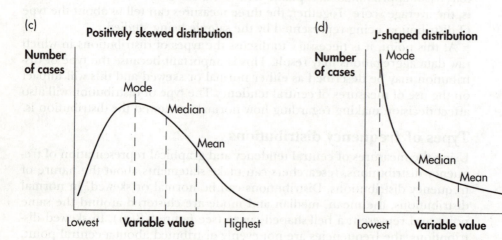

■ **Figure 9.8** *Examples of frequency distributions*

Measures of variation

There are three measures of variation:
- range
- percentile and
- standard deviation.

Range

Range is the amount of difference between the smallest score and the largest score being measured. This is easily calculated by examining your frequency distributions and locating the lowest- and highest-value scores. Range is associated with arithmetic calculations and so is not applied to nominal levels of measurement.

To provide an example of the calculation of range, consider the following raw data list representing the duration of stay at a destination by 10 tourists:

1 night, 2 nights, 3 nights, 4 nights, 5 nights, 6 nights, 7 nights, 10 nights, 21 nights, 35 nights

The range is determined by subtracting the lowest-value score from the highest-value score, in this case 35 nights is the highest-value score and 1 night is the lowest-value score. The range is the difference between 35 and 1, that is 34 nights. The range for duration of stay is subsequently 34 nights.

Percentiles

'Percentiles tell the score at a specific place within the distribution' (Neuman 2000, p. 320). The median is the 50th percentile; other percentile scores that are used are the 25th and 75th percentiles or the 10th and 90th percentiles.

As measures of variation, range and percentiles are used for ordinal, interval and ratio level data. Percentiles enable researchers to break the distribution into smaller sections to examine what is happening at these points. For example, if you refer back to figure 9.8, what could you say about the 10th percentile in each of the distributions presented? You should be able to 'eyeball' the data to answer the question. However, in practice it would be calculated exactly. Looking at the curves to answer the question, not many of the population are represented in the normal distribution at the 10th percentile, although this could not be said of the J-shaped curve.

Standard deviation

Standard deviation involves a higher level of arithmetic skill than the calculation of range and percentiles (Neuman 2000). Although it is more involved in its calculation, it is the most used measure of variation. Standard deviation requires measurement at the level of interval and ratio and uses the mean. Essentially, the standard deviation identifies the difference between all scores and the mean. Standard deviations are used in comparisons between groups, to see if the groups are similar as a result of comparing standard deviations. Moreover, standard deviation is used in the calculation of *t*-scores and *z*-scores (outlined at the end of this section).

To determine the standard deviation, researchers must:
1. calculate the mean
2. subtract the mean from each score
3. square the difference between the mean and each score
4. sum the differences
5. divide the sum by the number of cases
6. determine the square root of the value from step 5 (which gives the standard deviation) (Neuman 2000, p. 321).

The following example demonstrates how to calculate the standard deviation using the above steps. The raw data list is based on hypothetical values for air travel time for visitors to Adelaide on a specific day, for the purpose of this example — assume it is today. The data for air travel are: 1 1 1 1 1 2 2 2 2 2 3 3 3 3 3 5 10 hours. The data are related to 17 travellers as there are 17 units of data.

• *Step 1: Calculate the mean*
  45 (hours) divided by 17 (travellers) = 2.7 hours. The mean is 2.7 hours.
• *Step 2: Subtract the mean from each score*

HOURS	HOURS – MEAN
1	1 – 2.7 = –1.7
1	1 – 2.7 = –1.7
1	1 – 2.7 = –1.7
1	1 – 2.7 = –1.7
1	1 – 2.7 = –1.7
2	2 – 2.7 = –0.7
2	2 – 2.7 = –0.7
2	2 – 2.7 = –0.7
2	2 – 2.7 = –0.7
2	2 – 2.7 = –0.7
3	3 – 2.7 = 0.3
3	3 – 2.7 = 0.3
3	3 – 2.7 = 0.3
3	3 – 2.7 = 0.3
3	3 – 2.7 = 0.3
5	5 – 2.7 = 2.3
10	10 – 2.7 = 7.3

- *Step 3: Square the difference between the mean and each score*

HOURS	HOURS – MEAN	DIFFERENCE SQUARED
1	1 – 2.7 = –1.7	2.89
1	1 – 2.7 = –1.7	2.89
1	1 – 2.7 = –1.7	2.89
1	1 – 2.7 = –1.7	2.89
1	1 – 2.7 = –1.7	2.89
2	2 – 2.7 = –0.7	0.49
2	2 – 2.7 = –0.7	0.49
2	2 – 2.7 = –0.7	0.49
2	2 – 2.7 = –0.7	0.49
2	2 – 2.7 = –0.7	0.49
3	3 – 2.7 = 0.3	0.09
3	3 – 2.7 = 0.3	0.09
3	3 – 2.7 = 0.3	0.09
3	3 – 2.7 = 0.3	0.09
3	3 – 2.7 = 0.3	0.09
5	5 – 2.7 = 2.3	5.29
10	10 – 2.7 = 7.3	53.29

- *Step 4: Sum the differences*
  This means summing the values in column three:
  $(2.89 \times 5) + (0.49 \times 5) + (0.09 \times 5) + 5.29 + 53.29 = 75.93$
- *Step 5: Divide the sum by the number of cases*
  75.93 divided by 17 (the number of travellers) = 4.47
- *Step 6: Determine the square root of the value from step 5*
  This establishes the standard deviation. The square root of 4.47 is 2.11.
  The standard deviation of travel time is 2.11 hours — that is, the standard
  deviation from the mean is 2.11 hours.
  The formula for the standard deviation is:

Standard deviation = $\sqrt{\dfrac{\sum (X - \bar{X})^2}{n}}$ where X is the score of the unit, $\bar{X}$ is the

mean, $\sum$ is sigma (means sum of) and n is the number of cases.

While the above calculations were done manually, computer software programs do this in a fraction of the time.

Standard deviation is also used to calculate z-scores and t-scores. Both of
these enable the comparison of raw scores from different distributions

using calculations that standardise the scores. Specifically, '[s]tandard scores or (z-scores) transform raw scores from different distributions into a common distribution, which has the same mean (a mean of zero) and the same standard deviation (a standard deviation of 1)' (Sarantakos 1998, p. 380). The formula for calculating z-scores is:

$$Z = \frac{\bar{X} - \mu \bar{x}}{\sigma \bar{x}}$$

t-scores use the same principle as z-scores, but t-scores are determined using a mean of 50, while the standard deviation is 10. 'As virtually all scores will fall within plus or minus 5 standard deviations from the mean, they are therefore within a range from 1 to 100, a range that is often easier for many people to understand. It avoids the use of decimals and negative scores, which occur with z-scores' (Sarantakos 1993, p. 364). The formula for determining t-scores is:

$$t = \frac{\bar{X} - \mu \bar{x}}{\tilde{\sigma} \bar{x}}$$

■ 9.4.2 Bivariate *analysis*

Bivariate analysis considers the relationship between two variables, which may or may not be related to each other. Variables that are related are described as demonstrating covariation; variables that are not related in any way are described as having an independent relationship. There are a number of ways to determine relationships between two variables: cross-tabulation, scattergrams and measures of association.

Cross-tabulation

Cross-tabulation enables the researcher to present information on two variables simultaneously and to determine whether any relationship exists between the two variables. Such relationships can be determined using bivariate tables — that is, bivariate tables enable the researcher to cross-tabulate two variables. Bivariate tables can be constructed with variables measured at any level (nominal, ordinal, interval and ratio). When preparing bivariate tables, the independent variable is presented in the columns and the dependent variable is presented in the rows.

An example of cross-tabulation follows. Assume that the researcher hypotheses that increases in waiting time will increase the number of cancellations for an air transport operator. The independent variable, or cause variable, is the waiting time and the dependent variable, or affected variable, is the number of cancellations. Over the period of a day, the researcher collects data and then aggregates them into a bivariate table as shown in table 9.3.

Table 9.3 demonstrates a positive measure of relationship. An easy way to identify this is to highlight the largest percentage in each line to determine if a linear pattern emerges in regard to each of the cells identified with the largest percentage. In table 9.3, as one variable increases (waiting time), so does the other (number of cancellations) — that is, the variables are demonstrating positive covariation. A negative relationship would be indicated when one variable increases as the other decreases. The positive relationship in table 9.3 is demonstrated in table 9.4.

■ Table 9.3

Example of a bivariate table

Length of waiting time by number of cancellations for air transport operator X on (the date is inserted here) at transport terminal Y (N = 100 travellers)
Column percentaged table

	WAITING TIME			
NUMBER OF CANCELLATIONS	LESS THAN 1 HOUR	1 HOUR– 2 HOURS 59 MINUTES	3 HOURS– 4 HOURS 59 MINUTES	5 HOURS– 6 HOURS 59 MINUTES
Nil	100	40	30	10
1–50	0	10	0	0
51–100	0	50	0	0
101–150	0	0	70	0
201–250	0	0	0	0
251–300	0	0	0	90
TOTAL	100	100	100	100

■ Table 9.4

Example of a positive relationship between two variables

Length of waiting time by number of cancellations for air transport operator X on (the date is inserted here) at transport terminal Y (N = 100 travellers)
Column percentaged table

	WAITING TIME			
NUMBER OF CANCELLATIONS	LESS THAN 1 HOUR	1 HOUR– 2 HOURS 59 MINUTES	3 HOURS– 4 HOURS 59 MINUTES	5 HOURS– 6 HOURS 59 MINUTES
Nil	100	40	30	10
1–50	0	10	0	0
51–100	0	50	0	0
101–150	0	0	70	0
201–250	0	0	0	0
251–300	0	0	0	90
TOTAL	100	100	100	100

If you are using variables measured at the interval or ratio level, it is best to group them, as done in the above example, in order to clearly demonstrate relationships.

Note several aspects about tables 9.3 and 9.4:

1. The title of each table is shown in full and enables the tables to stand alone away from the text and be meaningful. The tables are not dependent on the text that precedes or follows them.
2. The sample size is indicated (N = 100).
3. The reader is informed as to whether the tables are row or column percentaged.

4. No other comments are required to assist the reader, so there is no need for footnotes beneath the tables to explain, for example, the number of missing data sets.

Scattergrams

Scattergrams can also be described as a graph or plot of a relationship. In generating a scattergram, the researcher investigates each case individually and plots it on the scattergram. When preparing graphs to represent a scattergram, ensure that you place the independent variable on the X axis (the horizontal axis) and the dependent variable on the Y axis (the vertical axis). Furthermore, the lowest values for a variable are located at the intersection of the X and Y axes, and the highest scores are located towards the outer ends of the axes. A positive relationship is demonstrated when a line of best fit through the plots on the graph is positioned in an upwards direction, moving from the bottom left to the top right of the graph (see figure 9.9(a)). A negative relationship is demonstrated when the line of best fit is positioned running from the top left to the bottom right of the graph (see figure 9.9(b)). No relationship is demonstrated when the points on the graph are plotted all over the place (see figure 9.9(c)). A curvilinear relationship is demonstrated when the points on the graph form around a centre point in either a U shape (which may be inverted) or an S shape (not shown) (see figure 9.9(d)).

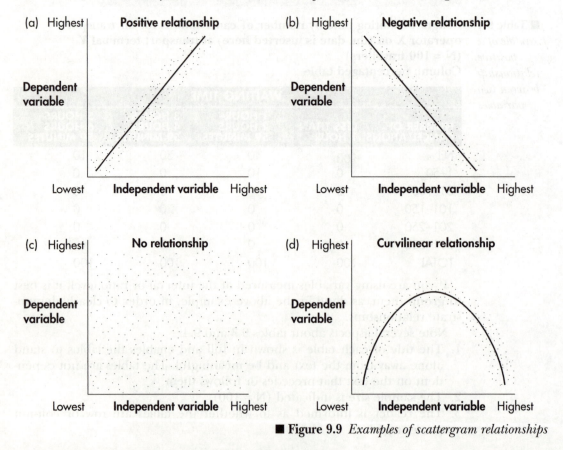

■ Figure 9.9 *Examples of scattergram relationships*

Measures of association

Measures of association reduce information about a bivariate relationship into a single numerical representation. Measures of association indicate whether there is or is not a relationship between the variables through the use of statistical calculations. There are a number of measures such as lambda, gamma, tau, rho and chi-square. An overview of each is presented in table 9.5.

■ **Table 9.5** *Overview of the measures of association*

MEASURES OF ASSOCIATION	LEVEL OF MEASUREMENT OF THE DATA	HIGH STRENGTH OF ASSOCIATION LEVEL WHEN:	INDEPENDENCE WHEN:	FORMULA
Lambda (λ)	Nominal	1.0	0	$\lambda = \dfrac{\sum f_1 - F_d}{N - F_d}$
Gamma (γ)	Ordinal	+1.0, −1.0	0	$\gamma = \dfrac{n_s - n_d}{n_s + n_d}$
Tau (τ)	Ordinal	+1.0, −1.0	0	$\tau_\alpha = \dfrac{n_s - n_d}{N(N-1)/2}$
Rho (ρ)	Interval, ratio	+1.0, −1.0	0	$\rho = 1 - \dfrac{6\Sigma d^2}{N(N^3 - 1)}$
Chi-square (χ²)	Nominal, ordinal	Infinity	0	$\chi^2 = \sum \dfrac{(O - E)^2}{E}$

Source: *Babbie (1995, pp. 416–20); de Vaus (1995, pp. 168–71); Neuman 2000 (pp. 330–2); Sarantakos (1998, pp. 384–400); Tilley (1999, pp. 179–226)*

While the formula for each test has been provided in table 9.5, many of the computer software packages available to quantitative researchers can perform the statistical analyses associated with each of these tests, as well as the following tests. Other tests that researchers can use include Yule's *Q*, contingency coefficient *C*, Tschurprow's *T*, Cramer's *V* and phi coefficient for associations measured at the nominal level (Sarantakos 1998, p. 384). At the ordinal level, other tests include Spearman's rank correlation and Sommer's *d* (Sarantakos 1998, p. 384). At the interval and ratio level, another test is Pearson's product–moment correlation (Sarantakos 1998, p. 384). It is important to remember when using these tests that the measures show association only, not the causes. In particular, they identify the existence of a correlation, the direction of the correlation (positive or negative) and the strength of the correlation, but not the cause of the relationship. Additionally, another test — regression analysis — enables the researcher to make statements about the value of one variable when the other variable is not known (Sarantakos 1998, p. 398). Neither regression analysis nor the measures of association noted above are explained in great detail here as the teaching of these skills is beyond the scope of this textbook.

■ 9.4.3 **Multivariate** *analysis*

Multivariate analysis involves the analysis of more than two variables at the one time. The researcher holds one variable constant (as a control) and examines an independent and a dependent variable. The researcher tests to see if the association between the independent and dependent variable is the same for different categories in a variable. For example, gender may be the constant and the researcher may test for an association between gender and the dependent variable being studied. Researchers use multivariate analysis to ensure that any bivariate relationship is not 'spurious' (Neuman 2000, p. 333). Trivariate analysis may be conducted using tables or multiple regression analysis. A trivariate table is made up of bivariate tables that represent the values 'of the independent and dependent variables for each category of the control variable' (Neuman, 2000, p. 333). Tables that are constructed in regard to each category of the control variable are called partials (Neuman 2000, p. 333). You also need to be aware that multivariate analysis goes beyond the analysis of three variables at once, although representing this in table form becomes more complex.

Table 9.6 demonstrates an example of a trivariate table. The independent variable is age, the dependent variable is satisfaction level with a travel experience and the control variable is gender. The table comprises two partial tables, one for women and one for men. Together, the two tables display the three variables of gender, age and satisfaction. Both partial tables are required to determine the impact of gender on the relationship between age and satisfaction. In this table, the introduction of the control variable (gender) has no impact on the relationship between the independent variable and the dependent variable. In both partial tables, younger age groups were more satisfied with the travel experience than older age groups, so gender had no impact on the satisfaction level of the travel experience.

■ **Table 9.6**
Example of a trivariate table

PARTIAL TABLE FOR WOMEN						
SATISFACTION LEVEL	**AGE GROUP**					
	14–17	**18–24**	**25–39**	**40–54**	**55 AND OVER**	**TOTAL**
Very satisfied	20	10	5	2	1	38
Satisfied	18	8	3	1	0	30
Undecided	0	0	0	0	1	1
Dissatisfied	1	0	2	9	15	27
Very dissatisfied	0	2	5	10	12	29
No opinion	0	1	0	0	0	1
Number of women	39	21	15	22	29	126

PARTIAL TABLE FOR MEN						
SATISFACTION LEVEL	AGE GROUP					
	14–17	18–24	25–39	40–54	55 AND OVER	TOTAL
Very satisfied	21	12	3	2	1	39
Satisfied	20	9	1	1	0	31
Undecided	0	0	0	1	0	1
Dissatisfied	1	2	2	8	13	26
Very dissatisfied	1	1	2	9	15	28
No opinion	0	0	0	1	0	1
Number of women	43	24	8	22	29	126

Multiple regression is another form of multivariate analysis. Multiple regression investigates the effect of several independent variables on a dependent variable. It is used with data measured at interval and ratio levels and is generally calculated using statistical software packages. The method of multiple regression is beyond the scope and intent of this textbook and so is not explained in further detail here.

Researchers can also undertake a number of other types of multivariate analysis:

- *path analysis* — this generates a causal model regarding variable relationships and uses regression analysis (Babbie 1995)
- *time series analysis* — this uses regression analysis to understand changes in variables over time (Babbie 1995)
- *factor analysis* — this determines patterns in the variations of a number of variables and uses complex statistical calculations to determine the patterns and, subsequently, is best performed using statistical software packages (Babbie 1995).

9.5 INFERENTIAL STATISTICS

Inferential statistics are based on probability sampling and are important when testing a hypothesis and making statements about the sample in relation to the population being studied. When considering inferential statistics, the researcher focuses on statistical significance, levels of significance and Type I and Type II errors.

■ 9.5.1 **Statistical** *significance*

There are a number of tests of statistical significance. Different tests have different applications depending on the level of measurement and the number and type of samples. Sarantakos (1998, p. 403) provides a summary of the more common tests of significance, and this is illustrated in table 9.7.

■ **Table 9.7**
Examples of tests of significance

SAMPLE NUMBER AND TYPE	NON-PARAMETRIC TESTS	PARAMETRIC TESTS	
	NOMINAL LEVEL	ORDINAL LEVEL	INTERVAL/RATIO LEVEL
One	Chi-square test (goodness-of-fit test)	Kolmogorov–Smirnov test	*t*-test
Two independent	Chi-square test (test of independence) Fisher's exact test *z*-test for proportions	Mann–Whitney U-test Wald–Wolfowitz runs test	*t*-test
Two dependent	McNemar test	Sign test Wilcoxon test	*t*-test
More than two independent	Chi-square test	Kruskal–Wallis *H*-test	ANOVA
More than two dependent	Cochran Q-test	Friedman test	ANOVA

Source: *Developed by Sarantakos (1998) based on: S. Siegel. 1956.* Non-Parametric Statistics for Behavioural Sciences. *London: McGraw-Hill; and R. G. Knapp. 1985.* Basic Statistics for Nurses. *New York: Wiley & Sons*

Tests of significance enable the researcher to determine statistically whether a relationship between variables is a chance one in the sample as opposed to being probable in the population (Neuman 2000, p. 338; Babbie 1995, pp. 431–6). Sarantakos (1998) refers to non-parametric and parametric tests in table 9.7. Parametric tests assume that the variable being studied reflects a normal distribution in the population. Non-parametric tests assume that the variable being studied does not reflect a normal distribution in the population.

■ 9.5.2 **Levels** *of significance*

Statistical significance is generally described with respect to levels of significance (Neuman 2000). One of three levels of significance is usually reported: 0.05, 0.01, or 0.001 (Babbie 1995; Neuman 2000). Respectively, the levels refer to a 5 in 100, a 1 in 100 or a 1 in 1000 chance of an association between the variables being a result of sampling error. Levels of

significance enable researchers to make statements about findings, such as (Neuman 2000, p. 338):
- findings are due to chance only 5 in 100 times
- there is a 95% chance that the sample findings reflect the population.
These sample statements assume a 0.5 level of statistical significance.

■ 9.5.3 Type I *and Type II errors*

Type I and Type II errors are associated with research projects that state hypotheses. In the analytical phase of a research project, having aggregated the data, the researcher is able to test hypotheses. There are several types of hypotheses that the researcher uses, primarily the null hypothesis and the alternative hypothesis:
- Null hypothesis (Ho) — the null hypothesis is a hypothesis that assumes that there is no relationship between the variables being tested for relationships.
- The alternate hypothesis — the alternate hypothesis states the opposite of the null hypothesis. There are a number of other terms that are used for the alternate hypothesis, such as the research hypothesis or the experimental hypothesis (H1).

Testing hypotheses

As Kumar (1996, p. 69) notes, a hypothesis is an assumption about which the research process gathers data to prove whether it can be supported or not. However, Kumar (1996, p. 69) cautions that the validity of a hypotheses may by incorrectly determined because of:
- an improperly developed research design that contains faults
- an inadequately and improperly conducted sampling process
- inaccuracies in data gathering
- improper analytical processes
- inappropriate statistical processes being used
- unsound findings or conclusions.

These items introduce error into a research project and the findings are rendered useless. In any study, there is always a possibility of error being introduced in the testing of hypotheses. The errors may be described as one of two types — Type I or Type II. Type I errors occur when the null hypothesis is rejected when in fact it is true. Type II errors occur when the null hypothesis is accepted when in fact it is false. Table 9.8 outlines the types of error that may arise in hypothesis testing.

■ Table 9.8
Types of errors associated with hypothesis testing

	IF A NULL HYPOTHESIS IS IN FACT:	
	TRUE	**FALSE**
And you decide to accept	This acceptance is correct	This is a Type I error
And you decide to reject	This is a Type II error	This acceptance is correct

Source: *Kumar (1996, p. 69)*

COMPUTER PROGRAMS FOR QUANTITATIVE DATA ANALYSIS

Computers have assisted greatly in the analysis of quantitative data. Nowadays, most quantitative data are turned into 'machine-readable form — a form that can be read and manipulated by computers and similar machines' (Babbie 1995, p. 363). There are a number of quantitative software packages available to assist researchers, such as the Methodologist's Toolchest Version 3.0, SphinxSurvey, SPSS (Statistical Package for the Social Sciences), Minitab, SAS (Statistical Analysis System), and winMAX. Several of these software packages are aids for research design rather than solely analytical packages. A brief description of these packages follows, so that you have an understanding of the diversity available to you, rather than a comprehensive summary of all the features of each package.

9.6.1 Methodologist's Toolchest *Version 3.0*

This software package is designed to assist researchers from the very beginnings of a research project to the final presentation of the findings. The package assists you with writing proposals, and developing budgets and timelines. It does not, however, assist with the analysis of data. In particular, the Methodologist's Toolchest (2000) enables researchers to:

- organise thinking processes and text into the following areas — research aims, background and significance, content of the study and relevant experience of the researcher, research design and methods, ethics and management issues
- simulate peer review of research proposals
- generate summaries
- track progress of proposal development
- determine appropriate sample size
- select the appropriate statistical analyses for the proposal being developed
- check the research design matches the aims of the research proposal
- develop relevant measurement and scales for the responses sets to be used in the study
- consider the ethical implications associated with the research project, such as use of informed consent
- select the appropriate graphical representation of the data to be analysed in the project
- be aware of definitions and find suitable research references.

9.6.2 SphinxSurvey

SphinxSurvey has already been discussed in chapter 7. SphinxSurvey assists researchers in the analysis of quantitative data sets (particularly SphinxSurvey Plus[2]), qualitative data sets (particularly SphinxSurvey Lexica) and mixed data sets. SphinxSurvey Plus[2] facilitates the preparation of questionnaires, and supports data entry and analysis. The software works on a PC platform using Windows. It has specific hard disk space and free memory requirements and requires a 3.5" floppy drive. In particular, SphinxSurvey Plus[2] enables researchers to:

- generate questionnaires
- import and export data from and to other applications
- analyse data using univariate, bivariate and multivariate statistics
- create tables and graphs to match the analyses
- generate reports.

9.6.3 SPSS

Statistical Package for the Social Sciences (SPSS) is, as the name asserts, a package that enables researchers to conduct statistical analyses of quantitative data. Many universities hold site licences for SPSS. It is one of the most frequently used software packages for quantitative data analysis. SPSS allows researchers to:

- enter and store data
- analyse data using univariate, bivariate and multivariate statistics
- generate data files, output files and graphics
- print tabular results
- prepare graphs and charts.

9.6.4 Minitab

Minitab is another statistical analysis software program. Minitab enables researchers to:

- design experiments
- calculate sample size
- conduct basic statistic and advanced statistical analyses
- conduct regression analysis and ANOVA
- perform multivariate analysis
- prepare graphs and charts
- import, export and manipulate data.

9.6.5 SAS

Statistical Analysis System (SAS) is predicated to data access, management, analysis and presentation. The software package enables researchers to:

- enter and store data
- utilise retrieval strategies
- engage in statistical analyses
- generate graphics and reports
- manage research projects
- write reports.

As noted in chapter 7, winMAX operates in conjunction with Windows 95 or 98 or Windows NT and PC platforms. winMAX allows researchers to:

- work with multiple texts
- work with text files, generate memos, use qualitative and quantitative procedures and undertake file exchange
- code and retrieve and analyse text analysis using Boolean and lexical searches
- identify relationships and display them visually.
- export and import into SPSS.

As Brent and Thompson (1996, p. 5-1) note:

> There are literally hundreds of forms of statistical analysis available today. Powerful packages such as SPSS, SAS, SYSTAT, CSS, StatGraphics, BMDP, and others provide an embarrassment of riches to the user in the form of possible forms of statistical analyses.

As researchers, you need to familiarise yourself with the various programs. At the end of this chapter there are a number of Web sites for quantitative data analysis as well as some demonstration Web site addresses. You should conduct your own investigation of the various software packages and make your own decisions regarding the choice of software package to be used in any project. The guidelines developed by Miles and Weitzman (1994) for evaluating software that were included in chapter 7 are presented again here to assist you to make informed decisions about appropriate software for your project. Having answered these questions you will be in a better position to select an appropriate software package for your project.

When selecting quantitative software packages, consider:

- What are your current computer literacy skills?
- What type of platform are you going to be operating on?
- How would you define your research project?
- How do you need data managed for the project?
- What analytical procedures do you need to undertake?
- What are the quantitative data analysis features of the software package?
- Is the package user-friendly?
- Is there any software support available either locally or electronically?

9.7 SUMMARY

Preparing and coding quantitative data ready for analysis
Coding data involves the development of codes, data entry and data cleaning. Data entry can be undertaken using transfer sheets, edge-coding,

direct data entry, scanners, spreadsheets and manual tally sheets. Data cleaning is associated with code cleaning and contingency cleaning.

The role of descriptive statistics in quantitative data analysis

Descriptive statistics involve the researcher in univariate, bivariate and multivariate analysis. Descriptive statistics enable researchers to describe trends in the data and also to determine whether relationships exist between variables.

The procedures to establish measures of central tendency

The three measures of central tendency are the mean, the mode and the median. The mean is the average of all scores; the mode is the variable that has the highest level of frequency; and the median is the middle score.

Measures of association

Measures of association identify the existence of relationships between variables. The measures articulate relationships in terms of a single numerical representation. Some of the measures of association include *lambda* (nominal level), *gamma* (ordinal), *tau* (ordinal) *rho* (interval and ratio level) and chi-square (nominal and ordinal). Measures of association determine the existence of a relationship, its strength and direction.

The key elements of inferential statistics

Inferential statistics require the use of probability sampling and are important to test a hypothesis and its relationship to the overall population being studied. Tests of inferential statistics include chi-square (used with nominal levels of measurement) and ANOVA (used with interval levels of measurement). Inferential statistics also involve researchers in tests of statistical significance, consideration of levels of significance, and Type I and Type II errors.

Ways to display quantitative data analysis findings

Quantitative data analysis findings may be displayed in tables (univariate, bivariate and multivariate tables), as scattergrams or as a single number through the use of measures of association. Graphs may also be used such as histograms, pie charts and bar graphs.

The range of computer programs available to quantitative researchers

There is a vast range of computer programs available for researchers. Some focus on research design, such as the Methodologist's Toolchest and SphinxSurvey, while others are more focused on statistical analysis, such as SPSS, Minitab, SAS and winMAX.

Questions

9.1   Develop a table summarising the various types of coding procedures that a researcher may undertake in analysing quantitative data.

9.2   Which do you think would be a better to way to display research results, tables or graphs? Justify your answer.

EXERCISES

Exercise 9.1

Using the following raw data, prepare a raw count frequency distribution table and a percentage frequency table that represent the data. The raw data are responses regarding purpose of visit to a destination:

conference, business, visiting friends, visiting relatives, private business, other, pleasure, conference, business, visiting relatives, private business, visiting friends, pleasure, conference, business, pleasure, pleasure, visiting relatives, conference, business, other private business, pleasure, visiting relatives, pleasure, pleasure, conference, business, conference business, visiting friends, visiting relatives, private business, other, pleasure, conference, business, visiting relatives, private business, visiting friends, pleasure, conference, business, pleasure, pleasure, visiting relatives, conference, business, other private business, pleasure, visiting relatives, pleasure, pleasure, conference, business.

Exercise 9.2

Determine the mode, median and mean for the following raw data. After you have determined the measures of central tendency,

- plot the frequency distribution in a bar graph
- join the midpoints of the bar graph to determine the type of distribution.

Comment on the type of distribution portrayed in the graph. The raw data for this exercise represent the ages of visitors to a rural destination:

56 35 57 45 23 31 57 66 64 61 25 10 3 2 71 75 80 45 32 77 63 57 49 51 62 65 69 71 71 75 80 45 32 56 35 57 45 66 64 61 10 71 75 80 77 63 57 62 65 69 71

Exercise 9.3

Locate the latest data from the Bureau of Tourism Research in either hard or electronic copy that provide you with bivariate tables or multivariate tables relating to travel variables. Then generate other visual displays or analyses of the data using the various methods of analysis discussed in this chapter.

Exercise 9.4

Investigate each of the Web sites discussed in this chapter (the addresses are at the end of the chapter) and complete your own evaluation of the software programs using the following criteria. The criteria are based on those used by Miles and Weitzman (1994, p. 316):

- identify the version of the software program
- identify the operating system
- identify the activities the program will perform
- rate the user-friendliness of the program
- comment on its appropriateness for your own study in this course.

Having collected data on each program, prepare a table that overviews the software programs and take it to your next tutorial for sharing and discussion with your peers.

RESEARCH PROJECT ··

If your own research project is a quantitative project, what levels of measurement did you use and how might those variables be analysed and represented using visual representations? Write a summary of 500 words outlining your selection of methods and the reasons that informed your decision making regarding your analytical methods. If your project uses a qualitative methodology, what methods of data collection and analysis could you use if you chose to include a quantitative method to make your approach mixed method?

REFERENCES ··

Babbie, Earl. 1995. *The Practice of Social Research*. Seventh Edition. Belmont: Wadsworth.

Brent, Edward & Thompson, Alan. 1996. *Methodologist's Toolchest™ for Windows: User's Guide and Reference Manual*. Columbia, MO: Idea Works.

Bureau of Tourism Research (BTR). 1996. Domestic Tourism Monitor, 1994–95. Canberra.

de Vaus, David A. 1995. *Surveys in Social Research*. Fourth Edition. Sydney: Allen & Unwin.

Frazer, Lorelle & Lawley, Meredith. 2000. *Questionnaire Design and Administration*. Brisbane: John Wiley & Sons.

Jennings, Gayle. 1998. *Recreational Usage Patterns of Shoalwater Bay and Adjacent Waters*. Research Publication No. 50, Townsville: Great Barrier Reef Marine Park Authority.

Killion, G. L. 1998. *Research in Tourism: Study Guide*. Rockhampton: Central Queensland University.

Kumar, Ranjit. 1996. *Research Methodology: A Step-By-Step Guide for Beginners*. South Melbourne: Longman.

Miles, Matthew & Weitzman, Eben. 1994. 'Appendix: Choosing Computer Programs for Qualitative Data Analysis'. In Miles, Matthew & Huberman, A. Michael. (Eds) *Qualitative Analysis: An Expanded Sourcebook*. Second Edition. Thousand Oaks, CA: Sage, pp. 311–17.

Neuman, W. Lawrence. 2000. *Social Research Methods: Qualitative and Quantitative Approaches*. Fourth Edition. Boston, MA: Allyn & Bacon.

Sarantakos, Sotirios. 1998. *Social Research*. Second Edition. South Melbourne: Macmillan.

Tilley, Andrew. 1999. *An Introduction to Research Methodology and Report Writing in Psychology*. Brisbane: Pineapple Press.

FURTHER READING

Green, S. B., Salkind, N. J. & Akey, T. M. 1997. *Using SPSS for Windows: Analyzing and Understanding Data.* Upper Saddle River, NJ: Prentice-Hall.

Pelosi, Marilyn & Sandifer, Theresa. 1999. *Doing Statistics for Business.* New York: John Wiley & Sons.

Wild, Christopher J. & Seber, George A. F. 2000. *Chance Encounters: A First Course in Data Analysis and Inference.* New York: John Wiley & Sons.

WEB SITES

Methodologist's Toolchest (link from http://www.sagepub.com)

SphinxSurvey
(http://www.lesphinx-developpement.fr/en/download/overview.htm);
demonstration site
(http://www.lesphinx-developpement.fr/en/download/download.htm)

SPSS (http://www.spss.com)

Minitab (http://www.minitab.com/global/index.asp); demonstration site
(http://www.mintab.com/products/13/demo/index.htm)

SAS (http://www.sas.com); online sample site
(http://www.sas.com/service/library/onlinedoc/code.samples.html)

winMAX (http://www.winmax.de/)

10
Tourism research
proposals and reports

'Writing is a form of thinking, not simply a mechanical process of presenting results. There are, consequently, many different styles of writing and no absolutely "right" way. Initially, you should try simply to write up results of research and not worry about how you are writing. Little can be done with your writing until your ideas have been committed to written words.'

(Jorgensen 1989, pp.119–20)

LEARNING OBJECTIVES

After studying this chapter, you should be able to:

- describe the purpose of a research proposal
- outline the structure of a research proposal
- comment on the overall presentation of a research proposal
- discuss audience considerations in research proposal writing
- review the procedures for ethical clearances
- outline the purpose of research reports
- identify the differences between qualitative and quantitative research reports
- list the various types of research reports
- discuss audience considerations in research report writing.

Research involves two elements: the research process and the production of written documents such as research proposals and research reports. Consequently, research is both process (the conduct of research) and product (proposals and reports) based. So too is the process of writing — there is the act of writing itself (the process) and the product that the writing generates (proposals and reports). Before addressing the nature of writing research proposals and reports, this chapter overviews the writing process, to reinforce that the written products of research require sufficient attention to ensure that they are quality products. In the act of writing research proposals and reports, you convey to the reader your knowledge and understanding of the research process and your knowledge and understanding of the tourism phenomenon you are about to study or have studied. When preparing research proposals and reports you need to allow sufficient time to move through each of the writing stages. One-shot writing rarely results in a quality product. Quality writing requires drafting and redrafting, as well as revision, to clarify the meaning being communicated.

You will recall from chapter 1 that the writing process involves five stages: rehearsal, drafting, revising, proofing and publishing (see figure 1.6 on page 25).

- The rehearsal stage enables you to brainstorm, prepare an outline, and collect and organise relevant materials, literature and models. At this stage, you also need to consider your audience, the purpose of the writing, the topic and the type of text to best convey your meaning.
- In the drafting stage, you refine your text to make it clearly convey your intent.
- In the revising stage, you may allow a critical reader to respond to your text or you may re-read the text to ensure that all the sections are cohesively linked and your intent and content match. You need to allow time between the drafting and revising stages so that you can come to the text with fresh eyes. Often, when you have been working on a text for a period of time, you may think it says what you want when it does not, as you have become too close to the text. Time between drafting and revising enables you to look at the text more critically, and you need to plan your time schedule to allow this to happen.
- In the proofing stage, the focus moves from the clarity of your message to the proofing issues of spelling, punctuation and grammar.
- The publishing stage is associated with the preparation and presentation of the writing product upon which you have been working.

Any writing that you undertake needs to follow these stages to ensure that the final product is coherent and polished and clearly and effectively conveys your intent to the reader. Ensure that you allow yourself enough time to draft and review your writing through several iterations.

THE PURPOSE OF A RESEARCH PROPOSAL

The purpose of a research proposal is to convince the reader that you have the knowledge, skills and expertise to either engage in or be selected for a proposed research project. This expertise is determined in three ways:

1. by the overall presentation and content of the proposal
2. by the curriculum vitae or résumés that are appended to the proposal
3. by the process of peer review.

Research proposals convey information about a proposed research study or project to one of several audiences, including:

- an academic supervisor overseeing your research studies for under-graduate or postgraduate study
- a supervisor for whom you are working
- an ethics committee
- a government agency that may be considering providing you access to a study site or visitors
- a client for whom you have been contracted to work
- peer reviewers who examine the research merit of the proposal
- an individual or group of individuals who have requested tenders (research proposals) for a project in either the pubic or private sector.

THE STRUCTURE OF A RESEARCH PROPOSAL

A research proposal consists of seven sections: an introduction, a literature review, a methodology section, a time line, a budget, a reference section and the attached curriculum vitae or résumé for each researcher. Research proposals are generally between 1000 and 2000 words in length. Sometimes, proformas are provided by granting agencies, clients or stakeholder bodies for use by researchers in the preparation of research proposals. Depending on the audience, different requirements will be imposed on the writing of the research proposal. The influence of audience on the proposal is discussed later in the chapter.

■ 10.3.1 Introduction

The introduction and background section establishes the context for the proposed research study. It provides information on the setting being studied, such as its geographical location, and the location of the study's focus within various types of tourism products (e.g. cultural tourism, indigenous tourism, adventure tourism, independent tourism, domestic tourism, international tourism, special events tourism, business tourism or some combination, such as international cultural tourism trends) or within the hospitality sector (e.g. accommodation, transportation, food and beverage, management, customer service). The key concepts that are associated with the study are also introduced (e.g. motivation, the travel experience, satisfaction, conflict or leadership or management styles) and definitions of variables may be presented (e.g. the definition of a tourist, the local area, a business traveller, an independent traveller). Definitions should apply national standards or international standards rather than being generated by you. However, if you are studying a concept that has not been studied before, then you may have to provide non-standard definitions of variables.

The introduction and background section should also state:
- the aim and/or objectives or the study if the study is a qualitative study, or
- the hypotheses if the study is a quantitative study.

If the study is going to use mixed methods, then the type of mixed method needs to be stated (refer to chapter 5 for comments on the types of mixed methods). There may be a presentation of the aims (and objectives) as well as the hypotheses, although not necessarily in that order depending on the type of mixed method that is being applied. The overlying research approach should be identified, such as a descriptive or comparative research. The contribution of the study needs also to be stated and noted in the introduction.

■ *10.3.2* **Literature** *review*

Neuman (2000, p. 446) suggests that there are four purposes associated with conducting a literature review:
- to demonstrate a familiarity with a body of knowledge
- to show the path of a priori research
- to integrate and summarise what is known
- to learn from others and to stimulate new ideas.

These purposes should guide the conduct of your literature review. Furthermore, as researchers, you need to consider the following six types of literature review (Neuman 2000, p. 446):
- self-study reviews, which familiarise you with the literature and simultaneously educate you regarding the status quo of the topic being researched
- context reviews, which enable you to situate the current study within the overall literature and identify the current project's contribution
- historical reviews, which enable you to critically analyse the development over time of different theoretical frameworks that have been used to explain a phenomenon
- theoretical reviews, which enable you to compare and contrast different theoretical perspectives on the same study phenomenon. Sometimes, this review and the historical review are combined to create an historical-theoretical review
- methodological reviews, which enable you to critique the methodologies of past research studies
- integrative reviews, which enable you to examine and analyse a new research area and to identify the current status by drawing together as yet unconnected studies into one whole — which may be published as an article.

How to conduct a literature search

In preparing your literature review, you need to conduct a literature search. A literature search requires you to investigate and exhaust all possible sources of literature that are accessible to you. With the development of electronic databases, electronic journals and academically rigorous Web sites, literature searches have become easier tasks for researchers to complete. It is possible to conduct your literature search without having to physically visit a library. All searching, ordering and downloading can be conducted from your computer via modem access or networks to an Internet server. However, there are times when researchers have to access literature via inter-library loans because of the limited dissemination of the document, such as conference proceedings that are only distributed to attendees and a local library. In other circumstances, a major holding of documents may be restricted to on-site access only, due to, for example, document fragility or the holdings being the only copies. In these circumstances, you may have to travel to the site where the documents are held in order to access them.

The work sheet presented in figure 10.1 outlines an approach you might adopt to guide your thinking regarding accessing relevant literature and to take you through the process of commencing a literature search. The steps involve you identifying your topic, key words and related words, and focusing your search on library catalogue holdings, statistical references, reference section holdings, government strategies, electronic sources (e.g. government and tourism sites, electronic databases and electronic journals) media sources and other sources.

■ Figure 10.1
Literature search work sheet

1. State your proposed research topic

2. Identify the key concepts/words associated with your topic

3. Identify synonyms and related concepts and words for each of the key concepts/words

Look in thesauri, key word databases and subject dictionaries. (For example, in the literature, tourist could be described as domestic tourist, international tourist, traveller, visitor, daytripper or excursionist, and motivation for travel could be recorded as reasons for travel or purpose of visit/trip. So think laterally. Your first key word choice may draw a blank in a search, and you need to think of alternative ways of describing your concept.)

(continued)

■ Figure 10.1
*Literature
search work
sheet
(cont'd)*

Concept one	Concept two	Concept three

Concept four	Concept five	Concept six

4. Identify current library catalogue holdings and their availability
(Place a loan request if necessary.)

5. Identify specific sources for statistical references
Look up, for example, the Bureau of Tourism Research (BTR), Australian Bureau of Statistics (ABS) and the World Tourism Organization (WTO) and identify relevant publications or Web sites that provide statistical data relevant to your topic.

6. Identify suitable reference section sources in library holdings
Investigate, for example, subject dictionaries, year books, almanacs and subject abstract indexes.

7. Identify relevant government strategies

Consider local, regional, state, national and internationally produced documents.

8. Government sites on the Web

Investigate various government sites and linked sites.

9. Tourism sites on the Web

Investigate various tourism sites and linked sites.

10. Identify relevant and associated databases

List the databases that you consider may contain information appropriate to your topic (e.g. APAIS, Uncover, Firstsearch). Also consider related disciplinary databases, such as psychlit and sociofile.

11. Identify electronic journals located on the Web

Investigate, for example, ABI/Inform.

12. Other sources

Consider, for example, media sources in both hard copy and electronic format.

Source: *Developed from James Cook University*

Recording your literature research results

As you commence gathering relevant literature and documents, you should start a bibliographic index, or a bibliographic card/book system. The system can be created manually by handwritten methods or by using software programs such as Endnotes. Such programs are very useful, as you can integrate and merge text between the bibliographic program and your word processing program. Figure 10.2 illustrates examples of bibliographic index cards for book references, edited book references, journal references and Web sites.

Book reference

```
Author(s):
Title of book:
Year of publication:
Publisher:
Place of publication:
Key words:
Comments and quotes (including page
references):
```

Edited book reference

```
Author(s) of chapter in edited book:
Title of chapter in edited book:
Year of publication:
Title of book:
Editor(s) of book:
Publisher:
Place of publication:
Page numbers:
Key words:
Comments and quotes (including page
references):
```

Journal reference

```
Author(s):
Title of article:
Year of publication:
Title of journal:
Volume:
Number/issue:
Page numbers:
Key words:
Comments and quotes (including page
references):
```

Web site reference

```
Author(s):
Title of Web site:
Year of publication:
Publisher:
Place:
URL address:
Date downloaded:
Key words:
Comments and quotes (including 'page'
references):
```

■ **Figure 10.2** *Examples of bibliographic index cards for book references, edited book references, journal references and Web sites*

Once you have gathered the relevant literature, the next step is to 'write it up'. A literature review consists of an organised discussion and synthesis of the literature. It is not a listing of books or an evaluative comment on the contents of the various pieces of literature you have gathered. A literature review must be an integrated and properly referenced piece of writing. Figure 10.3 illustrates two examples of a literature review. Both types are submitted as literature reviews; however, in reality the first is not technically a literature review (it is a listing), whereas the second example approximates the textual style of a literature review.

■ **Figure 10.3**
Two examples of literature reviews: example (a) is really a listing, but example (b) approximates the correct style of a literature

(a)
The following literature will be useful for my study:

Alston, Margaret (1995) 'Women and their work on Australian farms'. *Rural Sociology*, Vol. 60, No. 3, Fall, 521–32.

Bell J. H. & Pandey, U. S. (1989) 'Gender-role stereotypes in Australian farm advertising'. *Media Information Australia*, no. 51, 1989, 45–9.

Blackman, Graeme (1998) 'Home paddock'. Paper presented at *Showcasing the stories of success from rural and regional Australia*, Video-conference workshop, hosted by Monash University, Tuesday 10 November 1998.

Collie, G. (1999) 'Women forced to work off the farm'. *The Courier Mail*, 28 January, p. 7.

Craik, Wendy (1997) 'Missed opportunities, harnessing the skills of rural women for economic, environmental and social change'. Paper presented at *International Women's Day Celebrations*, Dubbo, March.

Gilbert, David & Tung, L. (1990) 'Public organizations and rural marketing planning in England and Wales'. *Tourism Management*, March, pp. 164–72.

Gray, Ian & Phillips, Emily (1996) Sustainability and the restructuring of tradition: A comparative analysis of three rural localities. In Geoffrey Lawrence, Kristen Lyons & Salim Momtaz (eds) *Social Change in Rural Australia*. (276–89). RSERC Press, Rockhampton.

Jennings, Gayle & Daniela Stehlik (1998) 'Agriculture women in Central Queensland and changing modes of production: a preliminary exploration of the issues'. Paper presented at *The Australian Sociological Association's Conference, TASA '98, Refashioning sociology: Towards the new millenium*, Brisbane, December.

Kieselbach, Scott & Long, Patrick (1990) 'Tourism and the rural revitalization movement'. *P & R*, March, pp. 62–6.

Leckie, Gloria J. (1993) 'Female farmers in Canada and the gender relations of a restructuring agricultural system'. *The Canadian Geographer*, Vol. 37, No. 3, 212–30.

Lyon, Neil (1995) 'Farm tourism makes its move'. *Australian Farm Journal*, January, pp. 34–7.

Petterson, Liv Toril (1997) 'Women for agriculture — the empowerment of farm women'. Paper presented at the *XVII Congress of the European Society for Rural Sociology*, Crete, August.

Rosenfeld, Rachel Ann (1985) *Farm women: work, farm and family in the United States*. University of North Carolina Press.

Rural Women's Unit 91998) *A Vision for Change. National Plan for Women in Agriculture and Resource Management*. Commonwealth of Australia, Canberra.

Sachs, Caroline, (1983) *The invisible farmers: women in agricultural production*. Rowan and Allanheld, Totawa, New Jersey.

Shortall, Sally (1992) 'Power analysis and farm wives, an empirical study of the power relationships affecting women on Irish farms'. *Sociologia Ruralis*, Vol. XXXII, No. 4, 431–51.

Smith, Valene (1977) *Hosts and Guests: The Anthropology of Tourism*. University of Philadelphia Press, Philiadelpha.

(continued)

■ **Figure 10.3**
*Two
examples of
literature
reviews:
example (a)
is really a
listing, but
example (b)
approximates
the correct
style of a
literature
review
(cont'd)*

(b) BRIEF LITERATURE REVIEW

Off-farm labour has been a well-documented phenomenon among male farmers in Australia (Ian Gray & Emily Phillips 1996) and overseas (Gloria Lecke 1993). The impacts of globalisation on the farm sector and the relationships between family/community/work is now becoming an important one for this region. Many family operators are considering alternative approaches to income generation and 'women in the bush are increasingly being forced to seek work off the farm to help keep the family properties afloat' (Collie 1999, p. 7). Some of those innovations include farm tourism and cottage industry production (Graeme Blackman 1998; Rural Women's Unit 1998; Rural Tourism Conference 1995). In general, these activities while undertaken on the farm, remain outside of farm production and have been classified as off-farm production (Gayle Jennings & Daniela Stehlik 1998). Some other innovations constitute value-adding such as knitwear businesses (Wendy Craik 1997) and thereby are classified as on-farm activities.

Currently, most literature focuses on the difficulties related to operating farm tourism as a business (Neil Lyon 1995; Scott Kieselbach & Patrick Long 1990). In this regard business skills and marketing expertise is often lacking by the innovators (David Gilbert & L. Tung 1990). While the business issues have been addressed to some extent, knowledge of host–guest interactions (Valene Smith 1977) and the impacts on the host family remain under-investigated. Such knowledge would assist innovators in preparing a family plan to minimise the social impacts associated with the introduction of farm tourism. Further, the Commonwealth Tourism Strategy stated that 'the social impacts of tourism, whether from tourism infrastructure or the tourists themselves, affect Australians in their communities. The positive social impacts can be significant provided the appropriate community consultative, educative and information processes are followed ... *It is important to gauge tourism's social impacts on a community so that negative impacts, where possible, can be avoided, alleviated or overcome'* (Commonwealth Department of Tourism 1994, p. 8; emphasis added).

Further, the distinct lack of studies on tourism from a gendered perspective is a well lamented fact, and this project would contribute to increasing the attention which studies consider the impact of gender on tourism. Already it has been noted that women are the key decision makers in holiday-destination choice (Jones 1989; US Travel Data Center 1991; Fodness 1992) and this study would contribute to understanding the key role farm women play in the enterprises of farm tourism. In addition, this project would serve to break down the invisibility of farm women's work, another well-documented issue (Bell & Pandey 1989; Margaret Alston 1995a; Caroline Sachs 1983; Rachel Rosenfeld 1985; Sally Shortall 1992; Liv Toril Pettersen 1997).

■ 10.3.3 **Methodology** *section*

The methodology section needs to state the overlying methodology that is informing the research data collection and analysis (qualitative, quantitative or mixed methods). It also needs to state why that methodology has been chosen, and how that methodology enables the researcher to best gather the required data and analyse that data. Once the methodology has been identified, the selected methods for data collection and analysis need to be briefly outlined and justified. Any limitations to the study should be clearly stated. Limitations might include:

• time available for the research project
• monetary resources available
• number of personnel able to be involved in the project
• infrastructure limitations.

The methods should also describe the sampling procedure and outline the proposed conduct of the pilot study.

The important thing to remember here is that both the data collection and data analysis methods must be addressed. Ethical considerations also need to be addressed, including the ethical issues associated with the project and with whom ethical clearance will be obtained or how ethical issues will be addressed if there is no ethics body associated with the management of the project or auspicating body.

At this stage of the project, there is usually no need to attach the main data collection tool to the proposal — the main data collection tool is developed after the project has been sanctioned. The reason is simple: if you submit a tender and prepare the questionnaire, but do not get the tender, then you have contributed a lot of your time for no return.

■ 10.3.4 Time line

Time lines can be presented in several ways. You may choose to use a matrix to gain an overall view of the tasks by days, weeks or months, or you may choose to use a milestone technique. Both techniques are illustrated in figure 10.4. When preparing a time line, ensure that you provide enough detail — sometimes the tasks noted are very general and do not enable a reader to determine the overall effectiveness of your planning ability. On the other hand, you should not be so prescriptive that you are presenting a minute-by-minute account of the timing for the project.

Time line — matrix

TASK	Weeks: 1	2	3	4	5	6	7	8	9	10	11	12
Meet with client	→→					→→						→→
Literature search												→→
Prepare research proposal	→→→											
Submit proposal			→→									→→
Meet with client to refine research design				→→								
Apply for ethical clearance			→→									
Prepare data collection tool(s)				→→								
Peer review of data collection tools					→→							
Pilot test tools						→→						
Data collection phase								→→				
Data coding										→→		
Data analysis										→→		
Prepare seminar paper										→→		
Prepare draft report										→→		
Respond to peer reviews to seminar and draft report											→→	
Revise and submit final report												→→

(continued)

Time line — milestone

Early February 2000	Apply for ethical clearance (BC/EF)
Weeks: 20–31 March	First series of focus groups (BC)
Weeks: 27 March–14 April	Transcribe focus group texts (HI)
	Analyse transcriptions (BC/EF supervising HI)
	Literature search (BC/EF)
	Draft introduction, literature review and methodology sections of report (BC/EF)
Weeks: 17 April–12 May	Second series of focus groups (BC)
Weeks: 8–13 May	Transcribe focus group texts (HI)
	Analyse transcriptions (BC/EF and HI)
June 2000	Progress report (BC/EF)
Week: 3–7 July	Third series of focus groups (BC)
Weeks: 10 July–11 August	Transcribe focus groups (HI)
	Analyse transcriptions (BC/EF and HI)
Weeks: 14 August–8 September	Draft findings and discussion sections of report (BC/EF)
September/October	Revise final report (BC/EF)
November	Prepare journal articles (BC/EF)
December	Submit articles to nominated journals (BC/EF)
	Submit final report (BC/EF)
2001	Submit conference papers to TTRA (BC/EF)
	Present findings in Autumn seminar series (BC/EF)

BC and EF are the two researchers, and HI is the research assistant.

■ **Figure 10.4** *Examples of time lines*

■ *10.3.5* Budget

The budget section, like the time line, differs in style from the introduction, literature review and methodology sections. The budget section does not contain a lot of textual description. You should commence the section with an overview statement that indicates the complete budget amount and indicate if any quotes have been included in the appendices. Organising the budget into a simple line item budget is the easiest representation of the individual budget items. When completing tenders, you may be asked to rank the budget items as to their priority for funding, as often budgets will be cut by the tender receivers to reduce the overall cost of the project. Justification of budgetary items needs to be completed either within the budget section or as a separate section entitled 'Justification of the budget'. An example of a budget is illustrated in figure 10.5.

BUDGET ITEMS	PRIORITY	AMOUNT ($)
Personnel		
Research assistant (RW, Level 3.1) (200 hrs @ $14.39 plus 11.9% on costs)	A	$3 221
Research/clerical assistant (RW, Level 3.3) (40 hrs @ $15.26 plus 11.9% on costs)	A	$684
Literature search costs		
(a) Photocopying of articles ($0.10/page × 1000 pages)	B1	$100
(b) Ordering of articles (30 articles × $14.00)	A	$420
Mailing stationery costs		
(Envelopes and reply-paid envelopes, approximately 2000 envelopes)	A	$100
Survey printing costs		
Survey covering letter (1 × 2000 sheets)	A	$65
Reminder cards (1 × 2000 cards)	A	$148
Surveys (2000 × 5 pages)	A	$480
Postage costs		
Initial mail-out costs (2000 envelopes including weight of contents @ $0.75/package)	A	$1 500
Reminder postcard mail-out costs (2000 × $0.45/card)	A	$900
Incoming mail (reply-paid costs based on best-case scenario, i.e. 100% return rate, 2000 returns × $0.75/package)	A	$1 500
Advertising		
Advertisements in magazines and papers (two × page 3–5 advertisements @ $241 per advertisement, five corporate advertisements @ $94.64)	A	$482
	A	$473
Telephone, fax costs		
Telephone costs (100 min × $0.30/min)	B3	$30
Fax costs (20 min × $0.50/min)	B2	$10
TOTAL		$10 113

■ **Figure 10.5** *Example of a budget*

■ *10.3.6* **Reference** *section*

References are those documents that you have accessed and noted in your introduction, literature review and methodology sections. The references should not include works you have read but did not cite. References should be listed in alphabetical order and presented in the style that your university or the client requires. This textbook follows the author–date system used in the Australian Government Publishing Service, *Style Manual*, Fifth Edition.

When preparing your research proposal, ensure that you provide information on all sections: the introduction, literature review, methodology, time line, budget, references and curriculum vitae. Ensure that the proposal is submitted on time, as late submissions are generally not accepted. Furthermore, ensure that the proposal has been professionally presented and all attachments have been included. To complete the overall proposal, prepare a covering letter indicating your interest, key skills and contact details.

10.4.1 Audience *considerations*

When preparing a research proposal, you need to be aware of your audience. The audience may be the general public, tourism organisations and associations, government agencies, business managers, other researchers or academics. Each audience will require a specific style of writing (tone, tenor, mode and genre). This is discussed in detail in the report section later in the chapter.

10.4.2 Ethical *clearance*

When preparing a research proposal, it is sometimes expeditious to simultaneously apply for ethical approval for your research, so that there is enough time for the ethical clearance to be processed and hopefully approved. By doing this, should your proposal be accepted, your research will not be held up waiting for ethical approval. Remember, ethical clearance is needed for research involving human and/or non-human participants. Consider the ethical issues noted in chapter 4 — such ethical considerations should be included in your research proposal.

In particular, ethical clearance requires the researcher to provide information about the purpose of the research, the hypotheses, aims or objectives, the methodology, and data collection and analysis, as well as procedures for administering and maintaining data sets and confidentiality or anonymity issues (refer to chapter 4). Ethical clearance may also require an indication of the type of consent to be used (either informed or written). Issues of reciprocity and, in particular, the sharing of research findings should be discussed. Some human research ethics panels may request the attachment of questionnaires or interview schedules, informed consent texts and/or written consent sheets. Make sure that you familiarise yourself with all the requirements requested by the ethics panel to which you are applying and that you respond to all the requirements the panel expects to be addressed.

10.5 THE PURPOSE OF RESEARCH REPORTS

The purpose of writing of a research report is sevenfold. As noted in the introduction to this chapter, research involves both process and product, and research reports are one of the ways of representing the product of research. The following are the main purposes of research reports:

- *To conclude the research process.* As a researcher, you have planned the research, collected the data, analysed the data and established your results. These parts need to be pulled together into a whole — the research report.
- *To engage in peer review.* When you prepare a research proposal it will be peer reviewed. This provides a quality check on your skills and ability to conduct the research. The research report is also peer reviewed, and this provides a second quality check on the research conducted. Peer reviews are obligatory for academic research work and for research completed for clients such as government agencies, tourism associations and tourism businesses.
- *To validate the work.* Peer review determines whether the work is valid (accurate) and whether the measures used do in fact measure the variables being studied. Client and academic works require peer review as a validity check.
- *To determine reliability and whether the research is replicable.* Peer review also determines the reliability of the measures used and whether the research is replicable.
- *To enable the research to go 'public'.* In conducting tourism research, researchers are studying the public or phenomena that impact on the public, so researchers should give something back. Disclosure of research findings is associated with research ethics, particularly reciprocity. Research reports also enable researchers to disseminate their findings to a wider audience.
- *To enable the researcher to provide a basis for further research.* The findings may suggest further areas for study or provide the tools for replication of the study for comparative research. Reports also enable another researcher to repeat the study to test the validity and reliability of the study and the recommendations made.
- *To enable plans and programs to be initiated based on the research findings and recommendations.*

10.6 TYPES OF RESEARCH REPORTS

Reports may be presented primarily in two styles: a document that is a 'report' of events or a 'narrative' of events. Reports are used for quantitative research approaches and narratives are more the realm of qualitative research.

■ 10.6.1 Narrative *reports*

Narrative reports differ from scientific reports, which have the following structure: statement of problem, conceptual framework, research questions, methodology, data analysis, conclusions, discussion (Miles & Huberman 1994, p. 298). The qualitative researcher is more inclined to use a narrative report style as it is less 'schematic and constraining' (Miles & Huberman 1994, p. 298). As Dey (1993, p. 240) notes: 'Stories are also accessible because the separate elements of the story blend together into a satisfying whole which is more than the sum of the parts ... [t]he story is not just a juxtaposition of individual parts, for these have to be organized in a way which makes it in some sense holistic and indivisible. The story moves us in its entirety.'

Van Maanen (1988) identifies a variety of narrative genres:

- realist tales
- formal tales
- confessionals
- literary tales
- impressionist tales
- jointly told tales.
- critical tales

Essentially, '[t]here are ... many different styles of writing and no absolutely "right" way' (Jorgensen 1989, p. 119) of writing up qualitative research in the narrative style. However, in selecting an appropriate genre, Webb and Glesne (1992, p. 803) note there are three sets of issues qualitative researchers must consider in relation to their writing:

- power, voice and politics
- authorial authority, assemblage of evidence and researcher–participant relationships
- first or third person voice, tone used for data and theory, and overall genre applied.

On the other hand, Miles and Huberman (1994, pp. 298–306) suggest that the following issues need to be addressed when preparing a qualitative research report: audience; voice, genre and stance; style; and format and structure. Key advice in regard to a narrative report is noted in the following recommendation by Dey (1993, p. 239): 'A good story is like a journey, in which we travel with the characters through the intricacies of the plot, to arrive at the conclusions.' Make sure your story has a beginning, a middle and a conclusion. More details of the narrative style are outlined in the discussions of various qualitative research reports later in the chapter.

■ 10.6.2 Qualitative *research reports*

Zeller (1991) suggests that qualitative studies don't report out 'data'; they report 'scenes' — that is accounts of researchers' engagements over time with informants in their surroundings. ... Zeller asks further whether qualitative field studies are different from the nonfictional novel, or from slice-of-life case studies from the New Journalism. Do qualitative studies have a distinctive reporting style? ... a set of field observations can be rendered differently — in poetic form ... or as a series of vignettes ... or as scenes or stories. A blurring of the frontiers seems to occur between social scientific reporting and 'figurative' or 'rhetorical' renditions of aesthetic material (Miles & Huberman 1994, pp. 298–9).

The following sections discuss case study reports, ethnographic reports, participant observation reports and action research reports.

Case study reports

The reporting of a case study can take written or oral forms. Regardless of the form, however, similar steps need to be followed in the compositional process; identifying the audience for the report, developing the compositional structure, and following certain procedures (such as having the report reviewed by informed persons who have been the subject of the case study) (Yin 1994, p. 127).

Stake (1995) suggests the following structure for a case study report:
1. opening vignette
2. issue statement, study purpose and method
3. narrative of case, including context
4. discussion of the issues
5. case study evidence
6. synthesis
7. closing vignette
8. references.

Case study audiences include: research peers; decision makers in government, organisations and the community who are not versed in case study methods; academic departments and divisions such as research service offices which administer postgraduate dissertations and theses; research clients; and the general community.

Case studies may be written, oral or visual presentations (Yin 1994). Written cases studies may be one of four types: the classic single-case study or the multiple-case study using narrative form; and the single-case study or multiple-case study using question–answer mode rather than narrative form, with single cases being presented in question–answer format, which enables the reader to also construct a cross-case analysis throughout the report (Yin 1994). Yin (1994) also suggests that any of these four types may use one of following six structures to compose the report:

1. *Linear-analytic structure* — this structure follows the scientific experimental report. The issue/problem is stated, followed by the literature review, discussion of methods, findings and analysis and, lastly, recommendations. This structure is used for exploratory, descriptive and explanatory case study reports.
2. *Comparative structure* — comparative case study facts are presented using different theoretical or conceptual models. The case study is presented several times, each time with a different theoretical lens being applied. This structure may be applied to exploratory, descriptive and explanatory case study reports.
3. *Chronological structure* — the case study is reported using a temporal organisation. Data about the beginning, the middle and the most recent historical phases of the case study are used to organise the report. The chronological structure is appropriate for explanatory,

descriptive and explanatory case study reports. Yin (1994) suggests that the writer should compose the report backwards, starting with the most recent phase before attending to the middle and beginning phases. He makes this suggestion as writers tend to get 'bogged' down in the background and history and write too much or spend too much time on these phases, leaving the most recent phases poorly or briefly discussed.

4. *Theory-building structure* — the case study is designed to progressively construct the overall theoretical argument. Each chapter presents a part of the overall theory, with the concluding chapter drawing the threads together. This structure is appropriate for exploratory and explanatory case studies.

5. *'Suspense' structure* — the case study 'answer' is presented in the first chapter and the remaining chapters discuss the rationale for the answer and apply, consider and dispose of alternative explanations along the way. This is an innovative structure to use with explanatory case studies.

6. *Unsequenced structure* — the case study report contains chapters that are self-contained units and can be reorganised without detracting from the report. This structure is only useful with descriptive case studies.

Ethnographic reports

The ethnographer 'inscribes' social discourse; he [sic] writes it down. In so doing, he [sic] turns it from a passing event, which exists only in its own moment of occurrence, into an account, which exists in its inscriptions and can be reconsulted (Geertz 1973, p. 19).

The distinguishing features of ethnographic reports are the use of thick descriptions (Geertz 1973) and verbatim quotations (Fetterman 1989). Ethnographic reports also use 'the ethnographic present' and the role of the researcher or the researcher's 'social situatedness' is also presented (Fetterman 1989). Thick descriptions enable the ethnographer to recreate the phenomenon being studied with clarity for the reader. Thick descriptions are developed from field notes and transcriptions. 'Ethnographic writing is a process of reduction, as the ethnographer moves from field notes to written text' (Fetterman 1989, p. 115). The use of thick descriptions and long verbatim quotes enables the reader to become a co-analyst and consequently determine whether the ethnographer's interpretations are sound and valid (Fetterman 1989; Reinharz 1992).

A number of literary conventions and writing techniques are available for the ethnographer to use. The author may assume the voice of different speakers, may appear omniscient or transparent. The author can expand or contract through narrative pace. Use of concrete metaphors, rich similes, parallelism, irony, and many other devices on a larger plane convey the true feel, taste, and smell of a moment (Fetterman 1989, p. 118).

Participant observation reports

Becker (1986) offers the following advice regarding writing:

- use the active rather than the passive voice
- use fewer words rather than more words
- ordinary words are preferable to jargon
- avoid repetition
- use concrete and specific language rather than abstract and general language
- exemplify and illustrate ideas
- use metaphors carefully and for impact.

There is no one way to present participant observation reports — the writing style will depend on the nature of the setting studied, the purpose of the study and the style of the ethnographer. However, Jorgensen (1989) makes the following suggestions for participant observation report writing:

- state the issue being studied
- comment on the relevant literature
- iterate the study focus
- identify relevant study ideas and concepts
- discuss research methods (e.g. the setting, access, rapport, 'participant role, data collection, analysis and theorising' (Jorgensen 1989, p. 122))
- discuss the findings
- state the contribution of the study.

As you can see, this is a relatively close structure to that of the scientific experimental report. What distinguishes the participant observation report from the former is the use of the features described by Becker above. And you should remember that:

> although chapter two is a favourite spot for the traditional literature review, there is no ironclad rule — even in the otherwise totally inflexible graduate school at my university — that chapter two must be a literature review. Nor is there any rule insisting that chapter one be devoted to the topic at all. I expect my students to know the relevant literature, but I do not want them to lump (dump?) it all into a chapter that remains unconnected to the rest of the study. I want them to draw upon the literature selectively and appropriately as needed in the telling of their story. In our descriptive and analytical accounts, the most appropriate place for examining the literature seems to me to be in consort with the analysis of new data. Ordinarily this calls for introducing related research toward the end of a study rather than at the beginning, except for the necessary 'nesting' of a problem in the introduction (Wolcott 1990, p. 17).

Action research reports

Researchers who engage in action research may choose to use written, oral or visual reports, and, for some, the change in the issue being studied may be the only outcome required and no report eventuates. However, a suggested format for action research reports is provided here. As with case studies, the report may be based on the scientific experimental model (introduction, literature review, method, findings and analysis, and future action plans), but there are alternative models. These models are based on the discussion of action research by Kemmis and McTaggart (1988). One alternative model involves the chronological reporting of the action research process; a second involves the reporting of the initial analysis of the issue, the plan for improvement, the implementation and evaluation of the plan, a reflection on the overall process and issues for future reflection and engagement in action research. Participatory action research may also be reported using the six structures presented in the case study section.

■ 10.6.3 Quantitative *research reports*

Science is a public affair and well-written reports must ensure that it remains so. The purpose of a report is to communicate ideas and relay empirical observations and findings. The main principle to follow in writing up a report is that it must include, in a clear, precise and concise manner, every relevant aspect of the study so that another researcher wanting to replicate or challenge the results could repeat the study solely on the basis of your report (Tilley 1999, p. 385).

Quantitative research reports follow the tenets of scientific experimental report writing — that is, the report consists of a cover, a title page, a contents page, an abstract, an introduction, a methodology section, a results section, a discussion section, a conclusion, recommendations, references and appendices.

Cover

On the cover, you should identify the title of the report, the author(s) and the host institution. Generally, this is the norm for covers; however, clients may have different requirements by which you must abide.

Title page

The title page includes the title of the report, the author, the sponsor or client, the date of the report and any special conditions such as 'Report-in-confidence', 'Commercial-in-confidence' or 'In-house distribution only'.

Contents page

The contents page lists the following items: executive summary, preface/foreword, acknowledgments, list of tables and list of figures, chapters, subsections, references and appendices. Roman numerals are used for pages from the executive summary through to the acknowledgments section. The contents page itself is not listed on the contents page, and chapters are organised into subsections (see figure 10.6).

■ **Figure 10.6**
Example of a contents page

Source: *Australian Tourism Commission (1995)*

Appendices should be titled and a page reference should be provided so that the reader can easily locate them. Tables, figures, maps and appendices should be listed as in figure 10.7. Note that for tables, figures and maps the first numeral relates to the chapter number in which the item is located and the second numeral after the full stop relates to the order in which the material is presented in each chapter — first, second, third, and so on.

Source: *Jennings (1999) and Jennings (1998)*

Acknowledgments page

Acknowledgments are a polite way to extend a vote of thanks to all those who have assisted in the research process and reporting. It is a courtesy to thank, in particular, those who participated in the study. However, you need to consider all those who contributed to your research: people who assisted in data collection, access to references and funding, clerical and technical assistance, and supervisors, as well as peer reviewers, known and unknown.

Foreword

Forewords are generally written by eminent or important people in the field. An example of a foreword is included in the following Industry Insight.

INDUSTRY INSIGHT

The following example of a foreword is drawn from the government sector. The foreword is written by the then Minister for Tourism, Michael Lee, on the establishment of the Tourism Forecasting Council and the release of the Forecast reports.

Message from the Minister

Few major industries in Australia can boast the growth rates achieved by tourism in recent years. For example, in 1993 inbound visitor arrivals increased by 15 per cent and tourism export earnings accounted for one-fifth of the growth in Australia's total export earnings.

The industry continues to offer outstanding potential for economic growth, but it is essential that we have policies in place to support this growth. The Commonwealth Government's commitment to tourism is clear. In 1994–95, we will provide $79 million to the Australian Tourist Commission to promote Australia as an international tourist destination.

In addition, $42 million has been allocated over the four years to 1996–97 to diversify and preserve the Australian tourism product through programs that encourage the growth of tourism in regional areas, develop Australia's potential for ecotourism and extend opportunities in the rural, backpacker and cruise shipping markets.

A key component of our strategy is to ensure that we have the infrastructure necessary to cater to the needs of increasing numbers of tourists. New investments will only occur in response to realistic expectations of sustainable profitability. Getting the right level of future investment in the tourism industry will therefore depend on the availability and use of accurate and timely forecasts of the balance between supply and demand.

Reflecting the need for the Government and industry to act in this complex area, the Tourism Forecasting Council was established and structured to draw on the combined expertise of the private and public sectors in tourism, construction, property investment and finance.

A key role for the Council is to encourage awareness among investors that, like other opportunities, investment in tourism facilities needs to be based on professional business planning, long-term operating viability and an achievable vision of the industry's future.

I am proud of the establishment of the Tourism Forecasting Council. It illustrates that this Government is taking a longer term view of the industry's prospects by providing a sound basis for future industry planning. It is also indicative of the results that can be achieved when Government and industry work together in productive partnership.

MICHAEL LEE
Minister for Tourism

Source: *Commonwealth Government of Australia (1994)*

Preface

The preface should be written by the author(s). The preface explains the history of the research project, its background or the impetus for the research. It also outlines limitations and qualifications regarding the research, such as funding and time. The preface may also include an acknowledgment section if there is no acknowledgments page. The following Industry Insight demonstrates the use of a combined preface and acknowledgments section.

INDUSTRY INSIGHT

PREFACE
The original idea for this book was generated in the back of a bus and over a number of beers during the 1992 International Geographical Union Commission on Tourism and Leisure Symposium in Telluride, Colorado. During our conversations on issues of sustainable tourism development it became readily apparent that there was a substantial gap in the available literature and knowledge on touristic activities in the northern and southern polar regions. It is hoped that this book will now fill some of that gap.

(continued)

Over the past two years numerous people have assisted us with research, advice and the production of the book. Help with research and the development of ideas has come from Dick Butler, Thor Flogenfeldt, Geoff Kearsley, Kohn Marsh, Brian and Delyse Springett, Valene Smith, Arvid Viken and Mariska Wouters. Further help with research, comment on drafts and the all-important moral support has come from Nicolette Bramley, Brenda Daugherty, Helen Gladstones, John Jenkins, Vanessa O'Sullivan, Jacqui Pinkava, Christine Petersen, Jane Saunders, Dave Twynam and Josette Wells.

Financial and administrative support has been kindly provided by the Lakehead University Centre for Northern Studies, Lakehead University Department of Geography and the Faculty of Communication, University of Canberra. Roberta Ferguson and Janice Hunt assisted with typing and organisational assistance at Lakehead University, while Anne Applebee, Stuart Christopherson, Susan McDougall, and Sue Wright assisted likewise at the University of Canberra. Maps were produced by Cathy Chapin and photographic reproduction was by Peter Puna both at Lakehead University. Robert Clarke, Pierre Germain, Sandra Haywood, Frigg Jorgensen and Laura Seddon helped with research and/or the reading of parts of the draft manuscript.

We would like to give a great deal of thanks to Iain Stevenson and everyone at John Wiley for their continued support. The editors would also like to give special thanks to the International Association of Antarctica Tour Operators (IAATO) for permission to reproduce IAATO's guidelines for tour operators and visitors to Antarctica. Finally, we would like to thank all the contributors for their support of the project and making the job of the editors that much easier.

C. Michael Hall   Margaret E. Johnston
O'Connor   Thunder Bay

Source: *Hall & Johnston (1995)*

Abstract

The abstract is perhaps the most difficult part of a report to write. The abstract provides the reader with a summary of the content of the report. This means that the abstract should state the problem or issues being studied, provide some background, briefly address the methods used, state the significant findings, and provide a brief discussion of the findings and the consequences of those findings. Abstracts are usually only 150–200 words in length, so the writing style must be clear, precise and informative. Your abstract will be read more times than your report will be read. A poorly written abstract may mean that a well-written report is never referred to, since the reader of the abstract may discount the report based on the quality of the abstract. Abstracts should not read like a table of contents. Figure 10.8 provides a discussion about abstracts.

A SCRUTINY OF THE ABSTRACT, II[1]

KENNETH K. LANDES[2]

Ann Arbor, Michigan

ABSTRACT

A partial biography of the writer is given. The inadequate abstract is discussed. What should be covered by an abstract is considered. The importance of the abstract is described. Dictionary definitions of 'abstract' are quoted. At the conclusion a revised abstract is presented.

For many years I have been annoyed by the inadequate abstract. This became acute while I was serving a term as editor of the *Bulletin* of The American Association of Petroleum Geologists. In addition to returning manuscripts to authors for rewriting of abstracts, I also took 30 minutes in which to lower my ire by writing, 'A Scrutiny of the Abstract'. This little squib has had a fantastic distribution. If only one of my scientific outpourings would do as well! Now the editorial board of the Association has requested a revision. This is it.

The inadequate abstract is illustrated at the top of the page. The passive voice is positively screaming at the reader! It is an outline with each item in the outline expanded into a sentence. The reader is told what the paper is about, but not what it contributes. Such abstracts are merely overgrown titles. They are produced by writers who are either (1) beginners, (2) lazy or (3) have not written the paper yet.

To many writers the preparation of an abstract is an unwanted chore required at the last minute by an editor or insisted upon even before the paper has been written by a deadline-bedeviled program chairman. However, in terms of market reached, the abstract is the *most important part of the paper*. For every individual who reads or listens to your entire paper, from 10 to 500 will read the abstract.

If you are presenting a paper before a learned society, the abstract alone may appear in a preconvention issue of the society journal as well as in the convention program; it may also be run by trade journals. The abstract which accompanies a published paper will most certainly reappear in abstract journals in various languages, and perhaps in company internal circulars as well. It is much better to please than to antagonize this great audience. Papers written for oral presentation should be *completed prior to the deadline for the abstract*, so that the abstract can be prepared from the written paper and not from raw ideas gestating in the writer's mind.

My dictionary describes an abstract as 'a summary of a statement, document, speech, etc. . . .' and that which *concentrates in itself the essential information* of a paper or article. The definition I prefer has been set in italics. May all writers learn the art (it is not easy) of preparing an abstract containing the *essential information* in their compositions. With this goal in mind, I append an abstract that should be an improvement over the one appearing at the beginning of this discussion.

ABSTRACT

The abstract is of utmost importance, for it is read by 10 to 500 times more people than hear or read the entire article. It should not be a mere recital of the subjects covered. Expressions such as 'is discussed' and 'is described' should *never* be included! The abstract should be a condensation and concentration of the *essential information* in the paper.

[1] Revised from K. K. Landes, 'A Scrutiny of the Abstract', first published in the *Bulletin*, in 1951 (*Bulletin*, vol. 35, no. 7, p. 1660).

[2] Professor of geology and mineralogy, University of Michigan. Past editor of the *Bulletin*.

■ **Figure 10.8** *A discussion of abstracts*

Source: *Landes (1964)*

In some reports, an executive summary may be required. Executive summaries can vary in length depending on the length of the overall report. For example, 20-page reports usually have an executive summary of one or two pages, 50-page reports three or four pages and 100-page reports five or six pages (Ticehurst & Veal 1999, p. 237). Reports longer than 100 pages have an executive summary of approximately six pages — anything over six pages is moving into a short article on the report itself. Furthermore, executive summaries longer than six pages defeat the purpose of the executive summary, which is to provide a summary for executives to understand and make decisions on the report without necessarily having to read the report. The executive summary also includes the report's recommendations.

Introduction

There are a variety of other headings that may used in conjunction with or as a substitute for the introduction, including: background, research problem, aims of the research, review of the literature or literature review, and hypotheses and definitions. Whatever terminology is used, the introduction section needs to address:

- the background to the research, that is the research rationale
- the anticipated contributions that the research will make
- the aims, objectives or hypotheses of the research
- the theoretical constructs that will be applied
- relevant definitions
- the current status of the literature in regard to the research problem.

Often, the introduction is separated from the literature review. However, these two sections usually account for 10% of the overall word count for a report (Sarantakos 1993, p. 427).

Methodology section

The methodology section is referred to more often than not as the methods section. Based on our earlier discussion regarding the terms 'methodology' and 'method', the use of the term 'methodology' is advocated here as it is the correct usage of the appropriate term. The purpose of the methodology section is to inform the reader of the research design and to demonstrate the methodological ability of the researcher. The methodology section should contain the following elements:

- The nature of the overlying theoretical paradigm utilised. This is particularly true for academic reports and professional reports, but less so for reports for general practitioners, tourism stakeholders groups and some government agencies and the general public. For example, if you use the terms ontological, epistemological and methodological perspectives in a report for the general public, you would 'turn the readers off' and effectively demonstrate that you are incapable of changing your writing style to match your audience. All reports should state the type of methodology used (quantitative, qualitative or mixed method) and your justification for the selection you made.
- The methods used — that is, your data collection tool(s) (e.g. in-depth interviews or self-completion questionnaires distributed by mail) and your justification for using them.
- The data collection schedule and any strategies used to increase response rates.

- The sampling procedure used, as well as justifications for the procedure. Sampling frames should be identified, as well as populations and their definitions.
- The pilot test procedures used.
- Methods of data analysis used and justification for the analytical procedure.
- Ethical issues, any guidelines followed by the researcher, any approving bodies that granted approval, gatekeepers and access issues, and confidentiality or anonymity issues.

The methods section constitutes approximately 20% of the word count for the overall report.

Findings/results section

The largest part of a report is the findings/results section (Sarantakos 1993, p. 428). This section usually commences with the response rates, non-response and refusals. The representativeness of the results is also affirmed. This section includes a description of variables and their relationships. The description of the results includes textual statements, tables, figures and graphs. Tables and graphs are introduced with brief sentences both before and after the tables and graphs are presented. This section only presents the results and findings — it does not analyse, interpret or discuss results.

There is a difference in opinion as to the overall presentation of findings. Sarantakos (1993) suggests that the order of the discussion of the findings should follow the order of the questions on the survey instrument. However, Ticehurst and Veal (1999) disagree and suggest that the question order in an interview or questionnaire is to facilitate the flow of data collection and the results do not follow that pattern. Instead, they believe the results should follow the statement of hypothesis or the aims and objectives stated at the beginning of the report. Whichever way you choose to present you results, it must be logical and coherent.

Discussion section

In the discussion section, the main findings are summarised and interpreted. You should link back to theoretical constructs and other studies introduced in the literature review section and to the main hypotheses and aims. In the discussion of the results, you must to be ethical: there should be no selective treatment of results or bias. The discussion should be frank and honest, especially when the results are contrary to expectations. Contrary results should be discussed and unusual results, weaknesses and alternatives clearly discussed (Neuman 2000). Neuman (2000) suggests the easiest way for novice researchers to present the discussion of the results is to use the hypotheses or aims as the organisers. An alternative is to merge the findings and discussion sections together and simultaneously present the results and discuss them at the same time. The findings and discussion sections constitute the largest sections of the report — each is 30% of the word count.

Conclusion

The conclusion section may also be referred to as the summary (Neuman 2000), 'conclusion and summary', 'conclusion and recommendations' or 'summary and conclusion' (Sarantakos 1993, p. 428). In this section, the research problem is restated and the findings are summarised. Conclusions may be described as first and second order conclusions. First order conclusions are statistical statements, such as '79% of daytrippers were satisfied with the facilities at Horseshoe Bay'. Second order conclusions link the statistical or factual statements to other research, such as 'While 79% of daytrippers were satisfied with the facilities available at Horseshoe Bay, this is higher than the number identified by Grimshaw (1996), who reported that 47% of daytrippers were satisfied with the facilities available at Horseshoe Bay'. The conclusion section summarises the report and comments on future directions.

Recommendations

Recommendations are grounded in the research findings and the research hypotheses and/or aims and objectives. If the recommendations are adopted, then the reason for the research being conducted in the first place should be solved by the implementation of the recommendations. Recommendations should include a range of alternatives from which the client can choose, as personnel, monetary and time constraints may influence which recommendations are adopted and why.

References

The reference list is a list of all works cited in the report. These are listed in alphabetical order and a specific style should be used based on the preference of the supervisor, client, researcher or government body. It is important to reiterate here the earlier comments on plagiarism presented in chapter 4. Plagiarism entails the use of other texts as if they were your own without acknowledging the original author(s).

Figure 10.9 provides some examples of inappropriate use of other works. Compare the original text with example 1. What do you notice about the text? You should have noticed that it uses end-of-paragraph referencing, which is inappropriate, and that the text is actually a direct quotation of the original without the use of quotation marks. This is unacceptable — it is akin to plagiarism. Compare example 2(a) and example 2(b) with the original — again, the text is inadequately referenced. Example 2(a) primarily uses the original text without referencing it, and example 2(b) presents the same text as in example 2(a), although in this case the writer has used end-of-paragraph referencing to identify the author. However, once again the presentation of the text is inadequate and amounts to plagiarism. The correct referencing style is used in example 2(c). This example demonstrates the correct use of punctuation for adding words not in the original text, as well as deleting words from the original text. However, you can see that the text becomes clumsy with punctuation. As a consequence, the use of indirect quotation is better. Example 3 uses indirect quotation and a clear citation style.

■ Figure 10.9
Examples of inappropriate use of other works

Original

'Tourism trends are determined by four interrelated factors: the economic, political and social environments, and technology (see Figure 1.1). The level of economic development will determine the availability of tourism infrastructure in a destination and the capacity of individuals to travel in a generating region. Economic growth also leads to changing spending patterns and shifts in social behaviour. Social change has a major influence on the shape of the tourism market because of the effect it has on individual consumption and demand ... The interaction of different cultures and societies will also have substantial impacts on host communities and travellers alike.' (Hall 1997: 2)

Example 1

Tourism trends are determined by four interrelated factors: the economic, political and social environments, and technology (see Figure 1.1). The level of economic development will determine the availability of tourism infrastructure in a destination and the capacity of individuals to travel in a generating region. Economic growth also leads to changing spending patterns and shifts in social behaviour. Social change has a major influence on the shape of the tourism market because of the effect it has on individual consumption and demand. The interaction of different cultures and societies will also have substantial impacts on host communities and travellers alike. (Hall 1997)

Example 2(a)

Tourism trends can be determined by four interrelated factors: the political, social, and economic, environments, and technology (see Figure 1.1). The degree of economic development will also determine the availability of infrastructure in a destination and the ability of individuals to travel in a generating region. Economic development also leads to changing spending patterns and shifts in social behaviour.

Example 2(b)

Tourism trends can be determined by four interrelated factors: the political, social, and economic, environments, and technology (see Figure 1.1). The degree of economic development will also determine the availability of infrastructure in a destination and the ability of individuals to travel in a generating region. Economic development also leads to changing spending patterns and shifts in social behaviour. (Hall 1997)

Example 2(c)

'Tourism trends [can be] determined by four interrelated factors': political, social, and economic environments, as well as technology (see Figure 1.1) (Hall 1997: 2). 'The ... [degree] of economic development will [also] determine the availability of ... infrastructure in a destination and the ... [ability] of individuals to travel in a generating region. Economic ... [development] also leads to changing spending patterns and shifts in social behaviour.' (Hall 1997: 2)

Example 3

There are four factors that may affect tourism patterns: social factors, political factors, economic factors and technological factors (Hall 1997: 2).

Source: *Hall (1997)*

Appendices

Appendices are adjunct pieces of data, material or text that have been incorporated to complement the main body of the report. Researchers must be judicious in their use of data and text within the body of the report. Material that is not imperative for the main report may be added to the end of the report immediately following the reference section (in the appendices section). Appendices should be individually labelled and titled. To assist the reader in directly finding an appendix, you should use page numbers and/or footers. Appendices should also be identified and listed with page references on the contents page.

10.7 AUDIENCE CONSIDERATIONS FOR RESEARCH REPORTS

There are a number of audiences for research reports. Ticehurst and Veal (1999) identify three: the general public, decision makers and professionals (experts). Neuman (2000) identifies five: instructors, students, scholars, practitioners and the general public. Regardless of how you classify audiences, in reporting your research you need to be cognisant of your audience, as this will influence the tone and tenor of your writing, as well as the specific genre (type or form of writing) that will be selected. It is necessary for you to write for your audience, so that your audience is able to read and comprehend your work. Some considerations regarding the style of language, the content of the report and the genre are described below in regard to each of the three audiences identified by Ticehurst and Veal (1999).

10.7.1 The general *public*

For the general public, the language used needs to be easily understood, so your text should be free from jargon and wordy statements. The directions noted in chapter 8 for question design also apply here: use simple and succinct language and avoid technical or ambiguous terms. In preparing reports for the general public, the level of the language should be equivalent to the language level in most tabloid newspapers. Special interest groups with technical knowledge may require more technical and detailed texts. This is not to suggest that the general public have poor language skills. Rather, these guidelines are offered to help you gain the maximum coverage for your report by ensuring that the reading level is appropriate and that the language is clear and unambiguous.

The content of the report should be focused on the facts, and any practical application of the research and the possible benefits of the research findings for the public. The report should not focus on the overall research design in great detail unless the public represents a special interest group and may want to lobby government or business based on the report. In preparing reports for the general public, do not make any unsupported claims.

Reports for the general public can be drawn from several genres: media reports, newsletters, bulletins, presentations at meetings, journal articles or addresses at public meetings.

In preparing written reports for the general public, remember to make the reports short, and readable in one sitting.

■ *10.7.2* **Decision makers**

The content of reports for decision makers should include a short summary of how the study was conducted. The main focus should be on the results. Visual inputs should be used to assist the communication of the results, such as graphs and tables (Neuman 1994, p. 473). Specifics of research design and findings can be situated in the appendices so that those who are interested in reading these sections will be able to access them (Neuman 2000). Technical reports for decision makers will generally follow the structure of the scientific research report detailed earlier.

The types of genres used to report research to decision makers include: position papers, issue papers, market profile reports and feasibility study reports. The length of the document is often determined in the research brief or contract and is negotiated prior to the commencement of the research.

■ *10.7.3* **Professionals**

In reports for professionals the language should be technical. Writing for professionals should exhibit 'a sound grasp of the theoretical and methodological concepts' (Neuman 1994, p. 473). Professionals 'like a compact, tightly written, but extensive section on data analysis, with a meticulous discussion of results' (Neuman 2000 p. 465). The length of the report should be appropriate to disseminate the information. A variety of genres are used including reports, books, journal articles and conference papers.

Regardless of the audience, there are several points that require emphasising when reporting research findings in writing:

- presentation should be approached professionally — that is, you should provide clear, typed copies free from typographical errors
- the text should be cohesive and succinct
- all sections should contribute to the telling of the research process, and there should be no omissions (e.g. referring to appendix one when appendix one has not been included with the report)
- text type, table construction, referencing and the use of headings should be homogeneous
- the report should be supplemented with visual aids (tables, graphs, diagrams, maps and images) in the body of the text itself and in the appendices
- statements should be grounded in the data.

Be aware that a glossy, good-looking report may belie the nature of its content. A professional-looking document should be complemented by text that matches the quality of the visual presentation.

The purpose of a research proposal

The purpose of a research proposal is to demonstrate to an intended readership that you have the research skills and expertise, as well as the appropriate knowledge, to conduct the research effectively.

The structure of a research proposal

Research proposals should contain the following components: a cover sheet, an introduction, a literature review, a methodology section, a time line, a budget and a reference list. Sometimes, proformas will be provided by granting agencies, clients or stakeholder bodies for use by researchers in the preparation of research proposals.

The overall presentation of a research proposal

Writing style should be clear, concise and written to match the audience's needs. Care should be taken with proposals and their visual presentation as this also reflects on the professional quality of your work. Ensure you allow yourself sufficient time to prepare proposals as submission dates are rarely extended for late submissions due to your poor time management.

Audience considerations in research proposal writing

The audience determines the language, content and genre used.

The procedures for ethical clearance

Ethical clearance for research involving human and non-human participants/subjects usually involves researchers in stating the research aims and objectives or hypotheses, the methodology and methods of the research, protocols for administering and maintaining data sets and confidentiality or anonymity issues. The type of consent (informed or written), and aspects of reciprocity associated with the research, may also be required. Some ethical panels desire the inclusion of questionnaire or interview schedules, informed consent texts and written consent sheets. It is best to apply for ethical clearance when the research proposal is submitted, so that the processing of the clearance is timely.

The purpose of research reports

Research reports provide closure to the research process, allow peer reviews of the research and report the findings.

The difference between qualitative and quantitative research reports

The difference between qualitative and quantitative research reports is the style of writing and key genres used. Qualitative reports adopt a narrative style, whereas quantitative reports use the style of scientific writing. Both include the following structural elements, though not always in the same order: introduction, literature review, findings, discussion, conclusion and/or recommendations.

The various types of research reports

Reports may be either 'report' or 'narrative' in form. Specifically, quantitative reports tend to adopt the scientific research report style, whereas qualitative reports tend to use the narrative style (such as realist tales, critical tales, formal tales).

Audience considerations in research report writing

The audience is particularly important when writing reports. The audience determines the level of language used, the style of writing adopted, the genres selected, the length of the report and the type and amount of information provided.

Questions

10.1 Why is it necessary to include a literature review in a research proposal? Why not use a list of possible literature resources?

10.2 Prepare a checklist of the key items that the researcher must attend to when preparing a research proposal and a report, including audience considerations. Share these in your next tutorial session.

10.3 Write a 250-word summary detailing the similarities and differences between quantitative and qualitative research reports.

10.4 Prepare a table overviewing the various types of qualitative research reports.

EXERCISES

Exercise 10.1

Assume that you have accepted an invitation to be a peer reviewer for a small grant body, which has just closed its call for research proposals. Examine the following research proposal, and comment on the quality of the presentation and the proposed research.

Research proposal outline: Mt Prichard

Mt Prichard is biggest and closest recreational and environmental park to Hanaman. The Cooperslea Tourism Strategy suggests that greater intensive use and management of Mt Prichard is needed. This study aims to establish current usage patterns of the Mt Prichard area as well as community expectations regarding usage.

Aims

1. To determine local recreational usage patterns of the Mt Prichard Environmental/National Park;
2. To determine non-local recreational usage patterns of the Mt Prichard Environmental/National Park;
3. To determine the values held by the local community members towards the Mt Prichard Environmental/National Park;
4. To determine the values held by the non- local community members towards the Mt Prichard Environmental/National Park;
5. To gather information regarding possible improvements for the Mt Prichard Environmental/National Park including physical and activity based improvements.

(continued)

Relevance

As mentioned in the introduction, this study has direct relevance to the Cooperslea Region Tourism Strategy, specifically:

Cooperslea Tourism Strategy

Objective 1: Develop and co-ordinate tourism management planning and tourism monitoring.

Actions and Recommendations

1. *Prepare a management plan for the Mt Prichard area in Hanaman.*

Methodology

This study applies descriptive, comparative and evaluative approaches. The descriptive approach will describe current usage patterns, the comparative approach will compare holiday usage patterns with the weeks prior to and following the Easter period, the evaluative approach will evaluate the current management of Park usage as well as suggesting some future directions for Park managers to consider.

The methodology for this study will be primarily quantitative in nature with data collected at user-sites by interviewer-conducted surveys. A time period will be selected for the interview period which accounts for the maximum visitation possible to the area by both locals and non-locals. This will include weekend periods and some holiday times. A period of one month's duration will be used for data collection.

Ethical considerations

- Free and comprehending consent must be gained.
- Minimal disturbance to the park experience.
- Assurances of anonymity and security of data collected.

The study will apply the standards of the Ethics Committee, West Coast University.

Analysis

Simple statistical analyses and chi-squared tests.

Budget

Surveys

Printing of survey recording sheets (500 × 3 page surveys @ 10c/page)	$ 150.00
Report printing	$50.00
Travel costs	
University to Mt Prichard return [30 km return @ 0.48c/km (over 2000cc) × 2 trips/weekend × 4 weekends]	$115.20
University to Mt Prichard return [30 km return @ 0.48c/km (over 2000cc) × 10 week days]	$144.00
TOTAL	**$459.20**

Exercise 10.2

Examine the following research budget. What are your comments as a peer reviewer? The budget is part of a research proposal that uses a case study design, specifically a multiple case study to examine senior citizens' travel behaviours from the date of retirement for a period of 20 years following retirement. Citizens are to be drawn from the states and territories of Australia and will be interviewed in these capital city centres: Brisbane, Melbourne, Sydney, Adelaide and Perth. The researcher lives in Rockhampton. Focus groups are to be held every five years. The proposed budget has been prepared for the duration of the project.

Rockhampton–Brisbane–Sydney–Melbourne–Rockhampton airfares × 3 [3 fares × $1451.40 (full economy fare)	$4 354.20
Per diem 3 days × 3 trips 3 × Sydney $166.8 = 500.4 3 × Brisbane $152.1 = 456.3 3 × Melbourne $152.1 = 456.3	$1 413.00
Mackay travel and accommodation (3 trips) Travel ($229.40 [21 days advance purchase] + $25.20 tax × 3 trips)	$763.80
Daily allowance (3 × $113)	$113.00
Morning/afternoon tea (12 people × 3 panels × 5 locations × $5.00/person)	$1 650.00
Research assistant 3.1 hours × (transcriptions and analysis)	
Literature review (research documents)	Nil cost
Travel for participants	$10 000.00
Meals	$2 000.00
Miscellaneous	$3 500.00
Total	$23 794.00

Exercise 10.3

From the following data prepare a table and a graph, and then write two brief paragraphs to accompany your table and graph to report the findings. Ensure that you title the table and graph based on the data that you are given. Remember, the table and graph should be able to stand alone, away from the supporting text. Compare your work with the work of others in your tutorial group and seek feedback from your lecturer.

Raw data representing the main activity engaged in at Horseshoe Bay (only one response per person)

ACTIVITIES	RAW COUNT	TOTAL
Camping	11111 11111 11111 11111 1	
Recreational shell collecting	11111	
Recreational fishing	11111 11111 11111 11111 11111 1111	
Sport fishing	111	
Spearfishing	11111 11111 11111 11111 11111	
Snorkelling	11111 11111 11111 11111 11111 11111 11111 11	
Diving	11111 11111 11111 11111 11111 11111 11111 11111 1	
Photography	11111	
Sailing	11111 11111 11111 11111 11111	
Windsurfing	11111 11111 11	
Coral viewing	11111 11111 11111 11111 11111 11111 11111 11111 11111 11111 11111 11111 11	
Waterskiing	11111 11111 11111	
Jetskiing	11	
Speed boating	11111 11111 111	
Swimming	11111 11111 11111 11111 11111 11111 11111 11111 11111 1111	

Exercise 10.4

Read the following constructed interview extracts generated to exemplify qualitative case study interview data. Then write a brief narrative (200 words) summarising the key themes evident in the transcripts associated with multigenerational holidays.

Rhona (female, single, employed, two children, aged 40 years)
I go on holidays with my Mum and Dad; it allows them to have time with the grandkids and me to have a break from doing all the chores. The caravan gets a bit cramped sometimes, especially when it rains — then we can't use the lean-to area and we all have to squash inside.

Val (female, retired pensioner, married, mother of Rhona, aged 62 years)
To tell you the truth, I am getting a bit sick of it. I love Rhona and I know she is battling to bring the kids up all right and work at the same time; however, the kids run a bit wild sometimes, when she gets run down. I love the kids too, but I have done all that. I brought up Rhona. I don't want to bring up another set of kids; if I wanted to do that, I would have had more kids myself. When we go on holidays, I really dread it; some days are great, when it's not raining, but when we get

cooped up inside I nearly go mad. But generally I end up doing all the work and Rhona rests and I come home needing a holiday to get over the holiday.

Dave (male, retired pensioner, married to Val, father of Rhona, aged 65)
Holidays, well, let me see, they are often a challenge, but it's great to have the family all together — Val, Rhona and the two kids, Vicky and Rob. Poor Rhona is always exhausted coming up to the holidays, she does her share, she buys all the tucker and pays for the caravan site. Val and I both take turns in looking after the kids to give Rhona a break. I try to help Val out and cook barbeques for tea each night so she doesn't have to worry about the evening meal.

Vicky (female, daughter of Rhona, studying at high school, aged 16)
It gets a bit boring sometimes, but its great to all be together and to have time together. Usually we are all so busy rushing to get homework done and Mum's doing all the household chores after a full day at work and trying to study as well. Rob and I help with clearing up and our own rooms and that. I guess soon it will all change. I'll leave and want to do other things, so these holidays are really important to me.

Rob (male, son of Rhona, studying at primary school, aged 11)
Holidays are the best. Nan, Pop, and Mum and Vicky; it's really cool. Everyone gets on real well, and Vicky and I know that if Nan and Pop didn't let us come with them, we wouldn't have a holiday; we've told them how much we appreciate it. Pop teaches Vicky and I all sorts of things and Nan is the best fisher — she's ace, she's taught me heaps, we get up early and fish before breakfast when the tide is right.

RESEARCH PROJECT

As you have already considered the development of a research proposal in chapter 1, you should think about the reporting process for your research project. You will have conducted a quantitative, qualitative or mixed method research project. Now consider what main headings and subheadings you could use to organise your report. By doing this you are already beginning to think about the development of your contents page. Remember to consider any lists of tables and/or graphs, as well as appendices.

REFERENCES

Becker, H. S. 1986. *Writing for Social Scientists*. Chicago: University of Chicago Press.

Commonwealth Government of Australia. 1994. 'Foreword: Message from the Minister'. *Forecast*, vol. 1, no. 1, August.

Dey, Ian. 1993. *Qualitative Data Analysis: A User-Friendly Guide for Social Scientists*. London: Routledge.

Fetterman, David. 1989. *Ethnography, Step By Step*. Applied Social Research Methods Series, Volume 17. Newbury Park: Sage.

Geertz, Clifford. 1973. *The Interpretation of Cultures: Selected Essays*. New York: Basic Books.

Hall, Colin Michael. 1997. *Tourism in the Asia Pacific Rim; Development, Impacts and Markets*. Second Edition. South Melbourne: Longman.

Hall, Colin Michael & Johnston, Margaret E. 1995. *Polar Tourism: Tourism in the Arctic and Antarctic Regions*. Chichester: John Wiley & Sons.

Jennings, Gayle. 1998. *Recreational Usage Patterns of Shoalwater Bay and Adjacent Waters*. Research Publication No. 50, Townsville: Great Barrier Reef Marine Park Authority.

Jennings, Gayle. 1999. Voyages from the Centre to the Margins: An Ethnography of Long-Term Ocean Cruisers. Unpublished PhD dissertation. Murdoch University.

Jorgensen, Danny I. 1989. *Participation Observation: A Methodology for Human Sciences*. Applied Social Research Method Series, Volume 15. Newbury Park: Sage.

Kemmis, Stephen & McTaggart, Robin (Eds) 1988. *The Action Research Planner*. Third Edition. Melbourne: Deakin University.

Landes, K. K. 1964. 'A Scrutiny of the Abstract'. *Bulletin of the American Association of Petroleum Geologists*, vol. 50, no. 9, p. 1992.

Miles, Matthew B. & Huberman, A. Michael. 1994. *An Expanded Qualitative Data Analysis*. Second Edition. Thousand Oaks: Sage.

Neuman, W. Lawrence. 1994. *Social Research Methods: Qualitative and Quantitative Approaches*. Second Edition. Boston, MA: Allyn & Bacon.

Neuman, W. Lawrence. 2000. *Social Research Methods: Qualitative and Quantitative Approaches*. Fourth Edition. Boston, MA: Allyn & Bacon.

Reinharz, Shulamit. 1992. *Feminist Methods in Social Research*. New York: Oxford University Press.

Sarantakos, Sotirios. 1993. *Social Research*. South Melbourne: Macmillan.

Stake, Robert. 1995. *The Art of Case Study Research*. Thousand Oaks: Sage

Ticehurst, Gregory W. & Veal, Anthony I. 1999. *Business Research Methods: A Managerial Approach*. Malaysia: Longman.

Tilley, Andrew. 1999. *An Introduction to Research Methodology and Report Writing in Psychology*. Brisbane: Pineapple Press.

van Maanen, J. 1988. *Tales of the Field: On Writing Ethnography*. Chicago: University of Chicago Press.

Wolcott, Henry F. 1990. *Writing up Qualitative Research*. Qualitative Research Methods Series, Volume 20. Newbury Park: Sage.

Yin, Robert K. 1994. *Case Study Research, Design and Methods*. Second Edition. Applied Social Research Methods Series, Volume 5. Thousand Oaks: Sage.

Glesne, Corrine. 1999. *Becoming Qualitative Researchers*. Second Edition, New York: Longman.

Kumar, Ranjit. 1996. *Research Methodology: A Step-By-Step Guide for Beginners*. South Melbourne: Longman.

Macrorie, Ken. 1980. *Telling Writing*. Rochelle Park, NJ: Hayden Book Company.

Patton, Michael Q. 1990. *Qualitative Evaluation and Research Methods*. Second Edition. Newbury Park: Sage.

Richardson, Laurel. 1994. 'Writing: A Method of Inquiry'. In Denzin, Norman K. & Lincoln, Yvonna S. (Eds) *Handbook of Qualitative Research*. Thousand Oaks: Sage.

Conference presentations,
posters and articles

'Research is a political act, involving power, resources, policy and ethics. Throughout the research process, the political context is generally limited to the research site(s) and the researcher's relationships with participants, and sometimes, with their supervisors (as well as the researcher's supervisors). Writing extends the complexity of research politics because it invites in a third party — the reader — with all the ramifications that inclusion of this invisible but vital participant may generate for both researcher and researched.'

(Glesne 1999, p. 173)

LEARNING OBJECTIVES
After studying this chapter, you should be able to:
- explain the purpose of conference papers
- outline the structure and style of conference papers
- explain the purpose of poster presentations
- prepare a conference poster
- explain the purpose of journal articles
- develop an outline for a journal article
- outline the influence of audience on each of the genres discussed in this chapter
- understand the process of getting your work accepted.

As was the case in chapter 10, this chapter continues to focus on the writing process presented in chapter 1 and, in particular, the 'publishing' stage of the writing process (and, by association, the research process). Although some forms of publication are presented orally, oral presentations still involve rehearsal, drafting, revising and then 'going public' with the research findings. In going public, researchers reiterate the 'political' nature of the research act, as their findings will have flow-on effects for themselves, the participants, the scientific community, sponsors and society at large. The discussion in chapter 4 on ethics is as pertinent to chapters 10 and 11 as it is to the consideration of research design and preparation for the research act. You will recall from chapter 4 that your ethical responsibilities to all the stakeholder groups should be in operation before, during and after the research act. The abridged quote by Glesne (1999) (opposite) re-emphasises both the ethical and political nature of the research act, especially in going public.

Within the overall structure of this textbook, this chapter concludes the discussion of the writing process as it relates to tourism research. The chapter discusses the purpose, structure and style of conference presentations and conference posters (both oral modes of disseminating your research findings), as well as one other method of disseminating your findings using written text through the genre of research articles. The chapter also identifies some of the audience considerations associated with these three genres.

11.2 ᑕONFERENCE PAPERS ·····················

The purpose of a conference paper is to inform a gathered audience of peers about the contents of your written research. The audience has assembled to hear you speak about your research and its key components. Conference papers should not be presented as a direct 'reading' of your research/conference paper. It is an insult to audiences to present your paper by reading out what you are going to hand out or what already appears in the conference proceedings.

■ 11.2.1 Structure *and style of conference papers*

Conference papers are composed of two elements: a performance and a written text. The performance is the element the audience will engage with at the time of the presentation. The written text is the element they take away with them or have already read in the conference proceedings. Ensure that you do not confuse the two elements of a conference presentation as being the same thing. They are not! The written text paper contains everything you want the audience to know about your research that you are unable to address within the time constraints of your oral presentation of the research. The oral presentation focuses on one or two of the highlights of the research and stirs the audience's interest so that they will engage with you at the conclusion of the presentation and ask you questions. Do not be surprised if not all the audience members engage with you immediately at the conclusion of your presentation. They have just absorbed a lot of new information — some people are extraverted thinkers and will ask questions or make comments immediately, and others will need time to reflect internally before they have questions or comments. The latter may come up to you after your paper to discuss your presentation. And, of course, some people may not engage with you at all, because the topic did not stir them or because the presentation was not effectively delivered.

◼ *11.2.2* **Types** *of conference papers*

There are two types of conference papers: working papers and research papers. Working papers report on research-in-progress, while research papers usually report on research that has been completed. Since working papers discuss research that is underway, the audience is expected to engage with the research and provide critical comments and suggestions. Although research papers report on research that has been completed, again the audience is expected to engage in the work, providing critical commentary on the research aims, the methods used and the findings.

◼ *11.2.3* **Conference** *paper selection*

Conference papers are selected for inclusion in a conference program primarily by one of four ways:
- submission of a short abstract (approximately 250 words), which is reviewed by a conference paper committee or a conference program chair
- submission of a two- or three-page abstract, which is double blind reviewed (neither the identity of the writer(s) nor the reviewer(s) is divulged to the other)
- submission of a full paper, which is double blind reviewed
- submission of a two- or three-page abstract, which is double blind reviewed, followed by a full paper, which is subsequently double blind reviewed.

There are other methods of paper selection, but as these four methods are the primary means, the others are not noted here. Essentially, the peer review process, whether by one person (the conference program chair) or by a number of reviewers (a paper review committee), is used to determine whether conference papers are worthy for inclusion in a conference program.

■ *11.2.4* **Changes** *to the genre*

The original purpose of conference papers was to share research findings. Initially, the findings were not supplemented with written text documents, unless there was a caveat on the paper saying 'not for quotation', since the research was still in progress and some findings might have changed once the analysis phase was completed.

Now, however, conference papers are moving beyond the original purpose of the genre, and there is a heavier focus on providing a written text document. Nationally, the change in focus is being driven by government funding to universities and the awarding of varying research points for different research genres. Greater points are earned for a conference paper that is a full paper and has been peer reviewed, as well as being published in conference proceedings. No points are earned for a conference paper that has been accepted based only on a short abstract and has not been published in conference proceedings. Internationally, financial support for conference attendance is also tied to written text outputs. Consequently, the original purpose of the conference paper genre is being manipulated by political machinations tied to university funding formulae.

■ *11.2.5* **Conference papers** *and written outputs*

As noted above, full papers may in fact go through two sets of refereeing — a review of the abstract and then of the full paper. The full paper may then be published in:

- conference proceedings
- an edited book produced by a commercial publisher
- a CD-ROM
- an electronic format on the Web.

Refereed abstracts may also develop into full papers that are printed in conference proceedings. Some papers in conference proceedings may also be requested or submitted for consideration for publication in journals. The journal review process is more demanding and time-consuming than the process for conference papers. Basically, conference papers provide an avenue for audiences to hear current research findings and trends, whereas journal articles report past findings and trends as journal articles may take up to two years to move through the peer review and revision process before being published. The introduction of electronic journals has served to shorten the publication process and thereby the release of research into the public arena.

■ *11.2.6* **Some considerations** *for conference paper submission*

When preparing an abstract for consideration as a conference paper, you need to ensure that you provide the reviewers with details, not intentions. The 'rules' for abstract writing noted in chapter 10 also hold true for conference presentations. Consider, for example, the two abstracts shown in figure 11.1. Abstract 1 provides the reviewer with data about the research, whereas abstract 2 provides one statement that is informative and then discusses intentions. A reviewer would be less inclined to accept abstract 2 since there is not enough evidence of the researcher's work available. Although abstracts are short, they must provide details.

■ **Figure 11.1**
Sample
conference
abstracts

Abstract 1

Appreciative inquiry (AI) is an alternative method to action research for facilitating organisational change. AI involves four stages: appreciating, envisioning, co-constructing and sustaining a collective vision. Use of appreciative inquiry in an educational organisation and heuristic research suggest that appreciative inquiry has the potential for application in the tourism industry, particularly in regard to transformational change, shared visioning, strategic planning, team development, focus group research and valuation.

Abstract 2

Appreciative inquiry (AI) is an alternative method to action research for facilitating organisational change. This paper will examine appreciative inquiry as a method for facilitating organisational change in the tourism industry. Possible applications will be discussed.

■ *11.2.7* **Conference paper** *content and preparation*

Follow exactly any directions provided by the conference organisers, such as font type, font size and type of margins to be used. Ensure you progress through the writing process fully, especially drafting, revising and proof-reading.

The checklist in table 11.1 is provided as a guide for preparing the content of a conference paper. As you can see, it is based on the scientific style of report writing. This has been done because most conference paper calls require information on the items nominated in the table. The checklist also reminds you that a conference paper involves an oral component, that is a performance, so the last checkpoints focus on that aspect. Remember, the performance mode of a conference paper is as important as any supporting written texts.

Presentation style is addressed in the next subsection and an example regarding conference dress is noted in the following Industry Insight. Be aware that different conferences may have different 'dress' requirements. These differences may relate to the conference venue and location, the style of the conference, and the conference attendees and sponsors, as well as the purpose or theme of the conference.

CONFERENCE PAPER CHECKLIST	CHECK
1. Introductory context of study provided, including linkage to conference theme	
2. Overview of paper contents provided	
3. Relevant literature briefly summarised	
4. Methodology used in the study identified	
5. Key findings stated	
6. Key discussion and recommendations considered	
7. Conclusion to presentation clearly stated	
8. Presentation skills rehearsed: Pace Audibility Modulation of voice Stance Eye contact with audience	
9. Inclusion of visual imagery, use of audiovisual equipment	
10. Knowledge of research and ability to answer questions	

INDUSTRY INSIGHT

Professional presentation includes your projection, stance and your attire. The following two excerpts from conference programs give advice on suitable attire.

Pretty in Pink

Attire at all events is business casual. (Marketing tours are casual; be sure to wear comfortable walking shoes.) The dress for the annual banquet is Island Beachwear! (TTRA 2000)

Dress Guide

"Smart casual" dress is appropriate for the conference day sessions and evening functions. (CRC Reef Research Centre 1996a)

■ *11.2.8* **Presentation** *style*

When making a presentation, you need to ensure that you are confident of your material and any audiovisual support. You should check the room that you are going to be presenting in so that you are aware of the physical layout, the audience seating arrangements and the area that you will be operating in. This will enable you to feel comfortable in the room before having to present to the audience. If you are using any technology, ensure that it has been organised or, if you are bringing your own, ensure that it is compatible with the fittings and other connectors in the room. If possible, during a break check that everything works and how it works. Nothing detracts more from a presentation than a presenter who indicates that they have no knowledge of how things work or what to do when things go wrong.

When the presentation commences, if there is no conference chair for the session, ensure that you introduce yourself and provide some background on yourself (briefly — do not use your time talking about yourself rather than the research topic). If there is a chair, ensure that you meet the chair beforehand and provide them with some brief biographical details about yourself and your research. Usually, a session chair will introduce you and then it is over to you to engage the audience. Once it is over to you:

- commence confidently (and continue to be confident)
- provide eye contact with all the audience
- if you have notes, ensure that you do not have your head down concentrating on the notes rather than the audience.

Remember, you are talking about your research — you should know it well enough to talk about it without constantly referring to notes. On the other hand, if you decide not to use notes, cue cards or prompts, have clearly organised in your head your key points and progress through those without sidetracking or losing your path.

During presentations:

- be aware that nervousness can be channelled into distracting behaviours, such as rocking back and forth, fiddling noisily with a pen (e.g. a pen that has a push-button top) or tapping a pen on the podium or table
- if you choose to hold your papers, hold them still and refrain from shuffling them backwards and forwards.

Ask a peer to provide you with feedback on your style in a rehearsal session so that you can work on removing any detracting behaviours prior to giving your presentation.

You should also rehearse your presentation several times so that you can time yourself and pace your presentation — this will also increase your confidence with your material. Although you may have prepared a 30-minute presentation, through nervousness you may present your material so rapidly that it is over in seven minutes. If you do experience nerves, ask a friend or colleague to sit in the audience in a position where you can see them. From this position, they can provide you with positive feedback and encouragement through non-verbals such as smiling or nodding their head to your points or even giving you an okay sign.

When preparing your presentation, remember that you are only presenting the key points, so make sure you have not chosen too many key points as this will take you beyond your allocated time slot. During the presentation, if there is a chair, the chair will let you know when you have 10 or five minutes or one minute remaining. If you find you will not be able to cover all the points that you want, take stock, revise in your head the main message you want to leave with the audience and do some mental gymnastics to revise the presentation and delete points. Do not try to speak faster to get it all in or keep telling the chair (and the audience) that you have just a few more points to go when you have something like 10 or 20. Be fair to other presenters — they need their amount of allocated time and to take time from them is extremely selfish. Some chairs will keep presenters to time, but others are more lackadaisical and this can throw the entire program out, and it can be especially annoying for participants who are hoping to move between sessions to catch papers in different streams.

■ 11.2.9 Use *of visual aids*

PowerPoint presentations are a variation on the traditional use of overhead transparencies and slide projections. There are a number of guidelines that apply when using PowerPoint presentations and overhead transparencies:

- Ensure that slides are not overwhelmed with text. Slides are used for making points, not for writing whole paragraphs — unless the paragraph is pertinent to a particular point used as an example.
- Ensure that the text is at least 18 points in size and is in a font that is easy to read.
- If you use colour, try not to use colours that are hard to focus on or are gaudy. Furthermore, some colour combinations do not work well, such as white on yellow or red on blue — the text gets lost.
- Try not to overuse different fonts and different styles such as italics, underlining and bold — the text becomes fussy and the message gets lost in all the styles.
- The slide is for the audience to focus on, not you — turning your head to read the points on the slide is as bad as reading your paper to the audience. You should have a copy of the slides in front of you so that you are constantly facing the audience.
- If you need to indicate something on the slide, use an infra-red or timber pointer or, if using an overhead, use a pen as a pointer on the slide.
- Remember not to turn your back on the audience — this often occurs when presenters choose to read from their slides on the screen. Another detracting habit is a presenter bowing their head to read from the slide placed on the overhead transparency. The audience ends up seeing only the crown of the presenter's head and not their face.
- Ensure that you are not blocking the view of the projection screen for anyone in the audience.
- Proofread your slides to ensure that there are no errors in them.
- Check that the slides are in the correct order.
- Be prepared for the unexpected. If the power fails or a globe in an overhead transparency projector fails and has no replacement, do not despair, it should be part of your planning. Carry on without the technical support. Remember, the research should be so much a part of you that you only use the audiovisuals to provide some colour and flavour to the presentation. You should be able to carry on without such prompts. Plan

simply so that technology does not become the focal point of the presentation. Technology should always be the support for the main focus of the presentation, the main focus being your message.

- Ensure that all texts and images are in focus.
- Ensure that all slides are positioned in correct alignment on the projector and are therefore not crookedly positioned on the screen.
- Check that the slide text is placed within the projection area.
- Ensure that overhead transparencies are placed on the overhead projector so that the text is presented in the correct position, not in mirror image on the screen, which is unreadable.
- One final point: if you are travelling to the conference, make sure that your presentation materials travel with you as hand luggage, in case your stowed luggage does not arrive at the same time as you. You may not have your professional attire, but you will have your paper and materials! Some conference-goers also travel with a small overnight bag with one change of conference attire just in case their luggage is delayed or lost.

■ 11.2.10 Modes *of presentation*

Conference papers may be delivered in a variety of modes: plenary sessions, individual stand-up sessions, round-table sessions and panel sessions.

Plenary sessions

Plenary sessions are usually allocated to key speakers or high-profile researchers or tourism- and hospitality-related individuals. Plenary sessions are prime-time sessions, and usually have audiences larger than conference paper sessions. Plenaries may last as long as 30 to 60 minutes. The session should stimulate and capture the attention of the audience. Controversial or groundbreaking information should be presented. After the plenary session, the conference sessions should further tease out the issues raised in the plenary session, otherwise the information provided to the audience becomes dislocated and unconnected.

Individual stand-up sessions

In individual stand-up sessions the presenters stand up at a podium or in front of an audience or, in some circumstances, sit at a table. However, the latter is the least-preferred option as audience members sitting beyond the third row cannot see you or engage in eye contact with you and will probably be bored by the lack of visual stimulation. If you sit down, you may as well provide them with an audiotape of yourself, since they are not able to see you during the presentation. Stand-up sessions may range from 15 to 40 minutes in duration (including question time).

Round-table sessions and panel sessions

Round-tables are essentially that — a group of people sitting around a table discussing their research (usually in progress) and a high level of interaction is expected. In total, round-table sessions may be scheduled for one to one-and-a-half hours so that full discussion can ensue.

Panel sessions involve a group of researchers from the same research project or similar research projects discussing their research findings. Different perspectives on the overall research topic should be elicited from such discussions and audience engagement and interaction should be higher than during a stand-up presentation. Panel sessions usually are allocated one to one-and-a-half hours to allow time for 'lively' debate.

■ 11.2.11 Audience *considerations*

Conference programs usually state their intended audience. For example:

> Who will be attending? Industry officials from the mining, tourism and agricultural industries, together with those from energy, transport and communications will be among those attending, as will business leaders, government representatives, regional and community development practitioners, local investors and members of the general community (Institute of Sustainable Regional Development 2000)

In reality, the audience may come from a variety of backgrounds, so you need to pitch your delivery to ensure maximum understanding by everyone in the audience. For example, technical terms may need to be briefly explained, discussion of complex and technical methodologies should be left to the full paper, only two or three key findings should be presented and there should be time for questions. If the audience comprises only technical experts, then the level of presentation will be different again. The level of presentation needs to match the background knowledge and expectations of the audience.

The style of presentation discussed here has been predicated to the scientific style, but you should be aware that non-verbal presentations may also be used to convey research findings, especially when the researcher has engaged in the use of qualitative methodologies. As noted by Glesne (1999) in regard to qualitative research reporting:

> While forms of writing dominate . . ., some researchers play with nonverbal representation as well. Blumenfeld-Jones (1995) describes using dance. Clark (1998) is exploring painting as one way to synthesize data from her research . . . Munoz (1995) uses photography as a form of representation. In these modes, as in creative verbal representations, the 'essences (as understood by the artist) are extracted and represented in concrete, condensed forms' (Blumenfeld-Jones 1995, p. 392) (Glesne 1999, p. 190).

'One practice these experiments have in common . . . is the violation of prescribed conventions; they transgress the boundaries of social science writing genres' (Richardson 1994, p. 520) and this can cause problems for acceptance in conferences run by those informed by the scientific model. Research findings may also be presented as poetry, drama, video clips, documentaries and multimedia presentations. If using such media, ensure that they are well developed and/or rehearsed as you are really moving into performance art in their use.

■ 11.2.12 Tips *for conference chairs*

As well as presenting a conference paper, as a conference participant, you may be asked to chair a conference session. 'Much of the success of a conference will depend on the quality of the chairing of individual sessions. Should this task fall to you, there are many responsibilities to fulfil. There are three categories of the task — responsibilities to the organizers, to the speaker, and to the audience' (Newble & Cannon, 1989, p. 35).

Some tips for chairing sessions:

- Meet the presenters prior to the session and ask for some biographical data to use when you introduce them.
- Detail how you intend to utilise the time and when questions can be asked (after each presenter or at the end of each session).
- Indicate how you will provide time cues, such as 10 or five minutes to go and finally one minute to go. If cue cards are used, they should clearly and boldly indicate how many minutes are to go, as well as 'STOP NOW'. You could also use a bell, or a utensil against a glass or jug of water. Let the person know the cue beforehand, so they are not put off when you use the cue.
- Describe to the presenter and the audience what you will do to prevent them going over time — such as standing up and interrupting the speaker.
- Remember to introduce yourself briefly to the audience so they know who you are.

Conference papers are not the only way to present research findings at a conference. Poster papers are another method to communicate your research.

11.3 POSTER PRESENTATIONS

A great poster is readable, organised and succinct. You have only 11 seconds to grab your audience's attention, then three to five minutes to hold their interest. Keep the main message brief, and include key ideas. Posters crammed with information are seldom read in their entirety (CRC Reef Research Centre 1996b).

Essentially, a poster is a quick and efficient way to succinctly report your research findings. It enables a larger audience to engage with your research findings than would be the case if the findings were presented during concurrent research presentation sessions (especially if there are no conference proceedings). One of the major problems associated with conference posters is related to researchers' desires to present an entire research paper in the small space allowed for a poster.

11.3.1 Structure *and style of poster papers*

When preparing poster texts, Macrorie's (1980, p. 43) advice about writing in general is equally as important for poster writing: '[T]he writer is under a fierce obligation to choose for his [sic] writing those facts that seem to him [sic] and will seem to his [sic] reader to belong on the same page ... only what fits is allowed. NORMAN PODHORETZ.' Text should be kept to a minimum, approximately 400–500 words. Specific aspects of structure and style are discussed below.

11.3.2 Size

Posters may be measured in metric or imperial measures depending on the country in which the conference is being held. For example, conference posters may be 1 metre × 1 metre, 1.3 metres × 1.3 metres, or 8 feet × 4 feet. Poster sizes vary depending on the display equipment that the conference organisers have hired or have available. Posters may be displayed on walls and or posted to display screens and boards. At some conferences, the materials required to attach a poster are the responsibility of the presenter, while at others they are the responsibility of the conference organisers. Take time to read conference poster information sheets so that you know who is responsible for what regarding poster organisation and display. To be really sure, you could take your own materials, even if the conference organisers have indicated that poster attachment materials will be their responsibility.

11.3.3 Structure

There is no set standard for the structure of a travel, tourism or hospitality poster, nor is there unanimous agreement between conference organisers regarding poster structure in general. However, suggestions include the use of visual aids to enhance the message such as graphs, photographs, tables and diagrams, as well as the judicious use of text. There are some key elements that need to be included in all posters: title of the research, name of authors and their affiliations and contact addresses, background or research aims or objectives, brief information on the method and greater focus on the findings and discussion or recommendations. Some posters focus on one key finding and focus on it to the exclusion of other findings. Some conference organisers draw on related disciplinary areas to specify the set-up for a poster, such as the Australian and New Zealand Association of Leisure Studies, which based it requirements for poster presentations on the guidelines from the Australian Psychological Association (see Industry Insight on the following page). Always check conference promotional materials to determine whether a set structure is required or not.

INDUSTRY INSIGHT
INSTRUCTIONS FOR THE PRESENTATION OF POSTERS

In order to raise the profile of posters at the ANZALS conference, delegates are encouraged to consider presenting their research through a poster presentation. To facilitate interaction and debate, times will be allocated in the program for poster presentation sessions. These time slots will provide opportunities for presenters to meet delegates who wish to discuss the work in more detail.

Poster guidelines
- The allocated poster board space is 1.5 m high and 800 mm wide. The boards are made of a material to which velcro tape can adhere. Velcro tape to affix your poster will be supplied.
- Poster material should be prepared in advance and should be large enough to be viewed from a distance of 1 m.
- Each poster should contain a section at the top containing title of paper, name(s) of author(s) and their affiliation(s). The size of the characters for the title should be at least 2.5 cm high.
- Drawings and charts should be clear and simple.
- Poster sessions will be interactive and authors are expected to be with their poster display during the assigned session.
- Presenters are expected to make good use of a variety of techniques, including different types of figures, graphs and illustrations, in order to make their posters interesting and easy to read.

Suggested arrangement for posters

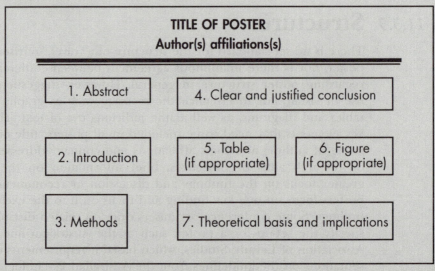

Source: *ANZALS (1997)*

■ 11.3.4 **Content**

Posters should contain a minimum of text. Only the key points should be presented. Do not attempt to put your entire paper into the prescribed dimensions of the poster. It will overwhelm the audience and is an inappropriate use of a poster. Posters are supposed to be eye-catching, draw the attention of the reader and briefly inform, so that the reader is able to pursue you for further information.

■ 11.3.5 **Visual** *layout*

The size of the text must be readable from a distance of one-and-a-half to two metres, otherwise the audience will have to get very close to the poster to read the text and this will reduce the number of people who can read the poster at any one time. In addition, if the print is too small, people will have their view of the poster blocked by others who are trying to read the poster and they will lose interest quickly. Ensure that you use diagrams, tables and images to supplement the text and to inform the reader. The text should be counterbalanced by visual items. The suggested text size is between 28 and 36 points.

■ 11.3.6 **Styles** *of presentation*

There are a variety of poster presentation styles used at conferences. These styles include:

- displaying the posters throughout the duration of the conference, so that interested people can seek out the poster presenters at suitable times, such as morning and afternoon teas, or lunch breaks
- displaying the posters in the refreshment precinct, during which time the poster presenters are required to stand near their poster
- displaying the posters in a designated conference area and providing a specific time in the conference program for each poster presenter to talk about their poster content
- displaying the posters during a specific time period in the conference program, as well as allocating a program session for the viewing of posters and discussion with poster presenters (either as a specific conference session or as a concurrent conference program session).

As a poster presenter, you need to read any instructions for poster presenters and know exactly what is expected of you regarding poster layout, presentation style and the area for poster display.

■ 11.3.7 **Audience** *considerations*

Know your audience. Just as chapter 10 discussed three types of audience for proposals and reports, similarly for poster presentations there are three types of audience — the general public, decision makers and experts

(Ticehurst and Veal 1999). The following discussion of audience considerations is based on the four styles of presentation mentioned above.

- *Displaying the posters throughout the duration of the conference, so that interested people can seek out the poster presenters at suitable times, such as morning and afternoon teas, or lunch break* — ensure that your poster can stand alone, that it is succinct and to the point, that the language is not overly technical or, if unusual terms are used, that definitions have been provided.

- *Displaying the posters in the refreshment precinct, during which time the poster presenters are required to stand near their poster* — still ensure that your poster can stand alone, as you are not going to be standing next to the poster to answer questions all of the time. Audiences can gain additional information by asking questions or you can provide a poster paper for collection near the poster itself.

- *Displaying the posters in a designated conference area and providing a specific time in the conference program for each poster presenter to talk about their poster content* — again the poster must stand alone, but you can formally provide additional information to expand on some of the points included in the poster. Ensure that what you present is not exactly the same as what the audience can read from the poster.

- *Displaying the posters during a specific time period in the conference program as well as allocating a program session for the viewing of posters and discussion with poster presenters (either as a specific conference session or as a concurrent conference program session)* — again the poster must be able to stand alone, but here you can expand on facts and methods or findings. However, do not overload people with too much technical detail. You may use a full paper handout to supplement your presentation. The full paper may also have been accepted for publication in the conference proceedings.

Having discussed two oral presentation modes, the remainder of the chapter focuses on an alternative written genre to the research report for the dissemination of research findings, that is journal articles. Articles may be a further development of a conference paper based on feedback received at a conference, or they may have been written without such a form of 'rehearsal'.

11.4 JOURNAL ARTICLES

The purpose of journal articles is to disseminate research findings to a wider audience. This may be national or international, depending on the scope of the journal. As noted in the article by Riley and Love (2000) (see chapter 5), most research reported in tourism and hospitality journals tends to be quantitatively based. As a consequence, the direction to authors by journal editorial boards and editors carries the bias of the scientific style of writing and is weighted against creative representations of findings. For example, *Annals of Tourism* requests texts presented in the following order: abstract, introduction, study, conclusion, acknowledgments, reference list, tables, figures. The *Journal of Travel and Tourism Marketing* and the *Asia*

Pacific Journal of Tourism Research advocate the use of the American Psychological Association (APA) style for manuscripts, as well as citations and referencing. *The Journal of Travel Research* uses the Chicago style. Most of these are based on the scientific report style. Adoption of the APA or Chicago style means that qualitative researchers are forced to use a style that is 'schematic and constraining' (Miles & Huberman 1994, p. 298).

■ 11.4.1 Structure *and style of journal articles*

Since most journals request the use of the APA style, the following text is presented based on the *Publication Manual of the American Psychological Association* (APA 1994). As the APA manual can be readily accessed as a hard copy in libraries or in electronic format via the Web, only a brief discussion is presented here.

■ 11.4.2 Manuscript *preparation*

Manuscripts should be prepared on A4 or US letter-sized paper, and text should be double-spaced using Times, Times Roman, American Typewriter or Courier in 12 point size. The manuscript should have 2.5 cm margins on all sides, the type should be left justified and no format characters should be used unless specified in directions or instructions to contributors. Text should be organised in the following order: title page, abstract, text, references, appendices, footnotes, tables and figures.

The specific sections of an article will now be briefly discussed in turn. You will note that there is similarity between these sections and those of a scientific report (see chapter 10).

Introduction

This section introduces the research 'problem' and presents background information drawn from relevant literature (consequently, the literature review is contained in the introduction section). The research aim and/or hypothesis should be stated and variables should be described.

Methodology

This is termed 'methods' in APA style since the overriding theoretical paradigm (positivism or postpositivism) is a given; therefore, only 'methods' need to be described. The details of how you conducted your study should be presented so the reliability and validity of your findings may be determined and/or your study repeated. APA style suggests the use of subsections that address participants (definition, sampling procedures, ethical procedures), data collection tools (what was used and why) and procedures (how, when and where the study was conducted).

Results

This section presents the reader with the statistical findings of your study. Findings that were contrary to the hypothesis or aims must also be presented. Tables and graphs may be used in this section and these must be cross-referenced to textual statements in the paper. Statistical analyses must be supported with statements relating to statistical power, statistical significance, and/or size and strength of relationships.

Discussion

Having presented the findings, you then interpret the findings and elaborate on your conclusions. 'In general be guided by the following questions:

- What have I contributed here?
- How has my study helped resolve the original problem?
- What conclusions and theoretical implications can I draw from my study?' (APA 1994, p. 19).

References

Only those writers whose works have been cited in the paper appear in the reference section. Each author is presented in alphabetical order. Several publications by the same author are presented in order of the year of publication. Several publications by the same author in the one year are differentiated by the use of a, b, c, and so on (e.g. 2000a, 2000b, 2000c). In-text citations use the author-date system (e.g. Glesne 1999).

Labelling of tables, graphs and appendices

All labels for tables, graphs and appendices should clearly and succinctly describe their contents. For example, 'Tourist numbers' is not as informative as 'Interstate tourist numbers in South Australia in 2000'. Remember that some tables and graphs may be removed from their context and used elsewhere, so the labels or titles should enable them to stand alone from the document from which they were drawn.

■ *11.4.3* **Audience** *considerations*

There are approximately 40 journals associated with travel, tourism and hospitality. Each has its own specific focus. However, there are some similarities:

- articles are written in the third person using the passive voice
- the preference is for scientific style research reports
- APA manuscript and citation/referencing is used
- articles are 3000 to 5000 words in length
- a double blind review process is used (the identity of the author(s) and the reviewer(s) are kept from each other, and no identifying features are noted on the documents)
- prescriptive instructions are provided for authors to follow and articles are rejected if the instructions are not followed.

It should be noted that some qualitative researchers publish their work outside tourism and hospitality journals, in disciplines that are more open to the narrative report style and to other alternative writing styles for journal articles. In particular, some of the styles of qualitative reporting do not lend themselves well to the 'schemata' and 'constraints' of the scientific model. For example:

In these postmodern times, the contextual nature of knowledge along with the role of language in creating meaning has become a focal point of thought and debate. Some critical, feminist, and interpretivist scholars highlight, in particular: (1) how the research tale cannot be separated from the teller, the researcher; (2) how the language the writer chooses carries with it certain values; and (3) how all textual presentations are 'fashioned' and thereby, in a sense, fictions. There are no 'true' representations (Glesne 1999, p. 176).

Subsequently, use of the narrative, multiple realities, the first person, the active voice and subjectivity can cause concern for some editors and editorial boards and reviewers of tourism and hospitality journals.

11.5 THE PROCESS OF GETTING YOUR WORK ACCEPTED

Regardless of whether you are submitting an abstract or paper for a conference presentation or poster presentation or submitting an article to a journal, there are a few points of which you need to be aware. When preparing the submission:

- take time to ensure that the overall preparation is professionally completed; give yourself enough time to prepare thoroughly
- check the directions given to you to ensure that you have attended to all the details required by the conference committee or the editorial board
- prepare a covering letter that clearly indicates that you are submitting the work for consideration in the conference program or journal.

Some journals and conference organisers request a declaration that the paper has not been submitted or presented elsewhere. Submission for conference papers may be delivered by electronic or hard copy (check conference guidelines); however, most journals require three hard copy sets of an article and an electronic version. The three hard copies save the journal editorial board from the cost of reproducing the article for the review process.

The review process for conferences is generally much faster than the review process for journals. Journals and conference committees usually engage experts to conduct the review process. These experts give their time and expertise voluntarily, so reviews have to be fitted into their normal commitments and busy schedules. Consequently, the review process for journals, in particular, can take some time — from three months up to six months or longer.

The first person to receive the paper (full paper or extended abstract, respectively) is the editor or conference program chair, who will determine whether the paper fits the scope of the journal or the conference. If it does fit the scope, then it will be forwarded to reviewers. The reviewers in turn assess the quality of the work and return their comments to the editor or conference chair. The editor or chair then determines whether the paper will be accepted for publication/presentation or rejected. There are several forms of acceptance:

- outright acceptance without any changes needing to be made to the manuscript
- acceptance pending major changes to the manuscript
- acceptance pending minor changes to the manuscript
- resubmission for another review after further changes have been made and following which a decision regarding acceptance will be taken.

The changes identified must be made or addressed prior to submission of the final paper, otherwise for both conferences and journals the paper will be rejected.

The aim of editors and conference chairs is to ensure that:

- papers fit the scope of the journal/conference
- the paper published/presented is the best that is possible.

The comments of the reviewers and the editors/chairs are there to help you to improve your text; they are part of the writing process and assist you in your revision of your text. Their comments are provided to ensure that your meaning is clear for the intended audience. If you disagree with some points from reviewers or editors/chairs, then discuss them with the editor or chair. When you resubmit your text, indicate in a covering letter which changes have been made and, if some were not made, the reasons why this is the case.

11.6 ᏚUMMARY

The purpose of conference papers

Conference papers enable you to present your research findings among peers and practitioners and interested members of the public in order to disseminate the findings and to receive feedback on the research processes and findings. Some conferences are specialist in nature and the audience could comprise: experts or practitioners; academics or educators; professionals in the tourism and/or hospitality industry; government agencies; or members of a specific association or society.

The structure and style of conference papers

Conference presentations involve two components: an oral presentation and a written support document that details the entire research project. The conference paper should never be a direct reading of the written support text.

The purpose of poster presentations

The purpose of posters is to succinctly inform an audience of the key aspects of your research. This may be done with a stand-alone poster or a poster and several supporting components such as the poster presenter providing responses to questions or providing a brief presentation and/or a formal presentation. The poster, however, must be able to stand alone and be meaningful without the assistance of the poster presenter being available.

Preparation of a conference poster

You need to ensure that you allow yourself enough time to prepare and produce the poster as well as your oral presentation (if applicable), including the written paper. Consider the following elements in the poster preparation:

- size
- layout
- content
- audience
- instructions from the conference organisers.

The purpose of journal articles

Journal articles are a way to present your work to an expert audience and to achieve a further process of peer review, as well as to reach a different and/or a wider audience.

An outline for a journal article

A journal article is usually between 3000 and 5000 words long. It should clearly articulate the purpose of the research and its contribution, and contain background information and/or a literature review, methodology, findings and discussion sections, as well as a reference section and supporting materials (for example, tables and appendices).

The influence of the audience on each of the genres

For conference papers, knowing your audience will assist you in the preparation of both the written and oral components of the conference paper. If the audience is diverse, ensure that you use language that all can understand. If the audience is comprised of experts, then you can use more technical terms. When presenting to academics and researchers, most will have a leaning to one type of methodology rather than another, so you need to ensure that you provide enough to inform but do not state the obvious.

Conference paper audiences may be diverse, and the poster should use language and text that is easily understood by the whole audience. The poster should also be readable from a distance of one-and-a-half to two metres.

For journal audiences, read a variety of articles already accepted by the journal to gain an understanding of the style, structure and level of language used. You should then investigate the readership of the journal, which is usually stated at the beginning or end of the journal or on the journal's Web site. The first reader will be the editor, then the peer reviewers, and then the journal readers themselves.

The process of getting your work accepted

Ensure that you follow the guidelines for submission to the letter. The review process can take time — several months for conference papers and up to six months or more for journal articles. Comments from the editor/chair and reviewers are there to assist the writing process and make your meaning clear. Take their comments as they are intended — to help you rather than as a personal criticism. The production of texts is a team affair — you (the writer), the editor/chair and the reviewers. If your paper is rejected, read the comments as they will assist you to rework the paper and/or improve your writing style.

Questions

11.1 Since the purpose of conference presentations, conference posters and journal articles is to disseminate information, as well as to achieve feedback, why are three different genres used to achieve the same ends?

11.2 Develop a table that identifies the similarities and differences between conference papers and conference posters.

11.3 Examine a journal article, then identify the key differences between the journal article and a research report (you may need to refer back to chapter 10).

11.4 Why is the audience so important to the writing process?

11.5 Which of the genres presented in this chapter do you feel most comfortable with using and why? Which genre do you feel the least comfortable with using and why? In conjunction with your peers during tutorial time, brainstorm a series of strategies to enable you to become more comfortable with the genre with which you least feel comfortable.

EXERCISES

Exercise 11.1

Locate a journal article that reports on research undertaken by the writers and that also focuses on a tourism or hospitality area or issue in which you are interested. Read the article several times to ensure that you have a clear understanding of the research, then prepare a conference poster about the research following the instructions in figure 11.2 opposite. You should also refer back to the text to refresh your memory regarding the style and structure of conference posters.

Exercise 11.2

Prepare an oral presentation reporting on the research from the article that you used in exercise 11.1. You have 15 minutes for your presentation. Consider the following:

- introduction
- background
- overview of presentation
- literature
- methodology
- findings
- discussion
- conclusion.

You are to prepare a poster that displays the main elements of your chosen journal article. The poster is to be prepared on an A3 sheet of paper. The overall word limit for the poster is 400 words, including your poster title, your name as the author and an abstract of 50 words. As you are restricted with text, consider the inclusion of maps, tables, diagrams, flow charts, illustrations and figures to convey your message. Your poster title should be in the largest font, followed by your name. Consequently, both are larger than the text in the poster.

The following is an example of a poster layout. **Remember this is only an example.** You are not required to number the various sections; however, you will need to provide headings.

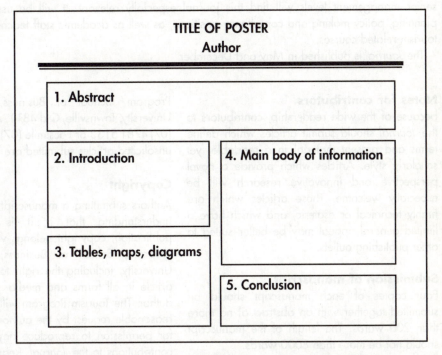

The function of a poster is to succinctly convey information to an audience. Usually, the author of the poster will be on hand to answer any queries that may arise after a person has read the poster. Make sure that your poster is clear and unambiguous and not overloaded with information. It must not exceed the word limit.

Exercise 11.3

Examine the two instructions for contributors in figure 11.3 on pages 370–3. What are the main differences in expectations regarding article submission between the two journals? What are the main similarities?

(a)

The Journal of Tourism Studies publishes articles on tourism from scholars and practitioners in a range of disciplines including economics, commerce, biological and physical sciences, social sciences and humanities. It aims to be international in scope and inclusive in its coverage. Articles are refereed and represent high standards of scholarship and research.

Material considered for publication includes original research reviews, issue-oriented papers and descriptive, analytic discussions which have a relevance to those involved in the practice of tourism.

The intended readership is expected to cover a wide range of personnel involved in the tourism industry. It is envisaged that those involved in tourism and tourism-related activities at the executive, senior management levels will find this journal especially relevant. It will be useful to those in planning, policy-making and consultancy positions, as well as academic staff teaching tourism and tourism-related courses.

The *Journal* is published in May and December.

Notes for contributors

because of the wide readership, contributors to the *Journal* should submit articles which define terms and present material in a readable, yet scholarly style. Articles which provide a novel perspective and innovative research will be especially welcome. Those articles which are highly technical or esoteric, and which have a limited general appeal may be better suited to other publishing outlets.

Submission of manuscript

Four copies of each manuscript should be submitted together with an abstract of no more than 200 words. The length of the manuscript should not be more than 8000 words.

The Journal of Tourism Studies requires that authors follow the style set out in the *1983 Publication Manual of the American Psychological Association* (3rd edn). All manuscripts should be typed double spaced on A4 paper with at least a one inch margin on all sides. Authors should keep a copy of the manuscript to guard against loss in the mail.

Any technical questions regarding manuscript preparation should be addressed to the Editor, *The Journal of Tourism Studies*, Tourism

Program, School of Business, James Cook University, Townsville, Qld 4811, Australia. Phone (07) 4781 5133 or Facsimile (07) 4781 4019. All unsolicited articles submitted are refereed.

Copyright

Authors submitting a manuscript do so with the understanding that if it is accepted for publication, copyright belongs with the Tourism Program, School of Business, James Cook University, including the right to reproduce the article in all forms and media, and not to the author. The Tourism Program will not refuse any reasonable request by the author and/or others for permission to reproduce any of his or her contributions to the *Journal*. Requests to reprint, cite excerpts, etc., are sent to the Editor, who must grant permission (and will usually consult with the corresponding author).

It is assumed by the editorial staff that the article is not under consideration for publication elsewhere and has not been published previously in another form.

Offprints

Ten copies of each article are supplied free to authors.

(b)

The objective of the *Journal of Travel Research* is to publish articles in the field of travel research and marketing, defining this field in the broadest sense. Its purpose is to serve as a medium through which those with research interests can exchange ideas and keep abreast of the latest developments pertaining to travel research and marketing.

The journal strives to advance the level and standards used in travel research by providing readers with new, helpful information about travel research and marketing; new techniques; creative views; generalizations about travel research and marketing thought and practice; and synthesis of travel research and marketing material.

Articles are encouraged from industry practitioners as well as academics, and authors are required to include a section in their manuscripts explaining the practical application of any research technique or set of findings for industry.

The procedures guiding the selection of articles for publication in the journal require that no manuscript be accepted until it has been reviewed by the editor and several (usually three) members of the Editorial Review Board. The editor's decision to publish a manuscript is influenced considerably by the judgments of these reviewers, who are experts in their respective fields of travel. It is journal policy to remove the author's name and credentials prior to forwarding a manuscript to a reviewer to maximize objectivity and ensure that manuscripts are judged solely on the basis of their content.

Two principal criteria are used by the editor and members of the Editorial Review Board in the judgment of a manuscript:

- Does it make a significant and substantive contribution to the literature of travel research and marketing? Does it contribute to the improvement of travel research and marketing practice?
- Does it convey its message clearly and concisely? Does it communicate technical information so that it is easily understood by most readers?

Manuscripts submitted to the journal can be processed expeditiously if they are prepared according to these instructions.

Manuscript preparation

Manuscripts should be typed double-spaced, including references. Do not use single spacing anywhere. Page numbers are to be placed in the upper right-hand corner of every page. A tab indent should begin each paragraph. Manuscripts ordinarily should be between 4000 and 6000 words (ca. 15 typewritten pages). Articles of shorter length are also acceptable and encouraged.

Submit four (4) copies of each manuscript. The author's name should not appear anywhere except on the cover page. The author should keep an extra, exact copy for future reference. Manuscripts are reviewed simultaneously by several different Editorial Review Board members who are geographically separated.

If a manuscript is based on survey research, please include a copy of the questionnaire with the manuscript.

For details of manuscript preparation not covered in the following sections, see *The Chicago Manual of Style*, 14th edition, Chicago and London: University of Chicago Press, 1993.

1. What goes where?

First page — Name of author(s) and title; author(s) note, including present position, complete address, telephone/fax numbers, e-mail address, and any acknowledgement of financial or technical assistance. (This page will be removed prior to sending the manuscript to reviewers.)

Second page — Title of paper (without author's name) and a brief abstract of no more than 150 words substantively summarizing the article. This should be informative, giving the reader a 'taste' of the article.

Body — The text, with major headings centered on the page and subheadings flush with the left margin. Major headings should use all uppercase letters; side subheadings should be typed in upper- and lowercase letters. The per cent sign (%) should be used.

(continued)

Tables and figures — Each table or figure should be prepared on a separate page and grouped together at the end of the manuscript. The data in tables should be arranged so that columns of like materials read down, not across. Nonsignificant decimal places in tabular data should be omitted. The tables and figures should be numbered in Arabic numerals, followed by brief descriptive titles.

When organizing tables, please keep *JTR*'s page dimensions in mind and avoid submitting very wide tables.

Additional details should be footnoted under the table, not in the title. In the text, all illustrations and charts should be referred to as figures.

Figures must be clean, crisp, black-and-white, camera-ready copies. Please avoid the use of gray-scale shading; use hatchmarks, dots, or lines instead.

References — References should be typed double-spaced in alphabetical order by author's last name (see 3).

2. Reference citations within text

Citations in the text should include the author's last name and year of publication enclosed in parentheses without punctuation, for example, (Kinsey 1960). If practical, the citation should be placed immediately before a punctuation mark. Otherwise, insert it in a logical sentence break.

If a particular page, section, or equation is cited, it should be placed within the parentheses, for example, (Kinsey 1960, p. 112). For multiple authors, use the full, formal citation for up to three authors, but for four or more use the first author's name with 'et al.'. For example, use (White and Smith 1977) and (Brown, Green, and Stone 1984). For more than three authors, use (Hunt et al. 1975) unless another work published in that year would also be identified as (Hunt et al. 1975); in that case, list all authors, for example, (Hunt, Bent, Marks, and West 1975).

3. Reference list style

List references alphabetically, principal author's surname first, followed by publication date in parentheses. The reference list should be typed double-spaced, with a hanging indent, on a separate page. Do not number references. Please examine reference lists in recent issues for specific examples. Be sure that all titles cited in the text appear in the reference list and vice versa.

Journal article:
Snepenger, David, and Laura Milner (1990). 'Demographic and Situational Correlates of Business Travel.' *Journal of Travel Research*, 28 (Spring): 27–32.

Book chapter:
Miller, Kenneth E. (1975). 'A Situational Multiattribute Model.' In *Advances in Consumer Research*, Vol. 2, edited by Mary Jane Schlinger. Chicago: Association for Consumer Research, pp. 455–63.

Book:
Gee, Chuck Y., Dexter J. L. Choy, and James C. Makens (1984). *The Travel Industry*. Westport, CT: AVI.

4. Mathematical notation

Mathematical notation must be clear within the text.

Equations should be centred on the page. If equations are numbered, type the number in parentheses flush with the right margin.

Unusual symbols and Greek letters should be identified by a marginal note.

For equations that may be too wide to fit in a single column, indicate appropriate breaks.

5. Permission guidelines

The author is responsible for obtaining all necessary permissions and for paying any associated fees. Permission must be granted in writing by the copyright holder and must accompany the submitted manuscript.

Permission is required to reprint, paraphrase, or adapt the following in a work of scholarship or research:

1. Any piece of writing or other work that is used in its entirety (e.g., poems, tables, figures, charts, graphs, photographs, drawings, illustrations, book chapters, journal articles, newspapers articles, magazine articles, radio/television broadcasts);

2. Portions of articles or chapters of books, if the portion used is a sizeable amount in relation to the article or chapter as a whole, or regardless of size, it captures the 'essence' or the 'heart' of the work;

3. Any portion of a fictional, creative, or other nonfactual work (e.g., opinion, editorial, essay, lyrics, commentary, plays, novels, short stories); and

4. Any portion of an unpublished work.

Source: *(a)* The Journal of Tourism Studies *and (b)* Journal of Travel Research

RESEARCH REPORT

At this stage, you may have conducted a small-scale research project, completed the entire process and be ready to write your final report, or alternatively, you may have already completed the report. Consider your overall research process, your research aims/hypotheses and your findings. Based on your own research project:

1. Prepare a conference poster on A3 paper that represents the main findings of your research report. Refer back to the text on conference poster preparation and presentation and prepare the poster to share with your peers in your tutorial.

2. Prepare a 15-minute oral presentation for your peers in your tutorial using only the guidelines provided for conference paper presentation.

3. Select the guidelines for submission of articles from one tourism and hospitality journal and prepare an outline of your research using the genre of a journal article. Then develop a first draft of the entire article. Ask for feedback from your peers or your supervisor and make revisions to the article. Engage in the entire writing process, then share the final article in tutorial time.

REFERENCES

American Psychological Association (APA). 1994. *Publication Manual of the Psychological Association.* Fourth Edition. Washington, DC: American Psychological Association.

Australian and New Zealand Association of Leisure Studies (ANZALS). 1997. Instructions for the presentation of posters. University of Newcastle: ANZALS.

CRC Reef Research Centre. 1996a. Program and abstracts for 'The Great Barrier Reef Science, Use and Management' conference, Townsville, 25–29 November, p. 4.

CRC Reef Research Centre. 1996b. Instructions for delegates to the 'The Great Barrier Reef Science, Use and Management' conference, Townsville, 25–29 November.

Glesne, Corrine. 1999. *Becoming Qualitative Researchers*. Second Edition, New York: Longman.

Institute of Sustainable Regional Development. 2000. Regional Outlook Conference brochure. Rockhampton: Central Queensland University.

Macrorie, Ken. 1980. *Telling Writing*. Third Edition. Rochelle Park, NJ: Hayden Book Company.

Miles, Matthew B. & Huberman, A. Michael. 1994. *An Expanded Qualitative Data Analysis*. Second Edition. Thousand Oaks: Sage.

Newble, David & Cannon, Robert. 1989. *A Handbook for Teachers in Universities and Colleges: A Guide to Improving Teaching Methods*. London: Kogan Page.

Richardson, Lynne. 1994. 'Writing a Method of Inquiry.' In Denzin, N. & Lincoln, Y. (Eds) *Handbook of Qualitative Research*. Thousand Oaks: Sage, pp. 516–29.

Riley, Roger W. & Love, Lisa L. 2000. 'The State of Qualitative Tourism Research'. *Annals of Tourism Research*, vol. 27, no. 1, pp. 164–87.

Ticehurst, Gregory W. & Veal, Anthony J. 1999. *Business Research Methods: A Managerial Approach*. Malaysia: Longman.

Travel and Tourism Research Association (TTRA). 2000. Travel and Tourism Research Association 2000 Conference preliminary program and registration materials. Boise, ID: TTRA, p. 11.

FURTHER READING ·····················

Behar, R. & Gordon, D. (Eds) 1995. *Women Writing Culture*. Berkeley, CA: University of California Press.

Ellis, C. & Bochner, A. (Eds) 1996. *Composing Ethnography: Alternative Forms of Qualitative Writing*. Walnut Creek, CA: AltaMira Press.

van Maanen, J. 1995. *Representation in Ethnography*. Thousand Oaks: Sage.

12
The future of
tourism research

'What, then, in the end, has this journey meant for us — these ponderings of ours on the foundations of . . . research? It should mean at least that we can look to the research task with greater clarity and a better sense of direction than we would otherwise have done.'

(Crotty 1998, p. 216)

LEARNING OBJECTIVES

After studying this chapter, you should be able to:

- reflect on the role of research in tourism
- discuss tourism research methodologies and methods
- outline the responsibilities of tourism researchers
- examine two case studies involving two different paradigms
- describe some future and continuing research needs of the travel and hospitality sectors
- identify employment opportunities in tourism research
- comment on tourism research for the future.

$\mathcal{I}$NTRODUCTION

This chapter concludes our journey into the rudiments of tourism research. As such, it reflects on our journey thus far and offers some suggestions regarding future directions for tourism research. Hopefully, your travels through this textbook have inspired you to further develop your knowledge and skills regarding the research process within a tourism context. You might, for example, consider further study that will develop your knowledge of the theoretical paradigms that inform tourism research and/or qualitative and quantitative methodologies (and mixed methods). Alternatively, your journey might have encouraged you to further develop your statistical skills. Or your journey may have presented another career option for you as a tourism researcher. Whatever your journey has been, along the way you should have acquired a rudimentary knowledge of skills for tourism research so that you can conduct small-scale projects, review and critique other researchers' work and build a framework upon which to further develop your tourism research knowledge and skills.

As this is the last chapter in the textbook, the role of research in tourism is reconsidered. The chapter also reiterates the three research methodologies and the range of methods available to tourism researchers, as well as re-emphasising the ethical responsibilities of tourism researchers. It also presents two case studies, one informed by an interpretive social sciences paradigm and one informed by a positivist paradigm. Both case studies focus on 'motivation' and, as you would expect, approach the research design from two entirely different perspectives. The chapter also overviews some employment opportunities in tourism research. Finally, the chapter concludes by considering the future of tourism research, especially in an e-world.

12.2 $\mathcal{T}$HE ROLE OF RESEARCH IN TOURISM

As stated in chapter 1, the role of tourism research is to:
- provide data for planning and management decision making ranging from local to international levels of administration
- establish data regarding the social, environmental and economic impacts of tourism
- understand the motivations, needs, expectations and satisfaction levels of tourists
- identify education and training requirements of tourism industry operators and service providers and their employees
- develop temporal databases
- facilitate the generation of specific disciplinary and sector requirements, such as marketing and promotion needs and product development

- provide data for policy development
- evaluate tourism activities across the tourism industry and within stake-holder groups.

In addition to discussing the role of tourism research, chapter 1 also noted that while tourism research is developing, there is a need to generate tourism-specific theory generated from interdisciplinary research contexts. As a novice tourism researcher, you have an important role to play in this development in order to continue the shift of tourism from a field of studies to a discipline in its own right. By engaging in quality research that is interdisciplinary in nature, you will facilitate this development. You will also be able to facilitate this by engaging in research that moves beyond exploratory and descriptive approaches and into explanatory, comparative, causal, evaluative and predictive research approaches.

In engaging in tourism research, remember that the overall research project will be informed by positivism (or postpositivism), the interpretive social sciences, critical theory, feminist perspectives, postmodern approaches or a chaos (or complexity) theory orientation. The selection of the theoretical paradigm that informs the research process subsequently affects the methodology that is used due to each theoretical paradigm's ontological (world view) and epistemological (relationship between knower and known) viewpoints, which in turn also influence methodological viewpoints. Depending on the theoretical paradigm, researchers may choose to use a qualitative, a quantitative or a mixed methodology.

12.3 *T*OURISM METHODOLOGIES AND METHODS

One of the key aims of this textbook is to make you aware of the need to link theoretical paradigms to the structuring of a research project. The links between theoretical paradigms, whether they are positivist, postpositivist or interpretive social sciences, critical theory, postmodern, chaos or complexity theory-based, will have implications for the selection of research methodologies so that the ontological, epistemological and methodological perspectives are in concert with the overall theoretical position of any research inquiry. You have been made aware of the difference between qualitative and quantitative methodologies, particularly in chapters 5, 6 and 8, and also through chapters 7 and 9 and to a lesser degree chapter 10. As a researcher, you should be aware by now that rather than view the selection of the research methodology based on any particular methodological bias, the decision should be based on the research purposes and any other influencing factors such as limitations of time, personnel, money and technology. The key differences between a qualitative and a quantitative methodology are inextricably linked to:

- the use of an inductive approach (qualitative) as opposed to a deductive approach (quantitative)

- multiple realities (qualitative) instead of causal relationships (quantitative)
- a subjective relationship between the researcher and the researched (qualitative) versus an objective relationship (quantitative)
- an emic (insider) perspective (qualitative) versus an etic (outsider) perspective (quantitative)
- emblematic themes (qualitative) versus numerical-stated relationships (quantitative)
- non-random sampling (qualitative) versus random sampling (quantitative)
- textual units of data (qualitative) versus numerical units (quantitative)
- key themes and motifs identified (qualitative) versus statistical representations (quantitative)
- narrative report writing in the first person (qualitative) versus third person, passive voice reports (quantitative)
- slice of life findings (qualitative) versus findings that may be inferred to the whole population (quantitative).

Qualitative methods include in-depth interviews, semi-structured interviews, participant observation, focus groups, longitudinal studies, the Delphic method, case studies, action research methods and documentary research. Analysis involves content analysis, constant comparative analysis, matrix building, mapping, successive approximation, domain analysis, taxonomy building, ideal type identification, event-structure building and modelling. Qualitative data analysis may also be facilitated by the following computer programs: ATLAS.ti, HyperRESEARCH™, winMAX, the Ethnograph, QSR NUD*IST, QSR NUD*IST Vivo and SphinxSurvey.

Quantitative methods include questionnaires and structured interviews, longitudinal studies, case studies, the documentary method, modelling, observation, the quasi-experimental method and impact assessment methods. Analysis involves descriptive statistics including measures of central tendency, measures of association and inferential statistics. Computers provide an additional tool in research designing and analysis, and some quantitatively based software packages include Methodologist's Toolchest, SphinxSurvey, SPSS, Minitab, SAS and winMAX.

12.4 RESPONSIBILITIES OF TOURISM RESEARCHERS

Researchers have ethical responsibilities to society, the scientific community, the research participants, the sponsors and themselves. The key governing documents regarding research ethics are the Nuremberg Code, the Declaration of Helsinki and the Universal Declaration of Human Rights. Researchers must guard against causing physical, psychological, legal and other harm to participants. Researchers must use either informed or written consent and, in most cases, must apply for ethical clearance through an auspicating body — in tertiary institutions, this is usually the ethics committee, which deals with research associated with both human and non-human participants.

CASE STUDY 1: AN INTERPRETIVE SOCIAL SCIENCES APPROACH

The first case study uses the genre of a research article to report tourism research conducted using an interpretive social sciences paradigm. As you read through the case study, you should:

- undertake a peer review of the contents
- make notes regarding aspects of the research that reflect the interpretive social sciences paradigm
- comment on the appropriateness of the methodology and the methods used
- evaluate the presentation of the findings and the discussion of the findings
- critique the literature review and its use in the beginning and end sections of the article
- comment on the style of writing used
- examine the referencing style: what style is used and why?

Finally, what suggestions would you make to improve the article?

Towards an understanding of travel motivations

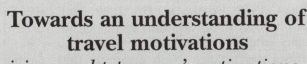

Cruising yachtspersons' motivations and the overall travel experience: a critique of theory and practice. A working paper.

Abstract

Within tourism literature, a variety of theoretical approaches has been used to study travel motivations. These approaches may be broadly classified into four groupings: quasi-(socio)-psychological theories; psychographic profiles; intrinsic motivation theories; and socio-demographic and economic profiles. The main criticisms of travel motivation studies relate to their unidimensional approach and subsequent unicausal analysis, as well as their predominantly etic (outsider's) perspectives.

(continued)

An ethnographic study of cruising yachtspersons conducted between 1992 and 1994 on the eastern seaboard of Australia demonstrates the need for a multidimensional approach and multicausal analysis to 'get at' the 'real' motivations of travellers using both emic (insider's) and etic perspectives. The study also found that cruising yachtspersons' travel motivations changed through the various stages of the overall 'travel experience'. Subsequently, motivation studies need to consider the episodic nature of the 'travel experience' instead of a singular snapshot of one phase of the travel experience, specifically the 'anticipation' phase. Key words: cruising yachtspersons/cruisers, travel motivation, travel experience.

Introduction

Tourism literature contains a variety of 'theories' — models and frameworks that have been used to interpret and/or understand travel motivations. Such literature may be classified into four groupings: quasi-(socio)-psychological theories; psychographic profiles; intrinsic motivation theories; and sociodemographic and economic profiles. The quasi-(socio)-psychological theories (Ross 1994) are based essentially on extrinsic motivations and are exemplified by the push–pull factor model (Dann 1977; Crompton 1979; Epperson 1983) or Gray's (1970) wanderlust and sunlust classificatory system. Psychographic profiles include Plog's psychocentric–allocentric continuum (1974, 1987, 1989) and the VALS typology of lifestyles (SRI International 1989). These profiles identify traveller types based on sets of personality or lifestyle attributes. Intrinsic motivation theories have been used to interpret the motivation of travellers based on either 'self-actualisation' experiences or 'optimal arousal' or 'flow' experiences (respectively attributed to Maslow 1943, 1954, 1970; Iso-Ahola 1976, 1980; and Csikszentmihalyi 1974, 1988). Aside from the previously psychologically based theories/models, sociodemographic and economic profiles have also been used to explain travel motivations (Nash & Smith 1991; Graburn 1983; Yiannakis & Gibson 1988 in Yiannakis & Gibson 1992; and Cohen 1972, 1984).

While the classification of the literature into the four groupings presents a simplistic perspective of travel motivations, various writers have developed models that reflect the complex nature of travel motivations. For example, Mill and Morrison (1992, p. 11) presented a model that highlights the interconnectivity of personality, culture and time, and social economic background, travel motives and vacation purchases. Goodall (1991) proposed a model that focuses on the relationship between social pressures, needs, extrinsic and intrinsic forces, motivations, preferences, goals and subsequent holiday choice. Ryan (1991, p. 48; 1997c, p. 50) identified personality, social class, lifestyle, past experiences, knowledge, marketing and expectations as influencing a person's motivation to engage in a travel experience. However, despite such models, which demonstrate the multiplicity and interconnectivity of factors influencing people to engage in travel experiences, tourism studies have tended to analyse travel motivations based on a unidimensional approach (Pearce 1993) and subsequent unicausal analysis (Ryan 1991). These studies have also primarily adopted an etic (outsider's) perspective (see Fetterman 1989 and Jorgensen 1989 regarding emic and etic perspectives), although tourism literature contains texts that advocate an alternative approach, an emic (insider's) one (see, for example, Graburn 1983, p. 28; Banner & Himmelfarb 1985 in Ross 1994, p. 15; and Ryan & Kinder 1996 in Ryan 1997a, p. 2). Furthermore, researchers have tended to study motivation in a snapshot manner, that is by focusing on only one phase of the travel experience, usually the anticipation or planning phase. Such an approach is problematic, for as Ryan (1997b, p. 41) noted, motivations change during the overall travel experience as 'initial needs are satisfied' and others emerge. Pearce (1993, pp. 114, 120) also purported that tourist motivation was 'dynamic' and multifaceted. Consequently, other phases of the travel experience need to be studied to gain a holistic understanding of people's motivations and their travel experiences.

The term 'travel experience' is often referred to in tourism literature. However, conceptually, there appear to be only two models that represent the experience. Both can be related back to Clawson's (1963 in Jubenville 1976) linear model of the recreation experience: anticipation; travel to; on-site experience; return travel; and recollection. Clawson's model has been modified by Killion (1992) into a circular model and renamed as the travel experience. The second model is a linear-repetitive model consisting of three stages: the anticipatory stage; the experiential stage; and the reflective stage (Craig-Smith & French 1994). This paper will utilise the Killion modification of Clawson's recreation experience in its discussion.

Literature review

Various writers have developed what Ross (1994) described as quasi-psychological theories. In this paper, the qualifier 'socio' has been added as some of the 'theories' are sociologically as well as psychologically based (for example, Dann 1977; Krippendorf 1987, Schmidhauser 1989). Furthermore, they are 'quasi' because they lack any real theoretical underpinning as they are founded on lists of motives or bipolar positions. The seminal work on quasi-socio-psychological travel motivators is attributed to Grinstein (1955). Grinstein (1955) identified 'change', ego-enhancement, relaxation and 'pleasure' as themes related to holiday taking. Later, these themes were iterated in the push–pull 'quasi-theories' of McIntosh (1977), Dann (1977), Crompton (1979) and Epperson (1983) and in Gray's (1970) wanderlust (push) and sunlust (pull) classificatory system. Primarily, 'push' factors induce a person to travel so as to escape routine and/or one's usual social milieu, and 'pull' factors draw a person to a specific destination or experience.

(*continued*)

However, while the push–pull 'quasi-theory' appears as a duality, it is important to note that Dann (1977) purported that there were essentially only push factors compelling a person to travel; it is only when such factors have manifested themselves that pull factors emanate. For Dann, travel was a result of 'anomie' and/or a need for 'ego-enhancement' (both push factors). Once away from the home environment, Dann noted that tourists could engage in 'fantasy' (a pull factor). Krippendorf (1987) similarly identified the need to escape the usual milieu of everyday life as the primary factor (push) in travel motivations. In their work, both Dann and Krippendorf drew on sociology to inform their conceptual frameworks, in particular the work of Durkheim on anomie. Another writer who drew on sociology in order to understand motivations was Schmidhauser (1989). Schmidhauser proposed a list of four sociological factors (Ross 1994). Those factors were compensation for deficits in everyday life, physical and psychological recovery, expanding one's horizons and self-reward (Schmidhauser 1989, p. 571).

As stated previously, the quasi-theories are based on bipolar positions such as Gray's (1970) wanderlust (push) and sunlust (pull) classificatory system or lists that reflect the push or pull tensions. For example, McIntosh (1977) generated a list of four sets of reasons for travel, while Crompton (1979) developed a list of nine socio-psychological motives for engaging in a travel experience. McIntosh's list included physical reasons, cultural reasons, personal reasons and prestige and status reasons, while Crompton's list contained seven push-related and two pull-related motives. The seven push-related motives were: escape from a perceived mundane environment; exploration and evaluation of self; relaxation; prestige; regression; enhancement of kinship relationships; and facilitation of social interaction. The two pull-related motives were novelty and education. However, despite the various presentations of the 'quasi-theories', there exist many similarities: '[t]he adjectives may differ, and the categorizations of tourists based upon motivations may differ in number, but recurrent themes emerge' Ryan (1997b, p. 27). For the quasi-theories, those themes were push and pull factors.

One of the most cited studies in the psychology of travel behaviour is the psychographic continuum of Plog (1974), which was developed from studies into people's reasons for choosing to fly or not to fly. The continuum ranges between two psychographic types: psychocentrics and allocentrics. Psychocentrics tend to be self-inhibited, nervous and non-adventurous people, while allocentrics tend to be self-confident, adventurous and interested in various activities. Between these two types appear the near psychocentrics, the midcentrics and the near allocentrics. Essentially, the model was promoted as a way to match the marketing of destinations to psychographic types.

In its original form, Plog's continuum was unidimensional until 1974 when he examined the effect of income level on psychographic type. His findings indicated that a relationship only existed at the outer limits of the continuum, that is within the allocentric and psychocentric types. An energy dimension was added to the continuum model in 1979. The resultant relationship between the energy dimension and allocentric/psychocentric dimensions was orthogonal (Nickerson & Ellis 1991). High energy levels meant high activity levels and low energy levels meant low activity levels (Nickerson & Ellis 1991). Plog's model has also been adapted by Slattery (1989). Slattery linked Cohen's (1972) traveller roles to each of Plog's (1974) psychocentric types.

Criticism of Plog's model has been based on the model lacking application in differing cultural contexts (Smith 1990a). This criticism sparked a debate between the two researchers (see Plog 1990; and Smith 1990b). Two other researchers, Nickerson and Ellis (1991), compared Plog's two-dimensional model of allocentrism/psychocentrism and energy using Fiske and Maddi's activation theory (1961). Their findings questioned the orthogonal nature of psychographic type and energy. The activation theory also generated more traveller types than Plog's original model. More recently, Ryan (1997c, pp. 59–60) found indirect evidence to support the normal distribution of Plog's psychographic continuum. However, a major criticism of Plog's model is that it does not account for the fact that people travel for different reasons at different times or that destinations may appeal to all the psychographic types depending on personal circumstances and on how the trip is planned (McIntosh, Goeldner & Ritchie 1995, p. 444). Furthermore, the model was developed in the late 1960s and as McIntosh, Goeldner and Ritchie (1995, pp. 173, 447) noted, travel and societies have changed since then.

Another psychographic model is VALS. '*Values and Lifestyles [VALS] is a way of viewing people on the basis of their attitudes, needs, wants and beliefs, and demographics*' (SRI International 1989, p. 207). Consequently, the model considers more than one dimension related to travel motivation. VALS is a hierarchical typology originally consisting of four key categorisations commencing with the need-driven group, the outer-directed group, the inner-directed group, and the combined outer- and inner-directed group. From these four categorisations nine lifestyle types emerged. The hierarchy was developed from Maslow's hierarchy of needs (Ryan 1991, p. 190; Ross 1994, p. 47). The original set of nine lifestyles has since been modified and now the hierarchy consists of eight different psychographic types (McIntosh, Goeldner & Ritchie 1995, p. 450). The new types are strugglers, makers, strivers, believers, experiencers, achievers, fulfilleds and actualisers. The VALS segmentation system is considered a useful marketing tool (McIntosh, Goeldner & Ritchie 1995, p. 449; and Ross 1994, p. 50). However, Ryan (1991, p. 192) cautions that potential users of VALS must determine whether the complexity of human motivations within large populations can be easily represented in eight lifestyle groups. VALS, like Plog's psychographic model, is primarily a commercial research tool and as Ross (1994, p. 48) noted, 'the proprietary' nature of the system has resulted in limited discussion in 'scholarly and scientific circles'.

(*continued*)

Primarily, three theories of intrinsic motivation are referred to in travel motivation literature: Maslow's hierarchy of needs (1943), Iso-Ahola's 'optimal arousal' theory (1976) and Csikszentmihalyi's theory of 'flow' (1974). Maslow's hierarchy of needs (1943, 1954, 1970) has been used in its own right by tourism researchers and also in the modified form developed by Pearce and Caltabiano (1982). The latter two created a travel career ladder based on Maslow's hierarchy. Ryan (1994 in Ryan 1997b; and 1997b, pp. 37–43) has questioned this modification of Maslow's hierarchy and its appropriateness to describe traveller motivations. Specifically, Ryan queries the soundness of the data on which the ladder is founded, the ladder's hierarchical nature and the ascending qualitative values assigned to traveller's positions on the ladder.

The work of Iso-Ahola in the leisure and recreation field has also been used in tourism studies. In 1980, Iso-Ahola (1980, p. 248) wrote that the '*fundamental motivator of leisure participation is a need for optimal incongruity or arousal, as determined by biological dispositions, early socialisation experiences, and social/situational influences*'. Iso-Ahola believed that intrinsic motivation regulated leisure encounters. His examination of motivation demonstrated that the best leisure activities were those performed for their own sake since they offered intrinsic rewards such as feelings of self-determination and competence. Iso-Ahola (1980) also suggested that leisure motivations should be ascertained by asking the person(s) engaged in the activity/activities (an emic perspective).

Iso-Ahola (1980) also provided a critique of Maslow's hierarchy of needs. Basically Iso-Ahola questioned the hierarchical nature of needs. He granted that Maslow wrote that the hierarchy was not as rigid as first implied; however, Iso-Ahola (1980) argued that the hierarchy is suspect due to research that shows that needs tend to overlap between adjacent and non-adjacent sets of needs. Research also showed that Maslow's prediction that security needs instead of social needs would be the most satisfied was unsupported (Iso-Ahola 1980). Further, self-actualisation and security were the least satisfied needs and social needs were the most satisfied. Iso-Ahola argued further that Maslow's idea of self-actualisation was an abstract concept and that the notion of it being inner-directed posed difficulties because self-actualisation was also socially motivated.

Another theory of intrinsic motivation is Csikszentmihalyi's optimal experience, which he calls a 'flow' experience (1974). Csikszentmihalyi developed his flow model from a study of people engaged in various activities. He ascertained the motive for involvement was the intrinsic reward that people gained from their participation. In his own words:

> *Flow refers to the holistic sensation present when we act with total involvement. It is a kind of feeling after which one nostalgically says: "that was fun", or "that was enjoyable". It is the state in which action follows upon action according to an internal logic which seems to need no conscious intervention on our part. We experience it as a unified flowing from one moment to the next in which we are in control of our actions, and in which there is little distinction between self and environment; between stimulus and response; or between past, present, and future.' (Csikszentmihalyi 1974, p. 58)*

Csikszentmihalyi (1988, p. 365) identified several dimensions of flow: '*intense involvement, deep concentration, clarity of goals and feedback, loss of a sense of time, lack of self consciousness and transcendence of a sense of self, leading to an autotelic, that is, intrinsically rewarding experience.*'

'Flow' has been applied in independent travel research (see the study of cruisers by Macbeth 1985), research into wilderness experiences (Mitchell 1983) and recreation studies (see Ryan 1997b).

Literature on the motivations for travel indicate that the propensity to travel and the type of travel experience engaged in can be influenced by gender, age, family life cycle, education, income and lifestyle pursuits (Cohen 1972, 1984; Iso-Ahola 1980; Graburn 1983; Pearce 1987; Yiannakis & Gibson 1988 in Yiannakis & Gibson 1992; Nash & Smith 1991; Mill & Morrison 1992; Fodness 1992, McIntosh, Goeldner & Ritchie 1995, McGehee, Loker-Murphy & Uysal 1996, Frew & Shaw 1997; Ryan 1997c). Leisure literature has also informed tourism research regarding the influences of sociodemographic and economic factors on travel motivations, for example the family life cycle and travel decision making (Godbey 1990; Levinson 1978; Rapoport & Rapoport 1975; Wells & Gubar 1986 in Mill & Morrison, 1992, pp. 81–7).

To reiterate, tourism studies have tended to utilise 'theories' from the four groupings in isolation from each other and primarily have adopted an etic perspective. This was not the approach adopted for the ethnographic study of cruising yachtspersons (cruisers) to be discussed in this paper. A contrary approach was applied and finds support in the writings of Witt and Wright (1990, in Ryan 1991), Ryan (1991), McIntosh, Goeldner and Ritchie (1995), and Pearce (1993). Specifically, Witt and Wright (1990, in Ryan 1991) advocated that research into travel motivation should apply multi-motivational models. Ryan (1991) also stated it was insufficient to apply 'unicausal theories' to the analysis of motivation instead 'multi-causal analysis' was required. Furthermore, McIntosh, Goeldner and Ritchie (1995, p. 175) iterated that sound theory development of tourist motivation depended on a multi-motive and dynamic approach, which considered both intrinsic and extrinsic motivation. To that end, the study of cruisers combined an emic and an etic perspective, utilised a post hoc analysis, as well as a multi-dimensional approach by looking at various aspects of motivation including intrinsic and extrinsic motivation throughout the course of cruisers' travel experiences. Figure 1 provides an overview of the approach taken. Pearce (1993) noted that a study with such attributes should develop good 'theory'.

(continued)

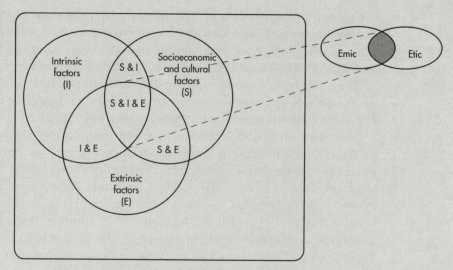

■ Figure 1 *Approach to studying travel motivations of cruisers*

Methodology

This research defined cruising yachtspersons or cruisers as people who had adopted a cruising lifestyle, who had lived aboard their own yachts, had independent means, were self-sufficient and had been away from their port of departure for an extended period of time. The cruisers who participated in this study were 42 women and 54 men drawn from 53 vessels, whose cruising (travelling) experiences ranged from one year to over 15 years. Primarily, cruisers constitute a subcultural lifestyle (see Macbeth 1985); however, cruiser self-reports intimated that they also shared characteristics with independent travellers. Subsequently, their similarity with independent travellers enables cruisers to become a lens through which to critique travel motivation research.

Formal fieldwork commenced in 1992. During 1993 and 1994, in-depth interviews with 96 cruisers were conducted at two locations, Brisbane and Townsville, along the Queensland coast in Australia. Both locations were stopover points for the cruisers while waiting out the passing of the cyclone season or for the taking on of provisions, or both. The in-depth interviews were semi-structured in nature and were supplemented by questionnaires relating to cruising and yacht inventories, tourism activities and budgetary items. These methods were complemented with periods of participant observation. During 1986 to 1992, the researcher was a 'complete'/'total participant' (Junker 1960; and Gans 1982) having 'complete membership' (Adler & Adler 1983). From 1992 to 1994, the researcher maintained 'active membership' and since 1994 has had 'peripheral membership' (Adler & Adler 1983). Consequently, I had no difficulty in accessing the cruising subculture as I had been a member of the subculture for seven years, had ocean cruising experience and was living aboard my yacht while engaging in the field work.

During field work, I would monitor yacht arrivals on a daily basis. Long-term ocean cruisers were discerned either by the flying of a courtesy flag from the yacht's rigging if an overseas yacht or by the general appearance of the boat, its equipment and the crew. All yachts that entered the study area were approached on the second day of their arrival to ascertain whether the crew would agree to participate in the study. The second day of arrival was chosen as the crew would have been rested from the previous day's passage and planning for the time in port would have been organised. During the first contact with the cruisers, the following ethics' principles were discussed: voluntary participation, informed consent (provided orally), no harm to the participants, anonymity and confidentiality issues (as there were several methods of data collection) (de Vaus 1995, pp. 330–50). Throughout the researcher's contact with the cruisers, transparency regarding the purpose of the study (Babbie 1990, pp. 343–4), respect and justice and debriefing (Sieber 1992, p. 18) were also part of the research process. Furthermore, the research followed the requirements of the Australian National Health and Medical Research Council's (NH&MRC) guidelines and standards for research on human subjects.

Of all cruisers approached, only four refused. Despite my assurances, one cruiser thought the interview would ultimately be used by government sources. The other three refusals occurred because one yacht was departing on the day the approach was made (thereby leaving no time for an interview), one cruiser failed to appear at the agreed time despite a follow-up which suggested that the cruiser did not really want to participate, and the last refusal was due to mechanical repairs not being completed as scheduled, resulting in a lack of time to participate in the study.

Also, at the first contact with the cruisers, questionnaires regarding yacht details and crew details were left for completion prior to the interview time. On the day of interview, the cruisers were re-acquainted with the purpose of the interviews and any queries were answered. The semi-structured interviews were tape-recorded in all but three cases where consent was refused and hand transcription was then utilised. The interviews lasted from two to three hours depending on the cruisers and had a break point in the middle. Interviews were conducted individually or in pairs or threes (this was determined by the cruisers and time available). The interviews focused on cruiser descriptions of their motivations for cruising, the cruising lifestyle, tourist experiences, and cruising impacts and cruisers' attitudes to regulation of yacht travel. For those who indicated that they adopted a cruising lifestyle in order to travel, the question 'why did you choose a boat as the means for travel?' was asked. During the course of the interview, cruisers also completed tourism-related questionnaires. These questionnaires took little time as a checklist format was used. Interviewing continued until 'qualitative informational isomorph' was achieved (Lincoln & Guba 1985, p. 233). Grounded theory (Glaser

(continued)

1992) was used to analyse interview data with the assistance of the NUD*IST software program. Throughout the research process, triangulation was also applied because '*no single method ever adequately solves the problem of rival causal factors ... Because each method reveals different aspects of empirical reality, multiple methods of observations must be employed*' (Denzin 1978, p. 28). Specifically, the ethnographic study of cruisers used five forms of triangulation: data triangulation, investigator triangulation, theory triangulation, methodological triangulation (Denzin 1978) and interdisciplinary triangulation (Janesick 1994, p. 251). Only the findings from the study that have relevance to travel motivations will be discussed in this paper. These findings are organised using each of the four 'theoretical' groupings previously discussed.

Findings and discussion

Quasi-(socio)-psychological theories

One of the tourism-related questionnaires used during interviewing was based on McIntosh's (1977) list of motivations for travelling. The data from this questionnaire would suggest that personal reasons and cultural reasons are primary motivations for cruisers (see table 1). Specifically, the questionnaire determined from an etically based and quasi-theoretical perspective that cruisers were motivated by a desire to achieve refreshment of body and mind, a desire for pleasure, specifically fun and excitement, curiosity about foreign countries, other peoples and places, a desire to seek new experiences in new environments, to meet new people, and to experience the personal excitement of travelling. The questionnaire, however, was unable to elicit the following reasons:

> '*I like the self-sufficiency, the comfort of the boat, it's almost womb-like, but it can be cramped. I suggested to 386m that we should go and sail around the world and 386m was reluctant at first but I gradually kept suggesting it to him and he became committed to it.*' (Cruiser 385f)

> '*Stress is the major problem in our lives today and I feel that getting away on a boat, there's only one thing you can worry about and that's the weather and you can't do anything about that anyway, so I think it's a great stress reliever.*' (Cruiser 392m)

Primarily, the questionnaire provided a reductionistic view of cruisers' motivations. Unless the interpretation of travel motivations is grounded in both an emic and etic perspective, the analysis falls short of determining the multiple realities of the cruisers' travel experiences and their motivations.

■ Table 1 *Cruisers' responses to McIntosh's (1977) reasons for travelling* N=93*

REASONS	NO.
A. Lifestyle reasons	
1. Refreshment of body and mind	36
2. For health purposes (i.e. either medically prescribed or undertaken voluntarily)	9
3. For participation, e.g. sports	12
4. For pleasure — fun, excitement	68
5. For romance	11
6. For entertainment	8
7. To shop	2
** To suit husband/partner/parents	4
B. Cultural reasons	
8. Curiosity about foreign countries	61
9. Curiosity about other peoples	60
10. Curiosity about other places	62
11. Interest in art	11
12. Interest in music	13
13. Interest in architecture	15
14. Interest in folklore	27
15. Interest in historical places (remains, monuments, churches)	28
16. Experiencing specific international events	7
17. National events, e.g. Oktoberfest	6
C. Personal reasons	
18. Visiting relatives and friends	5
19. Meeting new people and seeking new friendships	49
20. Seeking new and different experiences in different environments	51
21. Escaping from one's own permanent social environment (i.e. desire for a change)	29
22. Personal excitement of travelling	46
23. Visiting places and people for spiritual reasons (i.e. pilgrimages)	0
24. Travelling for travel's sake	23

(continued)

D. Other reasons	
25. Pursuit of hobbies	12
26. Continuation of education or learning	21
27. Seeking of business contacts and professional goals	0
28. Conferences and meetings	1
29. Ego enhancement	8
30. Fashion, i.e. 'keeping up with friends'	0
** Satisfy long-term goal/dream	2
** Challenge/adventure	2

* Three cruisers did not complete the questionnaire.
** Denotes additional reasons added to the questionnaire by some cruisers.

Psychographic profiles

In the study of cruisers, an attempt was made to critique Plog's psychographic types. Table 2 presents a list of travel characteristics that Plog deemed each of the psychographic types preferred (see Plog 1974).

■ **Table 2** *Travel preferences of psychographic types (Plog 1974)*

PSYCHOCENTRICS	ALLOCENTRICS
Familiar travel destinations	Non-touristy areas
Commonplace activities at destinations	Novel experiences in undiscovered tourist areas
'Sun'n'fun' and relaxation	New and different destinations
Low level engagement in activities	High level engagement in activities
Destinations within drivable distances	Destinations that involve flying
Sites with mass tourism facilities	Sites without mass tourism facilities
Familiar environmental bubble for tourist experience	Engagement with local people in their environments
Heavy reliance on tourist system for packaging and itinerary	Minimal reliance on tourist system for packaging and itinerary

Using the psychographic information in table 2 and etically determined data from the questionnaire based on McIntosh's list of travel reasons, cruisers may be classified as demonstrating allocentric characteristics, that is they seek adventure, prefer non-touristy areas, desire novel experiences and, by nature of their lifestyle, rely minimally on the tourism system to provide their travel requirements. However, using an emic perspective, self-reports of cruisers noted that their boats were considered as their homes (in fact, it was referred to by several cruisers as an environmental bubble that protected them and into which they were also able to retreat from the host communities). Based on Plog's work, this suggests a leaning towards psychocentrism. Furthermore, some of the women, despite crossing oceans in small vessels, might be considered to exhibit psychocentric traits as they were cruising only because of their partners and would have preferred to stay at home as this quote indicates:

> 'Okay, I guess I chose to go cruising because I married 306m, quite frankly, it wouldn't have been a choice if I were single or if I'd married a non-sailing person. I wasn't the sailor first in our relationship so, uhm, I went cruising because that was 306m's dream.' (Cruiser 305f)

In reality, the characteristics of the various psychographic types do little to inform us regarding cruisers and their travel preferences. Both emically and etically derived data indicate that cruisers could be interpreted as simultaneously exhibiting both psychocentric and allocentric traits. Moreover, cruisers could also be located at various positions on Plog's continuum. Still further, a cruiser's location along the continuum could also change during the course of their travel experience. For example, a cruiser may set out for adventure (an allocentric trait); however, they may end up pursuing a lifestyle that has become familiar, especially in regards to the home environment — the boat and mode of transport (a psychocentric trait). Furthermore, in order to determine personality types, five questions are used (Plog 1990). Do these questions establish 'intervening conditions' (Strauss and Corbin 1990)? See, for example, the following cruiser interview quote:

> 'When I was nineteen I saw, er, Eric Hiscock and his wife in our home town in the middle of winter. One winter, I got two tickets for his lecture, and I went along and I saw his first colour slides of the West Indies that he had taken on his first trip in Wander [Hiscock's yacht], I think it was the West Indies and that was the spark but of course the economics and sort of your life, it's taken all these years to get there.' (Cruiser 316m)

For this cruiser, cruising was not an option until he had enough money and had reached a certain stage in life when he was able to travel, that is there were intervening conditions that impacted on his travel preferences. Other cruisers also mentioned various intervening conditions that

(continued)

delayed their adoption of a cruising lifestyle. Such intervening conditions may mask a person's psychographic type. The study of cruisers did not draw on the five questions Plog uses to determine psychographic type (see Plog 1990). However, if Plog's characteristics are well founded then methodological triangulation using both etically and emically gathered data collected on cruisers should achieve a similar outcome. The psychographic continuum designed in the early 1970s does not account for the various forms of tourism now available to travellers/tourists in the 1990s. While Plog (1987, p. 204) has stated that researchers need to get inside the heads of travellers to find out their true motives, based on data gathered in this study of cruisers, psychographics with its unidimensional and/or two dimensional data does not fully explain the motivations of travellers, nor does it get inside the heads of cruisers.

Intrinsic motivation theories

An emic perspective was used to gain insight into the intrinsic motivations of cruisers. Drawing on Maslow's hierarchy of needs, cruiser self-reports reflected a need for belonging as one of the reasons for going cruising:

> 'It is my husband's dream, and I followed. ... Love is the biggest and strongest thing, I love him and he wanted to do it, so I followed. When I came on this boat it was like my home. I did courses — navigation and the certificate for a skipper ... We do not feel we have made a mistake, if we have it is the money that we have used. But we do not feel that we have made a mistake.' (Cruiser 357f)

Furthermore, a need for self-determination (Iso-Ahola 1976, 1980) was also a key reason for travelling by boat or cruising:

> 'You have a bit of independence; you don't get harassed by people knocking on your door or by people trying to sell you stuff and you are very much in control over your own destiny which is probably the major point. That's the big advantage of it [cruising], you haven't got someone telling you all day every day what to do. You've got a certain amount of control over your life, what you do with it and where you go and how you live and that's probably one of the major advantages ... you have grabbed your life and have said that I am in control.' (Cruiser 328m)

Cruisers intimated that 'intrinsically motivated leisure equals "self-actualising" leisure' (Iso-Ahola 1980, p. 248). Again, cruisers comment on reasons for going cruising:

> 'For me it is the challenge, because of a personal goal, it's a challenge for me to go Papua New Guinea. I've got to do it. I want to do it. It's my goal.' (Cruiser 351f)

Cruisers reported that they sought a lifestyle that provided them with intrinsically rewarding, and self-actualising or optimal arousing or 'peak' experiences, that also offered freedom and a sense of personal control. These peak experiences were achieved by travelling by their own boats, making their passages and getting themselves to destinations:

'There is the advantage of being able to leave and come and go when you want to, there's a certain amount of freedom associated with that, there is the satisfaction of getting, the personal satisfaction of getting to a place by your own means and away again.' (Cruiser 336m)

An earlier study of long-term ocean cruisers (Macbeth 1985) also found similar findings and evidence of cruisers experiencing 'flow' (Csikszentmihalyi 1974). Both studies found that these 'flow' experiences were episodic and did not occur for all cruisers or during all phases of their travel experiences.

Sociodemographic and economic profiles

Based on both emically and etically derived data, the study further found that the socioeconomic background of cruisers facilitated their propensity to adopt a cruising lifestyle. Of the long-term cruisers who were interviewed, 42 were women and 54 were men. Most men were aged between 55 and 64 years and most women were aged between 45 and 54 years. The women's ages ranged from 33 to 62 years and the men from 20 to 77 years. Most women had received a tertiary education, while most men had received either a tertiary education or high school education. The women had been formerly employed at the lower professional level and in the service industry. The men's work background was varied, from employers and managers to lower professionals, as well as workers in the service industry. The cruisers' nationalities were primarily Australian, American, New Zealand and British, with most participants in the study having been socialised in Western countries.

Seven cruisers were solo sailors (six men and one woman); the remainder were travelling with friends or were in stable heterosexual relationships. In regard to family life cycle, five yachts were cruising with children and could be classified as being in the middle adulthood (establishment stage) of the family life cycle (Rapoport & Rapoport 1975). Three boats were travelling with young children and three had teenagers aboard. The remaining yachts were travelling without children and these cruisers were in the middle adulthood (mid-establishment and late establishment) stage of the family life cycle (Rapoport & Rapoport 1975). Generally, most cruisers did not need to 'work' to sustain their cruising lifestyle. Cruisers had either taken early retirement packages, used superannuation funds or pensions, or had real estate investments or other investments. Several cruisers were planning to cruise and work along the way. The financial investment in the cruising lifestyle varied between cruisers. The majority of boats cost between AUS$50 000 and AUS$100 000. The range in the purchase price of boats varied from AUS$6000 to AUS$600 000. (These figures are raw figures and have not been indexed to take into account changes in the value of the dollar from the date of purchase.) Cruising budgets also varied between AUS$7000 and AUS$73 000. The average annual budget for two people on a boat was AUS$19 500 per annum.

(continued)

Cruisers also indicated that the decision to go cruising was related to technological factors, specifically:

- improvements in yacht design, especially sailing efficiency and the comfort of living on-board
- the increased affordability of navigation equipment, due to the innovation costs being carried by earlier adopters of the technological advances
- developments in telecommunications equipment, particularly wider-ranging satellite coverage, that provide greater contact with home bases and linkages to search and rescue facilities.

Primarily, the cruisers' ages, educational backgrounds, family life cycle stages, former work experiences and life experiences in Western societies, as well as their income bases, ensured that they had the financial and social propensity to adopt a cruising lifestyle.

Further findings

The study found that in most cases cruisers' motivations were multicausal in nature. This was specifically elicited during participant observation and in-depth interviews, as indicated by this cruiser's response to 'Why do cruising?':

'Well, in a few words, to escape stressful jobs, wanting to spend more time with a partner. We found out after about 10 years or so that which we have done in the last 10 years was not that, what we expected to do before we married. One of these evenings, winter time, open fire place, bottle of wine, a couple of friends, we started talking about the sense of your lives, what you did and your future, what you expect to do. Actually, on one of those evenings the idea was born that we might change. Whether the next five years, from then on, what we will do, and a few days later we both picked up that idea again and another few weeks later on we decided we would do it. We would stop the life we are living now with all the kind of consequences, which we didn't know at that stage, but we started thinking about the consequences. We decided to do it.

I've mentioned already two points, stressful jobs and to be willing to spend more time with a partner. Which might be an unusual reason, but in our case it was one of the major reasons because we figured out we divided out, husband, for example, 80 hours a week for my job and she did almost the same. We meet each other on Saturday, and on Sunday, we saw the husband, myself, already had to prepare for the week, so that was one of the major reasons. Another one based on a solid financial situation. We reduced expenses; we wanted to choose another lifestyle. We realised that we did not have to spend that much money for doing something, which might be fun for us, which we would enjoy. Another reason is to explore other countries, we both find out before we met each other that travelling is something we really enjoy, meeting other people. That's the next point to meet different people not only other but different ones, and generally that's it, those were the major ones.' (Cruiser 302m)

Another point that was consistently made by cruisers regarding their motivations was that their motivations changed during the course of their overall travel experiences. The following quotes indicate such changes:

'Mine [the motivation] was more [pause] I've never had a big yearning to see the world and the other things, [pause] mine was more the challenge of the trip. But I think that that's changed now that we've come this far. I'm beginning to know that it isn't the challenge any more. To go on around the world originally, I thought, boy, a trip around the world. What a challenge! Well, it's not a challenge any more. If you have come this far, what the hell! The rest isn't any worse than what you've come to. So now I am beginning to take-two [five]. My outlook is beginning to switch, it's what 371f's talking about. To see the world is becoming, [pause] and to meet different people and see the different countries, is becoming more important than the challenge of the trip but originally it was the challenge of the trip.' (Cruiser 372m)

'I think the reason why I started, the reason why, is because I am always game to do anything. I always have been and I hate sitting anywhere for any length of time. I just want to meet people. I mean that would be the reason why I did it in the first place ... I am one of those people who like to give anything a go. But now? Cruising? I love the lifestyle.' (Cruiser 339f)

Consequently, cruisers are articulating that as 'initial needs are satisfied', others emerge (Ryan 1997b, p. 41). A researcher would err if they considered that motivations remained constant throughout the travel experience or only considered motivations during one stage of the travel experience. The resultant data would only provide a snapshot view of travel motivations.

Findings from in-depth interviews regarding cruisers' motivations also contributed to a critique of society:

'I just wanted to get away from the city. I didn't want [pause] I just wanted to have some adventure. I've always wanted to travel. We have done a lot of travelling without being on a boat ... I just wanted to get out of town! I just wanted to get away from [my home city] and then have it be a lifestyle. It's fine going away for a two-week vacation to the Bahamas or something but that's just a little blast of unreality. I wanted to change my lifestyle completely. It took us 10 years basically to get everything together to go ... We worked a lot [pause] a long time, worked hard and we just wanted to get away and cruise, just to change our lifestyle.' (Cruiser 399f)

'You are not really totally, what should you say, a part of this society that we don't really want. The world is getting overpopulated, it is over populated, and with all laws and things on shore and things like that, it's really, it isn't what one really wants, you know and I just like the sea, it's wonderful ... Well, it's the last frontier of total freedom where, laws, I mean laws do exist for the sea obviously, but it's the freedom and you are really in touch with the elements this is what it is really about, when you are out at sea it is only you or the people aboard this vessel itself, you are in the hands, in the mercy [laughs] of the sea. And you really are in touch with nature, nobody can help you out there ...' (Cruiser 332m)

(*continued*)

Dissatisfaction with work, stressful jobs, daily routines and lack of personal control were constant themes noted by cruisers. Such themes begin to build a critique of the societies from which the cruisers were drawn.

Conclusion

The ethnographic study found that cruisers were motivated by a combination of extrinsic and intrinsic motivations and that motivations changed throughout the course of their travel experiences. It also found that while cruisers might initially be classified as allocentrics using an etic perspective, an emic perspective found that cruisers could be located along the various points of the psychographic continuum. However, the overall use of psychographic profiles was questioned. The study also found that cruisers' socioeconomic backgrounds influenced their decision to go sailing and their propensity to travel, that is to adopt a cruising lifestyle. Cruisers' decision making was also influenced by advancements in technology.

Overall, the study of cruisers has served a twofold purpose. It has provided insight into the motivations of cruisers, who may be considered as independent travellers, and it has also served to critique several approaches to gathering data on travel motivations. While various critiques of travel motivations already exist within the tourism literature (Graburn 1983; Smith 1990a; Smith 1990b; Ryan 1991, 1997c; Pearce 1993; Ross 1994; McIntosh, Goeldner & Ritchie 1995; McGehee, Loker-Murphy & Uysal 1996; Galloway 1998), this study of cruisers' motivations has added to those critiques of motivation theories and the conduct of tourism research. Specifically, the study of cruisers reiterates the need for a multidimensional approach and multicausal analysis in order to 'get at' the 'real' motivations of cruisers. It has also identified some alternative methodological applications for the study of travel motivations based on using both an etic and an emic perspective.

Subsequently, this critique has implications for travel and tourism industries and associated agencies when planning for and managing travel activities and experiences. It also has implications for marketing strategies that are solely developed on unidimensional and unicausal motivation studies. In addition, the critique has implications for travel and tourism educators and the travel and tourism curricula. Students need to be skilled in the use of multidimensional approaches and multicausal analyses that adopt both etic and emic perspectives for the study of travel motivations.

Finally, the study of cruisers and their varying motivations throughout their travel experiences has simultaneously contributed to a knowledge of mainstream and marginal Western middle class societies and the changing nature of those societies. Specifically, albeit briefly, the study has added to the examination of the '*linkages between changes in society, tourist motivation and the translation of motive and expectation into holiday experiences*' (Ryan, 1997b, p. 47).

References

Adler, P. A. & Adler, P. (1983). Shifts and Oscillations in Deviant Careers: The Case of Upper-Level Drug Dealers and Smugglers. *Social Problems*, Vol. 31, pp. 195–207.

Babbie, E. (1990). *Survey Research Methods* (2nd ed.). Belmont: Wadsworth.

Cohen, E. (1972). Toward a Sociology of International Tourism. *Social Research*, Vol. 39, pp. 164–82.

Cohen, E. (1984). The Sociology of Tourism: Approaches, Issues and Findings. *Annual Review of Sociology*, Vol. 10, pp. 373–92.

Craig-Smith, S. & French, C. (1994). *Learning to Live with Tourism*. Melbourne: Pitman.

Crompton, J. (1979). Motivations for Pleasure Vacation. *Annals of Tourism Research*, Vol. 6, No. 4, pp. 408–24.

Csikszentmihalyi, M. (1974). *Flow: Studies of Enjoyment*. Chicago: University of Chicago.

Csikszentmihalyi, M. (1988). The Future of Flow. In Csikszentmihalyi, M. & Csikszentmihalyi, I. S. (Eds) *Optimal Experience, Psychological Studies of Flow in Consciousness*. Cambridge: Cambridge University Press, pp. 365–83.

Dann, G. M. S. (1977). Anomie and Ego-Enhancement. *Annals of Tourism Research*, Vol. 4, No. 4, pp. 184–94.

Denzin, N. K. (1978). *The Research Act: A Theoretical Introduction to Sociological Methods* (2nd ed.). New York: McGraw-Hill.

de Vaus, D. A. (1995). *Surveys in Social Research* (4th ed.). Sydney: Allen & Unwin.

Epperson, A. (1983). Why People Travel. *Journal of Physical Education, Recreation and Dance — Leisure Today*, Vol. 54, No. 4, pp. 53–4.

Fetterman, D. M. (1989). *Ethnography, Step By Step*. Applied Social Research Methods Series, Vol. 17. Newbury Park: Sage.

Fiske, D. W. & Maddi, S. R. (1961). *Functions of Varied Experience*. Homewood, IL: Dorsey.

Fodness, D. (1992). The Impact of Family Life Cycle on the Vacation Decision-Making Process. *Journal of Travel Research*, Fall, pp. 8–13.

Frew, E. A. & Shaw, R. N. (1997). Personality and Tourism Behaviour: A Test of Holland's Theory. In Hsu, C. H. C. (Ed.). *Proceedings of Research and Academic Papers: New Frontiers in Tourism Research*. Vol. IX. San Diego: The International Society of Travel and Tourism Educators, pp. 32–45.

Galloway, G. (1998). Motivations for Leisure Travel: A Critical Examination. In W. Faulkner, C. Tidswell & Weaver, D. (Eds.). *Proceedings of the Eighth Australian Tourism and Hospitality Research Conference: Progress in Tourism and Hospitality Research*. Gold Coast, Queensland: Bureau of Tourism Research, pp. 99–108.

Gans, H. J. (1982). The Participant Observer as a Human Being: Observations on the Personal Aspects of Fieldwork. In Burgess, R. G. (Ed.). *Field Research*. Boston: George Allen & Unwin, pp. 53–61.

Glaser, B.G. (1992). *Emergence vs Forcing: Basics of Grounded Theory Analysis*. Mill Valley, CA: Sociology Press.

Godbey, G. (1990). *Leisure in Your Life: An Exploration* (3rd ed.). State College, PA: Venture Publishing.

Goodall, B. (1991). Understanding Holiday Choice. *Progress in Tourism, Recreation and Hospitality Management*, Vol. 3, pp. 59–77.

Graburn, N. H. H. (1983). The Anthropology of Tourism. *Annals of Tourism Research*, Vol. 10, pp. 9–33.

(*continued*)

Gray, H. P. (1970). *International Travel: International Trade.* Lexington, MA: Lexington Books.

Grinstein, A. (1955). Vacations: a Psycho-Analytic Study. *International Journal of Psycho-Analysis,* Vol. 36, No. 3, pp. 177–85.

Iso-Ahola, S. (1976). On the Theoretical Link Between Personality and Leisure. *Psychological Reports,* Vol. 39, pp. 3–10.

Iso-Ahola, S. (1980). *The Social Psychology of Leisure and Recreation.* Dubuque, IO: Wm C. Brown.

Janesick, V. J. (1994). The Dance of Qualitative Research Design. In Denzin, N. K. & Lincoln, Y. S. (Eds). *Handbook of Qualitative Research.* Thousand Oaks: Sage, pp. 209–19.

Jorgensen, D. L. (1989). *Participant Observation: A Methodology for a Human Studies.* Applied Social Research Methods Series, Vol. 15. Newbury Park: Sage.

Jubenville, A. (1976). *Outdoor Recreation Planning.* Philadelphia: W.B. Saunders.

Junker, B. H. (1960). *Fieldwork.* Chicago: University of Chicago Press.

Killion, L. (1992). *Understanding Tourism: Study Guide.* Rockhampton: Central Queensland University.

Krippendorf, J. (1987). *The Holiday Makers: Understanding the Impact of Leisure and Travel.* Oxford: Heinemann Professional Publishing.

Levinson, D. (1978). *The Seasons of a Man's Life.* New York: Alfred Knopf.

Lincoln, Y. S. & Guba, E. G. (1985). *Naturalistic Inquiry.* Newbury Park, Sage.

Macbeth, J. (1985). Ocean Cruising: A Study of Affirmative Deviance. Unpublished PhD thesis, Murdoch University, Perth.

Maslow, A. H. (1943). A Theory of Human Motivation. *Psychological Review,* Vol. 50, pp. 370–96.

Maslow, A. H. (1954). *Motivation and Personality.* New York: Harper & Brothers.

Maslow, A. H. (1970). *Motivation and Personality.* New York: Harper & Row.

McIntosh, R. W. (1977). *Tourism: Principles, Practices, Philosophies.* Columbus, OH: Grid.

McIntosh, R. W., Goeldner, C. R. & Ritchie, J. R. B. (1995). *Tourism: Principles, Practices, Philosophies* (7th ed.). New York: John Wiley & Sons.

McGehee, N. G., Loker-Murphy, L. & Uysal, M. (1996). The Australian International Pleasure Travel Market: Motivations from a Gendered Perspective. *The Journal of Tourism Studies,* Vol. 7, No. 1, May, pp. 45–57.

Mill, R.C. & Morrison, A. (1992). *The Tourism System: An Introductory Text* (2nd ed.). Englewood Cliffs, NJ: Prentice-Hall.

Mitchell, R. G. (1983). *The Psychology and Sociology of Adventure.* Chicago: The University of Chicago Press.

Nash, D. & Smith, V. L. (1991). Anthropology and Tourism. *Annals of Tourism Research,* Vol. 18, pp. 12–25.

Nickerson, N. P. & Ellis, G. D. (1991). Traveler Types and Activation Theory: A Comparison of Two Models. *Journal of Travel Research,* Winter, pp. 26–31.

Pearce, D. (1987). *Tourism Today: A Geographical Analysis.* New York: Longman Scientific & Technical.

Pearce, P. L. (1993). *Fundamentals of Tourist Motivation.* In Pearce, D. G. & Butler, R. W. Tourism Research. London: Routledge.

Pearce, P. L. & Caltabiano, M. L. (1982). Inferring Travel Motivations from Travellers' Experiences. *Journal of Tourism Research,* Vol. 17, pp. 337–52.

Plog, S. C. (1974). Why Destinations Areas Rise and Fall in Popularity. *The Cornell Hotel and Restaurant Administration Quarterly*, Vol. 14, No. 4, February, pp. 55–8.

Plog, S. C. (1987). Understanding Psychographics in Tourism Research. In Ritchie, B. J. R. &. Goeldner, C. R. (Eds). *Travel, Tourism and Hospitality Research: A Handbook for Managers and Researchers* (5th ed.). New York: John Wiley & Sons, pp. 203–13.

Plog, S. C. (1989). Two Decades of Travel Research. In Lyne, C. (Ed.). *Leisure Travel and Tourism* (2nd ed.). Wellesley, MA: Institute of Certified Travel Agents, pp. 227–34.

Plog, S. C. (1990). A Carpenter's Tool: An Answer to Stephen L. J. Smith's Review of Psychocentrism/Allocentrism. *Journal of Travel Research*, Spring, pp. 43–5.

Rapoport, R. & Rapoport, R. N. (1975). *Leisure and the Family Life Cycle*. London: Routledge & Kegan Paul.

Ross, G. F. (1994). *The Psychology of Tourism*. Melbourne: Hospitality Press.

Ryan, C. (1991). *Recreational Tourism: A Social Sciences Perspective*. London: Routledge.

Ryan, C. (1997a). The Chase of a Dream, the End of Play. In Ryan, C. (Ed.). *The Tourist Experience: A New Introduction*. Studies in Tourism Series. London: Cassell.

Ryan, C. (1997b). Similar Motivations — Diverse Behaviours. In Ryan, C. (Ed.). *The Tourist Experience: A New Introduction*. Studies in Tourism Series. London: Cassell.

Ryan, C. (1997c). From Motivation to Assessment. In Ryan, C. (Ed.). *The Tourist Experience: A New Introduction*. Studies in Tourism Series. London: Cassell.

Schmidhauser, H. (1989). Tourist Needs and Motivations. In Witt, S. & Moutinho, L. (Eds). *Tourism Marketing and Management Handbook*. Hemel Hempstead: Prentice Hall.

Sieber, J. E. (1992). *Planning Ethically Responsible Research*. Applied Social Research Methods Series, Vol. 31. Newbury Park: Sage.

Slattery, J. (1989). Road to Placelessness. In Lyne, C. (Ed.). *Leisure Travel and Tourism* (2nd ed.). Wellesley, MA: Institute of Certified Travel Agents, pp. 34–5.

Smith, S. L. J. (1990a). A Test of Plog's Allocentric/Psychocentric Model: Evidence from Seven Nations. *Journal of Travel Research*, Spring, pp. 40–3.

Smith, S. L. J. (1990b). Another Look at the Carpenter's Tools: A Reply to Plog. *Journal of Travel Research*, Fall, pp. 50–1.

SRI International. (1989). VALS — Values and Lifestyle of Americans. In Lyne, C. (Ed.). *Leisure Travel and Tourism* (2nd ed.). Wellesley, MA: Institute of Certified Travel Agents, pp. 207–14.

Strauss, A. & Corbin, J. (1990). *Basics of Qualitative Research: Grounded Theory Procedures and Techniques*. Newbury Park: Sage.

Yiannakis, A. & Gibson, H. (1992). Roles Tourists Play. *Annals of Tourism Research*, Vol. 19, pp. 287–303.

12.6 CASE STUDY 2: USING A POSITIVIST APPROACH

The second case study uses the genre of a poster paper to report tourism research conducted using a positivist paradigm. As you read through case study 2, you should:

- undertake a peer review of the contents

- make notes regarding aspects of the research that reflect the positivist paradigm
- comment on the appropriateness of the methodology and the methods used
- evaluate the presentation of the findings and the discussion of the findings
- critique the literature review and its use in the beginning and end sections of the paper
- comment on the style of writing used
- examine the referencing style: what style is used and why?

Finally, what suggestions would you make to improve the paper?

Recreational fishers in Shoalwater Bay and adjacent waters:
motivations and attitudes

Abstract

Recreational fishing is reported as a popular leisure time activity in national parks and wilderness areas (Borschmann 1987). While the desire to catch a fish is the primary goal of recreational fishers, there are non-catch related motivations associated with the experience (Dovers 1994). Non-catch related motivations may include a desire to escape from the everyday environment, a need to experience freedom and a need for rest and relaxation within a natural 'wilderness' environment. There are also social aspects associated with recreational fishing, such as being with friends and family (PA Management Consultants 1984).

Data collected in a recent mail survey of registered boat owners from Gladstone, Rockhampton, Yeppoon, Marlborough, St Lawrence, Sarina and Mackay found similar motivation patterns. The mail survey was part of a larger study of recreational users and their usage patterns of Shoalwater Bay and adjacent waters.

The mail survey also asked users about their attitudes towards various activities that might be conducted within the study area. A majority expressed concern about commercial extractive activities. This concern reflected the conflict of interests associated with the use of marine-based environments for recreational and commercial activities (Gartside 1986, Kenchington 1993 and Dovers 1994) and the continuous debate between recreational and commercial fishers regarding who is responsible for diminishing fishing stocks (Gartside 1986 and Dovers 1994).

From a management perspective, the registered boat owners noted the desire to experience a 'wilderness' setting while participating in outdoor activities and the need for the '*preservation of [the] environmental quality*' (Jackson 1986) of Shoalwater Bay and adjacent waters.

Introduction

To date, very few studies have focused on the recreational usage patterns of the marine areas of Shoalwater Bay. In fact, Gutteridge Haskins and Davey (1996) suggest none exist. Several studies of land usage patterns have been conducted as part of the Commonwealth Commission of Inquiry: Shoalwater Bay, Capricornia Coast, Queensland: A G B McNair conducted a study of Central Queensland residents and residents residing elsewhere in Queensland regarding their attitudes towards various land use issues related to the Shoalwater Bay Military Training Area; while Wood, Thompson, McIntyre and Killion (1994) developed a theoretical recreational and tourism opportunity spectrum for the Shoalwater Bay Military Training Area.

In order to obtain information on recreational marine usage of Shoalwater Bay and adjacent waters, a study was commissioned by the Great Barrier Reef Marine Park Authority. Part of the study investigated user motivations and attitudes. This paper will present and discuss the findings regarding the motivations and attitudes of recreational users, specifically fishers of Shoalwater Bay and adjacent waters, as determined by a mail survey of registered boat owners residing in Gladstone, Rockhampton, Yeppoon, Marlborough, St Lawrence, Sarina and Mackay.

Recreational fishing is viewed as a popular leisure time activity in national parks and wilderness areas (Borschmann 1987, p. 42). Dovers (1994, p. 103) highlights that while the desire to catch a fish is the primary goal of recreational fishers, there are non-catch related motivations associated with the experience. The importance of non-catch related motivations as part of the overall recreational fishing experience is also discussed by Fedler and Ditton (1994) in their 1978 to 1991 review of American recreational fishers. Johnson and Orbach (1986, p. 326) noted in an American study that non-catch related motivations included '*escape, freedom, relaxation and personal liberty*' as well as the desire to experience a '*frontier spirit*'. Such non-catch related motivations are also reported by various researchers in the Australian context. PA Management Consultants (1984, p. 38) found in a national Australian household study conducted during July 1984, that to '*relax and unwind, to be outdoors*', to enjoy the company of others, to experience the '*thrill/contest of catching fish*' and to obtain a source of food were the main reasons people reported for engaging in recreational fishing. Gartside (1986, p. 15) reported similar motivations ranging from a sense of '*escapism*' from daily life and work to '*enjoyment of the environment*'.

A social aspect of recreational fishing was also reported by PA Management Consultants (1984, pp. 38, 39), who stated that men favoured fishing with friends over fishing with their families, while women favoured fishing with their families than with their friends.

(*continued*)

Method

The Shoalwater Bay study area was defined as those waters located between the latitudes of 22° 08'S and 23° 00'S and the longitudes of 150° 02'E and 151° 02'E. See map one.

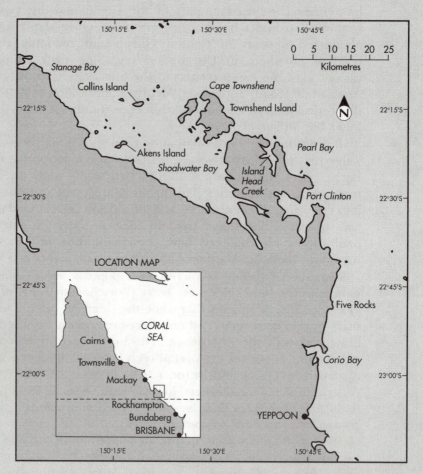

■ **Map one** *Shoalwater Bay Study Area*

Source: *Map courtesy of the Great Barrier Reef Marine Park Authority*

The mail survey component of the Shoalwater Bay and adjacent waters study targeted local recreational users who were registered boat owners of either motor- or sail-driven vessels. Expert opinion was used to identify the drawing areas in order to classify 'local' users. The experts contacted had either long histories as users or managers or executive positions in recreational clubs. According to expert opinion, local users were deemed to be those users located in coastal towns and cities along or east of the Pacific Highway between Mackay in the north and Gladstone in the south. The largest drawing areas were considered to be Yeppoon followed by Rockhampton. The sample for the mail survey was framed from boat registration records held by the Queensland Department of Transport. The sampling frame was received in late March 1996 and was up-to-date for the preceding six-month period. The sampling frame was proportionately stratified based on experts' opinions regarding usage of the Shoalwater Bay area by recreationalists from Mackay, Sarina, St Lawrence, Marlborough, Yeppoon, Rockhampton and Gladstone. After the proportions were determined for each of the locations, each location was further proportionally stratified by suburbs. The overall sample size was set at 1200 as this would provide a 95% confidence interval for a finding of 50% of ±3.0% (Veal 1992, p. 155).

Each person included in the sample was mailed a package that included a survey with a reply-paid envelope. Each survey included a covering page, asked 20 questions and utilised maps to orient the respondent to the Shoalwater Bay area. To improve the response rate, a reminder card was sent approximately one week after the survey was posted. Survey recipients were advised in the initial covering letter accompanying the survey that a reminder card would be used. The reminder served as both a thank you and as a reminder to those who had not yet returned the survey. It should be noted that surveys and reminders for Rockhampton residents did not arrive a week apart as mail deliveries did not occur on two days of one week due to two public holidays, resulting in some reminder cards arriving one or two days after receipt of the survey.

Of the 1200 surveys sent out, 50 were returned as a result of incorrect addresses and 50 telephone calls were received from people indicating that they did not use the area and would not be returning their surveys. Details of the latter were recorded on survey sheets and included in the analysis. In all, 400 surveys were completed and returned, giving a response rate of 33%. The proportions used in the stratified sampling were reflected in the completed and returned surveys. The response rate needs to be considered when discussing the results in relation to all recreational boat owners within the study area.

The returned surveys were coded, entered and analysed using the computer program SPSS.

Results

Of the 400 respondents to the survey, 256 indicated that they were users of the area, while 142 indicated that they did not use the area for recreational purposes and 2 respondents did not provide data regarding usage of the study area. Of the 256 users of the area, 245 respondents engaged in recreational fishing, that is 95.7% of respondents were fishers of the area. Some users indicated that they also engaged in other activities such as boating, camping and sightseeing.

(*continued*)

The reasons why the recreational users chose Shoalwater Bay and the adjacent waters as a recreational setting was related to the quality of the fish stocks (53.1%), followed by the amenity provided by the area (34.8%). When discussing the amenity of the area, users noted the scenic amenity, the wilderness settings, the peace, the quiet and the solitude. The proximity of the study area to mail survey respondents' residence was noted by 23.8% of the users.

While the opportunity to be with family and friends was noted specifically by three respondents, mail survey respondents reported that family and friends accompanied them on trips to the study area. The mode response for the type of passenger who accompanied the mail survey respondent was friends (68.4%), with family accompanying 62.1% of the mail survey respondents.

Survey respondents were also asked their opinion about various activities listed on the GBRMPA Shoalwater Bay BRA Q120 map (see map one). The activities listed were bait netting and gathering, camping, recreational collecting, commercial collecting, crabbing and oyster gathering, diving, commercial line fishing, recreational line fishing, research activities, boating activities, tourist activities, tourist and educational facilities/programs, spearfishing, commercial netting, trawling, and indigenous hunting, fishing and collecting. To this list were added sightseeing, photography and snorkelling. The study area was broken up into five sections in order to canvas the opinions of respondents. The sections were the northern section of Shoalwater Bay (section A), the southern section of Shoalwater Bay (section B), Island Head Creek and environs (section C), Port Clinton and environs (section D), and Cape Clinton to Little Corio Bay (section E).

In responding to the type of activities that the respondents thought were suitable for each of the areas, users and non-users were asked to comment. The following data represent the responses from approximately 78–85% of respondents to the survey, as some respondents did not provide data in various sections. In section A, the northern section of Shoalwater Bay, the following activities were considered to be unsuitable: trawling (68.3% of respondents); commercial collecting (66.5% of respondents); commercial netting (66.8% of respondents); and commercial line fishing (49.3% of respondents). Indigenous fishing, hunting and collecting received an almost divided response, with 41.2% of respondents noting that it should be allowed, while 36.8% considered that it should not be allowed.

In section B, the southern section of Shoalwater Bay, the activities that the mail survey respondents considered should not be allowed were: trawling (70.5% of respondents); commercial collecting (67.8% of respondents); commercial netting (67.8% of respondents); commercial line fishing (53% of respondents); and spearfishing (52.5% of respondents). Respondents were also divided between the appropriateness of indigenous hunting, fishing and collecting within this section (37.8% of respondents thought it was appropriate and 37.8% thought it was not).

Commercial collecting (66.5% of respondents), trawling (64.5% of respondents), commercial netting (64% of respondents), commercial line fishing (49.5% of respondents) and spearfishing (45.8% of respondents) were considered as inappropriate for section C, Island Head Creek and environs. Beliefs regarding the appropriateness of indigenous hunting were nearly divided: 37.9% thought the activity was inappropriate, and 39.5% believed the activity should be permitted.

In section D, Port Clinton and environs, the activities that the mail survey respondents considered should not be allowed were: trawling (69.3% of respondents); commercial netting (67.8% of respondents); commercial collecting (67.5% of respondents); commercial fishing (53.3% of respondents); and spearfishing (50.5% of respondents). Again there was division regarding the suitability of indigenous activities being conducted in the area: 39% thought it was appropriate, and 37% thought it was inappropriate.

The trends evident in sections A to D were reflected in mail survey respondents' attitudes regarding the various activities appropriate for section E, Cape Clinton to Little Corio Bay. Trawling (70% of respondents), commercial netting (73.3% of respondents), commercial collecting (68.2% of respondents), commercial line fishing (56.8% of respondents) and spearfishing (53.5% of respondents) were considered inappropriate. However, indigenous activities were marginally considered more appropriate in this section: 41.3% of respondents thought it was appropriate and 39.5% thought it was inappropriate.

Comments made by the mail survey respondents were related primarily to keeping commercial fishers out of the study area (46.0% of respondents). A range of activity controls was also suggested by 21.5% of respondents.

Discussion

The mail survey respondents indicated that the primary recreational activity pursued in Shoalwater Bay and adjacent waters was recreational fishing. The main reasons for the use of Shoalwater Bay and adjacent waters for recreational fishing were the quality of the fish stocks, the amenity of the area, the area's proximity to the user's place of residence and the provision of safe anchorages. The first two reasons or motivations supported those reported by Dovers (1994, p. 103), who stated that the primary goal of recreational fishers was to catch a fish, followed by non-catch related motivations. The non-catch related motivations reported in this study reflected the literature: to relax in the outdoors, to enjoy the environment and to get away from everyday life and work (PA Management Consultants 1984, p. 38; Gartside 1986, p. 15; and Johnson & Orbach 1986, p. 326).

(continued)

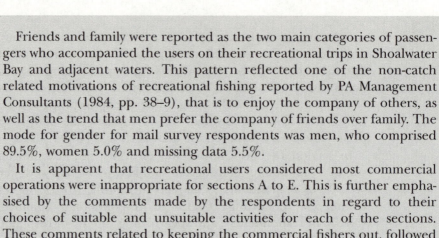

Friends and family were reported as the two main categories of passengers who accompanied the users on their recreational trips in Shoalwater Bay and adjacent waters. This pattern reflected one of the non-catch related motivations of recreational fishing reported by PA Management Consultants (1984, pp. 38–9), that is to enjoy the company of others, as well as the trend that men prefer the company of friends over family. The mode for gender for mail survey respondents was men, who comprised 89.5%, women 5.0% and missing data 5.5%.

It is apparent that recreational users considered most commercial operations were inappropriate for sections A to E. This is further emphasised by the comments made by the respondents in regard to their choices of suitable and unsuitable activities for each of the sections. These comments related to keeping the commercial fishers out, followed by suggestions for activity controls in Shoalwater Bay and adjacent waters. It should also be noted that other extractive activities such as spearfishing and indigenous activities received either negative attitudes or mixed attitudes relating to the conduct of those activities in the study area. The negative attitude to other extractive activities apart from recreational fishing highlighted the point made by Jaakson (1989, p. 96) that having to share an area had the ability to detract from users' satisfaction. It also reiterated the points made by Gartside (1986, p. 17), Kenchington (1993, p. 8) and Dovers (1994, p. 106) regarding a conflict of interests between commercial and recreational activities and the continuous debate over who is responsible for diminishing fish stocks.

In conclusion, recreational users of Shoalwater Bay and the adjacent waters were primarily fishers, who used the area because of the quality of the fish stocks and the desire to experience a 'wilderness' setting while participating in outdoor activities in the company of friends and family. These users expressed the need for the 'preservation of [the] environmental quality' (Jackson 1986) of Shoalwater Bay and adjacent waters. From their perspective, the preservation and/or maintenance of the quality of the fish stocks and the setting was best achieved through the exclusion of commercial operations. Having solicited this information on recreational users' motivations and attitudes, managers now need to provide such recreational experiences within the recreational and tourism opportunity spectrum to be developed for Shoalwater Bay and the adjacent waters, while simultaneously considering the perspectives of commercial fishing operators, indigenous users and other non-recreational users.

Acknowledgements

The study of *Recreational Usage Patterns of Shoalwater Bay and Adjacent Waters* was funded by the Great Barrier Reef Marine Park Authority and supported by Central Queensland University. Personnel from the Queensland Department of Environment and Queensland Department

of Transport provided data and/or feedback during the course of the study. Thanks are also extended to those persons who provided 'expert opinion' and to the recreational users of Shoalwater Bay who chose to participate in the study. Thanks also to Ray Berkelmans and Dominique Benzaken from the Great Barrier Reef Marine Park Authority, and Les Killion and Jillian Litster at Central Queensland University who provided comments and suggestions regarding this paper in its draft stages, as well as Leon Jackson at the Great Barrier Reef Marine Park Authority who prepared map one.

References

A G B McNair, 1994, 'Survey of Attitudes Toward Land Use Issues for Shoalwater Bay Military Training Area', Research Report 13, in *Commonwealth Commission of Inquiry into Shoalwater Bay — Research Reports, Report No. 5, Volume C,* Australian Government Publishing Service, Canberra, pp. 301–27.

Borschmann, R. 1987, 'Recreational Fishing in National Parks and Wilderness Areas', Conference paper presented at the Twenty-Second Assembly of the Australian Fresh Water Fishermen's Assembly, Khancoban.

Dovers, S. 1994, 'Recreational Fishing in Australia: Review and Policy Issues', *Australian Geographical Studies,* Vol. 32, No. 1, pp. 102–14.

Fedler, J. A. & Ditton, R. B. 1994, 'Understanding Angler Motivations in Fisheries Management, *Fisheries,* Vol. 19, No. 4.

Gartside, D. F. 1986, 'Recreational Fishing', paper presented to National Coastal Management Conference, Coffs Harbour, Australia in *Safish,* Vol. 11, No. 2, March/April, pp. 15–17.

Great Barrier Reef Marine Park Authority, Shoalwater Bay BRA Q120 Map, Great Barrier Reef Marine Park Authority, Townsville.

Gutteridge Haskins & Davey 1996, *Department of Defence: Shoalwater Bay Training Area Draft Strategic Plan,* Gutteridge Haskins & Davey, Cairns.

Jaakson, R. 1989, 'Recreation Boating and Spatial Patterns: Theory and Management', *Leisure Sciences,* Vol. 11, pp. 85–98.

Jackson, E. L. 1986, 'Outdoor Recreation Participation and Attitudes to the Environment', *Leisure Studies,* Vol. 5, pp. 1–23.

Johnson. J. C. & Orbach, M. K. 1986, 'The Role of Cultural Context in the Development of Low-Capital Ocean Leisure Activities', *Leisure Sciences,* Vol. 8, No. 3, pp. 319–39.

Kenchington, R. 1993, 'Tourism in Coastal and Marine Environments: A Recreational Perspective', *Ocean and Coastal Management,* Vol. 19, pp. 1–16.

PA Management Consultants, 1984, *National Survey of Participation in Recreational Fishing, Report No. 1 for the Australian Recreational Fishing Confederation,* PA Management Consultants, Melbourne.

Veal, A. J. 1992, *Research Methods for Leisure and Tourism: A Practical Guide,* Longman, Essex.

Wood, J., Thompson, D., McIntyre, N. & Killion, L., 1994, 'Recreation and Tourism Opportunities of the Shoalwater Bay Military Training Area and Environs', Research Report 7A, in *Commonwealth Commission of Inquiry into Shoalwater Bay — Research Reports, Report No.5, Volume A,* Australian Government Publishing Service, Canberra, pp. 282–331.

COMMENT ON THE TWO CASE STUDIES

As noted by Riley and Love (2000), most research in tourism and hospitality is predicated to a quantitative methodology; however, research informed by qualitative methodologically also has a part to play in understanding the phenomena of tourism and hospitality. Remember, it is not a question about which is the best methodology, but rather which methodology is the best way to gain the information required given the project circumstances.

12.8 CURRENT AND POTENTIAL RESEARCH NEEDS OF THE TRAVEL AND HOSPITALITY SECTORS

Prior to discussing tourism research in the future, the chapter focuses on the current and potential research needs of the travel and hospitality sectors. There is a large variety of research projects to be undertaken in both sectors. Some examples are presented below. The examples are suggestions only and do not represent a comprehensive listing of all research opportunities within each of the sectors identified. As you read through each sector, you should be able to think of other research opportunities.

■ 12.8.1 Travel retailers *and wholesalers*

Travel retailers and wholesalers provide travel products. In supplying products there is a need to understand market segments, changing societal trends, the preferences of travellers and levels of satisfaction with packages and service delivery. The following suggestions for research opportunities for travel retailers and wholesalers are based on Wohlmuth (1994). Travel retailers and wholesalers can use research to acquire:

- knowledge of the sociodemographics of generating areas
- knowledge of social, cultural, political and economic trends
- knowledge of leisure and recreation patterns and trends
- information regarding the acceptability of new packages
- knowledge of preferences regarding destinations, accommodation and modes of transport to access particular destinations
- feedback on various travel packages sold
- feedback on service delivery and satisfaction.

12.8.2 The meetings, *incentives, conventions and exhibitions industry*

The meetings, incentives, conventions and exhibitions (MICE) industry provides opportunities for a wide range of research projects that focus on the demand, supply and impacts of MICE industry activities. The following possibilities are informed by the writings of Abbey and Link (1994). The MICE industry requires information on:

- site decision-making processes by MICE organisers
- participant preferences regarding mode of transport and accommodation venues and preferences regarding prices of the same
- length of stay of MICE participants
- economic impacts generated by a MICE event
- social impacts on the resident population
- MICE industry requirements regarding flat space, tiered spaces, breakout areas, information technology needs, and so on
- impacts of teleconferencing and e-conferencing
- satisfaction of MICE organisers with suppliers
- satisfaction of MICE participants with MICE events and sites
- satisfaction of partners and families with add-on events and activities
- evaluation of pre- and post-tour opportunities and activities.

12.8.3 Special *events*

Special events range in size from local fairs to mega events such as the Olympic Games. The varying sizes and range of special events have ramifications for the scope (the drawing power) as well as the impacts of each type of event. Special events produce a range of research opportunities for tourism researchers. The following list is based on the work of Carey (1994) and McDonnell, Allen and O'Toole (1999). Special events research opportunities include:

- establishment of baseline data upon which to develop historical data sets
- identification of market segments for specific special event types
- social impact studies
- economic impact studies
- environmental impact studies
- nature of media coverage
- event evaluation.

12.8.4 Attractions *and destinations*

Attractions and destinations offer a plethora of travel experiences ranging from site-specific attractions to natural attractions, built attractions and human cultural/heritage attractions. There is a mix of interested stakeholders within the composite experience: travel suppliers, hospitality suppliers, residents and tourists, and government agencies and departments.

Research into tourism attractions and destinations enables a multidisciplinary perspective to be adopted, as well as the potential for interdisciplinary research. Some tourism attraction and destination research opportunities include:

- development of resource inventories
- social impact studies
- economic impact studies
- environmental impact studies
- planning and development studies
- establishment of baseline data for historical tracking
- identification of market segments
- evaluation of promotional packages
- motivation studies
- satisfaction with transport, accommodation, and food and catering services
- destination image studies.

■ 12.8.5 Restaurant *industry*

The restaurant industry is a sector in tourism and hospitality. The following list is based on the work of Olson and Blank (1994). Some restaurant industry research opportunities include:

- identification of market potential
- monitoring of operations
- economic impact studies
- health and safety capacities
- supply chains
- changes in social attitudes and trends
- evaluation of service and products.

■ 12.8.6 Transport *industry*

The following list is based on the work of Cunningham (1994). Some transport industry research opportunities include:

- private vehicle ownership demographics
- private vessel ownership demographics
- private caravan/mobile home ownership demographics
- the sociodemographics of generating regions
- planning and decision-making studies
- studies into the nature of trips (time of year, trip patterns, etc.)
- spending patterns of travellers
- market research
- evaluation of service delivery
- en-route surveys
- advertisement pre-testing and tracking
- forecasting sales
- studies of energy efficiencies
- evaluation of competition

- scheduling testing
- regulation and deregulation policy evaluations
- economic impacts of the transport industry
- environmental impacts of the transport industry.

■ 12.8.7 Accommodation *industry*

The opportunities listed below are based on the work of Hiemstra (1994). Some accommodation industry research opportunities include:
- occupancy rates over time
- planning and development of accommodation
- sales projections
- employment projections
- personnel studies (productivity, turnover, health and safety issues, training and development needs)
- impacts of bed, room and state taxes
- yield management studies
- market segmentation studies and specific needs of segments
- advertising and promotion studies.

12.9 EMPLOYMENT OPPORTUNITIES FOR RESEARCH IN TOURISM

There are a number of employment opportunities available to you as a tourism researcher depending on your skill level and the degree of research activity included in job descriptions. You may, for example, be employed to engage in tourism research 100% of your time or you may find that you engage in tourism research only 10% of your time. However, whether you intend to work within tourism research or not, a knowledge of tourism research is useful for you. Such a knowledge enables you to evaluate the research of others, which is useful if you have to subcontract out research activities, and a knowledge of research processes will enable you to evaluate research proposals and research findings. It will also enable you to develop research briefs for externally let contracts.

Overall, the growth of tourism, both nationally and internationally, opens up the potential for a range of jobs for which tourism and hospitality students may apply. Both public sector and private sector departments, agencies and organisations require research-capable employees for the study of tourism impacts, tourism patterns and trends, product development and assessment, as well as research associated with the various projects listed above.

Some public and private sector organisations have research departments. Some examples of public sector organisations are the Great Barrier Reef Marine Park Authority and quasi-government departments such as the

CSIRO and the Bureau of Tourism Research (BTR). Some university-located research groups include CRC Sustainable Tourism and CRC Reef Research Centre. Various private sector organisations also have research departments or personnel, as do numerous small business and local tourism associations.

Research positions may include:
- research assistants to a chief researcher or investigator
- data entry personnel
- data analysts
- experimental designers
- interviewers
- focus group facilitators
- impact assessors
- questionnaire designers
- proposal writers
- literature reviewers
- report writers
- peer reviewers (this would not be a full-time position unless you were a full-time journal editor and reviewer)
- IT developers for tourism research programs for data analysis
- IT developers for the conduct of online tourism research
- research project managers
- directors of research departments
- researchers in a research and development department of a government agency
- researchers in a private sector research department.

Furthermore, remember that the research skills that you have acquired throughout study of this textbook, although predicated on tourism and hospitality, are the same skills used in other disciplines. So the skills you have acquired are portable to other disciplinary areas and employment areas. And you may, as suggested at the beginning of this chapter, decide to engage in further study and acquire a stronger statistical analysis skill base than can be offered in this textbook.

12.10 TOURISM RESEARCH IN THE FUTURE

In the near future, tourism research will continue to be predicated on the use of the positivist paradigm and the application of a quantitative methodology. However, the use of a qualitative methodology should be considered as having a significant contribution to understanding tourism phenomena. Admittedly, a qualitative methodology is appearing within mixed method research, although it tends to be used as the exploratory phase rather than the major phase of data collection and analysis. However, as case study 1 indicated, to understand the full gamut of tourism phenomena involving humans, quantitative and qualitative methodologies should be used in concert with each other rather than in competition — using both enables an understanding of the tourism phenomenon under study of much greater depth and detail than is often currently achieved.

Tourism research in the future should also continue its shift in emphasis from multidisciplinary to interdisciplinary research in order to develop theories and methods that are attributable to tourism as a discipline. As a consequence, it will enable us to expand our understanding of tourism and the world in which we live.

Standardisation of definitions and measures where possible should continue so that research can be shared and used across disciplinary and national boundaries. Coordination and cooperation between research organisations should continue to be facilitated in Australia (and internationally), not only through the efforts of individuals and individual agencies and organisation but also via the tourism industry and its related sectors. In 1999, CRC Sustainable Tourism provided a national vehicle for cross-institutional and sector sharing and responsibility for tourism research. Such conduct, as well as the sharing and dissemination of tourism research, is vital for the sustainability of tourism and the resources upon which it draws.

Finally, tourism research will see an increasing use of information technology for research design, data collection (particularly, the addition of another mode of data collection: online data collection) and data analysis; access to participants will also widen through e-world connections. The future for tourism research is one of growth and you have the potential to play an important part and to make a significant contribution. I hope you continue your journey.

12.11 SUMMARY

The role of research in tourism

Tourism research provides data for:

- planning and management decision making
- policy development
- understanding the social, environmental and economic impacts of tourism
- insights into motivations, needs, expectations and satisfaction levels of tourists
- identifying education and training requirements
- developing databases for use in comparative studies over time
- facilitating industry requirements for product development and monitoring
- evaluating tourism activities across the tourism industry and within stakeholder groups.

Chapter 1, in particular, deals with the role of research in tourism in detail.

Tourism research methodologies and methods

There are two methodologies used in tourism research — qualitative and quantitative. These methodologies are associated with a number of theoretical paradigms that inform tourism research (these are outlined in chapter 2). Sources of data gathered using either a qualitative or quantitative methodology may be either primary or secondary or both (see chapter 3). Furthermore, some researchers use a mix of the two methodologies and this is called a mixed method approach (see chapter 5). Methods for qualitative data collection and analysis are outlined in chapters 6 and 7. Methods for quantitative data collection and analysis are outlined in chapters 8 and 9. Some methods are used for both qualitative and quantitative research, such as interviews and observation. However, the procedures for each differ depending on the methodology being used. The methodologies used will also influence the reporting of the research findings (see chapters 10 and 11).

Responsibilities of tourism researchers

Tourism researchers require ethical clearance to conduct research. The development of ethics in research is founded in the Nuremberg Code, the Declaration of Helsinki and the Universal Declaration of Human Rights. This is discussed in depth in chapter 4.

Current and potential research needs of the travel and hospitality sectors

Research needs are widely dispersed in the tourism and hospitality sector, including: travel retailers and wholesalers; the meetings, incentives, conferences and exhibitions industry; special events; attractions and destinations; the restaurant industry; the transport industry; and the accommodation industry.

Employment opportunities in tourism research

Employment opportunities exist in the public and private sector, ranging from the position of research assistant to director of a research department or organisation. Research could be a small part of your job responsibility or 100% of your job responsibility.

Tourism research in the future

Due to tourism's strong role in the nations and economies of the world, the need for tourism research is imperative. It is imperative to ensure that planning, management and service provision are effective and forward directed rather than reactive to past trends. Improvements in information technology are also impacting on the conduct of tourism research. IT is providing more sophisticated research planning and analysis software and tools for data gathering, as well as providing another medium for accessing research participants via online research technologies and methods of conducting research (see chapters 7 and 9). Overall, tourism research needs to move to the stage of being interdisciplinary as well as becoming a discipline in its own right. Finally, it needs to value qualitative as well as quantitative research methodologies in developing an understanding of this phenomenon called tourism.

Questions

12.1 Examine the employment sections in the Saturday newspapers and make a list of the employment opportunities available for tourism and hospitality research-trained personnel. Ensure that you examine the tourism and hospitality sections and the education sections, as well as the government sections.

12.2 Conduct a search of the following Web sites and identify research-based jobs available to you: www.monsterboard.com; www.istte.org.

12.3 As part of the preparation for your curriculum vitae or response to selection criteria, outline the research skills you have now developed. Share these in your tutorial and gain feedback from your lecturer and class peers.

12.4 What is your considered opinion regarding the future of tourism research?

12.5 What role do you see research contributing to sustainable tourism developments?

REFERENCES

Abbey, James R. & Link, Carl K. 1994. 'The Convention and Meetings Sector: Its Operation and Research Needs'. In Ritchie, J. R. Brent & Goeldner, Charles R. (Eds) *Travel, Tourism, and Hospitality Research: A Handbook for Managers and Researchers.* New York: John Wiley & Sons.

Carey, Carolyn. 1994. 'Research Needs for Developing Established Events and Attractions'. In Ritchie, J. R. Brent & Goeldner, Charles R. (Eds) *Travel, Tourism, and Hospitality Research: A Handbook for Managers and Researchers.* New York: John Wiley & Sons.

Crotty, Michael. 1998. *The Foundations of Social Research: Meaning and Perspective in the Research Process.* Sydney: Allen & Unwin.

Cunningham, Lawrence F. 1994. 'Tourism Research Needs in the Personal Transportation Modes: A 1990s Perspective.' In Ritchie, J. R. Brent & Goeldner, Charles R. (Eds) *Travel, Tourism, and Hospitality Research: A Handbook for Managers and Researchers.* New York: John Wiley & Sons.

Hiemstra, Stephen J. 1994. 'Research Needs of the Lodging Industry'. In Ritchie, J. R. Brent & Goeldner, Charles R. (Eds) *Travel, Tourism, and Hospitality Research: A Handbook for Managers and Researchers.* New York: John Wiley & Sons.

McDonnell, Ian, Allen, Johnny & O'Toole, William. 1999. *Festival and Special Event Management.* Brisbane: John Wiley & Sons.

Olson, Robert P. & Blank, Uel. 1994. 'Research Needs of the Restaurant Industry'. In Ritchie, J. R. Brent & Goeldner, Charles R. (Eds) *Travel, Tourism, and Hospitality Research: A Handbook for Managers and Researchers.* New York: John Wiley & Sons.

Riley, Roger & Love, Lisa L. 2000. 'The State of Qualitative Tourism Research'. *Annals of Tourism Research*, vol. 27, no. 1, pp. 164–87.

Robinson, Stuart N. (1994). 'Research Needs in the Intercity Bus and Rail Transportation Industry'. In Ritchie, J. R. Brent & Goeldner, Charles R. (Eds) *Travel, Tourism, and Hospitality Research: A Handbook for Managers and Researchers*. New York: John Wiley & Sons.

Wohlmuth, Ed. (1994). 'Research Needs of Travel Retailers and Wholesalers'. In Ritchie, J. R. Brent & Goeldner, Charles R. (Eds) *Travel, Tourism, and Hospitality Research: A Handbook for Managers and Researchers*. New York: John Wiley & Sons.

WEB SITES

Australian Tourist Commission (research and market intelligence)
http://www.atc.net.au/intell/intell.htm.

Australian Tourist Commission (external links) http://www.atc.net.au/links/links.htm#Article 4.

Tourism Futures International (home page)
http://www.tourismfuturesintl.com.

World Tourism Organization (information centre)
http://www.world-tourism.org:83/omt/which.

World Travel and Tourism Council (home page)
http://www.wttc.org/default.htm.

Inbound and outbound tourism data

COUNTRY OR DEPENDENCY	REGION	POPULATION (THOUSANDS) (1996)	OUTBOUND (THOUSANDS) (1996)	INBOUND (THOUSANDS) (1986)	INBOUND (THOUSANDS) (1996)	TOURISM AS % OF GNP (1996)
Afghanistan	SAsia	22 664	n/a	9	4	n/a
Albania	SEur	3 290	16	n/a	56	0.3^3
Algeria	NAfr	28 520	2126^2	949	605	$<0.1^3$
American Samoa[#]	AusSP	50	n/a	30^4	21	n/a
Angola	MAfr	11 090	n/a	n/a	8	0.4^2
Anguilla[*#]	Car	10	n/a	17	37	75.0
Antigua and Barbuda[#]	Car	70	369	159	220	54.6
Argentina	SA	35 080	n/a	1 774	4 286	1.5
Aruba[*#]	Car	80	n/a	181	641	36.1^2
Australia	AusSP	18 230	2 732	1 429	4 165	2.2
Austria	WEur	8 070	n/a	15 092	17 090	6.7^3
Azerbaijan	CEEur	7 590	424^3	n/a	145	4.0^3
Bahamas[#]	Car	280	n/a	1 375	1 633	40.8^3
Bahrain[#]	ME	590	n/a	96	1 757	5.5^3
Bangladesh	SAsia	121 570	935	129	166	$<0.1^3$
Barbados[#]	Car	270	n/a	370	447	37.9^3
Belarus	CEEur	10 350	703	n/a	234	0.1^3
Belgium	WEur	10 160	5 645	n/a	5 829	2.3^3
Belize	CA	220	n/a	94	133	15.6^3
Benin	WAfr	5 630	418^1	48^5	147	1.3^3
Bermuda[*#]	Car	60	95^1	460	390	29.6^3
Bhutan	SAsia	1 640	n/a	3	5	1.7^3
Bolivia	SA	7 590	269	133	313	2.5^3
Bonaire[*#]	Car	10	n/a	27	65	n/a
Bosnia/ Herzegovina	SEur	4 410	n/a	n/a	99	0.6

(continued)

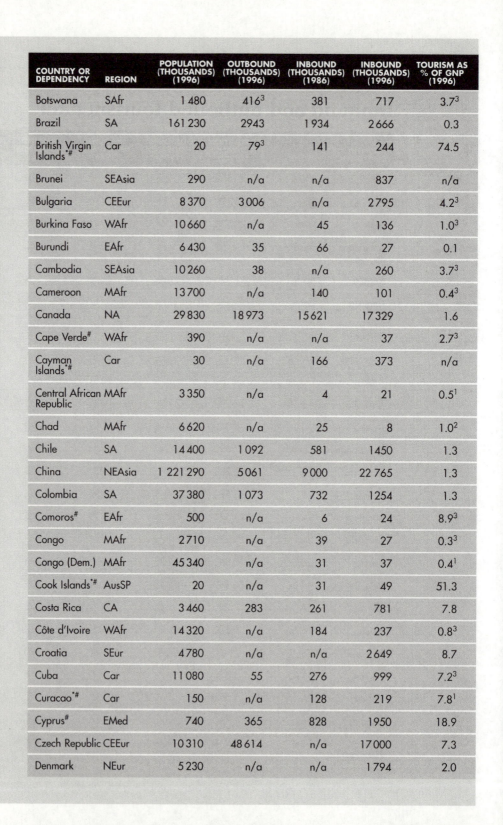

COUNTRY OR DEPENDENCY	REGION	POPULATION (THOUSANDS) (1996)	OUTBOUND (THOUSANDS) (1996)	INBOUND (THOUSANDS) (1986)	INBOUND (THOUSANDS) (1996)	TOURISM AS % OF GNP (1996)
Botswana	SAfr	1 480	416[3]	381	717	3.7[3]
Brazil	SA	161 230	2943	1934	2666	0.3
British Virgin Islands*#	Car	20	79[3]	141	244	74.5
Brunei	SEAsia	290	n/a	n/a	837	n/a
Bulgaria	CEEur	8370	3006	n/a	2795	4.2[3]
Burkina Faso	WAfr	10660	n/a	45	136	1.0[3]
Burundi	EAfr	6430	35	66	27	0.1
Cambodia	SEAsia	10260	38	n/a	260	3.7[3]
Cameroon	MAfr	13700	n/a	140	101	0.4[3]
Canada	NA	29830	18973	15621	17329	1.6
Cape Verde#	WAfr	390	n/a	n/a	37	2.7[3]
Cayman Islands*#	Car	30	n/a	166	373	n/a
Central African Republic	MAfr	3350	n/a	4	21	0.5[1]
Chad	MAfr	6620	n/a	25	8	1.0[2]
Chile	SA	14400	1092	581	1450	1.3
China	NEAsia	1 221 290	5061	9000	22 765	1.3
Colombia	SA	37380	1073	732	1254	1.3
Comoros#	EAfr	500	n/a	6	24	8.9[3]
Congo	MAfr	2710	n/a	39	27	0.3[3]
Congo (Dem.)	MAfr	45340	n/a	31	37	0.4[1]
Cook Islands*#	AusSP	20	n/a	31	49	51.3
Costa Rica	CA	3460	283	261	781	7.8
Côte d'Ivoire	WAfr	14320	n/a	184	237	0.8[3]
Croatia	SEur	4780	n/a	n/a	2649	8.7
Cuba	Car	11080	55	276	999	7.2[3]
Curacao*#	Car	150	n/a	128	219	7.8[1]
Cyprus#	EMed	740	365	828	1950	18.9
Czech Republic	CEEur	10310	48614	n/a	17000	7.3
Denmark	NEur	5230	n/a	n/a	1794	2.0

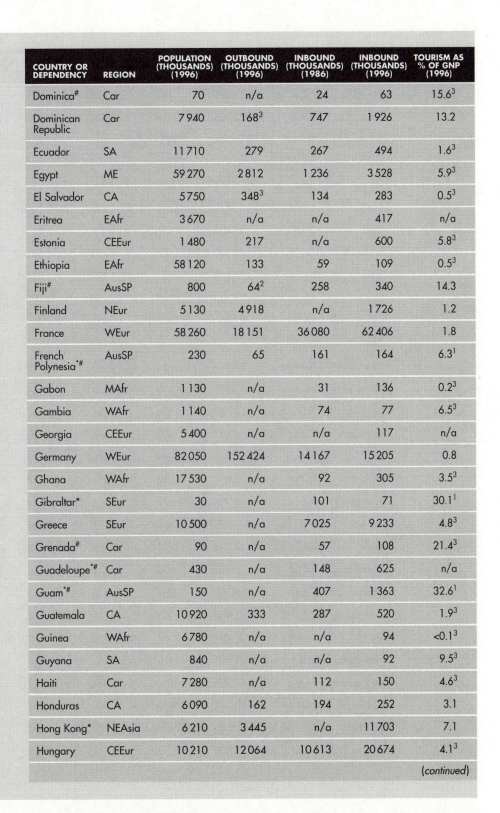

COUNTRY OR DEPENDENCY	REGION	POPULATION (THOUSANDS) (1996)	OUTBOUND (THOUSANDS) (1996)	INBOUND (THOUSANDS) (1986)	INBOUND (THOUSANDS) (1996)	TOURISM AS % OF GNP (1996)
Dominica[#]	Car	70	n/a	24	63	15.6[3]
Dominican Republic	Car	7 940	168[3]	747	1 926	13.2
Ecuador	SA	11 710	279	267	494	1.6[3]
Egypt	ME	59 270	2 812	1 236	3 528	5.9[3]
El Salvador	CA	5 750	348[3]	134	283	0.5[3]
Eritrea	EAfr	3 670	n/a	n/a	417	n/a
Estonia	CEEur	1 480	217	n/a	600	5.8[3]
Ethiopia	EAfr	58 120	133	59	109	0.5[3]
Fiji[#]	AusSP	800	64[2]	258	340	14.3
Finland	NEur	5 130	4 918	n/a	1 726	1.2
France	WEur	58 260	18 151	36 080	62 406	1.8
French Polynesia[*#]	AusSP	230	65	161	164	6.3[1]
Gabon	MAfr	1 130	n/a	31	136	0.2[3]
Gambia	WAfr	1 140	n/a	74	77	6.5[3]
Georgia	CEEur	5 400	n/a	n/a	117	n/a
Germany	WEur	82 050	152 424	14 167	15 205	0.8
Ghana	WAfr	17 530	n/a	92	305	3.5[3]
Gibraltar[*]	SEur	30	n/a	101	71	30.1[1]
Greece	SEur	10 500	n/a	7 025	9 233	4.8[3]
Grenada[#]	Car	90	n/a	57	108	21.4[3]
Guadeloupe[*#]	Car	430	n/a	148	625	n/a
Guam[*#]	AusSP	150	n/a	407	1 363	32.6[1]
Guatemala	CA	10 920	333	287	520	1.9[3]
Guinea	WAfr	6 780	n/a	n/a	94	<0.1[3]
Guyana	SA	840	n/a	n/a	92	9.5[3]
Haiti	Car	7 280	n/a	112	150	4.6[3]
Honduras	CA	6 090	162	194	252	3.1
Hong Kong[*]	NEAsia	6 210	3 445	n/a	11 703	7.1
Hungary	CEEur	10 210	12 064	10 613	20 674	4.1[3]

(continued)

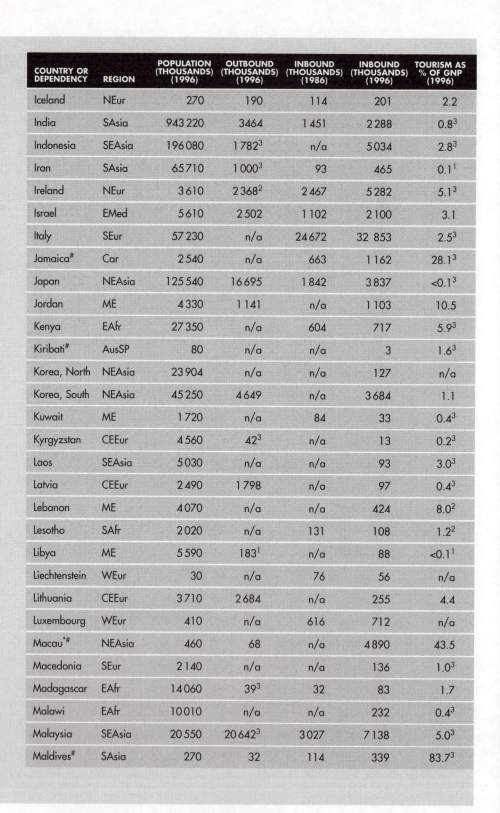

COUNTRY OR DEPENDENCY	REGION	POPULATION (THOUSANDS) (1996)	OUTBOUND (THOUSANDS) (1996)	INBOUND (THOUSANDS) (1986)	INBOUND (THOUSANDS) (1996)	TOURISM AS % OF GNP (1996)
Iceland	NEur	270	190	114	201	2.2
India	SAsia	943 220	3464	1 451	2 288	0.8[3]
Indonesia	SEAsia	196 080	1 782[3]	n/a	5 034	2.8[3]
Iran	SAsia	65 710	1 000[3]	93	465	0.1[1]
Ireland	NEur	3 610	2 368[2]	2 467	5 282	5.1[3]
Israel	EMed	5 610	2 502	1 102	2 100	3.1
Italy	SEur	57 230	n/a	24 672	32 853	2.5[3]
Jamaica[#]	Car	2 540	n/a	663	1 162	28.1[3]
Japan	NEAsia	125 540	16 695	1 842	3 837	<0.1[3]
Jordan	ME	4 330	1 141	n/a	1 103	10.5
Kenya	EAfr	27 350	n/a	604	717	5.9[3]
Kiribati[#]	AusSP	80	n/a	n/a	3	1.6[3]
Korea, North	NEAsia	23 904	n/a	n/a	127	n/a
Korea, South	NEAsia	45 250	4 649	n/a	3 684	1.1
Kuwait	ME	1 720	n/a	84	33	0.4[3]
Kyrgyzstan	CEEur	4 560	42[3]	n/a	13	0.2[3]
Laos	SEAsia	5 030	n/a	n/a	93	3.0[3]
Latvia	CEEur	2 490	1 798	n/a	97	0.4[3]
Lebanon	ME	4 070	n/a	n/a	424	8.0[2]
Lesotho	SAfr	2 020	n/a	131	108	1.2[2]
Libya	ME	5 590	183[1]	n/a	88	<0.1[1]
Liechtenstein	WEur	30	n/a	76	56	n/a
Lithuania	CEEur	3 710	2 684	n/a	255	4.4
Luxembourg	WEur	410	n/a	616	712	n/a
Macau[*#]	NEAsia	460	68	n/a	4 890	43.5
Macedonia	SEur	2 140	n/a	n/a	136	1.0[3]
Madagascar	EAfr	14 060	39[3]	32	83	1.7
Malawi	EAfr	10 010	n/a	n/a	232	0.4[3]
Malaysia	SEAsia	20 550	20 642[3]	3 027	7 138	5.0[3]
Maldives[#]	SAsia	270	32	114	339	83.7[3]

COUNTRY OR DEPENDENCY	REGION	POPULATION (THOUSANDS) (1996)	OUTBOUND (THOUSANDS) (1996)	INBOUND (THOUSANDS) (1986)	INBOUND (THOUSANDS) (1996)	TOURISM AS % OF GNP (1996)
Mali	WAfr	10090	n/a	51	101	0.8[3]
Malta[#]	SEur	370	163[3]	574	1054	21.1[3]
Marshall Islands[#]	AusSP	60	n/a	2	6	2.3[3]
Martinique[*#]	Car	380	n/a	183	477	n/a
Mauritius[#]	EAfr	1140	120	165	487	12.9
Mexico	NA	93420	9001	14625	21405	2.0[3]
Moldova	CEEur	4350	71	n/a	33	1.4[3]
Monaco	WEur	30	n/a	211	226	n/a
Mongolia	NEAsia	2510	n/a	199	71	2.7[3]
Montserrat[*#]	Car	10	n/a	16	9	35.8[2]
Morocco	NAfr	27060	1212	2128	2693	3.9
Myanmar	SEAsia	45900	n/a	41	172	<0.1
Namibia	SAfr	1580	n/a	n/a	405	7.2[3]
Nepal	SAsia	21980	119	223	394	2.7[3]
Netherlands	WEur	15530	10261[3]	3134	6580	1.6[3]
New Caledonia[*#]	AusSP	190	64	57	91	3.2[1]
New Zealand	AusSP	3670	1093	733	1529	4.2[3]
Nicaragua	CA	4490	282	n/a	303	2.8
Niger	WAfr	9330	10[3]	27	17	0.8[3]
Nigeria	WAfr	114400	n/a	340[4]	822	0.2[3]
Niue[*#]	AusSP	2	n/a	2	2	n/a
Northern Marianas[*#]	AusSP	50	n/a	n/a	729	n/a
Norway	NEur	4370	692	1637	2746	1.5
Oman	ME	2290	n/a	88	349	0.9
Pakistan	SAsia	133540	n/a	432	369	0.2[3]
Palau[#]	AusSP	20	n/a	n/a	69	n/a
Panama	CA	2670	188	308	362	4.2
Papua New Guinea	AusSP	4400	51[3]	32	61	1.2[3]

(continued)

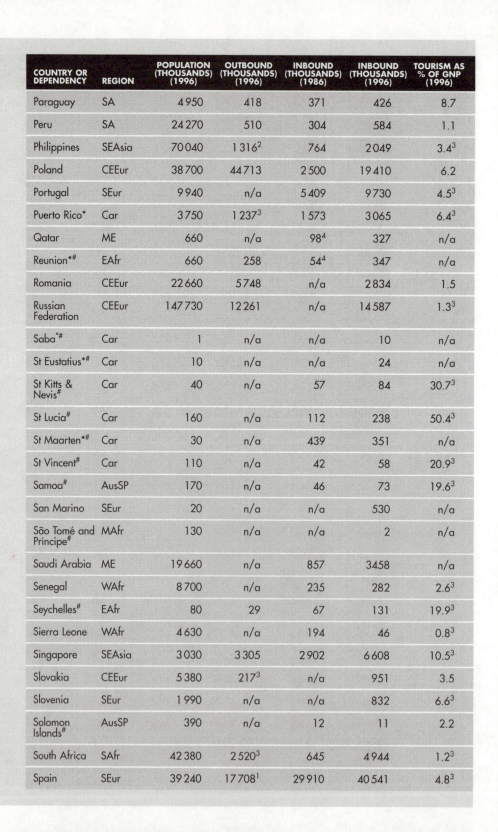

COUNTRY OR DEPENDENCY	REGION	POPULATION (THOUSANDS) (1996)	OUTBOUND (THOUSANDS) (1996)	INBOUND (THOUSANDS) (1986)	INBOUND (THOUSANDS) (1996)	TOURISM AS % OF GNP (1996)
Paraguay	SA	4950	418	371	426	8.7
Peru	SA	24270	510	304	584	1.1
Philippines	SEAsia	70040	1316[2]	764	2049	3.4[3]
Poland	CEEur	38700	44713	2500	19410	6.2
Portugal	SEur	9940	n/a	5409	9730	4.5[3]
Puerto Rico*	Car	3750	1237[3]	1573	3065	6.4[3]
Qatar	ME	660	n/a	98[4]	327	n/a
Reunion*#	EAfr	660	258	54[4]	347	n/a
Romania	CEEur	22660	5748	n/a	2834	1.5
Russian Federation	CEEur	147730	12261	n/a	14587	1.3[3]
Saba*#	Car	1	n/a	n/a	10	n/a
St Eustatius*#	Car	10	n/a	n/a	24	n/a
St Kitts & Nevis#	Car	40	n/a	57	84	30.7[3]
St Lucia#	Car	160	n/a	112	238	50.4[3]
St Maarten*#	Car	30	n/a	439	351	n/a
St Vincent#	Car	110	n/a	42	58	20.9[3]
Samoa#	AusSP	170	n/a	46	73	19.6[3]
San Marino	SEur	20	n/a	n/a	530	n/a
São Tomé and Príncipe#	MAfr	130	n/a	n/a	2	n/a
Saudi Arabia	ME	19660	n/a	857	3458	n/a
Senegal	WAfr	8700	n/a	235	282	2.6[3]
Seychelles#	EAfr	80	29	67	131	19.9[3]
Sierra Leone	WAfr	4630	n/a	194	46	0.8[3]
Singapore	SEAsia	3030	3305	2902	6608	10.5[3]
Slovakia	CEEur	5380	217[3]	n/a	951	3.5
Slovenia	SEur	1990	n/a	n/a	832	6.6[3]
Solomon Islands#	AusSP	390	n/a	12	11	2.2
South Africa	SAfr	42380	2520[3]	645	4944	1.2[3]
Spain	SEur	39240	17708[1]	29910	40541	4.8[3]

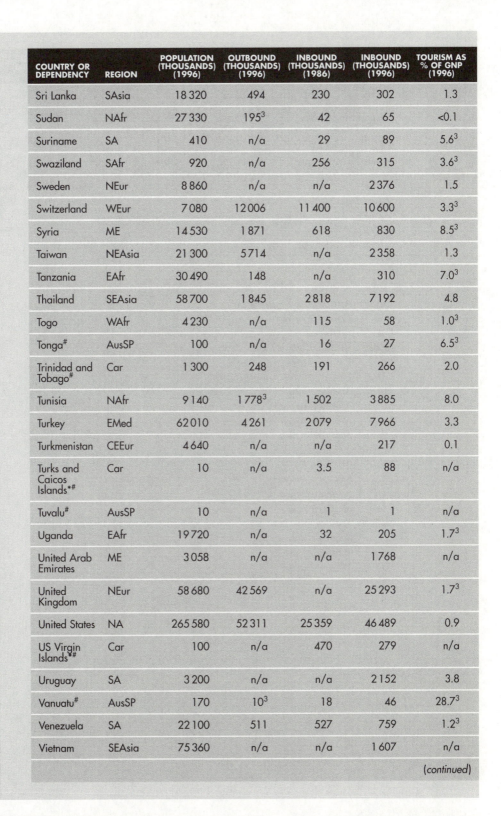

COUNTRY OR DEPENDENCY	REGION	POPULATION (THOUSANDS) (1996)	OUTBOUND (THOUSANDS) (1996)	INBOUND (THOUSANDS) (1986)	INBOUND (THOUSANDS) (1996)	TOURISM AS % OF GNP (1996)
Sri Lanka	SAsia	18 320	494	230	302	1.3
Sudan	NAfr	27 330	195[3]	42	65	<0.1
Suriname	SA	410	n/a	29	89	5.6[3]
Swaziland	SAfr	920	n/a	256	315	3.6[3]
Sweden	NEur	8 860	n/a	n/a	2376	1.5
Switzerland	WEur	7 080	12006	11 400	10 600	3.3[3]
Syria	ME	14 530	1871	618	830	8.5[3]
Taiwan	NEAsia	21 300	5714	n/a	2358	1.3
Tanzania	EAfr	30 490	148	n/a	310	7.0[3]
Thailand	SEAsia	58 700	1845	2818	7 192	4.8
Togo	WAfr	4 230	n/a	115	58	1.0[3]
Tonga[#]	AusSP	100	n/a	16	27	6.5[3]
Trinidad and Tobago[#]	Car	1 300	248	191	266	2.0
Tunisia	NAfr	9 140	1778[3]	1 502	3885	8.0
Turkey	EMed	62 010	4261	2079	7966	3.3
Turkmenistan	CEEur	4 640	n/a	n/a	217	0.1
Turks and Caicos Islands*[#]	Car	10	n/a	3.5	88	n/a
Tuvalu[#]	AusSP	10	n/a	1	1	n/a
Uganda	EAfr	19 720	n/a	32	205	1.7[3]
United Arab Emirates	ME	3 058	n/a	n/a	1 768	n/a
United Kingdom	NEur	58 680	42 569	n/a	25 293	1.7[3]
United States	NA	265 580	52 311	25 359	46 489	0.9
US Virgin Islands*[#]	Car	100	n/a	470	279	n/a
Uruguay	SA	3 200	n/a	n/a	2 152	3.8
Vanuatu[#]	AusSP	170	10[3]	18	46	28.7[3]
Venezuela	SA	22 100	511	527	759	1.2[3]
Vietnam	SEAsia	75 360	n/a	n/a	1 607	n/a

(continued)

COUNTRY OR DEPENDENCY	REGION	POPULATION (THOUSANDS) (1996)	OUTBOUND (THOUSANDS) (1996)	INBOUND (THOUSANDS) (1986)	INBOUND (THOUSANDS) (1996)	TOURISM AS % OF GNP (1996)
Yemen	ME	15 820	n/a	71	74	0.8[3]
Yugoslavia	SEur	10 540	n/a	n/a	301	n/a
Zambia	EAfr	9 180	n/a	123	264	1.3[3]
Zimbabwe	EAfr	11 210	256[3]	357	1 743	2.6[3]

Notes: **Source:** *WTO (1998a, 1998c)*

*Dependency.

#SISOD.

[1]1993.

[2]1994.

[3]1995.

[4]1985.

[5]1984.

AusSP   Australasia, South Pacific
CA   Central America
Car   Caribbean
CEEur   Central/Eastern Europe
EAfr   Eastern Africa
EMed   Eastern Mediterranean Europe
MAfr   Middle Africa
ME   Middle East
NA   Northern America
NAfr   Northern Africa
NEAsia   Northeastern Asia
NEur   Northern Europe
SA   Southern America
SAfr   Southern Africa
SAsia   Southern Asia
SEAsia   Southeastern Asia
SEur   Southern Europe
WAfr   Western Africa
WEur   Western Europe

·······························

Selected international and Australian tourism organisations

TOURISM ORGANISATION	DATE ESTABLISHED	PURPOSE	HEADQUARTERS
Australian Bureau of Statistics (ABS) http://www.abs.gov.au/	1976	Australia's official statistical organisation	Belconnen, ACT
Bureau of Tourism Research (BTR) http://www.btr.gov.au/	1987	A joint state and federal government agency that collects, analyses and disseminates information regarding the Australian tourism industry to government, industry and the general public.	Canberra, ACT
Ecotourism Association of Australia http://ecotour.csu.edu.au/ecotour/Pages/EAAHome.html	1991	Promotes an understanding of ecotourism and environmental issues in Australia, and aims to develop ethics and standards for the industry, and facilitate interaction between ecotourism stakeholders	Red Hill, QLD
Ecotourism Society http://www.ecotourism.org/index.html	1990	Founded to foster synergy between outdoor travel entrepreneurs, researchers and conservationists	Bennington, Vt, United States
International Academy for the Study of Tourism (IAST)	1988	A scholarly body that investigates the theoretical nature of tourism and its global role; interdisciplinary and international in scope, and limited to a membership of 75 scholars	Spain
Office of National Tourism http://www.tourism.gov.au/	1996	The main federal agency responsible for developing and implementing government tourism policy, managing Australia's participation in international expositions and delivering funding through the government's regional tourism program	Canberra, ACT

(continued)

TOURISM ORGANISATION	DATE ESTABLISHED	PURPOSE	HEADQUARTERS
Pacific Asia Travel Association (PATA) http://www.pata.org/patanet/psto.html	1951	A non-profit travel industry association that promotes travel and tourism destinations in the Asia–Pacific region through networking, marketing, promotion and sales, destination promotion and trade shows; consists of approximately 2100 organisations, including governments, travel organisations and companies	San Francisco, United States (administrative headquarters)

APPENDIX 3 ····································

Refereed English language tourism journals (1999)

JOURNAL TITLE	DATE OF FIRST ISSUE	COUNTRY OF EDITOR
Journal of Travel Research[1]	1962	United States
Annals of Tourism Research	1973	United States
Tourism Recreation Research	1976	India
Tourism Management[2]	1980	New Zealand
Anatolia	1990	Turkey
Journal of Tourism Studies	1990	Australia
Journal of Travel and Tourism Marketing	1992	United States
Festival Management and Event Tourism	1993	Canada
Journal of Sustainable Tourism	1993	United Kingdom
Journal of Vacation Marketing	1994	Australia
International Journal of Tourism Research[3]	1995	United Kingdom
Tourism Economics	1995	United Kingdom
Asia Pacific Journal of Tourism Research	1996	United States
Tourism Analysis	1996	United States
Pacific Tourism Review	1997	Australia
Current Issues in Tourism	1998	New Zealand
Information Technology and Tourism	1998	Austria
International Journal of Hospitality and Tourism Administration	1998	United States
Tourism Culture and Communication	1998	Australia
Tourism Geographies	1999	United States

Notes:
[1] Formerly Travel Research Bulletin.
[2] Formerly International Journal of Tourism Management.
[3] Formerly Progress in Tourism and Hospitality Research

Principles of ethical conduct

The primary purpose of this Statement of ethical principles and associated guidelines for research involving humans is the protection of the welfare and rights of participants in research. The ethical and legal responsibilities which researchers have towards participants in research reflect basic ethical values of integrity, respect for persons, beneficence and justice.

Integrity, respect for persons, beneficence and justice

1.1 The guiding value for researchers is integrity, which is expressed in a commitment to the search for knowledge, to recognised principles of research conduct and in the honest and ethical conduct of research and dissemination and communication of results.

1.2 When conducting research involving humans, the guiding ethical principle for researchers is respect for persons which is expressed as regard for the welfare, rights, beliefs, perceptions, customs and cultural heritage, both individual and collective, of persons involved in research.

1.3 In research involving humans, the ethical principle of beneficence is expressed in researchers' responsibility to minimise risks of harm or discomfort to participants in research projects.

1.4 Each research protocol must be designed to ensure that respect for the dignity and well being of the participants takes precedence over the expected benefits to knowledge.

1.5 The ethical value of justice requires that, within a population, there is a fair distribution of the benefits and burdens of participation in research and, for any research participant, a balance of burdens and benefits. Accordingly, a researcher must:

(a) avoid imposing on particular groups, who are likely to be subject to over researching, an unfair burden of participation in research;

(b) design research so that the selection, recruitment, exclusion and inclusion of research participants is fair; and

(c) not discriminate in the selection and recruitment of actual and future participants by including or excluding them on the grounds of race, age, sex, disability or religious or spiritual beliefs except where the exclusion or inclusion of particular groups is essential to the purpose of the research.

1.6 The proportion of burdens to benefits for any research participant will vary. In clinical research, where patient care is combined with an intent to contribute to knowledge, the risks of participation must be balanced by the possibility of intended benefits for the participants. In other research involving humans that is undertaken solely to contribute to knowledge, the absence of intended benefits to a participant should justly be balanced by the absence of all but minimal risk.

Consent

1.7 Before research is undertaken, whether involving individuals or collectivities, the consent of the participants must be obtained, except in specific circumstances defined elsewhere in this Statement.

The ethical and legal requirements of consent have two aspects: the provision of information and the capacity to make a voluntary choice. So as to conform with ethical and legal requirements, obtaining consent should involve:

(a) provision to participants, at their level of comprehension, of information about the purpose, methods, demands, risks, inconveniences, discomforts, and possible outcomes of the research (including the likelihood and form of publication of research results); and

(b) the exercise of a voluntary choice to participate.

Where a participant lacks competence to consent, a person with lawful authority to decide for that participant must be provided with that inforamtion and exercise that choice.

1.8 A person may refuse to participate in a research project and need give no reasons nor justification for that decision.

1.9 Where consent to participate is required, research must be so designed that each participant's consent is clearly established, whether by a signed form, return of a survey, recorded agreement for interview or other sufficient means.

In some circumstances and some communities, consent is not only a matter of individual agreement, but involves other properly interested parties, such as formally constituted bodies of various kinds, collectivities or community elders. In such cases the researcher needs to obtain the consent of all properly interested parties before beginning the research.

1.10 The consent of a person to participate in research must not be subject to any coercion, or to any inducement or influence which could impair its voluntary character.

1.11 It is ethically acceptable to conduct certain types of research without obtaining consent from participants in some circumstances, for example, the use of de-identified data in epidemiological research, observational research in public places, or the use of anonymous surveys.

1.12 A participant must be free at any time to withdraw consent to further involvement in the research. If any consequences may arise from such withdrawal, advice must be given to participants about these before consent to involvement in the research is obtained.

Research merit and safety

1.13 Every research proposal must demonstrate that the research is justifiable in terms of its potential contribution to knowledge and is based on a thorough study of current literature as well as prior observation, approved previous studies, and where relevant, laboratory and animal studies.

1.14 All research proposals must be so designed as to ensure that any risks of discomfort or harm to participants are balanced by the likely benefit to be gained.

(continued)

1.15 Research must be conducted or supervised only by persons or teams with experience, qualifications and competence appropriate to the research. Research must only be conducted using facilities appropriate for the research and where there are appropriate skills and resources for dealing with any contingencies that may affect participants.

Ethical review and conduct of research

1.16 Research projects involving humans must be reviewed by a Human Research Ethics Committee (HREC) and must not be undertaken or funded unless and until approval has been granted.

1.17 A researcher must suspend or modify any research in which the risks to participants are found to be disproportionate to the benefits and stop any involvement of any participant if continuation of the research may be harmful to that person.

1.18 The results of research (whether publicly or privately funded) and the methods used should normally be published in ways which permit scrutiny and contribute to public knowledge. Normally, research results should be made available to research participants.

1.19 Where personal information about research participants or a collectivity is collected, stored, accessed, used, or disposed of, a researcher must strive to ensure that the privacy, confidentiality and cultural sensitivities of the participants and/or the collectivity are respected. Any specific agreements made with the participants or the collectivity are to be fulfilled.

1.20 Where the records and results of research contain information of clinical significance it is the responsibility of both the researcher and the institution or organisation to maintain the security and storage of records and results so as to enable any necessary follow-up studies to be carried out.

1.21 Where research is conducted in an overseas country under the aegis of an Australian institution or organisation, the research must comply with the requirements of this Statement as well as the laws and guidelines of that country.

ANZALS Code of Ethics

Purpose of the code of ethics

1. This Code of Ethics has an advisory function and provides guidelines for ethical behaviour and decision-making with respect to research, teaching, publishing and professional conduct.

   Throughout this code the term 'researchers and scholars' is taken to include those who undertake research in the context of their profession (e.g. teachers, practitioners, administrators, scholars etc.)

   The statements in this code tend to refer specifically to the practice of research. However the spirit of the guidelines should be interpreted as applying to all forms of professional conduct of ANZALS members.

   Notwithstanding the advisory nature of this code, researchers additionally may be obliged to adhere to regulatory ethical codes and standards prescribed by other bodies when undertaking any research project.

   Ultimately, individual leisure researchers and scholars must take responsibility for their ethical behaviour.

   This code is not a fixed document. Its revision is an ongoing process.

The context of ethical judgements

2. The social, political and scientific context in which ethical judgements are made by leisure researchers and scholars is important. Due regard should be given to the following:

   i The social world is plural, contradictory and conflictual. It is hard to establish that there exists a singular, non-contradictory 'public good'.

   ii Relations of power exist in all social science research pursuits.

   iii Leisure researchers and scholars should recognise research as not neutral and should make explicit their epistemological postulates and assumptions. The research act is a gendered and political social act, shaped by the researcher's gender and personal biography (Denzin 1989).[1]

   iv Leisure researchers and scholars study sociological problems and topics rather than people *per se*; people should not be treated as objects in the process of doing research.

   v Research has effects at a wider social level, as well as on individuals, and these should be addressed.

   vi The Treaty of Waitangi has implications for both the production and dissemination of leisure research and scholarship in the New Zealand context.

---

[1] Denzin, N. K. (1989) 'On the ethics and politics of sociology', in *The Research Act: A Theoretical Introduction to Sociological Methods.* 3rd ed. New Jersey: Prentice-Hall, pp. 248–68.

(continued)

Ethical statement

3. Our responsibilities and obligations to colleagues, and hence to the field of studies are based both on the vital benefits of peer review of research and scholarship and on the desirability of maintaining accessibility to research.

4. Leisure researchers and scholars should report results honestly, avoid actions that will violate or diminish the rights of research participants or clients and avoid raising false hopes.

5. Researchers have a responsibility to raise ethical issues with all research team members prior to and while undertaking research.

6. Researchers should protect the welfare and privacy of the people or organisations participating in the research. People and collectives do not have an absolute right to privacy in their public capacity.

7. Researchers should protect privacy where appropriate by adequately disguising personal identities in written and oral reports of the research and by discussing only data germane to the purpose of research.

8. Researchers should not reveal information received in the course of the research where an assurance of confidentiality has been promised.

9. Researchers should inform research participants and funding agencies of any limits of confidentiality and anonymity.

10. Researchers should respect the right of funding agencies, host institutions and publishers to be given adequate information about the research and to have their contribution acknowledged.

11. Researchers have a responsibility to maintain high standards of competence and to maintain knowledge of current information methods in the areas in which they are involved.

12. Researchers should make full and honest disclosure in both written reports and to researched participants of financial and other forms of support of their research.

13. Researchers should given an account of their methodology and report the limitations of their research design.

14. Researchers should ensure that information of interest to individuals, groups and organisations be made available in a timely, acceptable and accessible manner, and where appropriate should return source material to its owner.

15. Any claims or conclusions presented by the researchers ought to be supported by the evidence.

Research participants

16. Where appropriate, and as a general rule, informed consent should be sought from those individuals directly involved in research to be undertaken. Where research involves a minor or a person unable to give informed consent, informed consent should be obtained from the guardian or other legal person(s) properly empowered to give such consent on behalf of the individual concerned. Thus, researchers should:

Inform participants about the purpose and nature of the research and its possible implications for them.

Make it clear that all have the freedom of choice to participate or not. This includes students.

Make it clear to research participants from whom informed consent has been obtained that they may withdraw that consent at any time.

17. Researchers should attempt to anticipate and avoid possible harm to participants. However, where harm occurs, researchers have an obligation to take all possible steps to minimise such harm, and to account for their actions.

18. Research participants are entitled to receive appropriate feedback on the outcome of research; researchers should make provision for this.

Contractual research

19. Before the research starts, the researcher should clarify with the client:

The right of the researcher to use the research results commercially or otherwise, or to publish research and information independently from the client.

The nature of the responsibility and liability of the researcher regarding the use made of the research results by the client once the research is completed.

20. When working for a multiplicity of clients which can be or are in competitive positions, the right to use information and results across projects should be carefully defined beforehand.

21. When research results are published independently by the researcher the institutional context within which the research took place should be made clear. This includes the objective of the client organisation, the nature and extent of funding and the role of the client in framing and defining the research.

Teaching and student research

22. Ethical consequences outlined in this document apply equally to student research and ethics should be included in the training of leisure researchers and scholars.

23. Teachers are responsible for the ethics of any research required of undergraduate students.

24. Supervisors have a responsibility to discuss with each graduate student the ethics of that student's research.

25. Students retain ethical responsibility for their own actions. Students should take account of the advice on ethics provided by their teachers and supervisors.

26. Supervisors and teachers have a responsibility to ensure that the community is not misused as a student resource. They must take care not to exploit groups through repetitive and burdensome demands.

27. When a student is funded by outside agencies, supervisors have a responsibility to ensure that a suitable research contract is agreed upon which provides appropriate remuneration, explicit agreements as to ownership and use of data produced, and protection against unethical pressures.

(continued)

Authorship

28. Leisure researchers and scholars (including students) must acknowledge all persons who contributed significantly to the research and publication process.
29. Material taken from published or unpublished work must be identified and referenced to its author(s).

Sponsorship

30. The receipt of financial support for research projects, such as grants, awards etc., should be fully acknowledged.

Procedures and conventions

31. This Code of Ethics has educational as well as exhortative and regulatory dimensions. We acknowledge that a major goal envisaged in the development and promulgation of this Code of Ethics is the enhancement of our collective knowledge of ethical issues and sensitivity to the various ways in which such issues may arise; and we affirm the responsibility of our Association to promote the development of such knowledge and sensitivity among all leisure researchers and scholars whether or not they are members of the Association.

32. When a researcher or scholar who is a member of the Australian and New Zealand Association of Leisure Studies violates ethical standards, those who know first hand of such activities should, if possible, attempt to discuss the situation with the member. Failing an informal solution unethical activities should be brought to the attention of the Board of Directors of the Australian and New Zealand Association for Leisure Studies. An Ethics Committee, a sub-committee of the Board of Directors, will be appointed to consider the matter and will forward a recommendation of advice to the Board of Directors of the Australian and New Zealand Association for Leisure Studies for consideration.

    In every case, including when the Ethics Committee concludes that the activity discussed was not unethical, a report is to be made to the membership and to the appropriate institution outlining the issues and describing the criteria by which the conclusions were reached.

    A member of the Australian and New Zealand Association for Leisure Studies may ask the Ethics Committee to consider (and the Board of Directors to make a statement on) the ethical standing of work presented as 'leisure research', or by people identifying themselves as 'leisure researchers' or 'leisure scholars'.

APPENDIX 6

A table of random numbers

10819	85717	64540	95692	44985	88504	50298	20830	67124	20557
28459	13687	50699	62110	49307	84465	66518	08290	96957	45050
19105	52686	51336	53101	81842	20323	71091	78598	60969	74898
35376	72734	13951	27528	36140	42195	25942	70835	45825	49277
93818	84972	66048	83361	56465	65449	87748	95405	98712	97183
35859	82675	87301	71211	78007	99316	25591	63995	40577	78894
66241	89679	04843	96407	01970	06913	19259	72929	82868	50457
44222	37633	85262	65308	03252	36770	51640	18333	33971	49352
54966	75662	80544	48943	87983	62759	55698	41068	35558	60870
43351	15285	38157	45261	50114	35934	05950	11735	51769	07389
11208	80818	78325	14807	19325	41500	01263	09211	56005	44250
71379	53517	15553	04774	63452	50294	06332	69926	20592	06305
63162	41154	78345	23645	74235	72054	84152	27889	75881	58652
17457	68490	19878	04981	83667	00053	12003	84614	14842	29642
28042	42748	55801	94527	21926	07901	89865	21070	80320	91153
32240	24201	24202	45025	07664	11503	97315	83178	26731	45568
87288	22996	67529	38344	29757	74161	16834	40238	48789	99995
39052	23696	42858	85695	50783	51790	80882	97015	81331	76819
71528	74553	32294	86652	15224	07119	45327	69072	64572	07658
76921	04502	78240	89519	02621	40829	88841	66178	01266	10906
45889	22839	77794	94068	85709	96902	19646	40614	03169	45434
10486	79308	75231	33615	42194	49397	91324	79553	66976	83861
42051	14719	80056	74811	58453	04526	90724	36151	09168	04291
47919	11314	80282	09297	02824	59530	31237	26311	62168	46591
19634	40589	28985	40577	33213	52852	17556	85342	66881	18944
10265	44549	38771	38740	48104	63990	73234	19398	33740	97345
74975	33526	36190	25201	19239	06254	02198	99109	01005	20983
37677	76778	15736	57675	81153	59651	69262	89250	75156	59164
18774	15979	26466	80236	65400	24272	02088	09307	33426	11230
93728	14965	85141	27821	53791	38728	66369	29415	55330	99228
34212	15590	41336	23614	26153	19466	44176	80885	00015	40077
81984	54478	45226	97338	14064	45768	13538	49093	05691	69720
72755	15743	00552	89374	85400	37392	26598	71917	64275	16125
13162	57044	75982	15819	23385	40860	51585	44542	39656	91139
64686	62224	34124	79171	73909	26196	54057	63264	72089	06658
00157	64594	03178	75774	32315	34443	37224	85593	55251	42666
84194	83591	82152	24311	22414	43244	81542	31491	42075	17275
05776	60399	65218	89299	20273	30071	53077	18853	56652	63896
33365	18314	81074	49433	10884	75467	56085	14731	98085	60895
67928	38976	38480	59980	23156	72665	33489	59420	67819	51874
64394	45154	81851	54228	73095	97217	16908	90242	92869	17311

Alternate hypothesis: An educated conjecture that sets the parameters that one expects to find. The alternate hypothesis is tested to see whether or not the null is to be rejected.

Ambiguous questions: Questions that are not clearly worded and likely to be interpreted by respondents in different ways.

Analytical study: A study that tries to explain why or how certain variables influence the dependent variable of interest to the researcher.

ANOVA: Stands for analysis of variance, which tests for significant mean differences in variables among multiple groups.

Applied research: Research that addresses some particular problem or attempts to achieve a particular set of outcomes; it is usually constrained by set time schedules.

Basic research: Research that is broadly focused on the revelation of new knowledge, and is not directed towards specific outcomes or problems.

Bias: Any error that creeps into the data. Biases can be introduced by the researcher, the respondent, the measuring instrument, the sample, and so on.

Case study: The documented history of noteworthy events that have taken place in a given institution, setting, community or environment.

Category scale: A scale that uses multiple items to seek a single response.

Causal analysis: Analysis done to detect cause and effect relationships between two or more variables.

Causal study: A research study conducted to establish cause and effect relationships among variables.

Census: Refers to the inclusion in a study of all possible units in a population. A census differs from a saturation sample (survey) in that a census is used with large populations and a saturation sample (survey) is used with unique smaller populations.

Chaos theory paradigm: Holds an ontological view that the world comprises open, dynamic, ever-changing systems that are non-linear in nature — where small changes can result in large-scale outcomes. Scientific research is based on descriptions of algorithms, whereas social science research utilises chaos theory as a metaphor. Chaos theory is being challenged by complexity theory as a way of explaining the world.

Chi-square test: A non-parametric test that establishes the independence or otherwise between two nominal variables.

Closed questions: Questions with a clearly delineated set of alternatives that confine the respondents' choice to one of them.

Cluster sampling: A probability sampling design in which the sample comprises groups or chunks of elements with intragroup heterogeneity and intergroup homogeneity.

Codes of ethics: Prepared by various organisations and institutions to set out the protocols to be followed when working with human and non-human subjects. Such codes outline the socially and morally acceptable norms of researcher and participant/subject interaction during the course of the research process.

Complexity theory: Holds an ontological view that the world comprises complex systems that rapidly move from a state of chaos to one of order as a result of interacting 'agents' in the systems being self-organising.

Computer-Assisted Telephone Interviews (CATI): Interviews in which questions are prompted by a PC monitor that is networked into the telephone system, to which respondents provide their answers.

Concurrent validity: Relates to criterion-related validity, which is established at the same time the test is administered.

Confidence: The probability estimate of how much reliance can be placed on the findings; the usual accepted level of confidence in social science research is 95%.

Consolidation stage: In the Butler sequence, as local carrying capacities are exceeded, the rate of growth declines; the destination is now almost wholly dominated by tourism.

Construct validity: Testifies to how well the results obtained from the use of the measure fit the theories around which the test was designed.

Content validity: Establishes the representative sampling of a whole set of items that measures a concept, and reflects how well the dimensions and elements thereof are delineated.

Control group: The group that is not exposed to any treatment in an experiment.

Controlled variable: Any exogenous or extraneous variable that could contaminate the cause and effect relationship, but the effects of which can be controlled through the process either of matching or randomisation.

Convenience sampling: A non-probability sampling design in which information or data for the research are gathered from members of the population who are conveniently accessible to the researcher.

Critical theory paradigm: Utilises a mid-point position between subjectivism and objectivism and sees the social world as constrained by rules. However, these rules can be changed by actors and their actions. Scientific inquiry in this paradigm attempts to elicit transformational change, particularly the social circumstances of those being studied.

Criterion-related validity: That which is established when the measure differentiates individuals on a criterion that it is expected to predict.

Criterion variable: The variable of primary interest to the study, also known as the dependent variable.

Cross-sectional study: A research study for which data are gathered just once (stretched though it may be over a period of days, weeks or months) to answer the research question.

Data analysis: The process by which the collected information is examined and assessed in order to identify patterns that address the research questions.

Data collection: The gathering of relevant information by way of the techniques identified in the research methodology stage.

Data interpretation: The stage during which some kind of meaning is extracted from the data.

Data presentation: The stage during which the results of the analysis are communicated to the target audience.

Decline stage: The scenario of declining visitor intake that is likely if no measures are taken to arrest the process of product deterioration.

Deduction: An approach in basic research that begins with a basic theory that is applied to a set of data to see whether the theory is applicable or not.

Demonstration effect: In economics, the tendency of a population, or some portion thereof, to imitate the consumption patterns of another group; this can result in increased importation of goods and services to meet these changing consumption patterns.

Dependent variable: *See* criterion variable.

Descriptive statistics: Statistics such as frequencies, the mean and the standard deviation, which provide descriptive information of a set of data.

Descriptive study: A research study that describes the variables in a situation of interest to the researcher.

Destination community: The residents of the destination region.

Destination life cycle: The theory that tourism-oriented places experience a sequential process of birth, growth, maturation, and then possibly something similar to death, in their evolution as destinations.

Development stage: In the Butler sequence, the accelerated growth of tourism within a relatively short period of time, as this sector becomes a dominant feature of the destination economy and landscape.

Domestic stayovers: Tourists who stay within their own country for at least one night.

Domestic tourist: A tourist whose itinerary is confined to their usual country of residence.

Double-blind peer review: A procedure that attempts to maintain objectivity in the manuscript refereeing process by ensuring that the author does not know the identity of the reviewers, while the reviewers do not know the identity of the author.

Electronic questionnaire: Online questionnaire administered when the micro computer is hooked up to computer networks.

Emic: The terms emic and etic are founded in anthropology and refer to ways of gathering data about a phenomenon. An emic perspective grounds the study in the setting being studied. It is sometimes referred to as 'insider' research as the researcher becomes as one with the research setting/group and uses the knowledge bases of the setting, the people and the latter's explanations and language to describe the phenomenon being studied. This represents a 'subjective' epistemology and is associated with the holistic-inductive paradigm.

Epistemology: The nature of the relationship between knower and known.

Ethics: Code of conduct or expected societal norms of behaviour.

Etic: An etic perspective utilises an 'outsider' perspective and is akin to the use of an 'objective' epistemology. Consequently, it is associated with a quantitative methodology.

Experimental design: A study design in which the researcher might create an artificial setting, control some variables and manipulate the independent variable to establish cause and effect relationships.

Experimental group: The group exposed to a treatment in an experimental design.

Exploratory study: A research study where very little knowledge or information is available on the subject under investigation.

External validity: The extent of generalisability of the results of a causal study to other field settings.

Face-to-face interview: Information gathering when both the interviewer and interviewee meet in person.

Face validity: An aspect of validity examining whether the item on the scale, on the face of it, reads as if it indeed measures what it is supposed to measure.

Family life cycle (FLC): A sequence of stages through which the traditional nuclear family passes from early adulthood to the death of a spouse; each stage is associated with distinct patterns of tourism-related behaviour associated with changing family and financial circumstances.

Feminist perspectives paradigm: The term feminist perspectives is used generically — there is no one feminist perspective but a number of perspectives (in this textbook — radical feminism, Marxist and socialist feminist perspectives, liberal feminism and postmodern feminist perspectives). The feminist perspectives paradigm aims to make visible the real-world experience of women and to break the dominant hegemony that is patriarchal in nature.

Field experiment: An experiment done to detect cause and effect relationships in the natural environment in which events normally occur.

Field study: A study conducted in the natural setting, with a minimal amount of researcher interference with the flow of events in the situation.

Focus group: A group consisting of eight to 12 randomly chosen members who discuss a product or any given topic for about two hours with a moderator present, so that their opinions can serve as the basis for further research.

Forced choice: Elicits the ranking of objects relative to one another.

Frequencies: The number of times various subcategories of a phenomenon occur, from which the percentage and cumulative percentage of any occurrence can be calculated.

Funnelling technique: The questioning technique that consists of initially asking general and broad questions, and gradually narrowing the focus thereafter on more specific themes.

Generalisability: The applicability of research findings in one setting to others.

Holistic-inductive paradigm: Studies the whole phenomenon and all its complexity rather than breaking down the phenomenon into parts and studying discrete variables and causal relationships (see hypothetico-deductive method for the alternative approach).

Hypothesis: An educated conjecture about the logically developed relationship between two or more variables, expressed in the form of testable statements.

Hypothesis testing: A means of testing whether the 'IF–THEN' statements generated from the theoretical framework hold true when subjected to rigorous examination.

Hypothetico-deductive method of research: A seven-step process of observing, preliminary data gathering, theorising, hypothesising, collecting further data, analysing data and interpreting the results to arrive at conclusions.

Inbound tourist: An international tourist arriving from another country.

Income multiplier effect (IME): A measure of the subsequent income generated in a destination's economy by direct tourist expenditure.

Independent variable: A variable that influences the dependent or criterion variable and accounts for (or explains) its variance.

Induction: An approach in basic research whereby the observation and analysis of data lead to the formulation of theories or models that link these observations in a meaningful way.

Inferential statistics: Statistics that help to establish relationships among variables and draw conclusions therefrom.

Indicators: A variable or parameter that provides information about some phenomenon in order to facilitate its management in a desirable way.

Interdisciplinary approach: Involves the input of a variety of disciplines, with fusion and synthesis occurring among these different perspectives.

Interpretive social sciences paradigm: Grounded in the social world of the actors and their everyday lives. This paradigm perceives that social actors are in control of their actions rather than pursuing their lives regulated by rules and actions without any agency of their own. Scientific inquiry in this paradigm is subjective and value-laden.

Interval scale: A multipoint scale that taps the differences, the order and the equality of the magnitude of the differences in the responses.

Intervening variable: A variable that surfaces as a function of the independent variable, and helps in conceptualising and explaining the influence of the independent variable on the dependent variable.

Interviewing: A data collection method in which the researcher asks for information verbally from the respondents.

Invivo: Associated with qualitative data analysis. Refers to the naming of theoretical concepts using the language of study participants instead of terms contrived by the researcher.

Irridex: A theoretical model proposing that resident attitudes evolve from euphoria to apathy, then irritation (or annoyance), antagonism and finally resignation, as the intensity of tourism development increases within a destination.

Leading questions: Questions phrased in such a manner as to lead the respondent to give the answers that the researcher would like to obtain.

Likert scale: An interval scale that specifically uses the five anchors of: Strongly Disagree, Disagree, Neither Disagree nor Agree, Agree and Strongly Agree.

Literature review: The documentation of a comprehensive review of the published work from secondary sources of data in the areas of specific interest to the researcher.

Literature survey: *See* Literature review.

Loaded questions: Questions that would elicit highly biased emotional responses from subjects.

Longitudinal study: A research study for which data are gathered at several points in time to answer a research question.

Market segmentation: The division of the tourist market into more or less homogenous subgroups, or tourist market segments, based on certain common characteristics and/or behavioural patterns.

Market segments: Portions of the tourist market that are more or less distinct in their characteristics and/or behaviour.

Mean: The average of a set of figures.

Measure of central tendency: Descriptive statistics of a data set such as the mean, median or mode.

Median: The central item in a group of observations arranged in an ascending or descending order.

Methodology: The way the researcher produces knowledge.

Methods: The tools a researcher uses for collecting and analysing data.

MICE: An acronym combining meetings, incentives, conventions and exhibitions; a form of tourism largely associated with business purposes.

Mode: The most frequently occurring item in a data set.

Modern mass tourism: The period from 1950 to the present day, characterised by the rapid expansion of international and domestic tourism.

Multiple regression analysis: A statistical technique to predict the variance in the dependent variable by regressing the independent variables against it.

Multistage cluster sampling: A probability sampling design that is a stratified sampling of clusters.

Nominal scale: A scale that categorises individuals or objects into mutually exclusive and collectively exhaustive groups, and offers basic, categorical information on the variable of interest.

Non-participant-observer: A researcher who collects observational data without becoming an integral part of the system.

Non-parametric statistics: Statistics used to test hypotheses, when the population from which the sample is drawn cannot be assumed to be normally distributed.

Non-probability sampling: A sampling design in which the elements in the population do not have a known or predetermined chance of being selected as sample subjects.

Null hypothesis: The conjecture that postulates no differences or no relationship between or among variables.

Numerical scale: A scale with bipolar attributes with five points or seven points indicated on the scale.

Objectivity: Interpretation of the results on the basis of the results of data analysis, as opposed to subjective or emotional interpretations.

Ontology: The nature of reality.

Open-ended questions: Questions that the respondent can answer in a free-flowing format without restricting the range of choices to a set of specific alternatives suggested by the researcher.

Origin region: The region (e.g. country, state, city) from which the tourist originates; also referred to as the market or generating region.

Outbound tourist: An international tourist departing from their usual country of residence.

Paradigm: The beliefs, assumptions and values that underlie the way that various perspectives interpret reality.

Participant-observer: A researcher who collects observational data by becoming a member of the system from which data are collected.

Population: The entire group of people, events or things that the researcher desires to investigate.

Population frame: A listing of all the elements in the population from which the sample is drawn.

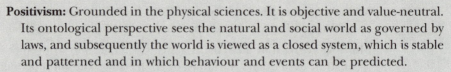

Positivism: Grounded in the physical sciences. It is objective and value-neutral. Its ontological perspective sees the natural and social world as governed by laws, and subsequently the world is viewed as a closed system, which is stable and patterned and in which behaviour and events can be predicted.

Postmodern paradigm: Debunks grand theory (no one theory has precedence over another) and attempts to deconstruct the surface features of phenomena to get to the underlying core reality.

Post-test: A test given to the subjects to measure the dependent variable after exposing them to a treatment.

Predictive study: A study that enables the prediction of the relationships among the variables in a particular situation.

Pre-test: A test given to the subjects to measure the dependent variable before exposing them to a treatment.

Pre-testing survey questions: Test of the understandability and appopriateness of the questions planned to be included in a regular survey, using a small number of respondents.

Primary research: Research that involves the collection of original data by the researcher.

Probability sampling: The sampling design in which the elements of the population have some known chance or probability of being selected as sample subjects.

Proportionate stratified random sampling: A probability sampling design in which the number of sample subjects drawn from each stratum is proportionate to the total number of elements in the respective strata.

Psychographic segmentation: The differentiation of the tourist market on the basis of psychological and motivational characteristics such as personality, motivations and needs.

Purposive sampling: A non-probability sampling design in which the required information is gathered from special or specific targets or groups of people on some rational basis.

Qualitative methodology: Does not place its emphasis on the collection and analysis of statistical data, and usually tends to obtain in-depth insight into a relatively small number of respondents or observations.

Quantitative methodology: Is based mainly on the collection and analysis of statistical data, and hence tends to obtain a limited amount of information on a large number of respondents or observations; these results are then extrapolated to the wider population of the subject matter.

Question formulation: The posing of specific questions or hypotheses that serve to focus the research agenda arising from problem recognition; these questions can be descriptive, explanatory, predictive or prescriptive in nature.

Questionnaire: A preformulated written set of questions to which the respondent records the answers, usually within rather closely delineated alternatives.

Quota sampling: A form of purposive sampling in which a predetermined proportion of people from different subgroups is sampled.

Range: The extreme values in a set of observations, the difference between which indicates the spread.

Rating scale: A scale with several response categories that evaluate an object on a scale.

Ratio scale: A scale that has an absolute zero origin, and hence indicates not only the magnitude, but also the proportion of the differences.

Reciprocity: Associated with the mutual exchange of information (usually during data collection, such as sharing information between participants and researchers as a two-way exchange, and also after data analysis, such as disseminating research findings to participants). It involves a win–win situation where both the participants and the researcher(s) gain from the research act. It is especially associated with the holistic-inductive paradigm (e.g. interpretive social sciences and feminist perspectives).

Refereed academic journals: Publications that are considered to showcase a discipline by merit of the fact that they are subject to a rigorous process of double-blind peer review.

Reliability: Attests to the consistency and stability of the measuring instrument.

Replicability: The repeatability of similar results when identical research is conducted at different times or in different organisational settings.

Representativeness of the sample: The extent to which the sample that is selected possesses the same characteristics as the population from which it is drawn.

Research: An organised, systematic, critical, scientific inquiry or investigation into a specific problem, issue, setting or phenomenon undertaken with the objective of generating knowledge about the same.

Research methodology: A set of procedures and methods that are used to carry out a search for knowledge within a particular type of research.

Research methods: The techniques that will be used to gather and analyse data for a research study.

Research process: The sequence of stages that are followed to carry out a research project from its origins to its conclusions.

Sample: A subset or subgroup of the population.

Sample size: The actual number of subjects chosen as a sample to represent the population characteristics.

Sampling: The process of selecting items from the population so that the sample characteristics can be generalised to the population. Sampling involves both design choice and sample size decisions.

Saturation samples: Also know as saturation surveys. Used with unique populations that are not large. All members of the population are studied. A saturation sample differs from a census in that the former is used with unique smaller populations, whereas a census is used with large populations.

Scientific paradigm: The currently dominant paradigm, which holds that reality is reducible and deterministic and can be understood through the application of the 'scientific method'.

Secondary research: Research in which the investigator uses previously collected data.

Simple market segmentation: The most basic form of market segmentation, involving the identification of a minimal number of market segments.

Simple random sampling: A probability sampling design in which every single element in the population has a known and equal chance of being selected as a subject.

Sociodemographic segmentation: Market segmentation based on social and demographic variables such as gender, age, family life cycle, education, occupation and income.

Standard deviation: A measure of dispersion for parametric data; the square root of the variance.

Stratified random sampling: A probability sampling design that first divides the population into meaningful, non-overlapping subsets, and then randomly chooses the subjects from each subset.

Structural interviews: Interviews conducted by the researcher with a predetermined list of questions to be asked of the interviewee.

Subject: A single member of the sample.

Systematic sampling: A probability sampling design that involves choosing every nth element in the population for the sample.

Telephone interview: The information-gathering method by which the interviewer asks the interviewee *over the telephone*, rather than face to face, for information needed for the research.

Theory: A model or statement that explains or represents some phenomenon.

_t_-test: A statistical test that establishes a significant mean difference in a variable between two groups.

Tour operators: Businesses providing a package of tourism-related services for the consumer, including some combination of accommodation, transportation, restaurants and attraction visits.

Tourism: The sum of the phenomena and relationships arising from the interaction among tourists, business suppliers, host governments, host communities, origin governments, universities, community colleges and non-governmental organisations, in the process of attracting, transporting, hosting and managing these tourists and other visitors.

Tourism industry: The sum of the industrial and commercial activities that produce goods and services wholly or mainly for tourist consumption.

Tourism product: Consists of tourist attractions and the tourism industry.

Tourism resources: Features of a destination that are valued as attractions by tourists at some particular point in time; a feature that was a tourism resource 100 years ago may not be perceived as such now.

Tourist: A person who travels temporarily outside of their usual environment (usually defined by some distance threshold) for certain qualifying purposes.

Tourist attractions: Specific and generic features of a destination that attract tourists; some, but not all, attractions are part of the tourism industry.

Tourist market: The overall group of consumers that engages in some form of tourism-related travel.

Travel purpose: The reason why people travel; in tourism, these involve recreation/leisure, visits to friends and relatives (VFR), business, and less dominant purposes such as study, sport, religion and health.

Unbiased questions: Questions posed in accordance with the principles of wording and measurement, and the right questioning technique, so as to elicit the least biased responses.

Unit of analysis: The level of aggregation of the data collected during data analysis.

Unobtrusive measures: Measurement of variables, through data gathered from sources other than people, such as examining birth and death records.

Unstructured interviews: Interviews conducted with the primary purpose of identifying some important issues relevant to the problem situation, without prior preparation of a planned or predetermined sequence of questions.

Validity: Evidence that the instrument, technique or process used to measure a concept does indeed measure the intended concept.

Variable: Anything that can take on differing or varying values.

Verstehen: Empathetic understanding of the group being studied by becoming one with the group —an 'insider' (see emic) perspective.

INDEX

mail surveys   230–2
manual entry   280–1
maps   329
matrices   207–8
mean   288–9
measures of association   297
measures of central tendency   286–9
measures of variation   291–4
median   288
meetings, incentives, conventions and
    exhibitions (MICE) industry, research
    needs   409
memos   197–8
method, definition   33
methodological triangulation   134, 151
Methodologist's Toolchest *Version 3.0*   302
methodology
    definition   33
    see also qualitative methodology; quantitative
        methodology
methodology section
    journal articles   363
    reports   334–5
    research proposals   318–19
mind maps   209, 210
Minitab   303
mixed method approach   22
mixed research methodologies   133–6
mode   286–8
multistage cluster sampling   144–5
multivariate analysis   283, 298–9

name method (sampling)   141
narrative reports   324
National Health and Medical Research Council
    (NHMRC), ethical guidelines   98
negatively skewed distribution   290
nominal group technique   261
nominal measures   253
non-parametric tests   300
non-probability sampling   138–40
non-random sampling, differences from random
    sampling   146–9
non-sexist research methods   182
normal distribution   290
null hypothesis   245, 301
number method (sampling)   141–2
Nuremberg Code   98

observation   255
    see also participant observation
omnibus surveys   240
on-site surveys   239
ontology, definition   33
open-ended questions   252
ordinal measures   253
other harm   107–8
outbound tourism data   417–24
outcome variable   244, 245
overhead transparencies   355

panel sessions   357
panel studies   174
paradigm
    choosing the 'right' one   55–6
    definition   33
    see also specifics, e.g. chaos theory
        paradigm
parametric tests   300
participant observation   169–70
    advantages/disadvantages   171–2
    steps   170–1
participant observation reports   327
participants, relationship with
    researchers   114–15
percentage frequency distribution table   284,
    285
percentiles   291
personal documents   67
phenomenology   159, 161
physical harm   106
pie charts   286, 287
pilot studies   152, 253
plenary sessions   356
polygons   286, 287
population   136
population pyramids   286, 287
positively skewed distribution   290
positivist paradigm   35–6
    case study   399–407
    consequences for tourism research   36
    potential areas of tourism research   37–8
poster presentations   358
    audience considerations   361–2
    content   361
    size of poster papers   359, 360
    structure of poster papers   359, 360
    styles of presentation   361
    visual layout   361
postmodern paradigm   48–50
    consequences for tourism research   50–1
    potential areas of tourism research   51
PowerPoint presentations   355
predictive research   20
predictive surveys   229
preface   331–2
primary data sources   63, 64
    advantages/disadvantages   64–5
    differences from secondary sources   83
    diversity in   83
primary documents   68
probability sampling   140–5
process of getting your work accepted   365–6
professionals (as audience for reports)   339
proofing stage (writing process)   25, 310
psychological harm   107
public documents   66
publishing stage (writing process)   25, 310
pure research   14
purposive sampling   139

QSR NUD*IST 4   216
QSR NUD*IST Vivo   216
qualitative content analysis   82–3